Understanding Language and Literacy Development

Understanding Language and Literacy Development

Diverse Learners in the Classroom

Xiao-lei Wang

WILEY Blackwell

This edition first published 2015
© 2015 John Wiley & Sons, Inc.

Registered Office
John Wiley & Sons Ltd, The Atrium, Southern Gate, Chichester, West Sussex, PO19 8SQ, UK

Editorial Offices
350 Main Street, Malden, MA 02148-5020, USA
9600 Garsington Road, Oxford, OX4 2DQ, UK
The Atrium, Southern Gate, Chichester, West Sussex, PO19 8SQ, UK

For details of our global editorial offices, for customer services, and for information about how to apply
for permission to reuse the copyright material in this book please see our website at
www.wiley.com/wiley-blackwell.

The right of Xiao-lei Wang to be identified as the author of this work has been asserted in accordance with
the UK Copyright, Designs and Patents Act 1988.

Library of Congress Cataloging-in-Publication Data is available for this book.

ISBN 9780470674291 (hardback); ISBN: 9780470674307 (papberback)

A catalogue record for this book is available from the British Library.

Cover image: Study group © sturti /iStockphoto; Girl reading © Aaraujo /Shutterstock; Mother and
baby © Evgeny Atamanenko /Shutterstock; School boy using tablet PC © michaeljung /
Shutterstock

Set in 10/12.5pt Galliard by Aptara Inc., New Delhi, India
Printed and bound in Malaysia by Vivar Printing Sdn Bhd

1   2015

Contents

Detailed Contents

Acknowledgments

I credit the existence of this book to Danielle Descoteaux, the senior acquisitions editor of psychology and linguistics of Wiley Blackwell. I received an email from Danielle on November 16, 2010, asking whether I was interested in writing a book related to language development. This invitation has turned out to be a great opportunity for me to produce a book that is much needed for preparing preservice teachers to meet the Common Core State Standards and edTPA requirements in teacher education programs. Danielle, thank you!

Working with the staff at Wiley Blackwell has truly been a pleasure. I would particularly like to thank Julia Kirk, the senior project editor, for your patience, constant help, and support in the writing process. Julia has never failed to check upon my progress. Julia, it is thanks to you that I was able to complete the book on time.

The input of the anonymous reviewers helped the book find its shape. For example, the idea of putting the theories at the end of the book instead of at the beginning was proposed by one of the reviewers. The reviewers have also provided valuable suggestions for the revision of the book. I am deeply indebted to you for your guidance.

I also would like to thank Dean Andrea Spencer of the School of Education at Pace University for granting me a semester of sabbatical leave and the Pace Kenan Scholarly Research Committee for granting me a course release to work on the book. Without your generous support, I would not have been able to find the time to write this book.

My ED 650 students in the 2013 spring semesters and ED 632 and TCH 452 students in the 2013 fall semesters have graciously "experimented" with the book drafts. Your feedback about the book has been most helpful. I would like to thank in particular Amelia Nelson, Shannon Melissa Summers, Keisey Igo, Amanda Eisner, Theresa Connelly, Danielle Frasca, Danielle Rodriguez, Mellissa Silva, Nora Rugova, and Alex Lengers for contributing your language samples.

I would like to express my appreciation to several of my present and past graduate assistants for helping me with the book at its different stages: Amanda Albano, Theresa Connelly, Jennifer Argenta, Deborah Hurdis, and Courtney Klein. Without your hard work, some tedious but important jobs simply could not have been accomplished.

Last, but not least, my gratitude goes to my husband, Philippe, and sons, Léandre and Dominique, for your moral support and humor. You always help me find meaning in what I do!

About the Companion Website

This book is accompanied by a companion website:

www.wiley.com/go/wang/langandlit

This website includes:

For Instructors
- Powerpoint slides for each chapter
- Sample Syllabus
- Suggested key activities

For Students
- A Summary of the Common Core K-12 Key Language And Literacy Standards

About the Book

Reasons to Read the Book

This book is about the language and literacy developmental characteristics of children and adolescents with different abilities. Especially, this book is about how to use effective supporting strategies in classroom settings to help all students learn across subject contents. Some of you may be eager to find out what is in it, whereas others would not have touched the book if it were not a course requirement. To those of you who are not so enthusiastic about the topic of language and literacy development and believe that it is seemingly unrelated to the subject area that you are teaching or plan to teach, I would like you to meet Peter, a new math teacher in Herald High School (see Box 0.1). I hope that the challenges he encountered will convince you to give this book a real try.

Box 0.1 Peter's Challenge – Student Diversity

Peter had looked forward to meeting his ninth-grade students in Herald High School since he was offered a teaching position in June. During the summer, he carefully studied the topics in the geometry textbook and prepared detailed lesson plans for the whole year. By the end of August, Peter was certain that he was more than ready to teach geometry! Indeed, Peter had all the reason to be confident; he received his Master's degree from a reputable teacher education program, had successfully completed his student teaching in a local high school, and was well prepared for the ninth-grade geometry content.

On the first day of school in September, Peter was excited. He put on his new outfit and headed for the school. While driving to school, he mentally went over what he had prepared to do in his first geometry class.

Understanding Language and Literacy Development: Diverse Learners in the Classroom, First Edition. Xiao-lei Wang.
© 2015 John Wiley & Sons, Inc. Published 2015 by John Wiley & Sons, Inc.
Companion website: www.wiley.com/go/wang/langandlit

When Peter entered his second period geometry class, 23 students eagerly checked him out with their curious eyes. Peter briefly introduced himself and began the class with a quiz to find out how well the students understood basic geometry concepts. While the students were completing the quiz, he noticed that some of them were staring at the quiz and appeared to be struggling. He approached one student and asked whether he needed any help. The young man told him that he did not understand what they were asked to do and he did not understand the problems in the quiz. Peter rephrased the quiz problems several times. However, the student showed no signs of understanding. Several other students in the class were also experiencing the same difficulty. Peter quickly collected the quiz and went on with the lesson he had planned. Thirty minutes into teaching, Peter was surprised to notice that some students seemed to have difficulties understanding what was written in the handouts. He was frustrated that he was not able to get through to his students with what he had planned.

He hurried to find out how his students did on the quiz immediately after his class left the room. To his dismay, half of his students completely missed the problems and gave wrong answers; some could not write coherent sentences. Peter had thought ninth graders should be able to read and write quite well.

When school ended at 2:30 p.m., Peter decided to find out some information about his students. He went to the Guidance Office and checked the students' files. The students in his second period geometry class were from diverse socioeconomic, cultural, linguistic, and developmental backgrounds. Fifteen of them had come to the country within the last three years from non-English speaking countries. Two were identified with autism spectrum disorder (ASD), one with Attention Deficit Hyper Activity Disorder (ADHD), and two with specific language impairment (SLI). Moreover, they were from a wide range of cultural backgrounds: White American, African American, Chinese, Thai, Tongan, Haitian, Ecuadoran, Mexican, Iranian, and Sudanese.

Even though Peter was informed during his interview that Herald was a culturally, linguistically, and economically diverse school and had students with different disabilities, he had decided to take the job because he wanted to make a difference. However, he was not prepared to encounter challenges of this magnitude on the first day. He was caught by surprise that many of them seemed to have language-related difficulties that were far deeper than understanding geometry concepts. The confidence he felt at the beginning of the day began to fade away.

Peter's experience indicates that teaching in a diverse classroom is particularly complex, multifaceted, and challenging. If you want to be successful in reaching all students in the subject content area, you must be ready to negotiate between teaching a subject and considering the learners' cultural, economic, linguistic, and developmental disparities. You must understand that the students' differences in the above-mentioned aspects often lead to their different abilities in reading, comprehending, and writing in the content area. Because students' language and literacy competence is critical to their academic content learning and social functioning, you must know how their language and literacy are acquired and developed before you can help them learn subject contents.

Peter's challenges are not his alone. The most recent National Assessment of Educational Progress report suggests that one-third of students in the United States failed to achieve the basic levels of reading competence by the fourth grade (National Center for Educational Statistics, 2011) and only 38 percent of high school seniors scored at or above proficiency (National Center for Educational Statistics, 2009). Moreover, the 15-year olds in the United States continue to perform poorly in reading, math, and science in the **Program(me) for International Student Assessment** (PISA)[1] compared with other industrialized nations.

The twenty-first century is characterized by significant cultural and linguistic diversity in schools, which requires teachers to have knowledge of their students' language and literacy development differences and to know how to respond to these differences in instruction. Therefore, ask yourself these questions: "Do I believe all students should benefit from learning?" "Do I want to create a learning environment that allows all students to participate fully and optimize their potentials?" "Do I believe all students can succeed?" "Do I want to be effective in reaching all students?" "Do I want to turn students' challenges into teaching opportunities?" and "Do I want to be more prepared than Peter when I walk into a classroom with diverse learners?" If your answers to these questions are yes, then read on; you are likely to find that the pages that follow will help you become more confident and competent in teaching your content area, whether it is math, science, social studies, or any other subject. In fact, a majority of teachers who have completed a course related to the basic linguistic principles found the information useful for their teaching, regardless of their specialty (Moats, 1994).

Your Turn

- Do you think some of Peter's students did not perform well because of their diversity or because our educational system has failed them? Research the term "deficit model in education" or "cultural deficit model" and discuss how we can explain the academic performances of Peter's students.
- If you were to give Peter some suggestions about the challenges he encountered in his first geometry lesson, what would they be and why?
- Visit a diverse classroom and fill out the demographic information of the students below (add more information if you want). What have you found? What does this demographic information tell you about the challenges of teaching and reaching these students?

Grade level
Student number
Student gender
Student ethnicity and race
Student cultural origin

Student social economic status
Student linguistic background
Student developmental and cognitive abilities
Other (include other information you observe in the classroom/school).

Unique Approaches of the Book

To better prepare you in responding to the challenges in diverse classrooms, this book takes the following unique approaches.

Paying balanced attention to all learners

When addressing language and literacy development, textbooks often tend to pay most attention to describing typical linguistic development characteristics while parenthesizing the characteristics of multilingual children and children with language and literacy learning difficulties. As you have observed in Peter's classroom, students with different language and literacy abilities often learn within the same classroom environment (i.e., the inclusive classroom environment). Therefore, it is unconscionable not to give enough attention to different language learners and not to address their characteristics concurrently. If we are sincere about providing equal opportunity for all students, we must have sound knowledge about their variations in language and literacy development. Thus, this book discusses the variations of language and literacy learners in parallel chapters to help you see the complexity of your students' language and literacy development and find effective ways to reach them based on their different strengths and needs.

Emphasizing language and literacy supporting strategies

This book not only provides you with information on language and literacy developmental characteristics in different populations, but also with information on how to support students' language and literacy development in the everyday classroom environment. Although many language and literacy supporting strategies can be used for students across various abilities, some are particularly emphasized for a specific population.

Encouraging thinking, questions, and explorations

Before you are introduced to the contents of a given chapter, you are asked to think about some important questions or carry out activities that are relevant to that chapter. These activities and questions will facilitate the development of your own perspectives in explaining the language and literacy development phenomena you have observed in life or classrooms. By doing so, you are likely to be more motivated to read the chapter and to bring in your own questions, thoughts, and observations. Consequently, your interaction with the chapter will be more in-depth. Similarly, you will have many opportunities to respond to important issues in the "Your Turn" sections (as you were just asked to do) and to ponder upon big questions in the essential question sections. Even though you often may not be able to provide all the answers and solutions to these questions, you are put in the thinking mode and are encouraged to search for the information constantly while reading.

Moreover, you are asked to be an accountable reader. This means that you are not spoon-fed the information. Instead, you are asked to engage actively in searching for answers to an issue. For example, in the "Your Turn" sections, you are sometimes required to research databases such as ERIC[2] and PsycINFO[3] to find more up-to-date knowledge on a topic under discussion. This practice will help you become an active consumer of research literature and continue to update your knowledge.

Unlike most of the textbooks on language and literacy development, which tend to introduce theories in the beginning, this book introduces theories in the last chapter. The purpose is to give you opportunities to come up with your own explanations about language and literacy development first. In this way, you are likely to be more critical in relation to the established theories with your own perspective.

My hope in doing the above is to help you form the habit of asking questions about what you see and do in your classroom, make an effort to explain the reasons behind the linguistic behaviors of your students, and plan your supporting strategies more thoughtfully.

Situating language and literacy development in students' cognitive and social development

Language and literacy development are not an isolated domain in human development. Instead, they are influenced by the development in other areas such as biological, cognitive, and social. Although in this book it is not possible to address all these areas due to space limitation, the cognitive and social developmental profile in a specific developmental period is discussed before the language and literacy development in that period is examined. The purpose is to remind you that you need to take into consideration your students' cognitive and social developmental characteristics at a given period when examining their language and literacy development to provide appropriate instructional support for them.

Your Turn

Seven-year-old Ben has trouble understanding the meaning of "Jonny is feeling *blue*." Do you think his limitation in appreciating the figurative use of the word *blue* can be explained only by looking at his language development? If not, what other developmental areas/domains do you need to consider? Make a list of the developmental domains (such as physical/neurological, cognitive, and social domains) that Ben needs to develop in order to understand the figurative meaning of *blue*. How does this exercise suggest the relationship between language development and biological, cognitive, and social development?

Teaching across ages

There is a general belief among educators that they teach students at their specific grade level or specific age groups, that is, high school teachers teach students at the high school level, elementary teachers teach children at the elementary level, and preschool teachers teach young children. A case in point is Peter, who thought his ninth graders should function academically as typical 14 and 15 year olds. However, in a diverse classroom environment, a learner may have reached a given **chronological age** (the amount of time that has elapsed since birth), but does not function at a given **developmental age** (a typical chronological age at which a student can perform a skill in a given area), and **language age** (the language ability and skills demonstrated at a certain age) (Gillam and Gillam, 2011). Some students at middle or high school level may still function at the elementary literacy level and some elementary children may perform at a higher age level. Therefore, regardless of what grade level you teach, you need to be knowledgeable about the language and literacy strategies for younger or older students. Teachers who teach younger students need to have a long-term goal for them, know what language and literacy skills their students will develop down the road, and begin to build those skills accordingly. Teachers who teach older students need to know the strategies for younger students because some of your students may not have developed literacy skills at the middle or high school level and you may have to use the strategies for younger children to help them.

Your Turn

- Amanda, a 17-year-old high-school student, has cognitive difficulties. Although she seems to speak quite well, she reads at the first-grade level. She also has a basic phonological processing issue. For example, she has trouble recognizing words such as *pine* and *mango*. How would you teach Amanda whose literacy level is far behind her chronological age and current grade level?
- Brian, a nine-year-old fourth grade student, is gifted. He reads at the level for eighth graders and performs math at the level for ninth graders. He often feels bored in class. How would you move Brian forward in his academic learning? Propose some ideas.

Treating language and literacy as an interrelated process

Language and literacy are closely related. The development of language and literacy should be considered complementary to each other rather than as two separate entities, although language and literacy do have their differences (e.g., spoken language in its early acquisition period is not formally taught, and literacy often needs to be explicitly taught). Research has shown that children's language skills influence their literacy skills in a significant way. For example, the properties of spoken words such as stresses in English, syllables in French and **morae** in Japanese (a mora is the basic timing unit in Japanese) are closely associated with written language processing (Wang,

Yang, and Cheng, 2009). A student's knowledge established in oral language, such as **phonological awareness** (the awareness of the sound structure of a given language), is closely linked to the student's ability to read. In this book, the development of **oracy** (oral language knowledge and skills) is treated as importantly as literacy.

Focusing on academic language and academic literacy

Academic language is the language used in school to learn content in various subject areas. Unlike everyday social language that students use, academic language is more purposeful and precise (E. Johnson, 2009). In everyday **social language**, you often hear students using words and sentences that are vague and imprecise such as *stuff* and *things*, "*They told me to do it*," "*The soda is better*; *I like it more*" (Costa, 2009). However, academic language must be used accurately to define terms, form concepts, and construct knowledge.

There are two types of academic languages: content language and general academic language. **Content language** provides essential building blocks from which conceptual knowledge can be built. The more a student understands the specific content language of a particular subject matter, the faster and more efficiently they can gain additional knowledge. Each subject area has its own unique academic language demands placed on students. These specific language demands set each content area apart from other disciplines and make each discipline unique. For example, *fraction*, *angle*, and *factor* are often used in mathematics; *photosynthesis*, *compound*, and *force* are frequently seen in science; *democracy*, *civilization*, and *legislation* usually occur in social studies; and *alliteration*, *plot*, *genre*, and *theme* are routinely used in language arts.

General academic language provides a foundation for educational success and can be applied to every content area. The words in general academic language such as *estimate*, *reduce*, *analyze*, *hypothesize*, and *conceptualize* act like mortar (E. Johnson, 2009). These words hold and bind specific content-area language and concepts together within the minds of students. General academic language helps students cement the building blocks of specific content language into conceptual knowledge. The words in academic language connect concepts, outline transitions, and demonstrate relationships. Developing academic language requires students to engage in abstract actions and to organize complex concepts. For these reasons, it is apparent why academic language is cognitively challenging for all learners (E. Johnson, 2009).

Moreover, academic language is the important groundwork for **academic literacy** (e.g., reading, writing, critical skills used to understand and analyze school subjects). Academic literacy is different from everyday literacy (for example, writing a letter, email or text to a friend). Academic literacy requires a more advanced level of cognitive function. To be able to do well in academic learning, students must be able to accurately express and justify their ideas and solutions. It is a known fact that the major cause of the academic gap between students, especially students from different socioeconomic groups, is the academic language and literacy gap (Hirsch, 2003; E. Johnson, 2009). If our students are going to meet the literacy demands of an increasingly global environment in the twenty-first century, they must master academic language and literacy (Wong-Fillmore, 2007). Therefore, this book provides supporting strategies to help students develop academic language and literacy, aiming to close the achievement gap between students with different backgrounds and abilities.

It is important to stress that focusing on academic language and literacy does not mean downplaying the everyday social language and everyday literacy. In fact, in later chapters, you will read about their significance in overall language and literacy development. However, as the alarming statistics from the Center for Educational Statistics show, our students as a whole are not doing very well in academic literacy. That is why we need to emphasize the support in this area because it takes a lot more time and effort to develop academic language and literacy abilities.

Your Turn

- Record a conversation during student recess and a classroom discussion and make a list of the words and sentences used in the two settings. Compare a text in a subject area and students' email and text message samples and make a list of the words and sentences used in the two genres. What have you found? Based on your findings, discuss whether every day social language and everyday literacy such as emails, text messages, and recess conversation can naturally lead to academic language and literacy development. Provide rationales to support your argument.
- Locate a text in a specific grade and in a specific subject. Identify the language demand in this text in terms of words and sentences. Discuss how these words and sentences affect a student's learning of the content.

Linking language and literacy development to identity and motivation

Motivation is an important factor in developing language and literacy (Wang, 2011a), especially for students who are learning the school language as a new language and for students who are facing language-learning difficulties. Furthermore, language and identity develop concurrently; it is not an exaggeration to state that the acquisition of a language is also the acquisition of one's identity. When students identify with school language in a positive way, they may do well in learning that language.

Therefore, supporting strategies are introduced to help you motivate your students for academic language and literacy learning, and at the same time promote their positive identity development.

Valuing different language acquisition experiences

This book also widens the language acquisition experiences by including various language acquisition circumstances, such as children who acquire more than one first language from birth or during early childhood (**multilingual first language acquisition**), children who learn a new language after they have already developed their first language (**new language acquisition**), children who acquire a manual language as a first language (**sign language acquisition**), and children whose language acquisition is compromised as a result of various disabilities. Considering different language acquisition experiences will help you see how your students started their language journey, the circumstances under which they acquired their language(s), and how their academic performance is influenced by their earlier different experiences.

Providing various linguistic experiences

Ideally, all teachers need to have experiences in learning other languages. Realistically, this is often not realized (unfortunately). However, a teacher's knowledge about his or her students' language background is useful (particularly in a linguistically diverse classroom). Throughout the book, you are given some exercises to develop basic knowledge about other languages. For example, in Chapter 2, when discussing the different writing systems, you are asked to research on the internet the different writing systems and get the basic information about these systems, and in Chapter 4, you are asked to research and compare Spanish and English *flaps*, *trills*, *affricates*, and *glides* (don't worry about these terms now; you will be introduced to them later. However, if you want to have a head start, go ahead and check them out). Little by little, you will become less ignorant about other linguistic systems. The information you accumulate will not make you speak these languages, but it will make you more knowledgeable when planning your instruction and helping your students with different linguistic backgrounds.

Your Turn

Thirteen-year-old Jeremy came to the United States two years ago from the People's Republic of China. He seems to be fine with his English speech communication in general. One thing his classmates noticed, however, is that he is often confused in using the pronouns "he" and "she." Find out what is the reason for Jeremy's confusion by conducting online research or asking a Chinese speaker.

Note on developmental stages

There are different ways to distinguish developmental stages. This book will divide the developmental stages into infancy and early childhood (birth to age 5), middle childhood (age 6 to age 11), and adolescence (age 12 to age 18). The rationale for dividing the age range in this way is to make clear the specific language and literacy supporting strategies relevant to early childhood, elementary, middle, and high school settings. Further, dividing the developmental stages in this way allows us to see the qualitative differences in language acquisition and learning at different ages. If children are exposed to one or more than one language before age 5, the acquisition process is regarded as first language acquisition, and after that, the process is treated as new language acquisition (traditionally referred to as second language acquisition or additional language acquisition). Unless new research proves it otherwise, the current evidence seems to indicate that the quality of language acquisition appears to be different before and after age 5 (see more discussions in Chapters 4, 7 and 10).

Overview of the Book

This book is organized in five parts according to the contents. At the end of each part, a language sample (either a speech or a writing sample of a child or student) is provided to help you apply the information you read and deepen your understanding of the reading materials.

Part I includes Chapters 1 and 2. Chapter 1 emphasizes the importance of teacher knowledge on language and literacy development and its impact on student content area learning. It introduces critical discourse analysis (CDA) as a guiding framework and transformative pedagogy (TP) as an instructional and assessment approach to help you reconceptualize the way you teach diverse students. It explores the evolving definition of literacy and its significance in the twenty-first century. It also discusses how the labels that you use to describe your students with different linguistic abilities can influence the way you interact with them. These reconceptualizations are highlighted to help you holistically view the complex elements involved in student language and literacy development and their relationship to subject content area learning.

Chapter 2 foregrounds the intricacies involved in the process of developing language and literacy. It discusses what it means to be a language and literacy learner in different socioeconomic, cultural, linguistic, and developmental circumstances. Further, this chapter analyzes the complex factors that influence language and literacy developmental outcomes among different learners, and suggests how the consequences of the varieties of language and literacy development can affect the academic learning of children.

Part II is comprised of Chapters 3, 4, and 5. Chapter 3 describes the language and literacy developmental characteristics of children with typical development during early childhood. You are informed about the crucial language abilities children need for developing emergent literacy skills. In addition, emergent digital-mediated skills and emergent critical literacy skills are identified as necessary literacy skills. Supporting strategies are suggested on how to choose stimulating language and literacy materials and design engaging activities.

Chapter 4 discusses the unique language and emergent literacy developmental characteristics of children who acquire more than one first language during the early childhood period. It addresses the complex factors involved in multilingual first language acquisition. Recommendations are made on how to support multilingual and emergent multiliteracy development.

Chapter 5 addresses the distinctive language and literacy development characteristics of children with language impairment during early childhood. Special attention is given to the children whose language and emergent literacy abilities can be improved with the support of parents and early childhood educators, such as children with autism, Down syndrome, sensory impairment, and specific language impairment. In addition, multilingual children with various language impairments are also discussed. Supporting strategies are proposed to help these children maximize their learning potential.

Part III contains Chapters 6, 7, and 8. Chapter 6 focuses on the language and literacy developmental characteristics in middle childhood. It addresses the essential language and literacy skills that children of elementary school age need to develop in order to function well in their academic learning. Effective strategies that incorporate language and literacy into subject-area learning are provided to ensure students' simultaneous development in academic literacy, multimedia literacy, and critical literacy.

Chapter 7 examines the language and literacy developmental characteristics of students who learn English as a new language (Ln) during middle childhood. It focuses on the unique challenges of Ln learners. Recommendations are made on how to help Ln learners develop academic language and literacy by incorporating their cultural and linguistic funds of knowledge.

Chapter 8 touches upon the language and literacy development characteristics of children with language impairment (LI) during middle childhood. Discussion focus is on how to assist students with LI in subject-area learning and how to help them maximize their learning potential.

Part IV consists of Chapters 9, 10, and 11. Chapter 9 identifies the language and literacy developmental characteristics during adolescence. It suggests how to motivate adolescents to continue with their language and literacy development when they are undergoing many changes in their lives. It offers useful strategies that aim to facilitate the development of self-motivated language and literacy learning behaviors. It also recommends literacy materials and activities that can foster sustainable interests in furthering language and literacy development throughout students' lives.

Chapter 10 concentrates on the language and literacy developmental characteristics of adolescents who learn English as a Ln during adolescence. It discusses the unique characteristics of learning a Ln later in life. Recommendations are made on how to help Ln learning adolescents develop academic language and literacy by using their cultural and linguistic resources.

Chapter 11 gives attention to the language and literacy developmental characteristics of adolescents with LI. Special attention is given to assisting adolescents with LI in developing academic language and literacy. Suggestions are made to help these students maximize their potential.

Part V consists of Chapters 12 and an exit self-evaluation. Chapter 12 introduces some important theoretical perspectives about how language and literacy are acquired in different populations. These theories serve three major functions: to help you predict what may happen in in the process of children's language and literacy development, to explain their language and literacy development distinctions, and to help you become more confident in evaluating your students' language and literature performances.

In the exit self-evaluation, you are asked to complete a self-assessment by examining a writing sample of a student. You are asked to demonstrate whether you know how to apply the CDA framework as well as the big "D" and little "d" analyses[4] to the student's work and whether you know how to use TP to help the student move forward in his or her language and literacy development. Through the exit evaluation, you are asked to confirm the belief that every student can learn with the right support, and you are encouraged to use this book as a starting point to continue to inform yourself as a teaching professional and to help your students grow.

Key Terms

academic language

academic literacy

chronological age

content language

developmental age

general academic language

language age

morae

oracy

phonological awareness

Program for International Student Assessment (PISA)

multilingual first language acquisition (MLFLA)

new language acquisition

social language

Notes

1. The Program(me) for International Student Assessment (PISA) is a worldwide study by the Organization for Economic Cooperation and Development (OECD) in member and nonmember nations of 15-year-old school pupils' scholastic performance on mathematics, science, and reading. It was first administered in 2000 and then repeated every three years. Its purpose is to help improve education outcomes.
2. ERIC stands for Education Resources Information Center. It is an online library of education research and information sponsored by the Institute of Education Sciences of the US Department of Education.
3. PsycINFO is an abstracting and indexing database with more than 3 million records devoted to peer-reviewed literature in the behavioral sciences and mental health from 1800 to the present.
4. The little "d" (discourse) means the discourse in its usual sense such as phonology, lexicon, semantics, morphology, and syntax in conversations or writings. The big "D" (Discourse) focuses on the analysis that is beyond the little "d." More will be addressed in Chapter 12.

Part I

Introduction

Part I includes two chapters, chapter 1 and chapter 2. The topics addressed in these two chapters lay a foundation for the rest of the book. Careful reading of the content will help you understand the importance of teacher knowledge regarding language and literacy and its relevance to teaching diverse learners. It will also help you become cognizant of the various complex factors that influence students' language and literacy development.

After finishing this part, you will have an opportunity to analyze a writing sample of a student by applying the information you read. You will learn how to use the critical discourse analysis (CDA) conceptual framework and the transformative pedagogy (TP) approach to help you put your students' language and literacy errors in perspective and turn their mistakes into teaching opportunities.

Essential Questions for Part I

- On what basis should a teacher make instructional decisions?
- Should "what works best for the individual student is the best pedagogy" be the motto for education?
- How can we reconceptualize literacy development in the digital age?
- How can the education process help students with various cultural, linguistic, and intellectual variations achieve language development potential and ultimately academic potential?

Understanding Language and Literacy Development: Diverse Learners in the Classroom, First Edition. Xiao-lei Wang.
© 2015 John Wiley & Sons, Inc. Published 2015 by John Wiley & Sons, Inc.
Companion website: www.wiley.com/go/wang/langandlit

1
Working with Diverse Students
Some Important Issues

Prereading Questions and Activities

The questions and activities listed in the beginning of each chapter throughout the book are meant to help you think about the important issues addressed in a given chapter. It is likely that you may not be able to answer or complete them fully. Nevertheless, by trying your best to reflect on the questions and carry out the activities, you will be more critical about what you will read.

- After reading Peter's challenges in the chapter "About the Book" (Box 0.1), you were asked to give him some suggestions. If you were able to provide suggestions, how do you know they would work? If you found it difficult to provide suggestions for Peter, what could be the reason? Would you feel more confident providing suggestions for Peter if you had sufficient information on the students' cultural, linguistic, and developmental backgrounds?
- What is your own definition of literacy? Do you think that how you define literacy will influence what you choose to emphasize in teaching your content area? Why or why not?
- What is in a label? Why are labels used to describe different student populations important for educators? Do you think the label you use to describe a student will affect the way you interact with that student? Why?
- Do you know what conceptual frameworks are? If not, research them. Do you have any experience in using a framework to guide you to do something? If so, what is the advantage of having a conceptual framework?

Topics to Be Addressed in This Chapter

- Importance of teacher knowledge of language and literacy development
- Critical discourse analysis (CDA) conceptual framework

Understanding Language and Literacy Development: Diverse Learners in the Classroom, First Edition. Xiao-lei Wang.
© 2015 John Wiley & Sons, Inc. Published 2015 by John Wiley & Sons, Inc.
Companion website: www.wiley.com/go/wang/langandlit

- Transformative pedagogy (TP)
- Evolving definition of literacy
- Reconceptualization of labels for diverse learners

Learning Objectives

After reading this chapter, you should be able to do the following:

- Understand the importance of teacher knowledge on language and literacy development in effective instruction.
- Become familiar with the CDA framework and TP and understand the advantage of using them to work with diverse students.
- Know that the words you choose to describe your students can influence your attitude toward and interaction with them, and exercise extra caution when using words and labels for diverse students.

Importance of Teacher Knowledge on Language and Literacy

Box 1.1 Peter's Challenge – Understanding the Nature of Student Language Difficulties

Two weeks after Peter had his first encounters with his Period 2 geometry class, the guidance counselor sent him an initial report from a language specialist regarding one of his students, Andrea. Andrea was not yet officially classified as a student with a particular kind of language impairment. However, since he came to the school district two years ago from Albania, he had had persistent difficulties in academic learning. He was referred to the specialist at the end of eighth grade. The report came to the high school counselor recently, and it contains some of the following information: "Student shows signs of dysgraphia … He has trouble organizing his thoughts … He seems to have impaired phonological memory … He has trouble understanding and producing complex syntax … He also exhibits difficulties in finite verb morphology …"

Peter read this report several times; he still did not understand some of the terminologies used by the specialist. What frustrated him most was that he had no clue how to provide specific instructional support for Andrea in his geometry class based on these linguistic and cognitive issues reported by the specialist. If he had to wait for the official disability classification report, the development of an **Individualized Educational Program** (IEP), and the assistance from a special education teacher, Andrea would fall further behind …

Peter is between a rock and a hard place. He is supposed to teach ninth grade math, yet the issues that he has to deal with in Andrea's case are far beyond his content area. To be able to help Andrea move forward in geometry learning, Peter must have sufficient knowledge of Andrea's linguistic and cognitive characteristics and know how to provide effective strategies to support him in learning the math content. This is indeed the challenge of teaching diverse students in the inclusive classroom environment.

However, if Peter were knowledgeable about Andrea's linguistic characteristics in the specialist's report, he would have an inkling of Andrea's condition; that is, he might have specific language impairment (SLI). He would have more effectively addressed Andrea's specific issues and utilized some of the instructional strategies recommended for students with SLI such as focusing on developing Andrea's skills in comprehending and producing complex sentences (which are prominent in academic texts; in this case, math reading materials). He could do this by modeling how complex sentence are used and scaffolding Andrea to recast the modeled complex sentences in his own production. Peter's experience reminds us that teachers must develop in-depth knowledge of their students' language and literacy development regardless of what content area they teach. There are at least three important reasons to do so.

Interpreting assessment results from specialist reports

As shown clearly in Peter's case, teachers need to have the ability to interpret specialists' reports and utilize the information to help their students learn. Reports from specialists often include language and literacy assessment results that contain terminologies about students' linguistic characteristics such as phonological abilities, fast naming, phonological memory, letter knowledge, alphabetic principle, sight word knowledge, pseudo word decoding, orthographic ability, morphosyntactic knowledge, and metalinguistic awareness. (Don't worry about these terms at this moment; you will know them after reading this book.) If teachers do not understand the relationships between these skills and the role each of these skills plays in students' learning, they are unlikely to help their students succeed in the content-area learning.

Identifying students' linguistic needs

In addition to knowing how to interpret the assessment results from specialists, teachers need to develop abilities to identify their students' linguistic difficulties and needs, and know how to address them in instruction and assessment. To simply wait for the specialist's assistance will not meet students' immediate learning needs (e.g., Soodak, 2003).

In the classroom environment, students need to have proficient language and literacy skills to function well in various content areas. In other words, language and literacy skills are the basis for content learning. Often, when students have difficulties learning a content area, they are also likely to have difficulties processing information (for example, being unable to comprehend what the teacher says or what is written in the text). Research in the past few decades clearly indicates that learners with linguistic processing difficulties often have challenges in processing meaning from texts efficiently. Most students who are identified with learning disabilities also have reading disabilities (e.g., Kavale and Forness, 1985). Thus, teacher knowledge of language and literacy development is crucial to improving students' academic performances in any content area.

Moreover, teachers' knowledge of their students' linguistic characteristics matters greatly in how they can provide focused instruction. There is clear evidence that students with difficulties in reading, for example, can significantly benefit from teachers' **intentional teaching**[1] (Moats and Foorman, 2003; Moats and Lyon, 1996). Even students with good literacy skills make rapid progress with teachers' intentional instruction (Moats, 1994). There is also evidence that when teachers are trained and have mastered specific linguistic knowledge, the reading scores of the students taught by these teachers also increase (e.g., McCutchen et al., 2002; Moats and Foorman, 2003; Spear-Swerling and Brucker, 2003) and reading comprehension improves (Carreker et al., 2007). If you are a teacher who wants to make a serious difference in students like Andrea, you must make efforts to understand their language and literacy developmental characteristics and know how to respond to their challenges in your content area instruction.

Meeting teacher education professional standards

Peter's inability in providing effective instructional support for students like Andrea draws attention to the problems in teacher education. It is a commonly recognized fact that many teacher education programs have not prepared teacher candidates well in knowing how to provide effective instructional support to help their students improve language and literacy skills (e.g., Bos et al., 2011; Joshi et al., 2009; Moats and Lyon, 1996; Moats, 1994). In response to this situation, many teacher education professional organizations now require teacher candidates to be efficient in their knowledge of students' language and literacy development. Some education professional standards also require language and literacy to be taught across the curriculum such as the Common Core State Standards (http://www.corestandards.org) adopted by 45 states. Moreover, the edTPA (Teacher Performance Assessment), which is now required by many states for obtaining teaching certification, asks for teachers to demonstrate competence in modeling academic language use in their classroom teaching (http://edtpa.aacte.org/about-edtpa).

Given these three reasons, teachers in any content area must develop knowledge and skills to be successful in teaching students with a range of abilities.

Your Turn

- Can you find *more* reasons why teachers need to have knowledge of their students' language and literacy development?
- It is a common misconception that teachers who teach math will not have much problem with students' issues related to language and literacy because math is a universal language. What is your take on this misconception? How do you address this misconception in reference to the Common Core State Standards (http://www.corestandards.org)?

- Locate a language assessment report of a student who has been identified as having a specific kind of language impairment and try to interpret it. What questions do you have?
- Identify 20 difficult words and complex sentences from a textbook in any subject area (you can decide a grade level). Discuss how these words and sentences can affect students' understanding of the content.
- Research the learning and teaching standards in your state and discuss how you can meet these standards by adding your knowledge on language and literacy development.
- Familiarize yourself with the Common Core State Standards (http://www.corestandards.org) and the edTPA (http://edtpa.aacte.org/about-edtpa). Identify the areas that require teacher knowledge of their students' language and literacy development.

Critical Discourse Analysis Conceptual Framework

In order to respond to the complexity of students with different cultural and linguistic backgrounds and abilities, it is important to have an overarching **conceptual framework** that can guide your instructional and assessment practices. A conceptual framework is like a road map or a compass that can point you in a general direction without getting sidetracked. In other words, with a general direction, you tend to be more focused on the important issues related to teaching diverse learners, and you do not waste time doing irrelevant things. Moreover, a conceptual framework can provide you with a basis to think about what you do and what it means. It can also assist you to connect and organize all related important ideas and to make these ideas easy to articulate. The advantage of having a framework is that it can help you predict the outcome of your actions, explain your rationale, become confident in your teaching, and minimize the impact the "trial and error" and "play by ear" practices tend to have at the expense of student learning.

The important conceptual framework used to guide your understanding of diverse language and literacy development and to direct you in working with diverse students is **critical discourse analysis** (CDA). CDA is based on the writings of many prominent and influential thinkers such as Norman Fairclough, Gunther Kress, and James Paul Gee. It is beyond the scope of this book to review the work that leads to CDA. For important literature on CDA, please refer to the recommended further readings at the end of this chapter. CDA is an interdisciplinary approach to the study of language and literacy, and it is particularly relevant to teaching diverse students. The appeal of CDA is that it is highly sensitive to cultures and classroom variations. This framework views language and literacy not as an isolated cognitive behavior, but as a form of social practice. It utilizes a learner's existing **funds of knowledge**[2] as resources of teaching and learning. It focuses on the ways social and political domination are reproduced by text and talk; that is, discourse is always tied to status and power relations, and it helps students develop critical thinking abilities. The essence of CDA is that it encourages teachers to analyze not only what is present in what students say and write, but also what is left out (e.g., Rogers, 2011), and that it encourages teachers to build a human relation with students and their families, to learn from their students, and to discover the resources students bring to the classroom so that students can be empowered to learn (Powell and Rightmyer, 2011).

Your Turn

- Some have criticized the CDA framework and referred to it as a chimera (i.e., something that is hopeful but impossible to achieve) (Edwards, 2010, p. 26). What is your take on this criticism based on what you have read so far? If you think that the CDA framework will not work in a diverse classroom, what is your alternative proposal to reach diverse learners?
- Comment on the following statement: "To become truly effective educators, we must 're-invent' ourselves as teachers. We must value the cultural knowledge of our students and families, and learn from those we serve" (Powell and Rightmyer, 2011, p. 5).
- Interview a student and fill out the following information:

  Student age
  Student grade
  Student gender
  Student developmental ability/level
  Student academic performance status
  Student ethnicity/race
  Student linguistic background
  Student hobbies and strengths (e.g., what the student does well)
  Number of siblings
  Number of people in the household
  Family print-related environment (e.g., Does the family have books and newspapers
      around? Does the student have internet access?)
  Parent education level
  Parent profession
  Parent ethnicity/race
  Parent cultural origin
  Other (include more information about the student and his or her family)

  Based on your interview, compile a profile about this student. What does this student's profile tell you about this student? Especially, what kinds of funds of knowledge does this student bring to academic learning?
- Discuss why understanding your students can help you empower them in their learning.

Transformative Pedagogy

A pedagogy that supports the CDA practice in diverse classrooms is **transformative pedagogy** (TP). The fulcrum of TP is that education has the potential to transform or change an individual over time. No matter what language and literacy backgrounds or abilities students have when they enter schools, the educational experiences they get in school should facilitate the achievement of their full potential. TP contains four important elements: situated practice, overt instruction, critical framing, and transformed practice (New London Group, 1996).

Situated practice stresses that knowledge should build on students' experiences in real-world contexts, not in an isolated environment (e.g., Lave and Wenger, 1991). Teachers need to help students make intuitive links with their prior knowledge (e.g., funds of knowledge) and lead them to the new topics (Mills, 2010). Learners do not learn well if learning activities are not meaningful to them and if they are not motivated. Therefore, effective teaching must consider the affective and sociocultural needs and identities of all learners (New London Group, 1996).

Your Turn

Support or dispute the following quote by using a concrete example.

> human knowledge, when it is applicable to practice, is primarily situated in socio-cultural settings and heavily contextualized in specific knowledge domains and practices. Such knowledge is inextricably tied to the ability to recognize and act on patterns of data and experiences, a process that is acquired only through experience, since the requisite patterns are often heavily tied and adjusted to context, and are, very often, subtle and complex enough that no one can fully and usefully describe or explicate them. Humans are, at this level, contextual and sociocultural "pattern recognizors" and actors. Such pattern reorganization underlies the ability to act flexibly and adaptably in context, that is, mastery in practice.

New London Group, "A pedagogy of multiliteracies: designing social futures," *Harvard Educational Review*, 66(1) (1996): 60–92.

However, situated practice is only the starting point of TP. If learners are left only at the stage of situated practice, school subject knowledge will not be obtained effectively. The New London Group (1996) expressed several concerns regarding situated practice. First, even though the immersion of learners in rich contexts can lead to knowledge mastery, learners vary significantly from each other in their experiences and some may even pursue "wrong" leads in their contexts. Second, much of the context immersion early in life such as that surrounding language acquisition is possible largely due to human biology and maturation in conjunction with adult socialization. However, in the school environment, context immersion alone is not enough to acquire academic language and literacy; learners must be taught overtly. Third, situated practice does not necessarily lead to conscious control of what one knows and does. Fourth, situated practice does not automatically make learners critique what they are learning in terms of historical, cultural, political, ideological, and value aspects. Finally, situated practice will not guarantee that learners will put their knowledge into action. Learners may be able to articulate their knowledge in words; they may not be capable of enacting their knowledge in practice.

Thus, it is clear that situated practice must be co-practiced with the other components (i.e., overt teaching, critical framing, and transformative practice) to ensure authentic learning.

Your Turn

Reflect how you acquired your first language(s) and your school language (academic language). Discuss the different nature of the supports you receive from your parents (at home) and your teachers (in school) as well as the different learning contexts.

Overt instruction guides students by using explicit instruction. It is different from teacher-centered direct instruction (which merely transmits knowledge from an expert to a novice). In contrast, overt instruction provides explicit instruction that can most usefully guide the learners' practice through utilizing students' funds of knowledge and scaffolding (Mills, 2010). Effective overt instruction must be enacted concurrently with other TP elements in a seamless way rather than as separated components (New London Group, 1996).

Your Turn

Compare an example of traditional direct teaching and an example of overt teaching. Discuss the differences in terms of students' learning.

Critical framing encourages students to interpret the social contexts and the meaning associated with texts. It encourages learners to explore alternative ways to read texts, to second-guess them, and to question the motives of the author. According to the New London Group (1996), the goal of critical framing is to help students to frame their growing mastery in practice (from situated practice) and gain conscious control and understanding (from overt instruction) based on the various perspectives (e.g., historical, social, cultural, political, ideological). Most importantly, teachers must help students to denaturalize and make strange again what they have learned and mastered. In this way, students can gain the necessary personal and theoretical distance from what they have learned and constructively critique it, and go on to the next step (transformative practice).

Your Turn

Read the following quote and discuss why it is important to include the component of critical framing in the teaching and learning process:

the claim "DNA" replicates itself framed within biology is obvious and "true." Framed within another discourse in the following way, it becomes less natural and less "true.": Put some DNA in some water in a glass on a table. It certainly will not replicate itself, it will just sit there. Organisms replicate themselves using DNA as a code, but that code is put into effect by an array of machinery involving proteins. In many of our academic and Western discourses, we have privileged information and mind over materials, practice, and work. The original claim foregrounds information and code and leaves out, or backgrounds, machinery and work. This foregrounding and backgrounding becomes apparent only when we reframe, when we take the sentence out of its "home" discourse and place it in a wider context. Here, the wider context is actual processes and material practices, not just general statements in a disciplinary theory…

New London Group, "A pedagogy of multiliteracies: designing social futures," *Harvard Educational Review*, 66(1) (1996): 60–92.

Transformed practice means that true learning transpires when students not only draw on their life, cultural, and community resources (situated practice), use knowledge appropriately (through overt instruction), and know how to critique what they have learned (critical framing), but also demonstrate a significant level of creativity and innovation and are able to put meaning to work in other contexts and to transfer existing meanings to design new meanings (Mills, 2010). According to the New London Group (1996), the key in transformative practice includes three aspects: juxtaposition, integration, and tension. It used the following example to illustrate the three aspects:

imagine a student having to act and think like a biologist, and at the same time as a biologist with a vested interest in resisting the depiction of female things – from eggs to organisms – as "passive." The student now has to both juxtapose and integrate (not without tension) two different discourses, or social identities, or "interests" that have historically been at odds.

Your Turn

Read the following quote and identify the elements of juxtaposition, integration, and tension.

how can one be a "real" lawyer and, at the same time, have one's performance influenced by being an African American. In his arguments before the U.S. Supreme Court for desegregating schools, Thurgood Marshall did this in a classic way. And, in mixing the discourse of politics with the discourse of African American religion.

New London Group, "A pedagogy of multiliteracies: designing social futures," *Harvard Educational Review*, 66(1) (1996): 60–92

With the guidance of CDA and the practice of TP, you will have a better chance of reaching diverse learners in your classroom by taking advantage of their funds of knowledge and by better motivating them to learn school literacy. Most importantly, you are likely to turn challenges into teaching opportunities and maximize your students' learning potential. Box 1.2 suggests the important components in implementing CDA and TP in your classroom teaching. You will have opportunities to apply them later in the book.

Box 1.2   Important Components in Implementing CDA and TP

- Discover your students' strengths, talents, funds of knowledge, and learning needs through a variety of methods such as observations, conversations, interviews, visiting families, talking to parents, and personal stories. Provide opportunities for them to demonstrate their funds of knowledge.
- Build on their funds of knowledge; provide responsive instructional support to meet your students' learning needs through situated practice, overt teaching, critical framing, and transformative practice.
- Help your students transform their learning by juxtaposing and integrating both their funds of knowledge and newly acquired knowledge.

(At this moment, these components may look abstract. Do not worry; you will have more opportunities later to develop the ability to use them.)

Your Turn

- Propose one concrete classroom instructional or assessment strategy for each of the four components in TP and share your strategies with your classmates (Note: be prepared to explain why you think your strategies will work.)
- Collect a student's writing sample in a content area and try to analyze it with the steps suggested in Box 1.2 and then try to propose some instructional strategies by using the four components in TP. Discuss why this kind of practice may empower students.

Evolving Definition of Literacy

The word "literacy" has taken on new connotations in the twenty-first century. Traditionally, literacy has been regarded mainly as the ability to read and write. As times have changed, the definition has also begun to shift from its narrow focus to encompass a range of other important areas. First, it is now generally agreed that literacy is a social and cultural practice rather than a context-free cognitive achievement (e.g., Diaz and Makin, 2002; Larson and Marsh, 2003; Street and Lefstein, 2007), and the beliefs of a culture and its **habitus** (the lens through which people interpret and relate to the world) play a central role in students' literacy development process and their approach to academic learning.

Your Turn

Select an article about a "controversial" issue and ask your students to discuss it (if possible, video- or audio-record the conversation). Observe the different habitus your students bring into the debate and discuss how your students' different habitus shape their approaches to literacy learning, including academic learning.

Second, the rapid development of information and multimedia technology has extended the meaning of literacy to a wider range of elements (e.g., visual, auditory, and spatial) than written words alone (New London Group, 1996). As Mills (2010) rightly points out, we are experiencing "a broader historical shift from textual culture of print, to one in which the visual mode is salient, assisted by novel technologies ..." A case in point: even the famous *Encyclopaedia Britannica* is now going out of print after 244 years and has changed to an online-only version with multimedia components (Bosman, 2012).

Reading and writing on the internet and through multimedia modality (**hypertext**) requires different ways of interacting with texts. When reading through multimedia, readers move away from the narrow, linear, print-only expectations of reading to a multidimensional and interactive context (Sutherland-Smith, 2002).

Your Turn

Observe a child's (student's) reading in the multimedia mode (e.g., surfing the internet) and in the conventional print mode (print text). Compare his or her reading characteristics in the two modes. What have you found?

Third, language is a social construct and never neutral (Freire, 1983). The texts students read are positioned. This means that writers shape texts based on their **positioning** (where they are in the world and where they are standing and how this position enables them to see and not see). A writer's positioning includes many aspects such as their beliefs, values, attitudes, social positions (e.g., age, race, class, and ethnicity), and experiences (e.g., education, languages, and travel) (Janks, 2014). Because a writer's positioning may be different from a reader's positioning, it is very crucial for students to develop critical literacy ability. **Critical literacy**, the ability to critique texts in different formats, to challenge the status quo, and to question authorities has been widely recognized as just as essential as the ability to decode texts (Kim, 2012; Stevens and Bean, 2007). With the easy access to information, students' ability to critique texts is ever more important, and critical literacy should be a part of every student's literacy pathway (Martello, 2002).

Your Turn

Read a fairy tale such as "Snow White" and ask yourself the following questions:

- What position does the writer construct for each of the characters?
- Which character does the writer want you to side with?
- How well does the writer use language to make an emotional impact on you as a reader?
- If you are asked to rewrite this story, what will you change based on your positioning?
- How does this exercise help you see the writer's positioning and your own positioning? What is the significance in identifying your own positioning in reading and learning?

As our society and technology keep moving forward, it is likely that the definition of literacy will continue to change. Thinking of literacy as an evolving concept encourages you to negotiate the digitalization of print in the classroom, school, and society. Treating literacy as an evolving concept also allows you to see cultural and linguistic diversity as a valuable resource for engaging students in new digital media, not as consumers, but as critical and creative producers so that students with different backgrounds and abilities can draw from a broader range of resources for making meaning.

In essence, being literate in today's society means being able to engage in a range of literacy practices and drawing on different sets of skills in different domains. Not being able to negotiate diverse modes of literacies will certainly prevent students from accessing a full array of choices.

Your Turn

Explain why the word "literacies" is used instead of the word "literacy."

Reconceptualization of the Labels for Diverse Students

The well-known German philosopher Hans-Georg Gadamer once cautioned us to be very careful in choosing our words. Whenever you use a word, don't use it lightly. You are not just using any tool that you could throw away when you are finished with it. On the contrary, you are positioning yourselves in a direction of thinking that precedes you and proceeds beyond you. Gadamer's advice contains two important messages. First, our words carry us as we think and express ourselves. Second, it is a worthwhile exercise and discipline to listen to our words, think about what we do with them, and contemplate what they do to us (Gadamer, 1993). If the kinds of words we use do influence our perception and action as Gadamer suggested, then teachers need to be extra cautious in using accurate and positive terms to describe their diverse students. Below are a few commonly used labels that warrant scrutiny.

Second language learners vs new language learners

Frequently, students who are learning a school language other than their heritage language or home language are labeled as second language learners (L2), such as English as a second language (ESL). In this book, these learners are generally referred to as **new language learners** (Ln learners). L2 learners will be used only when we are sure that the students we refer to are indeed learning English as a second language. The use of the general term Ln instead of L2 reflects the nature of many students' language learning experiences; that is, they are learning English not as a second language, but as a third or even as a fourth language. Although learning a second language may share similar characteristics with learning a third or fourth language, the complexity involved in learning two, three or more languages may be new and different (e.g., Wang, 2008).

Moreover, the term Ln learner recognizes the fact that although many children who enter our school system may go on to become fully bilingual or multilingual, some will stop before that point and will step in and out of different languages at different ages or stages of their school career (Gregory, 2008). Essentially, all children, whether or not the home language is the same as the school language, will have to learn the academic language as a new language.

Furthermore, although other terms such as "additional language" are used in the literature, the advantage of using the term "new language learning" foregrounds the fact that a student does not merely add a language (as the term "additional" implies) to her linguistic repertoire, she is in the process of making the new language part of her new self.[3] In addition, she is learning many new aspects associated with the new language. For example, she has to learn new conventions of communication, learn a new way of thinking in the new language, and develop a new linguistic and cultural identity.

Your Turn

What is your take on the argument for substituting the terms "second language learning" and "additional language learning" with the term "new language learning"? If you are not convinced by the idea, what term do you think best captures the nature of the student population who are in the process of learning English? Alternatively, you can also interview a student who is in the process of learning English and ask him to help you identify the *new* aspects that he has to grasp in learning English.

Bilingual vs multilingual

Traditionally, people who speak more than one language are labeled according to the number of languages they speak: bilingual (two languages), trilingual (three languages), or quadrilingual (four languages). However, some researchers suggest that it may be more accurate to use the word *multilingual* to describe people who know more than one language (e.g., Wang, 2008 and 2011a). Hoffmann (2001) suggested that the term *multilingual* is a more authentic term than *bilingual* or *trilingual* because it clearly distinguishes the macrolinguistic level (bilingual or trilingual) from the microlinguistic level (monolingual). Moreover, Martin-Jones and Jones (2000) provide additional reasons why it may be more accurate to use the term *multilingual* than *bilingual*. First, many people have more than two spoken or written languages and language varieties within their communicative repertoire. These include the languages and literacies associated with their cultural inheritance, the regional variety of dialects spoken in their local neighborhoods, and some form of "standard" language (such as "standard" English).

Second, the term *multilingual* signals the multiplicity and complexity of the communicative purposes that have come to be associated with different spoken and written languages within a group's repertoire. Third, the term *multilingual* takes into account the fact that in any linguistic minority household or local group (for example, among speakers of Welsh, Gujarati, or Cantonese), there are multiple paths to the acquisition of the spoken and written languages within the group repertoire, and people have varying degrees of expertise in these languages and literacies. Finally, the term *multilingual* is more useful than the term *bilingual* because it focuses attention on the multiple ways in which people draw on and combine the codes in their communicative repertoire when they speak and write.

In this book, unless the specific numbers of languages are actually referred to (*bilingual* or *trilingual*), the word *multilingual* is used as a generic term.

Disorder vs difficulty; symptoms vs characteristics

Students who have difficulties in processing linguistic related information are frequently labeled as having *language disorders* and show certain *symptoms*. Although the words *disorder* and *symptom* are commonly used in clinical literature and medical settings to describe a disease and an abnormal condition, it is important to avoid using them in educational settings because they sound negative and as if they require an action to *cure* them. Such a conception can affect our approaches to helping students. For these reasons, the word *disorder* can be replaced conceptually with *difficulty* and the word *symptom* may be replaced with *characteristic* in the classroom environment. *Difficulty* implies a challenge that calls for additional and different support, and *characteristic* indicates that students exhibit different attributes that require different instructional methods to promote development. Disabilities such as various language impairments are not diseases and thus cannot be cured, but the conditions can be improved with continuous support. The term *disorder* is occasionally used in the book when the intention is to describe a clinical situation or to refer to a conventional usage (e.g., children with autism spectrum disorders) or to quote research findings.

Delay vs deviant

There are debates on whether children with language impairment (LI) show deviant language acquisition patterns compared to children with typical development (TD) or whether they demonstrate similar language acquisition patterns to children with TD, but with a slower developmental rate (Paul, 2007). There are two opposite positions. One position sees the language acquisition pattern of children with LI as deviant. The evidence cited by the supporters of this position is based on the error patterns and grammatical features shown by children with language impairment that are not usually observed among children with TD. For example, the word-order errors and the grammatical structure features shown by German children with specific language impairment (SLI) are rarely observed among German children with TD (Grimm and Weinert, 1990; Hoff, 2009). However, current research evidence suggests that most children with LI follow the universal sequence of language development with a few subtle differences and with a slower rate (Fletcher, 2001; Paul, 2007).

Some researchers argue that if the **mean length of utterance** (MLU)[4] rather than age is compared between children with LI and children with TD, there is a similar tendency in language structure (except with a protracted rate); that is, a 4-year-old child with LI has a MLU equal to that of a 2-and-half-year-old child with TD. For example, some children with developmental dyslexia have a reading ability lower than would be expected on the basis of their IQ. These children do not appear to have a discrete difference but rather are at the low end of the normal distribution in reading skills (Hoff, 2009; Shaywitz and Shaywitz, 2004). Some also argue that the differences exhibited by children with LI are the result of their limited ability in reading performance (Fletcher, 2001). Some contend that the different representation shown by children with LI such as children with SLI is because these children have limited ability in processing information under the pressures of real-time language production, rather than representational deficiency (e.g., Bishop, 1994; Fletcher, 2001).

People-first language

The 1997 Public Law 101-336 (The American with Disability Act of 1990) recommends using **people-first language** in referring to people with disabilities. For example, the law suggests using "children with autism" instead of "autistic children" and "children with language impairment" instead of "language-impaired children." Using people-first language encourages respect for people with differences or disabilities. As our society moves forward, the terms and labels we use evolve as well. Thus, we need to constantly evaluate the words and labels we use.

The bottom line in choosing words

Having discussed choosing appropriate words to describe your students, I do not mean that you jettison some of the above terms entirely. Sometimes, labels do have a role in helping you communicate with other professionals (Paul, 2007) and in evaluating research focused on different student populations. The point of discussing label use and word choice is that you need to be cognizant of the words you use, because words can move one to action or stop one from taking action, and words can also evoke emotion (Edwards, 2010). The choice of words will make you do things differently. If you choose the term *language disorder*, you are likely to *correct* the *symptom* in your instruction. If you choose the words *language difficulty*, you are likely to realize the areas of need and turn them into teaching opportunities. Similarly, if you conceptualize some of your multilingual students as English as L2 learners (whereas they are simultaneous multilinguals), you are going to waste your time in focusing on the wrong areas when providing support.

Your Turn

- What is your opinion on the labels used to describe children with various abilities in the school setting? Explain your position.
- Suppose you are going to have a conference with a parent who has a child with language-related difficulties. Think about the words you plan to use to describe this student. Why do you decide to choose these words and phrases?
- Compile a list of words, terms, or labels that are used to describe people with disabilities by the general public. Discuss how these labels will affect your perception about people with disabilities and your way to interact with them.

Summary of Key Points

- There are three main reasons why teacher knowledge of language and literacy development can help reach diverse learners:
  - Know how to interpret disability classification reports from specialists.
  - Know how to identify issues with students in terms of their language and literacy characteristics and provide effective instructional support to help them learn the content area.
  - Fulfill the requirements of professional teacher organizations.
- The critical discourse analysis (CDA) conceptual framework and its companion pedagogy, transformative pedagogy (TP), are proposed for working with diverse learners. The essence of CDA is that it encourages you to analyze not only what is present in what students say and write, but also what is left out, and that it encourages you to build a human relationship with your students and families and to learn from your students and discover the resources (funds of knowledge) that students bring to the classroom so that students can be empowered to learn. The four components of TP (situated practice, overt instruction, critical framing, and transformed practice) can help you turn your students' needs into teaching opportunities by tapping into their strengths.
- Literacy is redefined to include not only the reading and writing process, but also the processes of digital literacy and critical literacy.

- Commonly used labels are scrutinized for their suitability in education settings. Emphasis is placed on using people-first language.
  - *New language (Ln)* learners is suggested to replace *second language (L2)* learners and *additional language* learners
  - *Multilingual* is recommended to replace *bilingual* or *trilingual*.
  - *Difficulty* is proposed to replace *disorder*.
  - *Characteristic* is advocated to replace *symptom*.
  - *Delay* is used to replace *deviant*.

Key Terms

Conceptual framework
Critical discourse analysis (CDA)
Critical framing
Critical literacy
Evolving definition of literacy
Funds of knowledge
IEP (Individualized Educational Program)
Habitus
Hypertext

Intentional teaching
Overt instruction
People-first language
Positioning
Mean Length of Utterance (MLU)
Multilingual
New language
Situated practice
Transformative pedagogy
Transformed practice

Notes

1. Intentional teaching means that a teacher carries out a teaching activity with specific goals in mind for his students, and organizes his teaching to accomplish the goals by using effective instructional strategies.
2. Funds of knowledge refer to the knowledge (or cultural capital) that students accumulate in the home and community environments (Moll et al., 1992).
3. Throughout the book, "she," "he," "her," "his," "him," and "her" are used interchangeably to avoid gender-biased language, and at the same time, to avoid the cumbersome use of "she or he," "her or his," and "him or her." However, "he or she" is used when the context requires.
4. Mean length of utterance (MLU) is used to measure children's language production. It is calculated by collecting 100 utterances (one utterance represents one idea) and then dividing the total number of morphemes by total number of utterances.

Recommended Further Readings

Edwards, J. (2010). *Language Diversity in the Classroom*. Bristol: Multilingual Matters.
Gregory, E. (2008). *Learning to Read in a New Language*. Los Angeles: Sage.
Janks, H. (2014). *Doing Critical Literacy: Texts and Activities for Students and Teachers*. New York: Routledge.

New London Group (1996). A pedagogy of multiliteracies: designing social futures, *Harvard Education Review*, 66 (1): 60–92.

Powell, R. and Rightmyer, E. C. (2011). *Literacy for All Students: An Instructional Framework for Closing the Gap*. New York: Routledge.

Rogers, R. (2010) An introduction to critical discourse analysis in education. In R. Rogers (ed.), *An Introduction to Critical Discourse Analysis in Education* (pp. 1–20). 2nd edn. New York: Routledge.

Snyder, I. (ed.) (2002). *Silicon Literacies: Communication, Innovation and Education in the Electronic Age*. New York: Routledge.

2

Complex Factors That Influence Language Acquisition and Literacy Development

Prereading Questions and Activities

- Reflect on how you acquired your first language(s). How did your parents and other adults around you talk to you? Did the ways your parent(s) talked to you influence your overall language development? If so, in what ways, and if not, why. Share your experience with your classmates. Compare your language-learning environment to theirs. What have you found?

- Reflect on how you learned to read and write. What roles did your family and school play and what role did you as a learner play? Share your experience with your classmates. Compare your experience to theirs. What have you found?

- Observe how a parent communicates to a prelinguistic infant or a young child (video- or audio-record the interaction if possible). Identify the communicative characteristics of the parent. If possible, find out the socioeconomic background and educational level of the parent. Based on your observation, discuss how the parent–child communicative style will influence the child's language acquisition and development.

- Observe a group or class discussion in a classroom. Write down part of what the students say verbatim (if possible video- or audio-record the conversation and then transcribe part of it). Have you observed any differences among the students (such as differences in pronunciation and grammar, or differences in language use by female and male students)? If so, what are the differences and what could be the reasons for them?

- In what ways does our biology contribute to our language acquisition? Give two examples to support your position.

- Do you know any writing systems other than English (i.e. the alphabetic writing system)? If so, what is the difference between the English writing system and the writing system you know? Discuss what could be the advantages and challenges in learning different writing systems. If you know only the English writing

Understanding Language and Literacy Development: Diverse Learners in the Classroom, First Edition. Xiao-lei Wang.
© 2015 John Wiley & Sons, Inc. Published 2015 by John Wiley & Sons, Inc.
Companion website: www.wiley.com/go/wang/langandlit

system, you can research on the internet one other writing system that you are unfamiliar with and discuss what could be the advantages and challenges in learning that writing system.

- Are you familiar with a signed language (such as American Sign Language)? If so, compare the structure of the signed language to the spoken language (such as English) and identify the similarities and differences. If not, research a signed language and compare it to a spoken language (such as English).
- What is the relationship between speaking and reading and writing? Support your argument with evidence.
- Identify the characteristics of conventional print (for example, the text you read in a paperback) and digital print (for example, the text you see on a screen with images and/or sound on the internet) and discuss the possible effects of these different types of text on a child's literacy development.
- What instructional advantages do you have by knowing your students' language and literacy developmental characteristics?

Topics to Be Addressed in This Chapter

- Important factors that influence language acquisition and literacy development
  - Language as a human universal
    - Pidgin
    - Creole
    - Deaf children of hearing parents
    - Nicaraguan Sign Language
    - Language acquisition trajectory of children with language impairment
  - Biological factors
    - Human brain: the neural underpinnings of language and literacy
    - Sensitive period in language acquisition
    - Hereditary and individual differences
    - Gender differences
  - Ecological factors
    - Parental cultural beliefs and childrearing practices
    - Parental socioeconomic status and education levels
    - Parental language input frequency and quality
    - Extended family and sibling support
    - Language use in sociocultural contexts
  - Language divergence factors
    - Language particulars
    - Orthographic differences
  - Modality factors
    - Spoken language vs signed language
    - Spoken language vs reading and writing
    - Conventional print vs digital print
  - Motivational and identity factors
  - Types of first language acquisition factors

Learning Objectives

After reading this chapter, you are expected to do the following:

- Understand various factors that contribute to language and literacy development, specifically
  - Why is language a unique human phenomenon?
  - How does the brain's anatomy affect its functions in language comprehension and production?
  - How does the sensitive period affect the language acquisition process?
  - How does our genetic inheritance affect our language and literacy learning, and how does gender affect our language development?
  - How do ecological factors such as parental sociocultural status and educational levels affect children's language acquisition?
  - How do the extended family members and siblings influence language acquisition?
  - How do children's opportunities to use language as well as their motivation influence the language acquisition process?
  - How do language acquisition and identity co-develop?
  - How does the linguistic feature of a language affect the rate of language acquisition and literacy development?
  - How do different modalities impact language acquisition?
  - How do the different types of first language acquisition experiences differ, and what are the linguistic manifestations of these different experiences?

Box 2.1 Peter's Challenge – Disparities in Language and Literacy Development

Peter divided the class into four groups based on the alphabetic order of their last name. He gave the students a handout with the following geometry problem:

Photographs of the Washington Monument are typically not taken from a bird's-eye view. Describe a situation in which you would want a photo showing a bird's-eye view.

He asked the students to brainstorm in groups first, and then to write their individual solutions based on the group discussion. Peter moved from group to group, listening to students' discussions. When he stopped at Group 5, he noticed a very different dynamic among the students: Amy, Michael, Ben, and Galo.

Amy and Michael were active in the discussion. They showed a clear understanding of the information in the handout and were able to refer back to it when needed. Both of them were on target and able to write their solutions within the 15-minute timeframe that Peter gave the class for the activity. Amy's and Michael's language and literacy development was what Peter expected for typical 14- and 15-year-olds. Nevertheless, Peter also noticed that there were differences between Amy and Michael. Although both were quite eloquent, Amy used richer vocabulary and more complex sentences than Michael in both speaking and writing.

Ben, a student identified with specific language impairment, tried to contribute to the discussion. However, his comments often missed the target, indicating that he did not understand the information in the handouts. At times, he seemed to have trouble understanding what Amy and Michael were saying. Occasionally, he stopped in the middle of his sentences, trying to clarify his ideas without avail.

Galo was silent during the discussion. He came to the school six months earlier from Ecuador and had been struggling with his academic work since his arrival. Although he was attentive to the discussion, he had trouble understanding the term "a bird's-eye view" and was unable to write the solution after the discussion. When Michael told a joke during the discussion, Amy laughed hysterically, and Galo was perplexed by Amy's reaction.

Having read these students' background information on his first day in the school, Peter was aware of the reasons for the language and literacy disparities among the four students. However, the challenge for Peter was how he could create opportunities to maximize their learning potential (Ben's and Galo's, in particular).

The performance snapshot of Amy, Michael, Ben, and Galo reflects the linguistic and cognitive disparities often observed in a diverse classroom. There were various complex factors over the course of these students' development that had contributed to the way they used language in academic learning. Therefore, the purpose of this chapter is to help you understand the reasons behind students' linguistic differences. By understanding how your students acquire and develop their language(s), you can reach them more successfully.

Language As a Genetically Predispositioned Human Universal

Language is a unique human capacity. Children who are exposed to any linguistic system learn to speak that language with relative ease (except in the case of disabilities or a severely impoverished linguistic environment). In the first three years from birth, a child typically progresses rapidly in acquiring one or more than one linguistic system. The language acquisition process of children across different linguistic systems is remarkably similar: from cooing and babbling to producing one-word utterances and then combining words together to form sentences. Even when no standard **language input** (language model) is available, children are able to actively create a communication system that reflects the universal features of human languages (Goldin-Meadow, 2011).

Children's extraordinary, robust language capacity led linguist Noam Chomsky to hypothesize that humans biologically process an inner or predisposed **language acquisition device** (LAD) that enables us to create language with the information available from the environment (even when language input is limited). Although there have been feverish debates on Chomsky's hypothesis as well as occasional controversial evidence arguing against the idea (e.g., see Everett, 2009 and 2012) and alternative proposals (e.g., see Tomasello, 2003 and 2008), ample evidence thus far has indicated that language is indeed an intrinsic part of human nature and that all humans have a similar innate **universal grammar** (UG). This universal grammar guides us in our language making and production. The foregoing cases illustrate how UG works from rudimental to more complex language-like creations and how children who come to the language acquisition task with impairment still follow a universal language acquisition path.

Pidgin

When people do not have a common language with which to communicate, they are inclined to create one. **Pidgin** is often the result of this situation. It is characterized by the use of words from two or more contact languages, but not by the use of the grammar. For example, an initial pidgin-like communication may take its shape in the following situation. Mary wanted to buy a souvenir cup from a vendor when she was in Paris. Because she did not know much French and the vendor did not know much English, they had to mix words from both languages to accomplish their goals (to buy a cup and to sell a cup). Below is the pidgin-like conversation they both created on the spot:

MARY: (Pointing at the cup) That cup, that, that *tasse* (cup), please.
VENDOR: (Pointing at two cups respectively) Cette (this) *cup* ou (or) cette *cup*?
MARY: (Nodding) *Oui* (yes) this one (pointing at the cup she wanted), please. How much?
VENDOR: Huit (eight) *dollars*, non (no), huit euros.
MARY: How much?
VENDOR: *Eight euros.*
MARY: Oh, yeah. Here you are …

Historically, there have been different kinds of pidgins created by humans stemming from the need to communicate. For example, Hawaiian Pidgin English was originally created on sugar cane plantations by immigrant workers from Japan, Korea, and the Philippines. When these workers initially met, they did not have a common language and thus had to invent a communication system by mixing words from their respective languages (Bickerton, 1981 and 1984).

Creole

When children acquire a pidgin as their primary language, they are said to speak a **creole** (nativization); that is, children make what they hear grammatically more complex by adding some grammatical features that resemble universal characteristics of human languages. Interestingly, adults who speak a pidgin show inconsistent use of many grammatical features, whereas when children are exposed to this inconsistent pidgin input, they tend to acquire a more regular system (the creole). Swahili is a good example of creolization. It evolved from a mixture of the Arabic and Bantu languages and added words from many languages such as Persian, German, Portuguese, French, and English throughout the centuries.

This is also true for deaf children who learned sign language from their parents who are not native signers. These children do not make the same errors as their parents. They seem to have the ability to surpass their parents by figuring out the regularities from an erroneous input model (Newport and Aslin, 2000; Singleton and Newport, 2004).

Deaf children of hearing parents

Approximately, 90 to 96 percent of children with hearing loss are born to hearing parents (Morgan and Kegl, 2006). This population initially receives neither oral speech input because they cannot hear, nor sign language input from their hearing parents who do not know a sign language. Despite lacking a conventional linguistic model, research shows that these children are able to create a gestural communication system that shares similar features of universal language (Goldin-Meadow, 2011). This phenomenon also has been found cross-culturally (Wang, Mylander, and Goldin-Meadow, 1993 and 1995). When analyzing the idiosyncratic manual gestures spontaneously created by American and Taiwanese children with hearing loss, researchers found that these children shared remarkably similar patterns to string gestures together into manual sentences. For example, they all produced spontaneous hand gestures with the same object and verb order, such as "apple eat": pointing at the apple and moving one hand toward mouth as if eating (e.g., Wang, Mylander, and Goldin-Meadow, 1993 and 1995).

Nicaraguan Sign Language

Another well-documented case of language creation is the birth of Nicaraguan Sign Language (NSL). In 1978, the Nicaraguan government opened a public school for children with hearing loss. When these children entered the school, they had no common manual language to communicate with each other except their idiosyncratic home signs. After staying together for a while, these children developed a communication system that is now called **Nicaraguan Sign Language** (NSL). Researchers have tracked the developmental process of NSL. They found that children who entered the school before 1983 (using pidgin-like signs) and after it (using creole-like or language-like signs) demonstrated differences in the complexity of using NSL. The younger the children were when they had exposure to NSL, the more they used spatial modulation in their signing (which did not exist in the beginning of the creation of NSL) (Kegl, Senghas, and Coppola, 1999; Kegl, 2002). This situation is similar to children who acquire creole from pidgin input; they apply universal grammar and make any inconsistent input language-like.

In short, all of the above cases suggest that human beings do have a genetically predispositioned universal language-making capacity. In a typical language acquisition process, adults provide input for children, and children modify and add to the language, thereby acquiring and developing a language. However, in the absence of an adult language model, children are able to create a language-like communication system with the help of their **language bioprogram** (the innate capacity to create a language structure even when the input is unstructured) (Bickerton, 1981, 1984, and 1988).

Language acquisition trajectories of children with disabilities

Sometimes children's language acquisition process is interrupted by various disabilities. Although these children come to the language acquisition task with difficulties, their general language acquisition path is more similar to than different from the typical language acquisition trajectory. For example, research suggests that the error patterns of children with cognitive impairment in narrative tasks were similar to those found in the narratives of young children with TD. Moreover, the syntactic structural types and the frequency of recruiting such structures increase with age in these children. Even though the children with impairment showed a slower rate in their development such as in morphology and syntax, they nevertheless were moving forward in the same language development course as those children with TD (Reilly et al., 2004).

Taken together, it is clear that language is indeed a robust and resilient human phenomenon; it will generally unfold even under the least favorable conditions.

Biological Factors

Biology plays a considerable role in language acquisition. In this subsection, several important biological factors for language acquisition are identified and briefly discussed.

Human brain: the neural underpinnings of language acquisition

The remarkable capacity for human language is attributed to a highly complex and specialized organ: the brain. By analogy, the brain is like the software in a computer that supports all human high-level functioning, including language. Understanding the brain anatomy will help you see how language works in different parts of the brain.

The largest part of the brain is the **cerebrum** (or the telencephalon), which consists of two halves or hemispheres: the left and right hemispheres, each tending to have its own separate functions. The two hemispheres are connected by a band of nerve fibers called **corpus callosum**, which delivers messages between the hemispheres. The left hemisphere mediates core aspects of language (i.e., phonology, morphology, and syntax) for 95 percent of the population, including sign language users (Reilly et al., 2004). The right hemisphere is primarily specialized for spatial and visual functions. It also plays a role in language functions. For example, adults with right hemisphere damage have troubles in nonliteral language (such as jokes and figurative language), discourse cohesion, and coherence (Reilly et al., 2004). The division of labor of the brain is called **brain lateralization** or localization. However, brain localization or lateralization is relative rather than absolute. In some people (usually some left-handed people), language is actually controlled by the right hemisphere (about 18.8 percent of left-handed people). In addition, about 19.8 percent of left-handed people have bilateral brain functioning. Also, for some people, more women than men, the right hemisphere shares language function with the left hemisphere (Hoff, 2009). When a certain part of the brain is damaged, an individual will reveal certain language deficits. However, younger children with brain damage do not show the irreparable language deficits that damage produces in adults. Although children with brain damage initially tend to score lower in narrative measures than children without brain damage, they usually score at the range that is compatible with children with typical development by age 7.

Our cerebrum is made up of four lobes: frontal, temporal, parietal, and occipital, each having different functions (see Figure 2.1). The **frontal lobe** takes care of our higher cognitive functions such as planning, organizing, problem solving, abstract thinking, attention, judgment, and emotion. The **temporal lobe** controls auditory and visual memories, language, and some hearing and speech, and some behavior. The **parietal lobe** integrates sensory information, and portions of it are involved with some language, reading, and visual functions. Finally, the **occipital lobe** controls vision. All four lobes work together to make language and literacy possible.

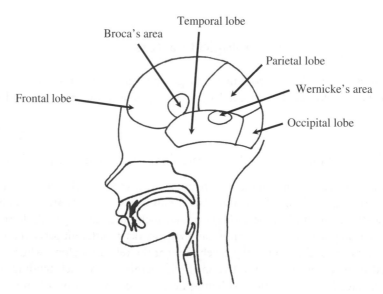

Figure 2.1   Location of lobes, Broca's area and Wernicke's area.

In the left hemisphere, there are two important areas that must be noted for human language: Wernicke's area and Broca's area (see Figure 2.1). The **Wernicke's area** (named after its discoverer, the Austrian neurologist Karl Wernicke) spans the region between the temporal and parietal lobes in the left hemisphere. It plays a key role (in tandem with Broca's area) in language comprehension (or processing meaning). People who have damage to the area may not have difficulty speaking, but much of their speech makes no sense. They also tend to have difficulty comprehending what people say to them. The **Broca's area** (named after the French neurologist Paul Broca, who discovered it in the late 1860s) is located at the back of the frontal lobe in the left hemisphere; it is an important region for speech production as well as **syntax** processing (assembling words into meaningful sentences). When people have damage to this area, they tend to produce telegraphic speech, using nouns, verbs, and adjectives while often omitting conjunctions and other important parts of speech.

Moreover, the structure of the brain that affects language is the gyrus and sulcus. A **gyrus** is the elevated surface of the brain. A **sulcus** is a groove-like depression on the brain's surface that separates the gyri. The left inferior frontal gyrus is in charge of functions such as meaning processing and speech sounds. The left middle temporal gyrus is in charge of processing meaning, and the left fusiform gyrus is in charge of writing processing (Brice and Brice, 2009).

Many of the structures used in reading are the same as those used for spoken language. There are two additional areas of the brain that are involved in reading: the **visual cortex** and the **angular gyrus**. The initial recognition of the visual pattern of a word begins in the visual cortex (Gazzaniga, 1998). The angular gyrus is located at the junction of the occipital and temporal lobes; it is the bridge between the visual word recognition system and the rest of the language processing system. It is here that written words are translated into the sounds of spoken language. Without this transformation, reading and writing would not be possible (Wolfe, 2001).

Although most brain cells are formed before birth, the majority of the connections between the cells are developed after birth, particularly during infancy and early childhood. Brain cells continue to mature until around age 15 (Hoff, 2009). Early stimulation of the brain enables neurons to fire together and form **synapses** (a junction between two nerve cells, which allows a neuron to pass information to another cell). Recent research evidence suggests that the human brain has a unique ability to constantly change, grow, and rewire itself to adapt to new situations over the course of a lifetime. This ability is referred to as **brain plasticity**. Thanks to the plastic nature of the brain, older children's brain potential may still be maximized through environmental stimulation.

Sensitive period of language acquisition

Germane to the brain's development, there is a span of time or window of opportunity in our lives when our brain is more receptive to environmental stimuli in signed and spoken language acquisition than in any other period. This period is referred to as the **critical period of language acquisition** or sensitive period of language acquisition. The term *critical period* was originally used by Canadian neurologists Wilder Penfield and Lamar Robers in 1959 and was later popularized by Eric Lenneberg in his 1967 book entitled *Biological Foundations of Language*. Although the terms *sensitive period* and *critical period* are used interchangeably in literature, some prefer to use the term *sensitive period* to accentuate that learning can still occur after the optimal time for language acquisition (e.g., Werker and Tees, 2005).

There are ongoing debates on what exactly is the cut-off age of the sensitive period for language acquisition. Different age limits have been put forward. For example, some researchers have proposed that the first six years in a child's life are optimal for language acquisition and learning; that is, if a child is first exposed to a primary language before 6 years of age, the child will acquire that language with native abilities, whereas if a child is first exposed to a primary language from 6 years of age and no later than 10 years of age, the child will acquire the language with near native abilities (e.g., Newport, Bavelier, and Neville, 2001). It seems that the peak for optimal language acquisition begins shortly before the age of 2 years and gradually ends during an age span approximately from age 7 through 10 years (Meisel, 2006, p. 104). Emerging literature on children who acquire signed languages seems to identify age 10 as a pivotal age for acquisition; that is, after age 10, children are unlikely to develop native language abilities (e.g., Morgan and Kegl, 2006; Mayberry, Lock, and Kazmi, 2002; Senghas and Coppola, 2001). In any case, the current state of evidence seems to indicate that if a person does not enter the threshold of a particular language acquisition process before the onset of puberty (roughly about 12 or 13 years of age), it is more difficult for them to be able to achieve full proficiency in that language, especially in phonology (e.g., accent) and grammatical structure.

Moreover, the age of exposure to a first language or languages also affects the way that language is represented in the brain. For instance, when a new language is learned after age 7, the regions and patterns of activation are partially or completely non-overlapping with those for the native (first) language (Newport, 2002). Early language learners showed the characteristic anterior left hemisphere **event-related potential** (ERP)[1] components, whereas learners with delays of four years (after 7 years of age) showed significantly more bilateral activation (Newport et al., 2001; Newport, 2002; Weber-Fox and Neville, 1996). The same was found in learners of signed languages (Neville et al., 1997).

The most noticeable effect of passing the sensitive period of language acquisition is a person's accent if a new language is learned after puberty. There are also a few known cases about feral children that can support the sensitive period hypothesis (for more information, please see the recommended readings at the end of the chapter). One example of particular interest is the case of Genie. Genie spent most of her first 13 years of life in isolation in her bedroom. She was harnessed to an infant's potty-chair most of the day and was placed in a sleeping bag at night. Her abusive father forbade her mother and brother to talk to her. Consequently, Genie did not have much language stimulation during her first 13 years. When she was rescued, Genie initially could understand only about 20 words and negative command intonations. She depended on gestures and other nonlinguistic cues to make sense of the speech directed at her. Because Genie began to learn her primary language at the age of 13 years and 7 months, she missed her sensitive period in language acquisition and displayed the negative impact in her language learning. For example, her frequent substitutions and deletions distorted the phonological structure to a degree that at times made Genie's speech almost impossible to understand. Although Genie could understand the meaning of everyday English sentences, she could not understand most grammatical rules. She was not able to put words together in a grammatical way. For instance, she might say something like, "Applesauce buy store," rather than "We need to buy applesauce at the store" (Curtis, 1977). This case shows that it is difficult to develop the full potential for acquiring a language if the optimal period for language acquisition is missed.

The sensitive period hypothesis is also shown in children who acquire sign language late in life. For example, research on American Sign Language shows that if children with hearing loss do not acquire it early in life, it will fundamentally affect their proficiency in the language as well as the subsequent language learned later in life (Mayberry, 2007 and 2010).

There are a number of caveats concerning the issue of the sensitive period hypothesis. First, the sensitive period does not end abruptly. Therefore, the window of opportunity does not shut itself overnight. All hope is not lost for children who missed the optimal time in language acquisition to learn and develop a language. Given the right maturation, environmental stimulation, and brain plasticity, children who are late on the language learning train for various reasons can still catch up and develop communication skills. Even in an extreme case like Genie's, we still observed some possibility in her language learning with intervention. Although her brain showed the characteristics of cognitive impairment, her **mental age** (the cognitive ability shown at a specific age, which may not match a child's chronological age) increased by one year every year after she had been found. This cognitive improvement is not a usual characteristic of cognitive impairment. Over the four years of language learning, Genie appeared to be "tuning in" to language by paying attention to conversations around her, and she began to use language in new ways by being able to reflect on past events. Moreover, Genie used many substitutions in her sound production, but interestingly, her substitutions were not random, her vowels were not substituted for consonants, and her consonants were not substituted for vowels. It shows that human language acquisition is so robust and deeply ingrained in our biological program that it is not easily abandoned (Paul, 2007).

Second, exposure to a language after the sensitive period does not affect all aspects of language learning equally. Even though late language acquisition may affect linguistic properties such as speech sounds and some features in grammar, it does not necessarily affect vocabulary and meaning processing (J. Johnson and Newport, 1989; Newport, 2002; Newport et al., 2001; Weber-Fox and Neville, 1996). The encouraging outlook is that when you have students who are learning English as a new language after the optimal window of opportunity in language acquisition, they will still have potential to develop proficiency in English, although they may have an accent and make some grammatical mistakes.

Heredity and individual differences

There are two kinds of **heredity** influences. One is specific to the genetic inheritance associated with the species of homo sapiens which makes us process certain abilities that other species cannot. For example, human children with typical development can learn to speak a language even with minimal linguistic input, whereas other species cannot. The other is the specific biological inheritance from our individual ancestors that is carried immediately by our genes and makes us different from one another (Black, 1979). About 60 percent of our individual differences can be accredited to our genes. Genetic inheritance (or genes) can make various impacts on our language and literacy learning and performances. For instance, over half of the variance in young school-age children's conversational language skills may be accounted for by genetic effects (DeThorne et al., 2008). Further, genetic factors play a dominant role in the relationship between early speech and reading (Hayiou-Thomas et al., 2010). Heredity may lead some children to be more responsive to caregivers' cues in communication. It can also play a moderate role in a child's ability to read, which may affect how a child processes information, including linguistic information, and may also determine the speed and quality of how a child learns to read. Research indicates that about half of our reading ability is genetically influenced (e.g., Smith 2007).

Moreover, heredity also plays a role in certain language disabilities. For instance, dyslexia tends to run in families. Children who have a parent or sibling with dyslexia are far more likely to have dyslexia than children without such a family history. Similarly, late-talking children with family histories of speech and language delay are also more likely to show delays than those without such family histories (Dale et al., 2003). It is important to note that genetic effects on child language abilities vary widely, ranging from 10 percent to 100 percent (DeThorne et al., 2008).

Although heritability can tell us whether a child has inherited a trait and whether the child will develop the trait in her encounters with the world, it cannot operate independently. Genetic predispositions can express themselves only through an individual's interactions with others in the environment. Therefore, it is important to emphasize that "genetic" is not a synonym for "unchangeable" (DeThorne et al., 2008). Understanding how generic factors affect the process of language acquisition can help us know how to support our students through preventing and intervening with the potential or existing language learning challenges.

Gender differences

As you observed in the beginning of this chapter, Michael and Amy were both typically developing students, yet they exhibited differences in their language performances. Amy used a wider variety of words and more complex syntax than Michael. Research suggests that girls tend to demonstrate linguistic superiority over boys from early on. For example, at age 2, girls know an average of 363 words versus 227 for boys, and these differences attenuate by ages 6–7 (Bornstein, Hahn, and Haynes, 2004). Some studies found that girls continue to hold advantages (though small) over boys for verbal and written language that persist through school years (e.g., Undheim and Nordvik, 1992) into adulthood (Parsons et al., 2005), although some researchers believe that current evidence does not show that differences in brain–behavior correlations persist into adulthood (Burman, Bitan, and Booth, 2008). Nonetheless, it seems that girls tend to achieve language milestones earlier than boys; they tend to talk earlier as well as produce more words and longer sentences than boys. They also tend to be more verbal and to demonstrate more facility with grammatical rules, making their speech more coherent in spontaneous language than boys (e.g., Bauer, Goldfield, and Reznick, 2002).

Some researchers also found that even though the linguistic advantage of girls appears early (usually between 17 months and 27 months), it becomes less evident from 28 months on, when boys seem to catch up with girls (Bouchard et al., 2009). Some believe that the verbal difference between boys and girls disappears in the first years of school and only reappears around age 10 or 11 (Coates, 1993).

Gender differences in language development seem to be ubiquitous cross-linguistically. For example, Canadian French-speaking girls produce significantly more words, a greater number of grammatical forms, and more complex sentences than boys. There are also qualitative differences between the genders in the acquisition of the first 100 words (Bouchard et al., 2009). For example, Dutch-speaking girls do better than boys in word decoding (Verhoeven and Van Leenuwe, 2011). They also tend to do significantly better than boys on the regular consonant-vowel-consonant word patterns (Verhoeven and Van Leenuwe, 2011). Taiwanese children exhibit gender differences in language development at 36 months (gender has a transient effect at 18 months) (Lung et al., 2011). Moreover, research shows that failure in reading tends to occur more frequently for boys than for girls in the early grades (Phillips et al., 2002).

However, the gender differences in language development are complex. On the one hand, there are biological reasons such as developmental differences in the maturation rate between boys and girls (e.g., Blanton et al., 2004) that account for the observed gender differences. For instance, girls' brains mature earlier than boys'. Brain activation is also different between genders. Girls show stronger bilateral activation in the frontal and temporal regions that are related to language processing skills across modalities (Burman, Bitan, and Booth, 2008). On the other hand, there are also possible different environmental influences. The way in which parents and caregivers interact with boys and girls may be responsible for gender-based language differences. For example, one study shows that when mothers interacted with their 2-year-old girls, they produced longer sentences, more repetition, more acknowledgment of the girls' answers and more turn-taking than when they interacted with their 2-year-old boys (Owens, 2012). Another case on environmental influences can be illustrated by the previously mentioned study conducted with Canadian French-speaking children. Even though girls in that study acquired the majority of the words (91.5 percent) before boys, boys produced transportation-related words before girls, except for the word *plane* (Bouchard et al., 2009).

In sum, although the various biological factors mentioned above may play important roles in our potential to acquire and develop languages and literacy, they are not destiny. We must be cognizant that much of what we know about the biological aspect of language development is only tentative and sometimes even controversial.

Your Turn

Based on the genetic factors that influence language acquisition, discuss how you as a teacher can beat the genetic odds of your students and help them develop language and literacy (provide at least one concrete example).

Ecological Factors That Influence Language and Literacy Development

Our biology can explain only part of our language differences; other aspects of our differences in language can be explained by our environment or **ecology** (our overall language acquisition settings). This subsection focuses on these ecological factors.

Parental cultural childrearing beliefs and practices

Every cultural and socioeconomic group has its own ideologies and beliefs about language learning, including when it begins and how children should learn it. This process is called **language socialization**. Caregivers' beliefs about child language learning and development (**cultural template**) will influence how they interact with their children (e.g., Donahue, Pearl, and Herzog, 1997), and subsequently, how children acquire and develop language.

Different cultures socialize their children differently in the early years of a child's life. For example, white middle-class caregivers believe that children are social and capable of acting intentionally. However, in the Kaluli culture (in the rain forests of Great Papuan Plateau in Papua New Guinea), infants are regarded as "soft" and "having no understanding" (Ochs and Schieffelin, 1984). The Kalulis also believe that language begins at the time when a child uses two critical words, *mother* and *breast* (Schieffelin, 1979). As a result of these different beliefs, caregivers in these cultures have different communicative exchanges with their young children. White middle-class caretakers treat infants as conversational partners and address them in dyadic fashion. Caregivers use two major communication strategies. One is the **self-lowering strategy** in which caregivers simplify words and sentences (baby talk or **motherese**). The other is the **child-raising strategy** in which caregivers expand on what a child is saying.

In contrast, the Kaluli caretakers do not gaze directly into their babies' eyes. The caregivers face the babies outward so that they can see and be seen by others. The Kaluli caregivers do not address infants directly. Instead, they talk to a third party such as an older sibling. Triadic exchanges are typical (e.g., mother–older sibling–infant). In addition, the Kaluli caregivers use direct instruction such as "say like this" to provide modeling to their young children, and they do not expand their children's speech (Ochs and Schieffelin, 1984).

Moreover, different cultures and socioeconomic groups have different beliefs about how reading and writing should be learned. Influenced by their different beliefs, parents and caregivers guide their children with different early literacy practices. For example, Chinese mothers reported using picture books and flashcards to teach new words to a greater degree than Western mothers. This practice indicates that in their opinion, children learn best through direct instruction rather than through play (J. Johnston and Wong, 2002). Gregory (2008) described the literacy behavior of a boy named Tony who immigrated to the United Kingdom from Hong Kong. In class, Tony only wanted to copy words rather than to experiment with writing them like other children. His behavior was exactly what his family expected of him. Tony's grandparents and parents believed that learning to read and write should follow a clear sequence: First, understand the meaning of the word; then, learn how to pronounce it correctly, repeat it, memorize it, carefully copy it, and use it to make different sentences. Once a child can prove competency in these aspects, he or she will be given a book to read. To have immediate access to books devalues both the book and the principle of hard work. Children must work their way toward knowledge step by step, and the book is a reward for a child's conscientious achievements. A love of books comes after reading is learned and not as a necessary prerequisite to it.

Parental socioeconomic status and education levels

Research has consistently shown that economic advantages or social stratum matters more than race/ethnicity, gender, and birth order in the kind of linguistic environment that parents provide for their children (Bloom, 1995). The socioeconomic status of parents (SES) is most strongly associated with differences in the amount of talk by parents (Hart and Risley, 1995). For instance, vocabulary growth at age 3 is strongly correlated with family SES, which could account for 42 percent of the variance in children's rates of vocabulary growth and 40 percent of the variance in their vocabulary use (Hart and Risley, 1995). Further, mothers with high SES backgrounds tend to use more conversation-eliciting questions, more complex syntax, and a greater diversity of vocabulary when talking to their toddlers compared with mothers from low SES backgrounds. In addition, parents' educational levels influence the language sample measure such as the number of different words (NDW) in children's spontaneous speech (e.g., Horton-Ikard and Weismer, 2007).

A well-known longitudinal study by Hart and Risley (1995) examined parental talk in the families of three different economic groups: professional, welfare, and working-class. The study found that parents from these socioeconomic strata have quantitatively and qualitatively different conversations with their children.

In the professional families, the parents, in an average hour, displayed to their children more words with more variety, more multi-clause sentences, more past and future verb tenses, more declaratives, and more questions of all kinds than the welfare and working-class parents. The parents from the professional families also gave their children more affirmative feedback and responses than the working-class parents and parents on welfare. Moreover, the professional parents provided richer verbal exchanges with their children. For example, they used more nouns, modifiers, past-tense verbs, auxiliary-fronted yes/no questions, declarative sentences, and affirmative feedback. They displayed less negative feedback to the children per hour. The professional parents gave their children an average of 5 prohibitions per hour, while the welfare parents gave 11. The professional parents gave their children affirmative feedback more than 30 times per hour, twice as often as the working–class parents and 5 times more than the welfare parents.

As a result of the children's different experiences in the first three years in these families, the average words children produced per hour were 2,150 in the professional families, 1,250 in the working-class families, and 620 in the welfare families. Hart and Risley extrapolated that by age three, the children from the professional families would have acquired more than 30 million words, children from the working-class families would have acquired 20 million, and children from the welfare families only

10 million. Such language development disparities will affect children's later language development. In fact, a study confirmed that the linguistic accomplishments identified in Hart and Risley's study predicted the language skills of children at ages 9 and 10 (Walker et al., 1994).

A recent study also showed that at 18 months, children from wealthier families could identify pictures of simple words much faster than children from low-income families. By age 2, children from affluent families had learned 30 percent more words than the children from low-income homes (Fernald, Marchman, and Weisleder, 2013).

Although children's earlier linguistic experiences are crucial in their later language development, intervention and support at the school level can make a difference. For example, recent studies found that even when toddlers from low SES homes performed significantly more poorly than those from middle-class homes on standardized receptive and expressive vocabulary tests and on the number of different words used in spontaneous speech, there were no significant SES group differences in their ability to learn new word meanings (Horton-Ikard and Weismer, 2007). This study indicates that given appropriate educational opportunities, children from low SES backgrounds can improve their language performance.

Parental input frequency

There is a general agreement among researchers that frequency of parental **language input** does matter greatly in children's language acquisition, notwithstanding the conflicting arguments (e.g., Goodman, Dale, and Li, 2008). Research has shown that parents who provide more input overall tend to have children whose early vocabulary grows more quickly. What parents said to their children in their early years has an enormous impact on how much language their children learn and use (Hart and Risley, 1995; Huttenlocher et al., 1991; Weizman and Snow, 2001), and frequency of parental input has shown to be highly related to children's language production (e.g., Moerk, 1980). Specifically, parental input is related to early acquisition of vocabulary and is significantly correlated with the acquisition of common nouns (Goodman, Dale, and Li, 2008). Parental input also provides pragmatic convention models for children (Becker, 1994).

Extended family and sibling support

In extended families, multiple members can provide extra support for children's linguistic development. In non-Western societies such as the Kaluli cultural community, it is typical that two or more extended families live in the same household; children are therefore exposed to multiple linguistic inputs from different adults (Ochs and Schieffelin, 1984). Moreover, grandparents can play a supportive role in children's language, including heritage language and literacy development (e.g., Mui and Anderson, 2008; Nolan, 2008; Wang, 2008 and 2011).

Siblings also play an important role in one another's lives (Caspi, 2011; Whiteman, Bernard, and Jensen, 2011), including language development (e.g., Barton and Tomasello, 1991; Brown, Donelan-McCall, and Dunn, 1996; Cicirelli, 1976; Jones and Adamson, 1987; Olsen-Fulero and Conforti, 1983; Pine, 1995; Steelman et al.,

2002; Woollett, 1986). A growing body of research suggests that siblings are "cultural educators" and "socializing agents," and they learn much from each other and contribute to one another's development (e.g., Reynolds, Dorner, and Orellana, 2011).

Older siblings can impact younger siblings' language development indirectly and directly in at least two ways. First, they provide the second–order effect (indirectly) on younger siblings' language development. For example, when older siblings are present, caregivers' language becomes more complex as well as more social, with more questions, answers, and feedback, and has less commentary on behavior than when younger siblings are alone with the caregivers. Caregivers also make greater reference to people and events beyond the immediate context (Woollett, 1986). Thus, in the presence of older siblings, the linguistic environment of younger siblings tends to be more stimulating (despite the fact that caregivers tend to be less sensitive to younger siblings) and the caregiver–older sibling communication offers linguistic models for younger siblings. In triadic interactions among caregivers and older and younger siblings, younger siblings are exposed to more pronouns in the overheard conversations than in speech directed at them alone. As a result, younger siblings such as second-born children are more advanced than firstborn children in personal pronoun production (Oshima-Takane, Goodz, and Derevensky, 1996; Woollett, 1986). Second, older siblings can provide different sources of language learning opportunities for younger siblings directly by using languages that reflect their shared experiences (e.g., Ortiz, 2009) and by using more directives that drive younger siblings to use more nonlinguistic forms of communication (Tomasello and Mannle, 1985). In some cultural communities where older siblings have to take the responsibility of taking care of younger siblings such as in some Latino families, older siblings have a greater influence on their younger siblings' language development (e.g., Maynard, 2004; Orellana, Dorner, and Pulido, 2003; Ortiz, 2009). In Central Mexico, for example, older siblings often provide explicit models of appropriate responses to parents' verbal instructions and help younger siblings to understand the verbal meanings of parents' instructions and how to respond to them (Zukow, 1989).

Although the majority of the literature suggests that older siblings tend to have more influence on younger siblings, younger siblings can also influence older siblings. For example, multilingual siblings influence each other with their mistakes. In a study of trilingual siblings, Wang (2008) found that the older sibling, Léandre, often copied the mistakes of the younger sibling, Dominique, in both French and Chinese.

Language use in sociocultural context

The process of acquiring language is deeply affected by the process of becoming a competent member of a society. The process of becoming a competent member of a society is realized to a large extent through language. In everyday language use, children acquire knowledge of its functions, social distribution, and interpretations in and across socially defined situations, that is, through exchanges of language in particular social situations (Ochs and Schieffelin, 1984). For example, the development of labeling (for example, naming objects in a child's immediate surroundings) is encouraged in middle-class families, and therefore, children in these families may develop the use of it earlier. In contrast, affect pronouns are encouraged in Kaluli and Samoan cultures, such as "poor-me" (Ochs and Schieffelin, 1984). Thus, affect pronouns will be more prevalent in these children's language use. In the Amazonian Pirahã culture, adults do not use the **phatic language** (social language) to communicate with each other. Therefore, words such as *hello* and *thank you* are nonexistent (Everett, 2009).

The ecological factors that we just discussed have a vital influence on how language and literacy are developed. Knowing these influences will help you to understand your students' current language and literacy abilities and to provide them with additional support that was not present in their previous environment.

Your Turn

- Ask someone from a culture other than your own to give you some language or communication examples that do not exist in English. Reflect on your findings.
- Interpret the following statement: "Genetic influences play a strong role in child language impairments, whereas environmental factors play a strong role in language learning within typical variations" (Crais, 2007, p. 158).

Language Divergence Factors

Language particulars

Earlier in the chapter, we touched upon the language universals, the idea that all human languages share a universal cognitive order of emergence in their acquisition (e.g., Clancy, Jacobsen, and Silva, 1976) or a common deeper structure. However, the properties of individual languages also pose different types of acquisition difficulties for their learners and thus influence the course of development (Slobin, 1985; Wang, 2008). For example, cross-linguistic findings have shown that the inflectional past-tense morphology of Danish children aged 4, 6, and 8 is delayed relative to Icelandic, Norwegian, and Swedish children due to the phonetic structure of the Danish language (Bleses, Basboll, and Vach, 2011).

Moreover, different languages present children with different learning tasks. For instance, children who acquire Chinese will have to learn how to use **classifiers** (measuring words). The classifiers are used along with numbers to indicate the quantity of objects, such as *kuai* (块) in "five *kuai* (块) of crackers" (five crackers) or classifiers can be used with demonstratives "this" or "that" to identify objects, such as *tou* (头) in "this *tou* (头) cow" (this cow). Children who learn French have to learn gender difference in words such as *une table* (a *table*, feminine) and *un verre* (a *glass*, masculine).

Orthographic differences

The speed of children's literacy development can also be affected by the differences in **orthographic systems** (the writing systems). Research suggests that each writing system is based on a different set of symbolic relations and requires a different set of cognitive skills (Bialystok, Luk, and Kwan, 2005).

The world's writing systems can be roughly divided into alphabetic (such as English), alphasyllabary (such as Korean *hangul*), and non-alphabetic (such as Chinese). Alphabetic writing systems can be further divided into different scripts such as Roman scripts (e.g., Spanish), Semitic scripts (e.g., Hebrew), and Cyrillic scripts (e.g., Serbian). Overall, the alphabetic system tends to have more phonology–orthography (sound–script) mapping than a non-alphabetic system. In other words, the alphabetic writing system has relatively more **transparency** than the non-alphabetic one. For instance, Finnish is a more transparent language than Chinese. Using the word "cat" as an example, the sound [*kisa*] and the script *Kissa* in Finnish correspond closely to each other, whereas, the sound [*mao*] and the script 猫 in Chinese are not pellucid. Thus, it takes different information processing skills for children to learn these different orthographies (Huang and Hanley, 1994; Wang, 2011b). Box 2.2 shows the degree of orthographic transparency of some languages.

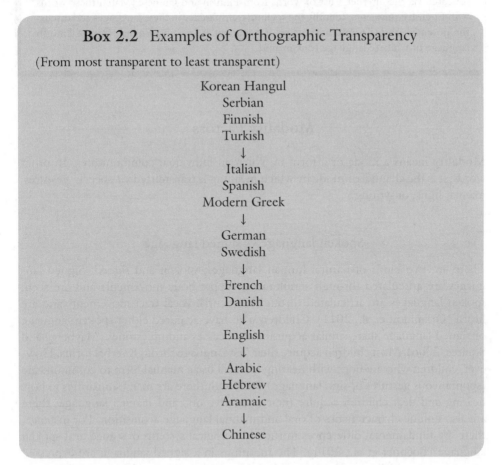

Box 2.2   Examples of Orthographic Transparency

(From most transparent to least transparent)

Korean Hangul
Serbian
Finnish
Turkish
↓
Italian
Spanish
Modern Greek
↓
German
Swedish
↓
French
Danish
↓
English
↓
Arabic
Hebrew
Aramaic
↓
Chinese

Moreover, even within the alphabetic writing system, different languages vary in their degree of transparency. English, for instance, is known to be less transparent than Turkish, Czech, Welsh, French, and German. Cross-linguistic studies have shown that English-speaking children consistently perform less well than those children from the relatively more transparent writing systems (such as Welsh and Turkish). Children learning relatively transparent writing systems appear to learn not only the basic phonological spelling more quickly, but also demonstrate more advanced conventional spelling skills than those learning English (Caravolas, 2004).

Such evidence has also been shown in children who simultaneously acquire three languages. For example, the siblings Léandre and Dominique who simultaneously acquired French, Chinese, and English from birth tend to be more proficient in English and French reading and writing than Chinese partly because of the orthographic differences (Wang, 2008, 2011a, and forthcoming).

Your Turn

Research via the internet a list of words from Finnish and Chinese. Match these words with English equivalents. Identify the spelling transparency in these languages and discuss the potential obstacles and advantages if a student is learning English from a Finnish language or Chinese language background.

Modality Factors

Modality means a mode or a form in which an individual communicates. In other words, it is the channel or mode by which meaning is transmitted via speech, gestures, manual signs, or writing.

Spoken language vs signed language

There are two kinds of natural human languages: spoken and signed. Signed languages are articulated through simultaneous upper-body movements and are seen; spoken languages are articulated through sequential vocal-tract movements and are heard (Orfanidou et al., 2011). Children who have acquired either spoken language or signed language share similar acquisition processes and milestones (Mayberry and Squires, 2006). Most children acquire their first language through verbal forms. However, children who are born with hearing loss will use a manual form to communicate (spontaneous gestures or sign language). Although there are many similarities in how hearing and deaf children acquire their respective oral and manual language, there are also unique characteristics of oral and manual language acquisition. For instance, there are fundamental differences in the phonological systems of signed and spoken language (Bochner et al., 2011). The meanings in a signed language are expressed through the modalities of hand shape, movement/motion, and location. For more information about sign language, please refer to the recommended reading list at the end of the chapter.

Spoken language vs reading and writing

Spoken language usually does not require intentional learning (given that it is a child's first language – L1). However, reading and writing are learned skills; they require conscious effort. There is a close link between children's oral language skills and their later reading and writing competence. Children with higher levels of oral proficiency and more elaborated vocabulary can read more easily than their less proficient peers (Bialystok, 2002). Children's knowledge established in oral language, such as phonological awareness and phonemic awareness, affects their ability to read. Phonological awareness and phonemic awareness are terms that refer to children's knowledge about words and their sounds. Phonological awareness is broader in scope and includes the ability to separate sentences into words and words into syllables. **Phonemic awareness** includes the ability to recognize that words are made up of a set of sounds and the ability to manipulate sounds. Phonemic awareness is an oral ability that allows a child to hear that words begin alike, that words rhyme, and that, for example, there are three sounds in the word *cat* (Cunningham and Hall, 2009). Research indicates that phonological awareness is highly correlated with success in beginning reading (Adams, 1990), even in non-alphabetic languages such as Chinese (M. Wang, Yang, and Cheng, 2009).

Conventional print vs digital print

Conventional print is printed text such as the print in traditional paper-format textbooks. **Digital print** (which also has other related terms such as multimedia text, electronic text, web text, hypertext, the internet-based system of communication, or new literacies) is text in conjunction with images and/or sounds. When communication is carried through the conventional print modality, it is linear, whereas when communication is expressed through digital modality, it is interactive and nonlinear with multimedia forms of pictures, video and/or sounds. As information technology increasingly advances, books and print media are no longer the sole source of reading materials. Nowadays, most students are actively engaged in multimedia text. As a *New York Times* article predicts, in a digital future, traditional textbooks could be history. Some educators have already noticed that students today do not engage with textbooks that are finite, linear, and rote (Lewin, 2009).

Multimedia text with its interactive features can facilitate children's literacy development. For example, preliminary evidence indicates that multimedia technology can help children who have reading difficulties make progress in reading comprehension (Coiro, 2003). However, reading hypertext requires high levels of visual literacy skills to enable comprehension of multimedia components. Successful hypertext reading requires evaluation of text and non-text (graphics, multimedia, and images), as readers must differentiate between important visual images and other information such as beautification of sites (Kress, 1997; Sutherland-Smith, 2002). Thus, although digital literacy affords new opportunities for children in learning literacy, it also presents a range of challenges such as the text formats, the speed of information, the purpose of reading, and the ways in which to interact with information; all these aspects require a different thought process and skill for making meaning compared with conventional print (Sutherland-Smith, 2002; Coiro, 2003). The multidimensional nature of digital text may make readers easily frustrated when not instantly gratified in their rapid search for immediate answers (Sutherland-Smith, 2002), because hypertext and interactive features have too many choices and too many animations that may distract and disorient otherwise strong readers.

Your Turn

- Locate an American Sign Language alphabetic chart on the internet. Try to use these signs to spell some English words. Describe your experience in doing these exercises.
- Verify the following statement by observing a student reading multimedia text on the internet.

> *The multidimensional nature of digital text may make readers easily frustrated when not instantly gratified in their rapid search for immediate answers, because hypertext and interactive features have too many choices and too many animations that may distract and disorient otherwise strong readers.*

Motivation and Identity Factors

Some believe that there is a difference between language learning and language acquisition. **Language learning** refers to the development of knowledge and skills that permit varying degrees of communication with others, while **language acquisition** involves making the language part of the self (Gardner, 2010). When young children acquire their first language(s), it is largely an unconscious experience; that is, they acquire the language(s) by interacting with people in their daily lives. However, learning a new language that is not in the same environment as one's first language(s) involves much more than the mere acquisition of a new set of grammatical rules. The language learners must be willing to take on features of another cultural community (Gardner, 2010; Gardner and Lambert, 1972). Therefore, motivation is the principal driving force in learning a new language. When language learners are motivated, they are likely to flourish in the Ln (e.g., Bialystok and Hakuta, 1994).

Motivation is goal-directed. It helps an individual make efforts, become persistent, attend to the task at hand, and use good strategies to help achieve the goal (e.g., Dörnyei, 2003). According to Robert Gardner (2010), motivation involves three components: the desire to learn the language, attitudes toward learning the language, and efforts extended to learn the language.

Individuals have different motives for learning a Ln. Some people exhibit a positive attitude or identification toward a language and its cultural community and are eager to learn the language. This kind of motivation is referred to as **integrative motivation**. Others want to learn a new language for practical purposes such as getting a job or relocating to a new place for necessity; this kind of motivation is called **instrumental motivation**, though Gardner (2010) argues that this kind of drive is only an orientation, not motivation. If individuals do not expend the effort, do not enjoy learning the language, and lack the desire, they are not motivated and only express an orientation, which is not a motive, but just a reason. When learners have integrative motivation, they tend to be more perceptive of the features of the language, including forms of pronunciation and accent (Gardner and Lambert, 1972).

As just mentioned, language acquisition involves making the language part of the self (Gardner, 2010). Language is intertwined with culture and identity. Identity provides a sense of grounding and belonging. How people feel about a language and how they identify with that language affects how they learn the language. Baker and MacIntyre (2000) state that mastery of a new language involves, to some degree, taking on the identity and culture of the **target language** (language being learnt). When children acquire their L1, the sociocultural knowledge is acquired simultaneously with the knowledge of the linguistic properties of the language. However, acquisition of a Ln may not necessarily follow the same model. The linguistic knowledge may precede the cultural knowledge (Ochs, 1997). The same mainstream language (e.g., English) will be affected according to the socialization experiences of children who belong to minority cultures, such as Native American and Australian Aboriginal, and who are not middle-class, compared with white, middle-class children. When new language learners interact with the Ln, they are engaged in identity negotiation and are constructing and reconstructing their identities.

Your Turn

Find evidence to support or dispute the statement "Acquiring a language is part of forming one's identity" by interviewing a person who acquired more than one language early in life.

Types of First Language Acquisition

When a child is exposed to a primary language from birth and continuously lives in the same linguistic environment until puberty, the child is said to acquire her first language. If only one linguistic system is acquired, the process is called **monolingual first language acquisition** (MFLA). If a child is exposed to two languages from birth concurrently, the process is called the **bilingual first language acquisition** (BFLA), and if three languages coexist in a child's linguistic environment, the process is called **trilingual first language acquisition** (TFLA). So far, there is no consistent research evidence indicating first language acquisition is beyond three languages, despite occasional reports (e.g., Dewaele, 2000).

Although there are similarities among MFLA, BFLA, and TFLA and there are no qualitative differences in the acquisition of one first language or more than one

(Meisel, 2006), the acquisition processes are not entirely the same. As soon as more than one linguistic system is present in the acquisition process, different factors will make the acquisition complex. In Chapter 4, more discussion will be devoted to this topic. For now, the major differences between MFLA, BFLA, and TFLA are addressed below.

First, the language acquisition environments for monolingual first language acquisition and multilingual first language acquisition (e.g., BFLA and TFLA) are different. Typically, monolingual children learn a language in an environment in which the family language and the environmental language is consistent, whereas the linguistic environment for children who acquire more than one language is different in one of several ways:

- Both parents' language (A) is different from the mainstream language (Alpha).
- One parent's language (A) is different from the mainstream language (Alpha), and the other parent's language is similar to the mainstream language (Alpha).
- One parent's language (A) is different from the other parent's language (Alef), and both parents' languages (A and Alef) are different from the mainstream language (Alpha).[2]

Second, the linguistic input frequency children receive as monolingual and multilingual varies. MFLA children have higher linguistic input frequency than BFLA and TFLA children. Simply put, MFLA children have 100 percent input from the linguistic environment, while the linguistic input for BFLA and TFLA situations is split between two and three languages. Therefore, the quantity of input per language is less for BFLA and TFLA children. However, less quantity may not necessarily affect the acquisition of the broader structure of the languages based on Chomsky's hypothesis discussed earlier. Given limited linguistic input, BLFA and TFLA children should have the capacity to acquire and develop the languages in their environment. The world's multilingual population is powerful evidence for this. However, input quantity limitation can affect the quality of BFLA and TFLA processes, particularly in the case of children's home languages in which only parents (frequently only one parent) are the major source of input. Some BFLA and TFLA children are able to understand and speak all their input languages, whereas others may have limited or no proficiency in one or all of their languages.

Understanding the different first language acquisition processes and types will help you see the strengths and challenges of different learners in your classroom and assist you in finding appropriate approaches to reach them.

Your Turn

The author used language "A," language "Alpha" and language "Alef" to describe the three *first* languages of a child. Can you explain why the author did not use Language A, language B, and Language C as alternatives?

You have so far learned in this chapter that language acquisition is intricate and that it is embedded in the contexts of biology and social interaction (Slobin, 1982). As teachers in the contemporary classroom, language diversity is the most challenging, yet exciting, area for you to tackle. In the remainder of the book, you will be introduced to language and literacy development at different developmental stages and the supporting strategies that you can use when interacting with diverse learners.

Summary of Key Points

Language acquisition and literacy development are affected by many intricate factors.

- Biological factors
  - Humans are biologically wired to create language in the absence of conventional linguistic input.
  - There is a division of labor in the brain for language functioning.
  - The sensitive period provides a window of opportunity for achieving a full language potential.
  - Our genes potentially influence how we acquire language and develop literacy.
  - Girls tend to have a slight advantage over boys in language performances.
- Ecological factors
  - Parents' cultural beliefs and childrearing practices influence how children acquire language and develop literacy.
  - Parental socioeconomic status affects children's language outcomes.
  - Parental linguistic input is related to children's linguistic production.
  - Extended family and siblings play an important role in children's language development.
  - Sociocultural contexts influence children's language acquisition experiences.
- Language divergence factors
  - Different languages pose different tasks for language-learning children and thus affect their language acquisition speed and quality.
  - Different writing systems also affect the speed and quality of children's literacy development. Some orthographic systems may help children learn them faster, whereas others may pose challenges and children may learn them at a slower pace.
- Modality factors
  - Spoken and signed language share many similarities, but also differences.
  - Speaking and literacy are connected. Spoken language abilities facilitate literacy development. However, speaking in its acquisition stage is effortless, whereas reading and writing are a learned behavior and need more intentional learning. In addition, spoken language skills affect reading competence.
  - Conventional print and digital print require readers to process information differently.

- Motivation and identity factors
  - Motivation influences new language acquisition.
  - Learning a language, including a new language, is part of identity formation.
- Types of first language acquisition
  - There are different types of first language acquisition (MFLA, BLFA, and TFLA). Although these first language acquisition types share many similarities, they also differ in the ways they are acquired.

Key Terms

Angular gyrus
Bilingual first language acquisition
  (BFLA)
Brain plasticity
Broca's area
Cerebrum
Child-raising strategy
Classifiers
Conventional print
Creole
Cultural template
Digital print
Ecology
Event-related potential (ERP)
Frontal lobe
Gender differences
Gyrus
Heredity
Instrumental motivation
Integrative motivation
Language acquisition
Language acquisition device (LAD)
Language bioprogram
Language input
Language learning
Language socialization

Left and right hemispheres
Modality
Monolingual first language
  acquisition (MFLA)
Motherese
Orthographic transparency
Parietal lobe
Phatic language
Pidgin
Phonemic awareness
Phonological awareness
Occipital lobe
Orthographic
Self-lowering strategy
Sensitive period of language
  acquisition
Sulcus
Synapses
Target language
Temporal lobe
Trilingual first language acquisition
  (TFLA)
Universal grammar (UG)
Visual cortex
Wernicke's area

Notes

1. Event-related potential (ERP) is a noninvasive means to evaluate the brain's response to an external event during cognitive and language processing.
2. "A" is the first letter in English alphabet, "Alpha" is the first letter in Greek, and "Alef" is the first letter in Hebrew. The rationale for using the first letters to represent different languages is to show that these languages are the first languages of a child.

Recommended Further Readings

Note: some of the readings listed are old, but seminal.

Barton, M. E. and Tomasello, M. (1991). Joint attention and conversation in mother-infant sibling triads. *Child Development*, 62: 517–529.

Brown, J. R., Donelan-McCall, N., and Dunn, J. (1996). Why talk about mental states? The significance of children's conversations with friends, siblings, and mothers. *Child Development*, 67: 836–849.

Cicirelli, V. G. (1976). Mother-child and sibling-sibling interactions on a problem-solving task. *Child Development*, 47: 588–596.

Curtis, S. (1977). *Genie: A Psycholinguistic Study of a Modern-Day "Wild Child."* New York: Academic Press.

Everett, D. L. (2009). *Don't sleep, there are snakes: Life and language in the Amazonian jungle.* NY: Vintage.

Everett, D. L. (2012). *Language: The Cultural Tool.* New York: Pantheon.

Hart, B. and Risley, T. R. (1995). *Meaningful Differences in the Everyday Experience of Young American Children.* Baltimore: Paul H. Brookes.

Heath, S. B. (1983). *Ways with Words: Language, Life, and Work in Communities and Classroom.* New York: Cambridge University Press.

Jones, C. P., and Adamson, L. B. (1987). Language use in mother-child and mother-child-sibling interactions. *Child Development*, 58: 356–366.

Jourdan, C. (2006). Pidgins and creoles genesis: an anthropological offering. In C. Jourdan and K. Tuite (eds), *Language, Culture and Society* (pp. 135–155). New York: Cambridge University Press.

Klima, E. S. and Bellugi, U. (1979). *The Signs of Language.* Cambridge, MA: Harvard University Press.

Kyle, J. G. and Woll, B. (1985). *Sign language: The Study of Deaf People and Their Language.* Cambridge: Cambridge University Press.

Lenneberg, E. H. (1967). *Biological Foundations of Language.* New York: John Wiley.

Ochs, E. and Schieffelin, B. (1984), Language acquisition and socialization: three developmental stories and their implications. In R. LeVine and R. Shweder (eds), *Culture Theory: Essays on Mind, Self, and Emotion* (pp. 276–321). New York: Cambridge University Press.

Maynard, A. E. (2004). Sibling interactions. In U. P. Gielen and J. Roopnarine (eds), *Childhood and Adolescence, Cross-Cultural Perspectives and Applications* (pp. 229–252). Westport, CT: Praeger.

Olsen-Fulero, L., and Conforti, J. (1983). Child responsiveness to mother questions of varying type and presentation. *Journal of Child Language*, 10: 495–520.

Orellana, M. F., Dorner, L., and Pulido, L. (2003). Accessing assets: immigrant youth's work as family translator or "para-phrasers." *Social Problems*, 50(4): 5005–5024.

Oshima-Takane, Y., Goodz, E., and Derevensky, J. L. (1996). Birth order effects on early language development: do second born children learn from overheard speech? *Child Development*, 67: 621–634.

Pine, J. M. (1995). Variation in vocabulary development as a function of birth order. *Child Development*, 66: 272–281.

Sacks, O. (1989). *Seeing Voices: A Journey into the World of the Deaf.* Berkeley: University of California Press.

Steelman, L., Powell, B., Werum, R., and Carter, S. (2002). Reconsidering the effects of sibling configuration: recent advances and challenges. *Annual Review of Sociology*, 28: 243–269.

Tomasello, M. (2003). *Constructing a Language: A Usage-Based Theory of Language Acquisition.* Cambridge, MA: Harvard University Press.

Tomasello, M. (2008). *Origins of Human Communication.* Cambridge, MA: MIT Press.

Tomasello, M., and Mannle, S. (1985). Pragmatics of sibling speech to one-year-olds. *Child Development*, 56: 911–917.

Language Sample Analysis I

In Box 1.2 in Chapter 1, important components regarding how to implement the critical discourse analysis framework and its companion pedagogy, transformative pedagogy, are shown. In the following writing sample analysis, you are asked to do the following:

- Read the writing sample of a student. (The writer is a 7-year-old second grader from an upper-middle-class background. She enjoys writing and dreams of growing up to be an author.)

My Name Is Ted

My name is Ted I always have a sock on my head. When I woke up I bumped my head on my small, small bed. Ted went downstairs to have some bread. he met a girl. Soon thay wed. It was winter Ted went for a slead he saw his old friend his name was med soon Ted found out that med was wed! Then he saw he had a son named zed together they went to slead they slead all morning amost all night! Ted took his slead he said goodbye to med and zed and went back home he had some Hot coco and went back to bed. the next day he bumped his head again I know it souds crazy but peaple aways bump their heads when there in their bed

Sample collected by Amelia Nelson.

- Discuss what other information you need to know before you can adequately evaluate this student's writing (make a list).
- Does your list include these elements: student age, grade level, parental socioeconomic status, and educational level, linguistic background, ethnic background,

Understanding Language and Literacy Development: Diverse Learners in the Classroom, First Edition. Xiao-lei Wang. © 2015 John Wiley & Sons, Inc. Published 2015 by John Wiley & Sons, Inc. Companion website: www.wiley.com/go/wang/langandlit

developmental and linguistic ability, and funds of knowledge? Before you look at the student's information, what are your inklings about this writer's background based on her writing?

- Based on the student information provided, identify the strengths of this student's writing and her needs by focusing on the following:
  - What is not revealed in the actual writing about this student's knowledge of writing and her funds of knowledge? (Revisit the CDA approach.) Can you try your best to discover the student's potential from her writing by drawing information from her background? What does this level of analysis help you see about the student's strengths?
  - What are the needs of this student with regard to her writing? (Identify the general error patterns.)
- Propose how you can empower the student by using the four components in transformative pedagogy (situated practice, overt instruction, critical framing, and transformed practice).
- Reflect on your experience of doing this analysis and discuss whether evaluating students' work beyond errors will help you reach them better.

Part II
Developing Language and Emergent Literacies
Divergent Abilities in Infancy and Early Childhood (Birth to 5)

Part II focuses on how infants and young children acquire language and develop **emergent literacies** (i.e., emergent conventional print literacy, emergent digital literacy, and emergent critical literacy). Chapter 3 addresses the typical characteristics of acquiring one linguistic system, Chapter 4 examines the attributes of acquiring more than one linguistic system, and Chapter 5 highlights the language-learning patterns of children with various language impairments.

Understanding young children's different processes in developing language and emergent literacies will help you see where your students have been, where they are now, and where they are going in their academic language and literacy development. More importantly, your knowledge about your students' early linguistic development divergence will help you anticipate potential advantages and challenges your students may have and reach them effectively.

At the end of Part II, you will have an opportunity to analyze some language samples by applying the information you read.

Essential Questions for Part II

- Why is it problematic to categorize language and literacy learners as "typical" or "atypical"? Is there any advantage to treating different language and literacy experiences as unique characteristics rather than "typical" and "atypical?"
- What is the educational significance of considering the early language experiences of children who are learning English as a Ln and children with LI?
- What should be the guiding principles when providing support for children with different linguistic needs in early childhood?

Understanding Language and Literacy Development: Diverse Learners in the Classroom, First Edition. Xiao-lei Wang.
© 2015 John Wiley & Sons, Inc. Published 2015 by John Wiley & Sons, Inc.
Companion website: www.wiley.com/go/wang/langandlit

3

Acquiring One Linguistic System
First Language Acquisition

Prereading Questions and Activities

- Video- or audio-record a short spontaneous talk of two children with typical development at ages 2 and 5 (one child at each age). Transcribe the conversations verbatim. Analyze the transcripts at the level of words and sentences (e.g., how many words have they produced? How many different words have they produced? How many words have they produced in a sentence on average?). Develop a language development profile for the two children and identify the differences you have found.
- Read the following sentences to a 4-year-old child and ask the child to identify the sentence that he or she thinks is correct. What is the child's choice? How do you explain this child's choice?
  - (a) That it is lost pet Amy is sad.
  - (b) Amy is pet lost that it is sad.
  - (c) It's sad that Amy lost her pet.
  - (d) Her pet is lost that Amy is sad.
- What do children bring to the task of language learning? Support your answer with concrete examples.
- If you do not teach young children, will your knowledge of early language development help you teach older children? If so, how? If not, why?

Topics to Be Addressed in This Chapter

- Typical developmental profile during infancy and early childhood
- Developing essential language abilities
  - Phonology (sound system)

Understanding Language and Literacy Development: Diverse Learners in the Classroom, First Edition. Xiao-lei Wang.
© 2015 John Wiley & Sons, Inc. Published 2015 by John Wiley & Sons, Inc.
Companion website: www.wiley.com/go/wang/langandlit

- ○ Lexicon and semantics (words and meaning)
- ○ Morphology and syntax (language structure)
- ○ Pragmatics (language use)
- ○ Metalinguistic awareness
- Special issues
  - ○ Private speech
  - ○ The role of gestures in language acquisition
  - ○ Dialect
- Developing emergent literacies
  - ○ Emergent print literacy
  - ○ Emergent digital literacy
  - ○ Emergent critical literacy
- Supporting strategies for language and emergent literacy development in infancy and early childhood

---

Learning Objectives

After reading this chapter, you are expected to do the following:

- Understand the cognitive and social development characteristics of young children with typical development and how these characteristics affect their language acquisition and emergent literacy development.
- Understand the typical path of language acquisition.
- Understand typical emergent literacy achievements of young children (emergent print, digital, and critical literacy development).
- Understand some important issues related to language development such as the functions of private speech, gestural development, and the different linguistic features of dialects.
- Understand that different cultures have different early literacy practices.
- Understand the focus and the general approaches in working with young children with regard to their early language and emergent literacy development.
- Know how to use various strategies to support children's early language and emergent literacy development holistically.

Typical Development Profile in Infancy and Early Childhood

Infancy and early childhood are marked by curiosity, exploration, and discovery (Copley, 2000). As a result, young children have natural learning drives and are always ready to explore and learn as long as there are opportunities (Wang, 2011a).

Infants and young children go through several remarkable cognitive changes. In the first year of children's lives, infants tend to focus on objects, events, and people in their immediate environment; learning is context-bound. "Out of sight and out of mind" is the hallmark of infants' cognitive characteristics. In the later part of the first year, infants show early signs of **symbolic thinking** (Piaget, 1962), but it is only toward the end of the second year that they begin to truly talk and think about things that are beyond their immediate experience or environment.

Young children's thinking often lacks **reversibility**; that is, they cannot see that a certain quantity remains the same despite a change in the shape or size. For example, a 4-year-old child is likely to insist that a tall container contains more water than a short one even though she saw the same amount of water being poured into the two containers.

Moreover, children's thinking at this stage is **egocentric** by nature, and they are likely to evaluate others and events based on their own viewpoint. For instance, 3-year-old Dana told her older brother Chris that the moon was following her while they were walking outside one evening. Likewise, children at this stage have a hard time understanding the function of rules. You have probably noticed that young children often change the rules of a game to suit their needs.

Even though young children have some cognitive constraints, they are not passive in the language acquisition process. For instance, they compensate for their limited linguistic capacities by employing different strategies such as bootstrapping to increase their language-learning possibilities. **Bootstrapping** means that a child learns something new by relying on knowledge in other domains. For example, toddlers learn new words and sentences by paying attention to phrasal prosody (e.g., rhythm, stress, and intonation) and function words (e.g., determiners,[1] auxiliaries,[2] and prepositions) without much knowledge of their ambient language (Christophe et al., 2008).

Your Turn

Use a few key words or phrases to summarize the developmental profile of children during infancy and early childhood (For example, *curiosity, eager to explore, lack reversibility, egocentric thinking,* and *bootstrapping*). Try to predict how these characteristics are connected to young children's language acquisition and emergent literacy development.

Developing Essential Language Abilities

To become competent language users and effective communicators, the major language acquisition task for infants and young children is to learn the sound system (**phonology**), words (**lexicon**), meanings (**semantics**), and structure (**morphology** and **syntax**) of their environmental language and to use the language appropriately in social interactions (**pragmatics**). They must also develop knowledge of the relationships and functions between the different language elements (metalinguistic knowledge). These different language components that children have to acquire are

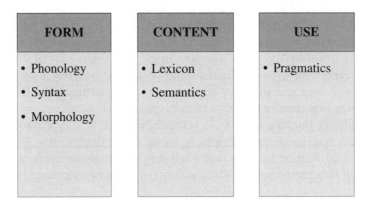

Figure 3.1　Language components

traditionally categorized as language form, content, and use based on their functions (See Figure 3.1).

In the following sections, you will develop knowledge on how these language components are acquired in infancy and early childhood.

Phonological development

Phonology refers to the sound system of a given language. When acquiring a language, one important task for a child is to develop knowledge of rules that govern the sound structure and to understand how sounds are used to carry meaning.

Three areas of phonological ability are essential to develop during infancy and early childhood: receptive phonological knowledge, productive phonological knowledge, and early phonological awareness. **Receptive phonological knowledge** refers to the ability to distinguish and understand the phonological information in a language, and **productive knowledge of phonology** is the ability to articulate the sounds in a language. **Phonological awareness** in its early form is the ability to attend to the phonological segments of speech and to be aware of the relationship between sounds in words (see Chapter 6 for more discussion). For instance, a child is cognizant of the sound /æ/ in *cat* and *bat*.

Receptive phonological knowledge development

When discussing phonology, it is important to understand the concept of phoneme because it is a basic unit of a language's sound system. A **phoneme** is the smallest meaningful unit of sound that allows an individual to make distinctions between words. For example, when the words *cat* and *sat* are said, listeners can distinguish one word from the other based on the contrast between the two phonemes /k/ and /s/.

Early in life, infants are capable of discerning differences among the phonetic units of all languages (Kuhl, Feng-Ming, and Huei-Mei, 2003). At 4 weeks of age, infants can already distinguish specific phonemes (Aslin and Pisoni, 1980), such as /i/ versus /a/ contrasts and /p/ versus /b/ (Aslin, Juczyk, and Pisoni, 1998). At 5 months,

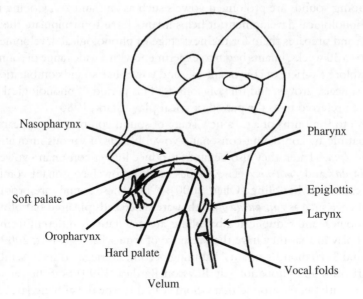

Nasopharynx

Pharynx

Soft palate

Epiglottis

Larynx

Oropharynx

Hard palate

Vocal folds

Velum

Figure 3.2 Human vocal tract

infants can recognize the same phonemes regardless of changes in a speaker's intonation or pronunciation by different speakers (de Boysson-Bardies, 1999). However,
between 8 and 10 months of age, some believe between 6 and 12 months of age (e.g.,
Kuhl, Feng-Ming, and Huei-Mei, 2003), infants' ability to discriminate the phonetic
units not in their environmental language sharply declines. They begin to pay more
attention to phonemes and sound contracts in the language they often hear (Werker
and Tees, 1984; de Boysson-Bardies, 1999), and they begin to lose the ability to detect
the contrasts in the languages that are not in their daily environment.

One important aspect that is critical in children's growth of receptive phonological
knowledge is the development of prosody. **Prosody** is the rhythmic structure (Lust,
2006) or sound pattern such as stress, pitch, tempo, rhythm, and pause of speech.
Prosody plays a significant role in attracting the attention of infants to processing
speech sounds (Otto, 2009). Infants can use the prosodic cues such as the word-
stress patterns to locate boundaries between words in adult speech (Pence and Justice,
2008). For example, when infants hear "You little cutie," they are able to use the
word-stress cue to help them isolate *little* and *cutie* as separate words.

Productive phonological knowledge development
Compared with receptive phonological development, productive phonological development comes later due to physical constraints. It takes a while for a child to be able to
coordinate the different parts in the vocal tract (see Figure 3.2) and learn to produce
different sounds in a language.

In the first months or so, infants produce vocalizations in the form of crying, coughs,
and hiccups, and these vocalizations are reflexive in nature. Starting from 6 to 8
weeks, infants begin to produce nonreflexive vocalizations such as cooing (e.g., Reich,

1986). **Cooing** sounds are prolonged vowels such as /a/ and /ɛ/. Cooing is significant for phonological development; it helps infants learn to manipulate their tongue
and mouth and prepares them for the next stage of phonological development.

From 16 to 30 weeks, infants begin to experiment with a wide range of sounds. They
begin to explore a variety of consonant-like and vowel-like sound combinations. They
also make squeals, growls, and friction sounds. This period of phonological development is often referred to as the period of **vocal play** (Stark, 1986).

Around 6 to 9 months of age, a new stage of sound combination appears. Infants
begin to **babble** by combining consonant–vowel blends of various intonations such
as /da/ and /ma/. Later, they also begin to produce longer consonant–vowels blends
such as /da-da/ and /ma-ma/. These types of clear vowel–consonant combinations
are called **canonical babbling** (Oller, 2000). When these sounds are produced in a
longer sequence such as /da-da-da-da/, they are called **reduplicated babbling** (Stark,
1986). Canonical and reduplicated babblings are qualitatively different from the previous vocal play in that they have the presence of true syllables (Hoff, 2009). Somewhere around 8–10 months, infants' babbling becomes variegated and resembles adult
speech in rhythm and phonation (de Boysson-Bardies, 1999) as if they are having a
conversation with people around them. Some call this type of babbling **jargon** (Sacks,
1989), and others call it **intonated babble** (Stoel-Gammon, 1998).

As children move toward toddlerhood, they are able to produce a range of words
when their phoneme perception becomes more advanced. However, some toddlers
still have trouble pronouncing some difficult or long words such as *spaghetti* (Hoff,
2009) and *hippopotamus* (Gillam, Marquardt, and Martin, 2011). Toddlers often omit
certain syllables, saying *bee* for *bambi* (first syllable is deleted) and *appe* for *apple* (last
syllable is deleted) (De Houwer, 2009). This phenomenon is referred to as **truncation**
(deletion of syllables). Toddlers also tend to omit some sounds like /s/ in *spill* and
in *store*. Sometimes they change word pronunciations, such as pronouncing *blanket*
as *banke* (Otto, 2009). By 6 years of age, children will have mastered the majority
of sounds in the English language, with exceptions such as /s/, /z/, and /ð/ (e.g.,
Goldstein, Fabiano, and Washington, 2005).

Your Turn

Listen to the babbles between the twins in the following YouTube link: http://
search.yahoo.com/search;_ylt=AuOQpP5M0WXe1eUbgEXAfVCbvZx4?p=youtube+
infant+twin+babbling&toggle=1&cop=mss&ei=UTF-8&fr=yfp-t-701

Based the information you just read, describe the nature of the babbling produced by
the twins and discuss the relationship between such babbling and language development.

Phonological awareness

Phonological awareness is the ability to recognize, identify, or manipulate sound units
in a language (Yeong and Liow, 2012). Around 2 years of age, some children begin to
show signs of phonological awareness. For instance, they begin to appreciate rhymes

in children's books and songs. They also spontaneously rhyme or produce a string of words that begin with the same sound (Hoff, 2009). In a study conducted by Liberman and associates, 50 percent of 4- and 5-year-olds can count the syllables in a multisyllabic word (Liberman et al., 1997). In addition, young children show awareness that a syllable can be further broken into two constituents: the **onset**, which consists of the initial consonant or consonant cluster, and the **rime**, which consists of the vowel plus any following consonants (Treiman, 1985). For example, in *cat*, /k/ is the onset, and /æt/ is the rime. However, 4-year-olds find it hard to recognize initial consonants when they are part of cluster (Treiman, 1885), and the ability to recognize phonemes as units (phonemic awareness) will develop later (Hoff, 2009).

Young children's phonological awareness typically goes through the stages of developing word-level awareness skills followed by syllable-level skills, onset-rime level skills, and finally phonemic-level skills (Yeong and Liow, 2012). These phonological skills are not just important for language development; they are also crucial for a child's later reading development. In fact, research has consistently suggested that phonological awareness is a robust predictor for reading success.

Many factors can influence children's emergent phonological awareness before they receive formal literacy instruction later in school. These factors are listed in Box 3.1.

Box 3.1 Factors That Influence Emergent Phonological Awareness

- Vocabulary development
- Knowledge of nursery rhymes
- Letter–name knowledge
- The quality of a child's phonological representation of spoken words
- Parental educational levels and socioeconomic status
- Language learning experiences

Modified from R. J. McCauley and M. E. Fey, *Treatment of Language Disorders in Children* (Baltimore: Paul H. Brookes, 2006), p. 287.

Therefore, when looking at young children's phonological awareness, it is important to take into consideration these factors and avoid making judgment before you know a child's background and her experiences with language.

Your Turn

Review the information on the complex factors in language and literacy development in Chapter 2; discuss how these factors can influence a child's phonological development.

Lexical-semantic development

To be able to communicate effectively in a language, a child must also develop knowledge about words (lexicon) and learn their meanings (semantics).

Lexicon

The lexicon is the volume of words in a language, and it is the building block of a linguistic system.

Lexicon comprehension

Infants exhibit signs of understanding words used in their daily lives typically around 6 to 9 months. By the end of the first year, infants typically understand about 15 words used frequently in their environment.

Lexicon production

A child's word production is usually later than his word comprehension. Several noticeable aspects of lexicon production are addressed below.

Rate of production   Toward the end of the first year (by about 10 to 12 months of age), children typically produce a few single words that are frequently used in their environment (usually one or two words). By about 15 months children have an average of ten words in production. Initially toddlers add about one to three words per week to their lexicon. Much of their early vocabulary contains social words (e.g., *bye* and *hi*). By the time children reach a vocabulary size of 50 words (at about 18 months of age), social words decrease, and other types of words increase. Overall, girls tend to be a little bit faster in their lexical development than boys (De Houwer, 2009).

Between 18 and 24 months, some children begin to undergo a period of **vocabulary spurt**; that is, they experience a rapid increase in vocabulary size (they usually gain one or two words per day). However, some researchers have questioned whether a vocabulary spurt is a widespread phenomenon. One study shows that only a minority of children (1 in 5) had a vocabulary spurt, and most children increased their vocabulary steadily (Ganger and Brent, 2004). Whether there is a vocabulary spurt or not, children's vocabulary increase during early childhood is impressive. By 24 months, children's productive lexicon reaches 300 words on average (Fenson et al., 1993).

Young children's vocabulary increase can be attributed to several factors. First, it is due to their cognitive advancement such as memory improvement (e.g., they develop a better ability to recall words) and categorization ability development. Second, it is because their life experiences begin to widen. Children now need more words to describe and label these experiences. Third, it is their environmental input change. Parents or caretakers use more words to talk with them (Huttenlocher et al., 1991; Pence and Justice, 2008). Fourth, as mentioned earlier in the chapter, young children increase their vocabulary learning by utilizing the bootstrapping strategy such as relying on knowledge in other domains (e.g., phrasal prosody) (Christophe et al., 2008). Finally, children learn words through **fast mapping**; that is, when children are first exposed to a new word, they make a prediction about the word's meaning based on clues available in the context (see more discussion in Chapter 6).

However, there is a wide variation in young children's vocabulary production. For example, at 16 months some children already produce 154 words, whereas others may produce none (Bates, Dale, and Thal, 1995; De Houwer, 2009).

Idiomorphs Initially, children may produce vocalizations that are word-like forms with recognizable and consistent sound patterns, but are not conventional. They are referred to as **idiomorphs** (Reich, 1986), which has other synonyms such as **protowords** (Bates, 1976), **vocables** (N. Nelson, 2010), and **quasiwords** (Stoel-Gammon and Cooper, 1984). Children's idiomorphs typically include the following categories (Otto, 2009):

- Sounds that accompany gestures (for example, *mlk* with a drinking gesture, meaning "I want milk").
- Imitation of environmental sounds such as animals, vehicles, and motors (for example, *choochoo*, referring to a train).
- Self-imitation sounds that occur naturally and then are repeated when a certain outcome is desired (such as *Achoo*, meaning "I need a handkerchief").
- Imitation of adult speech.

Although these idiomorphs are often only understandable in context, they help young children transition from babbling to using conventional words.

Categories of early words The early words of English-speaking children tend to be nouns. In general, their early words are related to people, animals, and objects in their immediate environment. About half of their early lexicon (51%) contains general nominals (names), 14% specific nominals, 13% action words, 9% modifiers, 8% personal and social words, and 4% function words (K. Nelson, 1973; Pence and Justice, 2008).

Lexicon innovation Sometimes, young children create new words to fill in their communication gap. Their word invention tends to include three types: denominal verbs,[3] object nominal, and agent and instrument nominal. Most of these invented words need to be interpreted in context. There are several needs for young children to coin words to overcome their vocabulary limitation. First, because they have few verbs available early on for talking about a large range of actions, many of them take up the option of coining new verbs from nouns to communicate about particular actions. These innovations allow young children, as young as 2, to be very precise about the actions they are talking about in context. Clark (1988) provided two good examples to illustrate young children's lexicon innovation. A child (2;4)[4] wanted to have some cheese weighed, and said, "You have to *scale* it." Another child (3;0) watched a truck passing and said, "It's *trucking*."

Second, because young children lack well-established terms for subcategories, they may opt to coin new compound nouns; that is, combining two or more nouns with the appropriate stress pattern and modifier-head word order. For example, in Clark's study (1988), a 2-year-old child could distinguish *fried eggs* from *boiled eggs* with the expressions *plate-egg* and *cup-egg*. Other 2-year-olds could also distinguish kinds of smoke such as *house-smoke* (chimney) from *car-smoke* (exhaust).

Third, young children also invent words to talk about agent and instrument nouns to compensate for their lack of words in conversation. For example, 2-year-old children can construct new compound nouns such as *fix-man* for a car mechanic and *garden-man* for a gardener. Three to 5 year olds also produced some instrument nominal such as jumping-thing (things for jumping with), eating-thing (things for eating with), and package-machine (machine for pushing things) (Clark, 1988).

What is remarkable about young children's lexical inventions is that they are rule governed, reflecting their notice of the general rules in their ambient language. For example, *-er* in English often signifies a person such as *worker*. Young English-speaking children's lexical inventions include the rules such as *hitter-man* (someone who hits things), *reader-man* (someone who reads things), and *kicker-man* (someone who kicks things).

Your Turn

Compile a list of words that young children invent (you can research literature or listen to young children's conversations) and discuss the significance of word invention in young children's communication and overall language development.

Semantics

Semantics refers to word meaning. For a child to learn a word, she needs to understand the relationship of a word in different contexts rather than just label it. For example, the word *cat* changes functions in different situations: *The cat is chasing birds; The dog is running after the cat; The cat is cute.* In the first example, cat is performing an action. In the second, cat is a recipient of an action. In the last, cat is an entity that is being described.

By ages 4 and 5, children have quite sophisticated semantic knowledge. For example, in a study, 4- and 5-year-old children were able to focus on the intended meaning by ignoring the semantic errors purposely made by adults, such as calling a *comb* a *brush* (Kondrad and Jaswal, 2012).

Semantic network   The meanings in a child's lexicon are not organized randomly, but in a **semantic network**. Words are organized and stored according to their phonological, semantic, and syntactic features. For example, the connection between *bib* and *bit* is their shared phonological features (both words have /b/), the association between *whale* and *dolphin* is their semantic similarities, and the link between *him* and *her* is their similar syntactic roles. Some researchers believe that our access to lexicon is based on the strength of connections among words. For instance, when the word *bird* is activated, a number of additional entries in the semantic network are also activated, such as the words *wings*, *robin*, and *canary*, because of their semantic similarities. This is referred to as **spreading activation** (e.g., Pence and Justice, 2008).

When young children learn new words, they go through an interesting process; they may first call a *kangaroo* a *mouse*, or a *saddle* a *chair*, because these two words are stored closely, and the lexical representation of the word *mouse* is stronger than the word *kangaroo*. As the child's lexical representation of *kangaroo* strengthens, accuracy is achieved. (e.g., Pence and Justice, 2008).

Semantic transparency   **Semantic transparency** refers to the consistency between the meaning of a compound word and its constituent morphemes. For example, *tooth* and *brush* in *toothbrush* are transparent constituents from which one can easily infer the meaning of *toothbrush*, but *dog* in *hotdog* is opaque, and one cannot infer the meaning of *hotdog* directly from *dog* (Cheng, Wang, and Perfetti, 2011). Young children usually have an easier time understanding and using the compound words that are semantically transparent.

Overextension, underextension, and overlap   In the second year of children's lives, they are often observed extending the meaning of words. Children usually tend to extend word meaning in three ways. First, they overextend word meaning based on their categories. For example, a child calls the neighbor's *cat* a *dog* because the cat resembles his dog (four-legged and furry). Second, they extend word meaning by focusing on the perceptual similarities. For example, they may call anything round a ball such as *moon* and *orange*. Finally, children may extend word meanings based on their relationship with other objects. For example, a child may use the word *flower* for *watering can* or *flowerpot* (Pence and Justice, 2008). This phenomenon is called **overextension** (using words in an overly general manner). Toddlers overgeneralize about one-third of all new words. Overextension such as the examples described above may actually represent strength in a child's ability in analogical processing for applying a reasonably close term when an exact label is unavailable (N. Nelson, 2010).

Children are also observed using **underextension** strategies in their communication. That is they use words to refer to only a subset of possible referents. For example, a child might only use the word *book* to describe his own books, not the ones that belong to others.

Sometimes, children overextend words in one situation and underextend them in another. For example, a child calls jellybeans and his grandmother's pills *candy* (overextension), but he does not call chocolate bars *candy* (underextension) (Pence and Justice, 2008).

Your Turn

Read the following metaphors about *word* and discuss the importance of *word* in a child's language and cognitive development.

Words glisten.
Words irradiate exquisite splendor.
Words carry magic and keep us spellbound.
Words are like glamorous bricks that constitute the fabric of any language.
Words are like roses that make the environment fragrant.

J. Aitchison, *Words in the Mind: An Introduction to the Mental Lexicon* (Oxford: Wiley-Blackwell, 2012), p. 3.

Morphosyntactic development

Morphology

Another important task for infants and young children to accomplish on their language acquisition journey is to develop knowledge of morphemes. **Morphemes** are the smallest meaningful units of a language. Morphemes can be words (e.g. *class* and *room* in *classroom*), word stems (e.g., *play*), and affixes (e.g., *pre-* in *preschool and -s* as in *plays*). Morphological knowledge allows children to expand their vocabulary from a smaller set of root words to form more words. For example, morphological knowledge in English allows children to form more words from a single word, as is the case with the word *child*: *childless, childlike,* and *childish*; it also allows children to make grammatical inflections such as adding *-ed* to verbs to create past tense *worked,* and adding *-ing* to form present progressive *working.* Moreover, it allows children to produce plurals (*dogs*) and possessives (*Peter's*) and to create prefixes (*pre-read*) and suffixes (*friendless*).

By age 4, children are able to understand the morphological rules. For example, in a well-known study by Berko (1958), English-speaking children were presented with a set of made-up English words like *wug*. Children in the experiment were able to correctly indicate that the plural form for *wug* is *wugs*.

Young children's morphological development goes through different stages. They initially learn to use the morphological markers by memorization. They then learn the morphological rule generalization, and later they go through a stage of morphological rule overgeneralization before they acquire morphological rules. For instance, around 3 and 4 years of age, English-speaking children tend to overgeneralize morphological rules such as irregular verb past tense. You may often hear children adding *-ed* to irregular verbs for past tense such as *goed* instead of *went* and *taked* instead of *took*. Children seem to be insensitive to adult correction, as shown in the following example.

> CHILD: I *goed* to the park yesterday.
> MOTHER: You *went* to the park yesterday?
> CHILD: Yeah, I *went* to the park yesterday and I also *goed* to Aaron's house.

Likewise, children also tend to generalize rules for adjectives such as substituting *better* with *gooder* and *best* with *goodest* or *bestest*. Mistakes made by children such as the above are developmentally interesting, because they show that young children begin to notice the rules in the English language (the higher frequency of regular morpheme forms, such as adding *-ed* to a past tense verb), and they err on what is most likely to occur. Over time, children are usually able to use the correct forms.

Your Turn

What would be your approach in addressing the mistakes made by young children, such as *goed* and *taked*? Explain.

Syntax

Developing syntactic knowledge is an important endeavor in children's language acquisition process. **Syntactical knowledge** means the knowledge of how words and phrases are combined to form sentences or **utterances** (a sentence in context). Note that in the case of young children, an utterance means a spoken sentence or phrase that expresses an idea (e.g., "eat cookie"). During early childhood, children make three important achievements in their syntactic development.

First, by 2 years of age, children typically begin to combine words. They begin by combining two words together such as "mommy sock" and then three words together such as "I want cookie." Usually early word combinations involve uninflected word forms. Sometimes, young children produce longer multiword chunks, such as "Here-ya-go," "All-done," "All gone," and "there it is." These utterances appear to be multiword phrases. However, they are learned by children as **unanalyzed chunks** (N. Nelson, 2010) or **unanalyzed wholes** (De Houwer, 2009). Although the unanalyzed chunks are often the direct imitation of adults' speech, they are an important step in young children's syntactic development. By age 2, the MLU is about 2.0 and by age 2 and a half, the MLU is about 2.5.

Children continue to refine their productive morphosyntax over the next few years. Early on, simple sentences predominate. By age 3, mean length of utterance is about 3.2, and by age 5, the MLU is about 5.7. By age 6, children can produce utterances as long as those of adults, such as "No, put that one over there, there on the blocks I set up" (Pence and Justice, 2008).

Second, children progress to produce different sentence types. By age 3, children can produce simple declarative sentences such as "I am working!" They also begin to use negative sentences such as "I'm not doing that!" "Don't touch that!" However, the negative sentence development goes through several phases. Initially, children place "no" at the beginning of sentences, as in "No eat that." Later, the negative word moves inside the sentence near the main verb, such as "I not eat that." By age 4 years, many children begin to use conventional auxiliary verbs, such as "You can't do that" and "I don't want to go." However, other types of negative sentences such as sentences containing "won't" and "I am not sure" may not emerge until several years later. Moreover, children also begin to produce interrogative sentence such as "Why is that light green?" "What is that?" "Who did it?" "Where are you going?" and "He is sad, isn't he?"

Third, children start to produce complex sentences. Starting from age 3, children begin to increase syntactic complexity, such as "Julia is hungry *but* I'm not" and "The girl *who* is my friend didn't come." Moreover, around 2 and 2 and a half, English-speaking children master the active voice use. Passive voice usually tends to appear late (typically after 3 years of age), with short sentences containing noun+be / get+verb (*-en/-ed*), such as "*It was crushed*" or "*It got broken.*" In these early passives, the noun or pronoun subjects are almost always inanimate. According to Owens (2012), these forms may be based on the adjective form of the copula (e.g., "He was sad"). Also, verbs of state (e.g., *lost*, *left*, and *broken*) tend to be predominant in these short passives. Later, children use action verbs, such as *killed*, *hit*, and *crashed*, in both short and full passive ("He got *hit*").

Children's difficulties with passives are well known (Lee and Lee, 2008). The early passives by children have some particular properties. At first, before ages 4–5, children produce and comprehend actional passives (e.g., *catch*) better than non-actional passives (e.g., *see*). Later, short passives (passives lacking the *by-phrase)* are produced and comprehended better than long passives (Lee and Lee, 2008). Also, children use truncated passives that omit overt agents. A recent study suggests that the event structure of predicates plays an important role in the development of passives. If a predicate has a result state, its passive counterpart is easily acquired, whereas if a predicate lacks a result state, its passive counterpart is acquired less easily. Children performed well on passives of accomplishment predicates since they make a good adjective (due to a result state in their event structure), whereas they performed poorly on passives of activity and state predicates since they do not make a good adjective (due to the lack of a result state) (Lee and Lee, 2008).

The input in children's environment has an impact on how children acquire passive voice. In a study, 4-year-olds were asked to listen to stories containing either a high proportion of passive voice sentences or a high proportion of active voice sentences. Children who heard stories with passive sentences produced more passive constructions (and with fewer mistakes) and showed higher comprehension scores than children who heard stories with active sentences (Vasilyeva, Huttenlocher, and Waterfall, 2006).

Your Turn

Document a speech sample of a 3-year old, a 4-year old, and a 5-year old and compare the differences in their use of passive voice.

Pragmatic development

Even if a child masters the sound, meaning, and structure of a language, it is not enough for him to be an effective language user in social contexts. A child must master the knowledge on how to use language appropriately in interpersonal communication; this ability is called **pragmatic competence**. Pragmatic development is closely tied to children's **theory of mind** development (Tager-Flusberg, 2001); that is, children need to understand others' mental status (such as intents, desires, and beliefs) in order to communicate with them successfully.

There are two components in pragmatic knowledge: **pragmalinguistics** and **sociopragmatics**. The former refers to the linguistic resources for conveying communicative acts (e.g., how to make requests, how to apologize, and how to refuse) and interpersonal meaning (one's knowledge of the means to strengthen or weaken the force of an utterance), whereas the latter refers to the social perceptions underlying a person's interpretation and performance of communicative acts (one's knowledge of the particular means that are likely to be most successful for a given situation) (Soler and Martínez-Flor, 2008). Box 3.2. shows an example of the importance of pragmatic ability in communication.

Box 3.2   Example of a Young Child's Pragmatics

One day when Léandre (3;4) entered a tram in Basel, Switzerland with his family, a frail old lady stood up to let Léandre have her seat. Instead of saying "merci" (thank you), Léandre called out to his younger brother, "Eh, Dominique, regarde la petite vieille qui m'a donné son siège!" (Eh, Dominique, look at the little old woman who gave me her seat!).

Example from X.-L. Wang, *Growing up with Three Languages: Birth to Eleven* (Bristol: Multilingual Matters, 2008), p. 80.

Although Léandre used correct French pronunciation, meaning, and grammar, he failed to use the language appropriately in the social interaction; that is, according to the Western tradition, it is very impolite to call a woman *a little old woman* to her face (in French, *la petite vieille* sounds even worse than the English term), especially because the lady just did him a favor. Léandre learned the term *La petite vieille* in the fairy tales his father read to him. However, he had yet to learn how to use this phrase in its proper context. Thus, **pragmatic development** is the process in which children learn to use language to communicate successfully with others in social interactions.

There are several important pragmatic skills children need to develop in early childhood: using language for different functions, using decontextualized language, learning how to communicate with others successfully, understanding extralinguistic cues (e.g., facial expressions), learning how to communicate in a culturally appropriate way, and learning how to tell personal stories (narratives).

Learn to use language for different purposes
Halliday (1986) described seven functions that children use in oral communication (see Box 3.3) during early childhood. The first four functions (instrumental, regulatory, interactional, and personal) serve the functions of helping young children satisfy physical, emotional, and social needs. The remaining three functions (heuristic, imaginative, and representational) serve the functions of helping young children grapple with their environment. The instrumental function (I want) usually appears first in children's communication, and the representational function (explanation) is observed last. However, the other functions do not necessarily appear in hierarchical order. Moreover, these communicative functions do not naturally appear on their own in children's language acquisition process; environmental influence such as adult input is important.

Box 3.3 Oral Communication Functions in Early Childhood

Function	Description	Example
Instrumental (I want…)	Use language to express preferences, needs, and wants.	"Want apple."
Regulatory (Do as I tell you)	Use language to influence others' behavior, feeling, or attitude	"Go away!"
Interactional (Me and you)	Use language to make contact and develop social relationships.	"Love you."
Personal (Here I come)	Use language to express feelings, opinions, and individual identity.	"Me, good girl."
Heuristic (Tell me why)	Use language to gain knowledge about the environment.	"Daddy, why cloud is white?"
Imaginative (Let's pretend)	Use language to create, explore, and entertain.	"I am a superman."
Representational (I've got something to tell you)	Use language to convey facts and information.	"It's plastic."

Based on M. A. K. Halliday, *Learning How to Mean* (New York: Elsevier, 1986).

According to Halliday (2003), among these functions, personal and heuristic are crucial for children's later school success; these two functions must be learned. Moreover, recent research indicates that children begin to develop the **persuasive communication** function a lot earlier than we used to believe (see Box 3.4). In fact, it starts to develop as early as infancy, when babies cry to get attention from a caretaker. Some toddlers use verbal and nonverbal tactics to get parents and siblings to share toys or food, relinquish favorite objects, and abandon bedtime rules (Bartsch, Wright, and Estes, 2009). To be able to verbally persuade others is important in social interaction. Children already have the ability to attend to others' psychological and mental states and perspectives at age 3. Children (3–5 years) frequently use six persuasive tactics: questioning, commanding, protesting, affirming, hinting, and explaining (Bartsch, Wright, and Estes, 2009). Understanding others' metal and psychological status (theory of mind) is a crucial ability to develop for further language, cognitive, and social development.

Learn to use decontextualized language

Through the preschool years, children tend to talk most often about here-and-now topics rather than distant past or future events and more about themselves than other people. This type of context-bound language associated with the immediate environment is called **contextualized language**. As children broaden their experience, they need to talk about many events that are not in their immediate surroundings; the

Box 3.4　Example of Young Children's
Pervasive Communication

CHILD (3;4):	Now, will you read that?
FATHER:	What about the Three Pigs? Do you want to go and get that book?
CHILD:	No.
FATHER:	Yeah, I like that book. Go get it. I don't want to read that. I want to read the Three Pigs book.
CHILD:	This one's a good one, it is.
FATHER:	It is?
CHILD:	Yeah.
FATHER:	How do you know?
CHILD:	Because, because it is from Sesame Street.

Examples from K. Bartsch, J. C. Wright, and D. Estes, "Young children's persuasion in everyday conversation: tactics and attunement to others' mental states," *Social Development*, 19(2) (2009): 394–417.

language they use that describes events that are not in the immediate environment is referred to as **decontextualized language**.

Even though contextualized talk is prominent in early childhood, decontextualized language is also observed with specific conversation partners, settings, and situations. For example, preschool children may carry on decontextualized conversation in their fantasy talks when playing with peers at school, use past tense references in the more familiar home settings with family members, and refer to people not present and events past, future, or make-believe during family meals and book readings (DeTemple, 2001) and travel in cars with parents and peers (Marvin, 1994).

Moreover, certain toys such as puppets may also facilitate greater use of decontextualized language during play because children can more readily have the toy assume multiple roles in various scenarios such as distant time or pretend play.

Research indicates that opportunities to hear and engage in decontextualized talk with others in the home are directly associated with young children's use of decontextualized language forms, subsequent emerging literacy abilities, and their ability to produce personal narratives at age 5 (e.g., DeTemple, 2001).

Decontextualized language is considered a precursor to the development of early literacy skills and is especially important for academic success (Marvin and Cline, 2010) because most of the school subjects deal with matters that are not in children's immediate environment.

Learn to communicate successfully with others

Learn to convey clearer messages　When children are younger, their major conversational partners are often their parents, caretakers, and immediate family members.

Because parents are familiar with the conversation context as well as the way that their children communicate, they tend to become indulgent in ratifying children's versions of events. For instance, when a child says, "I want that," a parent may know immediately the referent without pressing for clarity. As such, the child does not have to strive to make herself understood. Nevertheless, when different people are engaged in a conversation, there are different sources of challenges to the speakers. In a multiparty conversation, different people are likely to question or contest a particular presentation of reality. A child involved in such a conversation has to present arguments for her version of events or summon support for her interpretation and fill in many details (Blum-Kulka and Snow, 2002). In other words, the child is more accountable for clarifying her speech in such a conversational environment. As children widen their social networks, they must learn how to communicate clearly and effectively with a broader range of people, including their peers.

Develop conversational schema   In order to carry on a successful conversation, a speaker needs first to initiate and establish a topic. Then, the speaker needs to navigate a series of contingent turns that maintain or shift the topic. Finally, the speaker needs to resolve or close the conversation (Pence and Justice, 2008). All these skills are called **conversational schema**.

Developing the conversational schema begins with **joint attention** when caretakers and infants focus on mutual objects. In such interactions, infants learn to coordinate their attention between the caretaker and the object. Children then learn turn-taking, first for short period of time and then longer. By the end of age 6, most children can successfully enter peer conversation and are able to carry on a conversation with their peer interlocutors (Pence and Justice, 2008).

In addition, toward the end of the early childhood, children begin to develop other conversational strategies such as a turnabout (Berk, 2009). A **turnabout** means that a speaker not only comments on what has just been said but also adds a request to get the conversational partner to respond again (Berk, 2009). This important communication skill is gradually developed through interactions with adults (Martinez, 1987). Box 3.5 demonstrates how an adult used the turnabout technique to help the child engage in dialogue.

Box 3.5   Example of Turnabout

CHILD: We had pizza.
ADULT: Pizza! Hmmm, I bet you went to a _____
CHILD: Birthday party!
ADULT: I love birthday parties. Whose party was it?

Example from R. E. Owens, *Language Development: An Introduction* (Boston: Pearson, 2012), p. 174.

Learn to attend to extralinguistic cues

Young children begin to become sensitive to **extralinguistic cues** in communication such as intonation, degree of loudness, facial expressions, and gestures of their conversation partners. At 6 months, infants can follow the gaze of adults to map adult words onto objects in the environment (Morales, Mundy, and Rojas, 1998). Infants are also sensitive to the prosodic elements of caregiver speech, so they can make probabilistic estimates of where word boundaries occur in the speech stream (Jusczyk, Luce and Charles-Luce, 1994). By age 2, children use a softer tone with adults than they do with peers.

During the preschool years, children begin to use different styles to speak to different conversational partners. For example, in pretend play, children use higher pitches for mothers, louder voices for fathers, and higher pitches for children (Pence and Justice, 2008). In addition, children also use stress, loudness, hand gestures, and facial expressions to convey their intentions more effectively.

Learn cultural conventions

Pragmatic development is also culturally situated. Different cultural communities have different rules about how language should be used. For example, in Western cultures **phatic communication** (communication that primarily functions to maintain social and interpersonal relationships, such as "Thank you") is a very important social norm in interpersonal communication. However, in the Amazonian Pirahã culture in Brazil, phatic communication does not exist. In Pirahã, there are no words for "thank you" and "I am sorry." Instead, "transaction acknowledged" phrases such as "that's right" or "it's ok" are used if someone gives something to another person. The expression of gratitude can come later, with a reciprocal gift or some unexpected act of kindness, such as helping the gift-giver carry something (Everett, 2009).

Learn to narrate

Narratives are a form of decontextualized and extended discourse. A narrative requires the use of several utterances or turns that must be linked to build a coherent linguistic structure (e.g., Uchikoshi, 2005). Researchers have identified several crucial key dimensions of narrative characteristics in narrative development (Box 3.6), including **story grammar**.

Box 3.6   Key Dimensions of Narrative Characteristics

Story grammar (story structure)   Story grammar refers to the elements of a story. A well-formed story grammar (structure) includes an abstract (a summary of the narrative or a title), an introduction (a description of the characters, setting, time, and activity to set the stage for the narrative), events (actions that advance the storyline, including the problem), a resolution (a termination of complicating events), and a coda (an ending of the narrative).

Evaluation   The narrator uses various evaluative devices (e.g., identifiers, adjectives, negatives, references to emotional, cognitive, or physical states, intentions, causality) to signal the point of the story from the narrator's perspective.

Temporality and reference   Temporality and reference are the main elements in the narrative organization. A coherent narrative must follow a timeline by using temporal devices such as connectives (*and, then*). Also, a coherent story requires the narrator to introduce the story without assuming that the listener has prior knowledge. For example, to use "he" to begin a story is an unclear introduction, but "a bear" is clearer.

Storybook language   Use words that are more literary and varied and syntax that found in written text (e.g., use direct and indirect quotes from books).

Modified from Y. Uchikoshi, "Narrative development in bilingual kindergarteners: can *Arthur* help?" *Developmental Psychology*, 41(3) (2005): 464–478.

It is important to note that not all these narrative traits shown in Box 3.6 appear in the narratives of children before the age of 6. For example, narratives of 4- and 5-year olds contain little evaluation of story events. At age 4, children tend to jump from one event to another and leave out one major event and provide only a simple recounting of successive events. At age 5, they typically tend to include major events, but provide no resolutions. It is not until about age 6 that children's narratives tend to contain the elements listed in Box 3.6.

Young children's narrative development undergoes several stages. At around 20 to 24 months, children begin to demonstrate early narrative abilities. For example, they talk about objects from the past and future. In the early stages, young children are likely to use narrative discourse to talk about events that are unusual or that trigger an emotional response, such as a hurt knee or scrape on an elbow. Between ages 2 and 3 years, children also attempt fictional storytelling. Their narratives contain sound and prosodic play as well as a combination of verbal and nonverbal forms. The content of these early narratives is often about scary events that children face (N. Nelson, 2010).

Through joint linguistic interactions with adults, preschool children learn to tell stories with a plot and to include core story elements like a beginning, middle, and end (Stein, 1988). With the development of pragmatics, the conversational use of language, and the understanding of emotions, children transition from scripts to fictional stories and then to personal narratives. They learn to make their stories meaningful by organizing them around a high point (the pivotal event that signals the reason for telling the story). Therefore, narrative is conceptualized as a cognitive activity inseparable from its pragmatic and social dimensions (Goldman, 2008).

Finally, through interactions with adults, young children are gradually perfecting their native comprehension skills. **Narrative comprehension skills** refer to the ability to process a narrative, which is a series of actions and events that unfold over time according to causal principles. Children are surrounded by narratives from their earliest language experiences (Skarakis-Doyle and Dempsey, 2008). For instance, parents model the structure of narratives to their children by telling stories of personal experiences to others in their presence. Narratives become important for communicative comprehension, as they become the framework for the expression of daily experience, and are thus interwoven into everyday social interactions. While children have developed a repertoire of knowledge about narratives by the age of 3, there is a great deal of development in narrative skills between the ages of 4 and 8 years (Nuske and Bavin, 2011).

Your Turn

Record a personal narrative by children at ages, 2, 4, and 6. Analyze their stories by using the information in Box 3.6. What have you found?

Early metalinguistic awareness

Young children not only have to acquire the basic elements of language and know how to use them in social interaction, but they also have to develop knowledge of a language in order to move further in their later literacy development and academic learning. **Metalinguistic awareness** is the ability to see the relationship between different elements in a language.

Metalinguistic awareness may emerge as early as 2 years of age. By age 4, children can spontaneously rhyme and play with the sounds in words. By age 5 or so (usually when attending kindergarten), children have already developed knowledge of the genre conventions. For example, when they are asked to produce narratives, they are able to structure their narratives around their own or others' experiences and around known fairy tales. When they are asked to produce humorous stories, children are able to employ incongruity, use different forms, and violate common language rules (Loizou, Kyriakides, and Hadjicharalambous, 2011). By age 6, they begin to segment words into component sounds (a skill referred to as phoneme awareness). However, there are variations among children.

Moreover, children are quite sophisticated in their metalinguistic knowledge early on. For instance, they intuitively know which words go with *a* and which words go with *some*; they can be quite proficient in respecting co-occurrence patterns for grammatical gender, especially in languages for which the gender marking is fairly transparent (e.g., Spanish); they know that the question "What color is this?" goes with answers like "red," "blue," and "yellow" before they know what the referents of the color terms are; they may even know which words are nouns and which are adjectives (Gathercole and Thomas, 2005).

There is compelling evidence suggesting that early metalinguistic awareness is a good predictor for later vocabulary and grammatical development (e.g., Smith and Tager-Flusberg, 1982).

Your Turn

Revisit the narrative you recorded earlier and identify the places where the child demonstrates metalinguistic awareness.

Special Issues Related to Language Acquisition

Private speech

Starting around age 3, children often carry on monologues before they go to sleep, as they play or when they draw. This kind of talk that does not intend to involve others is called **private speech** (or **egocentric speech** or **inner speech**). At age 4, children's private speech becomes more selective and is often used in sustained, goal-directed activities such as drawing a picture (Winsler, Carlton, and Barry, 2000). About 20–30 percent of 4-year-old children engage in private speech (Schober-Peterson and Johnson, 1991).

There are two kinds of private speech: the audible egocentric speech (the overt verbal thinking) and the inaudible inner speech (soundless internalized speech). Children typically use audible egocentric speech first and use internalized inner speech later. Throughout early childhood, audible private speech declines with age, and inaudible private speech increases. Overall, children's private speech decreases after age 10, but it does not disappear completely (Owens, 2012).

Private speech is central to children's cognitive functioning and serves as a core mediatory tool in the formation and development of cognition (Damianova, Lucas, and Sullivan, 2012). It helps children to plan and self-regulate their actions to a goal. It has been reported that children's use of task-relevant private speech is positively related to task success and to self-controlled activities during problem-solving (Ostad and Sorensen, 2007).

Your Turn

Listen to the following private speech by a young child posted on You Tube and discuss the functions (please skip the advertisement and go to the clip immediately): http://www.youtube.com/watch?v=cZDf1cYMThU

Gestures

Young children's hand gestures and language development go hand in hand. It is reported that 88 percent of young children's early gestures are deictic gestures. **Deictic gestures** (e.g., pointing, reaching, showing, and giving) emerge between 7 to 9 months of age. Another type of gesture produced by young children is the **representational gesture** (indicating the shape or movement; e.g., moving hand to mouth indicating drinking), which appears around 12 months of age. By 16 months of age, children use gestures and words interchangeably to name objects. By 20 months, children begin to use fewer gestures or stop using them in favor of words. However, gestures and words again emerge in parallel sometime later. Research suggests that young children's hand gestures (especially deictic gestures and representation gestures) often precede the emergence of naming and first words, and gestures often share similar content or meaning (Crais, 2007).

Moreover, hand gestures can help young children comprehend what is said (Iverson et al., 1999), and they can also facilitate young children's vocabulary gain. In a study by Goodwyn and Acredolo (1998), when parents were instructed to use symbolic gestures in addition to words, their children not only used more gestures themselves, but also showed greater vocabulary gains than children whose parents were encouraged to use only words or were not trained at all. Further, when children produced many different gesture types, they also produced many different types of words. This is perhaps because gestures serve as a symbol for children early. When young children have a symbol (gesture) for something, they can comment on it, ask questions about it or request it, and they can also gain increased information about it through interactions with other people.

Your Turn

Observe the gesture use of a young child and discuss the functions of their gestures in relation to their speech.

Dialect

Although many children develop the mainstream spoken language, some children grow up learning the dialect of a mainstream language. For example, in the United States, African American children often acquire a dialect called **African American English** (AAE) or **Nonmainstream American English** (NMAE) (see Terry et al., 2013) that is spoken in their communities. AAE or NMAE is a systematic and rule-governed dialect and it has distinct phonological and morphosyntactic features (see Box 3.7).

Box 3.7   Phonological and Morphosyntactic Features of AAE or NMAE

AAE features	Examples
Phonology	
Syllable deletion	*ar* (our)
Monopthongization of diphthongs	*hiss* (his)
Voiceless/voiced final consonants	*sa-* (sat)
Postvocalic consonant reduction	*jumpin'* (jumping)
"g" dropping	*wif* (wife); *wit* (with)
f/θ,v/ð, and t/θ in intervocalic and postvocalic positions	*dare* (there) *pos* (post)
d/ð in prevocalic positions	*aks* (ask)
Consonant cluster reduction	*pin* (pen)
Consonant cluster movement	*I* (ɛ)
Morphosyntactic	
Zero copula (auxiliary)	We __ goin' to the store.
Subject-verb agreement	They *was* lookin' for the little one.
Fitna/sposeta/bouta	We *fitna* play outside. They *bouta* ride bikes.
Undifferentiated pronoun case	*Him* callin' *him* brother.
Multiple negation	He *don't never* wanna buy *no* candy.
Zero possessive	I went to my Big *Mama* house.
Zero past tense	He said he already *call* his Mama.
Invariant "be"	He *be* tryin' to write all neat.
Zero "to"	He wanted his dog __ run.
Zero plural	His hand fit in his gloves.
Double model	*I'm am* going to look for another one.
Regularized reflexive	They went to the store by *theyself.*
Indefinite article	I want *a* apple for my lunch.
Appositive pronoun	*My daddy he like* to go fishin'.
Remote past "been"	We *been* knowin' how to put that together for a long time.
Preterit "had"	We *had* got his bike fixed already.
Completive "done"	You *done* broke that one.
Existential "it"	It was two cars parked in front of my house.

Modified from J. A. Washington and S. Thomas-Tate, "How research informs cultural-linguistic differences in the classroom," in S. Rosenfield and V. Berninger (eds), *Implementing Evidence-Based Academic Interventions in School Settings* (New York: Oxford University Press, 2009), p. 148.

Young children who grow up acquiring AAE go through the same universal language acquisition process. Research shows that young AAE-speaking children may exhibit a relative strength in oral narrations (e.g., Gardner-Neblett, Pungello, and Iruka, 2011). Some studies found that the children (between ages 4 and 6) who produced larger amounts of AAE fared better in their narrative structure than those who produced smaller amounts of AAE (e.g., Ross, Oetting, and Stapleton, 2004), and preschool children who produced **fictional narratives**[5] with high or low levels of dialect density demonstrated stronger early literacy skills (e.g., letter–word recognition and phonological awareness) than children who produced fictional narratives with moderate levels of dialect density (Connor and Craig, 2006). However, children who speak AAE do tend to produce narratives that are different from children who speak mainstream American English (MAE). For example, their narrative production is characteristic of the African American oral tradition that values audience participation (e.g., call and response), nonlinearity (e.g., linking events thematically rather than temporally), and stylistic embellishment (e.g., verbal dueling) (Mills et al., 2013). Often such differences are regarded as narrative deficiencies in the literature.

Recently, some researchers have suggested that the findings of these earlier studies only focused on the assessment of one distinct aspect of narrative abilities, that is, the use of decontextualized language in story telling (Terry et al., 2013) and these studies neglected to explore other aspects of AAE-speaking children's narratives. Through using a comprehensive measurement of AAE-speaking children's narratives such as **narrative assessment protocol** (NAP),[6] **high point analysis** (HPA),[7] and **narrative scoring scheme** (NSS),[8] researchers recently found that 3- to 5-year-old AAE-speaking children preformed, on average, within age-appropriate expectations on each narrative **macrostructure** (story grammar) and **microstructure** (syntactic and semantic production, complexity, and accuracy in bringing words and utterances together cohesively). Even though at the end of pre-K, the children included in the study produced fewer sentences in their narratives, the quality of their story was not affected (Terry et al., 2013). Thus, some researchers have recently called for using culturally sensitive and culturally fair assessments to evaluate children's narratives with diverse populations (e.g., Mills et al., 2013).

Chapter 6 will further discuss AAE and how it will affect children's academic learning in school settings.

Your Turn

- Analyze the following story told by a 5-year-old African American girl. Identify the variations with regard to grammaticality in comparison to the standard American English. Do you think that the dialect influences the clarity or the completeness of her narrative? Why do you think you are asked to carry out this activity and what is the teaching implication of this analysis?

> When my mamma went to the store with my auntie I stayed over to my Big Mama house with my cousin and my baby brother. We was watchin' t.v. and eatin' cookies. We was playin' with our toys and ridin' bikes too. My mama came home and she said "this a really fun day." I laughed. 'Cause I was thinkin' the same thing.

- What is your take about the following research findings? If you want to learn more about this research, you can check out the reference at the bottom.

Using a wordless picture book, researchers compared the narratives of a group of African American, Latino, and White children. They found that there were no race group differences in the children's organizational style and use of paralinguistic devices (such as prosody, pitch, volume, intonation, and nonverbal behavior). Children in all groups produced narratives that were topic centered and topic associated, with or without story conclusions that were linear, cyclical, or neither. However, the groups did differ in dialogue and character referencing. African American children used dialogue and fantasy embellishment more frequently; Latino children named characters more frequently; and White children referencing character relationships more frequently.

First example from J. A. Washington and S. Thomas-Tate, "How research informs cultural-linguistic differences in the classroom," in S. Rosenfield and V. Berninger (eds), *Implementing Evidence-Based Academic Interventions in School Settings* (New York: Oxford University Press, 2009), p. 147; second example from B. K. Gorman et al., "Oral narrative skills: implications for the reading development of African American children," *Child Development Perspectives*, 6(3) (2011): 218–224.

Developing Emergent Literacies

Once upon a time, children before age 6 and a half were viewed as not ready for reading and writing (McGee, Richgels, and Charlesworth, 1986). It is now a common understanding that, like learning how to speak, children learn about print in the home and community from birth. In a print-rich environment, young children begin to understand that words and sounds can be presented by symbols (such as letters), and they also begin to detect word boundaries and rhyme, and manipulate words as objects in language play. This initial awareness about the relationship between sounds and print in their ambient language before they are formally taught is referred to as **emergent literacy** knowledge (see the first two stages in Box 3.8 for the characteristics of emergent literacy development and Box 3.9 for emergent literacy accomplishments).

Box 3.8   Typical Stages of Literacy Development

Stage 1: Early emergent literacy   This usually occurs before children enter kindergarten. During this stage, children develop the foundations of literacy such as oral language, writing by drawing or scribbling, and being curious about print.

Stage 2: Emergent literacy   This typically takes place by the end of kindergarten or at the beginning of first grade. During this stage, children become more interested in literacy. They begin to use more standard oral language patterns and forms, and name letters. Concepts about print, such as recognizing a letter or word, also develop during this stage.

Stage 3: Beginning reading and writing   This usually occurs through first grade for most students and into second or third grade for some. In this stage, oral language expands and students begin to actually read and write in conventional ways. They figure out the pronunciation of words and also gain **fluency** in reading (the ability to recognize words automatically, accurately, and rapidly). They understand the meanings of more words.

Stage 4: Almost fluent reading and writing   For most students, this occurs toward the end of second grade and many continue into the beginning of fourth or fifth grade. During this stage, children are growing more sophisticated in all aspects of literacy. They read silently more than in the previous stage, do more writing, and have a larger oral language vocabulary.

Stage 5: Fluent reading and writing   This stage for some students begins in fourth grade and continues through the upper elementary grades and into middle school and high school. In fact, fluent reading and writing development continues throughout one's life. By this stage, students are using reading, writing, and oral language for a variety of purposes. They have attained most of the skills of reading and writing.

Adapted from J. D. Cooper and N. D. Kiger, *Literacy: Helping Children Construct Meaning* (Boston: Houghton Mifflin, 2006), pp. 9–10.

Box 3.9   Emergent Literacy Accomplishments in Early Childhood

Birth to 3 years

- Recognize specific books by cover
- Pretend to read
- Enjoy word play and rhyming
- Listen to stories
- Begin to produce some letter-like forms in own "writing"

3 to 4 years

- Know that alphabet letters have names and are different from pictures
- Recognize some environmental print (e.g., EXIT signs)
- Notice rhyming words and alliteration (such as in Peter, Peter, pumpkin eater)

Kindergarten

- Recognize and can name all uppercase and lowercase letters
- Understand that the sequence of letters in a written word represents the sequence of sounds in the spoken word (the alphabetic principle)
- Can name some book titles and authors
- Make predictions based on illustrations or portions of stories
- Use invented spelling to write own messages
- Can write own name
- Can write most letters and some words when they are dictated

Adapted from E. Hoff, *Language Development* (Belmont, CA: Wadsworth, 2009), p. 359.

Below are three important areas of emergent literacy knowledge that lay the foundation for children's future literacy development.

Emergent knowledge of environmental print

By the time children enter kindergarten, most of them have developed **print awareness** (knowledge of print forms and functions) in their ambient language and can recognize the letters (in an alphabetic language) or characters (in an orthographic language) in their names. Some can also write their names. Children become increasingly interested in how letters (in an alphabetic language) or strokes (in an orthographic language) are combined to make words.

Emergent knowledge of print conventions

Children who live in a print-rich environment develop the knowledge about the print conventions in their ambient language. For example, they know print should be read from left to right in English and from right to left in Arabic. They know books must be read from front to back, whereas newspapers, cookbooks, and telephone books need not be. Many children are also aware of the functions of punctuation marks (for example, to signal a rising intonation or to pause) (McGee, Richgels, and Charlesworth, 1986).

Emergent knowledge of writing

When exposed to a print-rich environment, young children learn the purpose of writing for communication. You have probably noticed that as soon as children can grab crayons, many of them scribble or "write something" to convey their message. For instance, a 4-year-old child wrote, "RUDF" to his mother when he tried to get his mother's attention when he was ignored (Bissex, 1980). Typically, children begin to make attempts to write between the ages of 3 and 7 (Garton, and Pratt, 1998), though their writing is very different from conventional writing.

Research indicates that once children are past the initial scribbling stage, they can discriminate between drawing and writing (e.g., McGee, Richgels, and Charlesworth, 1986). One study observed that the writing of young children was usually linear, spaced, and off-center, whereas their drawings were usually a larger figure in the center of the page (see McGee, Richgels, and Charlesworth, 1986). These various early abilities, although not conventional, are important to children's later literacy development.

Your Turn

Analyze the following writing sample of a 5-year-old child. Discuss the metalinguistic knowledge (especially, phonological knowledge) that this child used.

"Weather today is Wentr." (Weather today is winter.)
"I like my flAmingo." (I like my flamingo.)
"I Caem bac." (I came back.)
"I Wos dawn Uar see." (I was under the sea.)

Examples collected by Nora Rugova.

Emergent digital literacy

Infants and young children also experience increasing exposure to digital technology and engagement in a range of digital practices in the home with siblings and parents, which include the use of an iPad and e-games. If you log on to YouTube postings, you will find ample examples of infants and young children using electronic devices such as an iPad. Young children are accessing the internet at increasingly younger ages. Many children have already developed skills to utilize a variety of digital texts with independence before they begin their formal education.

Young children experience meaning-making differently when reading onscreen than when reading on a page. Computer games for young children, for example, tend to foreground graphical information rather than print and provide narrative structures and cueing systems that differ substantially from those available in print-based texts offline. When interacting with hypertext, children do not follow a linear relationship with a text and they navigate the text instead (e.g., Davidson, 2011).

Although more research is needed to find out the relationship between emergent digital literacy and language development, some studies found that computer use in infancy appears to be negligible and therefore plays no part in explaining the development of receptive vocabulary (although their parents' use of the internet does seem to be positively related to the child's acquisition of vocabulary). Further, the growth of vocabulary as the child develops appears to be unaffected by older electronic media (e.g., television) and is more influenced by the parents' education and participation in their child's media use. Finally, computer access (but not computer games) at later ages was associated with increased traditional literacy. The timing of the effect of computers suggests a developmental sequence – that certain levels of linguistic capacity are necessary to facilitate use of this platform (Bittman, Rutherford, and Lens, 2011).

The bottom line is that it is not "exposure" to media or hypertext that harms language acquisition and literacy development, but it is the absence of age-appropriate, "guided interaction" (Plowman, McPake and Stephen, 2010) by adults that is problematic. Thus, adult scaffolding is critical in the process of developing digital literacy.

Your Turn

Look at this 18-month-old child at the following link: http://www.youtube.com/watch?v=qAMiNLOlwqI

Describe her ability in using the iPad and emergent digital literacy.

Emergent critical literacy

To be a successful literacy learner in a diverse society like ours, knowing how to evaluate print and digital print is an important ability that young children need to begin to develop. Many now believe that the ability to critique what one reads is just as essential as the ability to decode (Stevens and Bean, 2007) and that the ability to analyze what one reads should be a part of every child's literacy pathway (Martello, 2002).

From early on, young children demonstrate emergent critical literacy abilities, and they do not always accept what is read to them. For example, when 3-year-old Beth was read a book about Christmas by her babysitter, she commented that in her house, Christmas was not celebrated (her family is Jewish). At this early age, Beth intuitively knows that the author of the book does not talk about the holidays that she and her family celebrate, and she is able to see her own positioning and the author's positioning (see Chapter 1).

Special Issues Related to Emergent Literacy Development

Dialect and emergent literacy development

Some in the past believed that children who speak dialects such as AAE would have a barrier to the development of early emergent literacy skills (Cecil, 1988). However, in a study of AAE-speaking 4-year-old children, researchers found that children exhibited stronger phonological awareness, letter–word recognition, and sentence imitation skills with increased dialect use. The children who used the most dialect also had the best emergent literacy skills (Connor and Craig, 2006). In addition, other research also reveals that preschoolers whose dialect use was heaviest were also the most sophisticated language users (Craig and Washington, 1994). Nevertheless, using AAE when children enter school seems to hinder their academic literacy development. See Chapter 6 for more discussion.

Cultural differences in early literacy practice

There are cultural differences in early literacy interactions between parents and young children. In middle-class, educated American families, book-reading activities are commonly observed. However, in other cultural communities and socioeconomic groups, book-reading activities are replaced through daily activities such as making lists, completing forms (N. Nelson, 2010), personal story telling (Wang, Bernas, and Eberhard, 2002), dancing and music (Cusworth and Simons, 1997), and religious teaching. Thus, it is important to value these different cultural socialization practices in children's early years and use them as a base to support children's emergent literacy development.

Your Turn

Analyze the structure of the following personal story told by a Native American mother to her child. Compare this oral story to a written story in a conventional children's book. What have you found?

(The mother and the child were chatting in the kitchen)

MOTHER: Okay. What is your name?

CHILD: Tishipapa.

MOTHER: What does that mean?

CHILD: Mmm. Eye.

MOTHER: What?

CHILD: Eye.

MOTHER: And you're named kind of after your Grandma. Whose name was..? Which means Green eyes. Right?

CHILD: Mmm, huh.

MOTHER: Okay. And your Grandma Babe, how did you hear about her? Now is Grandma Babe, whose Grandma is? She, my Grandma.

CHILD: Mmm, huh.

MOTHER: Your Grandma Shelly's Mom. And she was really a strong woman. A long time ago, Grandma was young and she was having babies. She lived in a ranch. And they were way, way, way out in the country. You know what it is like when you're out in the country. Well, they didn't have any telephone or cars. You know who Aunt Joan is? Aunt Joan was a little girl. And you know who Uncle Bud is? He was just a little boy. And you know who Uncle John is? He was just a little boy. And Uncle Wayne was in Grandma's?

CHILD: Belly.

MOTHER: Yeah. Well one day Grandpa Frank. You know who he is.

CHILD: (Nods).

MOTHER: Okay. Well, he went off to work that day. And back then, it was very important for all the grandmas to get all of the housework and stuff done, so that supper was ready by the time Grandpa got home. And, Grandma Babe had many babies. Three babies already and she knew she was going to have this baby that day after grandpa left. And she was stuck down at the ranch by herself with these three little kids, gonna have this baby.

CHILD: (Giggles).

MOTHER: So, she told Aunt Joan to take care of the other kids, and

CHILD: Was she little then?

MOTHER: Your Aunt Joan was little then. So, she told 'em to take care of the other kids and she went into the bedroom for a while. Well, by the time Grandpa Frank came home that night – Grandma Babe – He didn't even notice that Grandma Babe wasn't pregnant (laughs) anymore. And, he had, she had supper and then realized there was a new baby there. So Grandma Babe had that baby all by herself. That's how strong she was. Down, down at the old place is what they call it. Did you ever see the picture of the white house? That's how your Uncle Wayne was born. That's pretty tough?

Example modified from X.-L. Wang, R. Bernas, and P. Eberhard, "Variations in maternal support to children's early literacy development in Chinese and Native American families: implications for early childhood educators," *International Journal of Early Childhood*, 34(1) (2002): 9–23.

Supporting Language and Emergent Literacy Development in Infancy and Early Childhood

General approaches in working with young children

Based on the development characteristics of infants and young children discussed in the beginning of this chapter, the following approaches are suggested as a general guideline when working with young children:

- Create a print-rich and digital-rich environment that encourages children to explore.
- Be responsive to children's questions and encourage questions.
- Explain concepts with concrete examples and through play activities.
- Help children expand their interests.
- Conduct activities that are meaningful to young children.
- Focus on positive feedback and avoid negative comments.
- Provide choices for children.

By doing so, it is likely that young children can start their initial life experience on a positive footing, as early experience is crucial for children's future academic development (language and literacy being an important part).

Focus of language and emergent literacy support in early childhood

During early childhood, children are not full-fledged speakers and have not developed full ability in conventional reading and writing either in print or in digital form. However, they are on their way to mastering linguistic competence and in the process of accumulating knowledge about print and other modalities in their environment.

Therefore, when supporting young children's language and literacy development, the focus should be on helping them build essential skills in speaking, listening, viewing, and understanding, as well as on assisting them with developing emergent knowledge and ability in conventional print, hypertext, and emergent critical literacy.

Holistic strategies in facilitating language and literacy growth

Children's early language development and their emergent and future literacy development are closely related. Therefore, when providing support for young children, we must take a holistic approach. Hence, the supporting strategies proposed below are not focused on only one aspect, but rather on speaking, listening, viewing, understanding, analyzing, reading, and writing; all these areas are intertwined later in children's academic learning (N. Nelson, 2010, p. 326; Silliman and Scott, 2009, p. 116).

Oral language

Children's beginning reading is a process through which they uncover their oral language (Cohen and Horowitz, 2002, p. 36). There is a strong connection between children's oral language and their later academic language and literacies. In fact, research has shown that the oral language skills developed in preschool is directly related to alphabetic knowledge in grade 1 and reading comprehension in grade 3. Children who have acquired a rich, everyday oral language are more likely to succeed in acquiring the more specialized academic language that then allows them to meet academic discourse demands in grades 1–3 (Silliman and Scott, 2009, p. 110). Children from homes in which there are more extended discourses and in which caregivers use a more advanced vocabulary when children are 3 and 4 have better skills at age 5 (Tabors, Roach, and Snow, 2001).

Moreover, when teachers in early childhood settings engage children in conversations during mealtimes, children are exposed to a variety of lexicons (words) and morphosyntactic structures (Cote, 2001). Below are some suggestions for prompting oral language development in early childhood.

Decontextualized talk Decontextualized talk is the foundation for children's future academic success. **Decontextualized talk** means that the conversation between parents and young children is not limited to the topics about here and now; it touches upon subjects that are beyond the immediate environment. Lunchtime or snack time is an ideal setting to chat with children and provide support for their decontextualized conversations. You can have conversations with children about the past (e.g., What did you do yesterday?) and future events (e.g., What will your mom make for dinner tonight?). When young children are engaged in one-on-one conversations with adults during events such as mealtime and family car trips, they tend to use more decontextualized and complex language because adults provide more conversational supports in these contexts.

2) *Mental lexicon* An important part of acquiring a language is building the mental lexicon. The **mental lexicon** is the mental storage of words that can be activated by a language user. In other words, the mental lexicon is an individual's knowledge of words in a given language and the ability to process these words in comprehension (understanding) or production (use). Research has shown that the mental lexicon, particularly the productive mental lexicon (especially shown in kindergarten) is a strong predictor of later reading ability and comprehension (Lugo-Neris, Jackson, and Goldstein, 2010). Thus, children's mental lexicon developed during early childhood is closely linked to their future academic learning.

One effective way to help children build their mental lexicon during early childhood is to expand their life experience because broader life experiences create opportunities for wider vocabulary acquisition. When children visit different places (e.g., zoos, markets, or museums) and engage in different activities (e.g., making cookies and playing soccer), they will hear different words used, and they will also need to use different words to describe their experiences. A variety of life experiences will help them develop a larger mental lexicon, and consequently, it will help them make progress in their language development.

3) *Narratives* Children's narrative skills have long been identified as playing an important role in academic achievement, not only as an explicit part of school curriculum (e.g., in sharing time or story writing in classrooms), but also as foundational abilities for later literacy development (Uccelli and Páez, 2007). Research has shown that story telling (compared to other emergent literacy experiences such as drawing and interactions with books) is one of the best predictors of later literacy success in schools (N. Nelson, 2010, p. 328).

Therefore, you can take advantage of the spontaneous personal stories told by young children and build on them to help them develop narrative skills. Some basic scaffolding strategies include expanding children's narratives by adding words, suggesting different words, using more advanced syntactic structures, and adding simple conjunctive links (such as *and*, *then*, and *but*). However, it is essential that you respect the original message(s) expressed in a child's narratives and do not change his ideas. Your role is to help him make his story richer linguistically and develop his narrative skills, but not to alter his ideas.

Your Turn

Read a story to a child between the ages of 3 and 5. Ask the child to retell the story. Video-record the story. Calculate the total number of words (TNW) and total number of different words (TDW) and analyze the story elements described in Box 3.6. What have you found? Develop some strategies as recommended above and use the strategies to scaffold the child (pay specific attention to the crucial narrative dimensions shown in Box 3.6 in your scaffolding).

After your scaffolding, ask this child to re-narrate the story to another person. Record the narration. Calculate the child's TNW and TDW and the story elements. Do you see any impact of your scaffolding?

Note that TNW and TDW are often used as measures for monolingual children's narrative production. See Chapter 4 for further discussion on whether this measure is sensitive for multilingual children from low SES families.

Environmental print

Young children can benefit from the print sources in their daily environment such as number plates, clothing labels, cereal boxes, road signs, and store logos. This kind of print is referred to as **environmental print**. Environmental print is usually contextualized, which provides clues for young children to derive meaning and learn the purpose associated with it (Barratt-Pugh, 2000). For example, each time 3-year-old Lori sees the GAP store sign, she calls out, "GAP!" She associates the letters G-A-P with the clothing store because she was in the store with her mother on many occasions. Her experience with the store helps Lori understand that the symbol GAP represents the name of the store (Wang, 2011a). Environmental print helps young children decipher the meanings of printed words in their everyday lives.

Because environmental print is everywhere in children's lives, you can deliberately draw children's attention to what they see, like the EXIT sign located near the walking path to the bathroom. You can also put all kinds of signs on the wall and let children tell each other what they see. You might also consider setting up a corner where you can assist young children while they look for environmental print on an iPad or similar electronic devices.

Using environmental print as a prompt can help young children develop the ability to speak, to listen, to view, to understand, to analyze, and to develop meaning and symbol association.

Play

Play is an essential way that young children learn during the early childhood period. Play provides holistic, natural and fun ways for young children to explore and to experiment in a safe and enjoyable setting (Ramey and Ramey, 1999).

There are many ways in which you can help young children develop the emergent literacy concepts and skills through play. This is not to say that you interfere with their spontaneous play. Rather, this means that you take advantage of their favorite activity form (play) and scaffold them to develop emergent literacy skills through what they like to do. Box 3.10 demonstrates how this can be done.

Box 3.10 Orientating Children to Print through Play

CHILD: People keep coming into the restaurant with all their animals. If they do it again I want you to come and put them in jail and tell them off, and not let them do it again.

TEACHER: Have you got any animals in the restaurant at the moment?

CHILD: No. Only babies. Darren's got a baby and it's not a dog any more...only babies.

TEACHER: What are you going to do if someone else tries to bring a dog in?

CHILD: I'm gonna get you. To tell you to tell them it's not allowed. It's breaking the law so we can phone the police.

TEACHER: *Have you got a sign which says 'No dogs allowed'?*

CHILD: You mean like...I know...You mean like when you tell people not to smoke and that. We've got "No smoking" sign.

TEACHER: *Do you think it would help if you had a "No animals" sign?*

CHILD: Yeah! Then they'd know cause it would say so.

TEACHER: *Why don't you make one then? If you think it would help.*

Modified from N. Hall and A. Robinson, "Play and literacy learning," in C. Barratt-Pugh and M. Rohl (eds), *Literacy Learning in the Early Years* (Buckingham: Open University Press, 2000), p. 95.

In this example, the teacher takes advantage of this child's spontaneous play and cleverly helps him understand what words can do; that is (in this case), influencing people's behavior (don't bring animals into the restaurant).

Children's literature

Research suggests that of all the factors involved in children's early reading success, early exposure to reading by parents and a literature atmosphere at home seem to be the most important (Owens, 2012). Thus, reading to children is essential in language and emergent literacy development during the early childhood period.

The literature written for young children is often a good source for promoting their language and literacy development. There are several important benefits about children's literature. First, the language, pictures, and content presented in children's literature are usually appropriate for children both in terms of age and interest. Second, children's literature can provide a framework for experience. Children can often use stories to relate to their own experience and talk about them. Many experiences with books help children understand their own emotional reactions and provide manageable context for their real experiences because young children often do not have the language to explain their emotional reactions or fear. The language in children's literature can allow opportunities for this expression. Literature also provides children with opportunities to experience excitement and fear in a safe environment, and it can push children's language development to the limit in their attempts to express their feelings (Sheridan, 2000; Wang, 2011a). Third, children's literature provides ample opportunities for decontextualized language use. Books contain vocabulary that parents are unlikely to use in the everyday routines of eating, bathing, and dressing. Moreover, books include language formulated in sentences and discourse structure that young children are unlikely to encounter (N. Nelson, 2010, p. 264). Children with rich early literacy exposure have a significant advantage in preparing for the decontextualized language of schooling.

However, not all children's literature benefits young children. Below are some tips for selecting literature for young children.

Developmentally sensitive literature   Literature that is developmentally sensitive can help elicit better responses from children. For young children, early encounters with books may determine whether they will stay on course with their literacy development. The best way to test the suitability of your choice of books is to observe children's reactions to the books and materials you select for them. If they embrace the books you choose, you have the green light to continue.

Infants tend to enjoy books that have strong rhythm and onomatopoeia. For example, infants often enjoy lullabies. Books that have simple texts accompanied by bright, primary colors or contrasting black and white images are ideal for infants (Neuman and Wright, 2007). In addition, books with the themes of family, friends, parents, animals, toys, and teddies are usually attractive to infants (Braxton, 2007).

Young children, while continuing to enjoy similar kinds of books to infants, can appreciate simple and repetitive texts with a clear beginning, middle, and ending. As time goes on, young children begin to enjoy books such as the popular *The Very Hungry Caterpillar* by Eric Carle. In this book, children learn how a caterpillar becomes a butterfly. The information is conveyed through simple narrative and vibrant, collaged illustrations (Wang, 2011a, p. 68).

Books with illustrations   Young children often rely on contextual cues to recognize and identify print (Romero, 1983). Visual texts such as books containing pictures can provide further layers of meaning that allow children's continued enjoyment of the interactions between the words and pictures. These books can help young children to remember and interpret. It also can help them express their cognitive, cultural, and affective (emotional) understanding before they can read the print and link it to their own experience to make meaning (Walsh, 2003).

A good book with funny and attractive illustrations is a rich resource and can often provide an impetus to help young children understand the content of a book. Moreover, books can also provide a good opportunity for you to model different kinds of narratives. When choosing books for young children, consider choosing ones that have pictures, which will help them understand and construct meanings of the books and their experiences.

Simple books, but not simplistically written   Reading materials selected for young children should be simple. But, simplicity of language does not imply simplicity and banality of ideas. Some literacy experts suggest that texts selected for young children should go beyond oversimplified language for the purpose of helping beginning readers, and they should challenge the readers and help them respond or contribute meanings (Paul, 2007). Texts for young children need to be simple, but the ideas conveyed between the lines should be profound. This means that texts should be written at the children's level, but should at the same time provoke their reactions and questioning as well as invite them to imagine and participate in meaning-making. A good criterion to measure an author's ability to convey profound meaning through simple texts is that the stories are very child-friendly, warm, charming, attractive and, most importantly, intellectually interesting. They present a challenge to the mind and return our attention continually to the contemplation of issues of the soul (Witte-Townsend and DiGiulio, 2004).

Good examples of simple texts that contain deep meaning and can elicit young children's responses are books such as *The Very Hungry Caterpillar*, *The Very Busy Spider* and *The Grouchy Ladybug* by Eric Carle; *Something from Nothing* by Phoebe Gilman; and *Joseph Had a Little Overcoat* by Simms Taback. You can use these books as a guide when selecting reading materials for young children.

Different genres   Books in different genres can provide different vocabulary for children and guide them to broader subject areas. Chances are that the more genres children are exposed to, the greater the variety of vocabulary and expressions they develop. For children who do not have many opportunities to hear different subjects being discussed in their immediate environment, books with different genres can help them build their mental lexicon.

Good quality scary books   Children, including young children, tend to be attracted to scary books. It is often the adults, not the children, who are scared when encountering these books (Stone, 1981). What makes a book scary for a child is quite different than what an adult interprets as scary (Kellerman, 1981). Many educational experts now try to allay adults' fear of scary books by providing the following advice: "Scary books themselves do not cause fear" (Lewis, 1996). Some believe that scary tales, books, and movies are popular because the world is an unpredictable place for children as well as adults (Tomlinson and Lynch-Brown, 1996). Young children typically tend to have imaginary fears, and some children may even have fears and worries because of their life experiences. Thus, quality scary books and tales can help children deal with their fears and anxieties (Crosser, 1994). In fact, using good quality chillers can promote children's early literacy skills (Richards et al., 1999).

Books that can help phonological awareness   Since phonological awareness is important for children's future literacy development, you need to intentionally choose books that can help young children develop overall phonological awareness such as books that will help children understand the symbol–sound relationship and the patterns in words. Books such as *The Cat in the Hat* and *Green Eggs and Ham* by Dr. Seuss or traditional nursery rhymes are the best books to help young children develop phonological awareness.

Children's choice   Young children usually have very little power over book selection (Sheridan, 2000). Adults (for example, publishers, booksellers, parents, and teachers) are usually the people who decide what is suitable for children. However, the most attractive and engaging early literacy materials for young children are those chosen by children themselves. Giving children opportunities to choose what they want to read during early childhood can motivate them to stay the course in literacy learning. It is a simple fact that people are more motivated to do what they have chosen, and young children are no exception.

Good strategies in reading

Reading to young children is an art; you need to attract them to print and help them pay attention to what you read. Below are a few recommendations.

Reading styles   Although frequently reading to young children can help them develop emergent literacy skills, the frequency of reading in itself does not necessarily predict children's language and literacy success. In fact, reading frequency is only moderately correlated to receptive vocabulary and book strategy sensitivity (N. Nelson, 2010). It is the quality of book reading that is more essential to children's language and emergent literacy development.

Thus, how you read to young children can influence their experience with early literacy. They can either find reading interesting or boring. There are different ways that you can make this early literacy experience enjoyable. You can role-play the story in the book, you can draw and paint the story together, and you can sing and dance the story with them. You can also let young children "read" (tell) the story to you and ask them to interpret the story in their own words. When you read to young children, sharing the meaning of the book is also a vital part in making reading attractive. For example, talking about the ideas can help them derive rich understandings of the meanings involved (Sheridan, 2000).

Your Turn

Select a children's book and propose several ideas about how to make this story an enjoyable experience for young children. Practice your ideas with a child; what have you found?

Print-focused reading   Since reading is a learned ability, explicit and print-focused interaction is particularly important. It has been recommended that adults use verbal and nonverbal techniques to heighten children's attention to and interest in print within the storybook. The simple techniques include *asking questions about print* (for example, "Do you see the letter S on this page?"), *commenting on print* (for example, "That word says SPLASH!"), and *tracing one's finger along the text while reading*. Researchers have found that when preschool children are exposed to this explicit print referencing style of reading, they tend to achieve significant gains in print concept knowledge, alphabetic knowledge, and name writing abilities as compared to the children who are not exposed to this reading style (Justice et al., 2009).

Moreover, you need to provide guidance for young children so that they can focus on print. For example, use model reading (reading to children) and guided reading (reading together with children). This kind of guidance eventually will lead to children's independent reading (children reading on their own).

Reading for pleasure   It is important to make initial reading an enjoyable experience. Reading for pleasure will ensure children's literacy-learning motivation. The following factors may increase the pleasure associated with reading:

- Find a comfortable place to read so that young children associate reading with relaxation.
- Relate the books to children's immediate experiences and talk to them about the book and their experience.
- Use reserved time for reading only for reading, and try to avoid other distractions.
- Try to avoid a monotone and use an animated voice when reading to infants and young children.

When children associate the reading experience with pleasure, they are likely to be engaged in such activities continuously.

Visual and multimodal activities

To help young children develop their emergent literacy skills, you may also consider encouraging them to explore a plethora of visual (such as drawing and painting) and multimodal activities (such as building blocks, playing video games, and e-books for young children). Through engaging in such visual representational activities, young children can learn how to manipulate an array of signs, icons, and moving and still images, which can help them understand how meanings are made and represented through different visual images (Martello, 2002). This process will eventually lead young children to understand how print works.

You can also paint together with young children and deliberately direct their attention to the fact that image and color can represent meanings (such as emotions). For instance, the color *blue* may express the sentiment *melancholy*. Suppose a little boy lost his favorite toy. You would then use the blue color to express his mood. Through exploration like this, young children will begin to understand that colors can be used to attract, persuade, or inform other viewers (Martello, 2002), and that images can represent meaning just as they will realize later that words can achieve the same effects.

Additionally, you can help young children take advantage of devices such as digital cameras and video cameras to develop their early language and literacy skills. For example, help children take pictures with a digital camera during a nature walk and download the pictures onto the computer. Then, allow the children to label their photos, compose stories about the pictures orally, and then show and tell the stories to their friends.

The advantage of encouraging visual and multimodal activities in early childhood is that these activities are enjoyable. Many young children are already spontaneously engaged in them.

Children's music

Research has long established a relationship between music and emergent literacy. Music and literacy (such as reading) require similar skills. Both music and literacy cultivate auditory and visual discrimination, eye–motor coordination, visual sequential memory, language reception, vocabulary development, phonological and phonemic awareness, and fluency (Wiggins, 2007). In early childhood, the engaging nature of music encourages young children to attend to the lyrics, invites them to be active listeners, and promotes comprehension, dialogue, the building of their mental lexicon, and the learning of morphosyntax. Box 3.11 shows the parallels between music and early literacy skills.

Box 3.11   Parallels between Music and Early Literacy

- **Phonological awareness**   Sensitivity to units of sound (generating and recognizing rhyme, syllables, beginning and ending sounds, etc.) as compared to sensitivity to all elements of musical sound (recognizing repeated or imitated sound patterns, sequences, stylistic nuances, etc.).
- **Phonemic awareness**   Identifying and manipulating the smallest sound units in written symbols (e.g. individual letters in "stop") as compared to emphasizing the smallest units of musical sound through musical notation (e.g. individual pitches within a musical phrase).
- **Fluency**   Ability to express ideas clearly as compared to the ability to express oneself musically, such as through singing songs.

Modified from D. Hansen, E. Bernstorf, and G. M. Stuber, *The Music and Literacy Connection* (Reston, VA: MENC: National Association for Music Education, 2004), pp. 8–9.

There are many music activities that you can engage young children in for literacy learning. For example, you can teach children songs that can help them learn rhymes, develop phonemic awareness and build vocabulary. You can provide children with opportunities to talk about what they have heard in the song (the lyrics). You can ask them to repeat the advanced sentence structure in the songs and experiment with them in new sentence constructions. You can also ask children to make their own new songs with the words they heard in the songs. These activities will help young children develop emergent literacy in a fun way.

Your Turn

Examine the lyrics of a famous children's song. Identify the following information in the lyrics and discuss how you can use this song to help young children develop emergent literacy.

- How do the lyrics help young children develop phonological awareness?
- How do the lyrics help young children build vocabulary?
- How do the lyrics help young children's morphosyntactic abilities?
- How do the lyrics help the other areas of language and emergent literacy development?

Children's own work

Children's early literacy work tends to be scribbles, drawings, paintings and nonconventional spontaneous writing. This kind of children's work often demonstrates their knowledge and understanding of the world, including literacy. Some believe that if such self-expression by children is not encouraged, children cannot easily demonstrate what they know, what they can do, and what they hold dear or are fearful of (Makin, Campbell, and Diaz, 1995).

Thus, you may want to take advantage of young children's spontaneous productions and use them as an opportunity to talk about the meanings that they want to represent and gradually help them move their nonconventional expression to conventional expression.

Critical literacy

It is never too early to help young children develop critical literacy abilities. As you read earlier in this chapter, young children such as Beth are able to ask good questions about the stories that are read to them. Thus, you can build on their questions and facilitate their emergent critical literacy development. You can encourage them to ask questions before, during, or after reading. For example, before you read a story, you can ask a child about the cover of the storybook. You can ask simple questions such as "Do you like the cover? Why or why not?" After reading the story, you can then ask the child to design his cover of the story. Based on what the child presents to you in his design, ask questions about his thinking behind the cover design. You can also ask the child what he wants to add to or delete from the story. The goal is to get the child thinking, asking questions, and challenging the status quo.

Your Turn

Study the covers of some Disney children's books. Prepare a list of questions that you think will help children ask questions and develop emergent critical literacy abilities.

Emergent writing

During the early childhood period, building knowledge about writing is key. Relevant basic knowledge includes the development of the concept of a writing system (scripts and concepts) and the function of communication through print or digital print.

Handwriting Experimentation with writing scripts is more important than correct script formation and neatness in early childhood. Researchers have shown that when children (as well as adults) consciously control their handwriting, it is detrimental to their handwriting automaticity, which is more important in overall handwriting competence (Tucha, Tucha, and Lange, 2008).

Composition The traditional view holds that children should not begin the writing process until they attend school. In reality, most children who live in print-rich environments do not wait until they go to school to write. They are already investigating the written world around them, finding out what graphic symbols stand for and figuring out how these symbols can be used to communicate with others. Taking advantage of children's early spontaneous writing attempts can help them move forward in their writing development (Martello, 2002).

During the early childhood period, helping children construct meaning in what they want to express is far more important than the writing mechanics (such as correct punctuation and spelling). The focus should be on helping young children discover

3 the principles in writing, building the concept of print, including digital print, and understanding the function and purpose of written communication.

Moreover, there is a great deal of overlap in the skills that children must master in language and emergent literacy development, and much of what a child learns while engaging in one of these activities will be of relevance and beneficial to the other skills such as speaking, listening, and understanding.

Co-writing   Co-writing is a good application of Vygotsky's scaffolding concept. It allows children to write at a level slightly beyond what they are able to do on their own by working with a more proficient and mature writer. By introducing frameworks through discussing the purpose, content and structure of the writing, children are able to organize their ideas, learn new vocabulary, and try out new language structures within a safe context (Barratt-Pugh, 2000). Hence, modeling writing is an excellent way of demonstrating the writing process as well as styles and genres.

Writing together with young children also helps them contrast different writing styles and understand conventional norms in writing. Early exposure to different writing styles can help broaden young children's cognitive horizon.

Your Turn

Practice co-writing with a young child by using the ideas suggested above. Reflect on your experience and discuss the impact of your scaffolding on this child's emergent writing skills.

Explicit orientation

Before we end this chapter, it is necessary to say a few words about the importance of the explicit nature of early language and literacy interaction support. Although children can discover linguistic and literacy principles on their own, explicit orientation to certain linguistic features is worthwhile for their future language and literacy development as well as their academic success.

Explicitly orienting children to certain linguistic knowledge such as phonological awareness and syntax is beneficial in their language and literacy progress. Research indicates that explicit training in phonological awareness has positive effects on the progress of children in reading when they enter elementary school (Yeong and Liow, 2012). You can provide a supportive environment in which children have ample opportunities to hear how words are pronounced and used. Further, you can deliberately draw their attention to the phonological structure of words through activities such as rhyming games (e.g., *cat* and *bat* share a similar phonological structure).

Another area of explicit orientation during early childhood is syntax. For a long time, syntax has been regarded as not being affected by environmental input (Vasilyeva, Huttenlocher, and Waterfall, 2006). Research has now suggested otherwise. For example, preschool teachers' use of complex sentences is correlated with the growth in children's comprehension of complex syntactic constructions (Huttenlocher et al.,

2002), and children who hear the passive voice used in the stories produce more passive constructions and make fewer mistakes (Vasilyeva, Huttenlocher, and Waterfall, 2006).

Your Turn

How do you balance spontaneous language and emergent literacy activities and intentional teaching in early childhood?

Summary of Key Points

- There are three areas of phonological knowledge that young children need to develop to acquire a language: receptive phonological knowledge, productive phonological knowledge, and early phonological awareness.
- To acquire a language, children also need to develop knowledge about words and learn their meanings. Lexicon comprehension usually occurs before lexicon production. The early words of English-speaking children tend to be nouns. Young children initially use various strategies such as idiomorphs, lexicon innovation, overextension and underextension to compensate for their lexicon limitation.
- Another important task for language acquisition is developing morphosyntactic abilities. Young children's morphological development goes through different stages. They initially learn to use the morphological markers by memorization. They then learn the morphological rule generalization, and later they go through a stage of morphological rule overgeneralization before they acquire morphological rules. At first, children's utterances and sentences are short, about two or three words. The sentences eventually grow in length and complexity at around ages 3 and 4. However, children still have difficulties in using the passive voice.
- Children also need to develop a range of pragmatic skills to communicate. They learn to use language for different purposes; learn to use decontextualized language; develop conversational schema; learn to attend to extralinguistic cues; learn cultural conventions in communication; and develop narrative abilities.
- Children show metalinguistic awareness early on. For example, they can spontaneously rhyme and play with the sounds in words.
- By the time children enter preschool, many of them are able to recognize the characters or letters in their own names. They also show emergent digital and critical literacy ability.
- Effective strategies that can support young children's early language and emergent literacy include:
  - Encouraging oral language development.
  - Engaging in decontextualized talk.
  - Building mental lexicon.
  - Developing narrative skills.

- ○ Using environmental print, play, music, children's literature, and children's own work.
  - ○ Helping children develop the writing concept through co-writing.
- Explicitly orienting children to certain linguistic knowledge such as phonological awareness, which is beneficial to children's future language and literacy development as well as their academic success.

Key Terms

African American English (AAE) or Nonmainstream American English (NMAE)

Babble

Bootstrapping

Canonical babbling

Contextualized language

Conversational schema

Cooing

✓ Decontextualized language

Deictic gestures

Egocentric

Emergent literacies

Environmental print

Extralinguistic cues

Fast mapping

Fictional narratives

High point analysis (HPA)

Idiomorphs (or protowords, vocables, quasiwords)

Intonated babble

Jargon

Joint attention

Lexicon

Macrostructure

Mental lexicon

✓ Metalinguistic awareness

Microstructure

Morphemes

Narrative Assessment Protocol (NAP)

Narrative comprehension skills

Narrative Scoring Scheme (NSS)

Onset

Overextension

Persuasive communication

Phatic communication

Phoneme

Phonological awareness

Phonology

Pragmalinguistics

Pragmatic development

Private speech (or egocentric speech and inner speech)

Productive knowledge of phonology

Prosody

Receptive phonological knowledge

Reduplicated babbling

Representational gesture

Reversibility

Rime

✓ Semantic network

Semantics

Semantic transparency

Sociopragmatics

Spreading activation

Story grammar (story structure)

Symbolic thinking

Syntactical knowledge

Syntax

Theory of mind

Truncation

Turnabout

Unanalyzed chunk (or unanalyzed wholes)

Underextension

Utterance

Vocabulary spurt

Vocal play

Notes

1. Determiners are used before a noun or noun phrase. They include articles *a*, *an*, and *the*; demonstratives such as *this*, *that*, *these*, and *those*; possessives such as *my*, *your*, *his*, *her* and *their*; and others such as *each*, *some*, *any*, and *few*.
2. An auxiliary verb (also called helping verb) is before a main verb to achieve a grammatical function (such as *have*, *can*, *may*, and *must*). For example, I <u>*have*</u> finished my homework.
3. Denominal verbs are verbs that derive from nouns. For example, the verb *school* is from the noun *school* and the verb *shelve* is from the noun *shelf*.
4. The conventional way in research literature to describe a child's chronological age is using (;) to separate years, months, and days. For example, if a child's chronological age is 2 years, 4 months, and 7 days, the convention is to put it as (2;4;7).
5. Fictional narratives are accounts that are presented about fabricated events and characters (see more discussion in Chapter 6).
6. NAP measures and monitors preschool children's use of semantic and syntactic forms by using a wordless picture book "*Frog, Where Are You?*" by Mercer Mayer. It is a cost-effective way to measure young children's narrative microstructure (Terry et al., 2013).
7. HPA is used to measure children's narrative structure completeness and complexity both in personal and fictional narratives (Terry et al., 2013).
8. NSS is used to measure narrative macrostructure (or story grammar). It evaluates children's narrative quality. This measure is designed to be sensitive to changes in the development of narrative skills across the early schooling years (Terry et al., 2013).

Recommended Further Readings

Bissex, G. L. (1980). *Gnys at Work: A Child Learns to Write and Read*. Cambridge, MA: Harvard University Press.

Dickinson, D. K. and Tabors, P. O. (2001). *Beginning Literacy with Language*. Baltimore: Paul H. Brookes.

Halliday, M. A. K. (1986. *Learning How to Mean: Explorations in the Development of Language*. London: Edward Arnold.

Heath, S. B. (1982). What no bedtime story means: narrative skills at home and school. *Language in Society*, 1(1): 49–76.

Morrow, L. M. (2012). *Literacy Development in the Early Years: Helping Children Read and Write*. Boston: Pearson.

Wiggins, D. G. (2007). Pre-K music and the emergent reader: promoting literacy in a music-enhanced environment. *Early Childhood Education Journal*, 35(1): 55–64.

4

Acquiring More Than One Linguistic System

Multilingual First Language Acquisition

Prereading Questions and Activities

- Do you speak more than one language or dialect? If so, when did you acquire them? Write down your experience and share it with your classmates. Alternatively, write down the questions that you would like to know about multilingualism and then interview a multilingual person with the questions. What have you found?
- What are the similarities and differences in acquiring one L1 and more than one L1 early in life?
- Do you think that young children can be confused if they are exposed to more than one language? Why or why not?
- Is it fair to use the language and literacy characteristics of monolingual children as a yardstick to measure multilingual children? Support your argument with examples.
- Do you think multilingual children can speak all their languages equally well? Why or why not?
- What are your criteria to determine whether a child is multilingual?
- What is your opinion on language mixing?
- What types of support does a child need to acquire and develop more than one language in early childhood?
- What could be the cognitive consequences of knowing more than one language?

Topics to Be Addressed in This Chapter

- Cognitive attributes of acquiring more than one L1
- Complex issues regarding acquiring more than one L1
  - The cutoff age of L1 acquisition and Ln learning
  - Input quantity and quality

Understanding Language and Literacy Development: Diverse Learners in the Classroom, First Edition. Xiao-lei Wang.
© 2015 John Wiley & Sons, Inc. Published 2015 by John Wiley & Sons, Inc.
Companion website: www.wiley.com/go/wang/langandlit

- ○ Multilingual acquisition setting differences
- ○ Multilingual competence divergence
- ○ Competence and performance discrepancy
- ○ Potential differences between different types of multilingual L1 acquisition
- ○ One system vs separate systems
- ○ Cross-linguistic interaction
- ○ Rate of multilingual acquisition
- ○ Language and thought
- ○ Language-specific issues
- Developing essential linguistic abilities in more than one L1
  - ○ Phonological development
  - ○ Lexical-semantic development
  - ○ Morphosyntactic development
  - ○ Pragmatic development
  - ○ Metalinguistic development
- Developing emergent literacies in more than one language
  - ○ Emergent print literacy
  - ○ Emergent digital literacy
  - ○ Emergent critical literacy
- Supporting strategies for developing more than one L1 in infancy and early childhood

---

Learning Objectives

After completing this chapter, you should be able to do the following:

- Recognize the cognitive characteristics of children who acquire more than one L1.
- Understand the complex issues in acquiring more than one L1.
  - ○ The cutoff age for multilingual L1 acquisition and Ln learning
  - ○ The concept of critical mass
  - ○ Differences between competence and performance
  - ○ Potential differences between bilingual L1 acquisition and trilingual L1 acquisition experiences
  - ○ Single-system hypothesis and dual-system hypothesis
  - ○ Cross-linguistic interaction
  - ○ Rate of multilingual L1 acquisition
  - ○ Relationship between language and thought
  - ○ Language-specific issues
- Be cognizant of the unique characteristics of acquiring more than one phonological, lexical-semantic, morphosyntactic, and pragmatic system as well as the metacognitive advantages of acquiring more than one language.
- Be familiar with young children's emergent development in multilingual literacies.
- Know how to support multilingual and multiliteracy development.

Cognitive Attributes of Acquiring More Than One L1

Human language faculty has an endowment for multilingualism (Meisel, 2006, p. 92). Most children are able to acquire more than one L1 when they are given adequate exposure. Although multilingual children share the universal learning characteristics with their monolingual counterparts, they may diverge from monolingual children in their cognitive development as a result of being exposed to more than one linguistic system. Knowing more than one language is much more than simply knowing more than one way of speaking. Because the mind of a multilingual speaker is exposed to more than one set of linguistic details and conceptual representations, a multilingual speaker can entertain possibilities that a monolingual speaker has no need to regale (Bialystok and Hakuta, 1994).

There are several unique cognitive attributes of multilingualism, among which two are noteworthy: selective attention (or attention control), and cognitive flexibility. **Selective attention** means that when more than one language coexists, one of the languages must be constantly inhibited to prevent ongoing intrusion (Bialystok and Martin, 2004). This may explain why children who speak more than one language are better at problem-solving, because tackling a problem successfully requires focusing on some aspects of the information and ignoring the others.

Also, by knowing more than one word for one object or idea, multilingual children may possess an added **cognitive flexibility**. The following example demonstrates how the knowledge of two words – one in English and one in Welsh – for a single idea (a school) could enhance one's concept of "school." In Welsh, the word *ysgol* not only means a school but also a ladder. Thus, a Welsh–English bilingual child has an added dimension of the word *school* (Baker, 2011); that is, school is a place to learn and it functions as a ladder for one's knowledge. Such cognitive flexibility can be manifested, for example, in multilingual children's superior story-telling skills, because they are less bound by words and are more elastic in thinking due to knowing more than one language (Baker, 2011).

One word of caution: it is important to keep in mind that we must be careful about drawing universal conclusions about the effects of multilingualism on cognitive and language development. We cannot expect a uniform pattern of development across all operations in multilingual children. It is likely that multilinguals may differ from each other in their patterns of development (Bialystok, 1991). Also, multilingual children may differ from monolingual children in some but not all of the constituents of thought.

Your Turn

As described above, if the cognitive characteristics of multilingual children are the result of exposure to more than one language, how can these cognitive characteristics in turn benefit young children's language and literacy learning?

Complex Issues about Acquiring More Than One L1

Before we discuss the linguistic development of multilingual children during infancy and early childhood, several complex issues need to be addressed first.

The cutoff age of multilingual L1 acquisition and Ln learning

There are two major dichotomies used in the literature to indicate the timing and nature of multilingual acquisition: *simultaneous* and *sequential* (or *subsequent*). Debates are continuous on the cutoff age of simultaneous and sequential multilinguals. Some researchers believe that the term *simultaneous* can only be applied to children who are exposed to more than one L1 from birth (e.g., Padilla and Lindholm, 1984). Others suggest that only those children who are exposed to more than one L1 from birth up to age 3 should be considered simultaneous multilinguals (e.g., McLaughlin, 1978). It seems that the word *simultaneous* is often used with different meanings in the published literature. To avoid the unclear definition of simultaneous multilingualism, some researchers propose using the following terms to describe multilingual children who acquire different languages from birth or shortly after until age 4 or 5: *bilingualism as a first language* (Swain, 1972), *two first languages* (Meisel, 2006), *bilingual first language acquisition* (BFLA) (De Houwer, 2009), *trilingual first language acquisition* (TFLA) (Dewaele, 2000; Wang, 2008), and *multilingual first language acquisition* (Wang, 2011a). Despite the divergent terms used, all these researchers agree that the multiple language acquisition during early childhood should be treated as L1 acquisition.

The advantage of considering multilingual acquisition as first languages, such as BFLA (bilingual first language acquisition) and TFLA (trilingual first language acquisition) or simply MLFLA (multilingual first language acquisition) is that the unique language acquisition characteristics of multilingual children are highlighted as a full-fledged and distinct language acquisition process. It warrants discussion on an equal basis with MFLA (monolingual first language acquisition) that has long been used as a norm to evaluate the language development of multilingual children. In the same vein, seeing the multiple language acquisition process as L1 foregrounds the point that MLFLA is a phenomenon that cannot be treated as first language acquisition in different languages. In other words, a BFLA child in Chinese and English cannot be equated with a child who acquired only Chinese as the first language, or with a child who acquired only English as the first language.

The issue remains of when to call a child's multiple language acquisition as a first language acquisition (L1) and when to call it a second language acquisition (L2) or a new language acquisition (Ln). Meisel (2006, p. 105) suggested a provisional distinction to help us look at the age distinction of L1 and Ln (L2) acquisition (see Box 4.1). He argues that there are qualitative differences in these multilingual acquisition experiences.

> **Box 4.1 Distinction of First Language and Second (New) Language Acquisition**
>
> **Simultaneous first language acquisition** A child begins to acquire more than one language during the first three or four years of life.
>
> **Child second (new) language acquisition** The onset of acquisition of the second (new) or further language happens between ages 5 and 10.

Adult second (new) language acquisition The acquisition of the second or more languages happens after the age of 10.

Modified from J. Meisel, "The bilingual child," in T. K. Bhatia and W. C. Ritchie (eds), *The Handbook of Bilingualism* (Oxford: Blackwell, 2006), pp. 91–113.

Unless future research provides different evidence that suggests otherwise, multilingual acquisition in early childhood (birth to 5) in this book is treated as multilingual first language acquisition. There are considerable supports for this decision. First, the completion of the brain lateralization is around age 5 (H. Brown, 2000, p. 55). Therefore, a language that is acquired during the first five years is within the optimal acquisition window of opportunity. It seems that the peak of language acquisition begins shortly before the age of 2 years, and the gradual decline sets in before the age of 5 (Meisel, 2006, p. 104). Children who simultaneously acquire two or more languages before age 5 can attain the same type of native grammatical and phonological knowledge as the respective monolinguals. Second, a similar pattern of brain activation is found in children with two languages before age 4 (Meisel, 2006, p. 110). Likewise, bilingual children's two languages overlap in the regions and patterns of activation during the early childhood period (Newport, 2002).

Input quantity and quality

Since multilingual children are exposed to more than one language, the natural question is, how much linguistic input does a child need to acquire a language? Researchers so far have not been able to pinpoint the exact amount of exposure to a language a child needs to acquire a language. However, there are some proposals that may help us think about the input quantity necessary for acquiring a language. For example, one proposal suggests that the input for a child needs to reach a critical mass (the minimum amount of input required for language acquisition or language maintenance) before the child can acquire a language. Some researchers indicate that the minimal amount of input in a single language needs to reach at least 25 percent for acquisition (Pearson, 2007 and 2008).

However, research also suggests that the input quality is more important. Infants do not necessarily need a long-term listening to a language to develop a perception of that language. The key is that the language input must be in a live social interaction situation. Adult input needs to include the following elements: infant-directed speech, a speech pattern that has been shown to attract and hold infant attention (such as exaggeration of phonetic units), exposure to multiple talkers, which increases variability in the acoustic cues to phonetic categories and results in better phonetic learning (Kuhl, Feng-Ming, and Huei-Mei, 2003).

Moreover, literature also suggests that the input from mothers and fathers may play a different role in multilingual children's language development. For example, bilingual children's mainstream language narrative abilities, such as English narrative abilities, tend to be influenced by mothers who attended schools in the mainstream language, such as English, because these mothers tend to spend more time reading books and telling stories to children (e.g., Bradley et al., 2001). In addition, these mothers are more cognizant of their children's abilities and elicit more complex language from their children (Tenenbaum and Leaper, 1998). However, research suggests that fathers, in general, tend to have more influence on children's language development than mothers. One study found that when fathers were English monolinguals, nearly half of the children were English monolinguals, even when mothers typically spoke Spanish. In contrast, when fathers usually spoke Spanish and mothers were English monolinguals, less than 20 percent of children were English monolinguals (Veltman, 1981). Another longitudinal study of two trilingual children suggested that the siblings chose to speak to each other in French (their input language from the father) rather than Chinese (their input language from the mother) (Wang, 2008) and they demonstrated a better proficiency in their French than their Chinese, even though they received more enriched input for Chinese (including attending Chinese language school) (Wang, 2011a).

Multilingual acquisition settings differences

The language-learning settings for multilingual children vary greatly. Some children learn their home language(s) (usually parental input language) mostly in the home environment and their mainstream language in preschool settings. Others learn their mainstream language via more passive input such as TV, overhearing people in their ambient environment (not directly engaged), and children's media. Still others receive more balanced input in their home language and mainstream language in bilingual preschool programs. As a result of divergent linguistic exposure to their different languages, multilingual children's language abilities in different languages vary significantly.

Different multilingual effects on language acquisition

There are two sides of the story about the effects of multilingualism on language acquisition. Some children who are actively engaged in learning more than one language may develop particularly strong phonological representation, storage, and retrieval systems as a by-product of multilanguage learning and use (Bialystok, Majumder, and Martin, 2003). Others may develop relatively weaker representations in one or all of their respective languages because input in each language is not necessarily evenly distributed (Gollan, Forster, and Frost, 1997).

Misconceptions about multilingualism

Equal competence is a misnomer
When addressing the linguistic abilities of children who acquire more than one first language, a term *balanced* multilingual is often used. This term is problematic and inaccurate. A *balanced* multilingual suggests that an individual's linguistic knowledge consists of perfectly equal parts, and the individual is able to function in precisely the same way in every aspect and in each situation (De Houwer, 2009, p. 93; Meisel, 2006). A multilingual person is not different monolinguals in one person (Grosjean, 1989; Grosjean and Li, 2013). In reality, few multilinguals have exactly

the same balanced competence in all their languages, and there are always degrees of competences in different languages (Wang, 2008 and 2011a). Multilinguals rarely use their languages equally in every domain of their social environment. Rather, they use them for different purposes, in different contexts, and to communicate with different people. Consequently, their abilities are different. Therefore, balanced multilingualism is rarely possible (Grosjean and Li, 2013; Meisel, 2006), although some multilinguals do function more efficiently in their respective languages than others.

Competence and performance are not the same
The words competence and performance regarding children's multilingual abilities are sometimes used unclearly in published literature. Strictly speaking, **competence** means what a speaker knows about a language (an individual's underlying knowledge of a language system such as grammatical rules), and it is often unobservable, and **performance** means what a speaker actually does in the use of a language (a person's actual language use in context), and it is observable (S. Brown and Attardo, 2008). It is usually very difficult to judge a young child's multilingual competence. Unlike adults, who can be asked, for example, whether it is better to say "two foots" or "two feet," young children may not be cognizant of what they are being asked for. Below is a good example (H. Brown, 2000, p. 31).

> ADULT: Now Adam, listen to what I say. Tell me which is better to say: some water or a water?
>
> ADAM: Pop go weasel.

This example reminds us that an inability in a child's language production does not necessarily indicate a lack of competence in a given language. It is likely that a multilingual child knows the rules of a language, yet he does not always perform according to the rules in real communication. For example, if the trilingual child Léandre was asked which Chinese words 穿 and 戴 to use before *wear* (穿) *jeans* and *wear* (戴) *sun glasses*, he would say it correctly (in other words, he knew the rule). However, in his conversation with others, he always used the wrong words (Wang, 2008, p. 18).

Potential differences between different types of multilingual L1 acquisition

Although we call all children who are exposed to more than one language multilingual children in this book (as explained in Chapter 1), we must also keep in mind that trilingual L1 acquisition experience is potentially different from bilingual L1 acquisition experience. Trilingualism is generally treated in the existing literature as another type of bilingualism and is frequently explained as a special phenomenon of bilingualism, and the findings about bilingualism are often assumed to be applicable to trilingualism by extension (e.g., Hoffman and Ytsma, 2004; Wang, 2008). However, being bilingual is not exactly the same as being trilingual (Quay, 2001). When two languages are involved, a child has three choices: speak language A, speak language Alpha, or speak a combination of languages A and Alpha in a sentence. However, when three languages are available for a child, he has seven choices: speak language A, language Alpha, language Alef, a combination of Language A and Alpha, A and Alef, or Alpha and Alef, or a combination of all three languages.

In addition, as we observed in Chapter 2, there are many intricate social, cultural, and other complex factors that may influence how children acquire different languages. Although we do not currently have enough research evidence to determine the exact differences between bilinguals and trilinguals, as a result of sample collection difficulties, it is important to note that potential differences between bilingual and trilingual children have been revealed in small-sample studies (Wang, 2008 and forthcoming). To use bilingual children's language development as a measure to evaluate trilingual children will possibly diminish the importance of the unique characteristics of trilingual children.

One system or separate systems

Because more than one linguistic system is acquired simultaneously, one important question that has been asked by researchers is, "Are these linguistic systems separate or shared?" There are two positions: one is the **single-system hypothesis** and the other is the **dual-system hypothesis.**[1] The single-system hypothesis suggests that multilingual children initially develop only one system before they succeed in differentiating the lexical and grammatical systems of their different languages (Meisel, 2006; Volterra and Taeschner, 1978). Much current evidence seems to reject this hypothesis.

The dual-system hypothesis proposes that children who hear more than one language regularly develop separate linguistic systems (de Houwer, 2009; Meisel, 2006). This hypothesis seems to be corroborated by growing evidence from phonological, lexical, and morphosyntactic studies of multilingual children. For example, even during the one-word stage (the holophrastic phase), young multilingual children typically use one-word utterances in their separate languages (Quay, 1995).

Cross-linguistic interaction

A number of terms are used loosely in the literature about the interactions between the respective languages of multilingual children such as *language transfer*, *cross-linguistic interference*, and *cross-linguistic influence*. However, it is important to clarify what these terms mean exactly, particularly in the case when more than one L1 is acquired. The terms *language transfer*, *cross-linguistic interference*, and *cross-linguistic influence* indicate that after a language system has already been established (usually L1), a learner uses the knowledge from her L1 system to work on or influence her Ln system. It seems that these terms may be more accurate to describe the relationship between L1 and Ln. By comparison, the respective linguistic systems that children are acquiring as L1 are in the process of developing simultaneously. Therefore, it is perhaps more accurate to use the term **cross-linguistic interaction** or **code-switching** (CS)[2] to describe the relationship between children's different languages.

As soon as more than one language is involved in the acquisition process, interactions between languages are unavoidable. Almost all multilingual children, even in the strictest **one-parent-one-language**[3] environment such as that of the multilingual children described in the work of Wang (2008), show some characteristics of cross-linguistic interaction between languages. Cross-linguistic interaction, often observed as language mixing, can occur in different aspects of language (phonology, lexicon, semantics, morphology, and syntax); however, it occurs most frequently in the phonological and lexical aspects (Salameh, Nettelbladt, and Norlin, 2003).

What is fascinating about cross-linguistic interaction is that it does not occur randomly. It actually requires a child to have a good understanding of the features of the given languages to "mix." Some researchers believe that a child's mixing ability is an evolving process. When children are younger, they tend to mix less because they have not fully developed the linguistic systems to have a sufficient "knowledge base" to mix languages (Hoffmann and Stavans, 2007). More discussion of this topic will appear later in the chapter.

Your Turn

What could be the advantage for a multilingual child to "borrow" words from another language in communication?

Rate of acquisition

There may be an overall tendency for a slower language acquisition rate in multilingual children (Meisel, 2006, p. 96). However, the notion *slower* needs to be scrutinized. First, when the word *slower* is used, we actually apply the norms of children who acquire one L1 to children who acquire more than one L1. This is not completely fair. Children with more than one language are not simply the amalgamated product of their different languages, and each language operates largely independently, with constraints from the specific ambient language being acquired (Goldstein, Fabiano, and Washington, 2005; Grosjean, 1989).

Second, because multilingual children work with more than one linguistic system, there are different constraints with which they are required to grapple. It is possible that the seemingly slower rate can be looked at as the distinct process in which multilingual children are figuring out their different linguistic systems. It is reasonable to think that when a child acquires more than one language, it may take him a little longer to sort out the systems, although this is not necessarily true for every child.

Third, it is also important to note that multilingual children may show different developmental patterns in their different linguistic systems (Gut, 2000a). Some features in a language may be developed earlier than the ones in the other language(s). For example, a German–English bilingual child in a study developed intonation patterns earlier in German than in English (Gut, 2000a and 2000b). More will be discussed later in the section on phonological deceleration.

Finally, some studies found that the grammatical development of multilingual children is not much delayed compared with monolingual children. Other studies indicate that delay is evident (Hoff, 2009, p. 307). The question here is whether it is really a matter of delay or whether there is simply a different timetable in multilingual children's language development.

Language and thought

Although the cognitive process of a multilingual child derives from one integrated source of thought (Pavlenko, 2008), the different languages of a child may influence his thinking differently through language structures, particularly through the customary discourse, concept, and meaning in different languages. Multilinguals may change their thinking when switching from one language to another. Translation of meaning occurs across languages; yet, some enduring relativity within a language source also transpires (Baker, 2011). Box 4.2 illustrates how Dominique (a simultaneous trilingual child) described his Paris trip to different language interlocutors (conversation partners) by focusing on different aspects and different representations of self.

Box 4.2 Recounting a Trip to Paris with Different Interlocutors

To the relative (the Dutch speaker, but also an English speaker)

We lived in a hotel called the Splendid Hotel the first night. It was not splendid at all! I don't recommend it. The rooms were too small…The breakfast was bad. We then moved to the Hilton Hotel the next night; it was the best in all of Europe.

To the older brother (the French speaker)

J'ai visité le Louvre et j'ai vu la Joconde. C'était super. Je vais pouvoir dire à mes copains d'école que j'ai vu la vraie! Papa m'a même pris en photo devant elle. Je n'oublierai jamais cette journée…J'ai aussi vu la Vénus de Milo. Tu sais pourquoi elle n'a plus ses bras? C'est un "hobo" qui les lui a mangés.

(I visited the Louvre and I saw the real painting of the Mona Lisa. It's fabulous. I can now tell my classmates in school that I finally saw the real thing. Dad took some pictures of me in front of her (the painting). I'll never forget this day…I also saw the Statue of Venus. (Laughing) Do you know why her arms were missing? They were eaten by a hobo.)

(Dominique wanted to make the similar kind of joke as the Belgian cartoonist Philippe Geluck in one of his comic books.)

To the mother (the Chinese speaker)

我们到一个中国人开的泰国饭店吃晚饭。我叫了咖啡冰淇淋, 可是那个中国招待员 给我巧克力的。她可能想小孩子不能吃咖啡, 可是她没有告诉我。她假装要给我, 可是她没有给我。

(We ate dinner in a Thai restaurant opened by two Chinese people. I ordered coffee ice cream, but the Chinese waitress gave me chocolate instead; she probably thought that children should not have coffee (caffeine). She didn't tell me that I couldn't have coffee ice cream. She pretended to take my order and then gave me a different kind of ice cream.)

X.-L. Wang, *Growing up with Three Languages: Birth to Eleven* (Bristol: Multilingual Matters), pp. 184–185.

Language-specific issues

When dealing with different linguistic systems, we must be mindful of language-specific issues. An example will be the concept of morphemes, which was discussed in the previous chapter. However, such a definition may not be accurate when considering the world's other languages such as Chinese. For example, a morpheme is the smallest meaningful unit in English. In contrast, the basic unit of written language in Chinese is the syllable (McBride-Chang et al., 2003). Further, in alphabetic languages such as English, morphemes can be words, word stems, and affixes. For example, plurality in English is marked by -s as in *books*. In logographic languages such as Chinese, each character represents both a syllable and a morpheme (McBride-Chang et al., 2003). Meanings of new vocabulary concepts in Chinese are generally more transparent than they are in English because more sophisticated concepts may be built from simpler (previously learned) ones. For instance, the meaning of the word *adult* in English is opaque. In Chinese, the word *adult* (大人) is comprised of two characters which separately mean *big* (大) and *person* (人) (McBride-Chang et al., 2003). Therefore, when discussing multiple L1 acquisition processes, we need to be knowledgeable about linguistic features in other languages and how they may affect multilingual children's language competence and performance.

Your Turn

Select at least two issues you read in this subsection and discuss how they have changed or confirmed your way of looking at the process of acquiring more than one language.

Developing Essential Multilingual Linguistic Abilities

The major language acquisition tasks for children who are exposed to more than one linguistic system during infancy and early childhood are learning the sound systems, meanings, and structures in their different ambient languages, using them appropriately in different social interactions, and developing knowledge about the different linguistic systems.

Multilingual phonological development

Perception
Children who hear more than one language need to develop different strategies for processing and perceiving them. They must develop knowledge in distinguishing different sound systems in their different languages and begin to develop phonotactic knowledge in their respective languages. **Phonotactic knowledge** refers to the ability to know the rules that govern the arrangements and constraints of speech sounds in a given language. For example, English does not allow a word that begins with the consonant cluster /zv/, whereas Russian does.

The first and foremost task for infants who are exposed to more than one sound system is to learn how to distinguish between the sounds of the different languages that they are acquiring. For instance, for a Chinese–English bilingual child, she must know how intonation patterns in Chinese work. Chinese is a tone language; a tone decides the meaning of a word. There are four tones or intonation patterns in Chinese: high-level tone, rising tone, falling-rising tone, and high-falling tone. For example, the sound /ma/ differs in meaning when it is attached to different tones. When /ma/ has a high-level tone /mā/, it means *mother*; when it has a rising tone /má/, it is a marker in a question; when it has a falling-rising tone /mǎ/, it means *horse*; and when it has a high-falling tone /mà/, it means *scold*. This Chinese–English bilingual child must learn the tone variations to acquire Chinese. However, the knowledge on tones she acquires in Chinese will not help her learn English. If you try to say the word "stop" in different tones in English, you will notice that the meaning remains the same. Therefore, this Chinese–English bilingual child must also learn the rules for English sound systems; for example, the phonemic order of "stick" is fine, but the order of "tsick" is not (De Houwer, 2009, p. 155).

In the first months or so, all children, monolingual and multilingual children alike, are able to distinguish sounds in the environmental language(s) they have heard from birth and other languages they have not heard before (De Houwer, 2009). However, as we discussed in Chapter 3, monolingual children gradually lose this ability as they become more tuned in to their environmental language. This process is called **perceptual narrowing** (King and Fogle, 2006). Multilingual children, on the other hand, continue to be able to distinguish different phonemes in their ambient languages as well as in other unfamiliar languages. For example, a study found that Spanish–Catalan bilingual infants aged 4 and a half months could respond to recordings of sentences in either of their own two languages differently from the recordings of English and Italian that they had not heard before (Bosch and Sebastián-Gallés, 1997 and 2005). Another study looked at the perception of French and English contrasts in English monolinguals and French–English bilingual infants. Monolingual infants aged 6 months were able to distinguish both contrasts, but 10-month-olds could not, whereas bilingual infants were able to distinguish both contrasts at both ages (Burns et al., 2007).

Production

Early vocalization   Studies on multilingual infants' early vocalization yield different results. Some found that multilingual infants coo and babble similarly to monolingual infants (Cruz-Ferreira, 2006; Wang 2008), whereas others found that multilingual infants babble differently when interacting with parents who speak different languages (De Houwer, 2009). Studies also found that only consonants produced by infants are language-specific. They show differences when they interact with parents who speak different languages (De Houwer, 2009). There is also evidence that bilingual children produce phonological features that belong to the other language they are acquiring (Bhatia and Ritchie, 2013). Although it is inconclusive at this moment, much evidence seems to suggest that if young children are consistently exposed to the designated language systems, their phonological productions in their respective languages are clearly distinct without confusion (Wang, 2008).

Multilingual infants begin to produce canonical babbling around 8 months old (De Houwer, 2009). But, there is a range of variations regarding the age of babbling, and some multilingual infants may produce canonical babbling earlier. For example, the trilingual siblings Léandre and Dominique produced canonical babbling at around 4 months (Wang, 2008, p. 74).

Place holder One interesting phenomenon to note is that multilingual children develop the ability to "fill in" language-specific intonation patterns early on, even when they are not completely able to do it. For example, the Portuguese–Swedish bilingual children in Cruz-Ferreira's study (2006) demonstrated that when they were not sure of a word in a particular language, they would often replace it with a humming tone so that the overall intonation pattern of their utterance would still sound either Portuguese or Swedish. At a later age, the children produced many types of fillers, attempting to replace the supra-segmental structure of the language in question; as such, fillers add prosodic fluency to utterances (Cruz-Ferreira, 2006).

Multilingual phonological error pattern Some researchers believe that multilingual children exhibit atypical phonological error patterns in comparison with their monolingual peers (e.g., Dodd, Hemsley, and Holm, 2006). Others found that multilingual speakers demonstrate different developmental patterns from their monolingual peers and exhibit more errors initially than monolingual speakers, but these differences decrease over time (Gildersleeve-Neumann and Davis, 1998). However, recent research suggests that 4- and 5-year-old Spanish–English bilingual children exhibit phonological skills that are more similar to than different from both Spanish and English monolingual children; that is, the bilingual children's phonological skills are within a similar range as monolingual children, although the phonological skills of monolingual and multilingual children are *not* identical. For instance, accuracy for the **flap** (a type of consonant produced by allowing the tip of the tongue to strike the alveolar ridge very briefly), **trill** (the pronunciation of a consonant, especially *r*, with rapid vibration of the tongue against the hard or soft palate or the uvula), and **spirants** (sounds uttered with a continuous expulsion of breath) was higher in the Spanish of the bilingual children than in the Spanish of the Spanish monolingual children. Also, the percentage of occurrences for unstressed syllable deletion was higher in Spanish than in English (Goldstein, Fabiano, and Washington, 2005). In addition, the phonological patterns in 4-year-old Spanish–English bilingual children had no significant differences between the two languages in terms of percentage of consonants correct, percentage of consonants correct for voicing, place of articulation, manner of articulation, or percentage of occurrence for phonological processes. However, the children showed different patterns of production across the two languages (e.g., fricatives were more accurate in the children's Spanish productions than in their English productions).

On the basis of retrospective comparisons, these bilingual children also demonstrated different patterns compared to those of monolingual children of either language. For example, the bilingual children showed higher consonant accuracy in English than did monolingual English-speaking children. Consonant accuracy for the bilingual children's Spanish productions, however, was lower than that of monolingual

Spanish-speaking children (Goldstein, Fabiano, and Washington, 2005; Goldstein and Washington, 2001). Similarly, Cantonese–English bilingual children's error patterns were different for their two languages. In a retrospective comparison to monolingual English and monolingual Cantonese children, the bilingual children's patterns were not typical for monolingual speakers of either language; that is, the bilingual children exhibited error patterns that the monolingual children did not show (e.g., initial consonant deletion, backing, aspiration, and frication) (Dodd, So, and Li, 1996; Goldstein, Fabiano, and Washington, 2005).

Truncation   Multilingual children may truncate according to the patterns of each of their input languages. For example, the Portuguese–Swedish bilingual child Karin (1;8) truncated the Swedish word *banan* (banana) to *nanu* and the Portuguese word *banana* to *nana*. What is significant in this child's examples is that she truncates by mirroring the adult stress patterns in her input languages (Cruz-Ferreira, 2006). Phonological production takes a long time to perfect; even by ages 5 and 6, children may still utilize truncation in phonological production (De Houwer, 2009).

Deceleration   At some points of development (somewhere between the ages of 3 and 4), some phonological skills in multilingual children may be acquired at a slightly slower rate than in monolingual children of the same age. For example, research shows that monolingual Spanish speakers are significantly more accurate than bilingual Spanish–English children on their productions of the trill, **fricatives** (consonants produced by forcing air through a narrow channel made by placing two articulators close together such as /f/ in English), and **glides** (sounds produced as the vocal organs move toward or away from articulation of a vowel or consonant, such as /w/ and /j/ in English). Monolingual English-speaking children demonstrate significantly higher accuracy than bilingual children on **stops** (a consonant in which the vocal tract is blocked so that all airflow ceases) and fricatives. Interestingly, the deceleration that occurs is not identical across the two languages. Specifically, the Spanish–English bilinguals show a slower rate of acquisition for glides in Spanish but not in English when compared with monolinguals. Similarly, Spanish–English bilinguals show a slower rate of acquisition for stops only in English, yet they show a slower rate of acquisition for fricatives in both languages (De Houwer, 2009). Again, it is an issue whether multilingual children have a slower rate or whether they need a longer time to work on different systems.

Additionally, language differences can also make one of a child's languages develop slower than the other. For instance, South American Spanish uses 5 vowels and 20 consonants, but English uses 13 vowels and 24 consonants. Thus, there are more possibilities for contrasting sound combinations in English than in Spanish. These phonological and phonotactic differences in Spanish and English can influence the acquisition rate of the sound system in each language. Children learning Spanish master the sounds of the language relatively earlier than do children learning English. In English, fricatives, **affricates** or **affricatives** (complex speech sounds consisting of a stop consonant followed by a fricative; for example, the initial sound of *ch-* in *child* and *j-* in *joy*), **liquids** (consonants such as /r/ and /l/ in English, which are articulated without friction in roughly the same manner as a vowel), and **velars** (consonants articulated with the back part of the tongue touching or near the soft palate, such as /*g*/ in *good* and /*k*/ in *king*) are later developing sounds and are mastered between ages 4 and 5 years. In contrast, children learning Spanish produce most Spanish consonants and sound combinations accurately by age 4 (Goldstein and Iglesias, 1996). These differences may be attributed to the number of sounds to be learned and the possible contrasts to be produced (Summers et al., 2010).

Your Turn

Research online and find at least two examples for each of the following terms in Spanish and English. Articulate these sounds in English and Spanish and compare the differences. If you do not know Spanish, ask someone who knows Spanish to pronounce the Spanish sounds for you. Describe the differences.

	English	*Spanish*
Flap		
Trill		
Spirant		
Fricative		
Glide		
Stop		
Affricate/affricative		
Liquid		
Velar		

Cross-linguistic phonological interaction   There is increasing evidence suggesting that multilingual children develop separate phonological systems early on. However, the differentiated systems are not autonomous and can exhibit influences from one language to the other. This phenomenon is referred to as **cross-linguistic phonological interaction**. For example, the stages in bilingual phonological development appear to be different compared to phonological development in monolingual children. In a longitudinal study, Holm and Dodd (1999) investigated the phonological development of two young Cantonese–English bilingual children, who were exposed to English at an early age. They found that both children, simultaneously with the emergence of spontaneous utterances in English, exhibited phonological patterns in their Cantonese not typically found in monolingual Cantonese children. This finding led Holm and Dodd to suggest that the bilingual child, for a short period of time, might reconsider established rules in the one phonological system, while establishing another phonological system (Salameh, Nettelbladt, and Norlin, 2003).

The phonological interaction of multilingual children may be manifested from one language to the other in different ways. For example, French–English child Tom had interaction of word stress patterns in his two languages (De Houwer, 2009, p. 183). The French–Chinese–English siblings Léandre and Dominique placed English word stress on French words, and slightly altered Chinese tones influenced by English (Wang, 2008).

Often, when languages share similar phonological features, letters, and sound correspondence (e.g., English and Spanish), cross-linguistic phonological interaction tends to occur (Bialystok, Luk, and Kwan, 2005; Berk, 2009). Paradis and Genesee (1996) hypothesized that consonants and/or vowels that are specific to one language will interact with productions of the other language. This is known as **segmental interaction**. For example, a bilingual Spanish–English-speaking child uses the approximant /ɑ/, a sound specific to English, in the production of a Spanish word *carro* (car). Cross-linguistic interaction has been found to occur in a bidirectional manner – that is, from language A to language Alpha as well as vice versa.

Even though cross-linguistic phonological interaction is common among multilingual children, a recent study suggests that only 25 percent of the bilingual children demonstrated bidirectional phonological interaction. For the most part, these children maintain separation between their different phonological systems (Fabiano-Smith and Goldstein, 2010).

Phonological awareness

Cross-linguistic studies show that phonological awareness is a language-general ability that can be applied across languages (e.g., Yeong and Liow, 2012). Although the sequence of phonological awareness development is similar across most alphabetic languages, the rate of development and the level of proficiency attained by children may vary (e.g., Yeong and Liow; 2012). Different orthographic (writing) systems pose different challenges to learners in terms of phonological awareness. Children from a language system in which the correspondences between sounds and letters are regular (such as Hebrew and German) tend to perform better in phonological awareness; for example, they have the ability to count the number of syllables in a word and to identify rhymes (Hoff, 2009). Research shows that children who are exposed to Turkish, Italian, or Greek develop syllable awareness earlier than children who are exposed to English and French. This is perhaps because Turkish, Italian, and Greek all have relatively simple syllable structures and well-marked syllable boundaries in speech, whereas English and French do not (Yeong and Liow, 2012).

Moreover, between alphabetic (such as English) and logographic languages (such as Chinese), children may also have differences in their phonological awareness. For example, Chinese is a morphosyllabic system in which each morpheme maps onto one syllable and one character. The clear syllable boundary between morphemes may make the individual morphemes more distinct compared to the English language system (Cheng, Wang, and Perfetti, 2011). The phoneme level is much less salient in spoken Chinese than in spoken English. Although children would have little difficulty in developing syllable awareness, the phonological structure of Chinese might offer less support than English for phoneme awareness (Yeong and Liow, 2012). Thus, the oral form of a child's language may have an impact on her development of phonological awareness.

As mentioned before, phonological knowledge is fundamental to linguistic abilities and is predictive of reading development (Oller and Cobo-Lewis, 2002, p. 255). Research indicates that phonological abilities appear to be especially acute in multilingual speakers, even at a very young age. Multilingual children may have more advantage in phonological translation than their monolingual counterparts. **Phonological translation** is the ability to hear a word in one language and to render that word, not its meaning but its phonological form, in the other language. For example, a Spanish speaker says "Fernando," pronouncing the name with Spanish pronunciation styling; an English speaker, hearing the name, repeats it with English styling. This phonological translation requires a mapping of sounds between the two languages (Oller and Cobo-Lewis, 2002, p. 256). In multilingual children's daily environment, it is common for them to use phonological translation for names and linguistic borrowings (words borrowed from one language to the other). Thus, they are not only capable of making their phonological translation freely, but are also capable of choosing whether to use it or not. As a result, multilingual children tend to have a leg up in their phonological awareness (Oller and Cobo-Lewis, 2002, p. 258).

Multilingual children's advanced phonological awareness also manifested in their abilities in nonword repetition tasks. **Nonword repetition** (NWR) requires children to repeat novel phonological forms such as *woogalamic* or *noitauf* (Archibald, 2008). In NWR tasks, children repeat increasingly longer nonwords comprised of syllables that conform to the phonotactic constraints of the target language. Immediate recall of not meaningful phonological sequences depends heavily on children's ability to perceive, store, recall, and reproduce accurately strings of phonological sequences. NWR tasks mimic one of the most basic and important language-learning mechanisms, namely, immediate repetition of unfamiliar words. A child's NWR is especially important because the skills used in repeating nonwords play an important role in learning new words and morphemes. Compared to traditional language measures such as standardized language tests, NWR relies less on a child's prior knowledge of events, vocabulary, or language structures. Numerous studies show that performance on NWR tasks can predict children's vocabulary development and syntactic development (although to a lesser degree) (Archibald, 2008).

Multilingual children rely on similar language-learning mechanisms to mediate the NWR tasks. For example, more exposure to Spanish may increase abilities to repeat longer nonwords. This knowledge may shift across levels of multilingualism. Past research shows that NWR performance was similar across English and Spanish, with differences in performance patterns based on accuracy. NWR performance in both English and Spanish was also significantly correlated to cumulative language experience. Further, there were significant correlations between NWR and morphosyntax in both English and Spanish, and no correlations with semantics.

Children learning languages in which multi-syllable words are frequent such as Portuguese and Greek appear to be better at producing longer nonwords (up to five- and six-syllable nonwords, respectively). Because longer words are more frequent in Spanish than English, those children exposed to Spanish are also able to produce longer nonwords (Summers et al., 2010).

Your Turn

- What kind of strategies do young multilingual children use to compensate for their "inability" in phonological production? What could be the significance of their strategies in language acquisition?
- Given what you have read about multilingual children's phonological knowledge, can you predict how such knowledge would help them develop future literacy skills?

Multilingual lexical-semantic development

Compared to monolingual children, multilingual children have a more complex task in their acquisition of word and meaning in their different input languages.

Comprehension

Timing and rate of word comprehension   There is great variation among multilingual children with regard to when they understand words spoken in their environment. At about 4 to 7 months, multilingual children can respond to words that are used in their immediate environment. For instance, trilingual children Léandre and Dominique could understand Chinese and French words used frequently in their daily environment at 4 and 5 months respectively (Wang, 2008). The three Portuguese–Swedish infants started to respond to simple commands at the age of 7 months, and they increasingly showed signs of understanding many more words just one month later (Cruz-Ferreira, 2006). By 13 months, multilingual children have been shown to understand 70 percent more labels than monolingual children (De Houwer, 2009, p. 208).

The rate of vocabulary comprehension in multilingual children can vary greatly depending on their unique input languages. So far, we have not been able to establish a norm. The variation sometimes can be drastic. For example, for 13-month-old bilingual children, the comprehension of words can range from 16 words to 564 words in total (De Houwer, 2009, pp. 200–201). Also, vocabulary comprehension varies between children's different languages; some children will understand more words in one of their languages than the other(s).

Cross-linguistic synonym comprehension   Much of multilingual learning involves learning to understand different words from different languages for the same thing (De Houwer, 2009, p. 193). Young multilingual children are used to hearing the same thing referred to in more than one way (**cross-linguistic synonyms**). Even though young multilingual children understand the cross-linguistic synonyms, they may initially attribute different meanings to them. For instance, a child may think that Dutch word *fles* (bottle) means the bottle he drinks his milk out of (his mother usually fixes the bottle for him), and when he hears English *bottle*, he may understands it to refer only to the kind of bottle that contains his favorite juice (his father usually gives him the juice) (De Houwer, 2009, pp. 204–205).

Production

Timing of producing first words   The timing when multilingual children produce their words varies across individual children. The available research shows that multilingual children begin to produce their first words between 8 and 14 months (Cruz-Ferreira, 2006; De Houwer, 2009; Wang, 2008).

Idiomorphs   Multilingual children also use idiomorphs in the way monolingual children do. Some may use them for a long time, and others may use them briefly. For example, the trilingual child Léandre used *doméfice* (initially as a result of truncation, but it later became his idiomorph) for a long time to refer to *dentifrice* (toothpaste) in French (Wang, 2008, p. 74).

Categories of early words   Like monolingual infants, multilingual infants' early words are related to things in their immediate environment such as their actions, needs, wants, and feelings. They also refer to classes of objects or use proper names to refer to specific individuals (De Houwer, 2009, p. 214). In addition, multilingual children use a lot of social words such as *bye* in their first stage of word production in their respective languages. Once they reach a total of 50 different words, their social words begin to decrease compared to other types of words (De Houwer, 2009).

However, studies show that multilingual children exhibit quite different lexical acquisition patterns across their languages (De Houwer, 2009). For example, a Chinese–English bilingual child used lots of names for objects and people in Chinese, but he used lots of *good* and *no* in English (De Houwer, 2009).

Lexical gaps in different languages   Multilingual children do not typically produce a similar set of first words (cross-linguistic synonyms) at the same time in their respective languages, even though they sometimes do. This is because different adults (usually at this stage parents and caregivers) provide different input to their children, and often, the interactive contexts are different. Research has demonstrated that there is a high correlation (r=0.81) between parental language input frequency and multilingual children's output (Pearson et al., 1997). The following example epitomizes the point. The multilingual child Dominique acquired the French verb *tomber* (tumble) at the age of 1;1, and he used the Chinese equivalent (摔跤) only at the age of 3;6. He heard *tomber* much more frequently than 摔跤, because *tomber* was used by his father 45 percent more frequently than 摔跤 by his mother. When interacting with his father, Dominique had much more freedom in climbing and running than with his mother. As a result, he also had more incidents of tumbling, and thus, he had more opportunity to hear and use *tomber* rather than 摔跤 (Wang, 2008).

The lexical gap in children's different languages also depends on how close the children's input languages are. For example, Spanish and Catalan are closely related. Therefore, children who acquire these two languages will tend to have a large set of **cognates** (words in different languages that share the same etymology; they tend to have similar form and meaning, but not always pronunciation, e.g., *activate* in English and *activer* in French). However, children who are acquiring Chinese and Spanish will have no cognates to share.

Your Turn

Research online and make a list of cognates that are shared in English, French, and Spanish. What have you found?

Rate of lexicon production   Learning to use different labels for the same thing is a remarkable ability of multilingual children. Contrary to what is often claimed, research shows that there are no major differences in the total number of words produced by monolingual children and multilingual children (De Houwer, 2009). However, the question is whether multilingual children have a similar rate of vocabulary development in their respective languages. Some research found that multilingual children have a similar acquisition rate in all their languages (Yip and Matthews, 2008). Other research shows that multilingual children have more words in one of their languages (see De Houwer, 2009). Moreover, some children gradually increase their use of words, whereas others seem to show a vocabulary spurt within a short period. For example, just before 21 months old, Jessie (a Japanese–English bilingual child) had a total of 28 words, and half of them were Japanese. On the day he became 21 months, he added 14 words to his vocabulary. After another month, his total numbers of words had more than tripled. By the time he was 22 months, he produced 94 different words (Wanner, 1996).

Two issues relating to multilingual children's lexical production warrant attention. First, there are huge variations among multilingual children. For instance, at 20 months, bilingual children's word production can range from 14 words to 1,234 words (De Houwer, 2009). Second, there is a gender difference. Multilingual girls are a bit faster in lexical development than boys (De Houwer, 2009).

It is interesting to note that in the second year of children's lives, word comprehension and word production seem to go different ways. The fact that they seem to represent different aspects of psycholinguistic functions may partly explain why it is possible that somewhat older multilingual children can consistently speak language A in response to utterances from language Alpha (De Houwer, 2009).

Cross-linguistic synonym production   Multilingual children sometimes produce cross-linguistic synonyms (same sets of words in different languages), often because of their communication needs. For example, if a child wants to talk to his monolingual English grandmother about something she knows in Spanish, it is to her advantage to learn to say the equivalent English words (De Houwer, 2009).

However, multilingual children vary greatly in their production of cross-linguistic synonyms, and the age to produce them can range from 10 months to the end of the second year (De Houwer, 2009). In some cases, cross-linguistic synonyms never occur in the first stage of word production for some multilingual children.

Semantic overextension and underextension   The meanings in young multilingual children's word use are fluid just as they are in monolingual children. Such semantic fluidity is reflected in their word meaning overextension and underextension. The children overextend meanings in different languages in different situations (De Houwer, 2009, p. 215). For example, at 11 months, the Portuguese–Swedish multilingual Mikael consistently said the same form of Portuguese *água* (water) to refer to any kind of drinkable substance (Cruz-Ferreira, 2006, p. 143). They also underextend meaning of words in their respective languages. For example, an English–Dutch bilingual child used *car* only for the family car, and *auto* (the Dutch word for car) to refer only to the car of his favorite aunt (De Houwer, 2009, p. 230).

Holistic look at multilingual children's lexical-semantic production   Overall, when their lexical comprehension and production are considered together, multilingual children understand many more words than they can speak It appears that good comprehension may not necessarily result in good production. Research in Dutch–French bilingual children suggests that comprehension at 13 months did not relate to these children's later word production at 20 months. However, word production at age 13 months does predict word production at age 20 months (De Houwer, 2009).

Another study comparing monolinguals and bilinguals (4 to 6 years of age) found that bilingual children were two to three years ahead of their monolingual peers in semantic development (Baker, 2011). Other studies have shown that children with more than one language tend to have a smaller vocabulary than monolingual children in a single language. However, the fact is that multilingual children may know more words when all the words they know in their different languages are combined together (Hoff, 2009).

Your Turn

What strategies do multilingual children use in making meanings in their different languages? How do these strategies help children develop communicative competence in their respective languages?

Multilingual morphosyntactic development

Word combination

Multilingual children with a total production of 50 words or more begin to combine words (usually between ages 1;9 and 2;1), and those who have fewer than 30 words usually do not combine words (De Houwer, 2009). In general, multilingual children start to combine words in each of their languages at around the same time. Children who add new words to their vocabulary repertoires faster are more quickly able to produce longer utterances (Conboy and Thal, 2006).

However, the vocabulary size in one language is only correlated with the sentence complexity of that particular language. In other words, an English–Spanish bilingual child's vocabulary in English and Spanish is correlated with the sentence complexity in the respective languages, not necessarily across languages (Marchman et al., 2004). Changes in one language are not correlated with changes in another language (Conboy and Thal, 2006). For instance, an English–Latvian bilingual child produced quite a lot of **bound morphemes**[4] as compared to **free morphemes** (unbound morphemes) in her early Latvian utterances but none in English (Sinka and Schelletter, 1998).

Your Turn

Research on the internet and make a list of bound morphemes and free (unbound) morphemes of English and another language. What have you found?

Multilingual word mixing in syntactic production

Mixing words in a sentence in different languages is a typical and ubiquitous pattern of language use among multilingual children and adults. The frequency of language mixing varies widely across individuals. Because multilingual children are acquiring more than one language, the words in the different languages will interact with each other. Depending on how a child is exposed to the different linguistic systems, multilingual children will use words from one language in another (usually from the more exposed language to the less exposed one) to fill in the communication gap. For example, the trilingual siblings Léandre and Dominique borrowed the French word *tartine* (a piece of bread topped with butter and/or jam) when requesting it from their mother in Chinese, "给我做 *Tartine*" (Wang, 2008). The reason for them to mix words in a sentence is that there is no equivalent word for *tartine* in Chinese.

Besides mixing words in syntactic production, multilingual children sometimes also create words by mixing parts of words from different languages. For instance, the German–English bilingual child Haggard created a new word *bydersehen* for *bye-bye* by mixing the English *bye* with German *auf Wiedersehen* (Leopold, 1970). Research shows that there is about 30–50 percent overlap (mixing) in multilingual children's communication (Pearson, Fernandez, and Oller, 1995). However, this may depend on the input environment and other factors. For example, the trilingual siblings Léandre and Dominique tended to mix a lot less English in their French than in their Chinese because there are fewer equivalents between Chinese and English than French and English, in addition to other factors such as cultural and parental interaction styles (Wang, 2008).

Young multilingual children do not mix words randomly. Wang (2008) found four situations in which the English–French–Chinese trilingual brothers Léandre and Dominique mixed words during early childhood. First, they were found to mix store or brand names that do not exist in the other languages. For instance, *Target*, *Wal-Mart*, and *Lego*. Second, they used mixed words to inform the listener what a particular object was called in another language (e.g., Léandre told his father in French that his mother called a doll 娃娃 in Chinese). Third, the brothers used mixed words by imitating the words used by their parents as euphemisms in public (e.g., using 大便 for bowel movement when speaking in public). Finally, the children borrow the words from one language to fill the gap in another language; for example 穿 *parka* (wear coat or jacket).

Other researchers provided additional reasons to explain why young children mix languages. For example, De Houwer (2009) suggests that mixing occurs because the adults who talk to the children mix languages themselves and don't mind when children do either. Research corroborating this view shows that young children tend to mix languages at a frequency similar to that found in their adult input by age 3 (Kay-Raining Bird, 2007).

Your Turn

What are the communicative advantages for multilingual children to mix languages in their communication?

Multilingual pragmatic development

Pragmatic differentiation

When young children acquire more than one language, the aspect of pragmatic development takes on a new dimension. Multilingual children not only have to develop conversation **implicature** (the ability to apply meaning beyond the literal sense of what is explicitly stated) and learn how to make requests, refusals, complaints, compliments, and suggestions in their respective languages, but also have to learn to use their languages in a way customarily accepted by their respective linguistic communities.

Most young multilingual children show an early capacity to use their different languages appropriately (also known as **pragmatic differentiation**) with their parents by using more of a parent's preferred language with him or her (e.g., Montanari, 2005; Quay, 2008). Research shows that multilingual children as young as 2;2 already show language accommodation when speaking directly with strangers, using more of the stranger's language during a free-play session than they would normally (Gelman and Tare, 2011). Young multilingual children respond to their different conversational partners in the language they are addressed in. Almost from the very beginning, young multilingual children rarely make mistakes and use the "wrong" language with the "wrong" person. They are capable of selecting the appropriate language according to the interlocutors' language from the age of 1 (Montanari, 2008).

However, switching to the "wrong" language is also observed due to vocabulary gaps, the interlocutors' acceptance of mixing, and the possibilities determined by the existence of multiple lexical resources as well as multiple language users. In fact, young multilingual children's mixing of languages can be seen as a sign of their increasing sensitivity to the linguistic behaviors of their environment (Meisel, 2006).

Multilingual narrative development

Research on multilingual children's early narrative development is scarce. However, we are beginning to understand several aspects of their early narrative characteristics. First, multilingual children's early narrative styles are associated with their early language socialization experiences (e.g., Q. Wang and Leichtman, 2000). For instance, in some Latino families, parents tell traditional stories which differ from the narrative styles in mainstream American families (e.g., González, 2005; Schecter and Bayley, 2002). Moreover, multilingual children's early narrative styles are also influenced by their socioeconomic status (e.g., Dickinson and McCabe, 1991).

Second, although their narrative styles may be influenced by cultures, multilingual children's narrative structure has universal characteristics and properties, which are language and culture independent (e.g., Kupersmitt and Berman, 2001).

Third, multilingual children's ability to produce a narrative is more dependent on cognitive processes than on the specific language (Schwartz and Shaul, 2013). Multilingual children's narrative structure in one language may benefit the development of narrative structures in the other language(s). Therefore, narrative scaffolding in one language may boost development in the other language(s). However, narrative transfer does not necessarily happen automatically. For example, one study noticed that Spanish–English bilingual children's English narrative performance did not impact their Spanish narratives (Hammer et al., 2012). Another study also found that bilingual Russian–Hebrew children who attended the monolingual Hebrew preschool did not show narrative transfer from their Hebrew to their Russian. The researchers of the study speculate that the possible reason for this is that parents in these children's families did not often use Russian to narrate certain events such as birthday parties, and instead, they used Hebrew to converse about the events (Schwartz and Shaul, 2013). In other words, these parents did not provide enough Russian narrative modeling at home. This same study also found that children who attended the bilingual Hebrew and Russian preschool programs developed narrative skills in both of these languages (Schwartz and Shaul, 2013). It seems that linguistic transfer in narratives may occur only when children receive linguistic and narrative support in all their ambient languages, and only in such an environment can children activate and consolidate their various linguistic knowledge in narratives.

Finally, multilingual children's early narrative development is closely associated with their later literacy development in schools.

Your Turn

- As you are reading this chapter, it is possible that new research on multilingual children's early narrative development has been advanced. Research the academic databases such as PsycINFO and ERIC to find out possible new information.
- Analyze a personal or book-based narrative of a 5-year-old multilingual child. Discuss the characteristics of this child narration.

It is important to stress that multilingual children's earlier pragmatic development ability is not all-or-none. Rather, the pragmatic skills evolve throughout early childhood (Tare, 2008).

Metalinguistic development

A child's metalinguistic knowledge bears relation to her language ability, symbolic development, and literacy skills (Bialystok, 1991). Multilingualism enhances many metalinguistic abilities, including sensitivity to the details and structure of language, early distinction of word-referents, recognition of ambiguities, control of language processing, and correction of ungrammatical sentences.

Children who are exposed to more than one language tend to develop metalinguistic awareness earlier than those who are exposed to only one linguistic system. Research demonstrates that multilingual children exhibit advanced metalinguistic abilities as compared to their monolingual peers (Bruck and Genesee, 1995). Besides the phonological awareness discussed earlier in the phonological development section, most multilingual children become aware of their multilingualism in the second half of their second year of life, possibly as early as 1;7, but certainly around age 2 (Meisel, 2006). Around the ages of 2 or 3, many children who have been brought up with more than one language are able to talk about their languages (Cunningham-Andersson and Andersson, 1999; Wang, 2008). This ability is often demonstrated in naming the different languages they are speaking (e.g., "I speak French and Chinese"), displaying sensitivity about non-native speakers, comparing the words used in different languages, and making jokes in different languages (Wang, 2008). Below is an account described by linguist Suzanne Romaine about the Spanish–English bilingual child Mario's metalinguistic awareness and his showing of interest in other languages:

> When he heard other speakers speaking different languages, he would often imitate their pronunciation. Once when hearing his father speak Portuguese to a friend, he asked his father, "*Por que habla asi chistoso, papa? Es payaso? Paerce payaso.* – Why does he speak funny like that, Papa? Is he a clown?"…Mario was always eager to try phrases in a new language. Once when a German couple visited the home, he asked them how to say various things in German… (Romaine, 2005)

Moreover, multilingual children's increased use of self-correction or use of repairs is another form of metalinguistic awareness (De Houwer, 2009). Multilingual children tend to learn early on to correct themselves when they use the "wrong" language to communicate to an interlocutor, or correct others. For example, at age 2;5, the German–English bilingual child Laura self-corrected, "Adam gibt-geht auf den tree" (Adam gives-goes on the tree) (Gut, 2000a). At age 2;7, a German–French bilingual child Louis corrected his mother when he thought she said something wrong (Ronjat, 1913).

Your Turn

Given the early metalinguistic ability developed by multilingual children, predict how this ability would affect their future academic learning in school?

Developing Emergent Multilingual Literacies

Emergent knowledge of print conventions in different languages

When multilingual children are exposed to print in any language in their environment, they begin to form basic emergent concepts about it. Children begin to recognize the letters in alphabetic languages or characters in logographic languages. They also begin to notice the different language conventions. For example, print is read from left to right in English and from right to left in Arabic. Although 3-year-old Ommar does not know how to read and write Arabic and English, he has developed the knowledge to distinguish the two different scripts. When his father asked him to fetch the Arabic newspaper, he successfully accompanied the task without confusing it with the English newspaper (Wang, 2011a, p. 64).

Emergent knowledge of multilingual writing

Multilingual children begin to experiment with different orthographies in their input languages by scribbling them to convey meaning. Sometimes, the "writing" may be a combination of more than one language. For example, a bilingual English–Chinese child combined English letters with Chinese strokes in his spontaneous writing.

However, many multilingual children, although they are exposed to more than one spoken language, are exposed to only a monolingual print environment. Unless parents are conscious about providing these children with a multilingual print environment, many of these children may speak different languages but only have monolingual print input. Therefore, it is likely that these children's emergent literacy ability is in one language, often the dominant language such as English.

Cross-language interaction on emergent literacy knowledge

Research suggests that there is a cross-linguistic interaction in multilingual children's early emergent literacy knowledge. For example, there are positive correlations between children's Spanish and English in the areas of phonological awareness, letter–word identification, memory for sentences, and concepts about print. Children who have strong English abilities in these areas also have the same abilities in Spanish (Tabors, Páez, and López, 2003).

Emergent multilingual digital literacy

With the advancement of communication technology, multilingual children have more opportunities to access multilingual digital print or hypertexts. When they are exposed to hypertexts, multilingual children are able to develop emergent knowledge and concepts about them. Although little research is being conducted in this area at this moment, observations reveal that young multilingual children do begin to form the basic concept of how hypertexts work. For instance, when they click or touch a screen, images and other information can appear or disappear, and they can find information online. The following example illustrates a young multilingual child's emergent knowledge about obtaining information from the internet. Four-year-old Ayati requested that her mother download a picture of a dish used to serve in the Indian Diwali celebration from the computer (the internet) so that she could use it in Show and Tell at her nursery school (Wang, 2011a, p. 64).

Emergent critical literacy

Young multilingual children often show emergent critical literacy ability that is superior to monolingual children's because they have the advantage of being exposed to different stories or different versions of stories in their input languages. For example, 5-year-old Kanya told her friends in kindergarten that the "Snow White" story she heard in Thai did not use the same words as the English version to describe Snow White (Wang, 2011a, p. 9).

Your Turn

What are the similarities and differences between monolingual and multilingual children in their development of emergent literacies? What could be the education implications for these early differences in children's future academic learning?

Supporting Emergent Multilingual and Mul Development in Early Childhood

The path to multilingual and emergent multiliteracy deve
Therefore, supporting strategies need to be mindful of the uni
children.

   Multilingual children tend to have proportionally less input per language compared to their monolingual peers. That is, a monolingual child is immersed in one language everywhere in her environment, at home as well as outside. However, a multilingual child may hear one of his languages only at home, oftentimes from only one parent. In such a case, the multilingual child has substantially less input than the monolingual child, particularly in his home language(s). Even though the multilingual child will have the capacity to acquire a language with limited input, sufficient language input is helpful to move the child forward. As mentioned before, children may need about 25 percent of input in one language to become competent users of that language. If this is true, some proactive actions must be taken to ensure that multilingual children have sufficient input in the language that is not spoken in the larger community. The following strategies may be helpful.[5]

Book reading

Multilingual children's vocabulary development and narrative skills, particularly for those children who receive limited input in one or more of their ambient languages, can be boosted through book reading (Wang, 2008 and 2011a). Frequent book reading has been shown to be associated with narrative (e.g., Purcell-Gates, 2001) and vocabulary development. For example, one study shows that when the Spanish–English bilingual children between 21 and 27 months old were frequently read aloud to in Spanish, they acquired more words in Spanish (De Houwer, 2009, p. 197; Patterson, 2002). Although research on how book reading affects young multilingual children's narrative development is limited, it is plausible to infer from other studies on how reading can facilitate children's narrative development. For example, well-read–to children can learn linguistic registers that are specific to social contexts and use more formal and book-like narrative language when pretending to read a story book (e.g., Uchikoshi, 2005).

Media

Media such as educational and book-based TV programs and other digital software can serve as additional resources for young multilingual children to build vocabulary and learn narrative structure. However, just leaving young children in front of the TV or computer will not achieve the purpose. The key is to provide scaffolding and ask both contextualized and decontextualized questions about what they see and hear and to help young children develop longer narratives and use more book-like language.

   In addition, research shows that book-based TV programs (such as *Arthur*) may have a positive impact on multilingual children's narrative development (Uchikoshi, 2005). Therefore, you may want to use these book-based TV programs to help multilingual children develop their narrative skills.

Your Turn

Analyze a book-based TV program and discuss why such a program may facilitate children's, including multilingual children's, narrative development.

 ## Explicit teaching

Although storybook readings and media exposure can be useful in teaching children new words (i.e., natural exposure to new vocabulary) and get them familiar with the narrative structure, the overt teaching approach, that is, focusing on new-word teaching in reading and specific mentioning of the narrative elements and structure via scaffolding, is necessary to promote a deep knowledge of new vocabulary and narration in multilingual children because they often have limited input in one or more of their home language(s). You may want to deliberately teach the words and narrative elements/style in storybooks and explain them in context to facilitate a greater multilingual vocabulary gain. Moreover, in everyday communication, when multilingual children overextend or underextend meanings, you can seize the moment by offering appropriate words directly in the context.

 ## Communication demand

Children learn words driven by communication demand. Therefore, when interacting with young multilingual children, providing more opportunities that require them to respond, describe, and argue may help them learn different words in different languages.

 ## Concept building

Because of the imbalance in multilingual children's input languages, they often may know words in one of their environmental languages and not in the other(s). Therefore, building concepts through one language or more languages is more important for young children's future academic success than matching the right label in different languages. A concept built in one language can help build the foundation for understanding the concept in another language. For example, understanding how an electrical circuit functions in a child's home language is the same understanding that can be transferred later to the child's school language. When learning about such concepts in school, a child who is already familiar with the concept in his home language may only need to learn the new vocabulary for talking about the concept in the school language (Giambo and Szecsi, 2005).

 ## Gesture use

Words are not the only channels we use to communicate; other nonverbal behaviors such as hand gestures, body postures, and facial expressions are an integral part of our communication system. Some researchers even indicate that most of our messages in communication are conveyed through nonverbal channels (Mehrabian, 1981). Because of their direct link to lexical meanings, hand gestures in particular have received increasing attention among researchers in recent decades. A growing body of research suggests that gestures can help promote language development, including multiple language development.

Young multilingual children should be encouraged to use hand gestures before they can sufficiently express themselves in a given language. One advantage of using gestures to fill the vocabulary gap is that young children will not get frustrated when they do not know a word. Instead of stopping communication because of linguistic constraints, children will have a way to convey their thoughts through hand gestures. Some may be concerned that if they encourage children to use gestures rather than words, children will become lazy and not use words. Research actually shows that the opposite is true. For example, studies show that when prelinguistic infants are taught to use a set of gestures to communicate their needs and wants, they tend to be less frustrated and show a greater gain in their language acquisition than their peers who are not trained to use gestures before they can speak (Acredolo and Goodwyn, 2002). However, one study did caution parents to be careful when teaching their infants to use baby signs (J. C. Johnston, Durieux-Smith, and Bloom, 2005).

Another advantage in encouraging young children to use gestures is that through their gestures, adults can detect what word or concept children do not know. For example, before the multilingual Léandre was able to say the word 剪刀 (scissors) in Chinese, he used to open and close his index finger and middle finger to express the meaning of 剪刀. His gestural clue gave his mother an opportunity to teach him the Chinese words 剪刀 (Wang, 2008).

Also, using gestures can help young children retrieve words (Özçalişkan, Gentner, and Goldin-Meadow, 2013). A study conducted to test the effects of hand gestures on young children's narratives suggests that when an adult read a book to bilingual children with a set of deliberately used hand gestures, these children could recall more words than when the adult read the story without using hand gestures (Wang and Eberhard, 2006).

Moreover, all cultures contain a set of gestures that are recognizable by people from that specific community (these types of gestures are called **emblems** or conventional gestures). Emblems are a very important part of acquiring a language. Knowing how to use conventional gestures in a language/culture can make a speaker look more "authentic." Does an Italian speaker sound authentic without using some well-known emblems in a conversation? Thus, multilingual children need to be informed and deliberately taught about these conventional gestures by modeling their use in the context (Wang, 2008).

Your Turn

Provide one concrete example to implement each of the strategies discussed above:

Book reading, including shared book reading
Overt vocabulary teaching
Increase communication demand
Concept building
Gesture use

Summary of Key Points

- As a result of their experience in acquiring more than one language, multilingual children have better attention control and cognitive flexibility.
- The cutoff age for deciding whether multilingual children's language acquisition belongs to first language (L1) or subsequent language (Ln or L2) is about ages 4 to 5. If a child acquires more than one language before age 5, the multilingual acquisition is considered multilingual L1 acquisition (MLFLA) and after 5, it is treated as L2 or Ln learning.
- A critical mass needs to be reached in each of multilingual children's perspective languages before they can acquire that language.
- The environments in which children are exposed to more than one language differ greatly. As a result, multilingual children's language abilities in their perspective languages vary significantly.
- Multilingualism may have different effects on children. Some may benefit from multilingual acquisition experience and develop particularly strong phonological representation, storage, and retrieval systems. Others may develop relatively weaker representations in one or all of their respective languages.
- Few multilinguals have balanced competence in all their languages due to imbalance in their linguistic input and opportunities in language use.
- Although bilingual and trilingual children share lots of similarities, they have different language learning experiences.
- Cross-linguistic interaction does not occur randomly. Children must have a solid understanding of the features of their languages in order to be able to mix them.
- Some multilingual children may show a slower rate in acquiring their respective languages. However, the slower rate may indicate that they need more time to figure out their distinct linguistic systems.
- Multilingual children develop phonotactic knowledge in their respective languages to distinguish between the speech sounds of the different language systems.
- Young multilingual children use distinct strategies in learning their respective languages. For example, if they do not know a particular word, they will fill in the space with an intonation that jibes with the phonetic structure of the language.
- Different languages may pose different challenges to learners. Thus, this may affect multilingual children's acquisition of these languages.
- Multilingual children typically begin to produce their first words between 8 and 14 months. Like monolingual children, their first words are often related to objects and people in their immediate environment. However, the word qualities they produce in their respective languages vary, depending on their degree of exposure to the input languages.
- Like monolingual children, multilingual children underextend and overextend the meaning of words, and they often comprehend many more words than they can produce.
- Multilingual children tend to borrow words from Language Alpha to Language A to fill in communication gaps. They also might create hybrid words that fuse portions of words from two different languages.

- Multilingual children have to learn how to use more than one language in more than one culturally appropriate way of communication.
- Multilingual children tend to exhibit metalinguistic knowledge earlier than monolingual children.
- Multilingual children demonstrate emergent concepts of multilingual print conventions and multilingual hypertext. They also show emergent critical literacy abilities.
- To facilitate multilingual L1 acquisition and emergent multilingual literacies, additional input in their ambient languages is essential. Several strategies are recommended:
  - Engaging them in shared book reading and other media resources
  - Overt teaching of vocabulary and narrative elements
  - Increasing communication demands
  - Focusing on building concepts
  - Observing and encouraging gesture use

Key Terms

Affricates/affricatives
Bound morpheme
Code-switching
Cognates
Competence
Critical mass
Cross-linguistic phonological interaction
Cross-linguistic synonym
Emblems
Flap
Free morpheme (unbound morpheme)
Fricatives

Glides
Implicature
Liquids
Morphemes
Nonword repetition (NWR)
One-parent-one-language
Perceptual narrowing
Performance
Phonological translation
Phonotactic knowledge
Pragmatic differentiation
Segmental interaction
Stops
Velars

Notes

1. The dual-system hypothesis is also called separate development hypothesis (De Houwer, 2009) or differentiation hypothesis (Meisel, 2006).
2. Code-switching describes when a multilingual child or person changes languages within the same conversation. It is typical for a multilingual to mix words, phrases, or complete sentences of one language with another language. For example, "Pass me that *placa*, please." In this sentence, the speaker mixed English with a Spanish word *placa* (plate).
3. One-person-one-language or one-parent-one-language means that in a multilingual family, one parent speaks only language A to a child and another parent speaks only language Alpha to the child.

4. A bound morpheme is a morpheme that only appears as part of a word and cannot stand alone (e.g., English prefix *pre-* and suffix -*ment*). In contrast, a free or unbound morpheme can stand alone or bound with other elements (e.g., *ship* and *shipment*).
5. Please note that the strategies suggested for multilingual children here, and later for children with language learning difficulties, can also be used for children with typical development. However, these strategies may be particularly helpful with these specific populations. This will be the same later in the book for elementary and secondary students.

Recommended Further Readings

Bhatia, T. K. and Ritchie, W. C. (eds) (2013). *The Handbook of Bilingualism and Multilingualism*. Oxford: Wiley-Blackwell.

De Houwer, A, (2009). *Bilingual First Language Acquisition*. Bristol: Multilingual Matters.

Wang, X.-L. (2008). *Growing up with Three Languages: Birth to Eleven*. Bristol: Multilingual Matters.

Wang, X.-L. (2011). *Learning to Read and Write in the Multilingual Family*. Bristol: Multilingual Matters.

5

Acquiring First Language(s) with Difficulties

Prereading Questions and Activities

- Children are often identified as having language impairment based on the errors they make. However, errors alone are not necessarily a definite indicator of impairment. Typically developing children sometimes make errors and children from different cultural and linguistic backgrounds sometimes do the same. How do you know whether the errors made by a child are a typical linguistic developmental phenomenon or whether they truly represent a language-learning impairment?
- Audio- or video-record a narrative of a child between 1 and 4 with language impairment. You can give the child a topic such as "Tell me what you did last weekend." Transcribe it verbatim. Analyze the transcript at the level of words and sentences (e.g., how many words has the child produced? How many different words has the child produced? How many words has the child produced in a sentence on average?) What is your finding about this child's language development?
- What impact could children's LI during early childhood have on their future academic learning and life?
- When providing support for young children with LI, should we only focus on their language difficulties or should we also focus on the language areas that are associated with their future cognitive and social development?

Topics to Be Addressed in This Chapter

- Definition of language impairment (LI)
- Types of LI covered in this book
  - ○ Down syndrome (DS)
  - ○ Autism spectrum disorder[1] (ASD)

Understanding Language and Literacy Development: Diverse Learners in the Classroom, First Edition. Xiao-lei Wang.
© 2015 John Wiley & Sons, Inc. Published 2015 by John Wiley & Sons, Inc.
Companion website: www.wiley.com/go/wang/langandlit

- ○ Specific language impairment (SLI)
- ○ Hearing impairment (HI)
- ○ Vision impairment (VI)
- ○ Multilingual children with language impairments (MLI)
- Developmental profiles of children with LI
- Language acquisition characteristics in each language impairment
  - ○ Phonological development
  - ○ Lexical-semantic development
  - ○ Morphosyntactic development
  - ○ Pragmatic and metalinguistic development
- Emergent literacies
- Supporting strategies for young children with LI

Learning Objectives

After reading this chapter, you should be able to do the following:

- Understand the nature of LI and its impact on young children's language and future literacy development.
- Recognize the cognitive and social developmental characteristics of children with LI.
- Know the specific language and emergent literacy learning difficulties of children with LI as well as their strengths.
- Become familiar with the suggested supporting strategies and be able to use them to help young children with LI.

Language Impairment in Infancy and Early Childhood

Most young children acquire one or more than one language with relative ease. However, a small group of young children encounter difficulties in their language acquisition process due to a variety of physical and/or neurological-cognitive conditions. In 2006, the US Preventative Task Force estimated that about 5–8 percent of children of preschool age had speech and language impairments.

The consequences of LI can disrupt the typical path of language acquisition and potentially affect children's future social development, academic performance, and ultimately, employment and quality of life (Schwartz, 2009). In fact, research has shown that LI identified in early childhood tends to persist in a majority of children, often resulting in diminished ability to acquire written forms of language. Thus, without adequate support and effective intervention, young children with LI are at risk of prolonged language and academic difficulties (Paul, 2007).

What is language impairment?

The American Speech-Language-Hearing Association (1993) has defined LI as

a disorder or a deviant development of comprehension and/or use of a spoken, written, and/or other symbol system. LI may affect the form of language (phonologic, morphologic, and syntactic systems), the content of language (lexical-semantic system), and/or the function of language in communication (pragmatic system) in any combination.

Although this definition is useful in that it is quite broad, covering not only spoken but also written language, Paul (2007) points out that it does not help decide what constitutes the "impairments" in acquisition. She proposed an alternative definition (see Box 5.1).

Box 5.1   Definition of Child Language Disability

Children have a significant deficit in learning to talk, understand, or use any aspect of language appropriately, relative to both environmental and norm-referenced expectations for children of similar developmental level.

R. Paul, *Language Disorders from Infancy through Adolescence: Assessment and Intervention*, 3rd edn (St. Louis, MO: Mosby, 2007), p. 3.

Paul (2007) further suggests that when identifying children with LI, it is more positive and useful to focus on building a profile of strengths and needs. She recommends using the World Health Organization (WHO) framework as a guide to conceptualizing children with LI (see Box 5.2).

Box 5.2   WHO Framework

Body structure and function   Impairments are problems, such as significant deviation or loss in the anatomical parts of the body (organs, limbs, and their components) and/or the physiological functions of the body, including psychological functions.

Activities and participation   Any restriction in a person's ability to address the needs of daily living or execute specific tasks; these can change in different situations or stages of life.

Contextual factors   The physical, social, and attitudinal environment in which people live and conduct their lives. Thus, an individual may be affected not only by his or her own impairment or disability but also by the attitudes and biases of others with whom the person comes in contact.

From www3.who.int/icf/.

According to Paul (2007), the advantage of using the WHO framework to examine the language development of children with LI is that by considering the body structures and functions, we are sensitive to the fact that the children with LI are different in some respects from their peers. By focusing on participation, we pay attention to the impact of children's impairments on activities of daily life. Finally, by looking at the contextual factors, we can take into consideration the environmental factors in children's lives, including both how the environment contributes to the difficulty and how to change the environment to maximize children's potential (Paul, 2007, p. 10).

Your Turn

- Try to rephrase the WHO framework in the context of children with LI and discuss how this framework can be used in young children with LI.
- Based on the information you have read so far and your observations and experiences, describe children with LI in your own words.

Types of language impairment covered in this book

LI is often categorized according to its causes. For example, Nickola Nelson (2010) categorized the factors that cause LI into three big categories: central processing factors, peripheral factors, and environmental and emotional factors. Central processing factors relate to the part of the brain that controls language and cognitive functioning. The types of LI in this category include specific language impairment, mental delay, central auditory processing disorder, autism, and brain injury. Peripheral factors directly cause impairment in the motor or sensory systems which influence how language is perceived and processed, and hearing impairment, visual impairment, hearing-visual impairment, and other types of physical impairments are examples. Although these factors may contribute to LI, their presence does not always cause LI. Environmental and emotional factors, such as neglect, abuse, behavior problems, and emotional problems, which do not have a physical cause, can also influence language development. It is important to note that many children with LI can fit into more than one of the above categories (Gillam, Marquardt, and Martin, 2011, p. 225).

In this book, five types of LI are identified as the focus of discussion. In addition, multilingual children with LI are also addressed.

- Down syndrome (DS)
- Autism spectrum disorder (ASD)
- Specific language impairment (SLI)
- Hearing impairment (HI)
- Vision impairment (VL)
- Multilingual children with language impairments (MLI)

The decision to concentrate on these types of LI is based on three reasons. First, there is enough research evidence on these impairments to support adequate discussion. Second, these language impairments are likely to impact children's academic learning. Finally and most importantly, teachers can provide instructional support for these children in the classroom environment.

Developmental Profiles of Children with LI

Most types of LI are not obvious at birth; awareness of problems appears insidiously over months and years, because a child is not talking like others do (Bishop, 2008, p. 67). Because of individual differences in the rate of language development, it may not always be easy to distinguish between a young child's language delay that represents a child at the bottom end of the typical distribution and a child who has genuine linguistic impairment (Fletcher, 2001, p. 364). As a result, many children with LI are not identified early in life until they enter preschool and elementary school. Thus, a great number of children with LI may have missed the opportunity to receive early support in language acquisition, consequently affecting their cognitive and social development later in life.

The most challenging aspect in examining the language acquisition of children with LI is that not all of them show exactly the same characteristics, despite obviously exhibiting difficulties in either or both areas of language comprehension and production. In fact, children with LI function quite differently depending on whether their disabilities are caused by environmental deprivation during early years, the faculty of learning, emotional issues, disease, or physical trauma (Hulit and Howard, 2006). However, the most prominent cognitive characteristic shared by children with LI is that they tend to lack the generalization ability. For instance, it is usually easy for children with typical development (TD) to create new sentences by utilizing the large variety of grammatical examples they have heard (generalization ability), whereas most children with LI cannot do so (Gleason, 2009). In the following sections, each type of LI is introduced briefly.

Children with Down syndrome

Children with **Down syndrome** (DS) have an IQ ranging from 40 to 70, have difficulties in their functioning of the general cognitive system, and exhibit significant limitation in auditory working memory or short-term memory (Tager-Flusberg, 2001). As a result, they have a specific impairment in the computational mechanisms that underlie the processing of grammatical information (Tager-Flusberg, 2001). Despite these restraints, the strength of children with DS is that they are interested in people and are often quite social.

Children with autism spectrum disorder

There are five subtypes in **autism spectrum disorder** (ASD): autistic disorder, Asperger syndrome, Rett syndrome, childhood disintegrative disorder, and pervasive developmental disorder not otherwise specified. These subtypes are differentiated from one another primarily by age of onset and severity of the manifestations. ASD is the name given to any of five related childhood neurobehavioral syndromes subsumed under the term **pervasive developmental disorder** (PDD).

ASD is characterized by impaired social skills, language impairment, difficulties in intellectual functioning, ritualistic and repetitive behavior patterns, and uneven development of skill acquisition. Although popularly portrayed in many movies (e.g., *Rain Man*), autistic savants are very rare. The essential difference between Asperger disorder and autistic disorder is that with Asperger disorder, there is generally no cognitive and language delay.

Children with ASD display a wide range of intellectual abilities, from profound cognitive disabilities to superior intellectual capacity. In general, they have social and communicative impairments and restriction in creativity, flexibility of thinking, and generalization. Infants with TD tend to focus on a speaker's eye region as early as 2 months of age, because a speaker's eyes convey the social information connected with verbal and nonverbal communication. In contrast, children with ASD tend to focus on a speaker's mouth region. Such early gazing behavior puts these infants at risk for difficulties in typical language acquisition. As such, children with ASD have serious difficulties in joint attention (a shared focus on an object) with their caretakers. The difficulty in joint attention leads to their underdevelopment in theory of mind, which plays a central role in language and communication. As discussed in Chapter 3, theory of mind is the ability to understand the other's mental state, to infer what another person knows or might be thinking, and to intuit his or her intention (N. Nelson, 2010).

Most infants with ASD tend to show little or no interest in people, and it is difficult for them to maintain eye contact or engage in interactions. Prelinguistic toddlers with ASD often show no preference for listening to their own mothers' speech and may have idiosyncratic means to communicate their needs, which their mothers find hard to interpret (Tager-Flusberg, 2001, p. 329). Consequently, children with ASD tend to lack a grasp of self and other in social interactions.

However, despite functional disability in general, about 1 in 10 individuals with ASD have specific skills in which they excel, far beyond the average population. For instance, some children with ASD have exceptional rote memory capacity. They can memorize large amounts of materials, store a huge quantity of information in their minds for extended periods of time, and repeat the data accurately. Moreover, some children with ASD have **splinter skills**, as manifested in their exceptional talent for playing musical instruments, drawing, and doing mathematical calculations.

Children with specific language impairment

Specific language impairment (SLI) impacts about 7.4 percent of the US English-speaking population (Peña and Bedore, 2009), and boys are affected slightly more than girls (Schwartz, 2009). SLI is impairment in language comprehension and/or language production in the absence of general cognitive impairment, sensory-motor impairment (such as hearing impairment), neurological impairment, social-emotional issues, and a general lack of exposure to language (Leonard, 1998). However, children with SLI have various limitations in general auditory and speech perception; limitations in central cognitive domains such as memory, attention, and executive functions; difficulties in other cognitive functions such as problem-solving, **mental rotation**, and mathematics; and deviations in neurological structure and functions. They also have a relatively high incidence of dyslexia and other more global reading and writing disabilities. Due to its complexity, it is a challenge to identify SLI among young children, and it remains difficult to identify even with older children (Girbau and Schwartz, 2008). See more discussion of this topic in Chapter 8.

Although children with SLI usually have typical cognitive function, they tend to have impaired working memory (short-term memory) as manifested in their poor **phonological memory** (the ability to repeat a sequence of sounds). Since mapping words to meaning requires holding new word forms in short-term memory while hypothesizing the meaning of the word form from contextual cues, the limitation in children with SLI makes them less successful in word mapping and results in semantic and grammatical difficulties (McGregor, 2009, p. 366). Research shows that children with SLI tend to be four years behind children with TD in working memory performance.

SLI is often hereditary. For example, half of the members in a 30-people, three-generation family in the UK were found to have experienced language impairment (Fletcher, 2001).

Children with SLI and children with DS sometimes share similar cognitive characteristics, such as their difficulties in working memory. As a result, children with DS also show semantic and grammatical difficulties similar to children with SLI.

Children with hearing impairment

Approximately, 1–3 children in 1,000 births are born with a congenital hearing impairment (HI) or hearing loss (HL) (N. Nelson, 2010). About 4–10 percent of children with hearing impairment or loss are born to deaf parents, and these children's sign language acquisition is similar to the oral language acquisition of hearing children with TD. However, 90–96 percent of children with HI and HL are born to hearing parents (Morgan and Kegl, 2006). Thus, a majority of children with HI and HL who do not have a conventional language input (either sign language or spoken language) initially develop the ability to engage in interactions with parents and people around them by using spontaneous gestures. Their gestural communication is in many ways language-like (Wang, Mylander, and Goldin-Meadow, 1996). However, despite these early communication inventions in the gestural modality, their spontaneous gesture systems do not make a fully developed language. Without support, the consequence of a lack of access to spoken input from the ambient language as well as sign language input will seriously inhibit these children's language development.

As technology advances, many newborns in the United States are now receiving hearing testing at birth. Some children with HI or HL receive a cochlear implant that can restore the function of the auditory nerve. However, there is a controversy in the Deaf[2] community about whether it is natural for children with HI or HL to receive a cochlear implant. Some activists in the Deaf community argue that deafness is not a disability in need of a cure and that sign language is the natural language for Deaf people.

Children with vision impairment

Although vision impairment (VI) and vision loss (VL) limit children's joint attention with their caregivers, research shows that most children with VI achieve the usual milestone of human attachment in the first two years of life. Preferences for their mothers are known in differential smiling and vocalizing, manual tactile seeking, embracing, and spontaneous gestures of affection and comfort seeking. From 7 to 15 months of age, toddlers with VI, like sighted ones, begin to avoid and manifest stress reactions to strangers and reject them as interactive partners. During the second year, the anxiety of children with VI at separation and comfort at reunion provide evidence that children with VI value their mothers as indispensable human partners in the same way sighted babies do (N. Nelson, 2010).

Children with congenital vision loss who have sensory input difficulties may be affected in their language acquisition. In particular, children with VL have challenges associated with acquiring concepts and vocabulary that depend on coordinating visual information with spoken language and with developing awareness of social interaction cues that are expressed nonverbally, such as facial expressions and eye gaze.

Your Turn

If you were a parent of a child with severe hearing loss, what would be your decision: to teach the child sign language, to implant a cochlear device, or to teach the child oral language? Explain your decision. Alternatively, if a parent of a child with sensory impairment asks for your advice on the same issue, what would be your recommendation and why?

Language Development Characteristics of Children with LI

In the following sections, the language developmental characteristics of children with various language impairments are highlighted to provide you with a general overview. It is important to keep in mind that children with LI follow the same universal principles that operate on the acquisition of phonology meaning and grammar as children without LI. Within each of these domains, there are uniform sequences of development and certain principles that constrain the process of development. However, as these components develop over time, they may become integrated in different ways, which led to specific profiles that are related to each type of various language impairments (Tager-Flusberg, 2001).

Children with Down syndrome

Phonological development

As mentioned in Chapter 3, canonical babbling marks the most important developmental precursor to meaningful speech. Infants with DS are about 2 months behind infants with TD in the onset of canonical babbling. Once the canonical babbling starts in the infants with DS, it is less stable compared to infants with TD (Tager-Flusberg, 2001).

Research shows that the phonological abilities of young children with DS are a little delayed, but are generally comparable to their counterparts with TD. However, children with DS tend to produce more phonological errors overall than children with TD (Tager-Flusberg, 2001).

Lexical-semantic development

Young children with DS acquire earlier object labels by following the typical operating principles. That is, they tend to acquire words first at the basic level (e.g., *car* and *dog*) rather than at the more specific subordinate level (e.g., *Volkswagen* and *terrier*) or more general superordinate level (e.g., *vehicle* and *animal*). They also follow the same operating principle in word categorization and sort all cars, all boats, all dogs, and so forth together into a group (Tager-Flusberg, 2001).

Young children with DS also tend to follow the typical principle in constructing word meaning by demonstrating the knowledge that words can be extended to objects beyond those initially labeled with that word and that all objects belong to a category or group of similar items. Like children with TD, children with DS begin to sort objects at the same point in time as they begin the naming explosion, and they are able to fast map names of objects. There are also variations among children with DS. Some young children with DS develop vocabulary at a rate that is comparable to their mental age level, while others are significantly delayed (Tager-Flusberg, 2001).

As a group, children with DS in general tend to have difficulties in expressive vocabulary (Miller, 1995). In contrast, their receptive vocabulary is a strength, often being on a par with or even in advance of nonverbal mental age (Feltmate and Kay-Raining Bird, 2008). Moreover, they tend to produce fewer grammatical or lexical verbs per utterance and fewer verbs of communication of mental state, but they tend to use higher verb diversity than their counterparts with typical development (Hesketh and Chapman, 1998).

Morphosyntactic development

Children with DS have delays or significant delays in their syntactic development, especially in expressive syntax. They tend to use simpler and shorter sentences in communication compared to children with TD. Most children with DS never acquire grammatical constructions such as sentence embedding or correct use of complex questions. Their mean length of utterance (MLU) rarely progresses beyond 3.0 (Tager-Flusberg, 2001)

Children with DS whose IQ scores are below 50 may not begin to combine words until the age of 5 or 6, and then they spend a period of time during which they use relatively few two-word utterances. Their rate of development is very slow, and these children may never develop beyond the early states of grammatical development (Tager-Flusberg, 2001).

Pragmatic and metalinguistic development
Infants with DS show delays in the onset of mutual eye contact and vocalize much less than infants with TD. As a result, their early interactions with their mothers are less coordinated. However, by the second half of the first year, children with DS catch up and show higher levels of mutual eye contact with their caregivers. At this stage, they tend to fixate primarily on the eyes rather than exploring other facial features. Further, they tend to vocalize more than infants with TD. This increased interest in people in the latter part of the first year, expressed through eye gaze, is accompanied by lower level interests in objects and toys. Thus, 1-year-old children with DS have difficulty interacting with their mothers while at the same time playing with objects. Consequently, children with DS show higher frequencies of social interaction behaviors, but lower frequencies of object request behaviors, and thus, they tend to produce less expressive language.

Overall, pragmatic ability is the strength of children with DS compared with their phonological and expressive language. For example, children with DS express the same range of **speech acts**[3] as children with TD. However, there are differences as well, particularly involving interpersonal functions (e.g., see this) and instrumental functions (e.g., request, want cookie). Children with DS make fewer requesting behaviors. In general, children with DS seem to focus more on the use of communication to interact and engage socially with other people than to regulate their environment. Also, children with DS use significantly more turns on the same topic than children with TD. In effect, they maintain a conversational topic at levels higher than children with TD (Tager-Flusberg, 2001).

Young children with DS have particular difficulties in developing phonological awareness skills (Bertelson, 1993; Kay-Raining Bird, 2007, p. 258; Byrne, 1993). This may affect their later reading development in school. As a result, their reading development tends to be delayed.

Compared with other populations with LI, children with DS exhibit distinct individual differences. Some researchers claim that pronounced individual differences are a hallmark of DS (e.g., Chapman, 2003).

Your Turn

In what ways will the strengths and difficulties in language acquisition and development of children with DS influence their future academic learning?

Children with autism spectrum disorder

Research has suggested that about 20–50 percent of the population with autism spectrum disorder (ASD) does not develop speech and one reason for this could be the range of IQ in this population (Tager-Flusberg et al., 2009). These nonverbal children with ASD will not be discussed further in this chapter, because these children need support that is far beyond what teachers can offer in educational settings and they need to receive special support and intervention by trained language and speech pathologists. Instead, the following sections will focus on the population with ASD who do develop language, but with various impairments.

Phonological development
There is little research on the early phonological development of children with ASD. This is simply because many children are diagnosed with ASD beyond the infancy stage. The few existing studies, however, do generally indicate that the phonological development of children with autism is relatively intact (Tager-Flusberg, 2001). See Chapter 8 for more discussion.

Lexical-semantic development
Children with ASD appear to follow the same universal principles in their acquisition of words and meanings. They begin their early word acquisition from the same basic level as children with TD. They also appear to have no difficulty extending words to a range of different exemplars, and their extensions are based on typical organization principles (Tager-Flusberg, 2001, p. 332).

In fact, vocabulary development is an area of relative strength for most children with ASD. Some children with ASD can even have unusually rich knowledge of words and score well above the mean (Tager-Flusberg, 2001, p. 333). But, children with ASD tend to misuse words and produce idiosyncratic terms. Although young children with TD also use idiosyncratic words (early meaning errors), these types of idiosyncratic words tend to persist in children with ASD because they are insensitive to the corrective feedback provided by parents due to their social impairment (Tager-Flusberg, 2001, p. 333).

Morphosyntactic development
Although the MLU rate of children with ASD is slower compared to children with TD, the grammatical structures are developed in the same order (Tager-Flusberg, 2001, p. 333). However, young children with ASD tend to use less complex grammatical structures than children with TD (Manolitsi and Botting, 2011).

Pragmatic and metalinguistic development
The most seriously affected aspect of language among children with ASD is their pragmatic language ability. Even high-functioning children with Asperger syndrome show the characteristic overliteral language and poor conversational skill seen in others with ASD, especially in the area of pragmatic skills such as inference (Manolitsi and Botting, 2011). **Inference** is the ability to fill in information that is not overt. Inference-making ability has been shown to be a central component for reading comprehension (Cain et al., 2001) as well as important for general social functioning (Nuske and Bavin, 2011).

From the very beginning, the pragmatic abilities of children with ASD are significantly impaired. This impairment hinders these children's social functioning, particularly the theory of mind development (Tager-Flusberg, 2001). Certain speech acts are completely absent in children with ASD. These include making comments, showing off, acknowledging the listener, and requesting information. In addition, children with ASD only use declarative sentences to directly respond to questions; they do not otherwise make declarative statements or comments. They also produce few affirming or agreeing utterances. The lack of joint attention prevents infants with ASD from communicating about an object that was the focus of their mothers' attention (Tager-Flusberg, 2001). Young children with ASD tend not to respond to their mothers in a topic-relevant way; instead, they tend to introduce irrelevant or repetitive comments. They also have a tendency not to develop the capacity to expand or elaborate on the information provided by their mothers.

Moreover, as a result of their impairment in the development of theory of mind, children with ASD tend to have difficulties in narratives (e.g., story narration) because theory of mind knowledge is particularly important for the interpretation of characters' intentions, motivations, beliefs, and reactions that must be woven into the depiction of event sequences within an overall story structure (Tager-Flusberg, 2001, p. 331).

Compared to their peers with TD, children with ASD tend to produce significantly shorter stories and often fail to describe the causal explanations for the events of a story (Tager-Flusberg, 2001, p. 331). Children with ASD might also experience difficulties in perceiving and/or adjusting to the perspectives of different figures within a narrative, and in shifting from one person-anchored perspective to another (García-Pérez, Hobson, and Lee, 2008).

However, children with ASD are relatively unimpaired in their use of language for requests for objects or actions, protests, and self-regulation (e.g., don't do that). Moreover, children with ASD have a relatively high rate of turn-taking at the low level of conversation (Tager-Flusberg, 2001, p. 330).

Overall, there are enormous variations across the spectrum of autism, ranging from having no functional language and very limited communicative ability to performing in the high normal range on standard language assessments. The most distinct aspect is related to the areas of language that require theory of mind. The aspects of language that are related to computations, lexicon, and semantics are relatively less impaired, at least among higher functioning children with ASD (Tager-Flusberg, 2001, p. 335).

Your Turn

How do the strengths and delays of children with ASD influence their future academic language and literacy development?

Children with specific language impairment

Phonological development

Children with SLI tend to have difficulties in discriminating and processing sounds adequately. They also have expressive phonological difficulties, often referred to as **verbal dyspraxia** (Bishop and Snowling, 2004; Verhoeven et al., 2011).

For many years, SLI and **dyslexia**[4] were not looked at together by researchers. Some researchers have noticed many commonalities between these two populations, and one example is the phonological awareness problems that are seen in both children with SLI and those with dyslexia (Bishop and Snowling, 2004). Nowadays it is common for SLI and dyslexia to be regarded as points on a continuum of language-impairment severity rather than as distinct conditions, and this view is supported with many studies (Bishop, 2008). Therefore, in this book, SLI and dyslexia are discussed together whenever it is relevant (also see Chapter 8).

Children with SLI also have an apparent impairment in **phonological working memory** (PWM) as exhibited in their poor ability in tasks such as repeating nonwords (NWR tasks), particularly as the length of the nonwords increases (Girbau and Schwartz, 2008). The poor ability in PWM not only affects children's acquisition of new words, but also the broader level of language processing (Girbau and Schwartz, 2008).

Lexical-semantic development

Children with SLI tend to have a delay in the development of their lexicon. They are usually 20 months behind children with TD in their receptive vocabulary development (McGregor, 2009, p. 366). They are one year behind children with TD in the first core single-word production, and their comprehension is six months behind (Gleason, 2009; Hoff, 2009). As a group, children with SLI begin expressing meaning with conventional words 11 months later than do children with typical development (McGregor, 2009). It is not unusual to find that 5-year-old children with SLI produce language at the level of 3-year-old children with TD (Hoff, 2009). It is often recommended not to diagnose a child as SLI until age 4 (Paul, 2007) because many children are late talkers, and they can make great progress from 2 to 4 years. Although many of these children catch up, up to 40 percent of them whose language is delayed at age 2 continue to experience language difficulty later (Gleason, 2009).

The lexicon delay in children with SLI manifests in the following areas: They tend to have difficulties in acquiring new words and in retrieving words from common concepts that they seem to understand. They often rely on smaller expressive lexicons and a higher proportion of general all-purpose nouns and verbs such as *thing* and *do*. Moreover, they are less accurate in naming tasks and have difficulties in processing ambiguous words or metaphoric uses of language. Furthermore, they tend to obtain one meaning for a word and cannot see that there are other meanings, leading to problems in inappropriate word use (Gleason, 2009, p. 351). In addition, children with SLI are less able to derive the meanings of new words by using syntactic cues. For example, children with SLI cannot tell whether a new verb such as a nonsense verb *zirp* is transitive or intransitive in the context of "The dog is *zirping* the cat" and "The dog and cat are *zirping*" (Gleason, 2009; Shulman and Guberman, 2007).

Despite the semantic difficulties described above, the semantic development of children with SLI is still stronger than their grammatical development (see discussion next).

Morphosyntactic development

SLI affects the acquisition and development of underlying grammar in a given language. The grammatical impairment is considered a hallmark of SLI (Leonard, 1998). Some researchers termed this issue a language acquisition device (LAD) deficit because one hallmark issue in SLI is difficulty with grammatical morphology (Leonard, 1998). In fact, most children with SLI are not identified on the basis of lexical performance, but by their failure to achieve typical syntactic production with or without deficits in comprehension (Leonard, 1998).

Children with SLI tend to have difficulties in mastering **finite verb morphology** (verb-making, such as past tense inflection and the third-person singular inflection), plural forms, possessives, articles, prepositions, auxiliary verbs, copula verbs (a connecting word such as "to be"), and they also have difficulties in nonword repetition and phoneme discrimination tasks (Gleason, 2009; Leonard, 1998).

Verb inflections are in general more difficult than noun inflections for all children, and children with SLI have proportionately more difficulty than their peers with TD. Certain semantic classes of verbs might also prove particularly difficult for children with SLI, namely those involving placement (e.g., Manolitsi and Botting, 2011).

Your Turn

Identify a list of noun inflections and verb inflections. Discuss why young children with SLI tend to have difficulties in mastering them.

Pragmatic and metalinguistic development

Children with SLI have some mild delay in pragmatics as a result of delayed language skills. For example, children with SLI tend to produce less appropriate requests and are less sensitive to the requests of others. They are less adept at entering or guiding conversations, tend to interpret language very literally, and are insensitive to the intended meaning behind many conversational ruses.

Moreover, children with SLI tend to have poor narrative skills and inadequate decontextualized language. They tend to struggle with using decontextualized language to talk about past or future events or experiences. They also have poor narrative abilities, particularly in receptive and expressive language.

Your Turn

How do the strengths and difficulties of children with SLI influence their future academic language and academic literacy development?

Children with hearing impairment

Hearing is critical for acquiring spoken language. Even mild to moderate loss of hearing during infancy and early childhood can interfere with language acquisition. Language development quality in general depends on the degree of hearing loss, which is measured with **decibel** (dB).[5] Even though many newborns now receive hearing screening at birth, one-third of those who are identified in infant screen programs have not received complete diagnostic evaluations by 3 months of age, and less than half who have been diagnosed have received early intervention services by the critical point of 6 months of age (N. Nelson, 2010, p. 157).

The discussion of children with HI in this section excludes children who acquire sign language from birth as a natural language. The population discussed below includes the language development process of those children with HL who acquire oral language.

Phonological development

Children with HI cry and coo like hearing infants prior to 6 months of age. After 6 months, infants with HI do not progress on to vocalizing syllables or series of syllables. They also decrease their vocalization. By the time children with HI babble, they sound different from hearing infants quantitatively and qualitatively. Children with HI do not produce the canonical babbling that is typical of hearing infants around 9–10 months. However, if infants with HI receive oral training, they do show phonological systems similar to hearing children.

Lexical-semantic development

There is a difference among children with HL in terms of their lexical and semantic development. If children with HL receive oral training and active parental support, they tend to have more typical lexical and semantic development. However, overall, children with HI tend to have a delay in their vocabulary development.

Morphosyntactic development

There is also a general delay in the morphosyntactic development among children with HI. They often make errors when producing sentences such as "John sick," "Him wanted go," and "Beth made candy no" (Hoff, 2009). They may not fully acquire the grammatical structure of a spoken language.

Pragmatic and metalinguistic development

Children with HI are more likely to use communication to direct others' behavior and are less likely to make statements or ask questions than hearing peers (Hoff, 2009).

Children with HI receiving oral training show some phonological awareness. For example, they can lip-read information to identify rhymes. Such awareness, even though minimal at times, may help these children learn to read later (Hoff, 2009).

Your Turn

How do the language delays of children with HI influence their future academic development?

Children with vision impairment

Vision plays a vital role in language learning. Vision is a distance sense that helps children coordinate spoken language input with images of objects and events as they are experienced. Sighted infants use finger pointing to perform speech acts that request toys, other objects, or food during infancy. They do so because they can see objects and establish joint focus with their caregivers (N. Nelson, 2010), whereas, children with VI have limitations in doing so; this puts them in a disadvantageous position to learn a language.

Phonological development

Visual information such as lip configuration contributes to phonological development. Because children with VI cannot see or see well how certain sounds are pronounced, they tend to make more errors than sighted children in producing speech sounds that have highly visible articulatory movements, such as /b/, /m/, and /f/. However, they do not have problems in producing speech sounds that require nonvisible artic-ulatory movements such as /t/, /k/, and /h/ (Hoff, 2009, p. 384).

Lexical-semantic development

It has been reported that children with VI tend to have fewer words for objects that can be seen but not touched (e.g., *moon* or *flag*), and more words for things that can be heard (e.g., *piano* and *drum*) (Hoff, 2009).

The meaning of the lexicon is typically acquired through touch, verbal descriptions, and vision. For sighted children, the concept of an apple is a semi-rounded, sweet-tasting, red thing, which also can be other colors; children who have severe vision impairment demonstrate difficulties in associating words with things or pictures. They may be able to state that an apple is red, but would more likely have encoded the con-cept of apple as a small, smooth-textured, semi-spherical, sweet-tasting object and lack a corresponding stored visual image. They may need to be exposed to more variations of an object before being able to generalize the concept (N. Nelson, 2010, p. 171). As a result, children with VI are less likely than sighted children to overgeneralize words, and they tend to underextend the meanings of words.

Vision also plays an important role in helping children learn about the meanings of verbs, prepositions, relational terms including pronouns (*I*, *you*, *he*, *she*, and *it*), and other forms of **deixis** (*here* and *there*; *this* and *that*). References to person and place are supported heavily by vision. The pronouns *I*, *you*, *he*, and *she* refer to different people, depending who is talking. The term *near* (or *this* or *here*) is used by one communicative partner, while *far* (or *that* or *there*) may be used by a distant partner to refer to the same object. Because visual cues to deixis are missing, young children with VI may go through a stage of referring to themselves in the third person; they can also have *I* and *you* confusions. Even after basic pronouns are acquired, children with VI may continue to demonstrate a self-referential way of viewing the world. This can make it difficult to acquire and talk about spatial concepts and to use frames of reference other than the child's own, which has implications for social functioning (N. Nelson, 2010, p. 172).

Morphosyntactic development

Children with VI have a delay in their acquisition of verbal auxiliaries such as *can*, *will*, and *do* (Hoff, 2009). Some researchers have attributed this delay to the caregivers' speech. They found in a study that the mothers of children with VI used more direct imperatives such as "take the doll" and fewer *yes* and *no* questions, such as "Can you take the doll" (Landau and Gleitman, 1985). The low rate of *yes* and *no* questions in mothers' speech may be associated with VI children's slower acquisition of auxiliaries (Newport, Gleitman, and Gleitman, 1977).

Pragmatic and metalinguistic development

Because children with VI have limited or no access to nonverbal cues (such as facial expressions), they are likely to encounter pragmatic difficulties in communication. Infants with VI have more trouble in establishing joint attention with caregivers, and young children with VI tend to have problems in turn-taking and partner responsiveness (N. Nelson, 2010).

Despite the above-mentioned difficulties, children with VI in general (if without other disabilities) demonstrate a language acquisition timetable that is essentially similar to the one of children without VI.

Your Turn

How will the language delays of children with VI influence their future academic language and literacy development?

Multilingual children with LI

Research on multilingual impairment (MLI) lags behind the research on monolingual impairment (Jacobson, 2012). Multilingual children with LI face at least three kinds of challenges. First, because of their language learning difficulties, they cannot develop typical language functioning in their respective languages. Second, they also tend to have restricted/limited input in one or more of their languages (Verhoeven, Steenge, and van Balkom, 2012) compared with their monolingual peers with the same language impairment. Third, each of their environmental languages poses different acquisition challenges (Wang, 2008 and 2011a). The complexity involved in multilingual children with LI explains why it is very difficult to identify language impairment among multilingual children (Peña and Bedore, 2009), and it also explains why research in the area of multilingual children with LI is scarce.

It is important to stress that multilingualism in itself does not exacerbate or cause LI. Rather, multilingual children and monolingual children share the same underlying roots for their LI (Kay-Raining Bird, 2007). Some children with LI may have difficulties acquiring more than one language. Others, such as children with Down syndrome, can acquire two or even three languages (Vallar and Papagno, 1993). Some studies even suggest that multilingualism may pose certain advantages for multilingual children with LI (e.g., Paradis, 2010) and that there may be potential benefits for maintaining home languages, even in situations of LI (Jacobson and Walden, 2013).

Phonological development

Multilingual children with phonological problems tend to display a higher degree of phonological simplifications in their respective languages that are sometimes similar to but also different from children with TD (Salameh, Nettelbladt, and Norlin, 2003). Some multilingual children with SLI have speech-sound difficulties and produce words that are unintelligible. The intelligibility of some multilingual children with Down syndrome may also be compromised due to a variety of factors such as **hypotonia** (low muscle tone), oral structure differences, and phonological delays (Feltmate and Kay-Raining Bird, 2008). This situation may pose a high risk in their morphosyntactic development (N. Nelson, 2010).

Lexical-semantic development

Multilingual children with LI also tend to make more naming errors and need more processing time to respond in comprehension compared to their monolingual peers with TD. Multilingual children with LI such as multilingual children with DS have significantly lower MLUs and lower expressive language compared to their peers with TD. However, these children employ a vocabulary acquisition strategy that is compatible to the one employed by their multilingual peers with TD (Peña and Bedore, 2009, pp. 290–291).

Multilingual children with LI also have difficulties learning and using naming strategies, and they seem unable to benefit from intervention in the short term (Peña and Bedore, 2009, p. 291). Overall, research shows that multilingual children with LI have a semantic system that is impoverished both in its breadth and depth, and as such, they tend to demonstrate inefficiencies in word learning (Peña and Bedore, 2009, p. 291).

Morphosyntactic Development

Multilingual children with LI in general exhibit morphological error patterns analogous to monolingual children with LI. However, multilingual children with LI tend to progress more slowly than do their TD peers. For example, a study looked at some Swedish–Arabic learning children with and without LI over a one-year period. Children with LI tended to perform at the most basic level, using mainly short words and phrases as well as lexical morphology, whereas their counterparts with TD used the most complex clausal level structures (Peña and Bedore, 2009).

Moreover, multilingual children with LI tend to show difficulties in overall morphosyntax, including low MLU, verb tense, article and clitic errors (such as *I'm*), and they omit grammatical morphemes including present- and past-tense verb forms (Peña and Bedore, 2009). For example, research found that bilingual Spanish–English speaking children with LI tend to produce similar errors in Spanish to those made by monolingual Spanish-speaking children with LI. They make mistakes on articles, gender and number assignment, and on verb inflections (though to a lesser extent) (Jacobson, 2012).

Pragmatic and metalinguistic development

There is limited research on pragmatic and metalinguistic awareness as well as on the narrative performance of young multilingual children with LI. Available literature suggests that the narrative structure (story grammar categories) of young multilingual children with LI is in general intact. Comparative studies of children with TD and multilingual children with LI showed no differences in their story grammar (e.g., Iluz-Cohen and Walters, 2012). Also, like multilingual children with TD, multilingual children with LI are sensitive to the narrative setting and interlocutor (Iluz-Cohen and Walters, 2012). However, young multilingual children with and without LI differ significantly on a variety of lexical and morphosyntactic aspects of their narratives. Multilingual children with TD tend to produce longer narratives than multilingual children with LI. Moreover, young multilingual children with LI tend to have proportionally more code-switching (CS) than their multilingual counterparts (Iluz-Cohen and Walters, 2012), although other studies suggest that the two groups essentially have no differences in their amount of CS (e.g., Gutiérrez-Clellen, Simon-Cereijido, and Erickson Leone, 2009).

Your Turn

Collect a narrative sample of a multilingual child with TD and a multilingual child with LI. Analyze their narratives at the story grammar level and the lexical and morphosyntactic level. Discuss the your findings with your classmates.

Development of Emergent Literacies

Because of language-learning difficulties exhibited by the children with LI, their early emergent literacy abilities are affected accordingly. Depending on language impairment types, different aspects of emergent literacy skills can be impacted.

Overall, the language impairments that are related to the central processing factors (such as DS, SLI, and ASD) and peripheral factors (such as HI and VI) will result in delays in some areas of emergent literacy development. For example, these children may have difficulties in rhymes and sound play. Nonetheless, young children with LI will still have the basic abilities to be sensitive to environmental print and to notice print conventions, although they may be less able to produce language features associated with written language compared to their peers with TD.

Currently, little research information is available about the emergent digital and critical literacy development of young children with LI. Based on the cognitive and language developmental characteristics of these children, the educated guess is that children with LI are most likely to experience difficulties in their emergent digital and critical literacy development. Future research may provide concrete information in this area.

Your Turn

- Show a multimedia game to a child with LI and a child with TD. Observe how these two children play the game. What have you found?
- Research databases such as ERIC and PsycINFO and find out whether there is new information on the emergent digital and critical literacy development of young children with LI.

Supporting Strategies for Children with LI in Early Childhood

Children who reach school age with residual language problems from early childhood may have an increased risk of deficient reading ability, poor oral and writing skills, and problematic social behavior and psychosocial adjustment (Gleason, 2009, p. 316). Therefore, it is very important to provide proactive linguistic and social support for children with LI during early childhood to optimize their future language and literacy development as well as to prepare them for academic challenges in school.

Several general principles need to be kept in mind when providing support related to language and emergent literacy for children with LI in early childhood. First, the support should focus on the underlying cognitive skills that are associated with language learning such as attention, memory, storage, processing, organization, retrieval, and self-regulation (Peña and Bedore, 2009, p. 295). Second, the support should emphasize helping them develop basic linguistic building blocks such as phonological skills and word-level knowledge. Third, the support should target their specific strengths and needs to get them to a better footing for future school academic demands. Fourth, the support should prioritize learning and using meaningful language rather than correct production of grammatical forms (Peña and Bedore, 2009, pp. 297). Fifth, it must be recognized that children with the same type of LI may have very different levels of functioning in everyday life, just as children with TD who have similar levels of functioning may have quite different speech and language profiles. Finally, other environmental and child-specific factors also need to be considered (Paul, 2007, p. 10) when providing support.

Your Turn

Provide concrete examples to elaborate on the six general principles of providing support for children with LI.

Use of narratives as a comprehensive measure to determine areas of support

In this section, we will focus on using narratives as a comprehensive measure to determine the areas in which children with LI need specific support. Narratives are complex tasks that require children to draw on a range of linguistic, cognitive, and social abilities. As Reilly and her colleagues put it rightly, in narrative production,

> Linguistically, children must lexically encode information about the characters and events of the story using the appropriate morphosyntactic devices to articulate the sequence of events and their temporal relations. Cognitively, children must infer the motivation for protagonists' actions, the logical relations between events and the theme of the story. These inferences might be considered one aspect of the evaluation function as they all reflect the narrators' assessment of meaning or significance of the events of the story. Finally, telling a story is a social activity, and an additional type of evaluation concerns the relationship of the narrator to the audience. These elements in a story we have termed social evaluative devices as they serve to engage and maintain the listener's attention (Reilly et al., 2004, p. 230).

In Chapter 3, we briefly touched upon three narrative measures: narrative assessment protocol (NAP), high point analysis (HPA), and narrative scoring scheme (NSS). Here, we will revisit these measures. Unlike the standardized tests and inventories, these three measures are more user-friendly and cost effective. More importantly, learning how to use them will help you monitor changes in children's narrative skills. With this information, you will know in which specific areas your students with language impairment will need support.

NAP measures children's narrative microstructure (e.g., the use of semantic and syntactic forms). The modified procedures for NAP are as follows. Children are asked to tell (narrate a story) based on the wordless picture book "*Frog, Where Are You?*" by Mercer Mayer, or you can also choose your own wordless book or pictures. You either video- or audio-record the children's narratives and transcribe them verbatim. You then examine the microstructure of a child's narrative by identifying various semantic and syntactic forms such as sentence structure (e.g., complex and negative sentences), phrase structure (e.g., prepositional and elaborated noun phrases), advanced verbs, modifiers, and nouns (e.g., copula, auxiliary verbs, and pluralized nouns). You then calculate how frequently the child uses each of the linguistic forms. You also calculate the total number of words used in the narrative, the total number of different words, the total number of utterances, and mean length of utterance. In fact, you can use this measure throughout the year to see whether children with language impairment make any progress. In general, you can identify areas of your concern in a child's language and use the modified NAP to elevate and monitor the changes in their micro narrative structure.

HPA measures children's narrative macrostructure (story grammar). It focuses on the quality of the story by analyzing children's narrative structure completeness and complexity both in personal and fictional narratives. You can try the following modified version of the measure. You first ask a child to make a personal or fictional narrative. Video- or audio-record the narrative and then transcribe it verbatim. You then analyze the child's story elements based on a 0–7 point scale (see Box 5.3). The more points a child gets, the better narrative structure development the child has.

Box 5.3 Narrative High Point Analysis Scales

Classic: logical sequence of events that build to a climax with evaluation and ends with a resolution (7 points).

End-at-the-high-point: logical sequence of events that build to a climax but with no resolution (6 points).

Chronological: logical sequence of multiple events but with no evaluation (5 points).

Leap-frogging: leaps from one event to another but not always in sequence (4 points).

Miscellaneous: Multiple events but no logical, causal sequences (3 points).

Two-event: two past tense events but no climax (2 points).

One-event: one past tense event (1 point).

Nonnarrative: no past tense events (0 point).

Modified from N. P. Terry et al., "Oral narrative performance of African American prekindergarteners who speak nonmainstream American English," *Language, Speech, and Hearing Sciences in Schools*, 44 (2013): 291–306, at 293.

NSS also measures narrative macrostructure. However, it evaluates more advanced elements of children's narrative quality beyond story grammar such as literal language, lexical, conjunctive, and referential cohesive devices as well as metacognitive and metalinguistic verbs (Terry et al., 2013). This measure is designed to be sensitive to changes in the development of narrative skills over time. A modified way of using this measure can look like this: You ask children to tell (narrate) a story based on the wordless picture book "*Frog, Where Are You?*" by Mercer Mayer or you can also choose your own wordless book or pictures. You either video- or audio-record the children's narratives and transcribe them verbatim. Then you analyze and score the children's narratives with the scale in Box 5.4.

Box 5.4 Narrative Scoring Scheme Scales

(Each of the story grammar elements such as literal language, lexical, conjunctive, referential cohesive devices, metacognitive verbs, and metalinguistic verbs is scored on a five-point scale. Five points indicates proficient narrative skills,

3 points indicates emergent narrative skills, and 1 point means inconsistent or immature narrative skills.)

Introduction: inclusion and description of character and setting (0–5 points)

Character development: recognition of character's significance in the story (0–5 points)

Mental states: frequent and diverse use of vocabulary to convey characters' thoughts and emotions (0–5 points)

Referencing: correct use of pronouns, antecedents, and clarifiers throughout the story (0–5 points)

Conflict/resolution: inclusion and development of conflicts and resolutions (0–5 points)

Cohesion: sequencing and transitioning between events (0–5 points)

Conclusion: closing the final event and entire story (0–5 points)

Modified from N. P. Terry et al., "Oral narrative performance of African American prekindergarteners who speak nonmainstream American English," *Language, Speech, and Hearing Sciences in Schools*, 44 (2013): 291–306, at 293.

For a detailed and complete description of these three measures (NAP, HPA, and NSS), please consult the references at the end of this chapter.

Your Turn

Practice the above three measures with a child who has any of the language impairments described in this chapter. With the result of the child's narrative measures, propose strategies that can help this child develop overall language and narrative skills.

Although narrative measures are introduced above as a comprehensive way to monitor and assess the overall language and narrative development of children with LI, it is important to note that teachers and parents should also become familiar with other standardized tests and inventories and use them to understand young children's language and early literacy development at different levels. Understanding the languages used in these tests and inventories will help you better recognize the nature of a child's LI, and the support you provide for her will be more focused and effective. It is beyond the scope of this book to provide a detailed introduction to these standardized language tests and inventories, but the Appendix provides some basic information about them.

Your Turn

Research the standardized tests in the Appendix and try to understand the languages used in them. Obtain some test results of children who were given these standardized tests or inventories and try to interpret the results and their relevance to these children's future language and literacy learning.

Reciprocal interaction and imitation

Imitation is a human instinct. Newborns with TD can imitate adult behavior such as tongue protruding shortly after birth. Children with TD can engage in reciprocal interactions with caregivers at a very young age. Thus, imitation and reciprocal interactive ability is fundamental in language acquisition.

However, infants with certain language impairments such as ASD may have difficulties in engaging in reciprocal interactions with people around them, and their language acquisition is affected. The support provided for these children needs to be focused on deliberately engaging them in reciprocal interactions such as constantly commenting on what they are doing (e.g., "You smile because you are happy, right?") and frequently stimulating them to have a vocal or behavior response (N. Nelson, 2010, p. 244).

Also, to help infants engage in reciprocal interactions, it is recommended to constantly imitate infants' vocal sounds and facial expressions and encourage them to imitate adult vocal and facial expression as well (N. Nelson, 2010, p. 245). These reciprocal activities will help infants with LI learn turn-taking (an important component in language use with others).

Your Turn

Based on the above recommendations, design one reciprocal and imitation game or activity and try to practice it with an infant or young child who has ASD.

Joint attention

Communication is essentially social. A communicator needs to solicit another's attention to an object or self. Shifting eye gaze between the object and the communicative partner provides a clear sign of intentional communication (N. Nelson, 2010, p. 246). This kind of joint attention is developed in infants with TD around 6 months of age. Infants with TD begin to focus on a speaker's eye region as early as 2 months of age, because a speaker's eyes convey the social information connected with verbal and nonverbal communication. In contrast, infants who tend to focus on a speaker's mouth region may be at risk for difficulties in typical language acquisition.

Therefore, helping infants with LI develop joint attention as well as intentional communication by stimulating them to focus attention on caregivers (particularly the eye region) and on the object may optimize their language development. For example, when communicating with an infant, oblige her to make a request that includes all three components required for establishing clear intentionality (look at the adult, look at the object, and vocalize or gesture). Any component that is not present should be prompted. If a child initiates a request by reaching and vocalizing, but fails to look in the adult's eyes, the child should be prompted with a direct request, such as "Look at me." If no request is initiated by the child, the child then can be asked, "What do you want?" (N. Nelson, 2010, p. 247).

When carrying out this type of interaction, make it as natural as possible in the context. One activity to promote joint attention in natural context is play. Activities such as peek-a-boo exchanges will help the joint attention development in infants with LI. Symbolic play routine with adults using toys in meaningful exchanges is particularly helpful for children with LI. In different play contexts, adults can model language use in different areas such as decontextualization (use one object to present another; e.g., use a replica banana to represent a phone), self–other relations (e.g., pretend to comb own hair), functions (e.g., request, command, and indicate personal feelings), and forms and meaning (e.g., demonstrate possession word use such as *mine*; recurrence use such as *more*) (N. Nelson, 2010, p. 254).

Your Turn

Based on the above recommendations, design one joint-attention game or activity and try to practice it with an infant or young child who has ASD.

Oral language skills

It has been generally agreed among researchers as well as educators that children must have a strong base of oral language knowledge to attain their proficiency in reading, spelling, and composing to meet the academic demands in schools (Silliman and Scott, 2009, p. 107). Because young children with LI need additional help in this area, the focus of support for them during early childhood should focus on the following.

Word learning

Words are the building blocks of language, and therefore, helping infants and young children with LI develop a large mental lexicon will enable them to develop functional grammar.

For young children with LI, focusing on target-word learning may be more effective. For example, a study involving late-talking children between 23 and 29 months and their mothers has shown that when the mothers learned the targeted vocabulary and used the words to engage their children in naturalistic and interactive language stimulation, the children not only gained the target vocabulary but they also increased their overall vocabulary and social skills (N. Nelson, 2010). Thus, it is clear that stimulating children with LI with targeted words and adult scaffolding are important ways for these children to learn the essential vocabulary needed in oral language development.

In general, it is important to carry out the targeted vocabulary learning in a naturalistic context and embed vocabulary learning in play and other routine activities when helping young children develop oral language abilities. However, for young children with LI, leaving targeted word learning to naturalistic settings may not be enough. Intentional scaffolding and focused stimulation on the targeted words' use and reference in meaningful contexts may be more useful (N. Nelson, 2010). Adults need to systematically comment on their own and children's activities to help children pay attention to word use in relevant contexts. For instance, one can comment on activities such as "I am making cookies, see? Making cookies." One can also comment on activities to provide direct prompts by, for example, shaking baby powder on a doll while saying, "Let's shake powder on the baby" and then holding out the powder and prompting the child, "What do you want to do?" (N. Nelson, 2010).

Because children with LI tend to have a slower rate for learning new words and need more time and more support (such as modeling) to map word to meaning, targeting new words and meaning in both comprehension and production is helpful. Engage children with LI in rich experiences and use focused stimulation to teach them target new words. New words can be introduced in repeated daily interactions by using contrast. For instance, the contrast words such as *hot–cold*, *red–green*, and *round–square* can be embedded in cooking and eating activities when talking about "stirring red and green Jell-o," "cooling the hot Jell-o," and "choosing *round* or squared cookies" (N. Nelson, 2010).

Finally it is important to pay attention to children's language growth by looking at the number of different words (NDW) rather than the traditional **type/token ratio** (TTR)[6] because TTR is less sensitive to children's language growth (it does not count the repeated use of the small set of functional words) than NDW (N. Nelson, 2010).

Your Turn

Record a naturalistic speech sample of a child with LI and calculate the NDW. Research a children's book and identify the words that you think are important for young children like your target child to master. Teach these words to this child by using the strategies suggested above for a period of one month. Record this child's naturalistic speech sample again. Calculate the NDW. Do you see the effect of your intentional vocabulary teaching?

Narrative engagement

Children with LI are often behind in their early spontaneous narrative productions due to language impairments. Since narrative ability is one of the best predictors of school success for children with learning disabilities and language impairment, it is essential to support these children early on.

One effective strategy is to use story recounts to help young children with LI to narrate events that happened in the past (decontextualized). **Story recounting** is a scaffolding process in which adults and children co-construct stories/narratives. For example, immediately after an event such as a fall or after reading a story, an adult scaffolds the child to tell the experience/story to another person. Story recounting is particularly useful for children at the level of one- and two-word utterances who otherwise will not be able to narrate their experience on their own (N. Nelson, 2010, p. 265).

Emergent literacy skills

Two areas in early emergent literacy need to be considered when providing support for infants and young children with LI: sound–word and sentence–discourse. Frequently engaging infants and young children in sound-word play such as rhyming play and interactive babbling such as "*Blah blah blah blaah blaaah*" with strong variation in intonation patterns can enhance their awareness of the relationship between sounds and words (N. Nelson, 2010, p. 266). Using shared book reading activities can help them learn how to use sentences to describe events and ask questions for story comprehension.

Art and music

Art offers children sensorial experiences and a sense of mastery and self-esteem, all of which have been proven to be of critical importance to all children. For example, researchers and professionals have successfully used art as a means of increasing social interactions among children with autism. Art offers other benefits such as positive emotional development to children on the autism spectrum.

Similarly, music is another engaging way to engage children with LI for language and early literacy development. Music can provide a structured medium to accentuate the prosody or meaning of language in the context of an enjoyable, motivating stimulus (e.g., Pelliteri, 2000). Geist and colleagues (2008) summarized some major areas in which music can help promote language/speech development of children with LI in published research literature. For example, music techniques can promote increased breath and muscle control, stimulate vocalization, help develop receptive and expressive language skills, and improve articulation skills. Moreover, music can help preschool children with LI develop social communication skills. Furthermore, together with the strategies of AAC (augmentative and alternative communication; see definition in next session), music can help children with severe LI point to music symbol pictures to contribute to group "story songs" and express their feelings. Children with autism can learn more signs when they are paired with music and speech than when they are taught with music or speech alone. Therefore, you can try to adapt elements of music such as tempo, rhythm, melody, harmony, and texture to help children with LI to develop effective communication skills.

Your Turn

- Select a children's song and use it to teach a child with LI in the following areas:
  - Receptive and expressive language
  - Social communication

  Do you see the advantage of using music to promote the language/speech development of children with LI?
- Ask a child with ASD to tell you a personal story verbally and through drawing? Analyze the two versions of the story. What have you found?

Augmentative and alternative communication

Augmentative and alternative communication (AAC) is a compensatory approach that provides a means of communication as a supplement to verbal communication. AAC is designed for children who are unable to use speech as their primary communication method. The fundamental goal of AAC is to be as natural and as functional as possible. Even for some children whose oral speech may eventually develop, AAC is still often used to prevent delayed communication development and to support communicative participation in daily activities (Batshaw, 2002, p. 239).

There are two categories of AAC: unaided and aided. Unaided AAC uses only the physical body for communication. Sign language, gestures, vocalizations, and facial expressions are examples of unaided communication methods. Being successful with this method usually requires familiarity with the person using AAC and some additional training (such as sign language). Aided AAC requires additional tools or equipment (such as using communication boards, computers, iPads, pens, or paper) to convey a message. Aided AAC is physically cumbersome, but it has the advantage of being easily understood by most listeners (Batshaw, 2002, p. 240).

AAC has been found to be useful and successful with a variety of communication difficulties. To familiarize yourself with the AAC method, please see the recommended reading at the end of this chapter.

Nonverbal use

Young children with and without LI use gestures to communicate meanings. As discussed in Chapter 3, nonverbal behaviors of young children serve several functions, and they are an integral part of learning language and communication. For young children with LI, the nonverbal cues may be even more important. Sometimes, a gesture may symbolize meaning that they may not know how to articulate. Training yourself to notice the nonverbal cues in the context may help you supply words for children with LI. For example, when a child with LI was telling a story about a rabbit running away when it saw a deer, he moved his right hand from one direction to another; his mother then asked him a question in the context by supplying words, "So, the rabbit ran away?"

Moreover, children do notice adult gestures and gain clues from them (e.g., Singer and Goldin-Meadow, 2005). Research suggests that the hand gestures deliberately used by adults in story reading help children with LI comprehend stories better and improve their narrative abilities (Wang, L. Eberhard, and Bernas, 2014).

Explicit support in concerned areas

Although we have discussed the general approaches to support children with LI, a specific type of language impairment also needs a specific type of focused support. Focusing on strengths and needs for different types of language impairments may be effective. Below are some suggestions.

Support for children with SLI

The central issue about children with SLI is their syntax, and in particular, children with SLI will have trouble understanding and producing complex sentences. Complex sentences are prominent in academic texts; therefore, it is critical to focus on building oral complex sentences in narratives during early childhood. To help young children with SLI develop syntactic skills, the best way is through imitation, modeling, focused stimulation, conversational recasting, expansion, and scaffolding (see Box 5.5).

Box 5.5 Approaches to Support Syntactic Development

Imitation   Children are asked to repeat model sentences presented by adult.

Modeling   Adult models a target sentence and children take turns creating utterances that include the target sentence.

Focused stimulation   Children are exposed to a large number of exemplars of target sentences; they are asked questions requiring use of the target exemplars.

Conversational recasting   Adult responds to children's spontaneous sentence production by rephrasing it to include the target sentence form.

Expansion   Adult responds to children's spontaneous sentence production by adding extra information.

Scaffolding   Adult provides target syntactic structure for children to try. When they begin to grasp the target structure, children are allowed to produce the target structure on their own.

Modified from J. B. Gleason, *The Development of Language* (New York: Pearson, 2009), p. 360.

Children with sensory impairment

Children with impaired sensory systems face special challenges in acquiring language and developing emergent literacy skills. Important supporting strategies for children who have HI are to talk to them in close proximity face-to-face and to use gestures to accompany directions and concept explanation. Important supporting strategies for children with VI are speaking slowly and clearly and using technology.

Multilingual children with LI

Multilingual children with LI should have opportunities to use both languages. Parents should be encouraged to support multilingual children's vocabulary development in the language with which they feel most comfortable. Similarly, children should also be encouraged to develop vocabulary in the language in which they feel comfortable. Benefits in one language can help the development of the others. Children, however, do need to have ample opportunities to hear the different languages to ensure that there is sufficient input for each language.

It is important to help multilingual children with LI use language in a functional and meaningful way and assist them with building basic skills, such as paying attention to what people say, focusing on meaning, and responding to communicative intent (Peña and Bedore, 2009, p. 297). Allowing for mixed knowledge across different languages may facilitate children's learning of new information, and developing knowledge in one language facilitates development in other language(s).

Some researchers suggest that multilingual children who have intellectual disabilities (ID) should have the input in two or three languages postponed until the preschool years and suggest providing these children with one input in the primary language (e.g., Rondal, 2000). However, this proposal is not corroborated by research evidence. Children with ID such as Down syndrome can actually benefit from learning more than one language. The language skills developed in one language can spread to another language (Kay-Raining Bird, 2007).

Support for children with ASD

The major difficulty that children with ASD have is in taking the listener's perspective and, thus, they make assumptions that are inaccurate. In addition, they tend to struggle to guess others' intentions. Therefore, you may want to focus on providing support that helps them build the ability of theory of mind. For instance, you can design activities that can help these children understand the emotions of others by showing them how to recognize other people's facial expressions from photos, drawings, and videos in different contexts. You can also use pretend play to help these children develop abilities to guess how others involved in the play will act and what they will do by asking questions. For more information on how to help children with ASD develop the ability of theory of mind, please refer to the recommended reading list at the end of this chapter. Even though some of these books are discussing activities and strategies for children beyond early childhood, they nevertheless demonstrate the areas that you need to pay attention to when helping children with ASD develop theory of mind abilities during early childhood.

Your Turn

Use the information in Box 5.5 to create a plan for all the six types of children with language impairments in the areas of phonology, lexicon, semantics, morphology, syntax, pragmatics, and metalinguistic awareness. Share your plan with your classmates and ask for their feedback. If you have an opportunity to work with children with impairment, try your plan and reflect on how it works.

Summary of Key Points

- When conceptualizing various language impairments, three areas need to be considered: the physical and psychological aspects of LI, how LI affects children's ability to participate in everyday activities, and how contextual factors affect children with LI.
- Language impairments may be caused by three major factors: central processing issues, peripheral factors, and environmental and emotional issues.
- Six language impairment categories are addressed in this book: Down syndrome, autism spectrum disorder, specific language impairment, hearing impairment, vision impairment, and multilingual children with language impairments.
- Children with different LI tend to have distinct characteristics.
  - Children with DS have cognitive and working memory deficits, but they are social.
  - Children with ASD have an underdevelopment in theory of mind. They tend to have impaired social skills, language impairments, difficulties in intellectual functioning, ritualistic and repetitive behavior patterns, and uneven development of skill acquisition. However, 1 in 10 individuals with ASD also has exceptional talent in a specific area.
  - Children with SLI usually have a typical cognitive functioning, except deficits in working memory. They have difficulties in language comprehension and/or language production, particularly in the areas of semantics and grammar.
  - Children with hearing impairment, who are born to hearing parents, can develop a spontaneous gesture communication system. However, they will not develop a fully functional language unless intervention is provided through a cochlear implant or other language support.
  - Children with vision impairment may encounter challenges in acquiring concepts and vocabulary that depend on coordinating verbal and visual communication. They may also have difficulties in picking up nonverbal social cues such as body language and facial expressions.
  - Multilingual children with language impairments may exhibit any one of these above-mentioned language impairments or a combination of them with added complications involving more than one language.
- Although children with LI exhibit different cognitive and social characteristics, the most prominent cognitive characteristic they share is that they tend to lack the generalization ability.
- There are different language acquisition characteristics of children with various language impairments:
  - Young children with DS are delayed in canonical babbling, and they make many more phonological errors than children with TD. They show difficulties in syntactical and semantic development, but their pragmatic development tends to surpass the other areas of their language development.
  - As for young children with ASD, their early phonological development seems to be intact. Although they may have difficulties in lexical, semantic, and morphosyntactic development, they are functional overall. The most affected area in their language development is pragmatics. They lack the ability to make inferences and produce complex narratives.

- ○ Young children with SLI have difficulties in learning new words due to the impairment in phonological working memory. They also have a delay in lexical and semantic development (although this area is their relative strength compared with the other areas of their language development). They have a delay in pragmatics and have poor narrative skills. However, the most serious challenge is in the morphosyntactic area.
- ○ Young children with HI do not produce canonical babbling like hearing infants, but with oral training or technology intervention, their phonological, lexical, and semantic systems can be quite similar to hearing infants', and they can even lip-read to identify rhymes. Overall, children with HI tend to have a delay in morphosyntactic and vocabulary development.
- ○ Children with VI are at a particular disadvantage in consonants that require seeing lip configurations in order to produce the sounds accurately, such as /b/, /m/, and /f/. Further, they also have difficulties in developing pronouns and concepts that are heavily reliant on visualization. Also, because children with VI cannot read facial expressions, they tend to have a problem with turn-taking and establishing joint attention with caregivers.
- ○ Multilingual children with LI share the same underlying causes for language difficulties with monolingual children who have LI. Overall, multilingual children with LI can exhibit challenges in any of the linguistic areas.
- Young children with LI may have delays and difficulties in their emergent literacy development. However, they can develop the emergent literacy knowledge in their ambient language.
- The supports provided for young children with LI should focus on developing cognitive, linguistic, and phonological skills, target their specific strengths and needs, prioritize useful and meaningful learning, consider that different children with LI will have varying levels of functionality in daily life, and take into account their environments and individual-specific issues.
- Specific areas of support include:
  - ○ Using comprehensive narrative measures to determine the areas that need specific support
  - ○ Encouraging reciprocal interaction and joint attention activities
  - ○ Enhancing oral language skills through word learning and narrative development
  - ○ Engaging in emergent literacy activities such as sound–word play and shared book reading
  - ○ Using art and music to promote language development
  - ○ Using gestures and AAC to enhance communication
  - ○ Providing overt support for children with LI in their specific areas of difficulty

Key Terms

Augmentative and alternative
communication (AAC)
Autism spectrum disorder

Clitic errors
Decibel (dB)
Deixis

Down syndrome
Dyslexia
Finite verb morphology
Hypotonia
Inference
Pervasive developmental disorder
  (PDD).

Phonological memory and
  phonological working memory
  (PWM)
Speech acts
Splinter skills
Story recounting
Type/token rate (TTR)
Verbal dyspraxia

Notes

1. We discussed before that teachers need to avoid using the word "disorder" to describe children. However, the term "autism spectrum disorder" used here is only a clinical term.
2. When the word Deaf is capitalized, it refers to a group of people who share a culture (Hoff, 2009, p. 382).
3. Speech acts include the area in communication which includes making comments, requesting information, promising, ordering, greeting, warning, inviting, acknowledging the listener, and congratulating.
4. Dyslexia is difficulty in single-word decoding, which causes insufficient phonological processing and results in additional problems in fluent reading, spelling and writing. Dyslexia may be the result of the visual-spatial processing deficit and perceptual-motor integration deficit (Nijakowska, 2008, p. 130).
5. Mild hearing loss (20–40 dB), moderate (41–54 dB), moderately severe (55–70 dB), severe (71–90 dB), profound (91 and greater dB), and total hearing loss (deafness) has no hearing at all.
6. The total number of words in a given utterance or a written text is often referred to as the number of *tokens*. The token/type ratio means the proportion of the number of total words and the total types of words in an utterance or written text.

Recommended Further Readings

Beukelman, D. and Mirenda, P. (2013). *Augmentative and Alternative Communication: Supporting Children and Adults with Complex Communication Needs.* 4th edn. Baltimore: Paul H. Brookes.

Faherty, C. (2000). *What Does It Mean to Me? A Workbook for Explaining Self-Awareness and Life Lessons to the Child or Youth with High-Functioning Autism or Asperger's.* Arlington: Future Horizons.

Gray, C. (1994). *Comic Strip Conversations: Colorful Illustrated Interactions with Students with Autism and Related Disorders.* Jenison, MI: Jenison Public Schools.

Heilmann, J., Miller, J., and Nockerts, A. (2010). Using language sample databases. *Language, Speech, and Hearing Sciences in Schools,* 41, 84–95.

Howlin, P., Baron-Cohen, S., and Hadwin, J. (1999). *Teaching Children with Autism to Mind-Read: A Practical Guide.* New York: John Wiley & Sons.

Justice, L. M., Bowles, R., Pence, K., and Gosse, C. (2010). A scalable tool for assessing children's language abilities within a narrative context: the NAP (Narrative Assessment Protocol). *Early Child Research Quarterly,* 25: 218–234.

Leonard, L. B. (1998). *Children with Specific Language Impairment.* Cambridge, MA: MIT Press.

McAfee, J. (2001). *Navigating the Social World: A Curriculum for Educating Individuals with Asperger's Syndrome and High-Functioning Autism*. Arlington: Future Horizons.

McCabe, A., Bliss, I., Barra, G., and Bennet, M. (2008). Comparison of personal versus fictional narratives of children with language impairment. *American Journal of Speech-Language Pathology*, 17: 194–206.

Nelson, N. W. (2010). *Language and Literacy Disorders: Infancy through Adolescence*. New York: Allyn & Bacon.

Paul, R. (2007). *Language Disorders from a Developmental Perspective: Essays in Honor of Robin S. Chapman*. 3rd edn. St. Louis, MO: Mosby.

Schwartz, R. G. (ed.) (2009). *Handbook of Child Language Disorders*. New York: Psychology Press.

Language Sample Analysis II

The following speech samples are taken from YouTube. When you watch the clips, please skip the commercial advertisements and go directly to the videos.

Speech Sample 1: Monolingual Child

In this speech sample analysis, you are asked to do the following:

- Listen to the following speech sample of an English speaking young child: http://www.youtube.com/watch?v=XuDeh_raBxM.
- Make an educated guess about this child's socioeconomic background and her language development characteristics by using the information you read in Chapter 3.
- Provide your assessment of this child's language development in the following chart.

Language components	Strengths	Needs	Other
Phonological development in English			
Lexical-semantic development in English			
Morphosyntactic development in English			
Pragmatic development in English			
Metalinguistic development in English			

- Review all the strategies introduced in Chapter 3 and select a few that you think will be particularly helpful for this child. If you had to give advice to her parents, how would you communicate it to them based on the strategies that you have selected?

Understanding Language and Literacy Development: Diverse Learners in the Classroom, First Edition. Xiao-lei Wang.
© 2015 John Wiley & Sons, Inc. Published 2015 by John Wiley & Sons, Inc.
Companion website: www.wiley.com/go/wang/langandlit

(Please note that the focus should be on the language skills that will help this child succeed in school later on.)

- Reflect on your experience of doing this speech sample analysis.

Speech Sample 2: Multilingual Child

In this speech sample analysis, you are asked to do the following:

- Listen to the following speech sample of a French-Spanish-English multilingual child: http://www.youtube.com/watch?v=yzCZuWXOnLk&list=UUKlly_Xbrsbr ZNRevzZpKAQ.
- Make an educated guess about this child's age, her socioeconomic background, and her multilingual characteristics by using the information you read in Chapter 4.
- Provide your assessment of this child's multilingual development in the following chart.

Language components	Strengths	Needs	Other
Phonological development in different languages			
Lexical-semantic development in different languages			
Morphosyntactic development in different languages			
Pragmatic development in different languages			
Metalinguistic development in different languages			

- Review all the strategies introduced in Chapter 4 and select a few that you think will be particularly helpful for this child. If you had to give advice to her parents, how would you communicate it to them based on the strategies that you have selected? (Please note that the focus should be on the language skills that will help the child succeed in school later on.)
- Reflect on your experience of doing this speech sample analysis.

Speech Sample 3: Child with Down Syndrome

In this speech sample analysis, you are asked to do the following:

- Listen to the following speech sample of a child with Down syndrome: http://www.youtube.com/watch?v=1MQEpBxScbU.

- Make an educated guess about this child's age, his socioeconomic background, and his language characteristics by using the information you read in Chapter 5.
- Provide your assessment of this child's language development in the following chart.

Language Components	Strengths	Needs	Other
Phonological development in English			
Lexical-semantic development in English			
Morphosyntactic development in English			
Pragmatic development in English			
Metalinguistic development in English			

- Review all the strategies introduced in Chapter 5 and select a few that you think will be particularly helpful for this child. If you had to give advice to his parents, how would you communicate it to them based on the strategies that you have selected? (Please note that the focus should be on the language skills that will help this child succeed in school later on.)
- Reflect on your experience of doing this speech sample analysis.

Part III

Developing Language and Literacies

Divergent Abilities in Middle Childhood (6–11)

Part III focuses on the different characteristics of language and literacy development, including academic language and literacy development, in middle childhood (elementary school years). Chapter 6 focuses on the typical language and literacy development characteristics. Chapter 7 addresses the process of learning English as a new language in elementary grades, and Chapter 8 discusses the language and literacy development of elementary school students who have various language impairments.

At the end of Part III, you will have an opportunity to apply the information you read in these three chapters by analyzing language samples produced by elementary school students.

Essential Questions for Part III

- What is the purpose of supporting academic language and academic literacy development across the curriculum?
- What is your position regarding the issue of language learnability? How does your position on this issue lead you in your instructional decisions?
- What do children's language error patterns tell us about their development? How can you turn children's language errors into teaching opportunities?
- What is the significance for understanding children's home language development, particularly when it is different from the school language?
- In what ways do students who learn English as a new language differ from those with language learning impairment and how do you respond to the differences in instruction?
- Are all students capable of language and literacy learning?
- Should children with divergent abilities have the same educational goals, in particular, academic language and literacy goals?

Understanding Language and Literacy Development: Diverse Learners in the Classroom, First Edition. Xiao-lei Wang.
© 2015 John Wiley & Sons, Inc. Published 2015 by John Wiley & Sons, Inc.
Companion website: www.wiley.com/go/wang/langandlit

- How do we make decisions on language and literacy instruction for all children?
- What does it mean to provide instructional accommodations for students who have language and literacy learning needs?   *subject*
- How can we support the language development needs of all children and at the same time help them develop knowledge in content areas?
- What does the least restrictive language and literacy learning environment look like and how can you help children with language difficulties thrive in such an environment?

6

Typical Development of Language and Literacies in Middle Childhood

Prereading Activities and Questions

- Identify ten multisyllabic words from a dictionary and ask a few first graders to pronounce them. What have you found? What does the children's performance tell you about their language development compared to children in early childhood?

- Find a spontaneous writing sample or record a speech sample of a first-, third-, and fifth-grade student respectively. What have you noticed about these children's language development in terms of lexicon, semantics, morphology, syntax, pragmatics, and metalinguistic knowledge? Alternatively, you can give a specific topic to these children at different ages and ask them to respond to it in oral and written forms.

- Ask a first-, third-, and fifth-grade student respectively to tell you the meanings of the metaphor "*Camels are the trucks of the desert,*" proverb "*falling raindrops will wear through a stone,*" and idiom "*paper over the cracks.*" What have you found about their understanding of the figurative use of language? Alternatively, find two idioms and read them to these children and ask them to interpret their meanings. What have you found?

- Select a book without words (e.g., "*Frog, Where Are You*" by Mercer Mayer) and ask a student from first, third, and fifth grades respectively to tell you the story (if you can, video- or audio-record the process). What have you found about these children's vocabulary and sentence use as well as their narrative structure (story grammar)? How does it vary between age groups?

- Analyze a text in math, science, and social studies used in the third, forth, and fifth grades and identify the typical patterns at the lexical, semantic, and morphosyntactic levels. What have you found about the language demand of these texts?

Understanding Language and Literacy Development: Diverse Learners in the Classroom, First Edition. Xiao-lei Wang.
© 2015 John Wiley & Sons, Inc. Published 2015 by John Wiley & Sons, Inc.
Companion website: www.wiley.com/go/wang/langandlit

- Record a sample of social conversations of children in first, third, and fifth grades respectively. Analyze the conversations and discuss what styles (including gender styles) and skills the children employ. What have you discovered?
- Observe a class in an elementary school and record a sample of the instructional and social language a teacher uses. Analyze what the teacher says in the two different situations at the lexical-semantic and morphosyntactic levels. Do you find any differences? If so, what are they?
- Teach a student between 6 and 10 years old five new words in two conditions: one through explicit teaching and the other through context (i.e., let the child figure them out in the context). Which way do the students learn the meaning faster and/or better? What is your take on these two vocabulary-teaching methods?
- Ask a fifth-grade student to research a topic on the internet. Observe the online reading behavior of this student. What have you found?
- Select a text and ask a first-, third-, and fifth-grade student respectively to interpret the underlying message(s). What have you found?

Topics to Be Addressed in This Chapter

- Typical development profile in middle childhood
- Major language achievements in middle childhood
  - Phonological development
  - Lexical and semantic development
  - Morphosyntactic development
  - Pragmatic development
  - Metalinguistic development
- Developing literacies in middle childhood
  - Print literacy development
  - Digital literacy development
  - Critical literacy development
- Special issues
  - Academic language and academic literacy development
  - Dialect use in the classroom
- Supporting strategies for developing academic language and academic literacy in elementary grades

---

Learning Objectives

After reading this chapter, you are expected to do the following:

- Understand the developmental characteristics of middle childhood and know how these characteristics will influence children's academic language and literacy development in elementary grades.

- Understand the typical language developmental characteristics in the areas of phonology, lexicon, semantics, morphology, syntax, pragmatics, and metalinguistic knowledge in middle childhood.
- Understand the typical developmental characteristics of print, digital, and critical literacies in elementary grades.
- Understand academic language and academic literacy development in the elementary grades.
- Understand dialect development and its influence on academic learning.
- Know how to apply effective supporting strategies to enhance elementary students' language and literacy development in content areas.

Typical Developmental Profile in Middle Childhood

Middle childhood is a distinct developmental stage between early childhood and adolescence, characterized by increasing cognitive advancement, emotional regulation, and relative social independence. Developmentally, the onset of middle childhood is defined by Piaget (1962) as "ages 5 to 7 transition" and the end is marked by the onset of puberty (Campbell, 2011).

During the middle childhood period, children develop logical and systematic thinking, are able to incorporate multiple pieces of information (**decentration**), begin to take the perspectives of others (**non-egocentrism**), and increasingly realize the underlying reality despite superficial appearance. This is also the time when children begin to understand, appreciate, and use rules. Most importantly, children begin to develop the ability to think effectively about their own knowledge and processes of thought (**metacognition**) (Dehart, Sroufe, and Cooper, 2004).

Middle childhood has been traditionally regarded as a major cognitive turning point. Children begin to make a striking transition from the preoperational stage (their thoughts are not yet logical) to the concrete operational stage (their thoughts become logical, flexible, and organized). Recent research, however, indicates that the transition from early childhood to middle childhood does not involve as dramatic a transformation in cognitive abilities as once thought. Instead, the major cognitive development of middle childhood appears to involve refinement and more widespread use of skills that existed in primitive forms during early childhood (Dehart, Sroufe, and Cooper, 2004).

Nevertheless, children show major improvements in their attention and memory in middle childhood. They develop increasingly effective strategies for directing and maintaining attention, and they also develop memory strategies to retain information.

However, despite all the cognitive advancements, children at this stage still have some cognitive limitations. For example, they tend not to think abstractly and hypothetically. Their reasoning tends to be confined to their own concrete experiences. They sometimes have trouble using a skill they possess as part of a larger problem-solving system. Thus, when solving problems, they tend to have, on the one hand, too narrow in scope and be tied to a particular experience or context (e.g., "an apple is something you eat for lunch"), and, on the other hand, have too broad in scope and be incapable of differentiating between words and other related concepts (e.g., "a cat is a pet") (Brice and Brice, 2009).

Socially speaking, children begin to identify with their same-sex peers, and these peer groups become increasingly important. They enjoy an audience and realize that others have different perspectives. They enjoy games, sports, and hobbies and are competitive. In addition, during middle childhood, children tend to look up to teachers as role models, and thus, teachers have a greater effect on them.

Overall, three factors influence children's self-confidence and engagement in tasks and activities during middle childhood. First, their cognitive change enables them to have the ability to reflect on their successes and failures. Second, their social circles broaden, encompassing peers, adults, and activities outside the family. Third, children are exposed to social comparison and competition in the classroom environment and peer groups (Eccles, 1999). As a result, children's self-perceptions begin to emerge and consolidate in middle childhood (Coll and Szalacha, 2004).

Your Turn

Based on the cognitive and social development characteristics of children at middle childhood, what kind of language and literacy achievements and limitations can you predict during this period?

Major Language Developmental Characteristics in Middle Childhood

Children with typical development (TD) have accomplished the major language acquisition tasks during early childhood. They are able to produce almost all the sounds of their primary language or L1, have mastered the basic syntactic structures, and can use language for a number of communication functions. However, they will continue to develop and refine their language skills as they enter middle childhood with the influence of the school language environment. The language input for children during middle childhood becomes more versatile and is shifted from mainly parent input during early childhood to teacher and peer input, and from solely oral input to both oral and writing input. Thus, the school environment plays a crucial role in children's continued language development.

Phonological Development

Most children with TD should have mastered the major part of the phonology in their L1 by about age 8. They are able to pronounce all the sounds in their ambient language. Children also show significant improvement in their speech production coordination and are able to produce a complex sequence of sounds and multisyllabic words (Hoff, 2009). However, some children may still have difficulties in articulating some longer words or blends (Owens, 2012). Moreover, prosodic development, especially consonant duration, may take up to ten years to acquire (Kent, 1976). Similarly, it may take ten years to master most of the rhythmic patterns of a language (De Houwer, 2009; Whitworth, 2002).

Children gradually learn the rules of sound modifications and begin to master the pronunciation rules in plurals. However, up until the third grade, children may still have difficulties pronouncing endings in –*sk* and -*st* clusters, and they may also have difficulties in pronouncing /əz/, as in *desks* (Owens, 2012).

Children begin to improve vowel shifting when a deviational suffix is used. Examples of vowel shifting include *divine–divinity, collide–collision, explain–explanation, decide–decision, sane–sanity*, and *serene–serenity*. Most children, however, do not completely master vowel shifting until 17 years of age (Owens, 2012).

During middle childhood, children continue to improve using stress and emphasis to distinguish phrases from compound words (*hot dog* vs *hotdog*) and to distinguish nouns from verbs (*record* vs *record*; *present* vs *present*), and by age 12 children usually master the stress and emphasis.

Improvement can also be observed in the areas of phonological memory (e.g., can repeat a novel sound sequence), **rapid naming** (the ability to rapidly retrieve and produce known words), and phonological awareness (the ability to analyze and consciously manipulate the sounds of a language as in rhyme generation, alliteration, sound elision, and sound blending tasks) (Kay-Raining Bird, 2007), all of which are associated with children's reading skills.

Your Turn

Why do you think phonological memory, rapid naming, and phonological awareness can predict children's reading skills?

Lexical-semantic development

During middle childhood, children's vocabulary size grows more rapidly than in early childhood. It is estimated that vocabulary size increases by 9,000 words from first grade to third grade and by 20,000 words from third to fifth grade (Hoff, 2009). It seems that the strategy that elementary children use to store words is often based on root words (e.g., day) and morphological variations (e.g., days and daily). Many words are added from context, often while reading, especially after fourth grade (Owens, 2012).

The quality of children's vocabulary also changes significantly compared with early childhood. These changes during middle childhood are demonstrated in three areas: increase in the **lexical diversity** (use of more different types of words), increase in the **lexical complexity** (use of more polysyllabic words), and increase in the **lexical density** (use of more different lexical items). The difference between lexical diversity and density is that lexical diversity measures how many different words are used, whereas lexical density measures the proportions of lexical items such as nouns, verbs, adjectives, and adverbs (Johansson, 2008).

In Chapter 3, we observed that young children are capable of fast mapping the meaning if they hear a word and see a referent, particularly in the situation when caregivers follow their children's focus of attention and then explicitly label objects they see. Elementary children continue to use the fast-mapping word learning strategy to learn new words. They sometimes are able to use semantic and syntactic clues available in the texts to figure out new word meanings (see Box 6.1).

Box 6.1   Examples of Using Semantic and Syntactic Context Clues to Figure out New Word Meaning

Using semantic clues for the meaning of "philanthropist"   The weatherman enjoyed raising money for many charities. He gave large sums of his own money to homes for orphaned children, soup kitchens, and shelters for the homeless. He also turned one of his homes into a wonderful school for needy children. He was one of the most well known *philanthropists* of our time.

Using syntactic clues for the meaning of "apothecary"   The *apothecary*, who mixed the different drugs, placed his jars on the counter.

Examples adapted from M. A. Nippold, *Later Language Development: School-Age Children, Adolescents, and Young Adults* (Austin: Pro-ed, 2007), p. 31.

Starting from 5 years of age, children are able to get the meaning by **quick incidental learning** (QUIL) (Hoff, 2009) in which they are able to pick up the new word meaning from incidental exposure. This ability allows them to acquire new words rapidly. Children get better at deducing word meanings from context by using fast-mapping and QUIL strategies in learning new words throughout the elementary school years.

Furthermore, elementary school children's definitions of words become more literate (dictionary-like) and more explicit. Around age 11, children acquire most of the definitions used by adults (Owens, 2012).

Children begin to understand that words are **polysemous** (have more than one meaning) and are able to provide multiple definitions for a word with several similar meanings. However, most children will initially have difficulty understanding the secondary meanings of words that bear little or no relation to the primary meaning (Pence and Justice, 2008).

Your Turn

- Use the speech and writing sample you collected (the activity you were asked to do in the "Prereading Activities and Questions" section). Calculate the lexical diversity, density, and complexity of the first-grade, third-grade, and fifth-grade students respectively. What do the students' lexical diversity, density, and complexity differences tell you about your instructional planning for these students?

- Identify a list of words that have primary and secondary meanings. Ask a second-grade student to explain the secondary meaning of these words. Explain why this child may have difficulty in understanding the secondary meaning of words that bear little or no relation to the primary meaning. (Hint: Review the "Typical Developmental Profile in Middle Childhood" section on the cognitive developmental characteristics of middle childhood.)
- Observe an early elementary-grade student and discuss whether this student uses the word-learning strategies described in the above section.

Morphosyntactic development

Derivational morphology

The major morphological development in middle childhood includes the use of the **derivational prefix** (prefix added to the beginning of a word such as *unhealthy*) and the **derivational suffix** (suffix added to the end of a word such as *encroachment*). You will notice that children begin to use derivational prefixes such as *dis-*, *non-*, *un-*, and *ir-* and derivational suffixes such as *-hood*, *-ment*, *-er*, and *-ly* later in the elementary grades and onward.

Verb tenses, auxiliary verbs, and adverbial modality

Children begin to add verb tenses such as the perfect tense "*I have finished*" and "*It has been eaten*," irregular past tense such as "*He went to the party yesterday*," and modal auxiliary verbs such as *can, could, may, might*, and *should*. In addition, children gradually begin to express the notion of modality in adverbs (*possibly, maybe*), adjectives (*possible, likely*), nouns (*possibility, likelihood*), verbs (*believe, doubt*), and suffixes (*-able*), although not all forms of modality develop simultaneously, and the process tends to take a long time. By the fourth grade, most children understand the different meanings of adverbs such as *definitely, probably*, and *possibly* (Owens, 2012).

Pronoun, gerunds, and participles use

There is a fundamental difference between children in early childhood and middle childhood in their use of pronouns. For example, a 4-year-old uses pronouns to refer to things in the world, whereas a 9-year-old uses pronouns to refer to things in other sentences, thereby creating a cohesive narrative (Hoff, 2009). In other words, young children use grammar to produce sentences, whereas children after age 8 use grammar to produce text (Berman, 2007) and narratives.

Less than half of first graders are able to produce correct pronouns (the "cause" clauses) and gerunds (a **gerund** is the "*-ing*" form; when the *-ing* is added to a verb, it becomes a noun such as *running*). Less than 20 percent of them can produce *if* and *so* clauses and **participles** (a verb that functions as an adjective by adding *-ing*/ present participles or *-ed, -t, and -en*/past participles such as *fishing* equipment, *unkept* house, and *broken* arrow).

Mass nouns and count nouns

The mass nouns and count nouns are acquired slowly throughout the school years. **Mass nouns** refer to homogeneous, nonindividual substances, such as *water* and *sand*.

Mass nouns use quantifying modifiers, such as *much* and *little*. **Count nouns** refer to heterogeneous, individual objects, such as *cup* and *house*. Count nouns take quantifiers such as *many* and *few*. Children must also learn that the determiners (*this* and *that*) go with count nouns, but not with mass nouns.

Grammatical structure

The grammatical structure during middle childhood becomes more complex with expanded noun phrases, adverbial clauses, and subordinate clauses, and language use becomes richer and more varied. As a result, elementary school children's sentences become longer, with more words, and embedded phrases and clauses. Because of the emergence of complex sentences among school-age children, many researchers use C-units or T-units to measure school-age children's syntactic complexity instead of MLU. **C-units** refer to the mean number of words in communication units, and **T-units** refer to terminable units.[1] Both C-units and T-units consist of an independent clause and any modifiers such as a dependent clause (e.g., "A frightening storm came up while we were on the river"). The only difference between C-units and T-units is that C-units can include incomplete sentences when used to answer questions (e.g., "*For 16 years*" is a C-unit when answering the question, "*How long have you lived in New York?*"). As children move up through elementary grades, their mean number of words per C-unit in spoken and written language increases steadily.

Passive sentence   About 80 percent of children aged 7 and a half to 8 produce full passive sentences. In general, a full passive sentence contains some form of *be* or *got*, a verb with past tense marker, and a preposition flowed by a noun phrase as in "*The window was broken by Diego.*" However, some passive forms do not appear until 11 years of age (Owens, 2012). There are three types of passives in general: reversible (e.g., in the sentences "*The dog was chased by the cat*" and "*The cat was chased by the dog*," either noun *dog* or *cat* could be the actor or object), instrumental nonreversible (the nouns cannot be reversed because the subject is an inanimate instrument, such as "*The window was broken by the ball*"), and agentive nonreversible (the nouns cannot be reversed because the subject is an agent, such as "*The window was broken by the boy*"). There is a noticeable increase in nonreversible passive production before age 8, agentive nonreversible passives emerge around age 9, and instrumental nonreversible passives appear most frequently for 11- to 13-year-olds (Owens, 2012).

Although use of the past tense -*ed* (*He kicked the ball*) is acquired by most children by age 4, development of the participles -*ed* (*He was kicked by his friend*) and -*en* (*we were beaten by East High School*) used in passive sentences takes until school age to be mastered (Owens, 2012). Moreover, errors such as applying regular rules (e.g., "He was *cutted* by the axe"; "It was *boughten* by her") may persist until early adolescence (Owens, 2012).

Conjunctive links   Throughout the school years, children's use of conjunctive links increases, although it is a long process. Initially, children use *and* in narratives. However, the use decreases with age and also in written form. Up until age 12, *because* and *when* predominate and *if* and *in order to* are also used frequently (Owens, 2012). Although children use the link *because* often, it takes them a while to understand its meaning. Understanding the link *because* requires not only the relationship between two events, but also their temporal sequence (this sequence is not the same as the order presented in the sentence). For example, in *"I went because I was asked,"* the speaker was invited before he or she actually left, although the linguistic ordering is the reverse. At first, children tend to be confused in the usage of *and, because,* and *then*; they use these conjunctive links in a similar fashion. True comprehension of *because* does not seem to develop until age 7. The real understanding of *because* may not occur until around age 10 or 11 (Owens, 2012). Usually *because* is learned before *if* and *although* and followed by *unless*. However, children typically rely on semantic cues to understand conjunctions even before they fully master them.

Embedded sentences Children's use of embedded sentences in narratives tends to increase by 20–30 percent throughout the school years. First, their use of relative pronouns expands (*whose, whom,* and *in which*). The most notable achievement is the use of multiple embedding. Children in early elementary school grades tend to have difficulties in understanding center embedding (e.g., the book *that Roger read* was exciting). Semantics plays an important role in interpretation. If the object of a center embedding is inanimate, it is less likely to be misinterpreted than an animated object is. In the following example, window cannot run, so there is no confusion in the first sentence, but the second example may be misinterpreted by early elementary children:

> *"The boy who broke the window ran away."*
> *"The boy who hit the girl ran away."*

Some researchers believe that the ability to understand center embedding depends on working memory development because comprehension of complex sentences needs both speed and attention control and allocation (e.g., Montgomery, Magimairaj, and O'Malley, 2008).

Your Turn

Write a paragraph or two using the following conjunctive links:

> *and, then, because, so, therefore, if, but, although, when, before, after, unless*

(or you can also look for a text that contains these conjunctive links) and ask a child in first, third, and fifth grades respectively to explain the relationships of the different sentences joined together by these conjunctive links. Discuss the differences you observed among these children.

Pragmatic development

Pragmatic use of language

By the time children enter kindergarten and first grade, most of them can easily carry out a conversation with their peers and produce many types of narratives spontaneously. This ability allows children to engage in social interactions in the classroom environment. However, the classroom environment also requires children to change the way they use language. In the classroom environment, children must negotiate a turn by seeking recognition from the teacher and responding in a highly specific manner to questions. Further, text-related language becomes relatively more important than social language. In classroom interactions, children are held accountable for their responses and are required to use precise word meanings (Owens, 2012). Thus, the pragmatic use of language is the most dramatic linguistic growth for children during elementary school (Owens, 2012). Moreover, children's contributions to conversation are more frequently relevant to the current topic, and from second to fifth grades, children can sustain longer conversations (Hoff, 2009).

There is also a gender difference. Boys and girls begin to involve themselves in different gender groups. Girls play in small groups or pairs, and the groups tend to be homogeneous in terms of social status and age of the group members. Within the group, play is cooperative and activities are generally noncompetitive (Hoff, 2009). In contrast, boys tend to play in large groups that include boys of different social status and even different ages. Within the group, a hierarchical structure places some boys on top and others on the bottom. Speech is used in three ways: to assert one's position of dominance, to attract and maintain an audience, and to assert oneself when other speakers have the floor (Hoff, 2009). As result, girls and boys may develop different conversational styles.

Narrative development

Narration or storytelling is a critical aspect of pragmatic development during the school years. Children's narratives or personal stories serve several functions. For example, they socialize by telling each other stories about their lives, they use stories as mental tools for remembering events, and they use narrative to learn to read and write stories. Over time, children learn how to create more elaborated episodes in their stories and develop the ability to weave multiple episodes into their narratives (Gillam, Marquardt, and Martin, 2011). Through constant practice, children's narratives become longer, more coherent, and more complex. Their story grammar has also made progress with age. From ages 6 to 10, children develop the ability to produce narratives with multiple coordinated events and embedded events. Unlike the stories told by young children (which tend to contain actions alone and with no account of why those actions were produced), elementary children begin to infuse reference to internal motivations or mental status (Hoff, 2009).

Children also show improvement in their comprehension monitoring skills. **Comprehension monitoring** is the ability to evaluate whether a message is accurate or not. It is a major component of communication skills. Children starting at second grade begin to have better comprehension monitoring skills than younger children, and they begin to understand that messages do not automatically represent the speaker's intended meaning. They are able to revise their own messages and to request others to revise theirs (Hoff, 2009).

Your Turn

Besides what has been discussed above regarding the pragmatic development of children during middle childhood, what else do you think contributes to children's advancement in pragmatics? (Hint: you may want to revisit the discussion on cognitive and social development characteristics such as non-egocentrism and decentration.)

Metalinguistic development

As you read in Chapter 3, children begin to develop initial/emergent knowledge about the language they speak during early childhood. However, it is during middle childhood that they make significant progress in their metalinguistic competence. Metalinguistic awareness such as phonological awareness is fundamental for reading development. When learning to read in an alphabetic system, it is necessary to be able to perform explicit phoneme awareness tasks, like segmentation, deletion, and counting of phonemes. Learning to read allows readers to consciously monitor phoneme manipulation. In other words, reading experience influences implicit phonological awareness, as measured by children's sensitivity to salient units as rime, and precipitates the development of explicit phonological awareness (Gombert, 2002). Metalinguistic development manifests in several important areas.

Phonological awareness

Children become aware of the smallest units of sound (phonemes) and are sensitive to the distinct sounds in syllables and words (usually around 5 and 6 years of age). They develop the ability to blend sounds to make words (e.g., "What word is /b/ /ae/ /t/?") and segment sounds from words (e.g., "What is the first sound in *car*?"). Children begin to know the spelling pattern of words such as *boat* and *coat* and are able to use this knowledge to infer how to pronounce the word *moat*. Around age 7, children also develop sound manipulation abilities such as, "*What do you have if you switch the /p/ and /t/ sounds in pat?*" (Pence and Justice, 2008).

Morphological awareness

Besides phonological (phoneme) awareness, other metalinguistic abilities such as orthographic awareness and morphological awareness have also been identified in the literature as contributors to children's reading development; that is, phonemic awareness, orthographic awareness, and morphological awareness have been identified as contributing to the acquisition of reading and spelling skills. However, recent research suggests that morphological skills seem to be the most crucial in children's spelling development. This is supported by a study conducted with second and third graders. The finding of the study suggested that morphological awareness was the sole contributor to children's spelling performance (Apel et al., 2011). Moreover, together with orthographic awareness, morphological awareness also contributes to children's word recognition. Thus, morphological awareness is significant in children's reading comprehension (Apel et al., 2011).

√ *Word formation knowledge*

As discussed before, children in middle childhood have rapid vocabulary growth (especially between the third and fifth grades). One explanation for this increase is due to children's increased awareness of the word formation process (Hoff, 2009). They now have the ability to figure out words they have never heard before by using their knowledge of root and affix meanings. This morphological awareness allows children to decipher what new words mean.

In addition, children in middle childhood have begun to master the rules of word formation. They continue to develop knowledge in derivational morphology (e.g., sadn<u>ess</u> and preach<u>er</u>), inflectional morphology (e.g., boy<u>s</u> and soak<u>ing</u>), and compound words (e.g., playground and payday).

Development of Literacies in Middle Childhood

As discussed in Chapter 1, literacy includes reading and writing in a social context and involves the cognitive process (thinking, memory, problem-solving, planning, and execution) as well as the critical stance. It also includes other domains such as the visual, audio, digital, spatial, and behavioral. Thus, when discussing the literacy development of middle childhood, all these domains need to be considered.

Reading and writing are language-based skills. When children enter kindergarten and first grade, they usually have a great deal of knowledge about the vocabulary, grammar, and use of their L1. This knowledge is based on their experiences with listening to and speaking the language that surrounds them. To learn to read and write, children must organize their knowledge of language at a new level. They need to figure out how to use sequences of letters to represent the phonemes, words, sentences, and stories that have been part of their oral language for some time. To read, children must decode their language into sequences of letters. To write, they must encode their language into sequences of letters (Gillam, Marquardt, and Martin, 2011, p. 252).

Reading

Reading is a secondary language skill and is built on the foundation of the primary language skills of speaking and listening (Hoff, 2009). The secondary language skills usually do not come naturally to most children as the primary language skills do. Reading requires considerably more effort than oral language. Deliberate instruction in the school environment is often required, even though some individuals may learn how to read on their own without the benefit of instruction. Reading development typically follows the stages shown in Box 6.2.

Box 6.2   Chall's Stages of Reading Development

Prereading stage (approximately birth to 5 years old)   Children begin to understand the sound structures of words. Most children also acquire some knowledge of print at this stage.

Stage 1 (approximately 5 to 7 years old)   Children begin to decode words by associating letters with corresponding sounds in spoken words. They usually move through three phases.

Phase 1 Children tend to make word substitution errors by making the substituted word semantically and syntactically probable.
Phase 2 Children tend to make word substitution errors by making the substitute word graphically resemble the original word, but it does not make sense.
Phase 3 Children tend to make word substitution errors by making the substitute word graphically resemble the original word, but it is also semantically acceptable.

Stage 2 (approximately 7 to 8 years old)   Children further sharpen the decoding skills developed in Stage 1 and begin to develop fluency (efficient, well paced, and free of error). They gradually transition from "learning to read" to "reading to learn."

Stage 3 (approximately 9 to 14 years old)   Children begin to learn new knowledge, information, thoughts, and experiences by reading.

Phase 3A (9 to 11 years old)   Children begin to move away from the egocentric perspective and can read about and learn conventional information about the world. By the end of this phase, they can read words of typical adult length, but not the adult level of reading difficulty.
Phase 3B (12 to 14 years old)   Children can read on a general adult level. They start to confront different viewpoints and begin to analyze and criticize what they read.

Stage 4 (approximately 14 to 18 years old)   Students learn to handle increasingly difficult concepts and the texts that describe them. They can consider multiple viewpoints.

Stage 5 (approximately 18 and onward)   Readers can read materials in the degree of detail and completeness that is needed to serve their purposes. They select materials to serve their purposes; they know what not to read as well as what to read. They analyze, synthesize, and make judgments about what they read. They balance their own comprehension of the words with their analysis of the content and their own ideas about the topic. At this stage, reading is constructive. The reader constructs knowledge and understanding from reading what others have written.

J. S. Chall, *Stages of Reading Development*, 2nd edn (New York: Wadsworth, 1995); K. L. Pence and L. M. Justice, *Language Development from Theory to Practice* (Upper Saddle River, NJ: Pearson, 2008), pp. 254–257.

Children in the first and second grades enter the initial period of reading. They can identify specific words in the printed form, such as names, labels, sight words, and high meaning words. They can also decode orthographically regular multisyllabic words (e.g., *capital*) and nonsense words (e.g., *zot*). From grades 2 to 5, children enter the transitional period of reading. They are able to use letter–sound correspondence knowledge and structure analysis to decode print, but they are not yet fluent readers. They are able to read and comprehend both fiction and nonfiction that is appropriately designed for their levels (Ashmore, 2001, p. 10).

Writing

Like reading, writing is also a secondary language skill, which does not usually happen automatically. Deliberate instruction is often necessary. Children become sensitive to conventional spelling in the first grade. However, they sometimes use invented spelling based on phonics knowledge. They gradually learn about spacing, sequencing, ways to represent phonemes, and the morpheme–grapheme relationships. Six-year-olds tend to learn morphological rules for spelling on a word-by-word basis. As children begin to recognize more word regularities, they become more efficient spellers (usually between third and fifth grade). Children's increased memory capacity for word regularities explains why they become better spellers as they progress through the grades.

It usually takes several years for children to develop many vowel representations, phonological variations (e.g., later–latter) and morpho-phonemic variations (e.g., sign–signal). Gradually, they learn about consonant doubling, stressed and unstressed syllables (*re*port–re*port*), root words, and derivations (e.g., add–addition) (Owens, 2012).

Most spellers shift from a purely phonological strategy to a mixed one between second and fifth grade. As words and strategies are stored in their long-term memory, the load on cognitive capacity is lessened and access becomes fluent (Owens, 2012). This ability allows children to focus on other writing tasks.

Initially, children's overall structure of writing and speaking is very close, and their writing lacks coherence and organization. At first, they may produce drawings to highlight what they want to express or to help organize what they want to write. Later, their writing may consist of a list of sequential events. After a while, simple **expository texts**[2] emerge, usually as a result of school demands and teacher modeling. Variety in sentences also begins to emerge. For example, passive sentences increase in writing, and clause length also increases.

Children's writing becomes more automatic, and vocabulary and sentences become more advanced. In general, by age 9 or 10, children's writing is moving away from many of the features of speech and their writing becomes more mature than speech (Owens, 2012). Elementary school children are also able to produce a variety of written genres, such as letters, reports, and journal writing (Ashmore, 2001). They also learn to compose drafts by planning, drafting, reading for meaning, and self-correcting. For reasons that are not clear, most children's writing tends to lag behind their reading comprehension (Owens, 2012).

Hypertext

Hypertext is a digital text displayed on a computer screen or other electronic device with active links to other texts, images, graphs, and information that readers can instantly access. There are differences between hypertext and conventional text. Hypertexts are multimedia and are characterized by multisequential text patterns, which present readers with an array of information options online. They are also highly interactive, allowing readers to make choices on the basis of personal interest or purpose. In hypertext reading, the reader's purpose and choices, rather than the author's, determine the reading sequence. In conventional text reading, the author determines the reading sequence (McNabb, 2005–2006).

There is little research on how children's hypertext literacy develops. Nevertheless, available literature suggests that reading hypertext requires students to develop sophisticated comprehension-monitoring abilities that involve reviewing, evaluating, and synthesizing various **lexias** (specific blocks of text). There are striking differences between how students read online text and how they read printed materials. Typically, the interactivity of hypertexts draws out students' natural curiosity as they forge their own reading paths on the internet. Although some students monitor their reading sequence and comprehension successfully, many others become disoriented when attempting to complete online reading assignments (McNabb et al., 2006). Box 6.3 illustrates a common experience that many children may encounter when reading hypertexts without adequate teacher guidance and monitoring.

Box 6.3 Example of Children's Difficulties in Reading Hypertext

Sara, an average reader, used the internet to research how lifestyle and personal attributes influence a person's health. As a starting point, Sara's health education teacher had pointed her to bicycle racer Lance Armstrong's official website. After staring at the screen for several moments, Sara clicked on the link "About Lance." She read about Armstrong's training with the US Olympic cycling development team during high school, and then clicked on "Key Stats" from another menu of topics and discovered such random facts as Armstrong's resting heart rate.

At this point, Sara was feeling confused. She clicked on "Links," faced another directory of topics, and aimed for the "Shimano Components" link, without knowing why or what she might find there. To her surprise, she found a website offering the link "Which Bike Is Right For You?" Sara's interest quickly perked up; she had been begging her parents for a new bike for her birthday. Later, after spending time on the Shimano website, Sara realized in frustration that she had not accomplished anything related to her assigned topic.

Sara, a novice hypertext reader with weak hypertext comprehension monitoring abilities, was confused by the many hyperlink options and made decisions that caused her to waste valuable time reading hypertexts unrelated to the assigned research objective. Her learning problem was compounded by the teacher's poor initial website selection.

Example from M. L. McNabb, "Navigating the maze of hypertext," *Educational Leadership*, 63(4) (2005–2006): 76–79.

Critical literacy

There is a difference between critical thinking in problem-solving and critical literacy. Critical thinking is reflective and reasonable thinking, which requires mental agility and thoughtful consideration. Critical literacy is the ability to critique the ideologies of reading texts and of such issues as social inequity portrayed in the texts and to challenge the status quo and question authority (Kim, 2012).

Although elementary school children become increasingly more critical in their ability to problem-solve, their critical thinking ability will not naturally lead to critical literacy ability. Moreover, because elementary school children's cognitive ability is in the concrete operational stage, they tend to read messages as they are. Without conscious support, elementary children may not always be able to interpret the underlying meaning of a text. Thus, they need teachers' help to evaluate what they read.

Special Issues

Academic language and academic literacy development

As mentioned in opening chapter, "About the Book," there are two kinds of academic language: general academic language and content-specific academic language. General academic language is different from the social language used for everyday communication. Teachers and students use general academic language in classroom settings to communicate content-related information and understand concepts. Content-specific academic language is the key terms and concepts of a particular subject area; it sets math, science, language arts, social studies and other subjects apart from each other. Academic language in general is decontextualized. Students often need to rely on language itself to make meaning without the aid of context clues.

General academic language development

The school environment has an impact on children's language development, especially phonological, syntactical, lexical, and word definition skills (Hoff, 2009). The school environment provides students with access to words and concepts that are not typical for everyday conversations, and the topics of conversations in school are mostly decontextualized. It may take a while for elementary school children to understand the academic vocabulary such as *doubt, conclude, assert, interpret, predict*, and *hypothesize*. It may also take them a while to develop a full understanding of the connectives (conjunctive links) such as *but, although,* and *however.* Further, the sentence structure used by teachers or in texts tends to be longer and includes more clauses. Most elementary school children will get used to the complex structure as they proceed in grades both in the area of comprehension and production.

Content-specific academic language development

As students advance through each grade level and the subject matter becomes narrower in focus, the specific content language increases in difficulty. Students need content-specific language as the key resource for developing concepts in specific subject areas. When children are introduced first to content-specific language, for example math words like *grid, factor, value,* and *tangram,* they may not understand them right away and they are usually able to get the meanings through explanation with concrete examples or demonstration.

Academic literacy development

Academic literacy tends to be abstract and involves more complex concepts, and therefore, it presents more challenges for elementary school students. Further, academic literacy requires that a student be able to coordinate multiple abilities in listening, viewing, inferring, thinking, understanding, speaking, writing, reading, expressing, and critiquing. It will take some time for elementary school children to develop this comprehensive ability. They may often exhibit competence in several of these areas, but not in all the areas. In addition, elementary school children make a big jump from oral narratives and reading narrative texts to expository texts, which inform or explain something.

Your Turn

Analyze the following math problem and determine what language, literacy, and cognitive ability a student needs to complete the task.

> *To make spaghetti sauce, add one can of tomato paste and two cans of water to one package of mix. Add a spoonful of salad oil. How many cans of water would you use with three packages of mix? How many cans of tomato paste would you use with eight cans of water?*

M. A. Nippold, *Later Language Development: School-Age Children, Adolescents, and Young Adults,* 3rd edn (Austin: Pro-ed, 2007), p. 16.

Dialect use in the classroom

In Chapter 3, we discussed the African American English (AAE) used among young African American children and suggested that their early emergent literacy skills are on a par with children speaking mainstream American English. Those young children who used more AAE tended to perform better in their narratives than those children who used less AAE. However, some have found that the early narrative advantage might diminish when AAE-speaking children enter elementary school. When children continue to use dialect at moderate to heavy levels, they are more likely to read and write below grade level. This is because of discrepancies between mainstream American English (MAE) and AAE. If a child uses AAE features in writing such as zero copular, zero plural, and zero regular past, these will be regarded as errors in MAE. Thus, the advantage in oral language in the early years of AAE-speaking children may become a disadvantage in the academic setting. Moreover, research suggests that boys use significantly more dialect than do girls, and children from low-income families use more dialect than middle-income children (Washington and Thomas-Tate, 2009). These differences are often reflected in their academic language and literacy performances.

However, some researchers believe that despite the microstructural level differences between AAC speakers and MAE speakers, children who speak AAC demonstrate greater microstructural competences in their fictional narratives. In fact, by age 7, one study suggested that AAE-speaking children produced more embellishment and fantasy than their MAE-speaking counterparts (Gorman et al., 2011).

Your Turn

Is there any way you can help children who speak AAE to continue to develop their AAE and at the same time to code-switch to MAE? What is the significance of encouraging the development of both types of English?

Supporting Language and Literacy Development in Elementary Grades

General principles

Based on the typical middle childhood cognitive and social development characteristics discussed in the beginning of this chapter, several general principles are summarized below as a guideline for working with children at this stage:

- Provide opportunities for children to engage in authentic language and literacy activities and situated practices (i.e., activities should be close to their real-life experiences. For example, write about a recent sport event, write an e-mail to a friend, or write a letter to a grandparent).
- Supply contextual clues and hints to help children understand reading materials.
- Introduce grammatical rules (this is a good time to introduce grammatical rules because children begin to understand the importance of rules in general).
- Help children perform challenging academic literacy tasks through **scaffolding** (assistance) and **apprenticeship** (Lave and Wenger, 1991; Rogoff, 1990) (help children practice academic literacy skills in the real world just as a master carpenter helps his apprentice learn carpentry skills by asking her to observe and practice).

- Allow children to **appropriate** (Rogoff, 1990) academic language and literacy knowledge (give children the freedom to apply academic language and literacy knowledge in their own understanding and manner).
- Teach academic language register and other important academic language and literacy skills overtly.

If you are cognisant of elementary school children's developmental characteristics when planning and conducting language and literacy learning activities, they will learn better.

Your Turn

Provide your own examples for each of the above-mentioned general principles of working with children in elementary grades.

Focus of literacy support

The focus of literacy support during early elementary grades should be on teaching children decoding skills (**decoding** is the ability to break the code of letter–sound combination) and making decoding skills more automatic. The focus for mid and late elementary grades should be on **reading fluency** (the ability to read quickly and smoothly and understand the ideas in the text) and using reading and writing as a tool for learning subject contents. However, it is important to note that focusing on different literacy skills support in elementary grades should mean they are regarded as different isolated skills. Reading development from the very beginning should be considered as an integrated process.

Supporting strategies

Overt teaching on academic language register
Variations in how language is used are referred to as language registers. There are differences in the **social language register** (the oral language used in the everyday context) and the **academic language register** (the language used in the school setting to meet academic discourse expectations). For example, in science, math, and social studies textbooks, language is more tightly packed into multiclausal constructions, and clauses are tied together with logical connectives (e.g., *unless, whereas, likewise*) rather than simple additive or temporal connectives (e.g., *and, then*) often observed in personal narratives (Silliman and Scott, 2009). Also, the academic language register is often decontextualized. Students must be able to make inferences based on the information that textbook authors and their teachers frame through language.

Thus, your task as a teacher is to help your elementary students develop the academic register by deliberately orienting them to academic language understanding and use. For early elementary students, you may want to explicitly call their attention to a comparison of the everyday use of certain vocabulary and the content use (e.g., What is the difference between a *table* used in the everyday context and a *table* used in math). Later, you may want to ask your students to identify the differences. Moreover, in your own classroom discourse, you may want to frequently model the use of academic register.

Your Turn

- Observe a teacher and students in an elementary classroom. Identify the academic vocabulary she or he uses. What is the frequency of the teacher's social language use and academic language use (calculate based on a five-minute sample)? Does the teacher explain the academic vocabulary to the students? Can you find any examples in which the students model the teacher's academic vocabulary use?
- In the ed-TPA (Teacher Performance Assessment), teacher candidates are required to demonstrate their ability in modeling academic language use. Design a lesson plan in a particular content area by incorporating academic language use. Practice your plan with a group of elementary grade students. Videotape yourself and evaluate how you are doing in modeling academic language use in your teaching.

Overt teaching on code-switching discourse styles

Academic language is new for all children. However, some children may have an easier time adjusting to the new language than others. In a middle class, educated family, the conversational style of parents tends to resemble the teacher language. Children tend to benefit more from teacher scaffolding when their home discourse style matches the teacher discourse style, whereas when children's home discourse style is different from their teacher's discourse style, they tend to benefit less from teacher scaffolding.

Children who speak AAE may have difficulties benefiting from the school language. Therefore, it is important to help these children learn to code-switch (use different language registers in different contexts). Research shows that explicit teaching in code-switching is useful. Attention needs to be paid especially to the distinct differences. For example, focus on possessive "s," third-person singular "s," indefinite article "a," subject–verb agreement, and other mainstream American English rules in writing; provide guiding practice in changing sentences from AAE to MAE; and expose children to story structure (Washington and Thomas-Tate, 2009). Box 6.4 lists the general strategies in helping children who speak AAE code-switch to MAE.

Box 6.4   Strategies to Help Students of AAE Code-Switch to MAE

- Challenge students and accept that they are competent and sophisticated language users who will benefit from being taught language change strategies.

- Start with the students' community language and teach students to contrast their typical language use with the forms being introduced in the classroom. It is not always clear which features are most important to target. It is often helpful to examine students' writing to determine which AAE forms are most prevalent across the group.

- Provide opportunities for active, repeated practice transforming AAE sentences to MAE. Practice can help improve students' ability in understanding noticeable rules in MAE.

- Use written language as a bridging context for teaching MAE in oral language. That is, teaching code-switching in writing provides a natural "bridge" for explicitly teaching MAE in oral language contexts.

- Provide instruction in use of MAE in ecologically valid, contextualized classroom contexts rather than in separate, decontextualized supplemental instructional contexts.

Above all else, affirm rather than devalue the language of the African American student.

Modified from J. A. Washington and S. Thomas-Tate, "How research informs cultural-linguistic differences in the classroom," in S. Rosenfield and V. Berninger (eds), *Implementing Evidence-Based Academic Interventions in School Settings* (New York: Oxford University Press, 2009), p. 159.

Overt teaching on foundational skills in academic literacy

Children must be supported to develop academic literacy abilities. The following strategies are suggested for the early elementary grades.

Phonological skills

Phonological awareness consists of many skills including syllabication, phoneme identification, alliteration, rhyming, segmentation, and blending. Not all these skills are required for reading. Of particular importance for the development of reading are the phonemic skills of segmentation (dividing words into their parts) and blending (creating a word from individual sounds and syllables) (Owens, 2012). It has been shown that when children are trained in phonological awareness (particularly in phonemic awareness), they experience an increase in letter knowledge, which benefits their reading ability (Lyytine et al., 2006). In fact, reading in its beginning stage is primarily a process of word recognition and decoding. Therefore, deliberate and targeted training in letter and sound association will help children's reading ability.

As children read more, their reading also influences their phonological awareness.

Your Turn

Select a text for first- and second-grade students and identify some key words you think are important for comprehension. Design a lesson plan on how to train children to segment and blend the words. If possible, have a couple of children in first or second grade try what you have planned. Are you successful? Explain.

Vocabulary knowledge

As children's word decoding becomes automatic, their vocabulary size and vocabulary knowledge become more crucial in their reading comprehension. Reading is obviously a major source for children's vocabulary exposure. Thus, you might want to help children build their vocabulary size by providing opportunities to read and including reading materials that contain a variety of words.

Moreover, word learning cannot just rely on children's spontaneous engagement with words on their own. Rather, effective word learning must be deliberately taught (Beck, McKeown, and Kucan, 2002). Research has shown that systematic, explicit and direct teaching of vocabulary can indeed enhance a child's reading proficiency (Bear et al., 2008). Below are some strategies that you can use to help your students build their vocabulary knowledge.

Use contextual clues   You can help your students learn the meanings of new words by using the contextual clues in the reading material. For example, if your students encounter new words, you can help them look for the clues such as illustrations and background information. You can also use guiding questions to help them understand the meaning.

Make connections   You can help your students expand their vocabulary by learning words connected by their specific features. You can help your children learn more words by building on what they already know and expanding on their word knowledge. Suppose a child already knows the word *act*; she can be now introduced to a new word, *interact* (Beck, McKeown, and Kucan, 2002).

Moreover, you can teach your children more words that logically belong together in the context. For example, *eavesdrop* and *gregarious* do not have an apparent connection. However, you can make them belong together by creating a context. Suppose if someone reports you to a teacher for talking to a friend; this person is *eavesdropping* and you are being *gregarious* (Beck, McKeown, and Kucan, 2002).

Furthermore, you can help your children learn more words by employing the idea of a **word web** (Beck, McKeown, and Kucan, 2002), a visual representation resembling a web of concepts and related ideas with connecting lines to show relationships (White, Anderson, and Carrico, 2009) or accumulative vocabulary teaching (Brice and Brice, 2009). Suppose you teach the word *shoe*; you can draw different kinds of connections with this word and help your students not only learn more vocabulary related to this word, but also increase their knowledge of the concept. This approach is illustrated in Figure 6.1.

You can extend the idea shown in Figure 6.1 and make your students' vocabulary learning more interesting. Their mental lexicon can be supported via a word web. Developing a larger mental lexicon will help your students progress faster in their academic language and literacy development.

Contrast synonyms and antonyms   Explicitly teaching students synonyms and antonyms can help elementary grade students consciously build a large mental lexicon. **Synonyms** are words that have almost the same meaning as other words. **Antonyms**

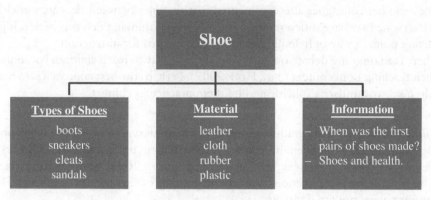

Figure 6.1   Word web

are words with opposite meanings (Ruddell, 2009). Take the following as an example: the word *kind* has several synonyms such as *nice, hospitable,* and *tender.* The antonym of *cruel* is *kind.* Using synonyms and antonyms can help your students enlarge their vocabulary. At the same time, it is also a meaningful way to help your students make connections between words. However, you might want to be cautious when teaching synonyms and make sure to explain the subtle semantic differences to your students.

Teach words selectively   Not all words need to be taught. According to Beck and her colleagues (Beck, McKeown, and Kucan, 2002), a mature literate individual's vocabulary is comprised of three tiers. The first tier consists of the most basic words such as *clock, baby, happy,* and *walk.* Words in this tier rarely require purposeful instruction because they are embedded in the everyday environment. The second tier contains words that are of high frequency for mature language users and found across a variety of domains. Examples of these include *coincidence, absurd, industrious,* and *fortunate.* Because of the large role these words play in a language user's repertoire, mastering them can have a powerful impact on the child's literacy development. Therefore, instructions directed toward second-tier words can be most useful. The third tier is made up of words that are not frequently used or are limited to a specific domain such as *isotope* and *lathe.* Beck and her colleagues suggest three criteria for selecting tier two words.

- *Importance and utility*   Words that are characteristic of mature language users and appear frequently across a variety of domains.
- *Instructional potential*   Words that can be worked with in a variety of ways so that children can build rich representations of them and of their connections to other words and concepts.
- *Conceptual understanding*   Words that can help children understand the general concept, and they can also assist children in describing the concept with precision and specificity.

Beck and her colleagues also commented that the lines between tiers are not clear-cut. Everyone may have different selections. However, thinking in terms of tiers is just a starting point, a way of helping choose targeted words for instruction.

There is an ongoing debate on what is an effective way to teach children vocabulary: explicit teaching or in context (e.g., Hoff, 2009). Perhaps the best approach is to teach children key vocabulary explicitly and let them practice in context.

Use dictionaries   You may gradually introduce a dictionary to mid and late elementary grade children and show them how to use it to help them understand texts. However, Beck and her colleagues (Beck, McKeown, and Kucan, 2002) warned that it might not be suitable to use a dictionary in the beginning of literacy development. They point out several potential pitfalls.

First, a dictionary often has weak definitions of words. For example, *conspicuous* is defined in a junior dictionary as "easily seen." This definition weakly differentiates *conspicuous* from the general domain of *visible*. Unless it is dark or someone has poor vision, nearly everything is easily seen. Something *conspicuous* is not just easy to see but rather pops out at you because of its size or color or inappropriateness to a situation.

Second, a dictionary definition is often stated in such vague language that it provides little information. For example, *typical* is defined as "being a type." A child might ask, "a type of what?"

Third, a dictionary definition may suggest a meaning that is not intended and it may lead a child to use familiar words in unfamiliar ways. For example, the word *devious* is defined as "straying from the right course; not straight-forward." The idea of straying from a course is likely to be interpreted in a concrete, physical way. A child in middle childhood (still in the concrete operational stage, as described by Piaget) may conclude that *devious* has to do with crooked walking or getting lost.

Finally, some dictionary definitions give multiple pieces of information, but offer no guideline on how they should be integrated. Using the word *exotic* as an example, the definition is "foreign; strange; not native." A child might wonder what relationship to draw among these parts. Is something exotic if it is strange but not foreign? Or only if it is both foreign and strange?

Even in grades 5 and 6, children may not have a complete understanding of some word meanings through consulting dictionaries. For example, when students were asked to learn the meanings of *stimulate*, *usurp*, and *erode* by using a dictionary and to make sentences, they understood as follows (Nippold, 2007):

> *Mrs. Morrow <u>stimulated</u> the soup (because the dictionary definition is "<u>to stir up</u>").*
> *The thief tried to <u>usurp</u> the money from the safe (because the definition in the dictionary is "<u>to take</u>").*
> *Our family <u>erodes</u> a lot (because the definition in the dictionary is "<u>to eat out</u>")*

Given these problematic features of dictionaries, elementary school children may not be able to learn effectively from dictionary definitions. One way to remedy this is to help your students get the initial word meaning in context and provide them with opportunities to use the words or observe the use of the words.

There are, however, good dictionaries that can help children study, discover, and follow up on interesting words. Checking more than one dictionary can help children see the openness and flexibility of language. It has been suggested that using learner's dictionaries is more beneficial to children. These dictionaries are tailored to language learners and provide discursive explanations unlike traditional dictionaries. You may want to research different dictionaries (including an online dictionary and thesaurus) before you encourage your children to use them.

Practice text talk   You can help your students develop vocabulary knowledge through **text talk** (Beck and McKeown, 2001; Beck, McKeown, and Kucan, 2002) – a method that is often used for young children. However, it is useful for older children as well. Text talk is an effective vocabulary teaching method in which teachers ask students questions regarding the ideas in a text, talk about them and make connections among them as the reading moves along, thus enhancing vocabulary development. There are different ways that you can help your students engage in text talk. For example, you can ask open-ended questions that encourage your students to move beyond simple responses and actively use more words they have read in dialogues. You can use follow-up questions that aim at assisting your students in thinking by encouraging them to elaborate and develop ideas they read in a book. You can ask your students to explain challenging words. You can also help your students understand vocabulary by tapping into their past experiences and knowledge. The advantage of this approach is that you can engage your students by actively using words through speaking, which enriches and deepens their understanding of word meanings.

Your Turn

- Select a text for second graders. Identify ten words from the text and do the following:
  - Develop guiding questions for these words
  - Identify words that are connected to these words
  - Develop a word web for each of the words
- Identify the second tier words in the same text and write a plan on how to teach them, including through the text talk method.

Grammatical knowledge
Children's grammatical knowledge will help them comprehend reading materials better and communicate (including writing communication) more effectively. Hence, explicit instruction on the difficult grammatical rules is useful. However, it is important to note that the goal for helping students develop grammatical knowledge is not just knowing the grammatical rules; rather it is to help them understand that grammatical rules can facilitate effective communication. Several strategies may help make grammar teaching effective.

Teaching grammatical rules   The first step in introducing grammatical rules is to draw students' attention to the materials they are reading. During middle childhood, children begin to understand the value of rules. Therefore, it is a good time to introduce grammatical rules. You can use guiding questions such as "*Did you notice something in this sentences? What would happen if the sentence were missing an element of ___ ?*" This can be done in all content areas. Drawing students' attention to grammatical rules in their readings is an efficient way to make them notice the grammatical rules.

Model the use of grammar   Modeling the use of grammatical rules is also beneficial. As mentioned before, elementary school children tend to look up to adults, especially teachers. Therefore, you may want to model the use of grammatical rules in your own discourse.

Use grammar in meaningful communication   Grammatical rules can quickly become boring if students do not see the purpose of it. Therefore, it is important to make grammar teaching meaningful in context and provide students with ample opportunities to use grammatical rules. It is usually effective to create a situation in which children can realize the need for grammatical rules.

Incorporate grammar games   Grammar games may be interesting for children. You can either create grammar games in your particular content areas or revise traditional games such as Monopoly and add the grammatical rules. For more information on how to design grammar games, refer to the recommended readings at the end of the chapter.

Your Turn

Identify one grammatical rule that you think is important for a specific grade in elementary school. Design a grammar game that aims to help children understand the rule and give them an opportunity to use the rule. Given that instructional time is limited, can you also incorporate this game for content learning?

Syntactic complexity

Research indicates that children's language productivity and syntactic complexity are strongly influenced by the genres of speaking tasks and familiarity with the topic (Nippold, 2009). Children tend to produce more complex sentences when they talk about expository topics (e.g., explaining the rules of a favorite game) or are engaged in narratives (e.g., retelling a story) than in general everyday conversation.. Children also produce longer MLUs when talking in narrative and expository genres than when talking in a conversational genre (Nippold, 2007). Therefore, when interacting with students, try to find out their hobbies and interests and ask them to explain these to you or to their peers. In these contexts, students will be more driven to use more complex syntactic structures.

Narrative skills

Narrative competence has practical significance for school-age children. A large part of elementary school curricula involves tasks that are narrative in nature, such as storytelling, summarizing, retelling, and reporting (Hughes, McGillivray, and Schmidek, 1997). The Common Core State Standards have used narration as an educational benchmark. For instance, by Grade 2, students are expected to "tell a story or recount an experience with appropriate facts and relevant, descriptive details, speaking audibly in coherent sentences" (Mills, Watkins, and Washington, 2013; National Governors Association Center and Council of Chief State School Officers, 2010).

Moreover, children's narratives can serve as an important index for language abilities because this genre provides a naturalistic and internal complex context for examining children's language use as well as their capability in organizing, comprehending, and producing language (Mills, Watkins, and Washington, 2013).

Therefore, it is important to provide adequate support for children to develop narrative skills in elementary school years. First, you may want to support their narrative abilities in both personal and fictional narratives. **Personal narratives** are accounts that are presented about specific, real-world events that have been experienced by the narrator or someone known to the narrator. **Fictional narratives** are accounts that are presented about fabricated events and characters. Research suggests that these two types of narratives have different cognitive demands on the narrator. Content knowledge is more easily accessed in personal rather than fictional narratives because of the narrator's familiarity with the events and characters in the story (Hudson and Shapiro, 1991). You may want to provide frequent opportunities for children to not only narrate their personal experiences in life, but also their experiences in learning. For example, recount their experiences in learning number concepts and their imagination on how others (fictional characters) learn to spell words. In late elementary grades, content such as social studies will be optimal for students to use genres such as history to practice narrative skills. The key in supporting elementary children's narrative development is to help them use their daily social life and academic subject learning to develop both micro and macro narrative structures.

Also, to help elementary school children develop narrative macrostructure, use picture books. However, not all picture books will help. Research indicates that children tend to use more sophisticated language and achieve cohesion when they are presented with pictures or picture books that provide the goal, the obstacle, and the solution rather than shown pictures that provide only a sequence of events (Hoff, 2009).

Your Turn

- Identify a text in social studies for fourth graders. Ask a student to read this text and then tell you a personal narrative and fictional narrative based on the text. Record the student's narratives and analyze them. Discuss strategies that may help this student move forward in terms of his or her narrative abilities.
- Research some picture books and identify some that will help children develop better narrative macrostructure.

Practice reciprocal teaching

Reciprocal teaching (Alfassi, 1998; Brown and Palincsar, 1987; Palincsar and Brown, 1984) includes four components:

- Predicting: anticipating what points an author is apt to make later in sentences or paragraphs.
- Questioning: asking questions to check comprehension of ideas.
- Clarifying: taking steps to better understand confusing points.
- Summarizing: identifying the main ideas of a text.

The reciprocal teaching approach (some people also used the term *guided* or *mediated* reading) requires that teachers and students read a piece of text together, occasionally stopping to discuss and process the text. Initially, teachers lead the discussion and help students make predictions, ask questions, clarify issues, and summarize main ideas. Teachers then gradually relinquish the teaching role to children and let them do the above steps. Eventually, children can read and discuss a text almost independently. Box 6.5 provides some sample questions for you to consider when using the reciprocal interaction approach with your children.

Box 6.5   Sample Questions for Reciprocal Teaching

Predicting	*Questioning*	*Clarifying*	*Summarizing*
Why do you suppose the author chose the title for the book? By looking at the title, can you predict what this text/story is about? After reading this first chapter or paragraph of the book/text, what specifics do you expect to learn from the information you read? What is likely to happen next? Can you predict how the main character will react to the situation?	How does the author's use of adjectives reveal her character's emotion? How does this chapter relate or connect to your life? Are you intrigued by what you read? Why?	Are there any words or phrases that confused you? Are there any cultural or religious references that you don't understand or you would like clarification for? How might you respond in that particular situation in which the main character found himself?	What is important and/or not important in this section of the text? What do you suppose was the author's intent in this chapter? How would you characterise the overall tone of the opening section?

Reciprocal teaching provides opportunities for teachers (more skillful readers) and children (novice readers) to work together, and teachers to offer modeling and guidance for their students (McDevitt and Ormrod, 2010).

Apply shared reading

Like reciprocal teaching, shared reading involves teachers and students reading books together. This approach can be used when your students are not yet able to read independently. In shared reading teachers usually read books aloud and model fluent reading. You read the materials again and again for a few days. The focus for the first reading is for enjoyment. During the next couple of readings, you draw attention to language features and comprehension (Tompkins, 2009). The benefit of shared reading is that children are actively involved in reading. They are encouraged to make predictions and pay attention to language features.

Encourage learning to read and reading to learn

It was once thought that in early elementary school (usually grades 1–3), the major literacy-learning goal was to learn how to read and write. From the fourth grade onward, children began to use reading and writing skills to learn about content areas (such as math, history, geography, and science). We now know that learning to read and reading to learn occur concurrently from the very beginning (Gambrell, 2009).

When helping your students develop academic literacy skills, focus on using reading to learn subject content and vice versa. Provide different topics and genres for your students to read. By doing so, your students will develop literacy skills and content knowledge simultaneously.

Writing support

Competent writers need to master several important skills: they must be fluent in handwriting or keyboard use, spell accurately, have adequate vocabulary, and have acquired cognitive strategies such as how to organize ideas before starting. All these skills do not usually come naturally and they require explicit instructions.

Handwriting   It is well established that handwriting fluency influences the quality of writing (Connelly, Gee, and Walsh, 2007) and affects a child's early writing development (Graham, 2009–2010). Just as young readers must learn to decode fluently so that they can focus on comprehension, young writers must develop fluent and legible handwriting (as well as master other transcription skills such as spelling) so that they can focus on generating and organizing ideas in writing.

During middle childhood, children's fine motor skills improve greatly compared with early childhood; therefore, this is the time when you can begin formal handwriting instruction. The focus is to help children develop fluency and legibility.

Young writers typically have to cope with the multiple demands of handwriting and composing by minimizing the composing process (for example, planning and organizing). As handwriting skills become more automatic and less cognitively demanding, children can focus more on reflection and careful composition. Some researchers believe that handwriting fluency needs to occur relatively early in a child's life, because the later handwriting fluency develops, the more difficult it is for the child to move to composing (Graham, 2009–2010).

There is considerable scientific evidence demonstrating that direct handwriting teaching enhances legibility and fluency (Peck, Askov, and Fairchild, 1980). Graham (2009–2010) suggests that the basic goal of handwriting instruction is to help children develop legible writing that can be produced quickly and with little conscious attention. A critical ingredient in achieving this goal is teaching children an efficient pattern for forming individual symbols (for example, letters).

You may ask how much time is needed for handwriting teaching. It has been suggested that during kindergarten and grades 1–3, about 50 to 100 minutes a week need to be devoted to the mastery of handwriting (Graham, 2009–2010).

Effective handwriting teaching does not mean only copying and rewriting; it involves other components. For example, observing parents' and teachers' writing, tracing scripts based on models or marked directions, dictations and real-life or relevant writing all play a part. The goal of handwriting instruction is to make it a fun experience and at the same time help children develop speed and legibility.

With the increasing use of keyboard writing in children's lives, you may ask whether it is necessary to practice handwriting at all. Research on this question is not conclusive. A study conducted on 300 primary school children does suggest that handwriting speed is consistently faster than keyboarding speed across all ages. Children's compositional quality is superior in handwritten scripts as opposed to keyboarded scripts. Keyboarded scripts tend to be up to two years behind handwritten scripts in development. In addition, writing with keyboards does not necessarily lead to improvements in script quality (Connelly, Gee, and Walsh, 2007). More research is needed for us to understand how handwriting and keyboard writing can contribute to children's writing (composition) development. Nevertheless, it is beneficial to help your students develop their handwriting fluency.

Spelling strategies   Good spellers use a variety of strategies. They rely on a combination of memory, reading experience, phonological indication, grammatical knowledge, orthographic information, mental grapheme representations, and analogy (Owens, 2012). Therefore, you may want to focus on helping children develop these strategies. For example, you can deliberately draw children's attention to the relationship between spelling and meaning. You can help children analyze the internal structure of words such as affixes (prefixes, infixes, and suffixes). You can encourage children to develop self-monitoring skills in spelling by asking themselves, "*Does that word look right?*" You can encourage your students to try to spell words using their prior knowledge of words that sound the same. Mostly importantly, children should have ample opportunities to be exposed to words and their spelling (Owens, 2012).

Invented spelling   As mentioned earlier, children who are exposed to a print-rich environment often spontaneously attempt to represent words in print through invented spellings. Initially the invented spellings bear little resemblance to conventional spellings. Over time, their invented spellings become more phonologically accurate and orthographically complex (Ouellette and Sénéchal, 2008a). In other words, their invented spellings look more and more like conventional ones. In fact, children's word inventions such as *MSTR* (monster) (Sipe, 2001) and *RUDF* (Are you deaf) (Bissex, 1980) tell us about the sophistication of their understanding of the way words work.

However, children's invented spellings are often regarded as spelling errors. Research findings show us otherwise. Invented spellings spontaneously produced by children are often principle-driven rather than random mistakes (He and Wang, 2009) as shown in "*MSTR*" and "*RUDF*." Children's early attempts to experiment with putting words into print can promote and facilitate literacy development. The invented spelling created by children may allow them to explore and analyze the written codes and begin to make important associations between phonology (sound) and orthographic or symbol (word in print) representation. Moreover, research confirms that children who are better at invented spelling are better readers in early grades (Richgels, 1995).

Furthermore, research shows that children can improve their phonemic awareness after invented spelling training (Martins and Silva, 2006). Thus, during the early elementary school years, you may want to create opportunities for your students to produce words on their own and then provide feedback. Box 6.6 provides an example of how you can do this.

Box 6.6   Example of Invented Spelling Training

To train children to increase the sophistication of their naturally occurring invented English spelling, the teacher presented the training words one at a time, in both picture and oral forms. Each word was spoken out loud by the teacher at a normal speech rate. It was then repeated in a stretched manner with exaggerated articulation but with no pausing between the phonemes. The teacher said the word a third time (at a normal speech rate), and the children were asked to repeat the word out loud. The word was said a fourth time and the children were each instructed to print the word in the notebook provided. Children were instructed to print the word as they thought it would look. They were repeatedly encouraged to do their best and told that their spellings did not have to be the same as the teacher's.

After each word was printed, the teacher offered individually tailored feedback in which each invented spelling was contrasted with a teacher-generated invented spelling (just a minimal increase in sophistication). The teacher's feedback included praising the child's invented spelling and showing another way to write the word. For example, a child who spelled *eel* as *ekxn* would be shown a teacher-generated spelling with one additional level of sophistication – in this example the correct final phoneme. The teacher would thus copy the child's spelling, replacing the last letter with a conventional representation of the final phoneme (*ekxl*). Following the fourth session, feedback also included drawing the children's attention to any extra letters within their invented spellings. Finally, the corrected feedback given to the child's *ekxn* was to add the final *l* and remove the unnecessary letters, yielding *el*.

Note that the procedure of providing feedback in the form of a model with one additional element of complexity resulted in providing the conventional spelling only when the child's production was one element away from being (conventionally) correct. For example, *eel* was only provided as the corrected spelling if the child produced *el* on his or her own; here, the one additional level of sophistication is to go from the accurate phonetic spelling to the conventional form.

G. Ouellette and M. Sénéchal, "Pathway to literacy: a study of invented spelling and its role in learning to read," *Child Development*, 79(4) (2008): 899–913; G. Ouellette and M. Sénéchal, "A window into early literacy: exploring the cognitive and linguistic underpinnings of invented spelling," *Scientific Studies of Reading*,1(2) (2008): 195–219.

The result of the teacher's practice in Box 6.6 shows that invented spelling coupled with feedback encourages an analytical approach and facilitates the integration of phonological and orthographic knowledge, hence facilitating the acquisition of reading. This kind of training in children's invented spelling has been successful with Portuguese-speaking children as well (Martins and Silva, 2006).

Language-experience approach   The **language-experience approach** (LEA) is a method in which children's own words are written down by a teacher and used as materials or background for literacy instruction (for example, reading, writing, spelling, listening, and speaking). The advantage of this approach is that it is personalized, meaningful and motivating (Gregory, 2008; Shanker and Cockrum, 2009). Try to use this approach to help beginning writers (you can certainly use the same approach to help your students develop abilities in other areas such as reading).

The basic procedure of the LEA method involves the following:

- Discuss with your students what to write about.
- Brainstorm with your students about the topic, title, and content of what they want to write.
- Dictate the story that your students narrate.
- Use your students' own words.
- Read and show the version of your dictation to your students (for example, spacing between words and conventional spelling).

You can help your students decide the topic, brainstorm what should be included in the writing and then record their narratives. You can write down your students' stories (narratives) mostly based on their vocabulary and sentence structure (even though they may not be the best). You basically use your students' own versions as a base for writing instruction. There are several pluses in this approach. First, you show your students that you value their versions/ideas (this step serves as a motivation). Second, your students are more interested in looking at their own stories/narratives (this step is relevant to what they want to write) than perhaps in other topics that you would ask them to write about. Third, you can draw your students' attention to the use of vocabulary by letting them know when they have chosen good words. You can also try to model the use of more precise words. Finally, you can insert some grammatical structures that your students are not using (such as the conjunctive link *because)* by still keeping the sentences they have produced.

One word of caution in using LEA: some people noticed that children might not be eager to do their own writing because they prefer the teacher's "perfect" writing to their own childish writing (Tompkins, 2009). To avoid this situation, you may want to gradually relinquish the writing task to your students. When they become more skillful in writing, you can scaffold them to move more toward conventional writing. For example, once a student decides a topic to write about, you can negotiate what should be put in writing, suggest better ways to express ideas, and guide the child throughout the sequence of ideas and writing mechanics (such as where to put a punctuation mark). Then, you can help the student revise and edit. All these guided efforts are called shared writing: you write together with your students and provide modeling and guidance.

Writers' workshop approach   The idea of the **writers' workshop** (or writing work-shop) is a well-known approach for writing instruction developed by Calkins and her colleagues. It is designed for use in all grade levels, and each grade has its specific units of study to meet the specific developmental and curricular needs. The writing workshop emphasizes the predictable and consistent writing environment and time (Calkins, 1994). There are five components in this method (see Box 6.7).

> ## Box 6.7   Components of the Writing Workshop
>
> - Mini-lesson
> - Work time (writing and conferring)
> - Peer conferring and/or response groups
> - Share session
> - Publication celebrations
>
> Adapted from L. M. Calkins, *The Art of Teaching Writing*, new edn (Portsmouth, NH: Heinemann, 1994), pp. 188–191.

In each writing workshop, students begin with a ritual of a mini-lesson. Students usually gather in a close circle. The teacher offers something to the group for the purpose of inspiring and instructing. For example, the teacher can begin by reading something interesting to prompt writing, "I want to read you something I found interesting. After reading, I want you to go back to your desks and begin to write." Alternatively, the teacher can also begin by referring to students' own writing; for example, "Last night, I was looking through your writing and realized that many of you are struggling with something that is difficult…" The mini-lesson can end with the teacher suggesting that each student spend some time doing a particular task related to writing. For instance, the teacher may introduce a strategy that will go onto a class chart or into student notebooks for future reference.

After the mini-lesson, students will spend time working on their individual writing projects. The whole idea is that everyone writes. The teacher writes alongside students for a few minutes, then moves among individuals, and confers with them. The conferences with students are the essential part of the teaching.

Students will confer with each other in response groups and peer conferences. Peer conferences are usually student-initiated short talks about each other's work in progress. Response groups are usually formed by students at the teacher's suggestion (four or five members in each group). The response groups begin with "status of the group" reports in which each member reports in a single sentence what he or she needs that day. The facilitator of the group sets up an agenda. For example, "Today we will help Tom get ideas for his writing." The student who is being helped will talk about his writing. The group will serve as a sounding board. At the end of each response group session, each group member will tell the group in a sentence what he or she will do before the group meets again.

The sharing session usually begins after the entire class has gathered. There are two purposes: one is to share as well as support work in progress, and the other is for the purpose of public, teacher-supported conferences. By participating in this session, students will learn how to confer with each other in one-to-one peer conferences. One format can be that each of three or four children takes a turn siting in the author's chair, reading aloud notebook entries or a draft and soliciting responses from listeners. Another format can be that the group shares its process of writing, such as how they brainstormed together on what individual writers could do when they got stuck. These formats provide models for what students can do in their response groups and peer conferences.

Finally, throughout the year, students come together to publish and celebrate their finished work at regular intervals. Parents, siblings, and grandparents can be invited for the celebration.

For more information about the writing workshop, please check the references listed at the end of this chapter.

Your Turn

Discuss the advantages of the writing workshop approach in helping students develop literacy abilities.

Learning to write and writing to learn   Promoting writing can help your students learn and develop in many areas. For example, writing can help children learn to read. Thus, when children write or observe you writing, you can purposefully help them pay attention to how letters form words, how words form sentences, and how words make meanings. You can help your students think about sequence, cause and effect, and other reading comprehension skills (Lamme, 1984).

Writing can help your students learn how to plan and make decisions. You can discuss how to plan writing and help your students think about not only what they want to write about, but also how they will write about it, who will read it and which words will communicate more effectively.

Writing can also help your students learn to become sensitive to the views of others. For example, when writing to someone else, a student may need to think about his audience's views. He has to be able to see another person's point of view to communicate effectively.

Finally, you can help your students express their emotions through writing. Children can learn to use writing as a medium to express their emotions and vent frustrations as well as anger in a more constructive way.

Your Turn

Review the language and literacy standards for the elementary grades in the common core standards (http://www.corestandards.org) and discuss how you can use the supporting strategies proposed in this chapter to achieve the common core expectations.

Retelling procedure as a comprehensive support for literacy development

The **retelling procedure** is an effective way to engage children in literacy learning by asking them to "spill over" what they read or what they hear when read to (Brown and Cambournes, 1990). The retelling procedure helps children develop their literacy abilities in listening, reading, speaking, thinking and writing simultaneously. The approach is easy to implement and can be used with children throughout the middle childhood period.

There are four forms of retelling. You can use any of them when you engage your students in content learning activities.

- *Oral-to-oral retelling* A child listens to a teacher reading aloud a text and then retells it orally.
- *Oral-to-written retelling* A child listens to a teacher reading aloud a text and then retells it in writing.
- *Written-to-oral retelling* A child reads a text and retells it orally.
- *Written-to-written retelling* A child reads a text and retells it in writing.

You can begin by either reading to your students or asking them to read a text; they then tell you either orally or in writing what they have heard or read. You can remind them to relax and not to worry about spelling and neatness. The goal is to tell or write whatever they are able to. Initially, your students' retelling (orally or in writing) may be very brief. Over time, their writing will become more sophisticated. You can also model the procedure by retelling the text yourself (orally or in written form). After your students retell, you may ask them to reread or relisten to the original texts and compare their version with the original texts (note that the purpose is not to make students feel bad about their version, but to expose them to a more sophisticated version). To avoid boredom, you can vary your request of their retelling by asking them to retell the texts to their peers.

Students who are immersed in the retelling procedure can gradually spill over the vocabulary, phrases, sentences and other "accouterments" of the text structure. This process in approaching literacy learning is natural in the sense that it is similar to how a child acquires oral language in a natural learning environment (Brown and Cambournes, 1990; Wang, 2011a).

Your Turn

Help a student in early elementary grades retell a text to you in any content area, using one of the four forms of retelling in the above session. Model the approach introduced. Share your experience in a group.

Hypertext use

Just because children are more motivated to read hypertext than conventional print, it does not mean that they know how to do it effectively. Research suggests that conventional reading strategies that are effective for reading a specific block of text (lexia) do not necessarily apply to reading hypertexts. When readers click on a hyperlink, it takes them to another lexia whose structure and content may be different from those of the lexia with which they began. Readers of hypertext continually face decisions about which hyperlink to click on next and why, and they are forced to make associations among lexias and create their own narratives as they go (McNabb, 2005–2006). Thus, you need to closely monitor students' hypertext reading activities to ensure that they help promote their literacy development. McNabb (2005–2006) suggested the following strategies for teachers to help students in reading hypertexts.

Suitable web sources   You need to spend time finding information on the internet before you give online assignments to students. You also need to thoroughly preview available web resources and find suitable web sources for your students, tapping into their developmental and reading abilities.

Guidance   Providing guidance while students initially engage in hypertext reading is important. For example, ask students to make predictions about what information various available links might lead to. You can call on students to summarize the meaning of texts on a single web page and to verbalize the associations they make as they move from one text-link to another. You can also model how to use the rich context of online hypertext to expand their knowledge of specialized words beyond those found in grade-level textbooks.

Monitoring   You need to monitor your students' online reading processes and intervene when you see a student becoming frustrated or taking an incoherent reading path. You need to watch for clues about whether or not their online reading leads to comprehension. Students who are monitoring their comprehension online will typically behave in ways that show that they are thinking about their reading choices, such as systematically assessing a website's breadth by visiting all the lexias one node away from the home page or backtracking when their narrative sequence no longer makes sense. Students should be able, when asked, to meaningfully summarize what they have read and why. You can use these clues as evidence that each student is actively monitoring his or her comprehension online. If a student clicks on links in seemingly random order, then that student may have underdeveloped hypertext comprehension-monitoring skills or lack the memory capacity to stay focused on a specific reading purpose during online time. Poor hypertext readers will often look perplexed when asked what they are reading. To monitor student online reading, you can create student login accounts and then access their search history through Google by going to www.google.com/searchhistory/login. Or if working in a password-protected collaborative learning environment, it may be possible to track each student's link log of hypertexts visited online. You can assign students to annotate their search history or link logs and explain the basis for their reading choices. This assignment could be paired with a short essay or oral presentation in which each student explains what he or she has read online. Information about how a reader selects from and connects the many reading options available online provides valuable data about that reader's comprehension-monitoring strategies, or lack thereof.

Once you identify a student who is struggling to read well online, you (the teacher) or a trained reading buddy can sit with that student and scaffold his comprehension monitoring during online reading tasks. For example, you can model how to think aloud and make semantic connections while navigating different lexias on a given topic. Once the student understands this strategy, you can observe the student's own navigational path without interrupting or making a judgment until the logic of his choices starts to break down. At that point, it is best to intervene by demonstrating how a more advanced reader would approach the same hypertext reading task.

Your Turn

Use the strategies recommended by McNabb and design a lesson plan that will help your students (you can decide a grade level) to read an assigned hypertext.

Critical literacy

The essence of teaching and learning critical literacy is about asking questions, seeking answers and challenging the status quo in an effort to discover alternative perspectives for self and social development (Kim, 2012). Therefore, you can help students develop critical literacy ability by providing them with opportunities to gain access to contradictory information and to deconstruct a wide range of texts. For elementary students, you can point out how certain words and ideas are used by the author to achieve a social or political purpose.

Also, reading online can give students new opportunities to identify biased language or compare different authors' perspectives on a topic. The rich, interactive multimedia context offered by online hypertext can enhance students' comprehension and build new knowledge that is complex or difficult to acquire from linear print alone. The multimedia features of online text illustrate meaning through audio, video, graphic, and kinetic text expressions as well as the printed word. Online readers can choose among vast resources for meaning making, which puts content control in the hands of students to a much greater degree than does a print-based curriculum. This requires you (teacher) to add strategies to your reading instruction so that students, instead of surfing aimlessly, effectively use that control.

Your Turn

- Select a text among the readings that teachers assign to elementary students. Analyze the text with a critical literacy lens. Try to answer the following questions:
  - Is this text politically or culturally neutral? Explain.
  - What messages are explicitly conveyed and what are not?

  If you have to use this text for your students, what questions do you ask to help them develop critical literacy abilities?
- Alternatively, locate a hypertext on the internet and check its suitability for a specific elementary grade level. Construct a series of questions that will help students develop hypertext critical skills.
- Locate a science text used in an elementary grade. Discuss in a group how you can use this text to help elementary students develop critical literacy ability.

So far, you have read many strategies for elementary children to develop language and literacy, including academic language and literacy. It is, however, important to note that no one strategy will be successful for all children all the time. Applying the above-proposed strategies eclectically may be more beneficial.

Summary of Key Points

- During middle childhood, children are able to pronounce almost all the sounds in their ambient language. However, they may still have difficulties with some longer words, consonant duration, rhythmic patterns, and word endings, rapid naming, and phonological awareness.
- Children's vocabulary increases more rapidly during middle childhood than in early childhood. These major increases occur in three areas: lexical diversity, lexical complexity, and lexical density. New words are learned through context, fast-mapping, syntactic and semantic clues, and quick incidental learning (QUIL). Children's definitions of words become more literate and explicit, and they understand that words have more than one meaning.
- The major morphological development in middle childhood includes the use of the derivational prefix and the derivational suffix. Throughout the school years, mass and count nouns are acquired slowly, and children begin to pick up verb tenses,

like the perfect and irregular past tense, as well as modal auxiliary verbs and some forms of modality. In addition, grammatical structure becomes increasingly complex during middle childhood, as children add to their repertoire noun phrases, adverbial and subordinate clauses, passive forms, conjunctive links, and more language variation in the form of embedded and passive sentences.

- The pragmatic use of language is the area that experiences the most dramatic linguistic growth for elementary school children. As they are held accountable for their responses, they must use precise language in a classroom setting, and have to seek specific recognition from their teacher. Children also use narratives to socialize, remember events, and read and write, and their stories become more complex and coherent as their story grammar and comprehension-monitoring skills improve.

- During middle childhood, children make significant progress in their metalinguistic competence, as shown in the advancement of their phonological awareness, knowledge of word formations, and comprehension of figurative language like metaphors, similes, hyperboles, idioms, irony, and proverbs.

- Children in the first and second grades enter the initial period of reading. They can identify specific words in the printed form, such as names, labels, sight words, and high meaning words. They can also decode orthographically regular multisyllabic words and nonsense words. From grades 2 to 5, children enter the transitional period of reading. They are able to use letter–sound correspondence knowledge and structure analysis to decode print, but they are not yet fluent readers. They are able to read and comprehend both fiction and nonfiction that is appropriately designed for their levels. In essence, elementary children are learning to read, but at the same time, they also read to learn.

- At first, structures for writing and speaking are very similar in young children, but gradually, their writing becomes more automatic as well as complex, coherent, and organized. By 9 or 10 years old, children's writing is free of many of the features of speech.

- Reading hypertexts requires students to develop sophisticated comprehension-monitoring abilities that involve reviewing, evaluating, and synthesizing various lexias. Teacher guidance is important in orienting online reading assignments.

- Academic literacy requires that a student be able to coordinate multiple abilities in listening, viewing, inferring, thinking, understanding, speaking, writing, reading, expressing, and critiquing.

- Subjects such as science, where the textbooks are highly expository and include a high volume of academic terms, require that students be more proficient in the academic register for comprehension.

- Some children have an easier time adjusting to academic language because their home language is similar to the teacher's. Those who speak AAE need to learn to code-switch to MAE for academic success.

- To support children's literacy development during early elementary grades, teachers must focus on enhancing phonological skills by training children in letter and sound associations as well as building vocabulary knowledge through teaching words via word webs; introducing children to synonyms and antonyms; and employing the text talk approach, among other methods.

- Teaching grammatical knowledge also helps children expand their academic literacy, as do picture books, good spelling strategies, and exposure to narrative and expository genres.
- Reading together through reciprocal teaching and shared reading are effective methods for getting students to think about material in a deeper, active, more independent way.
- In order for students to become good writers, children must first be explicitly taught good handwriting in middle childhood, when motor skills become more refined, so that they can focus on generating ideas rather than keeping their penmanship neat.
- Using the writers' workshop approach is an authentic way to help children move forward in their writing development.
- The retelling procedure is an effective way to help children develop their literacy abilities in listening, reading, speaking, thinking and writing simultaneously.
- There are three strategies that can help students read hypertexts in the classroom environment: finding suitable web sources, providing guidance to students, and monitoring students' online reading processes.
- Helping students develop critical literacy abilities through conventional print and hypertexts can provide them with new opportunities to identify biases in authors' works, offer them the chance to question writers' perspectives, and put content control in their own hands.

Key Terms

Academic language register
Antonyms
Apprenticeship
Appropriate
Code-switching
Comprehension monitoring
Count nouns
C-unit
Decentration
Derivational prefix
Derivational suffix
Expository text
Fictional narratives
Gerunds
Hypertext
Language-experience approach
Lexias
Lexical complexity
Lexical density
Lexical diversity

Mass nouns
Metacognition
Non-egocentrism
Participles
Personal narratives
Polysemous
Quick incidental learning
Rapid naming
Reading fluency
Retelling procedure
Scaffolding
Social language register
Story grammar
Synonyms
Text talk
T-unit
Word web
Writers' workshop (or writing
    workshop)

Notes

1. It is important to note that a T-unit is one main clause with all the subordinate clauses and nonclausal phrases attached to or embedded in it. All the coordinate clauses are separated out into separate T-units, unless they contain a co-referential subject deletion in the second clause (e.g., "*She swings and misses*"). Clauses that begin with the coordinating conjunctions *and*, *but*, and *or* would be considered to comprise a new T-unit (Paul, 2007, p. 587).
2. Expository text is a text that explains things.

Recommended Further Readings

Calkins, L. M. (1994). *The Art of teaching Writing.* New edn. Portsmouth, NH: Heinemann.
Calkins, L. M. (2011). *A Curriculum Plan for the Writing Workshop.* Portsmouth, NH: Heinemann.
Johnson, E. R. (2009). *Academic Language! Academic Literacy! A Guide for K-12 Educators.* Thousand Oaks, CA: Corwin.
Rinvolucri, M. (1996). *Grammar Games: Cognitive, Affective and Drama Activities for EFL Students.* Cambridge: Cambridge University Press.

7

Learning a New Language in Middle Childhood

Prereading Questions and Activities

- Video- or audio-record a speech sample of a child who acquired English during early childhood and a child who acquired English in middle childhood (to prompt the narration, you can give the children a topic such as "What did you do last weekend?"). Do you notice any difference between these two children? If so, identify the specific areas of difference with regard to phonology, lexicon, semantics, morphology, syntax, pragmatics, and metalinguistic knowledge.
- Obtain a writing sample of a student who is learning English as a new language in third, fourth, or fifth grade. Analyze the sample and identify the student's strengths (e.g., funds of knowledge) and needs (areas that need support). In what ways does this analysis help you?
- Use the same sample from above. Identify and analyze the errors the student made. What kind of error patterns have you found? Make an educated guess whether these errors are related to the student's L1.
- Why do students have different levels of success in learning a new language? What could be the factors that contribute to the learning differences?
- Identify the challenges of school-age children who are acquiring a new language and at the same time using the Ln for academic learning.
- What types of support do school-age children need to acquire and develop a new language?

Topics to Be Addressed in This Chapter

- Learning a Ln in middle childhood
  - Changes in L1 and Ln configuration
  - Important issues regarding learning English as a Ln in middle childhood
    - Language learning in home and school

- Brain capacity change
- Variations among Ln learners
- Interlanguage
- Language stabilization phenomenon
- Selective attention
- The explicit nature of Ln learning
- Markedness and unmarkedness
- Competence variety
- Discrepancy between Ln competence and performance
- Cross-linguistic interaction and skill transfer
- Deductive-inductive learning
- Individual factors
- Developmental sequence in Ln learning
- Specific features of English
- Developing a Ln in middle childhood
  - Phonological development
  - Lexical-semantic development
  - Morphosyntactic development
  - Pragmatic development
  - Metalinguistic development
- Developing literacy and academic literacy in a Ln
- Strategies for supporting academic language and literacy development in a new language

Learning Objectives

After completing this chapter, you should be able to do the following:

- Understand the changing configuration between children's L1 (home language) and the Ln (school language).
- Understand the distinctive characteristics of acquiring a language before and after the language acquisition sensitive period.
- Understand the important aspects that are related to Ln learning:
  - The brain is adaptable to learning a Ln beyond the sensitive period
  - Learning a Ln in middle childhood is different from early childhood, and many aspects of a Ln may need to be explicitly taught
  - The marked form in a Ln may be difficult to acquire
  - Ln learners may exhibit competency in a variety of areas
  - A learner's competence in the Ln may not manifest in her actual performance

- ○ L1 may interact with Ln and Ln learners may transfer L1 skills in Ln learning
  - ○ Ln learners may use deductive and inductive learning
  - ○ Ln learning may be influenced by individual differences in cognitive ability, aptitude, motivation, attitude, identity, personality, and learning styles and strategies.
- Understand phonological characteristics in learning a Ln.
- Understand the connections between developing phonological, lexical-semantic, morphosyntactic, and pragmatic knowledge in a Ln and academic language and literacy skills.
- Understand how metalinguistic knowledge as a result of being exposed to more than one language can potentially help Ln learners acquire academic language and literacy.
- Know how to use effective strategies to support students' Ln development.

Learning a Ln in Middle Childhood

More than 57 million American households (20 percent) with children over the age of 5 speak in a language other than English. Among which, Spanish is spoken in more than 35 million of these households (60 percent) (US Census Bureau, 2012). Thus, when these children enter our educational system, they present a linguistically and culturally diverse population that one cannot ignore.

In this chapter, we focus on children who have already developed their first language(s) or home language(s) and are beginning to learn English as a Ln in the elementary school environment. Before we discuss the specifics of Ln phonological, lexical-semantic, morphosyntactic, pragmatic, and metalinguistic development, several aspects related to Ln learning warrant our attention.

Changes in linguistic configuration

Typically, all children's linguistic environment changes when they enter elementary school. However, the change for children who are learning a Ln (in our case, English) is more drastic. The changes for these children bear several characteristics. First, over time, there is a change in the quantity configuration of these children's home language(s) and their Ln (English). As children progress in elementary school, they spend more time outside of the home and have increased exposure to English and English-speaking peers and decreased exposure to their home language(s). Second, there is a change in the input quality between their home language(s) and English. The home language input by parents is usually casual and mostly in spoken form; mistakes made by children are rarely corrected (with a few exceptions; see Wang, 2008). However, children's language is closely monitored by their teachers in school; formal language is learned not only in spoken form, but also in written form. As children move up in grades, writing increases. Third, children will increasingly receive a variety of other adult English inputs when they participate in social activities such as extracurricular activities. As a result of these changes, some children may experience **language attrition** (gradual loss of language abilities) in their home language(s). However, about 75 percent of these children may continue their home language development (Hoff, 2009, p. 309).

Your Turn

Besides the changes in the linguistic environment of Ln-learning children discussed above, can you think about some other changes in their linguistic environment?

Important issues regarding learning English as a Ln in middle childhood

There is a qualitative difference between children who learn a Ln in middle childhood versus those who learn in early childhood. As discussed in Chapters 2, 3, and 4, children who are exposed to one or more linguistic system during early childhood typically have an optimum chance of developing native-like competence in all language aspects without much effort (Meisel, 2006, p. 105). However, the optimum language-learning window begins to close in between the ages of 5 and 10, and the sensitive period in language acquisition gradually phases out in middle childhood (in the age range of 7 to 10) (Meisel, 2006). Following are some important characteristics of Ln language development.

Different language-learning environment
Acquiring a language in the school setting in middle childhood is different from acquiring a language (L1) in the home environment in early childhood. In the school environment, children not only have to engage themselves in the complex process of learning a language to interact with others both socially and academically, but they also have to understand and master various academic subjects. In contrast, the L1 language acquisition in the home environment focuses mainly on daily communication.

Brain's capacity change
Although at this moment we are unable to exactly pinpoint the timing of brain change, as discussed in Chapter 2, published literature suggests that the brain's capacity to acquire a language may be qualitatively different before 5 and thereafter. For example, the brain completes its lateralization around age 5 (H. Brown, 2000). It is likely that the gradual change in the brain's capacity may influence how children acquire a new language in middle childhood. It is important to stress that the window of opportunity to learn a new language does not shut abruptly, and recent brain research suggests that the brain has a lot more adaptability than we used to think. Therefore, those

children who begin to learn English (Ln) in the school environment can still develop proficiency in the language.

Variations among Ln learners

There tends to be great variation among Ln learners. That is, Ln learners tend to be from different cultural and linguistic communities. As you read in Box 0.1 in the opening chapter, the students in Peter's class came from a variety of backgrounds: White American, African American, Chinese, Thai, Tongan, Haitian, Ecuadoran, Mexican, Iranian, and Sudanese. Even though these students are all Ln learners, their cultural and linguistic differences may pose different challenges to English learning.

Interlanguage

The new language development process of Ln learners may be unique. This process is often referred to as **interlanguage** (IL). IL is a language learner's inner linguistic system in which the learner has not yet become fully proficient in the Ln. IL is a unique language developing process between the learner's L1 and the Ln (or target language). Some believe that IL has its own right to be regarded as a linguistic system, and it is Ln learner's own version of the target language (e.g., Selinker, 1972).

Language-learning stabilization phenomenon

Ln learners may experience an interesting phenomenon called **fossilization** (learners enter into a plateau and do not make further progress in language learning), whereas this does not usually happen among L1 learners. Ln learners' interlanguage continues to exist regardless of further exposure to the target language. Because it is difficult to determine when learning has ceased, this phenomenon is now often referred to as **stabilization**. Some believe that there is no solid research evidence at the moment to support the idea of fossilization and the focus should really be on stabilization (e.g., Long, 2003).

Selective attention

Learning a new language requires selective attention. Without selective attention, new language development will not take place. Ln learners need to notice the mismatch between the Ln input and their own organization of the new/target language (Gass and Selinker, 2001). Therefore, Ln learners who have a better ability in selective attention are likely to master the Ln more effectively.

The explicit nature of Ln learning

It has been proposed that there are three types of learning: implicit, explicit, and instructed learning. **Implicit learning** is a non-conscious and automatic abstraction of structure. In **explicit learning**, learners search for information and test hypotheses. **Instructed learning** occurs through explicit teaching (Ellis, 1994). L1 acquisition is mostly an unconscious operation (implicit learning), and Ln learning is mostly conscious learning. In Ln learning, learners need to search for the Ln structure, and many aspects of the Ln need to be taught explicitly.

Markedness and unmarkedness in a Ln

In general, the marked forms in a Ln are difficult to learn. **Markedness** refers to the aspects in a language that are difficult in comparison to more common or regular forms. For instance, the irregular verbs used in the past tense in English such as "went" and "took" are marked (i.e., difficult for English Ln learners), while regular verbs used in the past tense such as "worked" and "liked" are unmarked (i.e., easier for English Ln learners). Thus, it is likely that children who are learning English as a Ln in middle childhood will find it harder to learn the marked forms in English than to learn the unmarked ones.

Your Turn

Identify a list of marked forms in English in the areas of phonology, lexicon, semantics, morphology, syntax, and pragmatics. Think about how these marked forms can pose difficulties for students who are learning English as a Ln.

Competence variety

When looking at the language competence or proficiency of Ln learners, we should be mindful of the different competencies these learners develop in a broader sense. We may want to identify their competence by specifically looking at academic language competence (context-reduced) and basic interpersonal communication competence (context-embedded) (H. Brown, 2000). It is likely that Ln learners may initially demonstrate strength in one, but not both areas. Looking at competence in different areas may help us focus on differentiated assistance in a specific area, including linguistic competence (knowledge in the areas of phonology, lexicon, semantics, morphology, and syntax), discourse competence (connecting sentences to a meaningful whole orally and in writing), sociolinguistic competence (knowledge of the sociocultural rules of a language and discourse and using them successfully in the sociocultural communicative context), and strategy competence (the ability to make repairs by both verbal and nonverbal means to cope with imperfect knowledge and sustain communication) (H. Brown, 2000).

Your Turn

How do you interpret the point made in the above section about recognizing and differentiating Ln learners' competence in various areas in the context of teaching?

Discrepancy between Ln competence and performance

In Chapter 4, we observed that there is a discrepancy between a learner's competence and performance. We now extend this further and argue that competence and performance represent different abilities of a language learner. Competence is what speakers know about a language, and performance is what speakers actually do in the use of a language. An inability to perform in a Ln does not necessarily indicate a lack of competence in the Ln. It is likely that an English-language learner knows the rule to add -*s* in the third person, present tense in "She *works* at the clothing store," yet in actual performance, he may omit the -*s*. Because Ln learners have passed the sensitive period of language acquisition, it may be challenging for them to perform marked English grammatical features in oral communication, which requires quick real-time production. However, in written forms, Ln learners will have time to correct their errors with teacher scaffolding.

Your Turn

What is the teaching implication of a learner's competence and performance in learning a language?

Cross-linguistic influence

We discussed cross-linguistic interaction in Chapter 4 for children with more than one L1. In that chapter, we discussed the difference between cross-linguistic interaction and cross-linguistic influence (or cross-linguistic interference and cross-linguistic transfer). We used cross-linguistic interaction in Chapter 4 to describe the relationship between young children's different L1 acquisition. In this chapter, we are discussing children who have already acquired their L1 and are adding English as a Ln. In this case, language influence, language interference, and language transfer are more accurate terms to describe the process.

Students who are acquiring a Ln in middle childhood often experience cross-linguistic influence. The influence (or transfer) often occurs from their L1 to the Ln. L1 influence can happen in all language areas: phonetics, phonology, lexicon, semantics, morphology, syntax, semantics, and pragmatics. Perhaps two areas of transfer are most noticeable: "accent" and "vocabulary." For example, in Japanese, there is only one alveolar liquid (a sound represented in English transcription of Japanese as /r/). The English phonological system has two alveolar liquids, /r/ and /l/. It is likely a Japanese student learning English may have difficulty in distinguishing between /r/ and /l/. Also, Ln may have semantic transfer as a result of **false friends** (words that seem to be related, but are not). A case in point is the Spanish word *embarazada* (pregnant) and the English word *embarrassed* (S. Brown and Attardo, 2008).

Many people believe that L1 transfer is a barrier for learning a Ln. It is important to stress that while L1 transfer can interfere with Ln learning (in particular, when forms in L1 and Ln are not matched), it can also facilitate Ln learning via learners' linguistic funds of knowledge from L1. Many skills that Ln learners developed in learning their L1 can help them learn the Ln.

Moreover, students' L1 transfer can provide us with a window into their error patterns and help us target these mistakes more effectively in teaching. In fact, it has been argued that depending on the similarities of the languages, the knowledge transferred from L1 in the areas of phonological, lexical-semantic, or grammatical forms can serve as a useful basis for communication in a new language (E. White, Genesee, and Steinhauer, 2012).

One note of caution: even though the transfer from L1 to Ln is frequent, recent research suggests that transfer from Ln to L1 also occurs. In fact, Ln learning can have a huge impact on L1 (e.g., on lexical use). In extreme cases, significant influence of Ln on L1 may result in language attrition in the L1 (loss of productive use of L1) or shift the dominance from L1 to Ln (Li, 2013).

Your Turn

Revisit the error patterns you identified in the writing sample you collected in the Pre-reading Questions and Activity section. Can you try to guess the child's L1 interaction in his or her English?

Deductive-inductive dichotomy

Deductive language learning means to learn the general rules (whole) first and then learn the specific instances (parts). **Inductive language learning** refers to the process in which learners learn the specific instances (parts) and then the general rules (whole). Most children learn their first language by using the inductive learning approach (first learn sounds, then words, then sentences, and so forth), although some researchers believe the opposite. In Ln learning, learners may employ both strategies. Studies in the past seem to suggest that Ln learners whose left brain is dominant prefer a deductive style of teaching, and learners whose right brain is dominant tend to perform better with the inductive teaching style (H. Brown, 2000). Future research may provide more insight on this issue. However, sensitivity to the possible language-learning tendency in Ln Learners may help us address their language-learning needs better.

Individual differences in learning a Ln

Intelligence   There is a correlation between IQ and language aptitude test scores (0.60).[1] Although some suggest that IQ scores can only demonstrate an individual's cognitive or academic skills, but not his ability to communicate (S. Brown and Attardo, 2008), it seems that when students have a higher IQ score, they are likely to succeed better in learning a Ln. However, when they have a low IQ score (e.g., children with Down syndrome), language-learning is possible, but the quality may be compromised.

Aptitude   **Aptitude** means the cognitive ability which allows an individual to learn easily and quickly. Aptitude contains four aspects (see Box 7.1).

Box 7.1   Components of Aptitude

- Phonemic coding ability: the ability to associate sounds with symbols (such as letters).
- Grammatical sensitivity: the ability to recognize how words function grammatically in sentences.
- Inductive language learning: the ability to infer grammatical rules from language examples.
- Rote-learning ability: the ability to form and remember associations between sounds and meaning.

Modified from J. B. Carroll, "Cognitive abilities in foreign language aptitude: then and now," in T. S. Parry and C. W. Stansfield (eds), *Language Aptitude Reconsidered* (Englewood Cliffs, NJ: Prentice Hall, 1990), pp. 11–29.

It seems that there is a relatively high correlation between a learner's aptitude and his language aptitude test scores (0.40–0.60), although, as noted above, some believe that aptitude only demonstrates an individual's cognitive or academic skills, but not her ability to communicate (S. Brown and Attardo, 2008).

Motivation, identity, and attitude   As mentioned in Chapter 2, motivation and identity play a role in language learning. The effect may be more evident in learning a Ln. Integrated motivation shows the desire to become part of the Ln-speaking community, and instrumental motivation is to learn a Ln for practical necessity, such as passing exams and obtaining a degree. However, integrative motivation may initially be more favorable in learning a Ln than instrumental motivation. Nevertheless, instrumental motivation sometimes can facilitate a Ln learning, despite the fact that the learner may not have a favorable attitude toward the new language. There are also two other types of motivation: resultative motivation and intrinsic motivation. **Resultative motivation** emerges when learners begin to improve their Ln skills, and **intrinsic motivation** comes from within the students and is closely related to their genuine interest in learning the Ln.

Personality factors   A variety of personal factors can also play a role in learning a new language. First, when a student is outgoing and social, he is more likely to initiate contact with peers and teachers, thus creating more opportunities to use the Ln. Second, if a student is a risk-taker, she will initiate interactions with others more and have more opportunity to practice the Ln. Third, a student's ability to tolerate ambiguity is also important. **Ambiguity tolerance** means to avoid worrying about situations in which there are mixed messages (S. Brown and Attardo, 2008). Fourth, a person's ability to change may also affect Ln learning. Research shows that when a person is flexible, he is likely to develop a better accent in the Ln (S. Brown and Attardo, 2008). Fifth, a person's degree of inhibition is also important in Ln learning. If a student is too self-conscious about her mistakes, she is likely to avoid talking to others in the Ln. Finally,

affective filters (affects, feelings, emotions, and moods) can affect a person's performance in a new language. Affective filters determine which language models to adopt, which part of the language will be attended to, when attempts at acquisition will stop, and how fast a learner will acquire a Ln. If a student has anxiety toward using the Ln, that anxiety will block his ability to learn a language (S. Brown and Attardo, 2008).

Your Turn

Shadow a Ln learner in an upper elementary grade in a classroom for a few days. Identify the personal factors discussed above. Discuss how these personal factors can support and hinder a student's progress in learning a Ln.

Learning styles and strategies   As a result of the socialization process and various other complex reasons, learners may approach Ln learning with different styles and strategies; some may be more analytical, others may be more holistic, and still others may prefer to learn orally or visually. Being sensitive about these differences and learning approaches may help you reach these learners effectively.

Your Turn

Observe a Ln learner in the classroom setting. Try to understand how the learner approaches a problem. Characterize this learner's problem-solving strategies.

Developmental sequence   There are several developmental stages that Ln learners may go through. These stages should not be viewed as a disadvantage (see Box 7.2); rather they should be treated as the active language learning process. In addition, not all Ln learners show these characteristics.

Box 7.2   Possible New-Language Learning Sequence

- **Silent period** Some Ln learners may stay silent for a while when they are first exposed to the Ln. However, they are listening and learning.
- **Simplification and formulas period** Ln learners use one- or two-word utterances like "me no __" to communicate. They use the key words and omit the grammatical markers. They also memorize chunks of language such as "Can I have ___?" to communicate their basic needs.
- **Unpacking period** Ln learners begin to analyze the memorized chunks and break them down into Ln (target language) grammar.

Modified from S. Brown and S. Attardo, *Understanding Language Structure, Interaction, and Variation* (Ann Arbor: University of Michigan Press, 2008), p. 219.

Specific language features of English   English is a **deep orthography**; that is, the grapheme–phoneme (letter–sound) relationships are not always transparent, and thus are difficult to learn (e.g., the word *cough* is an example of an opaque relationship of sound and spelling). In English, a single sound can be graphically represented by more than one letter, and it can represented by different letters or letter combinations in different words (inconsistent spelling). Moreover, a given letter or combination of letters may represent more than one sound, and there are numerous exceptions and irregular words (Nijakowska, 2008). Consequently, language learners from other linguistic systems, especially those who are used to an orthographically transparent system, will find English difficult to learn.

Your Turn

Identify a list of English words where their sounds and letters mismatch. Discuss how these words would pose challenges for Ln learning students.

Ln Development in the School Environment

Phonological development

As a result of acquiring a Ln after the sensitive period, many children (with increased age of acquisition) tend to have cross-linguistic interaction in pronunciation. That is, the influence of phonological features such as an accent in one language will be heard in the other language. Ingram (1981) suggested that many Ln learners process the Ln via their L1 by retaining the phonological system of their L1, whereas children who acquire more than one language simultaneously (or multilingual first language learners) tend not to have this issue. However, the study by Wang (2008) reported that even though there were no cross-linguistic interactions between the children's trilingual phonology during the early multilingual acquisition period, their Chinese tones went through some changes as a result of more exposure to English. In particular, they began to show some signs of problems in pronouncing the third tone (the falling-rising tone), although not to the point of unintelligibility. Some researchers suggest that Chinese tones are especially fragile for children learning Chinese in an English-speaking environment (Erbaugh, 1992).

The impact of the cross-linguistic influence in accent for children in middle childhood is less distinct than during adolescence (see Chapter 10). Many children who acquire English in middle childhood can still develop a native-like or near native-like accent.

Lexical-semantic development

Vocabulary development discrepancy

When Ln learners enter school, their lexical knowledge in their L1 and Ln may have discrepancies. For example, a child may know a lot of words related to math in his Ln and a lot of words related to kitchen terms in his home language (L1). This is called **distributed characteristic of multilingual word learning** (Oller, 2005). Ln learners' home language vocabulary may stagnate when entering school. Unless enrichment in the home language continues through trips to places where the home language is spoken or through book reading, Ln learners will have less vocabulary in their home language(s) (De Houwer 2009; Wang, 2008).

Vocabulary discrepancy is also evident in Ln learners' receptive and expressive lexicon. It has been suggested that vocabulary growth may show in comprehension (receptive lexicon) before production (expressive lexicon). A discrepancy between receptive and expressive vocabulary growth has been commonly reported in monolingual lexical acquisition (Bates, Bretherton, and Snyder, 1988) as well as in children who are exposed to more than one linguistic system. A study examined the vocabulary growth of 147 primarily English-language-learning (ELL) preschool children following one year of attendance in Head Start. The children demonstrated significant gains in receptive vocabulary on a standardized measure but did not demonstrate comparable gains in expressive vocabulary (Barnett et al., 2007). This asymmetry of vocabulary development has also been noted by other studies in the past, which found greater initial linguistic crossover from L1 to Ln for receptive tasks than for expressive tasks. Production tasks in Ln required more lexical experience to support lexical acquisition (Magiste, 1979).

Language-specific lexical development rate
Although Ln learners' abilities in one language are related to their abilities in the other language(s) in most areas, vocabulary development often seems lopsided. For example, research in bilingual Spanish–English children suggests that children with higher vocabulary skills in English tend to have lower abilities in Spanish and vice versa (Tabors, Páez, and López, 2003).

Similarly, Ln learners' vocabulary seems to be associated with a particular language. For instance, research found that bilingual English–Spanish children's English expressive vocabulary was strongly associated with their English letter–word identification abilities, and Spanish expressive vocabulary predicted Spanish letter–word identification abilities. This research also showed cross-linguistic influence of children's phonological awareness abilities but not vocabulary abilities. That is, children's English vocabulary did not predict their Spanish letter–word identification abilities, and their Spanish vocabulary did not affect their English letter–word identification abilities. Therefore, language-specific relationships occur between vocabulary and reading outcomes (Lindsey, Manis, and Bailey, 2003).

Children who learn English as a Ln in the school environment may have challenges in their English lexicon development. For instance, a study shows that despite six years of formal schooling in English, including focused English as a Ln support, bilingual students from both Vietnamese and Samoan cultural backgrounds performed less well than their peers in their understanding and use of the English lexicon. This is perhaps because their language performance is affected by their different language experiences, such as in language opportunities, distribution of linguistic knowledge, and exposure across two languages (Tabors, Páez, and López, 2003; Windsor and Kohnert, 2004).

Ln learners may continue to require additional language support through upper primary schooling and beyond in order to access curriculum content and contribute at the level of monolingual peers.

Cross-linguistic influence

The L1 lexicon may influence the Ln lexical organization, and L1 may influence Ln learners' way of accessing English word meanings and selecting English vocabulary for expressing themselves (Tabors, Páez, and López, 2003). For example, in Chinese the word *cup* (杯子) is used to refer to all containers for drinking liquids, whereas the word *cup* in English is used for drinking liquids such as coffee or tea and the word *glass* is used for drinking liquids such as wine and juice. An English learner with Chinese L1 is likely to use *cup* for wine instead of *glass* (Li, 2013).

Moreover, it is common for Ln learners to borrow words from their L1 in Ln communication. The pattern of mixing varies based on the learners' L1 backgrounds.

Your Turn

What are the functions of word mixing? Explain with concrete examples.

Morphosyntactic development

Research suggests that the morphosyntactic development order of Ln is similar to that of L1, regardless of children's L1 background. In other words, whether children's L1 is Chinese or Spanish, they all follow the same universal morphosyntactic development order (see Box 7.3).

Box 7.3   Morpheme Acquisition Order for Ln Learners

- Pronoun case (he/him)
- Articles
- Copula (be)
- Progressive (-ing)
- Plural (-s)
- Auxiliary (be+V+-ing)
- Regular past
- Irregular past
- Plural (-es)
- Possessive ('s)
- Third person singular (-s)

Modified from S. Brown and S. Attardo, *Understanding Language Structure, Interaction, and Variation* (Ann Arbor: University of Michigan Press, 2008), p. 220.

However, depending on the learners' L1 backgrounds, English morphology may pose some difficulties for some English learners. Using English tense as an example, when expressing time in English, inflectional morphology is used (e.g., adding suffixes, *-ed* and *-ing*). In Chinese, however, there is no system of grammatical morphology for tense. Instead, temporal adverbs such as 昨天 (yesterday), 今天 (today), and 明天 (tomorrow) are used to indicate the time in the past, present, and future (Li, 2013, p. 162). It is possible that English-language learners with a Chinese L1 may have difficulties in learning the morphological rules related to temporal reference.

Pragmatic development

Cultural pragmatics

The process of acquiring a new language is not only a linguistic issue, but also a cultural issue. Box 7.4 lists two examples that illustrate the cultural misunderstanding beyond the linguistic form (H. Brown, 2000, p. 258).

Box 7.4   Misunderstanding

Example 1

American: What an unusual necklace. It's beautiful!
Samoan: Please take it.

Example 2

American teacher: Would you like to read?
Russian student: No, I would not.

H. D. Brown, *Principles of Language Learning and Teaching* (White Plains, NY: Pearson Education, 2000), p. 258.

The development of pragmatics in a Ln can be difficult in the areas of apologizing, thanking, face-saving, conventions, and conversational cooperative strategies. For instance, Japanese learners of English may express gratitude by saying, "I am sorry," a direct transfer from "Sumimasen" (conveys a sense of gratitude, especially to persons with higher status) (H. Brown, 2000). The **cooperative strategy** (people cooperate to achieve mutual conversation ends) (Grice, 1975) is the most difficult for Ln learners to master.

Your Turn

Explain what could be the reasons for the misunderstandings in Box 7.4.

Narratives in a Ln

It is complex to discuss the narrative development of children who are in the process of learning a Ln. Depending on children's ages, Ln learners' narrative development may fall into two categories. For those children who are at the beginning of elementary grades, their Ln narrative development may resemble the characteristics that are similar to monolingual children. Like monolingual children, Ln learners at the beginning of schooling are in the process of developing their narrative abilities. However, if a child who has already developed a narrative structure in her L1 learns the Ln in the mid or late elementary school years, her narrative structure may exhibit some different characteristics. Perhaps the question is whether Ln learners' narrative differences only show in some narrative domains or whether they demonstrate a wholly different narrative process. A study by Viberg (2001) can shed some light. The bilingual Swedish–Finnish children in the study tended to provide more detailed and concrete narrative versions in both of their languages than monolingual children. However, these children provided a similar narrative structure in both of their languages. Thus, it seems that narrative structure belongs to a general conceptual level, which is independent of individual languages (Viberg, 2001). Nevertheless, some narrative features produced by Ln learners may turn out to be distinct from the ones produced by their monolingual peers.

Metalinguistic development

As we discussed in earlier chapters, children with more than one language in general tend to have a metalinguistic advantage compared with their monolingual peers. For example, depending on their degree of competency in their various languages, research shows that both more proficient bilinguals and less proficient bilinguals outperformed monolinguals in some metalinguistic tasks such as attention control tasks, but only more proficient bilinguals outperformed monolinguals in cognitive tasks such as representation tasks (Bialystok, 1988). Moreover, research suggests that reading proficiency in children's L1 and L2 can facilitate their L3 reading proficiency, largely because the metalinguistic awareness abilities they developed in the L1 and L2 allow them to compare and contrast the respective grammars (Rauch, Naumann, and Jude, 2012).

Although there is little research on the link between Ln learners' metalinguistic knowledge and their academic language development, according to available research on Ln learners' metalinguistic development, particularly their possible advantage in attention control, Ln learners may potentially have a leg up in their academic literacy development if teachers can utilize their potentials.

Your Turn

Provide a grade-level appropriate text to an elementary Ln learning student and ask the student to identify the grammatical features that are different from his or her L1. What have you found out about this student's metalinguistic ability?

Develop Literacies in the New Language

L1 literacy skills transfer

The emergent literacy capacity built by children in their L1 will be helpful in supporting their literacy development in the Ln. However, some children who enter elementary school without L1 emergent literacy skills may face double challenges; that is, they must learn a new language and at the same time, develop literacy in the Ln. Even so, their oral language skills established in learning their L1 are still beneficial to their Ln literacy learning. Research seems to suggest that promoting children's L1 (or home language) development can help their Ln development. For instance, a study shows that when children were encouraged to further develop their home language, Spanish, the skills they built in Spanish helped their English (Ln) literacy development (Cohen and Horowitz, 2002). In fact, the longer children receive reinforcement in their home language, the better they learned English (Ln). Research has also shown that the most promising way to help children's long-term academic success is to promote both L1 and Ln literacy development in elementary school years (Cohen and Horowitz, 2002).

Your Turn

Suppose that no support is provided for English language-learning children to develop their L1 or home-language literacy skills in your school district. How would you, within your power as a classroom teacher, provide such support? What could be the value of doing so?

Ln reading characteristics

Depending on text genre, text difficulty, proficiency, and reading ability in Ln, children who are learning a Ln may have a slow reading speed because of new or difficult words, poor comprehension (vocabulary has a strong association with comprehension), and difficulties with unfamiliar concepts and conventions. Some Ln learners may prefer oral-like texts over expository texts. However, not all Ln learners will exhibit these characters in approaching reading.

Syncretic literacy

Literacy activities or performances are never pure linguistic events. Instead, they are always organized on the basis of the integration of a learner's cultural beliefs and values. In literacy practices, Ln learners always will incorporate more than one cultural value, belief, emotion, practice, identity, and resource into the organization of literacy activities. In other words, when different cultural and linguistic systems inter-act, a learner rarely simply replaces one linguistic system with the other, and their literacy activities tend to reflect the integration of more than one system. The creative forms of literacy practices and transforming literacy learning experiences in which chil-dren draw from the existing pool of languages and literacy practices in their homes, schools and communities and blend familiar practices with new forms are called **syn-cretic literacy** (e.g., Curdt-Christiansen, 2013; Gregory, Long, and Volk, 2004). A growing body of research has suggested that syncretic literacy is a common practice among children who are exposed to more than one linguistic system and culture (e.g., Curdt-Christiansen, 2013; Gregory, Long, and Volk, 2004; Souto-Manning, 2013).

Your Turn

Analyze a narrative or writing of an elementary student who is learning English as a Ln with the syncretic literacy lens. What have you found?

Supporting Strategies for Learners of English As a Ln

Despite some passible challenges, children who learn a Ln in middle childhood still have a great chance to acquire the Ln proficiency as long as they are provided with adequate support. There are two major goals in providing support for Ln learners in middle childhood. The first goal is to help them achieve **automaticity** in their Ln (the control that a child has over the Ln knowledge). The second one is to help them develop academic language in their Ln. While Ln learning children have to learn both social language and academic language, it takes considerably longer for them to acquire academic language. In general, it takes anywhere from five to ten years or more for English-language learning students to reach the necessary levels of academic language proficiency on a par with children whose first language is English (Cummins, 1981; Ovando, Combs, and Collier, 2006). Often, children who are more gregarious and social tend to advance more quickly in Ln learning than those who are shy and withdrawn (Wong-Fillmore, 1983).

Moreover, even though it is not an easy task for all children to learn to read and write, it is more challenging for Ln learning children when their L1 is inconsistent with the Ln. How Ln learners will move forward in their Ln literacy development depends on a variety of factors such as children's sociocultural and economic back-grounds, children's L1 language acquisition experience, students' familiarity with the L1 writing system, the L1 and Ln degree of similarity, children's overall cognitive and social characteristics, and motivation and identification with the Ln.

There has been continuous debate among researchers and educators about the best way to introduce these children to Ln literacy. There are at least four proposals that have been put forth (see Box 7.5).

Box 7.5 Various Ways to Introduce
Literacy Instruction

- Introduce literacy instruction in both L1 and Ln.
- Introduce beginning literacy in L1 and, after it develops, then introduce literacy in the Ln.
- Develop literacy skills in Ln and after its development work on the literacy skills in L1.
- Focus on literacy skills in Ln and exclude L1.

Modified from A. D. Cohen and R. Horowitz, "What should teachers know about bilingual learners and the reading process," in J. H. Sullivan (ed.), *Literacy and the Second Language Learner*, vol. 1 (Greenwich, CT: Information Age, 2002), p. 34.

Although there is strong research evidence suggesting the benefits of L1 development on Ln development, most public schools in the United States provide English-only instruction for children with other linguistic backgrounds. In such an educational climate, classroom teachers can try some of the following strategies to maximize English-language learners' potential. It is very important to stress that these strategies are not meant to be a panacea for every student, especially in the case of Ln learners whose backgrounds vary greatly. You are encouraged to explore your own strategies and help English-language learning students effectively communicate content-area concepts, carry out reasoning in speaking and in writing, and support the continued growth of their home language(s), if at all possible.

Tap into students' funds of knowledge

In Chapter 2, we discussed using TP (transformative pedagogy) to help reach students from different cultural backgrounds and with different abilities. Recall that the first step in implementing TP is to situate teaching and learning in social practices and to tap into students' funds of knowledge. A good example of tapping into students' funds of knowledge can been seen Box 7.6.

Box 7.6 Learning Module on Mexican Candy

Once teacher teams had visited the home of one of their students and saw the child exchanging Mexican candy with his neighbor, the lead teacher came up with a creative lesson plan to incorporate the child's background in Mexico with a classroom activity. In order to do this the teacher interviewed a parent from Mexico to learn all about the different kinds of candy that were made in Mexico.

To focus students on the theme, the teacher asked each child in the classroom to think about what type of treats "counts" as candy. Students had to use analytical skills to decide whether snacks like *picalimon* and *saliditos* counted as candy.

Once students had identified different types of candies, the teacher had students organize the candy into what candy types they wanted to know more about.

On the final day, students were asked to hypothesize about the ingredients in each candy. After they had created lists of ingredients, teachers passed out candy wrappers and had students identify what ingredients were in American candies and what ingredients were in Mexican candies. This gave them an opportunity to compare and contrast differences in the candy. Students learned that Mexican candy had fewer ingredients and used less artificial color than American candy.

The following day the mother of the Mexican child that had been interviewed came to school and taught a lesson on how to make *pipitoria*. Students utilized math skills when measuring out the recipe. When the candy was baking, the mother, through the help of a translator, was able to tell the kids about some of the differences in food habits between Mexicans and Americans.

The final day students made advertisements and posters for their candy and were able to actually wrap and price their candy to sell during the school's talent show. Students were also asked to write a summary of what they had learned and to formulate new questions about candy and the foods of different countries. From the questions the students came up with, the teacher was able to continue investigating using the children's research questions and help to develop critical thinking skills for a considerable part of the year.

This plan demonstrates how to create a lesson plan that not only utilizes immigrant students' funds of knowledge but benefits the entire classroom and serves as a unique learning experience.

J. K. Lopez, "Funds of knowledge," Learn NC, University of North Carolina School of Education, at http://www.learnnc.org/lp/pages/939.

This example illustrates that if teachers are willing to take time to learn about their students' background and situate their instruction in their students' funds of knowledge, learners will find learning (including language learning) meaningful and relevant.

Your Turn

Based on the example shown in Box 7.6, design a learning module in a content area by using students' funds of knowledge and discuss how this learning module can help your students develop their ability in the content area and in the English language.

Learn vocabulary through semantic mapping

Learning words in context has been shown to be effective in Ln vocabulary development. **Semantic mapping** is one choice for contextualized vocabulary learning.

Semantic mapping is a process in which students can relate new words to their own experiences and prior knowledge by using visual displays of categories and their relationship in a graphic form. Semantic mapping can help students learn new word meanings (academic word meanings) in a situated context. Box 7.7 demonstrates an example of semantic mapping.

Box 7.7 An Example of Semantic Mapping for Teaching the Word "Oyster"

Put the word "oyster" in a circle in the middle of the board. Ask students to brainstorm and think of the ideas that come to their head when they think of the word "oyster." Students may come up with words such as pearl, shell, ocean, sand, eat, stew, slimy, hard, gray, etc. Write these words on the board, and then show students how to categorize them. Branching off from the original circle, write the main categories surrounding the word. You may want to put a square around them. Categories for oyster could be habitat, food source, and physical characteristics. Now, you will have the words habitat, food source and physical characteristics in little boxes surrounding the circled word, oyster. Then you will list the words associated with each main category. For example, under the square that has the words "Physical characteristics" in it, you will list shell, gray, hard, slimy, and makes pearls. For "Habitat," you would list the words ocean, sand, and so on. Complete this process for each category. You may have some words/concepts that only have two categories, while others may have eight or nine.

To extend the semantic map-making process, and give students additional practice, you may want to divide students into pairs or groups and assign a word. You could assign a word that arose from the activity, such as pearls, or you could assign words related to the topic in general, such as sea turtle.

"Teachers: how to use semantic mapping to increase vocabulary," at http://www.essortment. com/teachers-use-semantic-mapping-increase-vocabulary-61369.html.

Your Turn

Select a word that is also a concept in a specific content area. Put the word in the middle of a circle on the board and ask your Ln learning students to contribute words (including words in their L1) related to this target word/concept by using their experiences. Write down the words that your students have contributed. Then ask them to categorize the words they contributed into categories.

Support syncretic literacy

To be able to participate successfully in school literacy activities, Ln learners must learn to utilize resources from their cultural and linguistic communities. They must be able to intermingle or synchronize their cultural values, beliefs, emotions, identities, and other resources into the organization of their literacy activities in the school context. Therefore, it is important for you as a teacher to find out and utilize various literacy activities that are practiced in Ln learning children's home and communities and to create a **third space**[2] in the classroom to allow Ln learners to draw on their cultural and linguistic resources to make sense of what they are learning. By encouraging Ln learners to practice syncretic literacy, tap into their rich cultural and linguistic resources, and connect their Ln to L1 and culture, you will help these students engage in meaningful and relevant learning and construct meaning at a deeper level. In fact, research shows that when students are encouraged to practice literacies by drawing on all their resources, or in other words, by drawing on all points on the **multilingual continua**,[3] children tend to have better chances for successful multilateral development (Hornberger, 2003).

It should be noted, however, that practicing syncretic literacy is not just blending different things from different languages and cultures. Rather, the goal is to help your students to transform their literacy practices and make new meaning by drawing on their multilingual and cultural resources. Moreover, it should also be noted that the literacy behaviors of students with more than one linguistic and cultural system are not static; they are always fluid, dynamic, multiplex, and changing. Thus, the syncretic literacy process is always evolving; there are no final products.

Your Turn

Ask a Ln learning student at the elementary level to write a story about a subject. Analyze the student's writing and discuss whether this student indeed practices syncretic literacy. If so, identify the areas where the student writes as both conservator (e.g., revealing L1 characteristics) and innovator (e.g., using innovative expressions in his or her writing) in relation to the student's L1 (and culture) and Ln (and culture).

Practice metalinguistic reflection

Metalinguistic reflection refers to any conscious act of reflection about language, including learners' planning of how to process it linguistically. In other words, metalinguistic reflection is the observable manifestation of language awareness. For example, encourage students to pay attention to aspects such as the third person singular -s at the end of verbs. Some studies suggest that the practice of metalinguistic reflection in classrooms facilitates Ln development, and there is a specific link between the activities that promote language reflection and learners' accuracy in grammatical decision tasks. However, other studies did not find an association between the metalinguistic reflection and the test performance of Ln learners in grammar and vocabulary (e.g., Simard, French, and Fortier, 2007).

Despite the research debates on the effectiveness of metalinguistic reflection for Ln development, it is helpful to raise Ln learning students' awareness of the Ln grammatical forms through metalinguistic reflection activities. Box 7.8 suggests some metalinguistic reflection activities that you can try in your subject area teaching.

Box 7.8   Metalinguistic Reflection Activities

Think aloud   Probe learners' intuition with questions about a specific grammatical point and ask them to verbalize the strategies they use to arrive at their understanding of the target grammar point.

Dictogloss   Dictogloss focuses on teaching grammatical structures. The teacher first selects a text that contains examples of the grammatical forms to be studied. Then, the teacher reads the text at a normal speed to students and asks them to identify and jot down these grammatical forms. After that, students work together in small groups to reconstruct the text from their shared resources. The final versions are then analyzed, compared, and presented to the class. There are several advantages in using dictogloss activities. First, they integrate the language skills of listening, reading, speaking, and writing. Second, they also provide students with opportunities to talk about both content and the language itself. Third, the activities are a useful way of presenting new factual information to students and encouraging them to listen for key points. Finally, they give support to less confident students, as they are encouraged to participate in their groups as part of the structure of the activity.

Textual enhancement   Provide explicit grammar instruction and typographically alter the appearance of target grammatical forms to increase learners' perceptual salience. However, some researchers believe that while textual enhancement may aid learning of the target grammatical forms, it has unfavorable effects on meaning comprehension.

Input flooding   Deliberately flood Ln input by using many exemplars of the targeted grammatical forms.

Processing instruction   Processing instruction involves grammar explanation and comprehension practice directed at altering the way Ln learners process input and make correct meaning–form connections.

Guided reflection   Guided reflection refers to techniques that guide learners to reflect metalinguistically on the nature and function of a particular grammatical point. These techniques include probing learners with questions about a target grammatical form, having them compare samples of language to arrive at a deeper understanding of the function of the form, and asking them verbalize the strategies they used to arrive at their understanding of the target grammatical structure.

Cross-linguistic exploration   This process involves leading learners to reflect on both the nature of language acquisition as well as multiple aspects of language on a more global level. In so doing, learners are expected to develop better strategies that can be applied to Ln learning. The rationale is that this type of reflection is built on the ability of learners to reflect on their L1 which simultaneously will project on their ability to reflect on different aspects of the Ln.

Corrective feedback   When a student makes a grammatical error, the teacher might ask the student to clarify what she just said, or the teacher simply tells the student that she made an error in her production.

Consciousness-raising   Teacher conducts activities in which students are asked to formulate rules about the Ln language after being exposed to a series of example sentences.

Garden-path technique   Learners are deliberately led to make predictable errors and the teacher then corrects the errors immediately. The idea behind the garden path technique is that when learners are allowed to make errors and then they are immediately corrected, they will learn the information better.

Journal or diary   Students are asked to reflect on their learning of the grammar and write their observations about the rules that they observed. They then submit their journals for teacher feedback.

Ideas are based on D. Simard, "Using diaries to promote metalinguistic reflection among elementary school students," *Language Awareness*, 13(1) (2004): 34–48; D. Simard and W. Wong, "Language awareness and its multiple possibilities for the L2 classroom," *Foreign Language Annuals*, 37 (2004): 96–110; M. Swain, "Three functions of output in second language learning," in G. Cook and B. Seidhofer (eds), *Principles and Practice in Applied Linguistics: Studies in Honour of H. G. Widdowson* (Oxford: Oxford University Press, 1995), pp. 125–144.

If you try these metalinguistic reflection activities consistently, your Ln learning students may have a better chance of focusing more on the Ln specific features and accelerate their progress in mastering them. However, when implementing the metalinguistic reflection method, you need to be mindful that simply prompting the children to identify differences or similarities between their L1 and Ln is ineffective. You need to provide lots of scaffolding to make it work.

Your Turn

Select two activities from Box 7.8 and discuss how you can implement them in a specific content area (such as math, social studies, and English language arts).

Use L1 knowledge for Ln learning

Children's levels of L1 language proficiency may help them develop proficiency in their Ln (Verhoeven, Steenge, and Balkom, 2012). L1 functions as a clothespin on which the learner can hang his Ln information; that is, the learner can make use of his already existing knowledge in L1 to facilitate his Ln learning (Ringbom, 1987, p. 134). Thus, you might want to take advantage of what children know in their L1 and facilitate their English learning. For example, if a student cannot express a concept or idea in English, ask her to say it in her L1. The point is not whether you understand her L1 but to help the student express herself in a language with which she is familiar. There will be a transitional period before a student can use the Ln. By providing students with opportunities to use their L1 in academic learning, you are helping them build a bridge to cross from L1 to Ln. Also, if you know that a student already understands the concept, you do not need to waste time explaining it. What you need to do is to provide the student with the vocabulary needed to speak about the concept in English.

Moreover, research suggests that there is a positive transfer of knowledge between L1 and Ln in word learning (Lugo-Neris, Jackson, and Goldstein, 2010). In other words, children can use their knowledge of L1 to enhance acquisition in Ln. A study conducted in Spanish L1–English Ln children suggests that the Spanish (L1) expansions of novel vocabulary words during English storybook reading resulted in comparable or greater growth in the children's expressive knowledge of the English vocabulary words. The L1 bridging may be a promising strategy for Ln vocabulary learning. Children with higher-level L1 (Spanish) proficiency and limited English skills outperformed the children with low-level skills in both English and Spanish. Children with better home language skills in Spanish demonstrated greater responsiveness to vocabulary expansions during shared book reading. However, children who had limited skills in their L1 were at a disadvantage for using bridging during Ln learning due to the lack of a conceptual base in their L1. In conclusion, those children who were more proficient in Spanish (L1) appeared to benefit the most from vocabulary expansions of unfamiliar vocabulary words during shared book reading despite limited English (Ln) skills (Lugo-Neris, Jackson, and Goldstein, 2010).

Use shared reading for Ln learning

Shared reading is a reading instructional approach in which teachers explicitly model the strategies of a fluent reader. This method can be used for all grade levels and for students with different abilities. It is introduced here to show that it can also help Ln learners in the elementary grades.

Shared reading usually begins with a teacher reading from a Big Book so that every student can see the text and the pictures clearly. During the first reading, students listen to the story. The teacher might use a pointer to demonstrate directionality in text and one-to-one correspondence. As the text is read multiple times, students should begin to participate in the discussion by chanting together, making predictions, providing key words that are important in the story, or participating in **echo reading** (the teacher reads one line and students repeat it) (Morrow, 2012, pp. 213–215).

In primary grades, the teacher reads while the children are encouraged to read along. The more familiar the text, the more the teachers asks of the students in terms of reading, talking, and answering questions about the reading. In upper grades, the teacher reads the text aloud after stating a focus, and then rereads the text, asking questions specific to the focus of choice (and may ask students to join in). The focus may include things like analysis, predictions, drawing inferences, grammar and punctuation, vocabulary development, questioning, literacy elements, critical thinking, phrasing, fluency, intonation, character and plot development.

Shared reading may be particularly helpful in facilitating Ln learning. In the shared reading environment, Ln learners have repeated exposures to words and syntactic structures in contexts. It is an effective way to expose learners to a Ln. Moreover, shared book reading is helpful for Ln learning because it creates a meaningful context that facilitates Ln vocabulary learning (Enguidanos and Ruiz, 2008) and provides additional information to help Ln learners understand new words in the story (Justice, Meier, and Walpole, 2005).

Your Turn

- If a Ln learning student does not know how to express a concept in the content area you are teaching in English, how would you help her transition from her L1 to Ln?
- Suppose one of your students is learning English as a Ln. He already understands the concept in your content area (e.g., math, science, and social studies). Identify ten key words (or whatever number of words you deem fit) and propose how you can help the student use these English words to express the concept that he already knows in his L1.

Apply instructional conversation

Research has indicated that there is a strong connection between oral language and literacy and oral language competence and academic success. Thus, building oral language skills in students' Ln is critical. Instructional conversation has been shown to help students develop literacy skills (Cohen and Horowitz, 2002), and it is particularly useful for Ln learning. **Instructional conversation** refers to the teacher–student conversation in content teaching and learning. Box 7.9 shows the important elements in instructional conversation.

Box 7.9 Important Elements of the Instructional Conversation

Instructional

Thematic focus   Teacher selects a theme on which to focus the discussion and has a general plan for how the theme will unfold, including how to "chunk" the text to permit optimal exploration of the theme.

Activation and use of background and relevant schemata   Teacher either "hooks into" or provides students with pertinent background knowledge and schemata necessary for understanding a text, weaving the information into the discussion.

Direct teaching   When necessary, the teacher provides direct teaching of a skill or concept.

Promotion of more complex language and expression   Teacher elicits more extended student contributions by using a variety of elicitation techniques: invitations to expand, questions, restatements, and pauses.

Promotion of bases for statements or positions   Teacher promotes students' use of text, pictures, and reasoning to support an argument or position by gently probing: "What makes you think that?" or "Show us where it says ..."

Conversational

Fewer "known-answer" questions   Much of the discussion centers on questions for which there might be more than one correct answer.

Responsiveness to student contributions   While having an initial plan and maintaining the focus and coherence of the discussion, the teacher is also responsive to students' statements and the opportunities they provide.

Connected discourse   The discussion is characterized by multiple, interactive, connected turns; succeeding utterances build upon and extend previous ones.

Challenging atmosphere   (but nonthreatening): Teacher creates a challenging atmosphere that is balanced by a positive affective climate. Teacher is more collaborator than evaluator and students are challenged to negotiate and construct the meaning of the text.

General participation   (including self-selected turns): Teacher does not hold exclusive right to determine who talks; students are encouraged to volunteer or otherwise influence the selection of speaking turns.

Modified from ERIC Clearinghouse on Languages and Linguistics, ED347850, Washington, DC, 1992.

The advantage of instructional conversation for Ln learners is that it is natural and spontaneous in teacher–student interaction; it is free from the didactic nature of formal teaching, and it is relevant and meaningful. Thus, the instructional conversation method (see Box 7.10) can activate students' schemata, promote complex language, create a nonthreatening environment, involve direct teaching, and include teacher responsiveness to students' ideas. These and other speech structures can be practiced to develop vocabulary and syntax and to activate different content area genres that will ultimately be processed as text content (Cohen and Horowitz, 2002).

Box 7.10 The Instructional Conversation Method

- Teacher weaves together the comments and contributions made by different students with the ideas and concepts that the teacher wishes to explore with them.
- Teacher weaves students' prior knowledge and experiences with new knowledge and experiences, thereby broadening the scope of their understanding while building upon understandings they already possess.
- During the course of the conversation, the teacher weaves together, in appropriate proportions and shadings, the ten elements of instructional conversation (see Box 7.9). While particular elements can be picked out and identified – just as threads of a different color can be picked out and identified on a cloth – instruction and conversation are woven into a seamless whole: the conversation is instructional, and the instruction is conversational.

Modified from ERIC Clearinghouse on Languages and Linguistics, ED347850, Washington, DC, 1992.

Your Turn

Identify a topic that you want to teach in your content area (e.g., social studies, language arts, math, science). Write a lesson plan, focusing on using the instructional conversation method discussed above. What do you think your plan will do for the English-language learners?

Explicit instruction

Because the Ln learning environment in school is different from the learning environment of young children acquiring their L1, research has shown that exposure to Ln in itself may not be enough (Soler and Martínez-Flor, 2008). Therefore, instruction in specific areas (such as in pragmatics) is both necessary and effective in Ln learning. Using pragmatics as an example, explicit and deductive instructions are more effective for pragmatic learning than implicit and inductive teaching. Attention-drawing activities are more helpful for pragmatic learning than exposure to positive evidence. Research shows that learners who received pragmatic instruction outperformed those who did not (Soler and Martínez-Flor, 2008). Several explicit instruction strategies are recommended below for your reference.

Explicit lexical explanation
It has been discussed before that vocabulary is important for academic success. Building a rich vocabulary will help Ln learners succeed academically. Research has shown

that explicit explanation of words, such as providing synonyms of words or using role-play in the context, can facilitate vocabulary learning in monolingual children's L1 and can double the number of words children learn. Ln learning students can also benefit from the same enriched experience in their Ln vocabulary learning.

Ln learners' lexicon errors often tend to outnumber their grammatical errors by a 3 to 1 ratio. In communication, native speakers find lexicon errors to be more disruptive than grammatical errors. Grammatical errors generally result in structures that are understood (e.g., "Can you tell me where *is* the train station?"), whereas lexicon errors may interfere with meaning comprehension; for example, "I feel sorry for people who live in the *suburbs.*" The word *suburbs* was misused by a L1 Spanish person as a result of the Spanish false friend *surburbio* (slum quarter). Listeners who hear this misused word will misunderstand the speaker's intended meaning (Gass and Selinker, 2001). Therefore, explicit explanation is particularly important in Ln vocabulary accuracy. It is helpful if you can elicit the vocabulary knowledge in Ln learners and use that to benefit their English vocabulary building. Because of the issue of false friends in different alphabetic languages, you may draw your students' attention to them.

Your Turn

Research via the internet the most commonly occurring false friends in alphabetic languages (particularly Indo-European languages or romance languages). Make yourself familiar with them. In your future interactions with students from different linguistic backgrounds, this knowledge may help you know the source of errors.

Language model
Providing children with a good target language model is an effective way of exposing Ln learners to a new language. Unlike children who acquire their L1, Ln learners need to develop Ln skills to learn content areas. You can, for example, draw children's attention to exemplary phrases and words used in the texts you want them to read, you can ask them to keep a notebook and copy good words and phrases when they see them, and you can speak to them with well-chosen words.

Model pronunciation
As stated before, Ln learning is different from L1. Explicit teaching is essential. To help Ln learners' phonological development, you may want to draw their attention to the pronunciation. It is natural that when a student first hears the word, she does not know how to pronounce it correctly. You can help her by guiding the student to listen carefully to the way her peers and TV anchors pronounce the words. You can intentionally segment the words and show the student how the sounds are articulated. By doing so, you are helping the Ln learner to be understood by her peers, and thus facilitate better communication and social relationships.

Cultural pragmatics

Also, new language learners may speak English but act "foreign." Children who acquire their L1 as English acquire the style of the language use in the process. However, children who acquire English in a new cultural environment need to be explicitly taught about the pragmatic rules. Therefore, overt teaching is essential in helping Ln learners learn English pragmatics.

Your Turn

Research some cultural pragmatic differences. Share your findings with your classmates.

Text simplification

The text level (such as vocabulary and grammatical structure) is important in determining whether a student can comprehend it or not. It has been said that if students recognize less than 90 percent of the vocabulary in a text, then the text is too difficult for them. To move ahead with their academic learning, Ln students must read. The question is how. One way to help these students learn content while they are developing their language-learning capacity is to simplify texts. If the texts are too difficult for Ln students, you may consider simplifying the original texts to help students understand content. However, simplification of a text for the purpose of helping comprehension needs to be done with caution. When you simplify a text, the purpose is to eliminate the barriers of understanding, but you may want to be careful not to make the text too explicit, which will hinder your students' ability to infer. Thus, it has been suggested that you should not insert explicit connectives such as *because* or *although* so that your student deduces the relationships between sentences without them. When you simplify a text, retain as much as possible of the quality and structure of the original text and remove only difficult vocabulary and complex sentences (Nuttall, 1996). See more discussion in Chapter 10.

Your Turn

Identify a short text that you think is difficult for Ln learners at a given grade. Ask a Ln learner to read it and tell you the gist. How does the student do? Select another short text at a similar level and simplify it based on the suggestions above. Give this simplified version to the student again. What have you found?

Figurative language

In Chapter 6, we discussed figurative language development. Children who are learning English as a Ln will have difficulties mastering the figurative language (such as metaphors, similes, hyperboles, idioms, irony, and proverbs). Gaining competence with all types of figurative language is an important part of becoming a culturally literate and linguistically competent individual (Nippold, 2007).

Your Turn

Identify a short text that contains figurative languages. Ask a Ln learner to explain them to you. How does the student do? If you think that the student does need your help in understanding their meanings, how would you provide support for them?

Metalinguistic feedback

Providing feedback for students such as comment on their writing is a form of overt instruction. There are two kinds of feedback: direct (explicit) and indirect (implicit) feedback. In **direct feedback**, teachers point out the mistakes to students directly. In **indirect feedback**, teachers only provide hints where students can find their mistakes. Indirect feedback can also be called **metalinguistic feedback**, which refers to a process that is the result of error/contrastive analysis on the part of the teacher, who hints at the type of error the student may have made but does not provide explicit correction. Research on this type of feedback has been successful with older students who learn a Ln (Mourssi, 2012). However, using metalinguistic feedback starting at the elementary level will help students get acquainted with this type of teacher–student interaction and benefit their academic learning.

Your Turn

Revisit the error patters you identified in the "Prereading Questions and Activities" section. Think about how you will use metalinguistic feedback to help your students learn from their errors.

Help Ln learners transform their skills

If you are conscious about making language-learning and academic content subject learning a comprehensive and coherent area learning process, you need to help your students apply the strategies they develop in learning the Ln to other areas such as social studies, math, and sciences. For instance, in learning a Ln, learners are often asked to pay attention to the linguistic rules. Similarly, you can help your students to pay attention to the principles in subject areas.

Also, when Ln learners apply and practice what they have learned, it is always helpful to provide them with some language problems that push them beyond what they are taught. By doing so, learners might take risks to use new forms that they have never used before.

Your Turn

Write or obtain a lesson plan in a specific content area that you plan to teach. Identify the areas that you want your students to learn. Can you point out whether you can teach your students the English language and at the same time, the content principles/concepts? Reflect on the significance of this kind of transformative practice.

Critical literacy support

Besides applying the strategies discussed in Chapter 6, you may want to focus on helping elementary-school Ln learners develop critical literacy abilities in the following areas.

First, support Ln learners in becoming informed critics by helping them first understand how, for example, a story works (the story grammar) in English and in their L1.

Second, use the reading materials that you selected to help them broaden their understanding of a subject, and, at the same time, encourage Ln Learners to think about what they read by considering different points of views. For example, you can ask them a series of questions that aim to provoke a critical stance.

Third, challenge them to question what they read in a different subject-content area. For instance, we may take it for granted that double-column addition or subtraction starts from right to left. However, questions like "Do all people practice in this way?" "How do young children start this process when no instruction is given?" can help Ln learners question what they have learned and in the end, learn better. It should be noticed that critical literacy abilities develop gradually. During the elementary school years, like all their elementary peers, Ln children are mostly in the concrete operational stage (thinking is based on concrete aspects); modeling is a good way to expose elementary children to this kind of thinking.

Finally, it is critical to help Ln develop critical literacy abilities through scaffolding and provide opportunities for them to practice. You can show Ln learners how critical literacy can be done by analyzing a text together with them and explaining why you think certain points made in the text need to be scrutinized. Students should have ample opportunities to practice critical literacy and make it their second instinct.

Your Turn

Select a text from any of the subject content areas you plan to teach. Read through it and identify the places where you can help your students develop critical literacy abilities. Reflect on this activity and its educational implications.

Digital literacy support

Many elementary students, including Ln students, are becoming burgeoning users of hypertext and digital devices. You can build on their abilities by first focusing on the strategies introduced in Chapter 6. You can then help Ln learners develop abilities to see how print and hypertext work in their L1 and in their Ln. You can encourage Ln learners to search information related to the content area by looking at the websites in their L1. You can then ask them to write about their experiences.

Your Turn

Assign a research topic in your content area that requires your Ln learning students to research different websites. Encourage them to search the websites in their L1 (if a student is not literate in their L1, they are encouraged to ask for their parents' help). Ask the students to reflect on their web-searching experiences in writing.

Be aware of the masking phenomenon

Before we leave this chapter, there is a word of caution about the masking phenomenon (Walters, 2011) of some Ln learners. In order to "fit in" with the class, Ln learners may mask their Ln difficulties (e.g., Ln reading difficulties) to "pass" as readers and successful students (this can also happen to other children in the classroom). This kind of masking phenomenon can prevent Ln children from receiving the language support that they need. Therefore, you need to pay attention to how they perform in various activities, know their needs, and provide adequate support in a timely fashion.

Your Turn

Discuss the ways in which you can detect the masking phenomenon of a Ln learner?

Summary of Key Points

- There are quantitative and qualitative changes in children's exposure to the home language and the Ln (school language) when Ln learning children enter elementary school.
- Several important issues related to learning a Ln in middle childhood need our attention:
  - Different language-learning environments of different languages
  - Brain capacity change

- ○ Variations among Ln learners
- ○ Interlanguage
- ○ Language stabilization phenomenon
- ○ Selective attention
- ○ The explicit nature of Ln learning
- ○ Markedness and unmarkedness
- ○ Competence variety
- ○ Discrepancy between Ln competence and performance
- ○ Cross-linguistic interaction and skill transfer
- ○ Deductive–inductive learning
- ○ Individual factors
- ○ Developmental sequence in Ln learning
- ○ Specific features of English
- L1 may impact Ln in the area of phonology, particularly in the area of accent.
- Ln learners' vocabulary discrepancies may show in several areas. A Ln learner may know more words in one subject in the Ln and more words related to daily life in his home language. Ln learners' home language vocabulary development may stagnate. Students may understand more words than they use. Students may show a lopsided vocabulary development pattern; that is, when they have more vocabulary in the Ln, they will have less in their home language and vice versa. Learners' Ln vocabulary may be influenced by their L1 vocabulary.
- Although the morphosyntactic development of Ln learners follows the universal L1 acquisition order, Ln learners also show distinct morphological developmental characteristics depending on their L1. If learners' L1 is non-alphabetical, they may encounter difficulties in mastering the morphological rules related to temporal references in English.
- Pragmatic development of Ln may reflect cultural and linguistic backgrounds.
- Ln learners have advantages in metalinguistic knowledge, which can be used in learning the Ln and to develop academic literacy.
- The literacy skills developed in L1 can be transferred to the Ln literacy learning. Ln learners may have slower reading speed and prefer certain text genres. Ln learners' literacy performances may also show syncretic characteristics by drawing on their different linguistic and cultural resources.
- The primary goals in supporting Ln learners in elementary grades are to help them achieve automaticity in their Ln and develop academic literacy abilities in their Ln. To achieve these goals, various strategies are proposed, which include:
  - ○ Tapping into students' funds of knowledge
  - ○ Learning Ln vocabulary through semantic mapping
  - ○ Supporting syncretic literacy activities
  - ○ Practicing metalinguistic reflection
  - ○ Using L1 to help learn concepts and vocabulary
  - ○ Practicing the shared reading approach
  - ○ Applying the instructional conversation method
  - ○ Using explicit instruction to target difficult areas

◦ Helping Ln learners transform their skills and practice critical and digital literacy skills
◦ Being aware of Ln learners' masking phenomenon

Key Terms

Affective filter
Ambiguity tolerance
Automaticity
Cooperative strategy
Deductive language learning
Deep orthography
Direct feedback
Distributed characteristics or multilingual word learning
Explicit learning
False friends
Fossilization
Implicit learning
Indirect feedback
Inductive language learning
Instructed learning
Instructional conversation

Interlanguage
Intrinsic motivation
Language attrition
Markedness
Metalinguistic feedback
Metalinguistic reflection
Multilingual continua
Resultative motivation
Semantic mapping
Shared reading
Silent period
Simplification and formulas period
Stabilization
Syncretic literacy
Third space
Unpacking period

Notes

1. A correlation means the cause–effect relationship. A correlation coefficient of 0 means no cause–effect relationship and a score of 1 indicates a perfect cause and effect relationship. In general, a correlation coefficient between 0.30 and 0.60 is usual in research, with 0.30 being weak and 0.60 and above being relatively strong (S. Brown and Attardo, 2008, p. 227).
2. Third space is a conceptual classroom space for learning that draws on the discourse of formal teaching as well as that of the students (Volk, 2013).
3. The multilingual (or bilingual) continua are an overarching conceptual framework developed by Nancy Hornberger (2003). There are nine continua in this framework: micro–macro, oral–literate, monolingual–bilingualism receptive–productive, oral language–written language, L1–L2 transfer, simultaneous–successive exposure, similar–dissimilar structure, and convergent–divergent scripts.

Recommended Further Readings

Dodd, B., Hemsley, G., and Holm, A. (2006). Diverse but not different: the lexical skills of two primary age bilingual groups in comparison to monolingual peers. *International Journal of Bilingualism*, 10(4): 453.

Ferris, D. R. and Hedgcock, J. S. (2014). *Teaching L2 Composition: Purpose, Process, and Practice.* 3rd edn. New York: Routledge.

Hoffmann, C. (2001). Toward the description of trilingual competence. *International Journal of Bilingualism,* 5(1): 1–17.

Martin-Jones, M. and Jones, K. (2000). Multilingual literacies. In M. Martin-Jones and K. Jones (eds), *Multilingual Literacies: Reading and Writing Different Worlds* (pp. 1–15). Amsterdam: John Benjamins.

Verhoeven, L. and Strömqvist, S. (eds) (2001). *Narrative Development in a Multilingual Context.* Amsterdam: John Benjamins.

8

Language Impairment in Middle Childhood

Prereading Questions and Activities

- Ask a first- or second-grade student with language impairment to read a grade-level appropriate text. What have you observed, especially regarding the student's word decoding ability?
- Collect a speaking or writing sample of a fourth-grade student who has language impairment. Analyze the sample at the syntactic level. What kinds of sentences does this student use? Does this student encounter any syntactic difficulties? If so, list these areas and propose some strategies that might help the student.
- Familiarize yourself with the Individuals with Disabilities Education Act (IDEA) through the following sources (you can also find your own sources):

    http://idea.ed.gov/explore/home
    http://www.doe.in.gov/sites/default/files/specialed/ideafaq.pdf

    Understand the process of creating and implementing an Individualized Education Program (IEP) via the following link or other sources:

    http://idea.ed.gov/explore/view/p/%2Croot%2Cdynamic%2CTopicalArea%2C1%2C

    Discuss how IEP can help students with LI move forward in their academic language and literacy development.

Topics to Be Addressed in This Chapter

- The focus of language and literacy development for students with language impairment (LI) during the elementary grades
- Language development characteristics of children with LI in middle childhood
  - Phonological development

Understanding Language and Literacy Development: Diverse Learners in the Classroom, First Edition. Xiao-lei Wang.
© 2015 John Wiley & Sons, Inc. Published 2015 by John Wiley & Sons, Inc.
Companion website: www.wiley.com/go/wang/langandlit

- ○ Lexical and semantic development
- ○ Morphosyntactic development
- ○ Pragmatic and metalinguistic development
- Literacy development characteristics of children with LI in middle childhood
- Supporting strategies for children with LI in the elementary grades

---

Learning Objectives

After reading this chapter, you are expected to do the following:

- Know the language and literacy development focus for students with LI during the primary grades.
- Understand the specific challenges that children with LI encounter in the areas of phonology, lexicon, semantics, morphosyntax, pragmatics, and metalinguistic knowledge.
- Understand how various language impairments can impact elementary school children's academic and literacy development.
- Know effective strategies to help children with LI develop language skills to meet the challenges in academic learning and prepare them for middle and high schools.

Language and Literacy Development Focus for Elementary Students with LI

We saw earlier that it is estimated that 5–12 percent of preschool children in the United States have speech and language impairments (for other statistics on voice, speech, and language, see National Institute on Deafness and Other Communication Disorders, 2014). Children who experience language difficulties in early childhood are likely to continue to exhibit social and academic difficulties into middle childhood.

Beginning at elementary school, language and literacy take center stage in academic content area learning. Children with LI will inevitably have a significant disadvantage since academic learning skills (such as reading, writing, and thinking) are language-based. Unfortunately, many language and literacy learning difficulties are only taken seriously when children with LI encounter academic learning difficulties. Therefore, to meet the academic demands as well as local, state, and national assessment requirements, the focus must be on helping them develop several critical language and literacy skills such as phonological awareness, vocabulary development, complex syntax comprehension and production, narrative development, and reading fluency in the elementary grades.

In Chapter 5, the specific characteristics of different types of LI were discussed. These children may continue to exhibit their unique language development characteristics throughout the elementary school years. Nevertheless, one thing they have in common is that they all have to face the challenges of learning academic language and literacy to be able to function in the elementary grades. Thus, in this chapter and, later, in Chapter 11, the discussion will be on the common challenges that students with LI face in the classroom environment. For example, both children with Down syndrome (DS) and children with specific language impairment (SLI) tend to share semantic processing deficits due to their working memory limitation, and both children with autism spectrum disorder (ASD) and children with SLI tend to encounter the same difficulty in using sentences and discourse to aid interpretation of meaning. However, whenever there is a distinct language impairment characteristic related to a specific type of LI, it will be addressed specifically.

Language Developmental Characteristics of Children with LI in Middle Childhood

Phonological development

Students with LI may demonstrate phonological processing difficulties in the areas of phonological production, phonological awareness, and phonological memory and retrieval. On the phonological production front, although the phonological production of most children with LI is intelligible, some may distort a few sounds or simplify them (Paul, 2007). The voice quality and intonation patterns of some children (e.g., children with ASD) may be strikingly different from children with typical development (TD), and these problems may persist through the school years and into adulthood (Tager-Flusberg, 2001). Students with LI may also have difficulties in pronouncing multisyllabic words and complex phonological production (e.g., some have difficulty pronouncing the word *statistics*) (Paul, 2007).

Children with LI in general have limitation in phonological awareness. They often have trouble with phonological tasks such as producing unfamiliar words, phrases, and complex sentences, even if they are doing fine with everyday conversations (Paul, 2007). For instance, the most pronounced difficulty in children with dyslexia is their struggle in phonological and orthographic awareness and their phonological and orthographic processing skills. These difficulties considerably affect their fluency in reading, spelling, and writing. Children with DS also have particular difficulties in developing phonological awareness skills (Bertelson, 1993; Kay-Raining Bird, 2007; Byrne, 1993). As a result, the reading development of children with DS is usually delayed. However, one study by Cossu, Rossini, and Marshall (1993) claims that the Italian children with DS whom they studied could read without mastering phonemic awareness.

Because of the short-memory disability, many children with LI consistently show difficulties in retrieving accurate phonological representations of verbal material (or segmenting words into sounds, then storing sound-by-sound auditory images and retrieving these images as a template for production). Some researchers suggest that some of these difficulties appear to be related to these children's limitation in memory or semantic ability (Paul, 2007).

Lexical-semantic development

Word recognition contributes to reading comprehension. It involves two important subskills: the development of **mental graphemic representations** (MGRs) and decoding. MGR ability allows readers to identify words almost instantaneously without the need to decode (sound them out). Fluent readers use MGRs most of the time when reading (only when a new or uncommon word is present do they need to use decoding).

In general, children with LI encounter word recognition difficulties. The time they spend at the decoding level will certainly hamper their ability to process the meaning of the text. It has been recognized that poor word decoding skills of children with LI lead to comprehension problems (McCauley and Fey, 2006). During the elementary school years, vocabulary difficulties in some children with LI, such as children with SLI, may become more noticeable, as demonstrated in their sparse lexical semantic representations, sparse semantic category knowledge, and difficulties in understanding the explicit and implicit meaning of stories (McGregor, 2009).

In addition, children with LI often have difficulties with receptive vocabulary, especially in understanding teachers' instructional vocabulary and textbook vocabulary. They may struggle in expressive vocabulary as well. For example, they produce less lexical diversity compared with children with TD; in particular, they produce fewer different words (NDW). Further, they may have word retrieving difficulties. Unlike children with TD who have the ability to learn new words quickly through quick incidental learning, children with LI are usually slower in this area (Paul, 2007).

As children move up the grade levels, they increasingly encounter sentences that contain more than one idea. Thus, their abilities to infer semantic relations between these ideas are essential for academic success. Children with LI, especially children with SLI, tend to have trouble in inferring semantic relations between ideas. Children with TD can often infer from a sentence with made-up words. For example, given a sentence with made-up words such as "The girl *glimmed* some *pov*," children with TD intuitively know that *glim* is an action and that *pov* is an object or substance. However, children with SLI are less able to make such inferences. Moreover, children with SLI also have difficulties in learning verbs. Some researchers believe that this is a result of their limitation in the **syntactic bootstrapping** ability (i.e., a student looks to contextual cues to help her determine the meaning when presented with an unfamiliar verb). Syntactic bootstrapping ability is believed to be more important in verb learning than noun learning (McGregor, 2009). Similarly, one of the challenges for students with ASD is their inability to infer meaning from the social cues expressed by other speakers. They often have difficulties in understanding and using words that express mental or emotional states such as *imagine* and *pretend*.

Students with hearing impairment (with a hearing loss ranging from mild to profound) may encounter difficulties in understanding emotional words (labels) as a result of their delay in theory of mind development (McGregor, 2009).

Morphosyntactic development

Sentence complexity is usually indicated in four areas (Silliman and Scott, 2009):

- The number of verbs
- The number of embedding
- The order in which major elements appear in the sentence ("*John kicked the ball*" versus "*The ball was kicked by John*" and "*It was the ball that John kicked*").

- The distance between crucial elements in the sentence (e.g., *the Union troops* (subject) *that had just marched across the state of Virginia were* (verb) *tired and sore*. In this sentence, nine words interrupt the main clause subject and verb).

Children with LI often have difficulties in syntactic comprehension when sentences become more complex with the above-motioned syntactic elements. For example, they have particular difficulties in understanding the following types of sentences (Paul, 2007):

- Passive sentences
  For example, "*A student is seen by a teacher*" (misinterpreted as "*A student sees a teacher*").
- Sentences with relative clauses embedded in the center between the subject-noun phrase and main verb
  For example, "*The boy who hit the girl ran away*" (misinterpreted as "*A girl ran away*").
- Sentences containing adverbial conjunctions
  For example, "*Before you eat your dessert, turn off the TV*" (misinterpreted as "*Eat your dessert and then turn off TV*").

Children with LI not only have difficulties in understanding complex sentences, but they also have trouble expressing themselves by using complex sentences. They use less complex sentences than children with TD and have problems in using the correct conjunctive links (e.g., *because* and *then*) to connect different and complex ideas.

In addition, students with LI may frequently use mazes when they produce complex sentences. A **maze** is a false start, hesitation, repetition, or a reformulation of a sentence. The following is an example of a maze (from Gillam, Marquardt, and Martin, 2011, p. 256).

> "*But on time, when I had a b-, when uh, when last Christmas, I, uh uh, my aunt Mary Ann, my aunt, she gave me a bird, and her, and I called him Tweetie Bird.*"

When children with LI try to organize what they want to say and fight for words and sentence structure to express themselves, they tend to produce more mazes. Although mazes are also common for children with TD when they are attempting to formulate long, complex utterances (Nippold, 2009), children with LI tend to have more excessive and consistent maze production than children with TD.

Further, children with LI in elementary grades (even later in secondary grades) often have difficulty with complex mapping and dependency relations in sentences. These include tense and agreement marking and sentences in which subject–verb–object (SVO) order is altered such as in a question, passives, and object relative clauses. They particularly have difficulties in sentences that are combined with various types of subordination and coordination, which are prominent in academic texts (Silliman and Scott, 2009).

Among all the children with LI, children with SLI are most vulnerable in the morphosyntactic aspect. As discussed in Chapter 5, young children with SLI demonstrate great difficulties in their syntactic aspect of language acquisition. When these children enter elementary school, their issues with morphosyntax become more visible. The more complex the sentence is, the greater the difficulty. The grammatical errors rates for children with SLI are high and they are exacerbated in written samples (Silliman and Scott, 2009). Children with SLI are more likely to omit grammatical morphemes than to misuse or misplace them. As time goes on, their morphological difficulties may become less obvious, while problems in the use of advanced sentence structures and narrative coherence may become more apparent. It is at that point that this impairment begins to affect academic learning significantly, particularly in the areas of reading, writing, and classroom discourse (Gleason, 2009).

Morphosyntactic difficulty is also an issue for children with ASD. They have a noted impairment in understanding what others say because they are unable to rely on contextual cues to appreciate the meaning of interactions (Lord and Paul, 1997). This is illustrated in their tendency to overinterpret messages literally without an awareness of a speaker's intention (Lord and Paul, 1997). In addition, children with ASD lack inferencing skills in syntax processing and are unable to fill in information that is not overt in a message.

Pragmatic and metalinguistic awareness

In narratives, not everything is stated explicitly; part of understanding a narrative is being able to infer some of the implicit information. Children with LI often have challenges in narratives. Their difficulties may be manifested in both narrative comprehension (particularly, inferencing) and narrative production. Although some children with LI are capable of making inferences, they do not always exhibit the ability spontaneously (Paul, 2007).

Children with LI tend to show three distinct narrative characteristics compared with children with TD (Paul, 2007):

- They have overall less maturity of narratives in the **story macrostructure** (degree of organization and number and type of story grammar elements).
- Use less clear and appropriate linguistic markers such as pronouns, prepositions, and articles to provide cohesive ties throughout the story.
- Employ less precise and diverse vocabulary, use less literate language style, and apply less advanced episodic structure and linguistic highlighting of the crux of the story to create a comprehensible and interesting tale.

Some children with LI, such as children with SLI, also tend to interpret language very literally and are insensitive to the intended meaning behind many conversational gambits. They sometimes have shallow knowledge of word meanings; for example, they might use the word *liar* to refer to anyone who says something that is inaccurate regardless of the intent to deceive, and thus, they tend to alienate their peers (Gleason, 2009).

Moreover, children with SLI tend to have poor narrative skills and inadequate decontextualized language. Engaging in extended discourse (talk) requires the use of vocabulary to refer to past, future, or abstract/hypothetical times and events and persons; these skills are closely associated with early literacy demands. Children who struggle with using decontextualized language to talk about past or future events or experiences have long been found to have difficulty understanding and producing narratives (a form of extended discourse that is commonly used in reading material for elementary students) (e.g., Curenton and Justice, 2004). Poor narrative abilities (both receptive and expressive) are associated with reading comprehension difficulties in school-aged children (Cain, 2003). Furthermore, the inability to use decontextualized language has been linked to academic struggles (Snow, Burns, and Griffin, 1998).

Children with ASD tend to have problems sustaining conversations and constructing coherent narratives because of their theory of mind disability (McGregor, 2009). Also, telling personal experiences poses unusual challenges for children with ASD because personal narratives, defined as the recounting of a personal experience, focus on points of interest usually unknown to the interlocutor. Lack of ability may affect **autobiographical memory**.[1] A study indicates that the stories told by 11-year-old children with ASD consistently lacked a **high point**[2] as a consequence of their lack of social understanding of narrative. Children with ASD are less attuned to emotional cues and lack an understanding of the social role of narratives. Thus, they may not be aware of the information required to follow their stories, resulting in impoverished personal narratives. Their limited ability to take into account others' points of view may affect their stories and conversations about events. However, their script knowledge about social situations appears similar to that of chronologically age-matched children with Down syndrome, but they express fewer empathic responses (e.g., Goldman, 2008).

Children with ASD may use bizarre information, describe facts rather than causal relationships, and are less likely to use the gist of the story to organize their narrative coherently. In addition, they have significant difficulty narrating personal experiences as a result of their limited social and emotional understanding of events (e.g., Goldman, 2008).

The distinct difficulty in understanding narratives among children with ASD may be the consequence of their inferential processing limitation. This disability affects not only their academic learning (e.g., narratives), but also their social functions. In particular, the lack of inferential processing ability may impair their comprehension when inferencing is required. Comprehension requires an integration of meanings of individual words, sentences and paragraphs, as well as key ideas and themes. General knowledge needs to be applied to varying contexts. Information from various sources needs to be incorporated into a whole, using "gestalt-like" global processing. Instead of processing information at a global level like individuals with TD, individuals with ASD tend to process information on a local level and pay particular attention to details. This local processing bias may account for some comprehension problems in autism.

For a narrative to be taken as a coherent unit, inferential processing skills are required to build a mental representation. Consider the following example from Charniak (1972):

Jane was invited to Jack's birthday party. She wondered if he would like a kite. She went to her room and shook her piggy bank. It made no sound.

Many inferences need to be made to appreciate this message fully: if the piggy bank made no sound, then there is no money inside it. If there is no money, a gift cannot be bought for Jack, whose birthday is coming up or has just passed since he is having a birthday party. To make an inference as to the meaning of Jane's actions, one must draw on **event schema** of birthday parties and associated conventions (event schemas include relational information of parts to the whole and to each other). Inferences based on event schemas are **script inferences**. As script inferences require global processing of event schemas, it can be hypothesized that inferences of this type would be harder for individuals with ASD. Children with ASD do not spontaneously integrate information to make script inferences, as children with TD do. Children with ASD are impaired in their ability to make inferences based on event scripts as they fail to integrate existing knowledge of events with the information described in the narratives (Nuske and Bavin, 2011).

Moreover, while children with ASD and those with SLI have both been shown to have difficulties with narrative, children with ASD tend to show typical performance at the micro-level (i.e., the sentence-level and structural language ability evident in the narrative), whereas children with SLI show continuing difficulty with structural language forms, and this may continue into adolescence (Manolitsi and Botting, 2011).

Germane to the challenges in the pragmatic aspect of language development, children with LI may also be less advanced in their metalinguistic abilities. For example, they may have difficulties in analyzing words into syllables and in understanding and producing language play (e.g., riddles, puns, and rhymes). Children with LI also perform more poorly than peers with TD on a wide range of metalinguistic tasks that emphasize phonological awareness. For instance, researchers often use **spoken word recognition** (SWR) as a way to measure children's phonological/phonetic skills. SWR is the process by which a listener uses the acoustic-phonetic information available in the speech form, in conjunction with a variety of other forms of information that may be available, to access an entry in her lexicon (Kohnert, Windsor, and Miller, 2004). Accurate and efficient spoken word recognition is a fundamental aspect of language comprehension. School-age children with primary or specific language impairment show deficits relative to their peers with typical development for their chronological age (Kohnert, Windsor, and Miller, 2004).

Multilingual children with language impairment

Research on multilingual children with LI in elementary grades is scarce. However, available research indicates that bilingual children with SLI perform at a lower level than their TD monolingual and bilingual peers in almost all aspects of their language performance. Multilingual children with SLI may have an additional disadvantage in language tasks related to the mental lexicon and grammar.

A study by Jacobson (2012) suggests that when support for the L1 (Spanish) was provided at home and taught at school, the bilingual Spanish–English speakers with LI showed continued development of the use of **object clitic pronouns** (OCP),[3] including gender and number agreement morphology. However, there was a period of suppression in their use of Spanish grammatical morphology during the early elementary grades, coinciding with increased exposure and use of English due to a complex interaction between languages that were being developed in contact situations.

Nevertheless, these children showed a continued development of grammatical morphology in later school years as long as there was L1 support at home and school.

Literacy Development of Children with LI in the Elementary Grades

The linguistic challenges that children with LI have in early childhood will continue in the elementary grades; the language impairments impact their ability in learning to read and write. Ultimately, the continued linguistic disabilities will hinder their academic content area learning. This section will focus on the areas of LI that will affect the initial reading process.

Phonological awareness

As defined before, phonological awareness is the ability to identify, reflect on, and manipulate sound units of a given language. When children with LI such as children with DS are introduced to words initially in kindergarten and first grade, they often lack phonological insight and skills. They have difficulty in recognizing syllables, the **onset and rime**, and the phonemes in a word. The limitation in their phonological awareness will in general affect their reading fluency, spelling, and writing.

Although language and literacy abilities are related, the relationship is complex. Some children with LI may have relatively strong phonological skills and word decoding abilities but still have difficulties in reading comprehension (N. Nelson, 2010).

Lexicon

Children with LI such as children with dyslexia or SLI tend to have difficulties in word retrieval and **rapid automatized naming**.[4] They may have a relatively well-developed receptive vocabulary but still have difficulties retrieving word forms for rapid-naming tasks or when reading or formulating language. Research suggests that when children at Grade 1 have rapid automatic naming difficulties, they are more likely to have difficulties with reading at Grade 2. However, phonological awareness and rapid automatized naming ability can only predict word recognition; they did not add anything unique to reading comprehension (e.g., N. Nelson, 2010).

Semantics and syntax

Compared with phonological awareness and rapid automatized naming abilities, the semantic-syntactic aspect of children with LI better predicts children's later reading comprehension. The evidence is that children with grapheme–phoneme difficulties but strong syntactic-semantic skills at age 6 are less likely to have reading problems at age 8, even if they have a familial risk for dyslexia (N. Nelson, 2010).

Supporting Strategies for Children with LI in the Elementary Grades

As discussed earlier in Chapter 6, the language used in schooling (academic language) is a register with distinct words, sentence structures, and discourse organizations.

Academic language is challenging for all children, continuing through adolescence (Silliman and Scott, 2009), and it is particularly difficult for children with LI. Without adequate support, these children will most likely lag further behind and fail in their subject content learning.

It continues to be a challenge to identify SLI in school years due to the complex nature of this kind of LI. Many children who have SLI will go unidentified. Sometimes even when teachers notice these children's difficulties in academic subject learning, the support provided for them is often focused on poor academic performance and reading disabilities (Girbau and Schwartz, 2008) rather than the specific language and literacy support that these students need. Therefore, in your specific content area, you may want to try the following recommendations and provide support that aims at learning subject contents via language and literacy.

Integrated and cross-curriculum support

Children with LI in elementary grades can benefit from integrated support across the curriculum (e.g., in math, science, language arts, social studies, arts, and physical education). The major advantage in integrated and cross-curriculum language and literacy support is that language and literacy learning is not an isolated endeavor. Rather, it is embedded in learning the academic contents. Children will have opportunities to be repeatedly exposed to the academic vocabulary, sentence structures, and discourse, and learn their usages through different subjects. Using the word *predict* as an example, students can acquire the enriched meaning in all their content areas and observe how the meaning of this word and its concept plays out across the curriculum.

Your Turn

Brainstorm with your classmates on the idea of integrated and cross-curriculum support for students with LI in the elementary grades. Identify one word or grammatical structure and discuss how you can teach it throughout the curriculum.

Focused stimulation

Focused stimulation (FS) provides language models of target forms at higher than normal frequencies within meaningful communication contexts. Research has shown that FS is particularly helpful for children with LI. For example, in a study with children with SLI who were between 8 and 19 years old, children were randomly assigned to two narrative retell situations. In the maximum support situation, between listening to the story and retelling it, participants heard each sentence of the story again and repeated it. These sentences were constructed to contain a variety of subordinate clauses characteristic of higher-level language. Compared with those who did not receive such maximum support, these children produced twice as many subordinate clauses when retelling the story (Silliman and Scott, 2009). Therefore, when you provide support for children with LI in your content area, try to provide models for your students and draw their attention to these language models.

Your Turn

Select a text in your content area for a grade level and identify five sentences or words that you believe to be important for students with LI to know (both in comprehension and in production). Propose a plan of how you can help your students with LI to understand and use the targeted words or sentences by applying the idea of focused stimulation.

Inferencing support

As discussed before, inferencing is a process of drawing conclusions by connecting related information that may be implicit. There is a connection between inferencing and reading comprehension (Silliman and Scott, 2009). Thus, inferencing abilities are crucial for academic learning.

Several factors can affect inferencing: vocabulary breadth, grammatical processing, and discourse compression (this is the most important). Children with SLI, for example, tend to find it difficult to deduct information separated by four or more sentences, and in such situations, their text comprehension will breakdown. Usually, it is less difficult for them to comprehend when the inference is supported by information contained within the same sentence or in an adjacent sentence.

Explicit and direct instruction on how to make inferences is beneficial to school-age children in general and children with LI in particular. There are several ways in which you can try to help your students develop inferencing capacity.

First, teach your students with LI inferencing strategies (see Box 8.1). Research has shown that these strategies, such as **lexical inferencing**, can improve students' narrative comprehension (A. McGee and Johnson, 2003; Silliman and Scott, 2009).

Box 8.1 Inferencing Strategies

Lexical inferencing This strategy teaches students how to search for key words that allow them to understand the text better and the kinds of inferences that can be made from these words.

Why-question generation This strategy encourages students to generate their own queries about the text by asking questions (*who, where, when,* and *why*).

Predictive inferences This strategy helps students to focus on sentence meaning by searching for key words surrounding covered sentences. For example, inferring that: Simon had hit the ball (the hidden sentence from the surrounding sentences, "It was Simon's turn to bat" and "It was a good hit").

Modified from A. McGee and H. Johnson, "The effect of inference training on skilled and less skilled comprehenders." *Educational Psychology*, 23(1) (2003): 49–59.

Second, the shared book reading activities in early elementary grades we discussed in Chapter 7 are also useful in helping students with LI build inferencing capacity. In the early elementary grades, you can increasingly ask questions that elicit inferential responses, such as "What do you think Bear is going to do with his arrow?" In the middle and upper elementary grades, you can help children pay attention to **predictive inferences** (Silliman and Scott, 2009), such as "What do you think will happen based on what you know?"

Third, thinking aloud can also help improve children's inferencing abilities (Silliman and Scott, 2009). You can ask students to tell aloud what they understand about the story after each oral sentence is read to them. The advantage of this strategy is that you can get direct feedback on how well your students are doing with inferencing and what you can do next to help them.

Finally, support can focus on developing a "map" of events, placing the core elements of an event in the middle, and the optional or nonessential details in the periphery. This kind of support can assist children with LI, such as children with ASD, develop script inferencing (Nuske and Bavin, 2011).

Your Turn

Select a text in your content area and explain how you can help your students with LI develop inferencing capacity by using the strategies described above.

Phonological awareness support

Phonological awareness is not only important for reading, but also crucial for spelling development. Children with severe phonological awareness deficits are at high risk for literacy difficulties. It is important to provide intervention in early grades for these children to avert the situation. Children with LI can benefit from direct and specific phonological awareness training. The most effective phonological awareness training has been shown at the phoneme level. Research suggested that children with LI who underwent phonological awareness training made accelerated progress in their phonological awareness ability, and the training effects were maintained over time (Gillon, 2000 and 2002; Warrick, Rubin, and Rowe-Walsh, 1993). Box 8.2 is an easy assessment task that you can use to get a feel of whether a student (usually second grade or up) is at risk for phonological and literacy acquisition deficits. If a student's errors amount to more than 20 percent, this student should receive direct phonological awareness help.

Box 8.2   Phonological Production Task

Naming task

Have students name pictures of the following:

Alligator
Stethoscope
Helicopter

Submarine
Kangaroo
Buffalo
Rhinoceros
Vegetables
Octopus
Dinosaur
Asparagus
Hippopotamus
Ornaments
Broccoli
Domino
Gorilla
Volcano
Ambulance
Aquarium

Word repetition task

Say each word, and have students repeat it:

Peculiar
Colorado
Orchestra
Animal
Catalog
Permanent
Navigator
Aluminum
Cinnamon
Symphony
Specific
Governor
Pistachio
Especially
Probably
Calendar
Syllable
Enemy
Fudgesicle
Pneumonia

Phrase repetition task

Say each phrase, and have students repeat it:

Fly free in the Air Force.

> A box of mixed biscuits.
> Six slim sailors.
> Have some fried flounder.
> Shiny seashell necklace.
> Big black bugs' blood.
> Wash each dish twice.
> He likes split peas soup.
> He skied down the snow slope.
> Tom threw Tim three thumbtacks.
>
> R. Paul, *Language Disorders from Infancy through Adolescence: Assessment and Intervention* (St. Louis, MO: Mosby, 2007), p. 471.

The phonological training for children with LI can focus on syllable awareness, onset–rime[5] awareness, onset–rime blending, segmentation, and phonemic awareness (bring children's attention to the initial phoneme in target words through repetition and prolongation of the phoneme, sound categorization activities, and phoneme segmentation with two- and three-phoneme words).

Using a phonologic strategy in spelling a word involves segmenting the target word into phonemes and applying knowledge of how individual sounds in words are presented in spelling. Encourage children with LI to listen for the first sound of the word, to break down a word into parts, and to sound out the word when spelling (McCauley and Fey, 2006).

Also, you can intentionally teach students to use analogy for word recognition and spelling based on their previous word knowledge. You can help students decode (recognize) and encode (spell) new words based on their knowledge of known words with similar spelling and phonological patterns. For example, when a student with LI first encounters the new word *fan*, he can be asked to think about whether he knows other words that have the same rime such as *man* and *can*. The student can be encouraged to analyze rime unit -*an* by using his prior knowledge of *man* and *can* (McCauley and Fey, 2006).

Further, children with LI, such as children with dyslexia or SLI, need explicit and structured instruction to help them build capacity in sound–letter association. Research has shown that a direct **multisensory structured learning** (MSL) approach is effective. MSL utilizes several sensory channels simultaneously and synthesizes stimuli coming from these channels. While being taught reading and writing, children can use the integration of visual, auditory, kinesthetic, and tactile stimuli. Children learn how to read and spell words by hearing, seeing, and pronouncing them, by shaping modeling clay, forming them from wooden, sponge, or plastic letters, by tracing them on various surfaces such as paper, carpet, floor, and sand, and by writing them. The underlying idea is that the more perceptual channels that are open, the greater the possibility of forming associations between the graphic (visual) and phonetic (auditory) aspects of a word as well as its meaning (Nijakowska, 2008).

Your Turn

Identify a list of words that you believe to be difficult for students with LI at an elementary level from a text in your content area. Suggest how you would use these words to help students with LI with their phonological awareness.

Lexical-semantic support

The lexical-semantic support that you provide for your students with LI can focus on two aspects: instructional vocabulary and text vocabulary. To help students understand the instructional vocabulary, you can use visual cues when introducing new and difficult words and give students with LI an extra chance to understand what you say by paraphrasing words. When helping students understand the text vocabulary, you may want to first identify difficult words from the text or use the glossary at the end of textbooks, and then find out your students' knowledge about these words by doing the following: asking them directly about the meaning of these words; asking them to identify these words in pictures, graphics, maps, or diagrams; asking them to act out and use other nonverbal means; and asking them to use manipulation (e.g., "show me division with raisins"). If students have problems, teach these words first before they read the text. Also, do not ignore common words such as *above, after, following, however,* and *consequently* when selecting words, because some students with LI may have difficulties with these words (Paul, 2007).

Moreover, since semantic relations are important in academic learning, you may want to help your students by identifying some sentences in the readings and intentionally pointing out the relations between them. You can also select some multi-idea sentences, delete the conjunctive links, and ask your students to add them back.

Furthermore, teaching secondary word meaning is also important. For example, the word *bank* has at least two meanings: the place to keep money (dominant meaning), and the edge of a river (secondary meaning). Children with LI often have trouble mastering the secondary meaning of words.

Your Turn

- If possible, audio- or video-record a lesson taught in a real elementary classroom. You can also locate a teacher speech sample from the internet or other sources. Transcribe a portion of the teacher's speech verbatim. Identify the teacher's instructional language (i.e., words, phrases, and sentences) that you think will be difficult for students with LI to understand. Suggest how you can help students with LI understand the teacher's instructional language.
- Identify a text in a content area and underline all the words that you think will be difficult for students with LI. Suggest ways to teach these words.
- Use the same text and this time, identify the complex sentences and delete all the conjunctive links. Ask a student with LI to put these links back. If the student is not able to accomplish the task, how do you assist him or her?
- Identify the words in the same text that may have a secondary meaning and discuss how you can help students with LI first comprehend and then use them.

Morphosyntactic level support

Research shows that explicit teaching of grammatical rules such as the study of clause and phrase structure, parts of speech, larger units (nouns, verbs, adjectives, adverbs, predicates, clauses), and other common structures and systems (such as pronouns, noun–verb agreement) does not help some children with LI. However, explicit **sentence combining training** (SCT) is more successful for children with LI. In SCT, children are asked to combine short kernel (one-clause) sentences into a longer and more syntactically complex sentence. For example, children are asked to combine three simple-clause kernels into one long and complex sentence (e.g., Silliman and Scott, 2009).

KERNEL 1:   The girl was a great pianist.
KERNEL 2:   The girl was very young.
KERNEL 3:   The girl took lessons from a famous teacher.
COMBINED: The very young girl, who took lessons from a famous teacher, was a great pianist.

The advantage of SCT is that it helps children with LI in several syntactic operations such as deletion, insertion, replacement, embedding, coordination, and subordination. SCT is particularly successful in children with LI in their writing. In the above example, three simple clauses are combined into one complex sentence with two clauses via operations that insert an attributive adjective (young) before the head noun (girl) and embed a relative clause. The combination of these operations eliminates two kernel sentences (the second and third kernels) (Silliman and Scott, 2009).

Also, the syntactical level support that you can provide for your students in the content area may provide targeted exposure for students with LI to complex sentences (e.g., select complex or difficult sentences from the required readings in the content area). You can deliberately draw their attention to the structures of these complex sentences and make sure that they understand the relationship expressed in the sentence, especially in multiclause and embedded sentences. You can find out whether students understand them by asking questions either verbally or in writing.

Your Turn

- Select a few kernel (one-clause) sentences from a text in your content area and explain how you can use these sentences to help a student with LI develop morphosyntactic ability by using the SCT method described above.
- Use the same text you identified in the last section, and identify the complex sentences. Develop a list of questions that you think will help you know whether a student with LI understands these sentences or not.

Discourse-level knowledge and skills support

As students increasingly need to use decontextualized language in their academic learning in the primary grades, students with LI may especially need support for several kinds of discourses in the following areas.

Academic discourse

Academic discourse typically involves sequences of initiate/inquire-respond-evaluate or initiate-respond-feedback. Students do not usually receive explicit instruction on how to interpret academic discourse. As a result, they may miss cues used by teachers in academic discourse. For instance, a teacher asked a student, "What sound does *cat* begin with?" The students answered, "C." In fact, the teacher wanted the answer of /k/ (N. Nelson, 2010). Usually students with TD can figure out these kinds of academic discourses on their own after a while. However, students with LI may need explicit instructions on how to understand academic discourse used in the classroom environment.

A scaffolding strategy called **MAP** (model, analyze, and practice) may be especially useful for helping students with LI to understand and use academic language. This strategy was originally used for peer modeling (Hess and Fairchild, 1988). MAP is an effective intervention model originally used for children who had communication difficulties. The procedures usually involve one-hour training sessions once a week for six weeks in which children view videotaped models of the target communication skills, analyze them and practice the skills. You can try to use the MAP strategy by modeling the target academic discourse (e.g., sample discourse in initiate/inquire-respond-evaluate or initiate-respond-feedback), helping your students analyze the modeled discourse, and then putting the target discourse into practice. In fact, the MAP strategies can be applied to all the areas where students with LI need intervention.

Your Turn

Observe a class interaction between a teacher and students in an elementary grade. Identify some academic discourse between the teacher and students (if possible, video- or sound-record a few minutes of the classroom discourse). Think about how you can use the MAP strategy to help students with LI develop academic discourse capacity.

Social discourse

Even though academic discourse is important for students in the school environment, social discourse skills are also crucial. In the classroom environment, there are many occasions when students need to work together collaboratively. Therefore, you need to support students with LI and help them participate in class activities successfully.

Students with LI, especially students with autism, hearing loss, vision loss, SLI, and DS, may not find it easy to get the social cues from conversation contexts. Thus, it is often difficult for these children to establish social relationships with their peers. Research shows that children with LI tend to have fewer friends and may be rejected. They may also have difficulties using language skills to negotiate with peers and to resolve conflicts (e.g., N. Nelson, 2010). Many children do not have the skills to enter a peer group or learning group on their own. Therefore, you need to help them build skills, especially social language skills needed for participating in social activities with peers. There are at least three ways in which you can help these students with LI develop social discourse. First, modeling social discourse in the daily context by focusing their attention on specific areas such as how to enter a social conversation, how to maintain the conversation, and how to respond to conversation by getting cues from their interlocutors. Second, you may want to help them become conscious of the rules for successful conversation by talking about the concrete steps. Finally, you need to create opportunities for them to practice and engage in social discourse with peers, and monitor their interactions and provide feedback.

Your Turn

Observe a student with TD and a student with autism in a peer conversation during recess and class discussion. What have you found? Based on your observations, discuss what the successful and unsuccessful aspects of peer conversation entail.

Narrative-text support

In general, narrative texts are easier to understand because children are familiar with this genre. This is perhaps why elementary children are first introduced to reading through this genre. However, children with LI often encounter problems in the narrative aspects both in comprehension and in production. Therefore, the support provided for children in this area needs to focus on developing knowledge in the five areas listed in Box 8.3.

Box 8.3   Knowledge Necessary for Successful Narration

- Content: ideas or experiences
- Framework: story grammar (beginning, setting, characters, plots/conflicts, and resolution or ending)
- Linguistic knowledge: lexical-semantic and morphosyntactic knowledge
- Communicative adequacy: pragmatic knowledge
- Cognitive process: activate the previous four knowledge sources simultaneously and strategically.

Modified from N. W. Nelson, *Language and Literacy Disorders: Infancy through Adolescence* (Boston: Allyn & Bacon, 2010), p. 391.

Children in general are not conscious of these narrative elements. However, the difference between children with TD and children with LI is that children with TD can figure out these narrative elements through frequent exposure and use them in their comprehension and production. On the other hand, children with LI may be slower in developing the ability without additional assistance. Perhaps a more effective way of doing this is to employ the MAP strategy; that is, explicitly model the narrative structure, help them analyze the elements, and let children practice by both identifying the elements in narrative texts and using them in their narration.

Also, for children with ASD, narrative analysis of personal events can provide an opportunity for identifying their specific issues related to language and social impairments. Interventions to foster autobiographical memory in children with ASD may assist in their self-awareness development (Goldman, 2008) and narrative abilities.

Your Turn

Ask a student with LI to write a narrative on the topic of "My Weekend." Analyze the narrative based on the five components in Box 8.3. Develop a set of questions that you want to ask a student with LI (note these questions should aim to help them build knowledge in these five areas).

Expository-text support

Compared to narrative texts, expository texts are even more difficult for students with LI. Most content-area textbooks (such as science and social studies) use the expository genre to convey information. The challenge of this genre lies in its use of complex syntactic structure, high-level and abstract vocabulary, and assumptions of background knowledge (N. Nelson, 2010).

Support provided for children with LI should focus on both expository text comprehension and production. For expository-text comprehension, the **multipass approach** may be useful. This approach consists of three passes: survey, size-up, and sort-out. In the survey pass, students look for information about the main ideas and organization by reading the text title and introduction, reviewing the relationship to adjunct paragraphs, reading subtitles, looking at illustrations and captions, reading summary paragraphs, and paraphrasing the information. In the size-up pass, students skim the text to seek specific information for answering questions at the end of chapter or questions they have formulated in their minds. In the sort-out pass, students test themselves by reading each question at the chapter's end and checking off those they can answer immediately. If not, they return to the text section where the answers might be found and read until they can answer the questions (N. Nelson, 2010). In order to make this approach successful, you may want to model it first by thinking out aloud so that your students will know what is involved.

It is also important to note that expository-text comprehension involves background knowledge. Using this textbook as an example, when you first read some of the terminologies and concepts in the first few chapters, you probably found them difficult to understand (e.g., morphosyntax and metalinguistic knowledge). By now, you perhaps feel a lot more comfortable in reading these terms because you have accumulated some linguistic knowledge (background).

Using a K-W-L chart will help students with LI build background knowledge. You can help them answer the questions of what they already know before the reading (K), what they want to know (W), and what they learned after the reading (L).

It is also crucial to help students with LI to construct expository texts in writing because children increasingly have to use this skill in their academic learning (e.g., reports and essays). Writing is an encoding process. Children with LI may continue to have difficulties well into their school years where impairments are often displayed more prominently in writing, such as children with SLI (Silliman and Scott, 2009).

Although grammar is an important component in writing, what is most difficult to develop is how to write. In other words, organizing ideas before writing is an essential ability that students need help in developing. You can help students develop the ability to organize main ideas by using graphics, or you can utilize computer software such as Inspiration and Kidspiration to help them organize what they want to write about. Moreover, it is helpful to provide students with a template so that they can use it as a guide to organize their ideas before writing.

Your Turn

Research some computer software that can help students, including students with LI, organize ideas in writing and familiarize yourself with the software.

Supporting multilingual children with LI

As mentioned in Chapter 5, the issue with multilingual children with LI is very complex, and thus far, we do not have much reliable research information about the effective strategies. In the absence of research evidence, several suggestions are extrapolated from published literature.

First, the Ln language and literacy support provided for multilingual children with LI should focus on helping these children improve their overall communication ability both in social settings and in academic settings.

Second, when providing support and intervention for multilingual children with LI, there are reasons to believe that the use of both home language (or L1) and school language (Ln) together may be more effective. The rationale for incorporating home language (L1) in interventions is because in many multilingual families, parents speak only their home language, which is the foundation of the child's sociocultural and emotional language. Moreover, L1 paves the way for Ln learning; children's many experiences are first built on their L1 and these experiences will help these children transfer their knowledge to the Ln. Further, using the home language in intervention facilitates the generalization of communicative gains across settings (Kohnert and Derr, 2012); that is, multilingual children with LI can use the language trained in the school environment in their home or other social settings and vice versa.

As mentioned earlier, multilingual children's phonological system may be influenced by their L1. Some research shows that intervention in only one language had a positive outcome for the other language(s). Holm and Dodd (1999) assumed that multilingual children are likely to use the same phonological planning to process the phonology of each language; therefore, generalization is likely to occur (Ray, 2002). Thus, you may want to educate yourself about the phonological structures that are common to your multilingual students' languages (e.g., stops and consonant-vowel syllables) and also understand the features that are unique to each of their languages (e.g., trill in Spanish and /θ/ in English). Research indicates that there is mastery of most, but not all, sounds and phonotactic patterns in Spanish or English by bilingual children with TD entering kindergarten at age 5. This information suggests that, in the absence of timely identification and appropriate intervention, Spanish–English bilingual children who are less skilled in phonological production in both of their languages may be at risk for delays.

When interacting with multilingual children, you should have knowledge about the phonological structure of their L1. As previously discussed, if you teach a child whose first language is logographic, you may want to deliberately teach phoneme awareness because learning to read and write **Putonghua**[6] does not require phoneme awareness. Research shows that children do benefit from being explicitly taught the sounds of the English language (Yeong and Liow, 2012, p. 124).

Your Turn

Search research databases such as PsycINFO and ERIC and check whether there are new studies conducted on the topic of multilingual children with LI. If you do find new research on this topic, discuss how it informs you about multilingual children with LI as well as the teaching implications.

Working with family

To help children with LI achieve optimum support, it is very important to involve the family in the process; parents are primary agents in providing early support in children's language development. Several components are key. First, the family is accepted as a team member. Second, educational decisions need to reflect the family's goals and needs. Third, the family is recognized as the key decision maker (Kay-Raining Bird, 2007, p. 267).

Your Turn

Elaborate the three areas with regard to working with families. Discuss why they are important.

In short, when supporting children with LI, it is important to become familiar with the Individuals with Disabilities Education Act 2004; to treat children with LI as people first, understanding their strength and abilities as well as impairments; value the input from parents and the children themselves whenever possible (N. Nelson, 2010, p. 157); and use supporting strategies that target their needs.

Summary of Key Points

- Phonological awareness is a common issue facing children with LI in elementary school.

- Children with LI often struggle to complete phonological tasks such as producing unfamiliar words, phrases, and complex sentences. This can occur even if they do not struggle with day-to-day conversation.
- Children with LI also struggle with word recognition that involves the development of two important subskills: mental graphemic representations (MGRs) and decoding.
- Children with LI struggle with understanding complex sentences and have trouble expressing themselves using these complex sentences.
- Children with LI demonstrate problems with the comprehension and production of narratives. In particular, they lack the ability to infer.
- Children with LI tend to have difficulties in a wide range of metalinguistic tasks.
- Multilingual children with LI tend to exhibit similar impairments to monolingual children with LI.
- Children with LI will benefit from integrated support across the curriculum and focused stimulation.
- There are several ways to help students develop their inferencing capacity: shared book reading activities, thinking aloud, and the development of a "map" of events for pupils to see visually.
- Intervention in phonological awareness can focus on syllable awareness, segmenting words into phonemes, or using analogies for word recognition.
- Lexical-semantic support can focus on two aspects: instructional vocabulary by using visual cues and text vocabulary by identifying difficult words first then finding out about prior knowledge.
- Explicit sentence-combining training can help children with LI develop more sophisticated syntax.
- The MAP strategy may be useful for helping students with LI to understand and use academic language.
- Students with LI need special support for different areas: academic and social discourse as well as narrative and expository text.
- Supporting multilingual children with LI needs to focus on their overall communication. It is more effective to use both the L1 and Ln language. Teachers need to have knowledge of these students' home language (L1) to help them effectively.
- Working with families should be an integral part of the support process for children with LI.

Key Terms

Autobiographical memory	Onset and rime
Event schema	Predictive inferences
High point	Putonghua
Lexical inferencing	Rapid automatized naming
MAP	Script inference
Maze	Sentence combining training
Mental graphemic representations	Spoken word recognition
Multipass approach	Story macrostructure
Multisensory structured learning	Syntactic bootstrapping
Object clitic pronouns	

Notes

1. Autobiographical memory is the ability to recall episodes, experiences, and events in an individual's life. It is central to an integrated and functioning self-system. People who have impairment in autobiographical memory often experience a breakdown of the relationship between the self and memory.
2. The high point of a story is the climax of the story; that is, it contains the most interesting, exciting, and important part.
3. A clitic is a morpheme attached to a word either in the beginning or at the end, such as -n't in English "don't." Clitics are syntactically independent but phonologically dependent constituents. Some languages such as Spanish uses a system of clitics for the object of a verb when that object is a pronoun. For example, "*te doy un libro*" (*I give you a book*).
4. Rapid automatized naming (RAN) measures how quickly a child can name letters, digits, pictures, or objects. RAN is a strong predictor of children's later reading abilities. RAN is independent from other predictors such as phonological awareness.
5. An onset is the part of the syllable that precedes the vowel of the syllable. A rime is the part of a syllable which consists of its vowel and any consonant sounds that come after it. For example, in the word *spoil, sp-* is the onset *-oil* is the rime.
6. Putonghua is the official language of the People's Republic of China.

Recommended Further Readings

Kornos, J. and Kontra, E. H. (eds) (2008). *Language Learners with Special Needs: An International Perspective*. Bristol: Multilingual Matters.
Paul, R. (2007). *Language Disorders from Infancy through Adolescence: Assessment and Intervention*. 3rd edn. St. Louis, MO: Mosby.

Language Sample Analysis III

The following four writing samples were produced by students from elementary grades.

Writing Sample 1: Monolingual Student

This sample was written by a 10-year-old fifth-grade student, Megan (not her real name), in the first half of the school year. She is typically developing and from an upper-middle-class background.

> The holidays are my favorite time of year. Starting with Halloween. Halloween is a fun holiday because you get to dress up in cool costumes. This year I am going to be a nerd. I have cool glasses and suspenders and a tie. For Halloween 2 of my aunts have parties. 1 party is a birthday party for my cusin Brendan. 1 is on Halloween at my aunt vals house. It is fun because lots of trickortreaters come to the house. I get to see alot of my cusins.
>
> At thanksgiving we go to my gramma's house. There are alot of people. All my cousins come and aunts and uncles. We eat a big turkey with green beans and potatos. We sit at a big table in the living room and 1 person gets to say grace. We also get chocolate turkeys to eat after dinner but I like to eat mine befor.
>
> Christmas is the big celebration. We go to Roccis for dinner with the hole family. There is like 35 people. We have lots of food and get to talk to every one. After dinner we go back to my house for dessert. Then Santa comes and brings all of the grand children a present. We take pictures with santa. On Christmas day we open presents at my house. It is so much fun. Then we go to my aunts house for dinner with everyone. We have a great time.
>
> Sample collected by Shannon Melissa Summers.

Understanding Language and Literacy Development: Diverse Learners in the Classroom, First Edition. Xiao-lei Wang.
© 2015 John Wiley & Sons, Inc. Published 2015 by John Wiley & Sons, Inc.
Companion website: www.wiley.com/go/wang/langandlit

Provide your assessment of this student's language development in the following chart based on the information you read in Chapter 6. Does this student meet the grade-level language and literacy expectations listed in the common core standards?

Language components	Strengths	Needs	Other
Lexical-semantic development			
Morphosyntactic development			
Pragmatic development			
Metalinguistic development			
Writing convention			
Organization of ideas			
Narrative ability/Story grammar			
Other			

- Review all the supporting strategies introduced in Chapter 6 and select a few that you think will be particularly helpful for this student and justify your selection.
- Reflect on your experience of doing this writing sample analysis.

Writing Sample 2: Monolingual Student

The following writing sample was by a 9-year-old fourth-grade female student, Christina (not her real name), in the first half of the school year (in October). Christina is a native speaker of English from a middle-class background. In this writing sample analysis, you are asked to do the following:

- Read the assignment requirement by the teacher and Christina's writing carefully (see the following box).

Assignment   Write a personal story about an important event in your life.

Student Writing Sample

It may Sound hard to Believe

It felt like I was a famous singer, standing on top of that stage, hearing the clapping and roar of the audience. I swear it was as loud an airplane flying through the sky. As soon as I hit that note everybody stood up and started clapping to the beat.

I was in second grade and had already developed a singing voice almost as desirable as the singer from the band called "Pink Martini." I know it may sound hard to believe but it's true. It was my first talent show and I was nervous as heck. I had butterflies in my stomach and I kept running to the bathroom to make sure my voice was faultless. I would sing a note and run back to the auditorium.

After waiting for about an hour, I saw Melinda (one of the show monitors) hold up my number. Each person in he talent show had a number. When Melinda held up your number up you would get in line and wait until it was your turn.

I got in line and waited. The act before me was pretty good but I was too nervous to pay attention. When that act was over, the curtains shut. I went on to the stage and got in position. The other two girls who were singing with me got in position too.

The curtains opened and in a whisper I said, "1,2,3," then we began to sing. We sang a civil rights song from he movie "Selma Lord Selma." The song was called "Aint Gonna Let Nobody." Well that's at least what we called it. We sang and sang. Finally the most important part of the song came. When I hit that note, that was the prime moment from the talent show.

Oh how I wish I could relive that one little moment, that one little moment of the clapping, the whisteling, and screaming for an encore. Oh how I wish that just for one second I could relieve that day. Putting aside the butterflies in my stomach, or the trembling in my knees. I just wish I could.

Sample collected by Keisey Igo.

- Provide your assessment of Christina's literacy development based on the information in Chapter 6. Does this student meet the grade-level language and literacy expectations listed in the common core standards?

Literacy components	Strengths	Needs	Other
Lexical-semantic			
Morphosyntactic			
Pragmatic			
Metalinguistic			
Story comprehension (including inference ability)			
Information recall accuracy			
Writing convention			
Organization of ideas			
Narrative ability/Story grammar			
Other			

- Compare the writing of Christina with the one of Megan. What have you found?
- Review all the strategies introduced in Chapter 6 and select the ones that you think will be helpful for Christina. Discuss how you can help her move forward in her academic literacy development.
- Reflect on your experience of doing this writing sample analysis.

Writing Sample 3: Ln Learning Student

The following writing sample was by a 9-year-old fourth-grade female student, Maria (not her real name), in the second half of the school year (in March). Maria's L1 is Spanish. She has been enrolled in a public school in first grade. She is from a working-class background. In this writing sample analysis, you are asked to do the following:

- Read carefully the assignment requirement by the teacher and Maria's writing (see the following box).

Assignment Write a letter to a magazine editor and argue why children should or should not have a cell phone. Support your argument with examples or evidence.

Student Writing Sample

Dear Editor,

I believe kids should have a cell phone.

Kids should have a cell phone in case of emergency.

What if you get lost and you can't call anyone because you don't have a cell phone.

What if you want someone to pick you up from where ever you are and if you don't have a phone and then you can not call no one.

You can contect with someone you no.

You could contect with your friened sometimes.

If you get lost you will no where you are because some phones have a phones have maps and if you don't have a phone you won't no where you are because you don't have a phone or anything.

You can text someone you need something.

You could text someone your lost and you need help.

You could text something you want to say to a friened.

As you can see why there is so many reasons kids shoud a cell phone because a lot of inpotant things can happen and you don't have a cell phone.

Sample collected by Amanda Eisner.

- Provide your assessment of Maria's literacy development by using the information provided in the following chart. Note that your assessment must be based on the information you read in Chapter 7.

- Review all the strategies introduced in Chapter 7 and select the ones that you think will be helpful for Maria. Discuss how you can help Maria meet the grade-level language and literacy expectations listed in the common core standards.
- Reflect on your experience of doing this writing sample analysis.

Literacy components	Strengths	Needs	Other
Lexical-semantic development			
Morphosyntactic development			
Pragmatic development			
Metalinguistic development			
Writing convention			
Organization of ideas			
Narrative ability			
Other			

Writing Sample 4: Student with LI

The following writing sample was by an 8-year old third-grade male student, Chad (not his real name), in the second half of the school year (in February). Chad is a native speaker of English from a middle-class family and he has been identified as having LI. In this writing sample analysis, you are asked to do the following:

- Locate the book *Horrible Harry and the Christmas Surprise* by Suzy Kline and get familiar with the story content (it can be found on the internet).
- Read carefully the assignment requirement by the teacher and Chad's writing (see the following box).

Assignment   Write a summary of the story *Horrible Harry and the Christmas Surprise* by Suzy Kline in your own words. Include the important characters, events, and details from the beginning, middle, and end of the story.

Student Writing Sample

The Horibel Harry and the christms

in the Beginning of the Store Horible Harry and his class are reading a book and then a fire-truck comes and the firetruck made a sound Dee doo, dee doo, dee doo. Harry jumped out of his sea to see it, then Miss. Mackle Said "HARRY SEAT!! Miss. Mackle called out. Then Miss Mackle's char was rocking a lot the she fell down! And the char broke! Miss. Marckle felt fin but she broke her knee-bone So she has to goto the hospital Afte that, Mir. Cardini (principle) came to use and told use that he was going to be our teacher because Miss Mackle broke her knee-bone and the class had a Christmas play, so mr. cardini (principle) had to play for Miss Mackle.

Sample collected by Theresa Connelly.

- Provide your assessment of Chad's literacy development by using the information provided in the following chart.

Literacy components	Strengths	Needs	Other
Lexical-semantic development			
Morphosyntactic development			
Pragmatic development			
Metalinguistic development			
Story comprehension (including inference ability)			
Information recall accuracy			
Writing convention			
Organization of ideas			
Narrative ability/Story grammar			
Other			

- Review all the strategies introduced in Chapter 1 and select the ones that you think will be helpful for Chad. Develop an IEP that will help him move toward the expectations specified in the common core standards.
- Reflect on your experience of doing this writing sample analysis.

Part IV

Developing Language and Literacies

Divergent Abilities in Adolescence (12–18)

Part IV focuses on the different language and literacy developmental characteristics, including academic language and literacy development, during adolescence. Chapter 9 examines the typical language and literacy development in adolescence, Chapter 10 discusses adolescents who learn English as a Ln, and Chapter 11 focuses on adolescents with LI.

At the end of Part IV, you will have an opportunity to apply the information you read in the three chapters by analyzing some language samples.

Essential Questions for Part IV

- What are the language and literacy goals for middle and high school students?
- How can language and literacy developmental goals in adolescence be linked to students' college, future career, and life?
- Why is it important to encourage code-switching in classrooms?
- How does literacy fit into the larger picture of communication, and the outcomes of educational intervention and support?
- Is it possible to have multiple paths for developing literacies? Can educators support multipath literacy development in the classroom environment?

Understanding Language and Literacy Development: Diverse Learners in the Classroom, First Edition. Xiao-lei Wang.
© 2015 John Wiley & Sons, Inc. Published 2015 by John Wiley & Sons, Inc.
Companion website: www.wiley.com/go/wang/langandlit

9
Typical Development of Language and Literacies in Adolescence

Prereading Questions and Activities

- Analyze a sixth-, ninth-, and twelfth-grade text in science, math, and social studies. Identify the linguistic features in the text (e.g., vocabulary use and sentence structure). What have you found?
- Tell a joke to a 14-year-old student. Can the student fully appreciate it? Alternatively, ask a 14-year-old student to make a joke. What have you found?
- Listen to adolescent girls and boys carefully for 20 minutes. Do you hear gender differences in their pronunciations? If so, what are they?
- Observe some 15-year-old male and female students' conversations with their friends and observe the same students and their conversations with adults (if possible, record a sample of the two conversations). Do the students adjust their speech in terms of content, style, choice of words, and complexity of syntax when they talk to different conversation partners? If so, show some examples. Also, have you found any gender differences? If so, compare the differences and think about what might have contributed to these gender differences.
- Listen to a conversation between African American English speakers. Identify the specific language features.
- Locate a college application essay by a high school senior. Analyze it in terms of lexicon, semantics, morphosyntax, pragmatics, and metalinguistic knowledge. What do you think this adolescent is able to do with language upon leaving high school? Compare this essay to the writing sample(s) you collected from children in early elementary grades before and discuss the achievements that an adolescent has made in the language and literacy development journey.
- Is language competence a fixed ability or is it relative depending on the communication context?

Understanding Language and Literacy Development: Diverse Learners in the Classroom, First Edition. Xiao-lei Wang.
© 2015 John Wiley & Sons, Inc. Published 2015 by John Wiley & Sons, Inc.
Companion website: www.wiley.com/go/wang/langandlit

Topics to Be Addressed in This Chapter

- Typical developmental profile in adolescence
- Major language developmental characteristics in adolescence
  - ○ Phonological development
  - ○ Lexical and semantic development
  - ○ Morphosyntactic development
  - ○ Pragmatic development
  - ○ Metalinguistic development
- Developing literacies in adolescence
  - ○ Literacy development
  - ○ Digital literacy development
  - ○ Critical literacy development
- Supporting strategies for developing academic language and literacy in secondary grades

---

Learning Objectives

After reading this chapter, you are expected to do the following:

- Understand adolescents' developmental characteristics and know how these characteristics will influence their academic language and literacy development.
- Understand that academic literacy development is a continuous and lifelong process.
- Understand the typical language developmental characteristics in the areas of phonology, lexicon, semantics, morphology, syntax, pragmatics, and metalinguistic knowledge during the adolescent period.
- Understand the gender differences in language use among adolescents and know how to address the differences in classroom interactions.
- Understand the typical characteristics in developing literacies during the adolescent period.
- Know how to support adolescents' academic language and literacy development effectively and prepare them for college, the workplace, and life.

Typical Developmental Profile in Adolescence

In the secondary grades, adolescents demonstrate increased ability in hypothetical (scientific) and logical thinking. They no longer require concrete objects or events as support for thought, but can come up with new and more general logical rules through internal reflection (Berk, 2009). Unlike children in the previous developmental stages (early childhood and middle childhood), adolescents can solve problems by beginning to think about possibilities and then proceeding to reality. In other words, they begin to reason more like a scientist by devising ways to solve problems and testing solutions systematically (Santrock, 2007).

Adolescents also begin to demonstrate **formal operational thought**; that is, they can make logical inferences merely through verbal representations. For example, children in the earlier developmental stages would need to see the concrete relationship between A, B, and C to be able to make the logical inference that if A>B and B>C, then A>C. Adolescents can reach the logical conclusion A>C without having to rely on concrete steps (Santrock, 2007).

Adolescents' developing power of thought opens up new cognitive and social horizons, and drives them to idealism. They begin to engage in extended speculation about ideas – a mental quality they desire in themselves and others. Such thoughts often lead adolescents to compare themselves to others (Santrock, 2007). Adolescents also tend to be self-conscious and self-focusing (with an exaggerated sense of personal uniqueness). As a result, they are sensitive to public criticism and prone to taking risks.

One important difference in adolescent friendship compared to young children is that young children's friendship revolves around shared activity. In contrast, talk itself becomes the major medium of social interaction among adolescents. Talking represents the new aspect of adolescent relation to the social world in which friendship is negotiated primarily by talking about shared intimacies and experiences (Paul, 2007).

In addition, peer influence plays a vital role during this period. Adolescents are likely to engage in behaviors that are condoned by their peers either in reality or in the media.

Language and Literacy Development Focus

Given the cognitive and social characteristics of adolescence, the language and literacy development focus of this period should be on helping adolescents become independent, critical readers, writers, and communicators, develop self-monitoring learning habits, and strive to be lifelong language and literacy learners.

Major Language Development Characteristics in Adolescence

During the adolescent period, language continues to develop, particularly in the areas of syntax, semantics, pragmatics, and metalinguistic knowledge. However, it is difficult to identify any point during adolescence (not even in the lifespan) when the language developing process is truly complete. Therefore, when you read the information about adolescent language development in this chapter, it is important to keep in mind that the human language development process has a protracted and continuous nature and it is a lifelong process (Nippold, 2007).

Phonological development

Although the sound system in a given language is mastered by children around age 8, it is not until late adolescence that the phonetic inventory is refined (e.g., Owens, 2012). For example, by ages 11–12, adolescents are able to use stress and emphasis to express precise intent, and by ages 16 to 18, they are able to use vowel-shifting rules (Pence and Justice, 2008). During the adolescent period, students increasingly gain articulatory control of the phonological system. However, there is a gender difference in the production of some phonemes /f/, /θ/,/s/,/ʃ/. These differences emerge around age 6 but become more pronounced in late adolescence and young adulthood (e.g., Owens, 2012).

Perhaps, the most important phonological achievement in adolescence is sophisticated decoding ability. This attainment allows adolescents to decipher complex new words that they encounter in various subject areas, such as *seismology* and *superconductivity* in science textbooks and *stockbrokerage* and *commodity* in economics textbooks.

One interesting area of adolescent phonological development is the change in accent and dialect. Research suggests that accent and dialect change is often a result of peer influence. It seems that the maximum sensitivity to peer influence regarding accent and dialect is between ages 4 and 14 (Hoff, 2009). Adolescents' phonological changes may be caused by moving to a new social circle. For example, Hewitt (1982) described a phenomenon common among black adolescents of Caribbean descent who were born and live in London. These native Londoners began to adopt the British Jamaican accent when they were teenagers because the use of this dialect expressed their identity and their affiliation. Some white teens who became friends with the black teens also sometimes adopted Jamaican pronunciation.

Your Turn

Aside from what has just been discussed, explain why adolescents change or adopt certain accent and dialect. (Hint: Use the information from the developmental characteristics discussed in the beginning of the chapter.)

Lexical-semantic development

Word-learning approaches

Upon graduation from high school, students usually have command over about 60,000 words (Pence and Justice, 2008). They acquire such a large vocabulary in three ways: direct instruction, contextual abstraction, and morphological analysis (Nippold, 2007). Some words such as polysemous terms and metacognitive verbs necessary for academic learning must be directly taught for students to have a full understanding of their subtle meanings (Nippold, 2007). However, students will not accumulate a large quantity of vocabulary through direct instruction only. They must use other strategies to expand their vocabulary; that is, they also use **contextual abstraction** (learn words by using context clues to determine the meaning of unfamiliar words) and **morphological analysis** (analyze the components of words and use that information to infer meaning of the entire word; e.g., learn the word *talkativeness* by analyzing the parts *talkative-* and *-ness*).

Improvement in lexical and semantic ambiguity
Students in the secondary grades have gradually improved their ability in understanding ambiguous words and meanings such as *Polar bear* (animal) and *bear weight* and a host of other lexical level ambiguities, such as **homophones**, **homographs**, and **homonyms**.[1] As a result, they not only understand humor and jokes that take advantage of lexical and semantic ambiguity, but they also make jokes by applying lexical and semantic ambiguity. This is a great achievement during adolescence (see more discussion in the metalinguistic section).

Your Turn

- Collect a few examples of jokes made by adolescents (specify the age and grade) and analyze what linguistic ambiguity they have used. Discuss how you can take advantage of this ability to help adolescents in academic learning.
- Research a list of homophones, homographs, and homonyms and think about how you can use these words to help adolescents develop academic language and literacy by tapping into their increased understanding of linguistic ambiguity.

Morphosyntactic development

One of the major linguistic achievements during adolescence is the ability to understand and use more complex sentence structure and passive sentences. Syntactic complexity arises particularly in persuasive writing because students must produce longer sentences that contain greater amounts of subordination and stronger linkages between sentences (Pence and Justice, 2008).

Sentences produced by adolescents become longer with more words, embedded phrases and clauses. In addition, their sentence complexity has increased considerably over the years. Most notably, by Grade 12, adolescents' mean number of words (MNW) per C-unit in writing (13.27) surpasses MNW per C-unit in speaking (11.70) for the first time. Moreover, students in secondary grades gradually increase their mean number of words per T-unit. The MNW per T-unit is the highest in the persuasive genre for Grade 6 (11.75) and Grade 10 (14.26), intermediate in the descriptive genre for Grade 6 (10.45) and for Grade 10 (12.81), and lowest in narrative genre for Grade 6 (10.13) and Grade 10 (11.15) (Nippold, 2007). Further, the mean T-unit length is greater in the expository discourse genre than in the narrative discourse genre (Nippold, 2007).

Even though adolescents use simple sentences when they talk to their friends and use telegraphic phrases when composing text messages, they produce cohesively linked complex sentences when writing a persuasive essay on controversial topics or explaining the rules of a game to adults (Nippold, 2007).

Another area of adolescents' syntactic achievement is the emergence of uncommon syntactic structures. These structures are not frequently used in everyday conversation or writing communication, but are more essential in academic writing. Box 9.1 shows some examples of these uncommon syntactic structures.

Box 9.1   Examples of Low-Frequency Syntactic Structure

Noun phrase expansion	**Examples**
Appositives	Margret, the corporate attorney, bought a town house.
Elaborated subjects	Dogs such as collies, cocker spaniels, and golden retrievers were at the show.
Postmodification via prepositional phrase	They knew the Italian cyclist in the lead pack would win the race.
Postmodification via nonfinite verbs	The next runner to compete would anchor the relay.
Verb phrase expansion	
Modal auxiliary verb	We should have gone skating.
The perfect aspect	She had been working all day.
The passive voice	The house was carefully designed by a famous architect.

Modified from M. A. Nippold, *Later Language Development: School-Age Children, Adolescents, and Young Adults* (Austin: Pro-ed, 2007), p. 265.

Adolescents also improve gradually in their use of subordinate, coordinate, and correlative conjunction sentence structures. Box 9.2 lists examples of the conjunctive links that are used to connect sentences. These conjunctions, in particular the correlative conjunction, are not often used in speech, but often used in the writing modality to indicate the sophistication of an individual's language ability. In addition, understanding these conjunctions is essential in academic literacy. A student needs to be clear about the meaning of conjunctions in text comprehension or problem-solving in a content area. The conjunctions of *although* and *but* are the most challenging to acquire, and by Grade 6, only 68 percent of students can correctly comprehend them (Nippold, 2007). Students' understanding of these conjunctions improves as they progress through the grades. By the time they are in college, almost all students use them correctly. Adolescents also improve in their use of conjunctions such as *even though* and *because* when they move up the grades.

Box 9.2 Examples of Subordinating, Coordinating, and
Correlative Conjunctive Links

Subordinating conjunctive links

After
Although
As
As if
Because
Before
Even if
For
If
Since
Unless
Until
Whatever
When
Whenever
Whereas
While

Coordinating conjunctive links

And
But
Nor
Or
So
Yet

Correlative conjunctive links

Both...and
Either...or
Neither...nor
Not only...but also

Modified from M. A. Nippold, *Later Language Development: School-Age Children, Adolescents, and Young Adults* (Austin: Pro-ed, 2007), p. 266.

Moreover, adolescents also make progress in **adverbial conjuncts** like *moreover, however, accordingly, hence, similarly, consequently, therefore,* and *furthermore,* and **adverbial disjuncts** like *in my opinion, to be honest, frankly,* and *perhaps.* These linguistic devices make written discourse more cohesive. They frequently appear in academic contexts such as textbooks, essays, lectures, and debates. Ability in both using and producing these linguistic devices is particularly important in academic success. Adolescents do not usually use these adverbial conjuncts in their spontaneous conversations. Even if they do, they tend to use some common ones (such as *then*, *so*, and *though*). Although adolescents tend to perform better than elementary children when asked to choose correct adverbial conjuncts in experimental studies (Nippold, 2007), they still do not fully use these conjuncts correctly.

Furthermore, adolescents are found to use more adverbial conjuncts when they are engaged in persuasive writing in which they need to make their points clear through analyzing, discussing, and convincing. At age 17, the mean use of adverbial conjuncts is 0.77, which is a significant increase from 0.33 at age 11 (Nippold, 2007).

Finally, passive sentences, especially the instrumental nonreversible passives (e.g., *The window was broken by the ball*) appear most frequently between the ages of 11 to 13.

Your Turn

- Collect some writing and speaking samples of students in sixth, ninth, and twelfth grades and calculate the mean number of words per C-unit. What have you found? How do you explain your findings?

- Collect a narrative writing sample and an expository writing sample from a grade of your choice in middle or high school. Calculate the mean number of words per T-unit. What have you found and how do you explain your findings? (You may want to revisit Chapter 6 on the definition of T-units under the heading of "Grammatical Structure" before you complete this assignment.)

Pragmatic development

Adolescents continue to refine their conversational abilities. Because peer interaction is important during this developmental stage, adolescents are generally able to stay on a topic, transition between topics, adjust topics, maintain or extend dialogues, make relevant and meaningful comments, and offer support for peers. Compared with elementary school children, adolescents (e.g., twelfth graders) are likely to respond to feelings or attitudes expressed by the previous speaker, whereas elementary children (e.g., fifth graders) are more likely to respond to the facts expressed by the previous speaker (Hoff, 2009).

Moreover, earlier when we discussed morphosyntactic development, we suggested that adolescents are increasingly capable of distinguishing syntactic complexity depending on the context. For example, they use more complex sentences in the expository genre, use simple sentences in casual writing (such as notes), and use telegraphic phrases in text messaging. In addition to those abilities, they are also able to adjust their conversation styles with peers and adults. This kind of communication flexibility demonstrates adolescents' progress in their understanding of different language registers.

Metalinguistic development

One significant area of metalinguistic achievement during adolescence is the development of figurative language. **Figurative language** is the language that is used in non-literal and often abstract ways. People often use figurative language to evoke mental images and sense impressions in other people. Figurative language includes metaphor, simile, hyperboles, idioms, irony, and proverbs (Pence and Justice, 2008). Figurative language competence reflects an individual's cognitive level, creativity, and abstract reasoning ability (Nippold, 2007).

There is a developmental pattern in figurative language development. Although 2-year-olds have already produced spontaneous metaphors, it is not until age 10 that children appear to have the true ability to interpret metaphors (Hoff, 2009). But, it is during adolescence that the understanding of figurative language becomes reliable. There is a U-shaped curve in the production of figurative language. During early childhood, preschoolers are commonly observed using imaginative expressions such as "The faucet is crying" and "Pretend the headlights are eyes." During middle childhood, the use of imaginative expressions decreases, but the expressions increase during adolescence (e.g., in the form of slang such as *"chillin' in the crib"*) (Nippold, 2007). Below are some areas in which adolescents have improved with regard to figurative language use.

Metaphors and similes
A **metaphor** is a type of figurative speech in which a word or a phrase that is ordinarily used to describe one thing is used to describe another to make a comparison; for example, *"She is the apple of my eye."* A **simile** is similar to a metaphor. However, it uses the words "like" or "as" when comparing, for example, *"like water off a duck's back."* Although adolescents have already begun to understand some metaphors and similes, they continue to improve their comprehension and usage throughout school years and beyond.

Hyperboles
Hyperbole is another form of figurative language that uses exaggeration for emphasis or effect. For example, *"I am so hungry, I could eat a horse."* Children between ages 8 to 10 may use two kinds of cues to understand hyperboles: paralinguistic cues (the speaker's intonation patterns) or pragmatic cues (the speaker's intent) (Pence and Justice, 2008), whereas adolescents begin to improve their ability to understand hyperboles both in comprehension and production.

Idioms
Idioms are expressions that contain both a literal and a figurative meaning. Examples include *"We are in the same boat," "It's raining cats and dogs,"* and *"I've put that on*

the back burner." Adolescents improve their understanding and production of idiom throughout school years and beyond.

Irony

Using **irony**, the speaker or writer speaks or writes about one thing, but means another. For example, a person says, "*What a nice day!*" when the day is in fact cold and windy. Although elementary school children can begin to figure out the meaning by using acoustic cues or contextual information, adolescents are better at understanding the underlying meaning of an ironic remark.

Proverbs

A **proverb** is a conventional saying (usually giving advice). Examples include "*A stitch in time saves nine*" and "*An apple a day keeps the doctor away.*" Proverbs are one of the most difficult types of figurative language to master (Nippold, 2007). Children during middle childhood tend not to use proverbs spontaneously but begin to understand them. Adolescents begin to improve their ability to understand proverbs and some adolescents can use them in their communication. Proverb attainment during adolescence is associated with their development in abstract thinking because proverb understanding requires students to know the abstract and metalinguistic aspects of language. Proverb attainment also relies on a supportive linguistic environment.

Your Turn

Compile a list of metaphors, idioms, and proverbs. Ask a child in the sixth grade, ninth grade, and twelfth grade respectively to interpret their meaning. Overall, can these students get the meanings? Have you observed differences between younger and older students? Explain what you have observed with the information on adolescent cognitive and metalinguistic development.

Special Issues in Adolescent Language Development

Genderlect

Girls and boys at a younger age already exhibit differences. However, it is during the adolescent period that gender differences become more noticeable. In fact, the language use and styles of adult women and men are observable among adolescents. The gender differences or **genderlect**[2] (Owens, 2012) are shown in several areas: phonology (see the discussion in the phonological development section of this chapter), lexicon, and conversational style.

There is a quantitative difference between females and males in lexical use. Males tend to use more swearing words and coarse language in conversation, while females use more polite words (e.g., *please*). Females use more descriptive words (e.g., *adorable*, *sweet*, *lovely*) and color terms than males. In addition, females use more emphatic expressions more frequently than males (e.g., *oh dear* and *goodness*) and men use more expletives (e.g., *damn it*) (Owens, 2012).

There are also some style differences. First, adolescent girls typically speak "standard" English more often than boys (this pattern continues through adulthood). Second, adolescent boys and men tend to be more verbose than adolescent girls and women, contrary to common belief. Third, adolescent girls and women tend to use language that expresses more uncertainty (e.g., ask more questions) than men. Fourth, adolescent boys and men interrupt to suggest alternative views, to argue, to introduce new topics, or to complete the speaker's sentence. In contrast, adolescent girls and women interrupt to clarify and support the speaker (Owens, 2012). Moreover, women tend to sustain conversation topics longer than men. For example, 96 percent of male-introduced topics are sustained by females and only 36 percent of female-introduced topics are sustained by males (Owens, 2012, p. 387). Finally, males place more value on status and report talk, competing for the floor in conversational interaction, while females value connections and rapport, fulfilling their role as more cooperative and facilitative conversationalists who are concerned for their partner's positive face needs (H. Brown, 2000).

Some attribute the gender differences in communication styles to the language socialization process. Research shows that parents speak to their girls and boys differently. As early as 2 years of age, daughters are imitated more by their mothers and talked to longer than their sons. Fathers use more imperatives and insulting terms (e.g., butthead) with their sons and address their daughters as honey and sweetie. Fathers also use the diminutive form (adding a smallness suffix to denote affection) more frequently with daughters and interrupt them more often than sons (Owens, 2012). There are also sociocultural factors that contribute to the gender differences. In some cultures such as Africa and the Caribbean, women interrupt men far more frequently than in the US.

Your Turn

- Do you think the research finding about the gender differences in communication apply widely or narrowly to adolescents across contexts?
- Listen to a conversation between adolescent girls and boys. Do you find any differences? If so, what are the differences? What is your take on gendered language and how would you address the differences in classroom interactions?

Bidialect

Bidialect is the term used to describe students who use African American English (AAE) and mainstream American English (MAE) in different situations (Godley and Escher, 2012), such as in peer communication and in academic learning. Some educators assume that bidialectal students are less academically capable (Godley and Escher, 2012) and that speaking AAE is ungrammatical, lazy, and unintelligent (Blake and Cutler, 2003). Many teachers tend to single out the grammatical "errors" of AAE speakers and focus only on correcting these students' grammatical "mistakes," even though research has clearly shown that teachers' correction of students' AAE grammatical features does not really help students learn MAE (Wheeler and Swords, 2010). When bidialectal students perceive that AAE is not acceptable in classrooms, they tend not to be motivated to learn (Dickar, 2004). Box 9.3 shows an account of an AAE speaking student and how her teacher's negative reaction to her grammar affected her motivation in creative writing.

Box 9.3   A Story about an AAE Speaking Student

I'd been given an assignment by Mrs. Brakett, my 5th-grade teacher, to write a creative story. I decided to write a story about my shoe. Well, it wasn't actually my shoe but an evil shoe that had the power to make me extremely clumsy. After having completed the story, I discovered it was a masterpiece (I mean that in the most humble way).

Unfortunately Mrs. Brakett didn't share in my enthusiasm. She praised the story, but said that the use of language was unsatisfactory because of the word "ain't." That one little word, that I only used once in the entire four pages of brilliant creativity "forced" her to give me a *B–*. Now I would've been able to understand her judgment if this had been a book report. But this was supposed to be a creative story. So it wasn't really me saying ain't, but it was my shoe saying ain't. Now I don't know about you, but I've never met a shoe with good grammar.

I think it took me a good 3 years to finally put that behind me, and start taking creative risks again.

A. F. Ball, "Expository writing patterns of African American students," *English Journal*, 85(1) (1996): 27–36.

Ball (1996) closely observed the expository text writing strategies of four high school AAE students. She found that these students were able to intersperse the African American discourse styles into their formal expository writing, such as creating an atmosphere of interactive audience negotiation by using phrases like "*I hope you've enjoyed my explanation*" and by shifting styles from a formal stance in the opening to a performative stance like "*I would like to relate.*" These strategies created a sense of orality or conversational involvement within these students' expository texts. Ball lists some of the culturally influenced discourse strategies these students used:

- Using repetition to create formulaic patterning.
- Establishing a link or sense of rapport with the audience through the use of inclusive lexical terms like "we're."
- Taking on a quality of performance in the style and delivery of the text.

- Using orally based organization patterns in addition to topic associations, compare and contrast patterns, and the traditional five-paragraph essay used in most classrooms.
- Using interactive dialogue with the audience with phrases like *"you know what I mean, man."*
- Using common African American idioms that assume mutual understanding based on similar cultural experiences.
- Linking topics through the use of personal anecdotes and narratives interspersed within expository texts.

Ball believes that these students successfully included culturally influenced strategies and styles of expression in their expository writing. Such inclusions do not represent random instances of poor writing; instead, they demonstrate AAE speaking students' syncretic features of language use.

It has been shown that encouraging students to code-switch, that is, use both their dialects such as AAE and MAE, in the classroom can motivate adolescent bidialectal students to learn their academic language and literacy well (D. Brown, 2009; Godley and Escher, 2012; Wheeler and Swords, 2010). For example, in content-area learning such as in English language arts classes, speaking AAE can allow bidialectal students to focus on generating ideas during class discussions without fearing of having their language corrected. Research has shown that encouragement in rich, student-centered discussions conducted in the language that students feel most comfortable with (either AAE or MAE) can have positive effects on their academic reasoning and literacy. Speaking AAE allows students to draw upon the stylistic features of AAE that are important for understanding the rich use of language such as evocative language, descriptive metaphors (Smitherman, 1994), and hyperboles.

Your Turn

- Analyze the vividness of the hyperbole used by an AAE speaker and discuss the linguistic effect beyond its literal expression: *"You're going to come back quick! Or I will hit you so hard that your offspring will feel..."*
- Encouraging students to use L1 (see Chapter 7) and AAE (in this chapter) in academic learning can motivate and facilitate their academic learning. Suppose you have students who are Ln learners and bidialectal. How do you help them learn the content area by encouraging them to use their L1 and bidialect? Propose some concrete ideas.

Academic Literacy Development in Adolescence

Academic content-area reading comprehension

Reading in middle and high school grades is situated in disciplines (e.g., in mathematics, science, and history). The disciplinary or content-area literacy is demanding for readers for several reasons. First, students typically have fewer experiences with expository texts. Second, content-area texts are often denser than narrative text. Third, the vocabulary in content-area texts is often technical and the organization is typically harder to follow, and the multipart words and unusual words found in social studies and science texts are difficult to tackle. Finally, discipline-based texts often require readers to have some prior knowledge of the topic under study (Marchand-Martella et al., 2013). Thus, in order to achieve the expected proficiency characteristics listed in Box 9.4, the majority of adolescent students need more specialized literacy support and explicit instruction when they are learning subject contents as they move through the secondary grades.

Box 9.4   Characteristics of Successful Readers

- Know how to monitor their comprehension and use a range of strategies when they realize they do not understand what they are reading.
- Are able to explain concepts in the text and relate different concepts within a text to each other and to relevant prior knowledge.
- Can generate self-explanations during reading, ask questions that probe the connections among parts of the text, or see explanations.
- Use cues to the logical organization of a text to guide their comprehension.
- Rely on multiple types of knowledge as they interpret texts by using information about words, concepts, sentence structures, text structures, and genres.

Modified from S. R. Goldman, "Adolescent literacy: learning and understanding content," *The Future of Children*, 22(2) (2012): 89–116.

Adolescents' reading development falls into Chall's Stages 3 and 4 and the beginning of Stage 5 (see Box 6.2 in Chapter 6). Adolescents typically become increasingly more mature and critical. With proper support, they are able to handle difficult concepts described in different text genres. They also begin to consider multiple viewpoints. By the end of high school (around age 18), adolescents typically can construct knowledge and understanding from readings that others have written (Pence and Justice, 2008).

Adolescents' reading skills increasingly improve as a result of the integration of vocabulary expansion, morphosyntactic sophistication, and pragmatic and metalinguistic development. By high school, adolescents usually can use higher-level skills such as inference and recognition of viewpoint to aid comprehension in science and social studies textbooks. Some adolescents can also use theme comprehension strategy to help their reading comprehension, although this is a more difficult skill to develop than inferential skills. **Theme comprehension** refers to the ability to derive a more general message from a passage of text (Nippold, 2007).

Academic writing

Typically, adolescents' writing ability develops and improves as they engage in a variety of writing activities (writing reports and essays; editing and revising their own or others' writings). By the middle school years, the length and diversity of children's productions increase. Advanced narratives and expository text begin to develop. Narrative essays by some adolescents can contain temporal events unified by a topic sentence, elements of story grammar, character development, plot, and dialogue. Their expository essays may include a unifying topic sentence, comments referenced to the topic, and elaborations on the comments. In these writings, the syntax production becomes increasingly more complex. For example, their clause length increases both in writing and speaking, as shown in their increase in the mean length utterance (7.7 for a 13-year-old and 8.6 for a 17-year-old). There is also an increase in embedded subordinate clauses and a decrease in coordination or compound sentences. Moreover, the use of relative clauses doubles between ages 7 and 17, and adverbial clauses, especially those signifying time (when ...), increase and diversify.

At the phrase level, there is an increase in pre- and postnoun modifiers. By adolescence, students typically can modify nouns with adverbs as well as adjectives and use four or more modifiers with a noun. Their verb phrases are expanded by the increasing use of modality, tense, and aspect. However, it is not until early adulthood that most people develop the cognitive processes and executive functions needed for mature writing. Adolescent students still need teacher guidance in planning and revising their writing. By junior high school, teens are usually capable of revising all aspects of writing (Owens, 2012).

Moreover, student background knowledge is important in determining their writing complexity. For example, in a study, a group of boys 9–14 years old were asked to write an essay on the topic of football. Half of the boys knew very little about it and the other half knew a great deal about it. The result showed that in terms of their writing organization and content the boys who knew about the sport wrote better essays than the ones who knew little (Nippold, 2007).

Compared with other writing genres, persuasive writing is more difficult and takes longer to develop. Even though persuasive writing is usually first introduced to children at Grade 3, it remains challenging well into adulthood. The reason for its difficulty is that persuasive writing requires a writer to integrate advanced syntactic, semantic, and pragmatic knowledge as well as flexible thinking, metacognitive skills, and a knowledge base. The writing needs to show organization, logic, and supporting facts. It must also be convincing and show consideration of opposing views (Nippold, 2007).

Your Turn

Locate a high-school senior's college application essay and analyze it on the basis of the characteristics described in the above section (pay particular attention to the syntactic-phrase level of analysis). Did you find any discrepancy between the student's writing performance and the characteristics discussed in the book? If so, how do you explain the discrepancy?

Hypertext

Although literacy learning via hypertext involves the basic processes of comprehending and writing text, it differs from print-based literacy in significant ways (McNabb,

2005–2006). Adolescents may be good at using hypertext for a variety of reasons, but they need guidance to use it more effectively in academic learning. For example, in a recent series of studies, researchers assigned adolescents and adults to visit informational, entertainment, and commercial websites to complete a series of tasks, including online reading. Adolescents generally performed less effectively (with a 55 percent success rate) than did adults (with a 66 percent rate). The researchers concluded that the difference between the performances of the adolescents and the adults was because the adolescents had insufficient reading and information research skills, as well as less patience. Teenagers in the study also exhibited less tolerance for websites that they considered boring or difficult to figure out. And they gave more credence to visually appealing sites than adults did (McNabb, 2005–2006).

Your Turn

Give a topic for an adolescent to research on the internet. Observe how this student performs the search. What have you found?

Critical literacy ability development

At the secondary level, students are increasingly exposed to readings that offer contradictory viewpoints. This requires students to critically sort through these different viewpoints and make their own judgment or conclusions about the message, in particular the underlying message. With increasing metacognitive development, adolescents are more able to ask questions spontaneously about what they are reading. However, adolescents still need teacher guidance to rethink their identity as readers and they still need teacher support in developing critical literacy ability.

Your Turn

Find a short controversial article and give it to an adolescent to read. Discuss the reading with the student (you may want to use some guiding questions). What have you discovered about this student's critical literacy abilities?

Supporting Strategies for Adolescents

General principles

To help adolescents continue to develop language and literacy, it is important to consider the following general principles:

- Refrain from criticizing adolescents in academic learning activities, including language-learning activities. In particular, do not do it in front of their peers. Try to be as positive and supportive as possible. Using humor to replace criticism tends to achieve better results.

- Value your students' opinions and allow choices and freedom when carrying out language and literacy learning activities.
- Provide opportunities for your students to take risks in their language and literacy learning and encourage self-exploration.
- Motivate your students to be **self-regulated learners**.[3]
- Encourage your students to work with other peers.
- Help your students develop critical thinking and critical literacy abilities while carrying out academic learning.
- Use innovative methods to engage your students in academic language and literacy learning.
- Link language and literacy development to needs in college, career, and life.

Support academic literacy

Academic reading and writing are a complex process which calls upon a student's advanced levels of linguistic and cognitive ability as well as their background knowledge, in addition to other factors such as affects, motivation, and identity. By the end of high school, adolescents need to develop sufficient knowledge and ability to carry out reading and writing tasks in order to function well in college, the workplace, and life in the twenty-first century. Unfortunately, two-thirds of eighth- and twelfth-graders in the United States read below grade level (Brozo, 2009) and only 38 percent of high school seniors scored at or above proficient level according to a National Assessment of Educational Progress report (National Center for Education Statistics, 2010), and 40 percent of high school graduates lack the literacy skills required by employers (Brozo, 2009). Moreover, 15-year-olds in the United States (with the exception of Connecticut) consistently perform poorly in reading, math, and science in the Program for International Student Assessment (PISA). Although the reason for these shocking facts is complex, they may be partly attributed to our educational system and to the fact that literacy skills are not deliberately taught after third and fourth grades. In fact, there is a widespread assumption that literacy instruction is only for early elementary grades (Snow and Moje, 2010). Thus, explicit literacy instruction must continue throughout the K-12 grades to ensure that adolescent students are able to navigate and understand advanced narrative and expository content-area texts (Marchand-Martella et al., 2013) and achieve the proficiencies described in Box 9.4.

Explicit teaching of reading comprehension
Recent research suggests that an explicit approach to teaching literacy skills may be more effective than the discovery-based approach (e.g., Alfieri et al., 2011). There are quite a number of explicit instructional approaches that have been discussed in research literature, among which three seem to be promising: strategy-based instruction, discussion-based instruction, and disciplinary content-based instruction.[4]

Strategy-based instruction   The major underpinning idea of **strategy-based instruction** (SBI) is to teach students reading comprehension by focusing explicitly on teaching them strategies to aid their comprehension. It has been shown that teaching a single strategy to students tends to have limited effects. Instead, teaching students multiple strategies, and especially teaching the coordination of different strategies, tends to have better results. Box 9.5 shows some SBI examples that you can try in your content-area teaching.

Box 9.5   Examples of Strategy-Based Instruction

Reciprocal teaching (RT)   RT teaches four strategies for processing both narrative and expository texts: clarification, questioning, summarization, and prediction. The basic steps are that students work in a small group. They monitor their reading to clarify that they understand the meaning of the text, ask questions they have about the content, summarize the content, and predict what will be next in the text.

Structure strategy training (SST)   SST teaches students how to use paragraphing and signaling cues to figure out the overall organization of the information they are reading. For example, they may use paragraph beginning words and phrases (such as *In summary, First, Finally, On the other hand*, and *The problems is*) to find out whether the text is presenting a problem and solution or is comparing and contrasting ideas.

Self-explanation reading training (SERT)   SERT uses explicit, direct instruction to show students the purpose and function of different strategies.[5]

Paraphrasing helps students to understand what the text says, i.e., what the basic structure and meaning of the words and sentences in the text are.

Putting into one's own words makes the content more familiar.

Elaborating and predicting asks readers to make inferences that connect what the text says to what they already know or expect based on common sense and general reasoning heuristics.

Bridging engages readers in understanding how different concepts and ideas in the text fit together. It also helps readers achieve more sentence-to-sentence connections as well as a more coherent grasp of the overall text.

Comprehension monitoring orientates students to thinking about what they do and do not understand and to using other strategies to repair problems they detect.

Modified from S. R. Goldman, "Adolescent literacy: learning and understanding content," *The Future of Children*, 22(2) (2012): 89–116.

When implementing SBI to help adolescent students improve reading comprehension, you need to be cognizant of the following. First, effective SBI involves teaching multiple strategies and ways to coordinate them. Some strategies involve explicit attention to features of texts as cues to important content and its organization. Other strategies connect pieces of information within the text. Yet other strategies build connections to readers' prior content knowledge and expectations regarding additional content. Second, coordinating multiple strategies requires students to assess their successes and failures in using particular strategies, seeing whether they have achieved sufficient understanding and what to do if they have not. Third, explicit teaching of strategies and their coordinated use is necessary for most students, especially when they are reading to learn. Moreover, students need opportunities to practice the explicitly taught strategies and get feedback on their performances before they acquire these strategies (skills).

However, the drawback for SBI is that it is hard for students to be able to coordinate multiple strategies. This is because SBI requires students to engage with the texts for a sustained period of time, which students sometimes either do not do at all, or do only in cursory ways. Moreover, when SBI is given as generic strategies, students may not be able to apply these generic strategies to different text formats such as newspaper articles, research reports, editorials, and web texts (Goldman, 2012). Therefore, when implementing SBI, you may want to make sure that students engage in doing the necessary work, provide ample opportunities for them to be exposed to a variety of text formats, and scaffold their comprehension by using different strategies.

Discussion-based instruction   **Discussion-based instruction** (DBI) is based on student discussions. This type of instruction focuses on using dialogues to explore ideas and develop understanding of different types of text in different subject areas. Box 9.6. suggests a list of DBI activities that you can try in your content-area teaching.

Box 9.6   Discussion-Based Instruction Activities

- Book club
- Collaborative reasoning
- Instructional conversation
- Grand conversation
- Junior great books
- Literature circles
- Paideia seminar[6]
- Philosophy for children
- Questioning the author

Modified from S. R. Goldman, "Adolescent literacy: learning and understanding content," *The Future of Children*, 22(2) (2012): 89–116.

DBI encourages students to become more active in articulating meaning in and around text and to enhance basic comprehensions of the meaning of the text and inferences based on the text. Below are some examples of using DBI in content areas.

Use cultural modeling in literature content   The cultural modeling method can be used in literature instruction to help students explicitly become aware of how they process a literary text. **Culture modeling** indicates that many of the literary devices that students need to know to engage critically with literature are already part of their repertoire, developed in an everyday context in their cultural communities. For example, evocative language and descriptive metaphors are often used in AAE. Students are already using them in their everyday communication. Teachers can help AAE speaking students realize how the same language techniques are also used by writers and how these devices can be used to interpret literature. Similarly, symbolism is another language device that students have been exposed in their daily lives. Suppose this literary device is critical for understanding a particular type of literary text. Teachers would begin by presenting a more familiar form such as the lyrics of a song, logos, or advertisements, since students already understand them. Building on their prior knowledge, teachers then ask students to discuss what the symbol means and how they know that it is a symbol. Through discussion (first led by the teacher and then by students), students have opportunities to give their views on the reasoning behind their interpretations. More importantly, by making their reasoning explicit, they are able to apply the same thinking as they approach the texts under study.

Promote mathematical thinking through discussion   DBI can be applied in mathematics instruction as well. For example, teachers can provide discussion prompts that are appropriate to math thinking. Teachers encourage students to provide answers to a problem and to explain how they got the answer, and why their method worked. If students get the same answers using different methods, teachers will ask why the different methods worked. If they arrive at different answers, teachers ask which answers are the most reasonable in math thinking. In such discussions, students are accountable to the subject matters and to their classmates for their thinking. This type of discussion is called **accountable talk**.

Teach science-specific discourse   In science class, teachers need to give explicit instruction and modeling of science-specific discourse. Teachers need to help their students, through discussion, with how to construct science arguments, which include recording, measuring, and repeating trials of data collection; noticing patterns in data; reasoning about data; and knowing how to argue on the basis of evidence instead of personal opinions. Teachers also need to help students to use, through discussion, different forms of data representation, as well as aids for presenting arguments, and help them clearly indicate claim and data, and the reasoning that connects data to claim.

Practice the reading apprenticeship approach in biology   The **reading apprenticeship approach** integrates biology content and literacy. Students learn to annotate biology text first by identifying key words or noting the main ideas and then talking to each other about the text using their annotations. The discussion process makes student thinking visible, that is, they share not only their interpretations, but also the processes by which they come to these interpretations. By doing so, students become more aware of the strategies they are using and the characteristics of texts to which they are responding (Goldman, 2012).

It must be mentioned that we currently do not fully understand how DBI relates to other features of effective classroom instruction such as the choice of texts and tasks, and student engagement. Moreover, we do not quite understand what is the minimal level of skilled facilitation needed for productive student discussion (Goldman, 2012).

Disciplinary content-based instruction **Disciplinary content-based instruction** (**DCBI**) engages students in problems and questions typical of a specific academic discipline and in the literacy practices in which students work on the content in the discipline and communicate about it.

Students are encouraged to read and communicate like a professional in a particular discipline. For example, in science classes, students are taught to read and communicate like a scientist (e.g., be able to translate among different representational forms to understand, reason about, and express key relationships among qualified variables), and in history class, students are taught to read and communicate like a historian (e.g., use provided documents and their knowledge of history to analyze or exemplify a historical event or policy).

Your Turn

Locate a SAT subject test in a specific discipline. Identify the areas that are specifically relevant to academic literacy skills. Try to link each of these areas to the three reading comprehension instructional approaches discussed above.

Support writing development

Writing, in particular academic writing, is an essential part of school experience. As students move up in grade levels, they are increasingly expected to compose texts to demonstrate and deepen their knowledge and understanding of their subject areas. In other words, students move from learning to write in early elementary levels to writing to learn in late elementary and secondary grades. Writing has become increasingly crucial for students to be successful in high-stake standardized tests such as SAT (the Scholastic Aptitude Test), and most importantly, high literacy proficiency is demanded by work and life in the twenty-first century. Therefore, educators must pay special attention to this aspect in order to educate a generation of students who can function well in the globally competitive environment.

Scaffolding writing Writing is a long, gradual, and continuous process. Even though adolescents typically have developed abilities in planning, organizing, and revising their writing, they will still need teacher scaffolding and opportunities to write. Benko (2012–2013) has suggested seven concrete steps in scaffolding students' writing:

- Give students writing tasks that are appropriately challenging for their level. If a writing task is too easy, students will not make an effort and if a writing task is too difficult, they will give up quickly.
- Encourage students to feel the ownership of what they are writing and inspire them to write things that matter to them.
- Help students focus on the most important parts of the writing task first by first simplifying the writing task and letting them practice and perfect the skills that they can manage (this is called **reducing degrees of freedom**). However, it is important to remember that you must help your students move on for new challenges as soon as they master the skills that they initially try to master. The goal of reducing degrees of freedom is to use a simple writing task as a stepping-stone for a more challenging task.
- Provide direct feedback for students to pay attention to the areas that need improvement so that they can continue to make progress. Teacher feedback should not only focus on the surface level correction such as punctuation, grammar, words, or phrases. Rather, teacher feedback should aim to help students improve the overall quality of their writing. For example, teachers can help students understand which parts of their writing need attention and provide guidance and examples of how they can revise.
- Mark critical features of writing for individual students. Students' progress in writing varies. Teachers need to help students understand important parts of the task and assess why they have difficulties by using mini-lessons to address areas that an entire group of students needs to better understand and using individual or small group conferences to mark critical features for individual students.
- Provide good samples of writing for students. There are different ways to do this. You can demonstrate how to write. You can use exemplary writings from newspaper, commentary, and peers. The goal is to show what exemplary writing should look like.
- Structure lessons to help students integrate what they know and what they will learn and avoid concentrating on writing skills that are irrelevant to the current task.

Box 9.7 summarizes the key concepts of these seven steps for scaffolding writing. Make sure to practice these steps in your classroom practice.

Box 9.7 Important Steps for Scaffolding Writing

- Provide a writing task that is appropriately challenging.
- Help students to feel the ownership of what they write.
- Practice the reducing degrees of freedom.
- Provide direct feedback for students to pay attention to the important parts of their writing.

- Provide individualized instruction to mark critical features for individual students.
- Provide good models of writing.
- Help students integrate old and new learning.

Modified from S. L. Benko, "Scaffolding: an ongoing process to support adolescent writing development," *Journal of Adolescent and Adult Literacy*, 56(4) (2012–2013): 291–300.

Engage writing with popular culture materials   Writing, particularly academic writing, can be a tedious process. Many adolescents can find it boring if they do not see a real purpose. One effective way to engage adolescents in writing is through popular culture since most of them show a special interest in it.

Fan fiction has recently been introduced and discussed in educational literature (e.g., Kell, 2009). **Fan fiction** is written by fans of the original work with their own versions of creativity and twist. It can appear as stories, novels, comics, games, or other media properties. Fan fiction writers post their work on the internet (www.FanFiction.net). Encouraging and scaffolding adolescents to participate in fan fiction writing can make adolescents more interested in writing and so develop skills necessary for academic writing. There are several unique advantages in fan fiction writing.[7] First, fan fiction writing motivates adolescents because it offers multiple modes of representation (e.g., stories, cartoons, novels, musicals) and diverse pathways to participation (participatory culture building as a writer, reader, or a critic). Second, it fosters an excellent learning community in the online affinity spaces, in which adolescents can share their work, build a peer social network, and develop collaboration abilities. Third, it helps adolescents to see a real purpose for writing. Fourth, it helps adolescents to know their strengths and the areas that need improvement through peer critique and interaction. Finally, it can help students develop literacy abilities such as creatively using supportive dialogue, strong vocabulary, cohesive storyline, and critical literacy.

Your Turn

- Provide two concrete examples for implementing the seven steps for scaffolding writing.
- Visit www.FanFiction.net and familiarize yourself with its contents and styles (books, cartons, comics, games, movies, musicals, and TV shows) and think about how you can use this particular internet affinity space to engage adolescents in developing reading and writing skills as well as critical literacy and digital literacy abilities.
- Biancarosa and Snow (2006) have developed a guideline for effective adolescent literacy instruction, which contain 15 important and effective practices (see below). Find one concrete example for each of these elements and discuss why they may be useful in helping adolescents develop content-area literacy abilities.
  - Explicit comprehension instruction
  - Effective principles embedded in content

- Motivation and self directed learning
- Text-based collaborative learning
- Strategy tutoring
- Diverse texts
- Intensive writing
- Technology
- Ongoing formative assessment
- Extended time for literacy
- Professional development
- Ongoing summative assessment of students and programs
- Teacher teams
- Leadership
- Comprehensive and coordinated literacy program

C. Biancarosa and C. E. Snow, *Reading Next: A Vision for Action and Research in Middle and High School Literacy: A Report to Carnegie Corporation of New York*, 2nd edn (Washington, DC: Alliance for Excellent Education, 2006).

Your Turn

Review the language and literacy standards for the secondary grades in the common core standards (http://www.corestandards.org) and discuss how you can use the supporting strategies proposed in this chapter to achieve the common core expectations.

Explicit teaching of content-specific vocabulary use

Explicitly teaching content-specific vocabulary can facilitate adolescent students' vocabulary development and content comprehension. Using vocabulary in science as an example, many words used in science are long and uncommon in everyday reading. However, most of these words are the combinations of word parts that students are already familiar with (prefixes, suffixes, and roots). Therefore, deliberately teaching students with the words parts can facilitate students in understanding scientific vocabulary. For example, you can create a list for students and help them learn the meanings of affixes (see Box 9.8), suffixes, and roots. Alternatively, you can discuss the meaning of word parts each time when they occur in the texts.

Box 9.8   Example of Affixes and Their Meanings in Science

Affix	Meaning	Affix	Meaning
ante-	before	ortho-	straight
aster-	star	per-	through
baro-	pressure	physio-	organic
chrono-	time	ultra-	beyond
circum-	around	vita-	life
omni-	all		

> ## Your Turn
>
> Research a textbook in your specific content area. Make a list of the key vocabulary in the text. Identify those words that you can preteach by using their prefixes, suffixes, and roots.

Increase the frequency of complex sentence use

As mentioned in Chapter 6, the discourse genre and communication context often determine the frequency of complex sentence use. As we read in the previous discussion in this chapter, adolescents produce the most words per T-unit in persuasive and descriptive genres. Research suggests that these two types of genres are more sensitive to developmental growth in T-unit length than the narrative genre (Nippold, 2007). Therefore, you need to create opportunities for adolescents to engage in the use of complex sentences through activities such as debates, book reports, and research project reports. It may be more effective for you to model presentation styles focusing on complex sentence use. In addition, you can also tap into college application essays, scholarship applications, mock college admission interviews, and resume writing in high-school junior and senior years.

> ## Your Turn
>
> Obtain a writing sample of a high school student and calculate its syntactic complexity by using T-units. What have you found? Discuss how you can use the strategies suggested above to help this student further increase his or her sentence complexity.

Support figurative language development

As discussed earlier in the chapter, figurative language comprehension and usage demonstrate an individual's high-level metalinguistic ability. Figurative language use can help a writer evoke mental images, create impressions, and make writing more interesting and persuasive. Therefore, when you teach a topic in a content area, you may want to provide students with some words that may have different meanings and ask them to play with the words and come up with jokes, ironies, advertisements, and comic strips. If you do this often, your students will not only improve their ability in using figurative language, but also be more motivated to learn the topic you introduce to them.

> ## Your Turn
>
> Select four words or concepts from your content area and think about how you can use them to help your students develop figurative language use.

Encourage code-switching

Since encouraging bidialect use in classrooms can facilitate academic content learning, several strategies have been suggested in the literature (e.g., Godley and Escher, 2012; Wheeler and Swords, 2010). First, at the beginning of the school year, discuss code-switching with your students. You can ask students to role-play talking about the same issue with a friend and with a teacher. Help students understand the different linguistic registers for different communication purposes.

Second, stop treating AAE features as errors and regard them as specific linguist patterns.

Third, do not "force" bidialectal students to speak MAE at all times. Doing so will likely reduce students' participation and negatively affect their motivation for academic learning. It may be more productive to encourage these students to use the language they feel most comfortable with in discussions.

Fourth, help students appreciate language complexity and diversity by comparing specific examples of language features in both AAE and MAE.

Finally, provide opportunities for students to practice using MAE in meaningful contexts such as class presentation and academic writing and help students understand language choices.

Your Turn

Use the above strategies to create a lesson plan. In particular, the lesson plan should highlight the opportunities for students to code-switch AAE and MAE.

Teach self-regulation

Teaching students self-regulation strategies in academic learning should be emphasized in the secondary grades. Students need to develop the ability to self-monitor their academic literary progress. For example, in reading comprehension, the class interactions, activities, and assignments that you provide for your students should aim to help them develop self-regulatory strategies in the following areas: search for the major purpose of a message, infer the author's assumptions about the topic, and know how well the author supports an opinion. These strategies will be needed for the SATs, which emphasize abilities in critical reading skills, vocabulary, and other areas.

In writing, the goal is to help adolescents continue to develop the strategies discussed in Chapter 6 and write effectively in a variety of genres. However, focusing on developing persuasive writing strategies required in the SAT essay is critical: organization, clarity, grammatical accuracy, vocabulary style, and the use of logic and convincing evidence. Activities and assignments in different content areas need to aim at developing these skills and helping students self-monitor their progress.

Your Turn

Locate a recent SAT essay topic and ask a high-school senior to compete the writing in 25 minutes. Analyze the student's writing in the areas of organization, clarity, grammatical accuracy, vocabulary variety, and supporting evidence. What have you found? If you have to design a plan to help this student develop self-monitoring strategies, what would that look like?

Summary of Key Points

- The phonetic inventory is refined during adolescence. Gender differences in the production of some phonemes become more pronounced in late adolescence. Adolescents demonstrate sophisticated decoding ability, which allows them to decipher complex new words in their different content areas. Some adolescents also experience accent and dialect changes due to peer influence.

- Adolescents enlarge their vocabulary size through direct instruction, contextual abstraction, and morphological analysis. Adolescents gradually improve their ability in understanding ambiguous words and meanings in homophones, homographs, and homonyms. They can not only understand humor and jokes, but also make jokes by applying lexical and semantic ambiguity.

- Adolescents increase their ability in understanding and using more complex sentence structures such as subordinate, coordinate, and correlative conjunction sentences and passive sentences. They also make progress in adverbial conjuncts and adverbial disjuncts. Syntactic complexity arises particularly in persuasive writing, as evidenced in the increase of the mean number of words per C-unit and per T-unit.

- Adolescents continue to refine their conversational skills. They develop the ability to stay on a topic, transition between topics, adjust topics, maintain or extend dialogues, make relevant and meaningful comments, and offer support for peers. They respond to feelings or attitudes expressed by the previous speaker. They are able to distinguish the syntactic complexity depending on the context and demonstrate understanding in using different language registers.

- Figurative language comprehension and production improve greatly during adolescence. For example, understanding of proverbs becomes more reliable.

- There are gender differences in word use and communication styles.

- Using bidialect in class discussion can generate rich ideas that will help AAE-speaking students improve their academic learning.

- Adolescents' reading development falls into Chall's Stages 3 and 4 and the beginning of Stage 5. Adolescents typically become increasingly more mature and critical. With proper support, they are able to handle difficult concepts described in different text genres. They also begin to consider multiple viewpoints. Around age 18, adolescents typically can construct knowledge and understanding from readings that others have written.

- Syntactic complexity increases during adolescence. Adolescents typically are able to write effectively in a variety of genres such as narrative, descriptive, expository. However, persuasive writing is more difficult and remains challenging for them.

- Although adolescents are actively engaged in hypertext use, research shows that they may not perform well using hypertext due to their insufficient reading and information research skills as well as their lack of patience.
- With increasing metacognitive development, adolescents continue to improve their critical literacy abilities. For example, they are able to ask questions spontaneously about what they are reading. However, they still need teacher guidance to rethink their identity as a reader.
- Content-area academic literacy development needs explicit instruction. Three promising instructional methods may be effective: strategy-based instruction, discussion-based instruction, and disciplinary content-based instruction.
- Popular culture such as fan fiction may be an attractive way to motivate adolescents to write and develop academic literacy skills.
- Explicit teaching of word parts such as affixes, suffixes, and roots can facilitate content vocabulary development and eventually help content comprehension.
- Increasing complex sentence use and figurative language talk through real life situations may facilitate adolescents' academic literacy advancement.
- Teaching self-regulation skills can help adolescents continue their literacy development in college, the workplace, and life.

Key Terms

Accountable talk
Adverbial conjuncts
Adverbial disjuncts
Bidialect
Contextual abstraction
Discussion-based instruction (DBI)
Disciplinary content-based
  instruction (DCBI)
Fan fiction
Figurative language
Formal operational thought
Genderlect
Homographs
Homonyms
Homophones
Hyperbole

Irony
Mark critical features
Metaphor
Morphological analysis
Proverbs
Reading apprenticeship approach
Reciprocal teaching
Reducing degrees of freedom
Self-explanation reading training
  (SERT)
Self-regulation
Simile
Strategy-based instruction (SBI)
Structure strategy training (SST)
Theme comprehension

Notes

1. Homophones are words that sound alike. They are sometimes spelled alike, such as *brown bear* vs *bear weight*, or are spelled differently, such as *brown bear* vs *bare hands*. Homographs are words that are spelled the same and may sound alike, such as *row* a boat vs *row* of

homes, or they may sound different from each other such as *record* player vs *record* a speech. Homonyms are words that are spelled and pronounced in the same way, but are different in meaning; for example, *brown bear* vs *bear* weight (Pence and Justice, 2008, p. 267).

2. Genderlect is the collective stylistic characteristics of men and women (Owens, 2012, p. 388).
3. Self-regulation is a form of self-control or self-monitoring in the learning process which consists of strategies such as setting standards and goals for oneself and engaging in self-motivated learning.
4. Note that most of the ideas discussed in this section are based on Goldman (2012).
5. SERT has now been extended into a computer-based automated intelligent tutoring system. iSTART (Interactive Strategy Trainer for Active Reading and Thinking)
6. In a Paideia seminar, students and teacher participate in a collaborative, intellectual dialogue facilitated with open-ended questions about a text. The teacher encourages students to talk about their learning and use questioning to learn how to solve complex problems.
7. Ideas inspired mostly by Kell (2009) and Curwood, Magnifico, and Lammers (2013).

Recommended Further Readings

Brown, D. W. (2009). *In Other Words: Lessons on Grammar, Code-Switching, and Academic Writing.* Portsmouth, NH: Heinemann.

Charity-Hudley, A. H. and Mallinson, C. (2010). *Understanding English Language Variation in U.S. Schools.* New York: Teachers College Press.

Nippold, M. A. (2007). *Later Language Development: School-Age Children, Adolescents, and Young Adults.* 3rd edn. Austin: Pro-ed.

McNabb, M. L., Thurber, B. B., Dibuz, P., McDermott, and Lee, C. A. (2006). *Literacy Learning in Networked Classrooms: Using the Internet with Middle-Level Students.* Newark, DE: International Reading Association.

10

Learning English As a New Language in Adolescence

Prereading Questions and Activities

- What advantages and challenges do older learners such as adolescents have with regard to learning a Ln?
- Do you think promoting home language development will hinder adolescent Ln development? Why and why not?
- Select a text and ask a student who learned English later in life to read it. Do you hear any difference in his or her accent? Identify the areas (such as words or stress) that are articulated differently and explain why.
- Analyze a text written by an adolescent Ln learner. Discuss the strengths and needs of this Ln Learner.
- What roles do motivation, identity, aptitude, anxiety, affect, and personality play in learning a new language during adolescence? Support your opinions with examples.

Topics to Be Addressed in This Chapter

- Characteristics of learning a Ln beyond the sensitive period
  - Age in acquiring a Ln and its impact on academic performance
  - Differences in the knowledge of the English language between learners whose English is L1 and those whose English is Ln
  - Reorientation in learning a Ln
  - Unique strategies in learning the Ln
  - Academic demands in the Ln
  - Uniform achievements in the Ln

Understanding Language and Literacy Development: Diverse Learners in the Classroom, First Edition. Xiao-lei Wang.
© 2015 John Wiley & Sons, Inc. Published 2015 by John Wiley & Sons, Inc.
Companion website: www.wiley.com/go/wang/langandlit

- ○ Ln learner ability diversity
- ○ Code-switching and cultural identity
- Acquiring a Ln in adolescence
  - ○ Phonological development
  - ○ Lexical-semantic development
  - ○ Morphosyntactic development
  - ○ Pragmatic development
  - ○ Metalinguistic development
- Developing academic literacy in a Ln
- Strategies for supporting academic language and literacy development in a new language

Learning Objectives

After completing this chapter, you should be able to do the following:

- Understand the distinct differences between English as a L1 and English as a Ln during adolescence.
- Understand that adolescent Ln learners must reorient themselves in using the Ln to communicate.
- Understand the unique language-learning strategies used by adolescent English language learners.
- Understand the challenges that adolescent English language learners face.
- Understand that different English language learners may have different difficulties in English due to the specific linguistic features in their L1.
- Understand English language learners' diversity.
- Understand how the cultural identity of English language learners can impact their English language learning.
- Understand that English as L1 students who learn a foreign language at secondary grades experience similar and different Ln learning experience to English language learners.
- Understand the distinctive features of adolescent English Ln learners in the areas of phonology, lexicon, semantics, morphology, syntax, pragmatics, and metalinguistic knowledge.
- Understand the characteristics of literacy development (including academic literacy) of adolescent Ln learners.
- Know how to support adolescent Ln learners not only in English language learning, but also in academic success, and how to motivate them to develop the literacy skills, including digital and critical literacy skills, necessary for college, the workplace, and life.

Characteristics of Learning a Ln beyond the Sensitive Period

There are a number of complex issues involved in learning a Ln after the sensitive period in adolescence. Several notable aspects are briefly mentioned before discussing the Ln acquisition characteristics.

Age in acquiring a Ln and its impact on academic performance

As we discussed in Chapters 2, 4, and 7, there is a sensitive period in language acquisition. Despite disagreement about the age when the sensitive period ends, it is generally agreed that beyond puberty, it becomes increasingly difficult for an individual to achieve native competence in a Ln. However, learning a Ln after the sensitive period may have some advantages. Although younger learners (e.g., in early and middle childhood) may have a better chance of achieving native competence, older learners (e.g., in adolescence) may compensate by using stronger cognitive skills such as better memory and metalinguistic abilities (Jia and Fuse, 2007). In fact, research shows that older Ln learners performed (at least, on tests) better in **suprasegmental phonology**[1] in syntax (Long, 1990; McLaughlin, 1978 and 1990), and in learning speed (Jia and Fuse, 2007).

Moreover, age also plays a role in academic performance. A study that looked at learners of English as a second language (ESL) suggested that the learners who entered the ESL program when they were between 8 and 11 years old were the fastest achievers, requiring 2–5 years to reach the fiftieth percentile on national norms in all the subject areas tested. Those who entered the program when they were between 5 and 7 years old were 1–3 years behind the performance level of their English language learner (ELL) peers who entered the program aged 8–11, when both groups had the same length of residence. Arrivals between 12 and 15 years old experienced the greatest difficulty and were projected to require as much as 6–8 years to reach grade-level norms in academic achievement when schooled only in the second language. Whereas some groups may reach proficiency in some subjects in as little as two years, it is estimated that at least 4–8 years may be required for all ages of Ln learning students to reach the national grade-level norms of native speakers in all subject areas of language and academic achievement, as measured by standardized tests (Collier, 1987).

Knowledge of the English language

There is a fundamental difference between an English L1 speaker and an English Ln learner in their knowledge about English. Native English speakers intuitively know which are possible sounds of English and which are not (e.g., /œ/ cannot be an English sound), when to combine sounds and when not to (e.g., What are you *gonna* do?), and which sounds can be blended and which cannot (e.g., /b/ and /r/ can be blended into *brain* and /b/ and /n/ cannot be blended into *bnick*) (Gass and Selinker, 2001). Similarly, a native English speaker will know intuitively which are correct English sentences and which are not, which morphemes can be used alone (e.g., free morpheme: *man* and *book*) and which morphemes cannot be used alone (e.g., bound morpheme: *un-*), which meaning of a word is acceptable and which is not (e.g., the *leaf* of a table vs the *leaf* of a hand), and how to communicate in a proper context. It will take a Ln learner a while to master the knowledge of a language, given that the Ln is motivated, makes an effort, and has ample opportunity to interact with the Ln.

Reorientation in the Ln

Learning a new language involves more than just language learning. To be a competent language user, a student must also acquire a new culture and a new identity. A Ln learner, especially an older Ln learner, must reorient herself in using the Ln to communicate. A reorientation of both things and feelings is necessary (H. Brown, 2000). Therefore, it may take a while for Ln learners to be competent in the area, even after they have mastered the linguistic aspect of English.

Your Turn

Interview an adolescent Ln learner. Based on the interview, identify the skills that a Ln learner needs time to master beyond the English language itself.

Strategies used in learning the Ln

Ln learners are not passive in learning a Ln. Instead, they use different strategies to reconstruct the Ln learning process. The common strategy found among Ln learners is the **transfer strategy** in which Ln learners apply their L1 knowledge to the Ln. There are two kinds of transfers: Positive transfer and negative transfer. **Positive transfer** refers to using knowledge in L1 to tackle Ln learning which results in correct Ln production. For example, a Ln learner might use the French word *nuit* to learn the English word *night*. **Negative transfer** refers to using knowledge in L1 to learn Ln which results in incorrect Ln production. For example, a learner uses the Spanish word *nudo* (knot) for the English word *nude*.

Ln learners also use the **avoidance strategy** to learn English. That means that when a Ln feature is beyond a learner's reach, he tries to use an alternative way to express the same meaning. For example, when a Ln learner does not know how to use the passive voice, he tries to find a different way to express his meaning.

Your Turn

Find two examples of *transfer* and *avoidance* by observing one or several adolescent learners of a Ln in a naturalistic classroom interaction. Discuss how these strategies used by Ln learners can promote and hinder their English language learning.

Academic demands in Ln

Learning a Ln and transitioning from L1 to Ln requires adolescent Ln learners not only to have oral language flexibility, but also to move beyond the personal, contextualized discourse of an immediate family and neighborhood. They need to use the Ln in formal academic settings and to obtain proficiency in academic literacy with the Ln. It is particularly challenging for those adolescent Ln learners who are from cultures where oral-based modality has been the primary vehicle for learning and expressing. These adolescents need to learn not only the Ln, but also the way to construct meaning from complex, written sources in school (Cohen and Horowitz, 2002). Thus, English Ln learners face double challenges: to learn English to communicate, and to learn academic content by using English.

Uneven achievements in the Ln

English Ln learners often do not have uniform achievements in all the areas of the Ln. For example, English learners with Chinese L1 and those with French L1 may have different advantages and difficulties in learning English. Chinese learners may have difficulties in learning the English tenses, whereas French learners may have difficulties in pronouncing the English *th* /θ/ sound.

Your Turn

Research the linguistic features in Spanish, Chinese, and Arabic (or any other languages that interest you). Discuss the advantages and challenges in learning English for Ln learners who are from these linguistic backgrounds.

Ln learners' ability diversity

English Ln learners are not a homogeneous group and they differ in myriad ways. For example, Ln learners vary in their rate of Ln acquisition and academic success depending on their age of arrival, English proficiency level upon arrival, basic literacy, math skills, and content knowledge in the native language upon arrival, number of years of schooling in English, their parents' educational levels, and the family's socioeconomic status. It is very difficult to generalize about them. The big challenge for a classroom teacher like you is that you must take into consideration each Ln learner's specific history when you plan your instruction.

Your Turn

Observe a class in middle or high school. Identify the Ln learners in the class. Interview these students with questions such as their age of arrival in the United States, their English and literacy proficiency level upon arrival, their subject content knowledge (such as math) in their L1 upon arrival, their number of years of schooling in English, their parents' education levels, and their family SES. What have you found?

Cultural identity

As discussed in Chapters 4 and 7, language mixing is the hallmark of multilingual individuals. However, language mixing is not always a linguistic phenomenon; it can also be intentionally used by multilingual speakers to reveal their cultural and linguistic identity. For example, a study that examined mixing patterns in a Puerto Rican Spanish-speaking community in New York City suggested that members of this community engaged in an especially fluent form of mixing, where the same utterance could include several switches from Spanish to English and back again. This kind of mixing can be an important marker of social identity in the Puerto Rican community; rapid, fluent mixing served to identify the speaker as both Spanish- and English-speaking and, thus, as both Puerto Rican and American. This kind of language mixing can be regarded as code-switching.

Box 10.1 Example of Code-Switching

But I used to eat the bofe, the brain. And then they stopped selling it because, tenian, este, le encontraron que tenia (they had, uh, they found out that it had) worms. I used to make some bofe! Después yo hacía uno d'esos (then I would make one of those) concoctions: the garlic con cebolla, y hacía un moho, y yo dejaba que se curare eso (with onion, and I'd make a sauce, and I'd let that sit) for a couple of hours. Then you be drinking and eating that shit. Wooh! It's like eating anchovies when they drinking. Delicious!

Example from S. Poplack, "Sometimes I start a sentence in English y termino en Espanõl: towards a typology of code-switching," *Linguistics*, 18 (1980): 581–618.

The adolescent period is the time when teens are exploring their identity. Ln learning adolescents may intentionally mix their L1 to reveal their cultural and linguistic identity.

English L1 speaker learns a foreign language

In Chapters 4 and 7, we have discussed children who learn English as a Ln in the school environment and use the Ln to learn content. However, at the secondary level, many students of English as a L1 will also begin to learn a foreign language. These English-native speakers who are learning a foreign language encounter similar and different Ln learning issues as those students who learn English as a Ln. The acquisition process is similar. However, the exposure and nature of learning are different. The Ln learners of English, in fact, have more exposure to English than students who learn a foreign language such as Spanish and French in school. Moreover, English speakers who learn a foreign language usually do not use the language to learn the content areas.

Your Turn

Ask a middle or high school student who is learning a Ln (often termed a foreign language) and a student who is learning English as a Ln to write a narrative about their language-learning experience. Compare the two writings and what have you found? How do your findings inform you about the same and different needs of these two students?

Acquiring a New Language in Adolescence

Phonological development

One of the most noticeable phonological aspects in adolescent Ln learners is their accent. The accent of a Ln speaker can often be attributed to her L1 origin. However, the degree of a learner's accent largely depends on the age when the learner is exposed to English. It is generally observed that the older a learner, the more pronounced the accent will be.

Other factors such as motivation and identity also play a role in a learner's accent. Some learners may want to maintain their cultural and linguistic identity by deliberately pronouncing English with their L1 accent. Other learners are more motivated to imitate an English native-like accent.

Also, research has suggested that a speaker of a language with a more marked L1 structure than the Ln will have an easier time learning the Ln structure than a speaker whose L1 is less marked. For example, an English L1 speaker will have no difficulty in producing German words where there is no contrast in final position. On the other hand, a German speaker learning English will have to learn how to make a contrast in final position (*tab* vs *tap*; a more marked structure than the German L1) and can be expected to make errors (Gass and Selinker, 2001).

Adolescents who are learning English as a Ln may have difficulties in certain English consonant clusters such as fi*fth* and fi*sts* and consonant clusters at the ends of the words (Gass and Selinker, 2001). Also, some Ln learners tend to use epenthesis (insert a sound in words). For example, when pronouncing the word *floor*, Iraqi-Arabic speakers tend to pronounce it as fi*loor* and Egyptian-Arabic speakers tend to say it as i*floor* (Gass and Selinker, 2001).

Sometimes Ln learners delete or add sounds to English. For example, Korean learners tend to add a final sound to the English word sack /sæke/. It is also usually difficult for Ln learners to combine sounds like native English speakers, such as "I'm gonna wriDa leDer" (I am going to write a letter).

Lexical-semantic development

There are several distinct features regarding the lexical-semantic development of adolescent Ln learners.

1) *Lexical discrepancy*
The lexicon discrepancy issue addressed in Chapter 7 still holds true for adolescent Ln learners. Adolescent Ln learners initially may have more English receptive lexicon than expressive lexicon. They may also have more social lexicon than academic lexicon.

2) *Cross-linguistic influence*
Because adolescent Ln learners have acquired L1 on a more solid footing than children who learn English in middle childhood, they are likely to have more L1 vocabulary than Ln vocabulary. As a result, when Ln learners do not have enough English words to use, they will naturally borrow from their L1 lexicon.

3) *Lexicon memory storage differences*
Recent research has shown that there is a difference in how words are stored in the memory system between L1 and Ln learners. For example, Ln language learners tend to store their words in the **episodic memory** (the memory of autobiographic events that are associated with contexts and emotions), and L1 individuals store their words in **lexical memory** (the ability to remember words and morphemes) (Witzel and Forster, 2012).

Your Turn

If L1 and Ln learners store their words differently in their memory, what is the indication for classroom instruction of Ln learners?

---

4) *Emotion and emotion-laden words in a Ln*
Research suggests that **emotion words** (words directly referring to particular affective states such as "*scared*" and "*anxious*" or processes such as "*to worry*") and **emotion-laden** words (words that do not refer to emotions directly but instead express emotion such as "*loser*" or elicit emotions from interlocutors such as "*malignancy*") are represented, processed, and recalled differently from **concrete words** (e.g., *cup*, *chair*) and **abstract words** (e.g., *myth*, *emancipation*) (e.g., Altarriba and Bauer, 2004). Some researchers suggest that emotion words and emotion-laden words should be separated as a distinct class of words because they are more deeply encoded in the L1 and depend more on context availability than other types of words (e.g., Pavlenko, 2008).

Ln learners are often hindered by their limited emotion and emotion-laden words in a Ln, especially when they need to express anger and frustration (Pavlenko, 2008). This is because L1 or the language learned early in life is more emotional than the language(s) learned later in life (Ln). At an early age, the development of the L1 linguistic system coincides with the development of concepts and emotional regulation. In the process of affective socialization in young children's L1, some words become stimuli for positive or negative arousal. However, when learning a Ln later in life (such as during adolescence), Ln learners need to develop such responses anew in the Ln. The school environment where most adolescents spend a substantial amount of time daily may not necessarily offer the same opportunities for affective linguistic conditioning as L1 learning in childhood. Because adolescent Ln learners' conceptual system and emotion regulation system may have already reached a more or less stable state, many emotion and emotion-laden words in the Ln may not trigger their personal and affective associations or sensory representations (Pavlenko, 2008). Many adolescent Ln Learners are likely to experience difficulty in expressing emotion-related vocabulary.

There are seven processes in Ln learners' emotional lexicon development (see Box 10.2).

Box 10.2   Ln Learners' Conceptual Processes in Emotional Lexicon

- **Coexistence**   Ln learners categorize emotion-eliciting situations in each of their languages similarly to monolingual speakers of the respective languages.
- **L1 conceptual transfer**   Ln relies on the L1 concept of emotions, and Ln learners have not internalized the representations of emotions in the Ln. (It is often beginning or intermediate Ln learners, in particular classroom learners, who have not had an opportunity to be socialized into the target language community. This reliance may result in positive transfer in the case of identical concepts in L1 and Ln, and it may also cause negative transfer in the case of partially overlapping concepts in L1 and Ln or language-specific concepts.)
- **Internalization of new concepts**   Ln language learners are socialized into the Ln community and use the emotional words in the right context. However, Ln socialization may not guarantee internalization. Internalization does not always happen. Ln learners may be aware of the core meaning but do not appeal to the words. This may be because they have not yet formed a unified conceptual category that allows them to identify this emotion and to use the words accurately.
- **Conceptual restructuring**   A previously existing L1-based concept has been modified but does not fully approximate the target (initiated but not completed).
- **Conceptual convergence**   Ln learners create a concept or category distinct from monolinguals of the respective languages.
- **Conceptual shift**   Ln learners have resided in the Ln context and their representations of partial concepts have shifted in the direction of Ln-based concepts (as opposed to restructuring, where the shift has been initiated but not completed).
- **Conceptual attrition**   As a result of living in the Ln environment, Ln learners have ceased to rely on particular conceptual categories to interpret their experiences. While it does not imply that they no longer recognize the

categories, it means that the categories cease to be central to their interpretation of the world around them. Conceptual attrition may be further accompanied by attrition of emotion vocabulary and difficulties in expressing one's emotions in one's native language.

Modified from A. Pavlenko, "Emotion and emotion-laden words in the bilingual lexicon," *Bilingualism: Language and Cognition*, 11 (2008): 147–164.

When examining the processes in Ln emotional lexicon development, we need to consider the following aspects (Pavlenko, 2008):

- The processes are based on late Ln learners and adults.
- None of the seven processes account for the whole emotion domain in the multilingual lexicon. Rather, they depend on individual learners' personal history and on the relationship between the concepts in question. Some conceptual representations may display evidence of restructuring and others may be evidence of attrition.
- The process is dynamic and not static. The conceptual configurations may change when Ln learners' experiences and speaking contexts change.
- These processes are context-dependent; different aspects and dimensions are activated in different settings and in different languages.

Your Turn

Make a list of English emotion words and emotion-laden words. Ask a Ln learning adolescent to explain the meanings of these words. What have you found?

5) *Targeted reading and Ln vocabulary increase*

Ln language vocabulary development, particularly academic vocabulary development, depends critically on the type of readings that learners are asked to read. Research indicated that learners who read a combination of expository and narrative texts gained more vocabulary than those who read only an expository or narrative text. Moreover, learners who read a text with target word–text ratios of less than or equal to 2 percent did not learn significantly more vocabulary than those who read a text with a ratio of 2–5 percent (S. Huang, Willson, and Eslami, 2012).

Your Turn

Analyze a narrative text and an expository text in a middle or high school textbook in a particular content area. Discuss how these two kinds of texts contribute to academic vocabulary development with regard to Ln learners in their unique ways and why a combination of the two kinds of text tends to yield better vocabulary gain for Ln learners.

Morphosyntactic development

English language learners may have difficulties in several morphosyntactic areas such as passive voice, adverbial conjuncts, regular and irregular past tense, third-person singular, progressive aspect -*ing*, copula *be*, and auxiliary *do*. Though these areas can be taught, adolescent English language learners may not always produce these correctly in spontaneous speech and writing. However, the morphosyntactic characteristics of English language learners are not uniform. Not all learners show the same kinds of difficulties in their English morphosyntactic structures. In general, if the learners' L1 is closer to English, they will produce fewer or no errors, and if their L1 is less close to English, they may have more difficulties in mastering the English morphosyntactic features. For instance, older Chinese L1 learners are likely to encounter tense difficulties because their L1 does not have verb tenses.

As a compensatory measure, Ln learners sometimes use avoidance as a strategy when they are unable to express themselves in English. As mentioned earlier, if they don't know how to use the passive voice, they may use an alternative sentence structure to express the same concept.

Pragmatic development

In different cultures, there are different styles of communication and different ways in which men and woman use language to communicate. For instance, among the Carib Indians in the Lesser Antilles, males and females must use entirely different syntactic and phonological variations. In Japan, women's and men's language is differentiated by formal (syntactic) variations, intonation patterns, and nonverbal expression (H. Brown, 2000). It is not an easy task for adolescent Ln learners to master the pragmatic aspect of the English language because learners may not know the idiomatic expressions or cultural norms in the Ln, or they may transfer their L1 rules and conventions into the Ln.

There are two commonly occurring pragmatic failures among Ln learners: pragmalinguistic failure and sociopragmatic failure. **Pragmalinguistic failure** occurs when the pragmatics used by Ln learners is systematically different from the one used by native speakers of the target language or when speech act[2] strategies are inappropriately transferred from L1 to Ln. Pragmalinguistic failure can be illustrated by the transfer of the Russian word конечно (of course) when it is used in place of *da* (yes) in English. For example, "Are you coming to the party?" "Of course." When конечно is transferred into English like this, it may be interpreted as a peremptory response or even as an insult, as if the first speaker is asking a question that is stupid to ask or to which the answer is self-evident. **Sociopragmatic failure** refers to the social conditions placed on a language caused by different beliefs in social interaction. An example of sociopragmatic failure would be where a Russian speaker asks an American for a cigarette on the assumption that cigarettes are virtually free in the United States as they are in Russia (Baba, 2010).

A speaker's emotive communication under given circumstances is in accordance with cultural expectation. However, many Ln learners tend to transfer their L1 cultural norms to the Ln. For example, research on Japanese Ln learners suggests that Japanese

English-language learners tend to have difficulties encoding affect appropriately in English. They frequently employ the following four strategies:

- They accommodate the English patterns.
- They avoid language-specific features unique to English. They avoid using hyperbole and curse words in English. When it comes to a situation that requires the use of hyperbole in English, they tend either to simply avoid using it or to find that they are not competent enough to express it.
- They overgeneralize English linguistic rules. They hypercorrect the tense match in English, which prevents them from effectively using historical present as a linguistic expression of affect in English. This is perhaps because tense matching is not part of Japanese grammar, whereas aspect is more predominant in Japanese.
- They demonstrate negative transfer from L1. They clearly indicate negative transfer in the area of correlation between the intensity of aggression and the use of **weakeners**[3] rather than **strengtheners**. They use more weakeners when the intensity level of aggression increases (Baba, 2010).

Your Turn

Explain why the Chinese speaker misunderstood the American English speaker's speech act:

SARAH: I couldn't agree with you more.
CHENG: Hmmm ... (Thinking: "She couldn't agree with me? I thought she liked my idea!")

Example from "What is a speech act," at http://www.carla.umn.edu/speechacts/definition.html.

Metalinguistic development

Figurative language development in the Ln

Unlike the younger Ln learner in elementary grades, adolescent Ln learners already possess a rich idiomatic knowledge base in their L1 in addition to their cognitive advancement (at the formal operational stage). They are able to detect idioms in readings with ease. However, they may not be able to understand and interpret the Ln figurative meanings right away. They may first use a literal interpretation, and after that fails, they may begin to try other strategies. Ln learners' ability to make sense of the figurative language largely depends on their mastery of the Ln. Research suggests that Ln learners use cues to understand and interpret figurative language such as vivid phrasal idioms in addition to the pragmatic system that they employ in order to construct the appropriate cultural meaning of a given idiom in the Ln.

Idiomatic understanding in a Ln is a continuous and interactive/integrative process. Ln learners transact and produce meaning from a text and from what they bring to the dynamic act of reading by way of their prior personal and cultural background knowledge, experience, interests, values, and societal paradigms (Liontas, 2002, p. 211).

Your Turn

Identify five English idioms and discuss what a Ln learner needs to know in order to understand them.

Nonverbal communication

Ln competency is not only restricted to the linguistic aspect, but also the nonlinguistic aspect. Every culture has its distinct emblems (conventional gestures) that can set it apart from others. The same hand gesture, for example, may have different meanings in different cultures. The famous American "OK" gesture is an obscene gesture in Latin American cultures. Box 10. 3 lists some areas of nonverbal communication.

Box 10.3   Nonverbal Communication

Hand gestures and body movements   Every culture has its distinct emblems (conventional gestures) and body movements. For example, rubbing one index finger on the other index finger means "shameful" in the US, whereas in Chinese culture, one scratches an index finger on one's cheek or nose. Nodding one's head means "yes" among most Europeans and Americans, but among the Ainu of Japan, "yes" is expressed by bringing the arms to the chest and waving them (H. Brown, 2000, p. 262).

Eye behavior   In American culture, avoiding eye contact is impolite, while in Japan, intense gazing may indicate rudeness.

Proximity   The comfortable physical distance between speakers differs from culture to culture. In the American culture, the safe physical distance between people is about 20 to 24 inches. If it is violated, people feel threatened. However, in Latin American and southern European cultures, this distance is too great.

Touching behavior   In some cultures touching signals a personal and intimate interpersonal communication.

Olfactory dimensions   In some cultures, odor such as perspiration is considered unacceptable, whereas in others it is acceptable and even attractive (H. Brown, 2000, p. 265).

Time orientation   Punctuality is understood differently in different cultures. "We start the meeting at 8:00 a.m." may mean different timeframes for people from different cultures. For North Americans, it means 8:00 a.m. sharp, but for some Arabs and Latinos, this may mean roughly at 8:00 a.m.

Artifacts   Clothing and jewelry signify a person's sense of self, socioeconomic class, and identity. North Americans tend to avoid being seen wearing the same clothes for two consecutive days and tend also to wear different clothing for different occasions. However, this may not be true in many other cultures.

To use a language authentically, a Ln learner must also understand and master these nonverbal behaviors. It usually takes a long time for Ln learners to achieve nonverbal communication proficiency in a Ln.

Your Turn

Research nonverbal communicative behaviors in different cultures and compile a list of these behaviors that differ among cultures. Share this with your classmates and discuss how these different nonverbal communication behaviors can impact Ln learners' communication in English.

Developing Academic Literacy in a Ln

In the following section, we will focus on how adolescent Ln learners develop their academic literacy in English.

The relationship between background knowledge and academic literacy comprehension

To comprehend what one reads does not only depend on literacy knowledge; it also depends on the background knowledge of the reader. A reader is likely to comprehend a text about the Roman Empire if he has knowledge of Roman history. Ln learners sometimes may encounter difficulty in English comprehension because they lack the cultural background knowledge.

The relationship between oral language and academic literacy

In Chapters, 3, 4, 6, and 7, we discussed the relationship between oral language and literacy. However, for some adolescent Ln learners, oral language development is not necessarily a prerequisite for written language development. Some of them can become higher-level readers in the Ln without being able to speak it or speaking it well, given that these students have established oral and written competence in their L1 (Cohen and Horowitz, 2002).

Impact of prior schemata on Ln academic literacy development

A learner's assumption and expectation about a text (academic text included) are largely influenced by his prior cultural and linguistic experience. Thus, Ln learners will unavoidably approach Ln texts, both in comprehension and production, with the schema they have formed in the process of acquiring their L1(s) and culture(s). In other words, Ln learners will approach Ln texts with expectations and assumptions that may be different from the ones intended by authors or schools.

There are at least four kinds of schemata that may influence a learner's approach to school academic literacy: content schemata, cultural schemata, formal schemata, and linguistic schemata. **Content schemata** refers to a learner's prior knowledge of the ideas expressed in an oral or written text. This schemata is crucial in reading and writing in any language, and it is even more vital for Ln learners, as incomplete content schemata in the Ln will cause a serious comprehension gap when they encounter unfamiliar texts (Ferris and Hedgcock, 2014). **Cultural schemata** (or abstract schemata) includes knowledge about cultural-specific practices, traditions, relationships, identities, beliefs, and values. Learners develop cultural schemata in the everyday routine interactions with people around them. Cultural schemata is an extension of content schemata, and they are inextricably intertwined; that is, in order to understand a text or participate in a speech event, a learner must have established a role as a member of the culture (Ferris and Hedgcock, 2014). **Formal schemata** means what a learner knows about how texts and speech events are organized. **Linguistic schemata** entails a learner's knowledge of the morphosyntactic properties and lexical choices associated with particular genres and speech events, as well as with particular topics (Ferris and Hedgcock, 2014).

Pioneering research in comparing cultural differences in rhetorical styles suggests that writers from different cultural and linguistic backgrounds exhibit different writing styles. For example, Kaplan (1966) found that Arabic-speaking writers made extensive use of coordination (using conjunctives such as "and," "or," and "so" to link sentences together), which was considered excessive by English academic standards. Chinese- and Japanese-speaking writers tended to circle around a topic and argument, rather than approaching it head-on or introducing an explicit argument in the way that is expected of English academic writing. French and Spanish writers tended to digress in exposing a topic or argument, often introducing extraneous material more frequently than did English-speaking academic writers. Subsequent studies supported Kaplan's earlier study. Hinds (1990) found that Anglo-American essay writers generally pre-reveal their purposes or arguments quite early in their texts, adhering to a predominantly deductive rhetorical structure. In contrast, Japanese and Korean writers consistently delay revealing the purposes of their writing until the end of their texts, preferring an inductive rhetorical pattern.

In recent years, some scholars have challenged the findings of the previous studies. They argued that the previous studies were culturally deterministic (e.g., Casanave, 2003), and the texts produced by Ln writers were treated as static (Kubota, 2010). In fact, some studies found that Japanese speakers could successfully transfer deductive features from Japanese into their English writing (e.g., Kubota, 2010). Thus, the current view regarding the rhetorical differences of Ln learners is that one should not presuppose that Ln learners from a given linguistic or cultural background will necessarily experience the same challenges from the rhetorical style in the Ln as reported in previous studies. However, knowing how patterns of organization in written language differ cross-culturally and cross-linguistically can help both teachers and Ln learning students understand the diverse ways in which writers make meaning in and across languages and literacies.

Your Turn

Obtain a few samples from Ln learning adolescents. Analyze the writing styles of these students. Have you found any differences? If so, explain how these differences may be a result of the learners' cultural and linguistic backgrounds.

Supporting Strategies for English Ln Learners in Adolescence

Motivation for reading and writing

All things considered, motivation is most important in ensuring that adolescents will continue to read and write throughout their lives. Research consistently suggests that motivation is essential for sustained learning. It leads to an increase in effort and energy, and it also increases initiative and improves performance (Wang, 2009). Thus, creating a need for your Ln learning students to read and write can help them discover the power of print and become avid language users.

Helping Ln learning adolescents realize that writing can be used as an effective tool or channel for self-expression (for example, to express emotions, thoughts, concerns and anxieties) is essential. Forming the habit of keeping journals and diaries may be a good way for Ln learning adolescents to find a safe place to express themselves. Writing responses to an issue of their choice may be another way for adolescents to express themselves. You can help your students by providing them with a sample (a model) initially.

Expression of emotion

Adolescents experience many changes and many emotions and Ln learning adolescents are no exception. As De Vries Guth and Pratt-Fartro (2010) commented, "Adolescents are a strange and wonderful mix of mature and child-like qualities, manifested in no particular order. They shift from serious, concerned citizens to teasing children with one comment and can be reduced to silence or tears with a look from a peer or teacher. It is very important to understand the variability of the adolescent years and enjoy the challenges if one is to be successful working with these demanding, yet giving adolescents."

Given these distinct characteristics, Ln learning adolescents need help in using the Ln to recognize and express their feelings and in learning how to identify and label their feelings (Greenspan, 2007), as well as in learning how to use words in the Ln to evoke emotions. Thus, you may want to intentionally help your students identify their emotions and label them with accurate words. For example, you can ask them to label the feelings of frustration, joyfulness or anger with accurate words. You can intentionally draw your students' attention to places where words and phrases are used to express emotions. You can also ask your students why they feel the way they feel and write their thoughts down and then discuss them.

When students feel the power of words, they will use them to express emotions more accurately (for example *moody* is not necessarily *depressed*). Identifying emotion through language use can help both students and teachers understand their emotions, which is important during adolescence. At the same time, emotional contexts like these will provide cues to help adolescents retrieve emotional words more readily.

Self-monitoring

Ultimately, the most sustainable way to ensure that adolescents want to continue with Ln development is to help them self-monitor. Self-monitoring is also called self-regulation. As mentioned in Chapter 9, self-regulation is a process of setting standards and goals for oneself and engaging in self-motivated learning. Self-regulation may not be achieved immediately. However, if you can incorporate this goal into your teaching plan, your students can become lifelong Ln language users.

You can begin by helping your students determine their own language and literacy learning goals by providing them with options. For example, when giving writing-related assignments, you can provide several choices for adolescent Ln learners. By doing so, Ln learners will feel empowered in their own learning.

Once Ln learners decide their learning goals, you may also need to help them self-monitor (self-observe) their progress. Research suggests that self-monitoring brings about changes in learning (McCombs and Marzano, 1990). Sometimes, Ln learners are not necessarily competent in observing their learning behaviors, and they may not necessarily know whether they make mistakes or not. What you can do is to help them reflect on what they have done and ask questions to help them observe their own learning behaviors.

To help Ln learners become self-monitoring, you may also want to help them develop self-instruction skills. This process requires you to demonstrate language-learning strategies. You can model self-instruction by showing (through thinking aloud, speaking out your thoughts) what you would do in a given learning task.

To help adolescent Ln learners develop self-monitoring in academic language learning, you may also want to help them self-evaluate their work. These questions can help: "Do you think you have put enough effort into this assignment?" "If you were to grade yourself, what grade do you think you would give yourself and why?" "Do you think that you have fulfilled the learning goals you set for yourself?"

Encouraging self-reinforcement is a good way to encourage self-regulation. For example, if a student has completed his assignments with great effort, he should be encouraged to treat himself to class activities he enjoys such as playing computer games. If he has not completed his assignments because of lack of effort, he should be encouraged to spend less time playing computer games. When learners begin to self-reinforce, their learning behaviors tend to improve.

Metalinguistic analysis

Adolescents who are learning English as a Ln will have developed metalinguistic knowledge in their L1. Thus, you can encourage them to take advantage of this ability to analyze their errors in English. For example, you can ask students to identify their errors or you can hint at their errors. Encourage them to reflect on the reasons for these errors.

Moreover, encourage Ln learners to notice the differences between L1 and Ln. An activity you can ask Ln learners to do is to record their own conversation about a topic with a native English-speaking peer, then analyze and compare the differences. The same can be done in writing, although you may want to look at the writing of the native English-speaking peer first to see whether mistakes are present (if so, eliminate those first).

Your Turn

Reread the section on metalinguistic refection in Chapter 7. Identify the English errors made by a Ln learning adolescent. Develop a step-by-step plan on how to help this adolescent self-monitor his or her errors by using the information in Chapter 7 as well as the information in this chapter.

Encourage the use of translanguage

Because English learning adolescents often have to do double work in learning the English language and in using English to learn subject content, and since it may take them 7 years or more to achieve academic English proficiency (Carhill, Suárez-Orozco, and Páez, 2008), it may be necessary to encourage them to use their L1 together with their Ln to achieve academic success. The use of L1 and Ln alongside each other in the classroom is called **translanguage**. Translanguage is often referred to as code-switching. For example, students use their L1 in discussion and use their Ln in writing or vice versa. Traditionally, translanguage use in educational settings is frowned upon. However, it has been gradually recognized that translanguage use is a creative, pragmatic, and safe practice (Creese and Blackledge, 2010) that promotes a deeper understanding of subject matter. Although this practice is used in bilingual programs, it is equally useful for any type of classroom setting at the secondary level.

A study on translanguage use suggested that the participants showed the following knowledge and skills through translanguage use (Creese and Blackledge, 2010):

- Students exhibited the ability to engage audiences through translanguaging and **heteroglossia** (the presence of two or more voices within a text).
- Students used translanguage to establish identity positions both oppositional and encompassing of institutional values.
- They recognized that languages do not fit into clear bounded entities and that all languages are "needed" for meanings to be conveyed and negotiated.
- The simultaneous literacies and languages used in more than one language kept the pedagogic task moving.

- Both teachers and students skillfully used their languages for different functional goals such as narration and explanation.
- Students used translanguage for annotating texts and had greater access to the curriculum, and lesson accomplishment.

Moreover, using the translanguaging approach can promote both L1 and Ln development simultaneously. In addition, the practice will make students feel that their L1 is valued, and thus they are more likely to continue the development of their L1.

Your Turn

Discuss how you can implement the idea of translanguage use in your content area teaching if you have no knowledge of your Ln learning students' L1 language.

Text comprehension

In Chapter 7, we introduced the idea of simplifying text to facilitate Ln learners' reading comprehension. We can continue to try this method in helping adolescent Ln learners. However, this kind of external manipulation of written input (text simplification) may have little effect on an adolescent Ln learner's intake. Research shows that text length has a significant effect on Ln intake (Sullivan, 2002). A shorter text length may result in better comprehension. More importantly, a learner's background knowledge as well as the use of pictures, graphs, charts, maps, highlights, margin notes, titles, and subtitles play a more predominant role in determining text accessibility (Sullivan, 2002). You can probably try to do all the above and see which one works better for your students.

Age-appropriate reading materials

Because Ln learners lack the proficiency to read grade-appropriate materials, the natural tendency is to provide them with simpler texts to compensate for their Ln level. Materials for younger readers often are the easy targets. As we described in the beginning of this chapter, adolescents are self-conscious; they may feel insulted when they are asked to read books intended for younger children. Therefore, when selecting reading materials for adolescent Ln learners, you may want to choose materials that are simple in vocabulary and grammar, but more sophisticated in content. If you cannot find such materials, use the text simplification techniques introduced in Chapter 7.

When choosing texts for Ln learning adolescents, you may also want to take into consideration their psychological needs and provide them with a variety of reading materials such as adventure, science fiction, biographies, mysteries, fantasy, romance, comedy, tragedy, and horror to help them find their place in the world and encourage self-discovery (for example, explore identity issues), build self-esteem and a healthy sense of self. Even though, in some content areas, you may not be able to find texts that cover all these genres, you can be creative. For example, in teaching the relativity theory in physics, you can ask students to read a biography of Albert Einstein. By doing so, you can achieve more than one purpose such as making a connection between the concept and the physicist, motivating students, and learning the language mechanics (e.g., vocabulary, syntax, and writing style).

Popular culture materials

Popular cultural materials (e.g., cartoons, comic strips, lyrics of rap, hip hop, rock, or metal music) are often deplored by parents and educators and denounced as a cause of violence and moral corruption by cultural watchdogs (e.g., Wang, 2010). Nevertheless, pop culture materials have a strong appeal to adolescents from all socioeconomic and cultural/linguistic backgrounds. In fact, pop culture materials are routinely appropriated by youngsters for pleasure, identification, and a sense of personal power.

Moreover, pop culture materials can help adolescents circumvent limits on learning and meaning. Despite some negative findings from research on pop culture materials and their association with violence and other behavioral problems, a growing body of literature examining the impact of such media on children's literacy development suggests that bringing pop culture, including pop music, into the classroom can motivate students' learning, as well as support critical literacy development (e.g., Wang 2010). It is now generally recognized among literacy researchers that critical literacy ability should be a part of every student's literacy pathway (e.g., Martello, 2002; Wang, 2011a). Pop music provides an ideal opportunity for students, including Ln learning adolescents, to cultivate critical literacy abilities because the content and language used in the lyrics of pop music are often sophisticated and intellectually demanding (Wang, 2011a). Despite the potential for improper language and messages in their content, popular culture materials may be a way to get Ln learning adolescents interested in reading and writing. Using pop culture reading materials can help you understand how your students construct meaning based on their personal interests and provide you with a window into how they form their identities.

Your Turn

Discuss whether it is possible to use pop culture genres such as rap to help Ln learning adolescents learn subject content. Visit the following link for an example of how rap can be used to learn math: http://mms.ucps.k12.nc.us/news/jump.php?news_id=35620.

Informal language register

During the adolescent period, peer influence is very important. Taking advantage of peer influence can help Ln learning adolescents develop language and literacy. With the availability of Facebook, Twitter, and texting, adolescents have more opportunity to socialize with other peers. You can take advantage of these informal language registers in online social networks and communication platforms and encourage adolescent Ln learners to use digital print to discuss ideas and thoughts about what they read. You can also take advantage of their favorite communication forms to encourage them to write. For example, text messaging is a popular communication tool among many teenagers. Despite the debate on whether text messaging prevents children from writing formally, many literacy experts now believe that it can promote overall literacy development. Moreover, communicating through text messages can support friendship, intimacy, and social networking, which are vital for adolescent development. Furthermore, text-messaging vocabulary in different languages is linguistically interesting, and it provides an opportunity for children to study the features in the texting language. For instance, discuss with your Ln learning students the interesting features in abbreviated words (e.g., *lol* – laugh out loud, *brb* – be right back, *gg* – gotta go, *mwah* – kiss, *yt* – your there, *Gr8* – great, and *Db8* – debate) and let them tell you the rules involved in the texting language. Then compare the abbreviations to the words used for formal writing. By treating text messaging as a legitimate way of communication, you can actually help your students understand that informal registers (such as texting) and formal registers (conventional writing) serve different purposes.

Innovative approach in writing

Using family photographs is an innovative approach to engaging Ln learning adolescents in writing in a purposeful and meaningful way.[4] Writing about family photographs is a good opportunity for Ln learners to explore their identities, including cultural identities. They can use family photos (including photos from older generations) to write in different genres such as a commentary about a historical event, a memoir, an autobiography, a short story, or an essay. It is likely that adolescents will be interested in this kind of writing if you offer them the opportunity. Initially, it may be difficult, but they can begin by labeling the photos and then writing first a sentence, then a paragraph, and eventually a narrative or an essay.

Intensive and extensive reading materials

There are two types of reading: intensive and extensive. Both are important for Ln learners in developing their literacy skills.

Intensive reading is slow and careful reading. In many ways, intensive reading is more of a method of language study than a form of reading. Intensive reading is useful for language study because its slow speed allows learners to stop and look up new words in the dictionary and allows them to pause and carefully study long or difficult sentences to get a better understanding.

However, intensive reading alone will not make Ln learners good readers. In fact, too much intensive reading may actually cause them to develop bad reading habits. For example, because intensive reading requires readers to pay attention to every detail, it often encourages the habit of paying more attention to the vocabulary and grammar of a text than to its overall meaning. It also encourages the habit of reading very slowly, and students who become accustomed to reading in this way often never learn to read any faster. Finally, intensive reading tends to be relatively boring, so students who fall into the habit of reading everything in this manner may ultimately grow to dislike reading.

The main purpose of most reading is to understand the meaning of a text, usually as quickly as possible. This kind of reading is called **extensive reading** – an approach that requires that a reader read fast in large quantities. Extensive reading is more like "real" reading than intensive reading. To become good readers, students need to read a lot (entire books or magazines) instead of just short articles or passages from textbooks. Just as a musician must practice sight reading in order to understand the meaning of the musical notes and demonstrate this understanding while playing a musical instrument, a good reader needs to read a lot to recognize the grammatical structure of a text and understand the meaning at the same time.

Moreover, extensive reading skills are essential to functioning in the real world (for example, to obtaining a general understanding of a subject or for pleasure). In a reading activity, speed, enjoyment, and comprehension are closely linked with one another (Nuttall, 1996). To achieve in these three areas, a proficient reader will not read word by word. Instead, she will read a meaningful unit at a time. If a reader reads too slowly, she will forget what she has read.

There are several benefits associated with reading extensively. It helps students

- build confidence
- increase motivation to read
- facilitate prediction skills
- develop reading automaticity
- enlarge vocabulary
- increase knowledge

Although it is useful for students to read intensively when studying a text's grammar and vocabulary to get a better grip of their heritage language, it is more important for them to spend time reading extensively, focusing mainly on the meaning of the text, not stopping to look up every new word. It has been suggested by experts that more access to books leads to more reading, and more reading results in higher levels of grammatical accuracy, a larger vocabulary, and greater reading comprehension (McQuillan, 1998). Thus, when you select heritage language reading materials for your Ln learning students, you may want to consider the balance between intensive reading and extensive reading materials.

Explicit instruction is crucial

Providing explicit instruction through scaffolding is crucial in helping Ln learning adolescents move forward faster. Ln learning adolescents need explicit instruction in several important areas.

Clear articulation

Even though after puberty, there are constraints on a learner's phonological development such as pronunciation, it is important to help Ln learning adolescents produce clear and understandable English pronunciation so that they can communicate effectively. Many people who have an accent in English can communicate clearly and effectively. When interacting with Ln learning adolescents in the classroom environment, you can encourage them to speak slowly if you do not understand them.

You can model the pronunciation, targeting the difficult sounds. However, you may not want to single a student out and put him on the spot.

You can also give assignments for a Ln learning student to listen to the radio or watch TV and report how anchors pronounce certain words. You can also use technology or computer devices to help students hear authentic English pronunciation. Remember that the goal is not to make an adolescent Ln speaker sound like a native English speaker (some of them will not be able to do so because they have passed the language acquisition sensitive period); the goal is to help them become understandable.

Prescriptive grammar and descriptive grammar

There are two kinds of grammar: prescriptive grammar and descriptive grammar. **Prescriptive grammar** is the grammar rules taught in school and in grammar books. Native speakers often violate these rules in the actual use of a language (e.g., don't end a sentence with a preposition and don't split infinitives). **Descriptive grammar** is the grammar rules that are actually used by native speakers (Gass and Selinker, 2001). On the one hand, the more education a person receives, the more prescriptive grammatical rules the person tends to observe. On the other hand, if a person speaks like a book, he sounds awkward. Therefore, it is important to help Ln learners to know the prescriptive English language rules, but the focus is to help them know how to use the descriptive grammatical rules. An overt comparison is helpful.

Academic literacy development strategies

Ln learning adolescents need assistance in developing academic literacy skills. You may want to consider the following approaches when helping your students read texts.

Text genres   Different types of texts are characterized by different organizational structures depending on their purpose and focus. Helping Ln learners recognize these different types of texts and knowing how to interpret them can not only increase their reading comprehension, but also promote their academic literacy development (Westby, 1994). There are seven types of academic texts (see Box 10.4).

Box 10.4 Types of Academic Text

- Descriptive texts (to describe what something is).
- Enumerative texts (to provide a list related to a topic).
- Sequential or procedural texts (to provide an overview of how to do something or a sequence of events that have occurred).
- Compare and contrast texts (to provide a comparison of how two or more things are the same or different).
- Problem–solution texts (to state a problem and offer solutions).
- Persuasive texts (to take position on a certain issue and justify it).
- Cause and effect texts (to give reasons why something happened).

Modified from A. E. Brice and R. C. Brice, *Language Development: Monolingual and Bilingual Acquisition* (Boston: Allyn & Bacon, 2009).

You can introduce these kinds of texts to your students and help them recognize the differences by looking for the clues that lead them to the type of structure being used and the cohesive ties that link structures to ideas both within and across sentences (Brice and Brice, 2009).

Nontextual information   Helping your adolescent Ln learners become conscious about nontextual information (Nuttall, 1996) can also help them become independent readers. Much of this kind of information may need to be consciously taught, particularly when learners' L1 print conventions are different from English. You may wish to try the following.[5]

Type style   You can deliberately point out the differences in type style to your students and indicate to them that the type styles may contain important information to help them understand a text. For example, headlines and footnotes often have a different typeface or size from the body of the text. Frequently, bold and italic styles may be used to indicate different kinds of prominence. Their function is often to make words easier to locate, define a technical term, emphasize something, or refer to something that is different from the rest. The conventions used in English may be different from the ones used in their L1 language(s).

Punctuation marks   There are different ways to use punctuation marks in different languages. Understanding their functions is important. For example, in English a period is ., whereas in Chinese it is o . In English, to quote someone, " " or ' ' is used and in German „ " or , ' is used. Consciously teaching adolescent Ln learners information such as the functions of punctuation marks will aid their English comprehension.

Reference aids (apparatus)   You can also draw your adolescent Ln learners' attention to reference aids such as titles, blurbs, author's biographic information, summaries, and tables of contents. Doing the exercises below may be helpful.

- Ask your students to match items in a list of titles with a selection of blurbs, arranged in random order.
- Ask them to match extracts from texts with a selection of blurbs and titles.
- Ask them to read one author's information and match it to a list of selected book titles, tables of contents, or summaries.

Diagrams   Diagrams such as illustrations, graphs, and tables can provide important information for comprehending and interpreting texts. You may be surprised that many students actually skip diagrams when reading texts. You can help your students pay attention to the information contained in diagrams by choosing one, supplying several statements, and asking them to match the statement with it. You can also provide several statements and ask your students to match them with one of several unlabeled diagrams. Alternatively, you can develop several questions and ask Ln learners to answer them with the information provided in the diagrams.

Index   Using an index to locate the information in the text is an important skill that will aid Ln learners' reading comprehension. Many students do not automatically use the index. You may want to purposefully point out the functions of the index as well as features such as abbreviations, definitions, and glossaries.

Different types of reading materials   To help your students become lifelong language users, you may want to teach them how to choose reading materials for different purposes. You can select different reading materials and ask them which ones should be used as intensive reading texts and which ones should be used as extensive reading texts.

Furthermore, you may want to teach your students the skills to prioritize certain reading materials and know that not every text deserves equal attention. Scanning and skimming to get the gist is good enough for some texts and reading the headlines to know what they are about is sufficient for other texts. However, going over the whole text carefully is important for some readings. Learning how to prioritize reading materials can help Ln learners avoid feeling discouraged about never finishing. Some people can never start a new book without finishing the previous one. This will prevent them from reading more. Ln learners need to be shown that reading can be used to find information or for personal enjoyment. If a book does not serve these functions, they can abandon it and look for a new one.

Reference materials   It is also a good idea to help your students develop research and reference skills and know where to find help when encountering learning difficulties. You can encourage your student to use different internet search engines and reference materials such as a thesaurus and a dictionary. You can also help them understand the different purposes of reference tools. For example, a dictionary is used to look up a word to find out its meaning, spelling, or pronunciation. A thesaurus is frequently used to look for different ways to express an idea (D. Johnson, 2001). If your students with English as a L1 learn a non-alphabetic foreign language such as Chinese, teaching them how to use the reference tools is necessary because the layout of Chinese dictionaries is different from an alphabetical language dictionary. In addition, students need to know when to use a dictionary and when to gather meaning from context. Checking every puzzling word in the dictionary will seriously slow down reading and take away all the joy.

Moreover, encouraging students to a use dictionary in their L1 is helpful. Some believe that if a student uses a dictionary in his L1, he will never learn English well. We now know that this belief is not corroborated by evidence. In fact, using a dictionary in a student's stronger language can help her understand the meaning in the Ln.

Figurative language

Since figurative language is important in students' academic literacy development, it is crucial to help Ln learning adolescents develop the ability to understand and use it. Research has revealed several effective strategies that teachers can use in their classroom practice.

Establish background knowledge   Figurative language interpretation is based on students' schemata. Therefore, explicit instruction is often needed to provide students with the knowledge necessary to understand not only the figurative language expressions but the context surrounding them as well (Palmer et al., 2007). Ln learners often lack the background knowledge to understand figurative language. Therefore, they need first to establish that background knowledge. Palmer et al. (2007) has recommended a three-step process to achieve this:

- Identify the figurative language in a written text.
- Determine if the literal meaning in the text makes sense.
- Find the intended meaning of the figurative language expression.

Provide real-life experience and ample exposure   Understanding figurative language depends on experience and exposure. Students often understand figurative language in real-life settings. It has been recommended that teachers can use real-life like experiences such as figurative posters which illustrate the literal and figurative meanings of idioms (Palmer et al., 2007).

Moreover, providing ample opportunities for Ln learners to be exposed to figurative language helps them learn it. You may want to select texts that use figurative language and make it a conscious learning process. You can also model the use of various types of figurative language in your oral instructions and you can deliberately choose reading materials that contain various figurative language uses. Moreover, you should also provide ample opportunities for Ln learners to use them.

Teach figurative language in context   You can teach figurative language by defining different types and providing examples of them in the context of a sentence or paragraph (Palmer et al., 2007).

Use inference   Teaching Ln learning students how to use inferencing strategies to understand the meaning of figurative language is useful. For example, you can encourage students to use their prior knowledge to try to unpack the meaning of a given type of figurative language. Students may not always be successful in doing so. Nonetheless, in the process, they develop inferencing skills, which are important for academic success.

Use elimination   To guess the meaning of a type of figurative language, you can teach your students to use the elimination strategy. By doing so, they can focus on a few possible meanings rather than being distracted by too many irrelevant meanings. The ability to use the elimination strategy will also help Ln learning students to perform better on standardized tests later, such as the SATs.

Use cues   You can also help Ln learning students understand figurative language by using contextual, graphophonic, syntactic, semantic, and pragmatic cues (Liontas, 2002, p. 211). If a student has problems understanding a type of figurative language, you can direct her attention to the above to look for clues.

Use visual images   Visual imagery can help Ln learners to comprehend figurative language. Art, for example, can help Ln learners to interpret figurative language in the text. Initially, art may give teachers an indication of how well a Ln learner understands the figurative language under study. For instance, when learning the idiom *raining cats and dogs*, a Ln learning student, Alejandro, interpreted this idiom literally with a sketch of cats and dogs falling from sky, and he drew his figurative interpretation with numerous falling raindrops (Palmer et al., 2007).

Use L1 to support Ln   You can also use Ln learners' L1 to support the development of Ln figurative language development. Figurative language is used in any language. If a Ln learner has entered the American educational systems in adolescence, he has already been exposed to figurative language in his L1. Using his figurative knowledge in his L1, is helpful for his Ln figurative language, despite admonitions that transferring students' L1 into figurative speech may result in language confusion and miscommunication when teaching in a multiple-language setting (e.g., Suleiman and Moore, 1995).

Your Turn

- Identify five English idioms and write down their literal meaning and intended figurative meaning. Find the real life connections to these idioms. Teach these idioms to a Ln learning adolescent by providing the real-life connection. Do you think that providing a real-life connection gave the student a better understanding of these idioms?
- Identify two types of figurative language and propose steps for teaching them in your specific content area by applying the strategies suggested above.

Cultural pragmatics

As we discussed earlier in the section on pragmatic development, many Ln learners bring the pragmatics from their L1 to their Ln. For them to be successful communicators in English, it is important to help them develop cultural pragmatics in English. Therefore, it is highly recommended that Ln learners be exposed to authentic interaction with native speakers and become familiar with cultural differences in order to avoid possible mistakes in the interpretation of affect. Special attention should be paid to hyperbole, intensified blame, and the effective use of the historical present, as well as to the possible misuse of the regular passive in English.

Explicit teaching of rhetorical styles in English writing

Ln learning adolescents need overt direction with regard to the rhetorical styles of English writing. There are several specific areas where Ln learners need explicit guidance:[6]

- Learners need to be shown a variety of ways of arranging textual elements and sequencing materials.
- They need to be guided in using divergent strategies for constructing arguments. For example, they need guidance on how to use the direct development of the

writer's position though deductive reasoning, in contrast to inductive reasoning achieved by indirect development of a position.

- Teachers need to model different methods of integrating evidence and source materials into writing. For example, show the extent of textual borrowing, paraphrasing, quoting, and stylistic imitating.
- Teachers need to explain different approaches to anticipating reader expectations and schematic knowledge. For example, develop assumptions about how much information the reader will require and the degree to which the reader will rely on implicit textual cues to connect points of information.
- Learners need to be taught to employ different ways to use devices for making cohesion (e.g., how to use pronouns, lexical variety and repletion,[7] transitional expressions) and coherence (the logical connections between ideas).
- Teachers need to scaffold for students how to practice divergent uses of linguistic structures and devices. For example, use less subordination, more conjunctions, less of the passive voice, less noun modification, use more commonly used vocabulary items, a narrower vocabulary range, predictable variation in grammatical structure, and a simpler style.

The advantage of practicing these strategies is that Ln learning adolescents are directly shown the core skills needed in academic literacy instead of trying to figure them out on their own. Many of them come to the US educational system late and must develop proficiency in their academic literacy in a short period of time before they enter college and the workplace.

Critical framing

As we discussed before, literacy is not neutral; students bring their personal perspectives when reading and writing. Although Ln learning students may already spontaneously question what they read (an advantage of being exposed to more than one culture and linguistic system), they still need to be oriented to analyze texts, including hypertext, with a critical lens so that they can actively question the stance (position and attitude) found within, behind and among texts. Critical literacy functions as an emancipatory endeavor that encourages adolescents, including Ln learners, to ask questions about the representation, benefits, marginalization and interests of texts (Stevens and Bean, 2007).

The English language and literacy limitations in Ln learners should not preclude them from developing critical literacy skills. Helping Ln learning adolescents become active readers and writers will help them create their own meanings to transform what they read and learn (Lau, 2012). There is evidence to suggest that engaging in critical literacy activities not only has an impact on Ln learners' linguistic skills, but also on the sense of their own voice.

Some have recommended that critical literacy activities include rewriting the characters in a story, reinterpreting a villain and a hero, and rewriting the ending of a story. However, others have cautioned that these activities are overly simplistic. The purpose of critical literacy is not to elicit the feeing of "us" and "them." Rather, it is to develop a different view of how people may act, provisionally, at a particular time and within particular conditions (Alvermann, 2006).

Most Ln learners and most students in general may not be able to do this high-level analysis at the beginning; you may want to provide a template first for them to fill in the information. They may begin by using key words or their L1 to draft the ideas. If you make this a constant classroom activity, adolescents will become critical language users.

Also, you can ask adolescent Ln learners to examine popular music such as Gangsta Rap.[8] Ask students to collect Gangsta Rap lyrics and discuss both the surface and underlying meanings they reveal. You can also ask them to write their own rap lyrics, incorporating their own experiences.

Further, in every culture, there are words or phrases that contain **semantic slanting** (a way of making statements to evoke emotional responses) or name-calling. These words and phrases will find their way into the Ln. To absolutely deny their existence will not work. Instead, discuss them and use the opportunity to help adolescents analyze the content of these negative terminologies and their influence on people's thoughts and actions. This is a more interesting way to do critical language learning.

Your Turn

Identify a lyric from pop music. Develop an activity that aims to help adolescents develop critical literacy abilities.

Application of divergent strategies

According to Ehren (2005), a good reader should be able to

- activate prior knowledge and relate it to a given text
- predict what will be addressed within a text given that knowledge
- ask important questions about the text
- use visual imagery to enhance comprehension
- paraphrase as well as summarize what has just been read
- monitor and repair breakdowns in comprehension
- integrate the use of these various strategies

These strategies are important for academic reading comprehension. Therefore, in your interactions with adolescent Ln learners, you need to deliberately help them use the strategies.

Reading aloud

Reading aloud has traditionally been an activity for young children. However, teachers who teach older students have found that reading aloud to them is still a favorite experience for adolescents (Zehr, 2010). There are many positive benefits associated with reading aloud for Ln language learning.

First, reading aloud can help Ln learners gain access to difficult texts that they cannot yet read independently.

Second, reading aloud to adolescents can help motivate them to read. If they enjoy what teachers read to them, they may be motivated to read.

Third, reading aloud can help Ln learners gain background information for their academic literacy development. It is likely that students will have an easier time in comprehending written texts if they have heard them before.

Fourth, reading aloud can model reading fluency and show Ln learners what reading should sound like (for example, what are appropriate pauses and what are inappropriate breaks).

Finally, reading aloud to Ln Learners can help them increase their vocabulary.

When reading to your adolescents, please pay attention to the following:[9]

- Select a text that is exemplary in language use, content, and style.
- Lead Ln learners into the text by setting the scene and generating interest in the context. Explain difficult vocabulary and background knowledge without letting go of the enjoyment.
- Pay attention to the use of your voice. Exude enthusiasm to attract your students and use clear enunciation. You can listen to professional recordings of read aloud sessions to improve your own reading skills.
- Use frequent eye contact to engage your students during reading. Observing their facial expressions is also a good way for you to measure their level of interest in the text and their comprehension.

Digital literacy

As mentioned before, literacy practice has experienced dramatic changes in confronting the challenges of space and time in the digital age. Technology such as the internet has provided new possibilities of thinking and communicating. Reading hypertext and writing with the help of the internet may be very different from traditional print and composition. A teacher's role may also change when providing guidance for adolescents, including Ln learning adolescents. Therefore, when helping Ln learning students digitally, the teacher's role changes from a director or choreographer to a facilitator (Lyman-Hager et al., 2002).

One example of teacher facilitation may be demonstrated by using the digital space to help student role-playing. For example, you can use online role-playing to facilitate Ln learning adolescents in developing ideas for a paper that debates school-wide internet policy. In the online role-playing process, students act in a variety of roles such as administrator, student, and parent. They assume multiple perspectives. In a certain period of time (e.g., two weeks), students can enter their stances on the issue and reply to others' views. This can help them advance their thinking and writing.[10]

Reflective reading response log

A **reflective reading response log** (RRRL) is a kind of journal in which readers write their reactions and opinions about the materials they read. This is particularly helpful for adolescent Ln learners in reflecting on what they read and seeking a deeper understanding of the texts. In addition, RRRL can help students develop writing fluency (Tompkins, 2009).

Initially, you can provide your students with a model chart to orient what they need to include in the reflective response log. The following is a template (you can add additional information based on your needs).

Identify the main points/ideas/issues in the text	
Enter your response or opinion on these points/ideas/issues	
Connect these points/ideas/issues to other texts you read in the pastw	
Connect these points/ideas/issues to your experience	
Identify words, phrases, information, or aspects that you do not understand	
Other thoughts or comments about the text	

If the Ln learners cannot fill in the whole chart with complete sentences, you can encourage them to put in what they feel comfortable with. Alternatively, you can fill in the log together (modeling).

Reading beyond texts

Helping adolescent Ln learners read beyond the text will help them become independent readers. You can help your students move from reading the lines to reading between the lines, to eventually reading beyond the lines. In other words, the goal is to prepare your students to make the transition from reading to inform (knowledge taking) to reading to transform (knowledge making). The benefit associated with this practice is that it may help your students take personal responsibility for their own meaning construction and become lifelong readers. The following are some suggestions for you to consider:[11]

- Ask for creative responses and questions, support your students' interpretation of a text, and avoid preaching and imposing your own ideas.
- Invite and welcome expressions of curiosity.
- Encourage students to consider issues from alternate perspectives by using the devil's advocate approach.
- Model how to give as well as receive creative critiques.
- Appreciate contrary or opposing views (ward off the "halo" effect; that is, just because it is in print and by an authoritative figure, it cannot be challenged).
- Provide critical-constructive feedback.

All the above suggestions are to encourage Ln adolescents to form the habit of reading beyond the lines and seek deeper meaning.

Summary of Key Points

- Typically, the later a student learns a Ln, the more difficult it will become. However, older learners may also have advantages. For example, they may perform better in suprasegmental phonology, in syntax, and in learning speed.
- There is a fundamental difference in English language knowledge between learners whose English is their L1 and those whose English is their Ln.
- Learning a Ln includes acquiring a new identity and cultural pragmatics.
- Transfer is a common strategy used by Ln learners to learn English.
- English Ln learners face double challenges: to learn English to communicate, and to learn academic content by using English.
- English Ln learners do not have uniform achievements in all the areas of the Ln.
- English Ln learners are not a homogeneous group, and their English ability differs in many ways.
- Language mixing is not always a linguistic phenomenon; it can be used intentionally by multilingual speakers to reveal their cultural and linguistic identity.
- At the secondary level, many students of English as a L1 will also begin to learn a foreign language. These native English speakers who are learning a foreign language encounter both similar and different Ln learning issues compared with those students who learn English as a Ln. The acquisition process is similar. However, the exposure and nature of learning are different.
- The most noticeable phonological aspect of a Ln learner is the accent. Motivation and identity also play a role in a person's accent.
- There are several distinct features regarding learners' lexical-semantic development. These are lexical discrepancy, cross-linguistic influence, how words are stored in a student's memory, and vocabulary gain through targeted reading. #4
- Ln English learners may have difficulties in several morphosyntactic areas such as passive voice, adverbial conjuncts, regular and irregular past tense, third-person singular, progressive aspect -*ing*, copula *be*, and auxiliary *do*. However, the morphosyntactic characteristics of English Ln learners are not uniform. Not all learners show the same kinds of difficulties in their English morphosyntactic structures.
- There are two commonly occurring pragmatic failures among Ln learners: pragmalinguistic failure and sociopragmatic failure.
- Ln learning adolescents may also encounter difficulties in figurative language use and culturally specific nonverbal use.
- Ln learning students may approach academic literacy in the Ln with four prior schema developed in their L1: content schemata, cultural schemata, formal schemata, and linguistic schemata. These schema may impact their Ln learning.
- Support adolescent Ln learners by doing the following:
  - Motivate Ln learners to learn English
  - Use Ln to help with expressing emotions

- ○ Self-monitor their progress
- ○ Use metalinguistic analysis to help students become conscious about their errors
- ○ Encourage the use of translanguage in academic learning
- ○ Use a variety of methods to assist text comprehension
- ○ Select age-appropriate reading materials
- ○ Use innovative approaches such as pop cultural materials and family photos to promote literacy development
- ○ Use informal registers such as texting, Twitter, and Facebook to help learners with academic literacy development
- ○ Use both intensive and extensive reading to promote academic literacy development
- ○ Explicitly teach skills in areas such as
  - • clear articulation
  - • prescriptive and descriptive grammar
  - • different text genres
  - • using nontextual information as clues to understanding reading
  - • figurative language understood through background information, real-life experience, ample exposure, context, inference, elimination, cues, visual images, and L1 background
  - • cultural pragmatics, rhetorical styles, and critical framing
- ○ Use diverse strategies
- ○ Read aloud
- ○ Use digital literacy such as online role-playing to help literacy development
- ○ Use reflective reading response logs
- ○ Encourage reading beyond texts

Key Terms

Abstract words
Avoidance strategy
Code-switching
Cognates
Concrete words
Content schemata
Cultural schemata
Descriptive grammar
Emblems
Emotion words
Emotion-laden words
Episodic memory
Extensive reading
Formal schemata
Heteroglossia

Intensive reading
Lexical memory
Linguistic schemata
Negative transfer
Positive transfer
Pragmalinguistic failure
Prescriptive grammar
Reflective reading response log
Semantic slanting
Sociopragmatic failure
Speech act
Suprasegmental phonology
Transfer strategy
Translanguage
Weakeners

Notes

1. Suprasegmental phonology (or prosodic properties) refers to rhythm, tone, pitch, stress, intonation, and length.
2. Speech acts serve a type of communication function in which we apologize, greet request, promise, congratulate, complain, invite, compliment, or refuse. Using speech acts in real-life communication requires not only knowledge of the language but also appropriate use of that language in a given culture.
3. Weakeners and strengtheners are discourse markers. Both can also be called either "intensifier" or "hedge." Examples of strengtheners are "really," "certainly," and "exactly." Examples of weakeners are "sort of" and "I think" (Baba, 2010).
4. The ideas suggested in this section are based on Van Horn (2008).
5. Ideas introduced in this section are based on Nuttall (1996).
6. These ideas are based on Ferris and Hedgcock (2014), p. 23.
7. Repletion means using two or more phrases in close proximity.
8. *Gangsta* is a non-rhotic pronunciation of the word *gangster*. Gangsta rap is a subgenre of hip hop music that evolved from hardcore hip hop and purports to reflect urban crime and the violent lifestyles of inner-city youths. Lyrics in gangsta rap have varied from accurate reflections to fictionalized accounts.
9. Ideas suggested in this section are based on Dwyer and Isbell (1990).
10. The ideas in this section are based on Benko (2012–2013).
11. Many of the ideas in this section are based on Manzo, Manzo, and Estes (2001).

Recommended Further Readings

Dewaele, J. M. (2012). *Emotions in Multiple Languages*. New York: Palgrave Macmillan.

Graves, M. F., August, D., and Mancilla-Martines, J. (2013). *Teaching Vocabulary to English Language Learners*. New York: Teachers College Press.

McKeough, A., Phillips, L. M., Timmons, V., and Lupart, J. L. (eds) (2006). *Understanding Literacy Development: A Global View*. Mahwah, NJ: Lawrence Erlbaum.

11

Language Impairment in Adolescence

Prereading Questions and Activities

- Listen carefully to the classroom discourse of one middle school and one high school student with LI. What have you observed, especially with regard to their vocabulary use and syntactic production?
- Collect a speaking or writing sample of one middle-school student and one high-school student with LI. Analyze the samples at the syntactic level. What are the distinct syntactic characteristics produced by these students?
- If you need to create an Individualized Education Program (IEP) for these two students, what aspects of these students' language difficulties do you need to consider in helping them move forward in academic content learning?

Topics to Be Addressed in This Chapter

- Language development characteristics of children with LI in adolescence
  - Phonological development
  - Lexical and semantic development
  - Morphosyntactic development
  - Pragmatic and metalinguistic development
  - Literacy developmental characteristics of adolescents with LI
- Language and literacy supporting emphasis for students with LI in middle and high school
- Supporting strategies for adolescents with LI

Understanding Language and Literacy Development: Diverse Learners in the Classroom, First Edition. Xiao-lei Wang.
© 2015 John Wiley & Sons, Inc. Published 2015 by John Wiley & Sons, Inc.
Companion website: www.wiley.com/go/wang/langandlit

Learning Objectives

After reading this chapter, you are expected to do the following:

- Understand specific challenges that adolescents with LI encounter in the areas of phonology, lexicon, semantics, morphosyntax, pragmatics, and metalinguistic knowledge and recognize how various language impairments in these areas impact adolescents' academic development.
- Know the critical language and literacy skills that you must help adolescents with LI develop during middle and high school.
- Know how to use effective strategies to help adolescents with LI develop language skills to meet the challenges in academic literacy and prepare them for college, the workplace, and life.

Language Developmental Characteristics of Adolescents with LI

When adolescents with TD enter middle school and high school, they typically can use language to learn different academic content areas. However, many adolescents with LI are still in the process of developing their basic language skills and some students with profound LI may still be at the emergent language learning stage. Their difficulties in language-related areas will most certainly affect their academic advancement if no adequate support and intervention are provided.

Phonological development

Although many adolescents with LI do not make a large number of phonological errors, some may continue to distort a few sounds and retain one or two phonological simplification processes in phonological production (Paul, 2007). Some adolescents with LI (e.g., students with autism spectrum disorder) may still encounter issues in voice quality and intonation patterns. This may affect their oral communication in classroom environments and in peer interaction.

The major issue for concern, however, remains limitation of their phonological awareness. Phonological awareness constraints continue to affect their fluency in reading, spelling, and writing. Moreover, some adolescents with LI may also have difficulties in retrieving phonological codes from memory (Paul, 2007).

Lexical-semantic development

Adolescents with LI tend to have a smaller vocabulary size and less lexical diversity, density, and complexity. They also have a limited capacity to process semantic information and a restricted knowledge base for multiple word meanings. For instance, they tend to have difficulty associating and categorizing words into semantic classes and exhibit problems with relational and abstract words. Word retrieval (or word finding) is also challenging for some students with LI. Some students may rely heavily on nonspecific terms such as *thing* and *stuff* (Paul, 2007). Many students with LI have a hard time producing accurate and complete definitions for words.

One major concern in the lexical development of adolescents with LI is that they have difficulty acquiring the content-specific vocabulary in math, social studies, sciences, and literature. Moreover, many adolescents with LI lag behind in their literate lexicon. A **literate lexicon** is the ability to use contextual abstraction to infer the meaning of new words from the linguistic cues that accompany them (Paul, 2007). Content-specific lexical difficulties of adolescents with LI hinder their learning in subject areas (Gillam and Petersen, 2011).

Moreover, adolescents with LI such as those with hearing impairment (HI) have great difficulty applying top-down, contextual strategies to pull implicit meaning from words in text. Adolescents with HI (with hearing loss ranging from mild to profound) may still have delays in theory of mind and have trouble comprehending emotion labels (McGregor, 2009).

Your Turn

Give a short text to a student with TD and a student with LI and ask them to respond to the text with a set of questions that designed to identify their ability to use a literate lexicon. What differences have you found in these two students?

Morphosyntactic development

Because students with LI are limited in the semantic process, they often cannot integrate information from a larger discourse unit that contains three or four sentences (Paul, 2007).

Some adolescents with LI may make fewer syntactic mistakes in oral communication but more syntactic mistakes in writing. Some are less sophisticated in their syntax, but do not show obvious grammatical errors. Most adolescents with LI produce less clause density in writing compared with their peers with TD. **Clause density** is another index to measure a student's syntactic complexity. It is the total number of clauses (main and subordinate) summed across T-units, and divided by the number of T-units in a sample (Paul, 2007).[1] This measure is often referred to as **subordination index figures**. Adolescents with LI have low subordination index figures (they either rarely or never use subordinate clauses). Box 11.1 lists the general trend of subordination index figures among students with TD from grades 6 to 12. This index will help you figure out where your students with LI are in terms of subordination index figures.

Box 11.1   Subordination Index Figures in Speech and Writing of Secondary Students with TD

Grade	Speaking	Writing
6	1.4	1.3
8	1.4	1.5
10	1.5	1.5
12	1.6	1.6

Modified from R. Paul, *Language Disorders from Infancy through Adolescence: Assessment and Intervention* (St. Louis, MO: Mosby, 2007), p. 589.

Box 11.1 shows that in early adolescence, the subordination index for students with typical development is higher in speech than in writing. In mid to late adolescence, the index in writing is similar to or slightly higher than in speech. However, the use of subordination depends heavily on the situation and audience. It is likely that adolescents use more subordination in literate and formal writing than speech (Paul, 2007). It is important to note that adolescents both with TD and LI need teacher guidance and opportunities to produce subordinate clauses, and adolescents with LI need more extra help in producing them.

Finally, morphological difficulties continue to affect the morphosyntactic development of many adolescents with LI. They may have difficulties in using plurals, possessives, third-person singular forms, comparatives, superlatives, irregular forms, and advanced prefixes and suffixes (-*ment*, -*able*, -*ness*, -*ly*, *un*-, *re*-, *dis*-,). They also show difficulties in pronoun reference, subject–verb agreement, and verb tense use.

Your Turn

Analyze a short writing sample of a student with LI and calculate the subordination index figures of the text. Based on your calculation, where do you place this student on the scales in Box 11.1?

Pragmatic and metalinguistic development

Some adolescents with LI may have limited verbal fluency. Their verbal discourse tends to be brief and unelaborated. Mazes occur frequently. Moreover, it has been reported that students with LI demonstrate significant delays in conversational pragmatics, as shown by their more hostile, less assertive, less persuasive, less polite and tactful, and less clear and complete use of language compared to that of their peers. Moreover, students with LI are less sensitive to their listeners, often give incomplete and inaccurate descriptions, or have trouble adjusting their speech to the age or social status of their audience (Paul, 2007, p. 437). Many students with LI have a hard time maintaining conversation topics.

Adolescents with LI continue to present difficulty in comprehending and communicating meanings through figurative language. They may still have trouble understanding implied meanings. They may still rely on literal interpretations when they encounter figurative language expressions. They rarely use figurative language in oral communication.

During the middle and high school years, there is a greater expectation for independence in academic learning. To be academically successful, adolescents must know how to acquire, store, recall, and use knowledge from assignments they complete outside of class. There are some metacognitive strategies that adolescents need to use to accomplish specific learning goals. For instance, if they do not completely understand a passage, they may reread it, take extra notes, memorize their notes by saying them out loud, or create their own practice tests. Adolescents with LI, however, tend to lack this kind of ability (Gillam and Petersen, 2011).

Your Turn

Listen to the class interaction of an adolescent with LI (e.g., a student with ASD). Identify the characteristics of this student's conversational pragmatics.

Literacy Development of Adolescents with LI

Adolescents with LI frequently encounter difficulty with both narrative and expository texts. However, they especially struggle in understanding the expository texts which they must read for their subject content areas. For instance, they may have trouble understanding cause-and-effect relationships that are expressed in their science or history textbooks. They may also struggle to compose the expository texts that are needed for completing assignments for class such as book reports, essays, and papers. As a result, they may experience academic failure (Gillam and Petersen, 2011).

Moreover, they often exhibit various other literacy related difficulties. For example, adolescents with HI are likely to have a low level of literacy proficiency. It has been noted that many students with HI encounter reading difficulties throughout the secondary school years. In fact, the average reading level of high school students with HI is roughly equivalent to that of students in the fourth to sixth grades. By contrast, students with HI who are born to deaf parents and acquired sign language from infancy do achieve a high level of reading (Hoff, 2009).

Adolescents with LI typically show strains in acquiring literate language forms in the following areas (Paul, 2007):

- advanced adverbial conjuncts (*similarly, moreover, consequently, in contrast, rather, nonetheless*)

- adverbs of likelihood (*definitely*, *possibly*) and magnitude (*extremely*, *considerably*)
- precise and technical terms related to curricular content (*abscissa*, *bacteria*, *pollination*, *fascism*)
- verbs with presuppositional (*regret*), metalinguistic (*predict*, *infer*, *imply*), and metacognitive (*hypothesize*, *observe*) components
- words with multiple meanings (*strike* the ball, *strike* at the factory; *run* for office, *run* the office)
- words with multiple functions (*hard* stone, *hard* water, *hard* feelings)

Also, the writing of adolescents with LI tends to be simple. They may use fewer complex sentences, less elaboration of noun phrases with multiple modifiers (e.g., *that big, red barn*), prepositional phrases (*the house in the country*), and relative clauses (*the house that's in the country*). They use fewer adverbs and combinations of auxiliary verbs (*could have been running*). Sometimes, sentences produced by these students may be longer than their peers with typical development because they use fewer complex forms to condense their expressions (Paul, 2007). They often cannot produce subordination and embedding in writing.

Supporting Strategies for Adolescents with LI

Critical language and literacy skills in the secondary grades

Like adolescents with TD, adolescents with LI must develop critical language and literacy skills in middle and high school to be able to meet academic demands, pass state and national standardized assessments, and be ready for college, the workplace, and life. Therefore, the support focus provided for secondary students with LI should be on three critical areas: academic and subject-specific lexicon, expository texts, and metacognitive strategies (Gillam, Marquardt, and Martin, 2011). Providing support in these areas can benefit these students in the development of memory, cognition, and academic language/literacy (Gillam and Petersen, 2011, p. 264). In addition, these students also need to have support in their social interaction and future life.

Support for academic and subject-specific lexicon development

#5.

Literate lexicon

Since a literate lexicon is critical for academic learning, you need to provide explicit support in this area.[2] Before you introduce a topic in a subject, you can select a paragraph that contains some unfamiliar and difficult words that are important for comprehending that topic and help your students with LI to study these words. Box 11.2 suggests some important literate lexicon categories that you need to consider when selecting words from texts for helping students develop literate lexicon ability. For example, you can first ask your students to guess what the difficult words mean and explain why they think so. You can then guide them by looking for the cues in the context to infer the meanings.

Box 11.2 Important Categories of Words for Developing a Literate Lexicon

- Nouns for technical and curriculum activities (e.g., *salutation, oppression, circumference, proton*).
- Verbs for the interpretation of and for talking about cognitive and logical processes. These include verbs used to refer to metacognitive activities (e.g., *remember, doubt, infer, hypothesize, conclude, assume*), to metalinguistic activities (e.g., *assert, concede, imply, predict, report, interpret, confirm*), and to presupposition (e.g., *regret, notice, forget, know, suppose, think, believe, guess*).

Modified from R. Paul, *Language Disorders from Infancy through Adolescence: Assessment and Intervention* (St. Louis, MO: Mosby, 2007), pp. 583–584.

Word definitions

To help students with LI develop accurate and complete word definitions, you can work on enhancing their understanding of word meanings by identifying words that they have problems defining and making a list of them. You then need to provide ample opportunities for them to work with these words by engaging them in activities such as looking up the definition in the dictionary, reading texts that expose them to the variety of word meanings, reproducing words, and generating word meanings.

Word relations

To be competent with words, students need to know more than what words mean. It is also necessary for them to know how words are related. There are several areas in which you may want to provide help.

You can help students with LI generate multiple meanings for words that often have more than one meaning by discussing them and asking questions. For example, "*Tell me what run means when you are talking about a race? What does it mean when you are talking about an election?*" You can also help them compare and contrast word meanings to choose the best words to express their ideas.

Many adolescents with LI use the same words repeatedly in writing. You can help them substitute words with the same or similar meanings. Help them develop a list of synonyms and refer to them in writing.

Finally, help your students with LI develop self-questioning abilities and encourage them to determine whether multiple meanings of a word need to be invoked to understand a word, an occurrence of figurative language, or a joke.

Overall, these strategies and skills need to be modeled first, taught explicitly, and practiced with your scaffolding.

Your Turn

Locate a text from a middle or high school grade level in a content area. Identify words that are critical for comprehension of the text. Design an activity that will help students with LI develop a literate lexicon and generate multiple word meanings.

Support academic literacy with literacy fiction

It has been suggested that literacy fiction can help promote the development of theory of mind (Kidd and Castano, 2013). It may be particularly useful to help adolescents with LI (especially students with ASD) to develop theory of mind abilities (which they often lack). By reading literacy fiction, students with ASD, for example, can learn to put themselves in the shoes of the characters, make inferences about them, and become more sensitive to emotional nuances and complexity. Through reading literary fiction, students with LI such as students with ASD can improve social skills and academic abilities.

Your Turn

Research a piece of literacy fiction at the reading level of a student with ASD. Prepare a list of questions that require the student to infer from the text.

Support for expository text development

Besides using the multipass approach introduced in Chapter 8 for supporting students in their comprehension of expository texts, another approach called **POSSE** can also be employed. Help students predict ideas (P), organize these ideas and background knowledge based on text structure (O), search for the text structure (S), summarize the main ideas (S), and evaluate comprehension (E) (N. Nelson, 2010, p. 406). The key in implementing this approach is that you need to model how to do it before you ask your students to apply it.

Another approach that you can try is **self-regulated strategy development** (SRSD). Box 11.3 shows the steps.

Box 11.3   SRSD Steps

- Help students develop background knowledge (e.g., use KWL chart).[3]
- Discuss with students the goals of the strategies they will use.
- Model the strategy.
- Encourage students to memorize it (e.g., by using cue cards).
- Scaffold students to practice it.
- Create opportunities for students to engage in independent performance.

Modified from N. W. Nelson, *Language and Literacy Disorders: Infancy through Adolescence* (Boston: Allyn & Bacon, 2010), p. 409.

You can also try the **EmPOWER** method to help students develop expository text production abilities through self-regulation. Students need to develop the complex process in expository writing. They need to learn to evaluate the writing assignment by first reading the instructions carefully (E), then to make a plan that is based on communicative purpose that will help them get started (MP), organize their ideas graphically using templates specific to the intended genre (O), work from the plan to represent the idea with written language (W), and evaluate and rework the draft with the purpose and audience in mind (ER) (N. Nelson, 2010).

Your Turn

Design a lesson plan in your content area by employing the POSSE, SRSD, and EmPOWER methods. Try your plan with a student with LI and discuss the learning results of this student.

Support for metacognitive strategies

Figurative language

An effective way to help adolescents with LI develop figurative language ability is to directly teach them. You can select a list of uses of figurative language from the texts they will read and reteach them. While teaching, you can ask students to explain what the figurative language means and why the authors chose to employ the specific device. You can also provide the context to aid their comprehension. The goal is to raise their metalinguistic awareness of the use of figurative language.

Verbal reasoning

The ability to use language to extend thinking, reflect on thinking, and entertain several cognitive viewpoints at once are hallmarks of formal operational thought. Many students with LI are unable to engage in this kind of language use. Helping these students develop verbal reasoning skills will allow them to learn academic content and pass standardized assessments. You can help students work on analogies and **syllogisms** (deductive reasoning). You can also use language to talk through logical problems.

Contexts that involve cognitive planning

To help students develop complexity in narratives and writing, you can choose contexts that involve cognitive planning because this will elicit complex syntactic forms from them. To enhance their oral narrative complexity, you can first discuss what a good narration involves, and then model a narration that uses those elements (e.g., tell them about a trip you recently took or a book you have read). You can then ask your students to do the same. While they are producing the narrative, try to ask questions and ask them to clarify, all the while asking them to follow the structure of good narration you modeled before. You can follow the same steps when helping them with writing.

Using literature to support language development

Book discussion has been shown to be effective in improving the spoken language, listening, reading, and writing of students with LI. In this approach, activities that facilitate semantics, syntax, morphology, narratives, and metalinguistic awareness are centered around a common theme in a story. Activities using this approach usually include prereading discussions about concepts that are contained in the books, reading and rereading the story on a number of occasions, retelling the story, conducting various language activities, and discussing a related book (Gillam and Petersen, 2011, p. 265). Because these kinds of activities tend to be engaging, you may want to use them for other content areas such as math, sciences, and social studies. For example, you can identify a biography of a scientist or an interesting article about a certain science phenomenon and follow the steps just discussed. By doing so, you will help your students learn the content, and at the same time, develop language and literacy skills.

Your Turn

Select a text that you want a student with LI to read. Based on this text, design an activity in your content areas using the literature supporting approach. Specify exactly what you need to do with these steps: prereading discussions about concepts contained in the books, reading and rereading the text on a number of occasions, retelling the story, conducting various language activities, and discussing related texts. Share your activity with a teacher and ask for her or his feedback.

Situated cognitive model of writing

Writing is an essential academic, employment, and life skill. In schools, students need to use writing to learn a variety of subject matter, to communicate with their teachers and classmates, and to express themselves. For students with LI, writing ability is particularly important because this modality can help them enhance their communication and learn to read. Moreover, when students with LI write well, they will have access to the world through the internet (Wollak and Koppenhaver, 2011). However, because writing is a complex interplay of cognitive processes, many students with LI will encounter tremendous challenges. Without proactive support, they will not be able to develop the writing abilities necessary to function well in content learning, in the workplace, and in life.

Drawing on the work of Hayes and Flower (1980), Wollack and Koppenhaver (2011) developed the **situated cognitive model of writing** to help students with LI improve their writing skills. This model includes the following components (see Box 11.4).

> ## Box 11.4   Components of the Situated Cognitive Model of Writing
>
> - Planning
> - Translating
> - Reviewing (revisiting and evaluating)
> - Production
> - Motivation
> - Social context
>
> Modified from B. A. Wollak and D. A. Koppenhaver, "Developing technology-supported, evidence-based writing instruction for adolescents with significant writing disabilities," *Assistive Technology Outcomes and Benefits*, 7(1) (2011): 1–23.

The first component in written communication entails planning. Planning requires a student to set goals, formulate ideas, and organize thoughts. During this phase, the writer has to address questions such as why she wants to write the text and what she wants to share. The second component in writing is translating, in which the writer needs to convert nonlinear and overlapping experiences and ideas such as sensory images, feelings, or impressions into linear, written language using print conventions. The third component of writing requires the writer to revisit and evaluate the text according to the plan. The fourth component, which especially considers the challenges for students with LI, involves production. It is a process in which students with LI must consciously attend to their writing tools (such as pencil, computer keyboard, and computer monitor). The fifth component involves motivation. Motivation influences the writer's willingness to actively engage in the writing process. Finally, the context of writing is crucial. Students need to know why they write and the relevance and meaning of their writing.

Your Turn

Based on the six components of the situated cognitive model of writing discussed above, provide one concrete example for each component. Justify why you think they may work for students with LI.

Supporting writing quality and motivation through interacting with mature writers

Wollack and Koppenhaver (2011) have found that pairing adolescent students who have LI with university preservice teacher candidates via e-pal exchanges can help these students improve their writing quality. The adolescent students with LI and the university preservice teachers became pals via email exchanges, and the preservice teachers served as models for writing. The e-pal program is a practical way to motivate adolescents with LI, increase their writing quality, as well as opening up explorations with new literacies. At the end of the program, all the students with LI showed significant improvement in their writing quality. For example, a student with ASD doubled his email in length and increased his word use from 30–40 words to 80–90 words at the end of the program. He began to feel comfortable expressing feelings and describing actions. The improvement in written communication also helped his ability to communicate face-to-face and understand "wh" questions. Another student with ASD improved his syntactic complexity through e-pal exchanges. Similarly, a student with DS improved his phonological awareness and could represent initial and final sounds logically when spelling unknown words. Moreover, this student could use humor in his emails. He could independently compose cohesive emails. Therefore, it seems that to pair students who have LI with more mature writers will increase their motivation and improve their writing quality.

Your Turn

If you know a student with LI, try to become an e-pal with him or her for the duration of one month on a daily basis. Compare the first email exchange and the last one. What have you found?

Making reading and writing enjoyable

In general, the incidence of reading for pleasure tends to decrease through adolescence, especially in male students (Owens, 2012). Academic writing is not a favorite for most adolescents (although they may be engaged in other types of writing). This trend may be more evident for adolescents with LI. Indeed, when an adolescent encounters challenges in unfamiliar vocabulary and complex sentences, they are easily disrupted by linguistic stress, and it becomes hard for them to associate reading and writing with pleasure. Therefore, it is important for you to engage adolescents with LI in reading with activities that are enjoyable. Adolescents often enjoy reading materials and writing on topics that are related to their interests and hobbies. This requires that you do some homework on what they like. If you can intentionally take account of what they like while selecting reading materials and assigning writing topics, there will more opportunities for adolescents with LI to read.

As we end this chapter, it is important to stress that the strategies we proposed in this chapter are provisional and they may not be applied to every student with LI. You must actively search for new research information and try it out in your classroom.

Your Turn

- Interview an adolescent with LI and make a list of her or his interests and hobbies. Research interesting reading materials that are related to this student's interests. Give some of the readings to this student to read and judge their effectiveness based on his or her feedback.

- Based on the list of the student's interests, think about a writing assignment that can incorporate those interests into a particular content area. Ask the student to write about this topic. What have you found?
- Research databases such as ERIC and PsycINFO on the topics that interest you about adolescent students with LI. Share your research with your classmates.

Summary of Key Points

- Some adolescents with LI may continue to distort a few sounds and retain one or two phonological simplification processes in phonological production. Students with ASD may still encounter issues such as voice quality and intonation patterns. This may affect their oral communication in the classroom environment and in peer interaction. The major issue for concern is their limitation in phonological awareness, which continues to affect their fluency in reading, spelling, and writing. Some adolescents with LI may also have difficulty retrieving phonological codes from memory.
- Adolescents with LI tend to have a smaller vocabulary size, and less lexical diversity, density, and complexity. They also have a limited capacity to process semantic information and have restricted knowledge of multiple word meanings. Many students with LI have a hard time producing an accurate and complete definition of a word. Many also have difficulty acquiring content-specific vocabularies and some are behind in their literate lexicon development. Some students with HI have difficulty applying top-down, contextual strategies to pull implicit meaning from words in written text and have trouble comprehending emotion labels.
- Students with LI often cannot integrate information from a larger discourse unit that contains three or four sentences. Some may make fewer syntactic mistakes in oral communication but more syntactic mistakes in writing. Some are less sophisticated in their syntax, but without obvious grammatical errors. Most adolescents with LI produce less clause density in writing compared with their peers with TD. These students have low subordination index figures. They may have difficulty using plurals, possessives, and the third-person singular, comparatives and superlatives, irregular forms and advanced prefixes and suffixes, and show difficulty in pronoun reference and subject–verb agreement.
- The verbal discourse of some adolescents with LI tends to be brief and unelaborated. Mazes occur frequently. They also demonstrate significant difficulties in conversational pragmatics and have trouble maintaining conversation topics. Adolescents with LI continue to present difficulty in comprehending and communicating meaning through figurative language.
- During the middle and high school years, adolescents with LI often lack the metacognitive strategies needed to accomplish specific learning goals.
- Adolescents with LI frequently encounter difficulties in several areas such as understanding expository texts and the cause-and-effect relationships that are expressed

in their science or history textbooks. They have trouble composing expository texts and acquiring literate language forms. The writing of adolescents with LI tends to be simple as they use fewer complex sentences, less elaboration of noun phrases with multiple modifiers, prepositional phrases, and relative clauses. They use fewer adverbs and combinations of auxiliary verbs. They often cannot produce subordination and embedding in writing.

- Adolescents with HL tend to achieve a low level of literacy acquisition. Reading difficulties remain an issue throughout the school years.
- The support focus provided for secondary students with LI should be on three critical areas: academic and subject-specific lexicon, expository texts, and metacognitive strategies.
- Concrete strategies of support include:
  - Support for academic and content-specific lexicon
  - Support for academic literacy skills through literacy fiction
  - Support for expository text development
  - Support for metacognitive strategies
  - Support for language development by using literature
  - Support for writing using the situated cognitive model of writing
  - Support for students' writing quality and motivation through interaction with mature writers.
  - Making reading and writing an enjoyable experience

Key Terms

Clause density

EmPOWER

Literate lexicon

POSSE

Situated cognitive model of writing

SRSD

Subordination index figures

Syllogisms

Notes

1. If a T-unit contains just one main clause, it receives a clause count of 1. For example, the T-unit in the following example, "*It was from monkeys and chimpanzees,*" contains one main clause; it receives a clause count of 1. The T-unit in the example "*Then after they graduated, they took them into this plane*" receives a clause count of 2 (1 for the main clause "they took them into this plane" and 1 for the adverbial clause "Then after they graduated"). The T-unit "*There was a boy who was about 21 who stole a plane with a woman and chimpanzee in the cockpit*" receives a clause count of 3 (1 for the main clause "*There was a boy,*" 1 for the relative clause "*who was about 21,*" and 1 for the relative clause "*who stole a plane with a woman and champanzee in the cockpit*").
2. Many ideas suggested in this section are based on Paul (2007).
3. KWL is an acronym for what students already know, what they want to know, and what they want to learn.

Recommended Further Readings

Gillam, R. B., Marquardt, T. P., and Martin, F. N. (2011). *Communication Sciences and Disorders: From Science to Clinical Practice*. 2nd edn. Burlington, MA: Jones & Bartlett.

Nelson, N. W. (2010). *Language and Literacy Disorders: Infancy through Adolescence*. Boston: Allyn & Bacon.

Language Sample Analysis IV

Three writing samples produced by adolescents are included in this language sample analysis assignment.

Writing Sample 1: Monolingual Student

This writing sample was by a ninth-grade female student, Amy (not her real name). Amy has typical development. She is a native speaker of English from a middle-class family. In this writing sample analysis, you are asked to do the following:

- Read Amy's writing sample carefully.

Writing Sample of a Ninth Grader, Amy

Romeo and Juliet

Throughout the play, "Romeo and Juliet" by Shakespeare, in the true lover's lives were impacted by many characters in the story, which had played both positive and negative roles therefore had a substantial impact on the outcomes. Some of the main characters who had a significant impact on Romeo and Juliet were Friar Lawrence and the Nurse. In this case these two characters had mostly a negative role toward Romeo and Juliet.

The first character that had greatly affected the outcome was Friar Lawrence. He had an enormous impact on the ending of the story. The Friar Lawrence

Understanding Language and Literacy Development: Diverse Learners in the Classroom, First Edition. Xiao-lei Wang.
© 2015 John Wiley & Sons, Inc. Published 2015 by John Wiley & Sons, Inc.
Companion website: www.wiley.com/go/wang/langandlit

was a great source for Juliet. He had provided all the negativity for Juliet. The Friar although comforted Juliet, he also gave her bad messages. First he helped Juliet and Romeo in getting married instead of going the right thing in telling the families. Friar Lawrence chose to keep the secrets between Romeo and Juliet. This all caused more ripples. Friar Lawrence also helped Juliet from getting married to Paris. This really brought a negative feedback toward the whole situation. The Friar had provided the sleeping position to Julie. When the situation occurred, it did not go as planned. The letter or note that the Friar intended was for it to go to Romeo, about the fake death that did not get delivered in time. By the time it got to the destination it was supposed t go to, Romeo but he had already been in the tomb with Juliet. Romeo had bought a poison after finding our that Juliet was "dead". Since the message never got to Romeo in time and Friar Lawrence after finding our Romeo was not aware that Juliet was not really dead. Romeo had killed himself with the poison Friar Lawrence did not get to the tomb in time to save the two lovers, the timing was really bad. The second Romeo drank the poison, Juliet woke up. Juliet then kills herself with a dagger for Romeo. They both end up dead together. The Friar helped with this whole event to take place. If he did not marry them and he hadn't kept this secret from their families then this death may have not occurs.

The second character that I had chosen was the Nurse. The nurse was the one who was supposed to take care of Juliet, to guard her and to make sure she was doing the right things. The nurse although sis help raise her well, she did not give her right judgments all the time. The nurse helped to deliver the messages between Romeo and Juliet. She should have not even let the marriage occur. She had kept the secrete of their marriage and the nurse did not even tell or warn Juliet parents about the love connection with Romeo and Juliet. The nurse even let Juliet have her night with Romeo in Juliet's house and at the same time the rest of Juliet's family was down stairs while they were having their night. The positive thing about the Nurse's action was that she let Romeo and Juliet been able to be in love, but the negative side was that the secrets caused a horrible ending.

Even though both Friar Lawrence and the Nurse did not mean to harm or affect Romeo and Juliet in a bad way, they still had a huge impact on the true lover's lives in negative and positive ways. They both had huge impacts on Romeo and Juliet, but they ended the feud between the two families.

Sample collected by Danielle Frasca.

- Based on the information you read in Chapter 9, assess Amy's literacy development by using the following chart. Does this student meet the grade-level language and literacy expectations listed in the common core standards?

Literacy components	Strengths	Needs	Other
Lexical-semantic development			
Morphosyntactic development			
Pragmatic development			
Metalinguistic development			
Writing convention			
Organization of ideas			
Narrative ability			
Other			

- Review all the supporting strategies introduced in Chapter 9 and select a few that you think will be particularly helpful for this student and justify your choice.
- Reflect on your experience of doing this writing sample analysis.

Writing Sample 2: Ln Learning Student

This sample was by a seventh-grade male student, Juan (not his real name). Juan is an English Ln learner with typical development. He is a native speaker of Spanish from a working-class family. In this writing sample analysis, you are asked to do the following:

- Read Juan's writing sample carefully.

Writing Sample of a Seventh Grader, Juan

Lost in Yonkers

Grandma is a perfect example why the title is Lost in Yonkers first all she lives at Yonkers New York and she is lost because she don't know how to love she is so tuff that when she was young a horse fell on her and she didn't go to the doctor everybody says that she have a steal heart all she's children never had love from her incluse one of them Bella say's that the lucky ones were her brother that pass the way and because of she because she never express love to them.

Louie is another example of the title Lost in Yonkers first all he is a criminal a ganster anybody in he's family know into what organization is he in jay things that he is henchcack or a bag man the one that kill's the people grandma never accepts his money because she know what he is in maybe he foundt he's place in the army.

Sample contributed by Danielle Rodriguez. *Lost in Yonkers* is a play by Neil Simon.

- Based on the information you read in Chapter 10, assess Juan's literacy development by using the following chart. Discuss how you can help Juan meet the grade-level language and literacy expectations listed in the common core standards.

Literacy components	Strengths	Needs	Other
Lexical-semantic development			
Morphosyntactic development			
Pragmatic development			
Metalinguistic development			
Writing convention			
Organization of ideas			
Narrative ability			
Other			

- Review all the supporting strategies introduced in Chapter 10, select a few that you think will be particularly helpful for this student and justify your choice.
- Reflect on your experience of doing this writing sample analysis.

Writing Sample 3: Student with LI

This writing sample was by an eighth-grade male student, Chris (not his real name). Chris is a student with SLI. He has been in special education since Grade 2. He has been in a resource room and specialized reading room for three years in middle school. Chris is from a middle-class family. In this writing sample analysis, you are asked to do the following:

- Read Chris's writing sample carefully.

Writing Sample of an Eighth Grader, Chris

Economy in the 1920's

One of the mainly thing that damage the economy of the 1920 was buying on installment plans. Burning the economic boom of the 1920 people were buying thing that they could not afford their loans and installment plan. In the 1920 there was many new products that makes life easier for the stay at home wives. They bought these things on installment plans which meant that they will give them produce and you will pay it off over time but when the stock market crashes and banks close they cannot. As a result debt rose and people did not have jobs so they cannot pay it back.

Burning the 20's stock sky rocketed stock rose beyond the villa of the compiles. Many people want to get in the market so they borrow up to 90% agents there total salary and as long as the stocks rose they can pay back the lion and make money. But tin the 20's there was a bull market to the stocks go up but the composes will stay the same. On October 29 the stock market fit rock bottom and people were not able to pay back there loans but all the creditors called back the loans.

During WWI many farmers take out loans to get more seed and erumpent. After the war however the demand for the crop declined so farmers could not pay back the loans. Most after wars farmers just grow less but in this case there had crushing debt so they cannot pay off the loan.

Sample collected by Melissa Silva.

- Based on the information you read in Chapter 11, assess Chris's literacy development by using the following chart.

Literacy components	Strengths	Needs	Other
Lexical-semantic development			
Morphosyntactic development			
Pragmatic development			
Metalinguistic development			
Writing convention			
Organization of ideas			
Narrative ability			
Other			

- Review all the supporting strategies introduced in Chapter 11 and select a few that you think will be particularly helpful for this student and justify your choice. Develop an IEP that will help the student move toward the expectations specified in the common core standards.
- Reflect on your experience of doing this writing sample analysis.

Part V
Theoretical Perspectives on Language and Literacy Development and Learning

Part V includes two parts. The first part (Chapter 12) begins with a brief discussion on the important functions of theories and their relevance to teaching practice. It then introduces the theories that explain how children acquire their first language, more than one first language, and a new language. It also touches on the theories about language impairment. The chapter concludes with the theories on narrative, literacy development, and classroom discourse. The goal of this chapter is to help you build a theoretical foundation for your teaching practice.

In the exit evaluation part, you are asked to complete a self-assessment by analyzing a writing sample of a student. You are asked to demonstrate whether you know how to apply the CDA framework as well as big "D" and little "d" analyses to the student's work and whether you know how to use TP to help the student move forward in his language and literacy development. Through the exit evaluation, you are asked to confirm the belief that every student can learn with the right support, and you are encouraged to use this book as a starting point to continue to inform yourself as a teaching professional and to help your students grow.

Essential Questions for Part V

- What is the use of theories?
- What would be the difference between instruction with and without the guidance of a theoretical framework?
- How can teachers decide which theories to use?
- What is more important than focusing on students' language errors?
- What is the significance of implementing CDA and TP in diverse classrooms? What will your instructional design based on CDA and TP look like?

Understanding Language and Literacy Development: Diverse Learners in the Classroom, First Edition. Xiao-lei Wang.
© 2015 John Wiley & Sons, Inc. Published 2015 by John Wiley & Sons, Inc.
Companion website: www.wiley.com/go/wang/langandlit

12

Theories That Explain Language Acquisition and Literacy Development

Prereading Questions and Activities

Now that you have read about the language and literacy developmental characteristics among learners with different abilities from infancy to adolescence and you have had many opportunities throughout the text to think about these issues, you may have already formed your own theories to explain why children and adolescents exhibit certain language and literacy characteristics. Before you proceed to read Chapter 12, please take a moment to think about the following questions:

- What do children bring to the language-learning task?
- What mechanisms drive children's language acquisition?
- What types of support do students need for their continued language progress and academic literacy development?

When you jot down your responses to these questions, proceed to read Chapter 12 and compare your own explanations to the established theories and perspectives.

Topics to Be Addressed in This Chapter

- Functions of theories
- Theories that explain L1 acquisition
- Theories that explain multilingual L1 acquisition
- Theories that explain Ln learning
- Theories that explain language impairment
- Theories that explain narrative development
- Theories that explain the literacy development process

Understanding Language and Literacy Development: Diverse Learners in the Classroom, First Edition. Xiao-lei Wang.
© 2015 John Wiley & Sons, Inc. Published 2015 by John Wiley & Sons, Inc.
Companion website: www.wiley.com/go/wang/langandlit

Learning Objectives

After reading this chapter, you are expected to do the following:

- Understand the functions of theories.
- Understand various theoretical positions on the language and literacy development of diverse learners.
- Know how to use theories to guide your instructional practice.

Functions of Theories

In Chapter 1, we discussed the functions of a conceptual framework. The difference between a conceptual framework and theory is that a theory describes a broader relationship of matters and is often supported by empirical evidence, whereas a conceptual framework describes a more specific relationship between things. Both a conceptual framework and a theory serve as compasses that guide our teaching beliefs and practice. There are at least three important functions of theories.

Prediction

The difference between the "trial and error" and "playing by ear" approaches in teaching and "using theories as guidance for teaching" is about efficiency. If you are well versed in theories of language and literacy development, you can predict the outcome of your teaching method and are better prepared for what you will encounter in the classroom. For example, if Peter (the new teacher you met in the beginning chapters of this book) had had a solid theoretical background in students' diverse language and literacy development, he would have better prepared himself before he entered the classroom. Thus, the first function of a theory is to predict what could potentially happen and make you more prepared. You will also be able to make a better decision on what to do and have a clearer focus by considering different theoretical perspectives. Most importantly, a theory will prevent you from wasting time. Students cannot afford the "playing by ear" approach when the time they spend in school is precious for them to learn and develop.

Explanation

The second function of a theory is that it can help you explain succinctly why students learn and perform in a certain way. It will also help you find a solution for a given issue that arises in learning, communicate with parents, and address their concerns about their children's learning more convincingly.

However, not all theories will work for your specific situation. When a theory does not work or is inadequate, you will be more motivated to search for an alternative explanation for your specific situation. This is one of the reasons why the theories are introduced toward the end of the book.

Confidence

What a theory can really do for you is give you confidence. Knowing what could potentially happen and knowing how to predict what will happen can help you save time and anxiety. For instance, if you know that English-speaking children at a certain time in early childhood will make "errors" in the irregular past tense verbs (such as use *goed* instead of *went* and *taked* instead of *took*), you will not be so anxious to correct them because you understand that they are actually making progress in their metacognitive development by noticing and applying the general rules (add *-ed* for past tense verbs).

Your Turn

Based on the functions of the theories you just read, provide concrete examples to argue why theories on language and literacy development would help Peter fare well in his first few weeks of teaching and thereafter.

Theories that Explain L1 Acquisition and Development

There are abundant theories that have been proposed to explain how children acquire their first language in early years. Two extreme theoretical positions along the nature–nurture continuum have been polarizing the field by repudiating each other. At one extreme, the **behaviorist perspective** emphasizes the dominant effect of the environment on language acquisition. At the other, the **nativist view** accentuates the effects of innateness. However, most other theoretical perspectives are somewhere along the nature–nurture continuum between these two extremes, recognizing in various degrees the importance of individual innateness and cognition (nature) as well as environmental support and experiences (nurture) in language acquisition.

Over the years, many names and labels have been used for the different theoretical views on language acquisition. They are often confusing. To help you form a better picture of the various theories, the two polarizing theoretical positions, behaviorism and nativism, will first be introduced and then other theoretical perspectives that are located at various points along the nature–nurture continuum will be briefly described. Please note that it is more important to understand the main points in a theory than get stuck in its label because sometimes people use different terms to name the same theory.

The polarizing theoretical positions

Behaviorist theory

The behaviorist view extrapolates that language acquisition, like any other behavioral learning, follows a stimulus-response-reinforcement model. That is, adults provide a language model for children, and children imitate the adult model. In the communication process, successful communication is reinforced (S. Brown and Attardo, 2008), and the mistakes are suppressed (Pence and Justice, 2008, p. 56). However, this theoretical perspective fails to explain why children produce errors that they cannot possibly have heard in their linguistic environment, such as "*I goed to the park*" and "*He taked my toy.*" Nor can it explain why children with TD acquire a language in a short period (usually over about four to five years) and are able to produce sentences that they have never heard before (S. Brown and Attardo, 2008; Owens, 2012).

Although the behaviorist theory's explanation of childhood language acquisition is limited, it should not be dismissed entirely, for two reasons. First, it has historically contributed to the development of sociolinguistic theories. Second, its emphasis on "stimulus (model)-response (imitate)-reinforcement" is still quite useful for children with LI (Owens, 2012).

Your Turn

What is your position on the behaviorist perspective of language acquisition? Support your position with examples from this textbook.

Nativist theory

As briefly mentioned in Chapter 2, Noam Chomsky proposed an opposite explanation to the behaviorist position regarding how children acquire a language. According to this theoretical perspective, language is a symbolic system that is innate, residing in the human genetic code. Language acquisition is a universal, stable, orderly, and stage-like process. He suggested that children are born with general grammatical rules and categories common to all languages (the universal grammar). With this inborn language acquisition device (LAD), children use environmental input to discover the parameters/framework their language uses to satisfy the general grammatical rules and categories they are born with. Such innate ability is especially evident in the acquisition of syntactic rules.

As suggested in Chapter 2, there is evidence to support this view such as situations where children acquire creole and deaf children of hearing parents create language-like gestural communication systems. However, the nativist theory gives less credit to the role of input in language learning. There is ample evidence to suggest that adult input does make a difference in the frequency and quality of children's language learning. For example, research shows that parental vocabulary input is connected to children's vocabulary growth and that talkative parents have more talkative children (e.g., Huttenlocher et al., 1991).

Your Turn

Discuss how the nativist theory can be applied to language and literacy development in the school context and support your position with examples from Chapters 2–11.

Other theories that explain language acquisition

The debate on the role of nature and nurture in children's language acquisition is still ongoing. The following theories provide different evidence to support either the nativist camp, the behaviorist position, or the interactions of both the environment and the individual. However, none are as extreme as the nativist or the behaviorist view.

Sociolinguistic theory of language acquisition and language socialization

The sociolinguistic theory emphasizes that language use in communication is central to the linguistic process and development. The overriding motivation for language and language acquisition is effective communication (Owens, 2012).

This theoretical position on language acquisition can be largely credited to the Russian psychologist Vygotsky (1986), who stressed the importance of social interaction for language development and proposed that language emerges through social interaction with capable peers and adults. The language skills move from a social plane to a psychological plane. With adult scaffolding (support), children can progress to the level that is ahead of their current developmental level (the **zone of proximal development**) (Pence and Justice, 2008).

The language socialization theory is an extension of the sociolinguistic theory. It proposes that language development is both socialization through language and socialization to use language. Children acquire tacit knowledge of the principles of social order and systems of belief (**ethnotheories**) through exposure to and participation in language-mediated interaction. The development of linguistic knowledge is facilitated by the communication between children and others. This perspective emphasizes that sociocultural information is generally encoded in the organization of conversational discourse; discourse with children is no exception. Many formal and functional features of discourse carry sociocultural information, including phonological and morphosyntactic constructions, the lexicon, speech-act types, conversational sequencing, genres, interruptions, overlaps, gaps, and turn length. These structures are socially organized. They are also culturally organized to express local conceptions and theories about the world. Children acquire a worldview as they acquire a language (Ochs, 1997).

The dynamic systems view of language acquisition

Some researchers believe that the language socialization perspective tends to treat the language acquisition process as relatively static, bounded, and unidirectional. They argue that the dynamic and interactive process of language development is fluid and extends throughout the lifespan as people come to participate in new communities, define and redefine themselves according to new roles, and either accept or challenge the definition and role relationships formulated by others (Schecter and Bayley, 2004).

The **dynamic systems view** of language acquisition has risen in prominence recently. This perspective proposes that children's language development is not simply the adults' version, but qualitatively different from it. The drive toward meaning-making and social connection continuously shapes more mature linguistic abilities. This position underscores that language development is not a static, abstract, or symbolic system, but it emerges over time as a property of the self-organization of a complex system. Moreover, language development is not a process of acquiring abstract rules, but the emergence of language abilities in real life.

The dynamic systems theoretical framework (K. Nelson, 2007) outlines four major developmental phases as young children progress from intrapersonal experience to interpersonal culture. In each of these phases, they increasingly "tune" their behavior and cognition to the social adults surrounding them (see Box 12.1).

Box 12.1 Four Major Developmental Phases in Children's Language Development Proposed by the Dynamic Systems Theory

Phase 1: Affective communication This is the stage when infants experience their first social communication. Infants begin to form communicative relationships with other people through joint attention and make connections between another person's body and their own through imitation. With both joint attention and imitation, infants start to shift away from their egocentric perspective and adopt a more social stance.

Phase 2: Mimetic cognition Mimetic cognition consists of exchanging social knowledge, typically marked with the beginning of language. Here, language is used only to replicate parental language. For example, parents often label objects in the environment for their children (look at the doggie!) and children practice this knowledge by repeating the label (Doggie!). Throughout this phase, children increase their productive vocabulary and are eventually able to use the label without adult prompting. For the first time the child is able to communicate intentionally and has vocabulary control over the transmission of her experience. Mimetic cognition serves as a way for children to express their private thoughts and to share these with the adults who are closest to them.

Phase 3: Symbolic system During this stage, children have honed their language system and are able to use grammar and complex sentence structures. These developments enable children to communicate effectively in groups, particularly with peers, widening their social network. Peer groups offer a setting in which children can engage in pretend play. For example, use a shoe as a phone (use symbols in lieu of the actual referent).

Phase 4: Shared meaning In this stage, children develop a theory of mind, allowing them to view the world both objectively and from another point of view. This skill contributes to sophisticated narration, as the child is able to tell stories from other perspectives or even from other time periods. Critically the advanced language memory skills associated with this phase enable children to position themselves within time and culture. That is, children become aware of history and traditions and broaden opportunities for social interactions. This last phase marks children's entrance into a culture of shared meaning and prepares them for entry into school.

Modified from K. Nelson, *Young Minds in Social Worlds: Experience, Meaning, and Memory* (Cambridge, MA: Harvard University Press, 2007).

Cognitive theory of language acquisition

The **cognitive theory of language acquisition** views children as active agents in constructing their own understanding and learning of language. One example is the production of egocentric speech (private speech or inner speech) when children bring their own perspectives into the language-learning process. For example, 4-year-old Jimmy said "Now, I go there" while playing with his toy truck. Children's egocentric speech will gradually lessen as they grow. They learn to internalize their thoughts by thinking first and then speaking.

Intentionality model of language acquisition

The theoretical focus of the **intentionality model of language acquisition** is on the **agency** of the children; that is, children themselves are the driving force for language acquisition. This model contains two important tenets. First, when children engage with people and objects in their environment, they are motivated to learn a language because they must learn how to express their intentions by using language (for example, to let adults know they are hungry). Second, to acquire language, children must then make an effort to construct linguistic representations for the ideas they want to express and act to express them (Bloom and Tinker, 2001).

Usage-based theory of language acquisition

Germane to the intentional model theory, the **usage-based theory of language acquisition** argues that the essence of language is its symbolic dimension, which rests on the uniquely human ability to comprehend intention. Grammar emerges as the speakers of a language create linguistic constructions out of recurring sequences of symbols; children pick up these patterns in the buzz of words they hear around them. As a child becomes aware of others' intentions, he begins to actively manipulate them – for example, by drawing his mother's attention to an object of interest. As children repeatedly and increasingly use their awareness of social conventions to engage with other people, their general language abilities emerge (Pence and Justice, 2008; Tomasello, 2003).

Modularity theory of language acquisition

The perspective of the **modularity theory of language acquisition** emphasizes the organization of the cognitive infrastructure of the brain as comprising a series of highly specialized modules, including modules for various aspects of language processing. Language modules operate independently to perform dedicated functions and can interact with one another at higher levels to produce combinations of functions. Because language modules operate independently, language development in different areas, such as lexicon, syntax, and morphology, is driven forward by different types of input.

Bootstrapping theory of language acquisition

As discussed in earlier chapters, bootstrapping is a metaphor used to describe when a child accomplishes a language-learning task with minimal assistance from adults. There are two major kinds of bootstrapping strategies that children use to acquire a linguistic system: syntactic bootstrapping and semantic bootstrapping.

Syntactic bootstrapping suggests that children approach language learning with knowledge of syntactic categories and use it to understand word meanings in sentences. For instance, children are able to utilize the syntactic structure as information to figure out what verbs mean (Landau and Gleitman, 1985). Through a study on the successful language acquisition process of a blind child, researchers realized that language acquisition could not be simply a process of mapping sounds onto the things and actions to which they refer. Otherwise, the unavailability of referents would prevent blind children from acquiring a language (Landau and Gleitman, 1985). Children rely on their knowledge of syntax to help them understand word meanings.

Children also acquire a language through **semantic bootstrapping**, which means that they deduct grammatical structures by using word meanings they acquire from observing events around them (Pinker, 1984). For example, once a child learns that *cup* describes a solid object, she may infer that *cup* is a count noun. Later, when the child understands the determiner *a*, she may infer that other words that include the determiner *a* (for example, *a* book and *a* chair) are also count nouns (Pence and Justice, 2008).

Competition model of language acquisition

The **competition model of language acquisition** views language acquisition as a process consisting of a series of competitive cognitive processes that act upon language. By applying general cognitive processes to the language stimulus in the presence of a rich and stimulating environment, children are able to connect intrinsically meaningless symbols (words and sentences) to their referents, allowing them to infer meaning. Thus, the competition model posits that language acquisition must be embodied and situated in addition to relying on traditional mechanisms of human information processing in order for learners to derive meaning from language. The phenomenon of overgeneralization for young children in using the form *goed* instead of *went* is a good example. When children who are learning English make an irregular past tense verb regular, they overgeneralize the past tense rule that applies to most verbs in the English language. Eventually, through ongoing exposure to the irregular form *went*, the correct past tense representation of the word is strengthened and the incorrect form *goed* disappears (Pence and Justice, 2008; MacWhinney and Bates, 1989).

Theory of mind perspective on language acquisition

Learning a language and using it to successfully communicate to others require the ability to understand others' mental state (their intention, desire, and beliefs, among others). It also requires that a communicator be able to predict how others will act, explain why others act in a certain way, and describe other people's psychological state. All these abilities are referred to as theory of mind. As we discussed in previous chapters, children's development of theory of mind begins with the establishment of joint attention with caretakers and emerges through interacting with people around them.

Your Turn

How do you use the following theories in your content area teaching? Support your position with the examples from Chapters 2–11.

- Sociolinguistic theory and language socialization
- The dynamic systems view
- Cognitive theory
- Intentionality model
- Usage-based theory
- Modularity theory
- Bootstrapping theory
- Competition model
- Theory of mind

Theories That Explain Multilingual L1 Acquisition

Overall, children who acquire and develop more than one L1 operate on the same universal principle in their multilingual acquisition. However, because more than one language is involved in the acquisition process, multilingual L1 learners also exhibit their unique language acquisition characteristics. Below are some theories that explain multilingual L1 acquisition.

The separate development hypothesis

The **separate development hypothesis** (De Houwer, 2009) or the **differentiation hypothesis** (Meisel, 2006) states that children with consistent input in two or more languages from birth who grow up according to the one-parent-one-language principle develop two or more distinct morphosyntactic systems (see also Chapter 4). Even children who consistently hear or overhear two or more languages spoken by the same adult develop two or more separate morphosyntactic systems (De Houwer, 2009).

The separate underlying proficiency model

The **separate underlying proficiency model** (SUP model) asserts that the different language systems of multilingual children operate separately without transfer. In other words, multilinguals are able to function at an equal level in their respective languages to achieve balanced proficiency.

Multilingual bootstrapping hypothesis

The **multilingual bootstrapping hypothesis** suggests that each of a multilingual child's languages develops at a different pace. The more advanced system will boost the development of the less advanced one. Thus, although the grammars of the child's different languages develop independently, the child occasionally produces sentences consisting of grammatical constructions imported into the use of the language that lags behind in development, as a "temporary pooling of resources" (Meisel, 2006).

Critical mass hypothesis

How much language input is needed for a child to acquire a language and obtain proficiency? Because multilingual children have more than one linguistic input, they proportionally have less input per language than monolingual children. Does the limitation of linguistic quantity affect their multilingual acquisition process? Some studies have found no qualitative differences between monolingual children and multilingual children (specifically bilingual children). Other studies have found that bilingual children, on average, have fewer words in a single language than monolingual children acquiring that same language. However, comparing average levels of multilingual L1 learners may mask the fact that at the individual level, multilingual children may do just as well in one or all of their languages as monolingual children (De Houwer, 2009), and some multilingual L1 learners may even surpass monolinguals (Wang, 2008 and forthcoming).

In Chapter 4, we discussed that as long as children receive a critical mass of language input a minimum amount of input of 25 percent has been suggested in each of their prospective languages), they are able to acquire a language.

Your Turn

How do you connect the following theories with your teaching practice? Support your position with examples from this textbook.

- The separate development hypothesis
- Separate underlying proficiency model
- Multilingual bootstrapping hypothesis
- Critical mass hypothesis

Theories That Explain Ln Learning

When children learn a Ln after developing the basic structure in the L1, the process of language learning is qualitatively different from that of both monolingual children and children who acquire more than one L1. There are several theories that explain the process.

The interdependent hypothesis

The **interdependent hypothesis** states that in the early stages of Ln language acquisition, the first or stronger language may guide development in the Ln. Children do not need to learn the basic categories of the Ln; they can transfer the skills from their L1 to the Ln and learn the language-specific devices of their Ln (e.g., Verhoeven, Steenge, and van Balkom, 2012). Ln learners use the knowledge of the structure and foundation of their L1 for the Ln (Peña and Bedore, 2009).

The ivy hypothesis

The **ivy hypothesis** (Bernardini and Schlyster, 2004) suggests that language learning is a competition between cues across phonology, lexicon, morphosyntax, and pragmatics. For learners to process information, they must store, chunk, and decode information. Decoding for Ln learners involves language transfer. Children learn their Ln through the filter of what they know about their L1, and they may retain certain information and associate it based on the language-learning strategies they already have available (Peña and Bedore, 2009). Also, Ln learners are likely to use high-frequency forms correctly, but will make mistakes in less frequent forms. Forms that are more similar between languages will be mastered sooner (e.g., Italian and Spanish), whereas forms that are less similar between languages will take longer time to master (Döpke, 2000; Peña and Bedore, 2009).

Markedness theory

The markedness theory proposes that marked items in a language will be more difficult to acquire than unmarked items and that degrees of markedness will correspond to degrees of difficulty (H. Brown, 2000; Eckman, 1981). One example is the order of morpheme acquisition in English: marked structures are acquired later than unmarked structures (Rutherford, 1982).

Common underlying proficiency model

Cummins (1981) used the image of an iceberg to illustrate the relationship between children's different languages. He suggested that the different icebergs are separate above the surface. That is, the different languages are evidently different in outward conversation. Underneath the surface, the icebergs are fused so that the different languages do not function separately. All the languages of a multilingual individual or Ln learner operate through the same central processing system or in one integrated source of thought (Pavlenko, 2008). This model is referred to as the **common underlying proficiency model** (CUP). The main points of the CUP model are summarized below (see Box 12.2).

Box 12.2   Major Points of CUP

- Humans have the capacity to store more than one language.
- When a person owns more than one language, there is one integrated source of thought.
- Information processing skills and educational attainment may be developed through two or more languages, as well as through one language. Cognitive functioning and school achievement may be fed through one monolingual channel or equally successfully through two or more well-developed language channels. All the channels feed the same central processor.
- The language the child is using in the classroom needs to be sufficiently well developed to be able to process the cognitive challenges of the curriculum.

- Speaking, listening, reading, or writing in the L1 or Ln help the whole cognitive system to develop. However, if children are made to operate in an insufficiently developed Ln, the system will not function at its best. If children are made to operate in the classroom in a poorly developed school language, the quality and quantity of what they learn from complex curriculum materials and procedure in oral and written form may be relatively weak and impoverished.
- When one or all languages are not functioning fully (e.g., because of pressure to replace the home language with the majority language), cognitive function and academic performance may be negatively affected.

Modified from C. Baker, *Foundations of Bilingual Education and Bilingualism* (Bristol: Multilingual Matters, 2011), p. 166.

Thresholds theory

The **thresholds theory** tries to explain how proficient a child needs to be in a different language to obtain cognitive advantages from multilingualism (Baker, 2011). This theory proposes that there are two thresholds in multilingual development. The first threshold is reached when a child can avoid the negative consequences of multilingualism. The second threshold is a level required to experience the possible positive benefits of multilingualism (Baker, 2011).

The educational implication is that children may have a temporary lag in achievement when the curriculum is taught through the Ln. Until the Ln has developed well enough to cope with the curriculum materials, a temporary delay may be experienced.

Developmental interdependent hypothesis

Built on the thresholds theory, the **developmental interdependence hypothesis** proposes that a child's Ln competence is partly dependent on the level of competence already achieved in the L1. The more advanced in L1, the easier it will be for a child to develop the Ln. When the L1 is at a low stage of development, it is more difficult to achieve multilingualism. Research has corroborated the hypothesis (Cummins, 2000). For example, Catalan–Spanish bilingual children who know more Catalan words also know more Spanish words and vice versa (Baker, 2011).

Social and academic language proficiency differential

There are two kinds of competence in Ln learning: the **basic interpersonal communicative skills** (BICS) and the **cognitive academic language proficiency** (CALP). BICS refers to basic proficiency levels that children use to carry out basic conversations in social contexts. Children are expected to acquire BICS over approximately two to three years of language use and exposure. Given the proposed reliance on L1 in the first two to three years of Ln learning, it is hypothesized that young sequential language learners would benefit from explicit expansions in L1 to promote lexical acquisition in Ln. CALP refers to later developing language skills used in higher level cognitive tasks such as analytical evaluations, reasoning, and the complex language skills needed for educational settings. It usually takes five to seven years or more to develop CALP. Using mathematics as an example, there are many words that have different meanings and concepts than their everyday uses such as *column, pattern, angle, plot, point, estimate, factor, root,* and *table* (Baker, 2011).

Expanded competition model in Ln learning

The competition model has been expanded to account for a number of psycholinguistic processes involved in Ln learning, including cues, storage, chunking, codes, and resonance. The expanded version of the competition model posits that each of these cognitive mechanisms controls the activation of representations in the Ln that compete in the mind of the learner during acquisition and usage of the Ln. As in the original version of the model, the weights of the competing representations are computed and adjusted based on the learner's experience with the Ln. Thus, the model infers that as the extensiveness of learners' exposure to the Ln increases, they will gain an increasingly complete and nuanced understanding of the meaning of sentences in the Ln.

Krashen's comprehension hypothesis model of Ln learning

Based on the research of his own and others, Krachen (1981 and 1988) developed a comprehension hypothesis model of Ln learning. This model consists of five important components (see Box 12.3).

Box 12.3   Krashen's Comprehension Hypothesis Model of Ln Learning

- The natural order hypothesis
- The acquisition/learning hypothesis
- The monitor hypothesis
- The input hypothesis
- The affective filter hypothesis

The **natural order hypothesis** suggests that children learn the rules of a Ln in a predictable order. Some grammatical structures tend to be acquired early, while others are acquired late. This order is independent of the Ln learners' age, their L1 background, and their exposure to the Ln.

The **acquisition/learning hypothesis** describes two ways of learning a Ln. One is through acquisition (using the Ln language for real communication) and the other is through learning (consciously learning the rules of the Ln). Krashen distinguishes the meaning of *acquisition* and *learning*. According to him, acquisition occurs in informal settings, and it is implicit and unconscious. Learning, on the other hand, occurs in formal settings, and it is explicit and conscious.

The **monitor hypothesis** describes the relationship between acquisition and learning. The acquisition system is the utterance initiator, and the learning system performs the role of the monitor or the editor. The monitor acts in a planning, editing and correcting function when three specific conditions are met: the Ln learner has sufficient time at her disposal, she focuses on form or thinks about correctness, and she knows the rule.

There is individual variation among language learners with regard to how the monitor or editor is used. The over-users use the monitor all the time, the under-users have not learned or prefer not to use their conscious knowledge, and optimal users use the monitor appropriately. Usually, a learner's personality will determine what group he belongs to. Extroverts tend to be under-users, and introverts, perfectionists, and learners who lack self-confidence tend to be over-users.

The **input hypothesis** implies that Ln learners improve and make progress when they receive Ln input that is one step beyond their current linguistic competence. For example, if a learner's current Ln competence is at stage "i," and if her Ln input is at the level of "i + 1," this learner will make progress in her Ln. However, Krashen cautioned that since not all learners can be at the same level of linguistic competence at the same time, the Ln input "i + 1" should be appropriate for their current level of Ln competence, and the key is that the input should occur in the natural communicative context.

The **affective filter hypothesis** states that a mental block, caused by affective factors, can prevent Ln input from adding to learning in the Ln.

Your Turn

Discuss the classroom implications of the following theories with the support of examples from this book and other sources.

- The interdependent hypothesis
- The ivy hypothesis
- Markedness theory
- Common underlying proficiency model
- Thresholds theory
- Developmental interdependent hypothesis
- Social and academic language proficiency differential
- Expanded competition model in Ln learning
- Krashen's comprehension hypothesis model of Ln/L2 learning

Theories That Explain LI

Theories that explain LI are scarce. Even when they are available, they tend to be restricted to explaining one specific kind of disability. Therefore, you are encouraged to research literature constantly for new information on LI.

The system model

The **system model** suggests that when working with students who have LI, we need to focus more on changing the environment of the students to facilitate their communication. (The ideas are based on Paul, 2007.) Suppose a child with ASD has difficulties in communicating his needs to his peers, and his frustration leads to aggressive or self-abusive behavior. Instead of blaming the child for his behavior, you, as a teacher, can modify the environment by providing means to help him to communicate, such as providing him with pictures, encouraging him to write down or draw what he wants, and modeling how to communicate needs to others. The purpose of the system model is to create a classroom environment that attends to the communication needs of the students with LI so that they can benefit from carrying on meaningful communication with the teacher and peers.

The categorical model

The **categorical model** attempts to group children with LI into similar etiological categories according to their impairment and their accompanying language-learning issues, and it also implies that the identified categories play a causal role in children's LI (Paul, 2007). In other words, this model describes how the language performance of students with LI within one category is similar to each other and different from that of typically developing students. For example, students with cognitive delay are put into one category and thus, teachers use strategies for students with cognitive delay when helping them. Students with SLI are considered in another category and strategies are used to help this group of students specifically. The advantage of this model is that it can help teachers distinguish how a child from one category is different from those in another category. It may be useful initially for you to have a general idea about your students with LI.

However, there are several concerns about this model. First, the problem with this model is that even when two students are categorized as having cognitive delay, in reality one student may be far more advanced in her language performance than the other. Further, we may be clear that a student's LI is caused by cognitive delay, but we may not know what caused her cognitive delay. Second, students do not often fit exactly into one category of LI. For instance, the majority of students with ASD have cognitive delay in addition to the specific characteristics of autism. Third, putting students into an etiological category does not inform us what kinds of language skills a student has. Moreover, putting students into the same category does not tell us what intervention goals are appropriate and what approach will work best for these students.

The specific disability model

Differently from the categorical model, the **specific disability model** postulates that students with LI differ in some underlying cognitive abilities (Paul, 2007). It focuses on the variations within a single student and how underlying strengths and difficulties influence a student's language development.

The descriptive-developmental model

The **descriptive-developmental model** is also called the **communication-language approach**. This model or approach posits that the language achievement target for students with typical development provides the best curriculum guide for teaching language for students with LI (Paul, 2007). In other words, this model emphasizes using the typical language development sequence to guide the intervention for students with LI. It focuses on identifying and describing in detail the current level of language function of children with LI in terms of the entire range of language performance (phonology, lexicon, semantics, morphology, syntax, pragmatics, and metalinguistic knowledge). With this detailed knowledge about a student's current language ability, teachers can provide focused and specific support in that particular language area to help the student in the direction of typical language development in the same area.

It is important to note that using this model does not mean that you expect that an eleventh grader with SLI to produce complex sentence structure in his writing through intervention because students with typical development can do so. Rather, this approach encourages you to use the typical language development trajectory as a guide and to guide the student with SLI to work on complex sentence structure (both in comprehension and production).

The weak central coherence theory

Children with ASD have a distinct difficulty in understanding narratives because of inferential processing limitations. This affects not only their academic learning (e.g., narratives), but also their social functions. This can be explained by the **weak central coherence theory** that suggests that individuals with autism are biased to process information locally. This cognitive style may impair comprehension, particularly if inferencing is required (the ability to fill in information that is not overt in a message). However, task performance may be facilitated by this cognitive style if local processing is required (Nuske and Bavin, 2011). Message comprehension requires an integration of the meanings of individual words, sentences and paragraphs, as well as key ideas and themes. General knowledge needs to be applied to varying contexts. Information from various sources needs to be incorporated as a whole, using "gestalt-like" global processing. Instead of spontaneously employing global processing (the default processing style in typically developing individuals), it is argued that individuals with ASD are biased when processing information on a local level, with particular attention to detail; they have "weak central coherence." By contrast, typically developing individuals are characterized by "strong central coherence". As comprehension requires global processing, this local processing bias may account for some of the comprehension problems in autism.

Sound discrimination disability

Spoken language relies primarily on the processing of auditory information. Thus, some researchers believe that the reason some children with LI have phonological difficulties is that they lack the ability to distinguish the brief, rapidly changing auditory signals that need to be processed in order to perceive, categorize, and recognize sounds. This has led to the belief that identifying and providing remedy in a specific auditory domain will result in improved language performance. For example, the **FastForWord program** (FFW program)uses intensive practice with computer-generated speech to teach children to gradually distinguish increasingly brief acoustic signals as a remedy for children with phonological difficulties (Tallal, Miller, and Fitch, 1993). Some studies support this explanation. Some children with documented phonological difficulties in temporal processing can benefit from FastForWord training (Habib et al., 2002). Other studies suggest that the FFW delivered at home by parents leads to improvement in children's performance on some structured language tasks, but not to broad changes in functional language use (Loeb, Stoke, and Fey, 2001). Many researchers dispute the effectiveness of this FFW program, and the jury is still out on determining its usefulness.

Your Turn

Discuss the classroom implications of the following theories with the support of the examples from this book and other sources:

- The system model
- The categorical model
- The specific disability model
- The descriptive-developmental model
- The weak central coherence theory
- Sound discrimination disability

Theories That Explain the Narrative Development Process

The filtering principle

The filtering principle suggests that in narratives, an individual's experiences are filtered into verbalized events through the choice of perspective taken on the experiences and the set of linguistic operations provided by the language in use (Verhoeven and Strömqvist, 2001).

The packaging principle

The packaging principle holds that a narrative does not involve a linear chain of successive events. Instead, there is a hierarchical set of events which are located in time and place with various event phases subordinated and interrelated (Verhoeven and Strömqvist, 2001).

Theories That Explain the Literacy Development Process

Natural literacy development theory

Teale (1982) suggests that some young children become capable emergent readers and writers before being formally introduced to the process or attending school. This phenomenon is sometimes referred to as **natural literacy development**. However, the natural literacy skills exhibited by some young children are, strictly speaking, not really natural. They are the result of being exposed to a rich literacy environment in which young children develop literacy skills through parental scaffolding. Moreover, it is not enough to develop literacy skills by just providing children with an enriched literacy environment; children must play an active role in their literacy development process. It is through their initiations, temperament, questions, and other actions that children affect the nature and frequency of adult mediated literacy activities.

Bottom-up and top-down reading processes

Reading can be described in two processes: bottom-up and top-down (Owens, 2012). The **bottom-up reading process** emphasizes that perceptual and phonemic skills influence higher cognitive functioning (such as reading); a student's knowledge of perceptual features in letters, letter–sound correspondence, and lexical retrieval aid her word recognition and decoding. In the bottom-up process, a child decodes print into speech. In English, a child must be able to segment or divide each word into phonemic elements and learn the alphabetic codes that correspond. Only when this process becomes automatic can a child give sufficient attention to the meaning. However, the bottom-up reading process cannot account for the entire reading process. In situations such as syntactic comprehension, the skills involved in the bottom-up reading process will not be sufficient. Readers must be able to use higher-level metacognitive strategies, hypothesis (such as inferencing through syntactic and semantic cues), and background knowledge to understand unfamiliar words, phrases, and sentences.

In contrast, **the top-down reading process** underscores the fact that higher-level cognitive functions such as concepts and inferences influence lower-level processes. A reader generates hypotheses about written materials based on her knowledge, the content, and the syntactic structures used. Again, the top-down reading process alone cannot adequately explain the reading process.

It is likely that reading contains both of these two processes at different levels. These processes are interactive and relatively rely on each other depending on an array of factors such as the reader's age, cognitive and linguistic abilities, and the difficulty of the text level.

Simple view of reading

The **simple view of reading** is a straightforward outline of the relationship between language and literacy (Gillam, Marquardt, and Martin, 2011). It suggests that reading is composed of two components: word recognition and language comprehension. Once these two processes are complete, reading comprehension happens.

Information processing theory of reading

The **information processing theory of reading** suggests that each word has a switchboard that activates all the visual, auditory, and semantic features associated with that word. If a reader has enough information from these features, the information is automatically presented to the other parts of the system for processing. It takes a child approximately 0.5 seconds to recognize a familiar word, and it takes an adult only half of that time (0.25 second) to do the same. If processing faculties are limited for a reader (e.g., early readers or children with difficulties in reading), he will spend more time on lower-level decoding and less time on higher-level comprehension (Owens, 2012).

Sociopsycholinguistic transactional theory of reading

The **sociopsycholinguistic transactional theory** of reading suggests that reading is making sense of text. In order to make sense, readers construct a text parallel to the author's printed text by using graphophonic, syntactic, and semantic cues from the printed text. When interacting with that text, readers also produce meaning through the personal and global knowledge they bring to the act of reading (Liontas, 2002).

Schema theory

Schema theory suggests that a person's expectations and assumptions about a text or speech event are externally constructed and impose external constrains on the ways in which learners understand messages Successful understanding of texts depends on the schema that a learner builds while growing up in a particular cultural and linguistic context. This schema helps the learner make sense of new facts, text types, formal patterns, and practices. It also triggers a learner's attitudes and feelings toward texts. In other words, a learner's schema explains the constitutive role of culturally organized experiences in her sense making (Ferris and Hedgcock, 2014).

This theory can be used to explain how Ln learning and bidialectal students approach school academic literacy practices. That is, they bring their cultural and linguistic schema initially to the learning tasks. Thus, you need to have a good understanding of your students' current schema and make them conscious about the different schema in their current schema and the school's academic literacy schema.

Individual-environmental model of the writing process

Hayes and Flower (1980) initially proposed three components that affect written communication: writing task environment, cognitive process of writing, and long-term memory. The task environment includes all the factors that can influence writing, such as social factors, teacher writing task assignments, and the text produced by a writer so far. The cognitive process in writing involves planning (deciding what to write and how to write it), translating (turning plans into written text), and revision (improving existing text). Long-term memory is the writer's knowledge about the topic, the audience of the writing, and the genre of the writing (Hayes, 1996).

Hayes later revised the model and made it clearer and simpler. The new model consolidates the previous three components into two big parts: task environment and the individual. Hayes called this new model "individual-environmental model of writing" (Hayes, 1996). In the task environment part, Hayes proposes the following aspects: the audience, the social environment, the other texts that the writer may read while writing, the text the writer has produced so far, and the writing medium such as a word processor. In the individual part, Hayes incorporates motivation, affective process, working memory and long-term memory. The new model has four important features. First, it emphasizes the role of working memory in writing. You will read why working memory is important in the next section on capacity theory. Second, it includes visual-spatial and linguistic representations, because graphs, tables, and pictures are essential in understating the text message in writings such as science journals, textbooks, and instructional manuals. Third, motivation and affect are important for the writing process. Finally, the three processes in the original model (planning, translating, and revision) have been significantly reorganized in the new model. Revision has been replaced with text interpretation. Planning is subsumed under the more general category of reflection, and translation is considered in the more general text production processes (Hayes, 1996).

Your Turn

Based on the individual-environmental model of writing described above, make a chart that indicates all the important components of this model. Using this chart that you developed as a reference, design a lesson plan to show how you will be able to use this model to help students improve their writing abilities.

The capacity theory of writing development

Some believe that writing development does not go in the order suggested by Hayes and Flower (1980) for the cognitive process: planning, translating, and reviewing. The process of translating usually tends to emerge first in beginning writers. The **capacity theory of writing** (McCutchen, 1996) suggests that beginning writers need to consume considerable resources of working memory when they engage in translating ideas directly into text through transcription; thus, the capacity limitations leave children with few resources for planning and reviewing. Young writers often require explicit instruction to help them develop the capacity of planning and reviewing.

By the age of 9 or 10, the resources demanded for transcription decrease so that children have more resources to manage text generation and become more efficient in it. However, children with learning disabilities, including LI, may continue to use most of their resources for the process of transcription.

Moreover, working memory limits the complexity of developing writers' text planning and reviewing when the resource demand is high. Children with larger working memory spans tend to do better in reviewing than children with smaller working memory spans.

The metacognitive theory of writing

Metacognition is a general concept. It can be broadly defined as one's knowledge of one's own cognitive and affective processes and states, as well as the ability to consciously and deliberately monitor and regulate those processes and states. Using this general concept to look at writing development, it can be defined as a process in which a student can make progress in writing when she becomes conscious about how she writes, including her strengths and needs. The **metacognitive theory of writing** contains two important components: self-regulation, and the motivational beliefs associated with strategy use (Borkowski, 1992).

As children mature, they acquire writing competency and self-regulatory skills at different rates and to different degrees. The competency and skills form the basis for planning, translating, and reviewing writing. However, self-monitoring in writing may need explicit teaching. Students need to develop the ability to monitor their own progress in the various areas that good writing requires.

Moreover, writing as a cognitive act has motivational consequences, which can potentially affect students' future self-regulatory action. As students' executive abilities become more refined, they come to realize the importance of the strategies they use in writing and how that will affect their writing performance. As a result, when students have a successful experience in writing tasks by using strategies, they are likely to have confidence in their writing ability. Over time, students' writing ability will improve as a result of being conscious of their mental action (Borkowski, 1992).

Your Turn

Discuss the classroom implications of the following theories with the support of examples from this book and other sources.

- Natural literacy development
- Bottom-up and top-down reading processes
- Simple view of reading
- Information processing view of reading
- Sociopsycholinguistic transactional theory of reading
- Schema theory
- Individual-environmental model of the writing process
- The capacity theory of writing development
- The metacognitive theory of writing

A Theory That Explains Discourse Analysis

There are many theories on how to analyze discourses in human communication. However, Gee's discourse analysis stands out because of its relevance to diverse learners in the classroom environment.

Gee's discourse analysis approach considers how language, both spoken and written, enacts individuals' social and cultural perspectives and identities. He capitalized the word Discourse and used the term big "D" to emphasize how language is used in communication that is beyond the little "d"s (e.g., phonology, lexicon, semantics, morphology, and syntax). There are seven important components in Gee's Discourse analysis (big "D"): significance, practice, identity, relationship, politics, connections, and sign systems and knowledge (Gee, 2011). In the significance aspect of communication, the focus of analysis is on how a particular piece of language (both in speaking or writing) is being used to make certain things significant or not. In the practice aspect of communication, the focus is on how this particular piece of language is being used to enact (i.e., get others to recognize what is going on). In the identity aspect of communication, the focus is on what identity this particular piece of language is being revealed to enact, what identity this piece of language is attributing to others, and how this helps the speaker or writer enact her own identity. In the relationship aspect of communication, the focus is on what sort of relationship this piece of language is seeking to enact with others (present or not). In the politics aspect of the communication, the focus is on how this piece of language is being used to phrase one's perspective (i.e., what is being communicated as to what is taken to be "normal," "right," "good," "correct," "proper," "appropriate," "valuable," "the way things are," "the way things ought to be," "high status or low status," "like me or not like me," and so forth?). In the connection aspect of communication, the analysis is on how a particular piece of language connects or disconnects things and how it makes one thing relevant or irrelevant to another. In the sign systems and knowledge aspect of communication, the analysis is on how this piece of language privileges or disprivileges specific sign systems (e.g., Spanish vs English, technical/academic language vs everyday language, words vs image, words vs equations, etc.) or how it expresses different ways of knowing and believing (e.g., science vs. the humanities, science vs "common sense," biology vs "creation science").

The advantage of using Gee's big "D" analysis to examine students' D̲iscourse (both in speaking and writing) is that it focuses on the messages beyond the surface and tries to understand how a student uses language to do things.

Your Turn

Ask two of your classmates to discuss a controversial topic. Video-record the debate. Ask one group to analyze the little "d" aspects of the debate and ask another group to analyze the debate with the seven components Gee's D̲iscourse analysis. Compare the analyses of the two groups and discuss which kind of analysis provides more information about the debaters, and the educational implications of such analysis.

The Bottom Line Regarding Theories

The various theories we have discussed so far have shown us that there is no simple and general way of explaining how children with different abilities acquire and develop language and literacy. However, theories – whether explicitly or implicitly held – have powerful effects on what we do in the classroom environment, how we do it, and how we determine if we are successful in reaching our diverse students.

There are several aspects that we must attend to when we consider theories. First, it is likely that one theoretical perspective alone may not necessarily explain what you encounter in your students' language and literacy development. Sometimes, the wise approach is to take the **eclectic approach**; that is, to take a bit from many perspectives and try them out to fit your learners' needs. Second, it is possible that you are not convinced by all the theories. Nonetheless, understanding even the theories that you disagree with can help you begin to think about why they may not work and, at the same time, broaden your perspectives on an issue that concerns you. Third, some people believe that new theories are always better than old theories. However, it is important to note that theories are built on each other; some old theories may have historical interest and they might help you see how current theories are formed. The criterion to determine a good theory is not when it is formed, rather whether it is supported by sound evidence and can withstand repeated scrutiny. Fourth, theories change and shift based on our continued understanding in a particular area. Finally, your knowledge about the established theories can help you discover, build, and artic-ulate your own theories and help you become reflective teachers (Ferris and Hedgcock, 2014). Teaching is a theoretical act.

Your Turn

- Identify the language and literacy development characteristics of children and ado-lescents from Chapters 3–11 and make a list of them by using keywords (it may be helpful if you reread the "Summary of Key Points" at the end of each of these chap-ters). Try to use some of the theories introduced in this chapter to explain these characteristics. What instructional insight did you get by carrying out this activity?
- Suppose you had a teacher–parent conference with one of the students whose writing samples were shown at the end of Parts I, II, III, and IV; how would you explain to the parent his or her child's language and literacy performance by using the theories in Chapter 12?

Summary of Key Points

- Theories serve at least three important functions: predict what will happen, explain what has happened, and boost teacher confidence.
- The behaviorist perspective emphasizes the dominant effect of the environment on language acquisition.
- The nativist view accentuates the importance of innateness in acquiring a language.
- Sociolinguistic theory emphasizes that language use in communication is central to the linguistic process and to development. The overriding motivation for lan-guage acquisition is effective communication. Building upon this framework, the language socialization theory proposes that language development is both social-ization through language and socialization to use language.
- The dynamic systems theory underscores the idea that language development is not a static, abstract, symbolic system, but that it emerges over time as a property of the self-organization of a complex system; language development is not a process of acquiring abstract rules, but is the emergence of language abilities in real life.
- The cognitive theory views children as active agents in constructing their own understanding of language.

- The intentionality model of language acquisition contains two important principles. First, children are motivated to learn a language because they must learn how to express their intention by using language. Second, children must make an effort to construct linguistic representations for the ideas that they want to express and act to express their ideas by using them (acquiring a language). In close relationship with the intentionality model theory, the usage-based theory of language acquisition argues that as children repeatedly and increasingly use their awareness of social conventions to engage with other people, their more general language abilities emerge.

- The modularity theory of language acquisition emphasizes the organization of the cognitive infrastructure of the brain as comprising a series of highly specialized modules. Each of these language modules operates independently, and language development in different areas (e.g., lexicon, syntax, and morphology) is driven forward by different types of input.

- The bootstrapping theory suggests that children acquire a language by using bootstrapping strategies. For instance, they use information in the syntactic structure of sentences as a significant source of information about what verbs mean. They also deduce grammatical structures by using the meanings of words they acquire from observing events around them.

- The competition model views language acquisition as a process consisting of a series of competitive cognitive processes that act upon language. By applying general cognitive processes to the language stimulus in the presence of a rich and stimulating environment, children are able to connect intrinsically meaningless symbols (words and sentences) to their referents, allowing them to infer meaning.

- The theory of mind perspective refers to the ability to understand others' mental state. It requires that a communicator be able to predict how others will act, explain why others act in a certain way, and describe other people's psychological states.

- The separate developmental hypothesis states that children with regular input in two or more languages from birth and who are growing up according to the one-parent-one-language principle will develop two or more distinct morphosyntactic systems.

- The separate underlying proficiency (SUP) model asserts that the different language systems of multilingual children operate separately without transfer.

- The multilingual bootstrapping hypothesis suggests that each of a multilingual child's languages develops at a different pace. The more advanced system will boost the development of the less advanced one.

- Although multilingual children, on average, may know fewer words in a single language than monolingual children acquiring that same language, no qualitative differences have been found between monolingual children and multilingual children. At the individual level, multilingual children may do just as well in one of their languages as monolingual children.

- The interdependent hypothesis states that in the early stages of a Ln language acquisition, children do not need to learn the basic categories of the Ln; they can transfer the skills from their L1 to the Ln and learn the language-specific devices of the Ln. Similarly, the ivy hypothesis suggests that children use the structure of the more proficient language (often the first or primary language) to support the less proficient language (often the Ln).

- The markedness theory proposes that marked items in a language will be more difficult to acquire than unmarked items and that degrees of markedness will correspond to degrees of difficulty.

- The common underlying proficiency (CUP) model proclaims that all the languages of a multilingual or Ln learner operate through the same central processing system or in one integrated source of thought.

- The thresholds theory proposes that there are two thresholds in multilingual development. The first threshold is reached when a child can avoid the negative consequences of multilingualism. The second threshold is a level required to experience the possible positive benefits of multilingualism.

- The developmental interdependence hypothesis asserts that a child's Ln competence is partly dependent on the level of competence already achieved in the L1. The more advanced a child is in L1, the easier it will be for the child to develop the Ln. When the L1 is at a low stage of development, it is more difficult to achieve multilingualism.

- The ivy hypothesis suggests that language learning is a competition between cues across phonology, lexicon, morphosynax, and pragmatics.

- There are two kinds of competence in Ln learning: the basic interpersonal communicative skills (BICS) and the cognitive/academic language proficiency (CALP). BICS refers to basic proficiency levels that children need to carry out conversations in social contexts, and it takes two to three years to develop the ability. CALP refers to later-developing language skills used in higher-level cognitive tasks, and it usually takes five to seven years or more to develop this ability.

- The expanded version of the competition model posits that as the extensiveness of learners' exposure to the Ln increases, they will gain an increasingly complete and nuanced understanding of the meaning of sentences in the Ln.

- Krashen's comprehension hypothesis model of Ln learning consists of five components:

  ○ The natural order hypothesis: Children learn the grammatical rules of a Ln in a predictable order. Some grammatical structures tend to be acquired early and others late.

  ○ The acquisition/learning hypothesis: There are two ways of learning a Ln. One is through acquisition (using the Ln language for real communication), and the other is through learning (consciously learning the rules of the Ln).

  ○ The monitor hypothesis: The acquisition system is the utterance initiator, and the learning system performs the role of the monitor or editor. The monitor acts in a planning, editing and correcting function when three specific conditions are met: the Ln learner has sufficient time at her disposal, she focuses on form or thinks about correctness, and she knows the rule.

  ○ The input hypothesis: Ln learners improve and make progress when they receive Ln input that is one step beyond their current linguistic competence.

  ○ The affective filter hypothesis: A mental block, caused by affective factors, can prevent Ln input from learning the Ln.

- The system model suggests that when working with students who have LI, we need to focus more on changing the environment to facilitate their communication.
- The categorical model describes how the language performances of students with LI within one category are similar to one another and different from those of typically developing students.
- The specific disability model postulates that students with LI differ in some underlying cognitive abilities. It focuses on variation within a single student and how underlying strengths and difficulties influence a student's language development.
- The descriptive-developmental model or the communication-language approach posits using the typical language development sequence to guide intervention for students with LI.
- The weak central coherence theory that suggests that individuals with autism are biased to process information locally. This cognitive characteristic may impair comprehension, particularly if inferencing is required.
- Spoken language relies primarily on the processing of auditory information. Thus, some researchers believe that the reason some children with LI have phonological difficulties is that they lack the ability to distinguish the brief, rapidly changing auditory signals that need to be processed in order to perceive, categorize, and recognize sounds. This has led to the belief that identifying and providing remedy in the specifically auditory domain will result in improved language performance.
- The natural literacy development theory suggests that some young children become capable readers and writers before being formally introduced to the process or attending school. In order to acquire language and literacy skills, young children must be exposed to a literacy rich environment in which they learn and in turn change the environment.
- The bottom-up reading process emphasizes that perceptual and phonemic skills influence higher cognitive functioning (such as reading).
- The simple view of reading suggests that reading is composed of two components: word recognition and language comprehension.
- The information processing theory of reading suggests that each word has a switchboard that activates all the visual, auditory, and semantic features of that word.
- The sociopsycholinguistic transactional theory of reading suggests that readers also produce meaning through the personal and world knowledge they bring to the act of reading.
- Schema theory suggests that successful understanding of texts depends on the schema that a learner builds while growing up in a particular cultural and linguistic context. This schema helps the learner make sense of new facts, text types, formal patterns, and practices. It also triggers a learner's attitudes and feelings toward texts.
- Hayes's individual-environmental model of writing has four important features. First, it emphasizes the role of working memory in writing. Second, it includes the visual-spatial and linguistic representations for understanding text messages. Third, motivation and affect are important for the writing process. Finally, the cognitive process of writing involves interpretation, reflection, and text production.
- The capacity theory of writing suggests that beginning writers need to consume considerable resources of working memory when they engage in translating ideas

directly into text through transcription; thus, capacity limitations leave children with few resources for planning and reviewing. Young writers often require explicit instruction to help them develop the capacity of planning and reviewing. As children get older (by the age 9 or 10), the resources demanded for transcription decrease so that children have more resources to manage text generation and become more efficient in it. Moreover, working memory limits the complexity of developing writers' text planning and reviewing when the resource demand is high. Children with larger working memory spans tend to do better in reviewing than children with smaller memory spans.

- The metacognitive theory of writing development suggests that writers can make progress in writing when they become conscious about how they write through self-regulation.
- Gee's discourse analysis approach considers how language, both spoken and written, enacts individuals' social and cultural perspectives and identities. There are seven important components in Gee's Discourse analysis (big "D"): significance, practice, identity, relationship, politics, connections, and sign systems and knowledge.

Key Terms

Acquisition/learning hypothesis
Affective filter hypothesis
Agency
Basic interpersonal communicative skills (BICS)
Behaviorist perspective on language acquisition
Big "D"
Bottom-up reading process
Capacity theory of writing
Categorical model
Cognitive academic language proficiency (CALP)
Cognitive theory of language acquisition
Common underlying proficiency model (CUP)
Connection aspect of discourse analysis
Descriptive-developmental model (communication-language approach)
Developmental interdependence hypothesis

Differentiation hypothesis (separate development hypothesis)
Dynamic systems view
Egocentric speech
Ethnotheories
FastForWord program
Identity aspect of discourse analysis
Independent hypothesis
Information processing theory of reading
Input hypothesis
Ivy hypothesis
Language socialization theory
Little "d"
Metacognitive theory of writing
Natural literacy development theory
Natural order hypothesis
Politics aspects of discourse analysis
Practice aspects of discourse analysis
Relationship aspects of discourse analysis
Separate development hypothesis (also see the differentiation hypothesis)

Separate underlying proficiency model (SUP)

Sign systems and knowledge aspects of discourse analysis

Significance aspects of discourse analysis

Simple view of reading

Sociolinguistic theory

Sociopsycholinguistic transactional theory

Specific disability model

Syntactic bootstrapping

System model

Thresholds theory

Top-down reading process

Usage-based theory of language acquisition

Weak central coherence theory

Zone of proximal development

Recommended Further Readings

Chomsky, N. (1975). *Reflections on Language*. New York: Random House.

Gee, J. P. (2011). *An Introduction to Discourse Analysis: Theory and Method*. 3rd edn. New York: Routledge.

Pavlenko, A. (2009). *Emotion and Multilingualism*. New York: Cambridge University Press.

Tomasello, M. (2003). *Constructing a Language: A Usage-Based Theory of Language Acquisition*. Cambridge, MA: Harvard University Press.

Exit Self-Evaluation

By now you should have attained the basic information about the language and literacy developmental characteristics of students with different abilities. You should also have built knowledge on how to provide differentiated language and literacy support for these learners in classroom settings. To help you assess whether you are indeed ready to apply what you have learned in this book to your teaching practice, you are now asked to conduct a comprehensive exit self-evaluation by doing the following:

- Read an essay written by Mario (not his real name), a 13-year-old Spanish–English bilingual student in the eighth grade, who has been enrolled in a diverse public school system since kindergarten.
- Evaluate the written comments made by Mario's teacher.

Essay by Mario

My personal memo

Everyone has experiences in life that create everlasting memories. One of my ever lasting memories is when I went to a soccer game with my dad, mom, and my brothers.

So we left Peekskill at 5:30 and we are going to city field home of the New York City mets in queens. When all of sudden it stares pooring rain and we got scared because I thought the was going to be cancelled and got there and it stopped for a little while, then my dad said let go grab a bite to eat. So we were eating then it started to rain really hard so we ran inside the stadium.

So we go inside take our seats but then my two big brothers said that the first three seat available so we went and so me and both of them and sat there so then

Understanding Language and Literacy Development: Diverse Learners in the Classroom, First Edition. Xiao-lei Wang.
© 2015 John Wiley & Sons, Inc. Published 2015 by John Wiley & Sons, Inc.
Companion website: www.wiley.com/go/wang/langandlit

they came out and stared getting ready by wornming up and a lot more stuff. So the game was Ecuador vs. Chile.

And so they go back inside to change until there uniform so we got ready to see the game and the game started and in the first 5 minutes we were winning 1-0 and everybody screaming goal everybody was happy. So they finish the first half and so they started the second half and they made another goal and everybody was going crazy screaming goal and it was crazy.

So the game ended and we won 3-0 and we went home and that was I was happy because I time to spend with my dad. So on the way home we stopped and got something to eat and we had a really good time on the way to and on the way back home and it good time because I spend with my dad.

Comments Made by Mario's Teacher

"So" is used too many times. PROOF READ!

Sample collected by Alex Lengers.

- Are the comments made by the teacher helpful for Mario to improve his writing.
- Mario has probably received comments like this throughout his schooling. However, he has not made much progress in his writing. It is likely that he will continue to receive this kind of feedback from his teachers through the remainder of his schooling. If you were Mario's teacher, what would you do differently to ensure that Mario would be empowered to improve his writing ability? It will be useful to consider the following questions:
  ○ What was not written in Mario's essay that will help you understand him and his writing better and how do you find out about it? (The following aspects will help you.)
    - The CDA framework (see Chapter 1) encourages teachers to be sensitive to students' cultural and linguistic backgrounds and uses their backgrounds as a basis to teach them effectively. How would you find out about Mario's background? Does Mario's writing reveal some information about him and his background?
    - Teaching is fundamentally about the human relationship (Powell and Rightmyer, 2011). How would you build a relationship with Mario?
    - Building a relationship with your students also involves letting them know you value their backgrounds and experiences. How would you show that to Mario?
    - All students come to school with strengths and motivations that can be used by teachers as a starting point to reach them (Powell and Rightmyer, 2011). To teach your students effectively, you need to know their strengths first, so that you can appreciate what your students bring to the learning process and know the areas where they need support. What are the strengths Mario

revealed in his writing? How would you find out his strengths beyond the writing?

- Analyze Mario's writing by using the seven elements in Gee's big "D" analysis (see Chapter 12). How did Mario use language to convey his messages? What would you have missed if you had not conducted the big "D" level of analysis?

- What are Mario's writing needs?
  - Identify Mario's writing needs by conducting the little "d" analysis (e.g., lexicon, semantics, morphology, syntax, and practices).

- How would you use the four elements in TP (see Chapter 1) to help Mario achieve the writing expectations for eighth graders specified in the common core standards (http://www.corestandards.org)?

- Are you convinced that by making an effort to understand what is not written by Mario, you are able to understand his writing better, and consequently, help him better?

- Do you believe that Mario has the potential to be successful in his writing if he is supported by a teacher who knows how to mediate the different knowledge from his home and community, who is able to evaluate his writing beyond writing mechanics and grammatical mistakes, and who is willing to use TP to help him move forward?

Appendix: Examples of Standardized Language Assessments

CDIs (MacArthur-Bates Communicative Developmental Inventories) asks parents to check off words their child says or signs, including vocabulary relating to things in the home, people, action words, description words, pronouns, prepositions, question words, sentences, and grammar.

CELF-3 (Clinical Evaluation of Language Fundamentals-Third Edition) measures abilities in word meanings, word and sentence structure, recall and retrieval of spoken language.

FLIT (Figurative Language Interpretation Test) is a multiple-choice, standardized test consisting of two equivalent 50-item forms that can be used to pre- and post-test students' figurative language progress. It can be administered in groups or individually during a regular 50-minute class period.

GMRT (Gates-MacGinitie Reading Test) assesses reading achievement.

LAB-R (Language Assessment Battery-Revised) assesses reading, writing, listening, comprehension and speaking in English and Spanish.

LAC-R (Lindamood Auditory Conceptualization Test-Revised) assesses the ability to perceive and conceptualize sound units and the changes in their number and relationship in spoken syllables and words.

MLAT measures metalinguistic awareness.

NAP (Narrative Assessment Protocol) measures and monitors preschool children's use of semantic and syntactic forms by using a wordless picture book, "*Frog, Where Are You?*" by Mercer Mayer. It is a cost-effective way to measure young children's narrative microstructure.

OWLS (Oral and Written Language Scales) measures listening, comprehension, oral expression, and written expression.

PPVT-III (Peabody Picture Vocabulary Test-Third Edition) measures receptive vocabulary achievement and verbal ability.

Understanding Language and Literacy Development: Diverse Learners in the Classroom, First Edition. Xiao-lei Wang.
© 2015 John Wiley & Sons, Inc. Published 2015 by John Wiley & Sons, Inc.
Companion website: www.wiley.com/go/wang/langandlit

SALT (Systematic Analysis of Language Transcripts) is a language-sampling tool that measures expressive language production such as utterance formulation, word finding, semantics, and pragmatics.

TOPA (Test of Phonological Awareness) measures ability to isolate individual phonemes in spoken words.

TWS (Test of Written Spelling) measures spelling ability.

WMLS-R (Woodcock-Muñoz Language Survey-Revised) measures cognitive-academic language proficiencies.

WLPB-R (The Woodcock Language Proficiency Battery-Revised) measures bilingual language proficiency.

WRAML (Wide Range Assessment of Memory and Learning) assesses verbal and visual memory skills in situations involving both immediate recall and acquisition of new information.

For more information about standardized language assessment, go to http://www.asha.org/assessments.aspx put together by the American Speech-Language-Hearing Association.

Glossary

abstract words Words used to represent intangible objects, such as myth and emancipation.

academic language Language used in school to learn content in various subject areas.

academic language register Language used in the school setting to meet academic discourse expectations.

academic literacy Reading, writing, and critical skills used to understand and analyze school subjects.

accountable talk Discussions in which students are accountable to the accuracy of the subject knowledge and to their classmates for their thinking.

acquisition/learning hypothesis Ln learning is through two ways: One is through acquisition (using the Ln language for real communication), and the other is through learning (consciously learning the rules of the Ln).

adverbial conjuncts Conjuncts that make written discourse more cohesive, such as *moreover, however, accordingly, hence, similarly, consequently, therefore*, and *furthermore*.

adverbial disjuncts Disjuncts that express a writer's mood, attitude, or sentiments, such as *in my opinion, to be honest, frankly*, and *perhaps*.

affective filter hypothesis A mental block, caused by affective factors, can prevent Ln input from learning the Ln.

affective filters Filters used by Ln learners to determine how to approach Ln learning.

affricates/affricatives Complex speech sounds consisting of a stop consonant followed by a fricative (e.g., the initial sound of *ch-* in *child* and *j-* in *joy*).

African American English (AAE) A systematic and rule-governed dialect spoken by the African American community in the United States.

agency Children themselves as the driving force for language acquisition.

ambiguity tolerance Ability to avoid worrying about situations in which there are mixed messages.

angular gyrus Area of the brain involved in reading.

antonyms Words with opposite meanings.

apprenticeship Learning academic literacy skills in the real world through observation and practice.

appropriate Applying academic language and literacy knowledge in students' own understanding and manner.

aptitude The cognitive ability that allows an individual to learn easily and quickly.

augmentative and alternative communication (AAC) A compensatory approach that provides a means of communication as a supplement to verbal communication.

autism spectrum disorder (ASD) The name for any of these childhood neurobehavioral syndromes: Autistic disorder, Asperger syndrome, Rett syndrome, childhood

Understanding Language and Literacy Development: Diverse Learners in the Classroom, First Edition. Xiao-lei Wang.
© 2015 John Wiley & Sons, Inc. Published 2015 by John Wiley & Sons, Inc.
Companion website: www.wiley.com/go/wang/langandlit

disintegrative disorder, and pervasive developmental disorder not otherwise specified.

autobiographical memory The ability to recall episodes, experiences, and events in an individual's life.

automaticity The control that a child has over the Ln knowledge.

avoidance strategy A strategy used by a Ln learner to find an alternative way to express the same meaning when a Ln feature is beyond a learner's reach.

babble Infants combine consonant–vowel blends of various intonations.

basic interpersonal communicative skills (BICS) The basic proficiency levels that Ln learners use to carry out basic conversations in social contexts.

behaviorist perspective A perspective that emphasizes the dominant effect of the environment on language acquisition.

bidialect Using both African American English (AAE) and mainstream American English (MAE) in communication.

bilingual first language acquisition (BFLA) Exposure to two languages from birth concurrently.

bootstrapping Learning something new by relying on knowledge in other domains.

bottom-up reading process The knowledge of perceptual features in letters, letter-sound correspondence, and lexical retrieval aid word recognition and decoding.

bound morpheme A morpheme that cannot stand alone (e.g., English prefix *pre-* and suffix *-ment*).

brain lateralization (or brain localization) The division of labor of the brain.

brain plasticity The unique ability of the brain to constantly change, grow, and rewire itself to adapt to new situations.

Broca's area The important region in the brain for speech production.

canonical babbling Longer and clear consonants–vowels blends such as /*da-da*/ and /*ma-ma*/.

capacity theory of writing Beginning writers need to consume considerable resources of working memory in translating ideas directly into text through transcription; thus, capacity limitations leave children with few resources for planning and reviewing.

categorical model Grouping children with LI into the similar etiological categories.

cerebrum The largest part of the brain.

child-raising strategy A strategy used by caregivers to encourage language learning by expanding on what a child is saying.

chronological age The amount of time that has elapsed since birth.

classifiers Measuring words used to indicate the quantity of objects in Chinese.

clause density An index to measure syntactic complexity.

code-switching Language mixing in which speakers switch between two or more spoken languages in communication.

cognates Words in different languages share the same etymology.

cognitive academic language proficiency (CALP) Language skills used in higher level cognitive tasks.

cognitive flexibility More elastic in thinking.

cognitive theory of language acquisition Children as active agents in constructing their own understanding and learning of language.

common underlying proficiency model (CUP) All the languages of a multilingual or Ln learner operate through the same central processing system.

communication-language approach (also descriptive-developmental model) Using typical language development sequence to guide the intervention for students with LI.

competence An individual's underlying knowledge of a language system such as grammatical rules (it is often unobservable).

competition model of language acquisition A theory that views language acquisition as a process consisting of a series of competitive cognitive processes that act upon language.

comprehension monitoring The ability to evaluate whether a message is accurate or not.

conceptual framework An overarching framework that guides what one does.

concrete words Words that represent tangible objects, such as *cup* and *chair*.

content language The language used in content areas to help build conceptual knowledge.

content schemata A Ln learner's prior knowledge of the ideas expressed in an oral or written text.

contextual abstraction Learning words by using context clues to determine the meaning of unfamiliar words.

contextualized language Language that is associated with the immediate environment.

conventional print Printed text.

conversational schema A schemata that a speaker uses to carry on a successful conversation, such as initiating and establishing a topic, navigating a series of contingent turns that maintain or shift the topic, and closing the conversation.

cooing Prolonged vowels such as /*a*/ and /*e*/.

cooperative strategy Cooperation to achieve mutual conversation ends.

corpus callosum The band of nerve fibers that connects the two hemispheres of the brain and delivers messages between them.

count nouns Nouns for heterogeneous and individual objects, such as *cup* and *house*.

creole Learning pidgin as a native language by making it grammatically more complex.

critical discourse analysis (CDA) A conceptual framework that encourages teachers to analyze not only what is present in what students say and write, but also what is left out, and that encourages teachers to build a human relation with students and their families, to learn from their students, and discover the resource students bring to the classroom so that students can be empowered to learn.

critical framing An approach that encourages learners to explore alternative ways to read texts, to second-guess them, and to question the motives of the author.

critical literacy The ability to critique texts in different formats, to challenge the status quo, and to question authorities has been widely recognized to be equally essential as the ability to decode texts.

critical mass The minimum amount of input required for language acquisition or language maintenance.

critical period of language acquisition A span of time or window of opportunity when the brain is more receptive to environmental stimuli in signed and spoken language acquisition than in any other period.

cross-linguistic interaction The relationship between the linguistic systems that multilingual children are acquiring as L1.

cross-linguistic phonological interaction. The relationship between the different phonological systems of multilingual children.

cross-linguistic synonyms The same thing is referred to in more than one way in different languages.

cultural schemata (or abstract schemata) The knowledge about cultural-specific practices, traditions, relationships, identities, beliefs, and values.

cultural template Caregivers' beliefs and practices about child language learning and development.

culture modeling The literary devices that students need to know to engage critically with literature are already part of their repertoire, developed in an everyday context in their cultural communities.

C-unit The mean number of words in communication units.

decentration The ability to incorporate multiple pieces of information.

decibel (dB) A unit to measure the intensity of a sound.

decoding The ability to break the code of letter–sound combination.

decontextualized language The language used to describe events that are not in the immediate environment.

decontextualized talk Conversation between parents and young children about subjects beyond the immediate environment.

deductive language learning Learning the general rules (whole) first and then learn the specific instances (parts).

deep orthography The grapheme–phoneme (letter–sound) relationship that is not transparent.

deictic gestures Gestures used to point, reach, show, and give

deixis Deictic words, such as *here*, *there*, *this*, and *that*.

derivational prefix The prefix that is added to the beginning of word, such as *unhealthy*.

derivational suffix The suffix that is added to the end of a word, such as *encroachment*.

descriptive-developmental model Using typical language development sequence to guide the intervention for students with LI.

descriptive grammar The grammar rules that are actually used by native speakers.

developmental age The typical chronological age at which a student can perform a skill in a given area.

developmental interdependence hypothesis The Ln competence that is partly dependent on the level of competence already achieved in the L1.

differentiation hypothesis Children with consistent input in two or more languages from birth who grow up according to the one-person-one-language principle develop two or more distinct morphosyntactic systems.

digital print The text that is in conjunction with images and/or sounds.

direct feedback A type of feedback in which teachers point out the mistakes to students directly.

disciplinary content-based instruction (DCBI) An instructional method in which students work on the content in the discipline and communicate about it.

discussion-based instruction (DBI) An instructional method that focuses on using dialogues to explore ideas and develop understanding of different types of text in different subject areas.

distributed characteristic of multilingual word learning The lexical discrepancies in L1 and Ln.

Down syndrome A disability that exhibits a significant limitation in general cognitive functioning and auditory working memory (IQ ranging from 40 to 70).

dual-system hypothesis Children who hear more than one language regularly develop separate linguistic systems.

dynamic systems view Regarding children's language development not simply as the adults' version, but as qualitatively different from it.

dyslexia Difficulty in single-word decoding, which causes insufficient phonological processing and results in additional problems in fluent reading, spelling, and writing.

echo reading The teacher reads one line and students repeat it.

eclectic approach An approach that takes a bit from many perspectives and tries them out to fit students' needs.

ecology The overall language acquisition environment.

egocentric Children evaluate others and events limited by their own viewpoint.

egocentric speech Monologues that are produced without the intention of involving others.

emblems Conventional gestures that are recognizable by people from a specific community.

emergent literacies Emergent knowledge about conventional print and digital print and the ability to ask questions about them.

emergent literacy Emergent knowledge about conventional print.

emotion-laden words Words that do not refer to emotions directly but instead express emotion (such as "loser") or words that are used to elicit emotions from the interlocutors (such as "malignancy").

emotion words Words that directly refer to particular affective states, such as "scared" and "anxious," or processes such as "to worry".

EmPOWER A method to help students develop expository text production abilities through self-regulation.

environmental print Print that is usually contextualized with clues for young children to derive meaning.

episodic memory The memory of autobiographic events associated with the contexts and emotions.

ethnotheories Knowledge of a social system and belief in a particular culture.

event-related potential (ERP) A noninvasive means to evaluate the brain's response to an external event during cognitive and language processing.

event schema The relational information of parts to the whole and to each other.

explicit learning Searching for information and test hypotheses in learning.

expository texts Texts that inform or explain things.

extensive reading Reading that requires that a reader read fast in large quantities.

extralinguistic cues Nonlinguistic cues, such as facial expressions, hand gestures, and body postures.

false friends Words that seem to be related, but are not.

fan fiction Writings by fans of the original work with their own versions of creativity and twist.

FastForWord program   An intensive practice with computer-generated speech to teach children to gradually distinguish increasingly brief acoustic signals.

fast mapping   Making a prediction about the word's meaning based on clues available in the context.

fictional narratives   Accounts that are presented about fabricated events and characters.

figurative language   The language that is used in nonliteral and often abstract ways.

finite verb morphology   Verb-making, such as past tense inflection and the third-person singular inflection.

flap   A type of consonant produced by allowing the tip of the tongue to strike the alveolar ridge very briefly.

fluency   The ability to recognize words automatically, accurately, and rapidly.

formal operational thought   Making logical inferences merely through verbal representations.

formal schemata   The ability to know how texts and speech events are organized.

✓ **fossilization**   Entering a plateau with no further progress made in Ln learning.

free morpheme   (or unbound morpheme) Morphemes can stand alone or bound with other elements (e.g., *ship* and *shipment*).

fricatives   Consonants produced by forcing air through a narrow channel made by placing two articulators close together, such as /f/ in English.

frontal lobe   The region that takes care of our higher cognitive functions, such as planning, organizing, problem solving, abstract thinking, attention, judgment, and emotion.

funds of knowledge   The knowledge (or cultural capital) that students accumulated in the home and community environments.

genderlect   The collective stylistic characteristics of men and women in communication.

general academic language   The language used to communicate across disciplines.

gerund   A word that is derived from a verb, but functions as a noun (or the "*-ing*" form), e.g., *run* (verb) and *running* (noun).

glides   A sound produced as the vocal organs move toward or away from articulation of a vowel or consonant, such as /w/ and /j/ in English.

gyrus   A ridge or an elevation on the surface of the brain caused by the folding in the cortex.

habitus   The lens through which people interpret and relate to the world.

heredity   The genetic inheritance as well as the specific biological inheritance from our specific ancestors.

heteroglossia   The presence of two or more voices within a text.

high point   The climax of a story.

high point analysis (HPA)   The measure that is used to understand children's narrative structure completeness and complexity both in personal and fictional narratives.

homographs   Words that are spelled the same and may sound alike such as *row a boat* vs *row of homes*, or they may sound different from each other such as *record player* vs *record a speech*.

homonyms   Words that are spelled and pronounced in the same way, but are different in meaning; for example, *brown bear* vs *bear weight*.

homophones   Words that sound alike and may be spelled alike such as *bear* vs *bear* or differently such as *bear* vs *bare hands*.

hyperbole   A form of figurative language that uses exaggeration for emphasis or effect.

hypertext   (also digital text) Text displayed on a computer screen or other electronic device with active links to other texts, images, graphs, and information that readers can instantly access.

hypotonia   Low muscle tone.

idiomorphs   (or protowords, vocables, and quasiwords) The vocalizations produced by young children that are word-like and with recognizable and consistent sound patterns, but are not conventional.

idioms   Expressions that contain both a literal and a figurative meaning.

implicature   The ability to apply meaning beyond the literal sense of what is explicitly stated.

implicit learning   Learning that occurs in a nonconscious and automatic manner.

indirect feedback   A type of feedback in which teachers only provide hints where students can find their mistakes.

Individualized Education Program   (IEP) IEP is mandated by the Individuals with

Disabilities Education Act (IDEA) in the United States. An IEP defines the individualized objectives of a child who has been found with a disability and helps him or her reach the educational goals more effectively.

inductive language learning   The process in which learners learn the specific instances (parts) and then the general rules (whole).

inference   The ability to fill in information that is not overt.

information processing theory of reading   Each word has a switchboard that activates all the visual, auditory, and semantic features associated with that word.

inner speech   (see egocentric speech)

input hypothesis   Ln learners improve and make progress when they receive Ln input that is one step beyond their current linguistic competence.

instructed learning   Learning occurs through explicit teaching.

instructional conversation   The teacher–student conversation in content teaching and learning.

instrumental motivation   The motivation to learn a Ln for practical purposes, such as getting a job or relocating to a new place for necessity.

integrative motivation   Eagerness to learn a Ln because of a positive attitude or identification toward the Ln and its cultural community.

intensive reading   Reading that is slow and careful.

intentionality model of language acquisition   A perspective that emphasizes children as the driving force for language acquisition.

intentional teaching   A teaching activity that is carried out with specific goals in mind for students and that is organized to accomplish the goals by using effective instructional strategies.

interdependent hypothesis   In the early stages of a Ln acquisition, the L1 or stronger language may guide the development in the Ln.

interlanguage   The process through which learners develop a Ln.

intonated babble   (or **jargon**) Infants' babbling that resembles adult speech in rhythm and phonation.

intrinsic motivation   The genuine interest in learning a Ln.

irony   Speaking or writing about one thing, but intending another.

ivy hypothesis   In the early stages of a Ln language acquisition, the first or stronger language may guide the development in the Ln.

jargon   (see intonated babble)

joint attention   Caretakers and infants' focus on mutual objects in order to develop the conversational schema.

language acquisition   Acquiring a language as part of the self.

language acquisition device (LAD)   The predisposition that enables humans to learn a language with the information available from the environment even when language input is limited.

language age   The language ability and skills demonstrated at an age that may not be the chronological age.

language attrition   The gradual loss of language abilities.

language bioprogram   The innate capacity to create a language structure even when the input is unstructured.

language-experience approach   A method in which children's own words are written down by a teacher and used as materials or background for literacy instruction.

language input   The language model provided to young children by their parents and other adults.

language learning   The development of knowledge and skills that permit varying degrees of communication with others.

language socialization   The ideologies and beliefs about language learning in different cultural and socioeconomic groups.

language socialization theory   Regarding language acquisition as the process of both socialization through language and socialization to use language.

lexias   Specific blocks of text.

lexical complexity   The use of polysyllabic words.

lexical density   The use of different lexical items.

lexical diversity   The use of different types of words.

lexical inferencing   The ability to understand a text better by inferring from words.

lexical memory   The ability to remember words and morphemes.

lexicon   The vocabulary that an individual knows.

linguistic schemata   An individual's knowledge of the morphosyntactic properties and lexical choices associated with particular genres and speech events, as well as with particular topics.

liquids   Consonants articulated without friction in roughly the same manner as a vowel, such as /r/ and /l/ in English.

literate lexicon   The ability to use contextual abstraction to infer the meaning of new words from the linguistic cues that accompany them.

macrostructure   The story grammar.

MAP (model, analyze, and practice)   A scaffolding strategy that is useful for helping students with LI to understand and use academic language.

markedness   The difficult features in a language.

mass nouns   Nouns used to refer to homogeneous and nonindividual substances, such as *water* and *sand*.

maze   A false start, hesitation, repetition, or a reformulation of a sentence.

mean length of utterance (MLU)   A measure used to understand children's language production (in particular, syntactic production).

mental age   The cognitive ability shown at a specific age, which may not match a child's chronological age.

mental graphemic representations (MGRs)   The ability to identify words almost instantaneously without the need to decode.

mental lexicon   The mental storage of words that can be activated by a language user.

mental rotation   How the brain recognizes objects in the environment.

metacognition   The ability to think effectively about their own knowledge and processes of thought.

metacognitive theory of writing   Writers can make progress in writing when they become conscious about how they write through self-regulation.

metalinguistic awareness   The ability to think explicitly about language as a system and to be aware of the relationship between different elements in a language.

metalinguistic feedback   A process that is the result of error/contrastive analysis on the part of the teacher, who hints at the type of error the student may have made but does not provide explicit correction.

metalinguistic reflection   Any reflection about language, including learners' planning of how to process it linguistically.

metaphor   A type of figurative speech in which a word or a phrase that is ordinarily used to describe one thing is used to describe another to make a comparison.

microstructure   The syntactic and semantic production, complexity, and accuracy in bringing words and utterances together cohesively.

modality   A mode or a form in which an individual communicates.

modularity theory of language acquisition   The perspective that emphasizes the organization of the cognitive infrastructure of the brain as comprising a series of highly specialized modules, including modules for various aspects of language processing.

monitor hypothesis   The relationship between acquisition and learning. The acquisition system is the utterance initiator, and the learning system performs the role of the monitor for planning, editing, and correcting.

monolingual first language acquisition (MFLA)   Exposure to only one linguistic input from birth and continuously living in the same linguistic environment until puberty.

morae   The basic stress units in Japanese.

morphemes   The smallest meaningful units of a language.

morphology   The study of the structure and form of words in a language such as inflection, derivation, and the formation of compound words.

morphological analysis   Analyzing the components of words and using that information to infer meaning of the entire word (e.g., learn the word *talkativeness* by analyzing the parts *talkative-* and *-ness*).

motherese   (also baby talk) Simplified words and sentences and the use of high pitch when talking to infants.

multilingual bootstrapping hypothesis   The more advanced language of a multilingual child will boost the development of the less advanced language.

multilingual continua   An overarching conceptual framework developed by Nancy

Hornberger to examine multilingualism, which contains nine elements: micro–macro, oral–literate, monolingual–bilingualism, receptive–productive, oral language–written language, L1–L2 transfer, simultaneous–successive exposure, similar–dissimilar structure, and convergent–divergent scripts.

multilingual first language acquisition (MLFLA) The acquisition of more than one first language simultaneously from birth or during early childhood.

multilinguals Individuals who have various degrees of command in more than one language.

multipass approach A reading instructional approach that consists of three passes: survey, size-up, and sort-out.

multisensory structured learning (MSL) An instructional method that utilizes several sensory channels simultaneously and synthesizes stimuli coming from these channels.

Narrative Assessment Protocol (NAP) A measure that is used to monitor preschool children's use of semantic and syntactic forms by using a wordless picture book "*Frog, Where Are You?*" by Mercer Mayer. It is a cost-effective way to measure young children's narrative microstructure.

narrative comprehension skills The ability to process a narrative that contains a series of actions and events unfolding over time according to causal principles.

Narrative Scoring Scheme (NSS) The measurement of narrative macrostructure (or story grammar).

nativist view A perspective that accentuates the effects of innateness.

natural literacy development Some young children becoming capable readers and writers before being formally introduced or attending school.

natural order hypothesis Children learn the rules of a Ln or L2 in a predictable order.

negative transfer Using knowledge in L1 to learn Ln and resulting in incorrect Ln production.

new language acquisition Learning a new language after a person has already developed a first language.

new language learner Learning a new language after a person has acquired his or her native language(s).

new language learning Learning an additional language after one or more than one L1 has been acquired.

Nicaraguan Sign Language (NSL) A sign language system originated from pidgin-like signs used by deaf children in Nicaragua and then evolved into a language-like system.

non-egocentrism The ability to take the perspectives of others.

nonmainstream American English (NMAE) (see African American English)

nonword repetition (NWR) The ability to repeat novel phonological forms.

object clitic pronouns (OCP) Languages that use a system of clitics for the object of a verb when that object is a pronoun.

occipital lobe The brain area that controls vision.

one-parent-one-language (OPOL) Receiving language A input from one parent and Language Alpha input from another parent.

onset The part of the syllable that precedes the vowel of the syllable.

oracy Oral language knowledge and skills.

orthographic systems The writing systems.

overextension Extending the meaning of words by their categories, by focusing on the perceptual similarities, or by their relationship with other objects.

overt instruction Explicit instruction that can guide the learners' practice through scaffolding.

parietal lobe The brain area that integrates sensory information, as well as involvement with some language, reading, and visual functions.

participles Verbs that function as adjectives by adding -*ing* (present participles) or -*ed, -t, and -en* (past participles).

people-first language Addressing the person first before his or her disability.

perceptual narrowing Gradually losing ability in perceiving sounds as an infant becomes more tuned in to his or her environmental language(s).

performance A person's actual language use in context.

personal narratives Accounts that are presented about specific, real-world events that have been experienced by the narrator or someone known to the narrator.

persuasive communication   Using verbal and nonverbal tactics to get others to do what one wants.

pervasive developmental disorder (PDD)   The term under which the five related childhood neurobehavioral syndromes of autism spectrum disorder are classified.

phatic communication   (see phatic language)

phatic language   Communication that primarily functions to maintain social and interpersonal relationships, such as "Thank you".

phoneme   The smallest meaningful unit of sound that allows an individual to make distinctions between words.

phonemic awareness   The ability to recognize that words are made up of a set of sounds and the ability to manipulate sounds.

phonological awareness   The awareness of the sound structure of a given language including the ability to separate sentences into words and words into syllables.

phonological memory   The ability to repeat a sequence of sounds.

phonological translation   The ability to hear a word in one language and to render that word, not its meaning but its phonological form, in the other language.

phonological working memory (PWM)   The ability in tasks such as repeating nonwords, particularly as the length of the nonwords increases.

phonology   The study of the sound system of a language.

phonotactic knowledge   The ability to know the rules that govern the arrangements and constraints of speech sounds in a given language.

pidgin   Using words from two or more contact languages, but not their grammar.

PISA   Program(me) for International Student Assessment.

polysemous   Words that have more than one meaning.

positioning   Writers insert themselves into their writing, including where they are in the world and where they are standing and how this position enables them to see and not see.

positive transfer   Using knowledge in L1 to tackle Ln learning and resulting in correct Ln production.

POSSE   A method that supports students in their comprehension of expository texts.

pragmalinguistic failure   The pragmatics used by Ln learners is systematically different from the one used by native speakers of the target language, or when speech act strategies are inappropriately transferred from L1 to Ln.

pragmalinguistics   The linguistic resources for conveying communicative acts.

pragmatic competence   The ability to use language properly in interpersonal communication.

pragmatic development   The process in which children learn to use language to communicate successfully with others in social interactions.

pragmatic differentiation   Using different languages appropriately.

pragmatics   The study of how language is used in a social context.

predictive inferences   The strategy that helps students to focus on sentence meaning by searching for key words surrounding sentences.

prescriptive grammar   The grammar rules taught in school and in grammar books.

print awareness   Knowledge of print forms and functions.

private speech   (see egocentric speech)

productive knowledge of phonology   The ability to articulate the sounds in a language.

prosody   The rhythmic structure or sound pattern such as stress, pitch, tempo, rhythm, and pause of speech.

protowords   (see idiomorphs)

proverb   Conventional saying that is known by people in a particular culture.

Putonghua   The official language of the People's Republic of China.

quasiwords   (see idiomorphs)

quick incidental learning (QUIL)   The ability to pick up the new word meaning from incidental exposures.

rapid automatized naming (RAN)   A measurement that enables researchers to find out how quickly a child can name letters, digits, pictures, or objects.

rapid naming   The ability to rapidly retrieve and produce known words.

reading apprenticeship approach   An approach that integrates biology content and literacy.

reading fluency The ability to read quickly and smoothly and understand the ideas in the text.

receptive phonological knowledge The ability to distinguish and understand the phonological information in a language.

reciprocal teaching Using four strategies for processing both narrative and expository texts: Clarification, questioning, summarization, and prediction.

reducing degrees of freedom Using a simple writing task as a stepping-stone for a more challenging writing task.

reduplicated babbling Sounds that are produced by infants in a longer sequence than canonical babbling, such as /da-da-da-da/.

reflective reading response log (RRRL) A kind of journal in which readers write their reactions and opinions about the materials they read.

representational gesture Gestures that indicate shape or movement.

resultative motivation Motivation to learn a Ln emerges when learners begin to improve their Ln skills.

retelling procedure An effective way to engage children in literacy learning by asking them to "spillover" what they read or what they hear when read to.

reversibility The ability to understand that a certain quantity remains the same despite a change in the shape or size.

rime The part of a syllable that consists of its vowel and any consonant sounds that come after it.

scaffolding Assistance from adults.

script inference Inferences based on event schemas.

segmental interaction Consonants and/or vowels that are specific to one language will interact with productions of the other language.

selective attention When more than one language coexists, one of the languages must be constantly inhibited to prevent ongoing intrusion.

self-explanation reading training (SERT) Using explicit, direct instruction to show students the purpose and function of different strategies.

self-lowering strategy A strategy in which caregivers simplify words and sentences.

self-regulated learner A learner who monitors his or her own learning.

self-regulated strategy development (SRSD) A strategy that creates opportunities for students to engage in independent performance by helping them develop background knowledge, discuss the goals, and model the strategies.

self-regulation A form of self-control or self-monitoring in the learning process.

semantic mapping The process in which students can relate new words to their own experiences and prior knowledge by using visual displays of categories and their relationship in a graphic form.

semantic network Words acquired by children are stored and organized.

semantics Word meanings.

semantic slanting A way of making statements to evoke emotional responses, also known as name-calling.

semantic transparency The consistency between the meaning of a compound word and its constituent morphemes.

sensitive period of language acquisition (see critical period of language acquisition)

sentence combining training (SCT) Training that requires children to combine short kernel (one-clause) sentences into a longer and more syntactically complex sentence.

separate development hypothesis (also see differentiation hypothesis) Development of two or more distinct morphosyntactic systems as a result of consistent input in two or more languages from birth.

separate underlying proficiency (SUP) model The different language systems of multilingual children operate separately without transfer.

shared reading A reading instructional approach in which teachers explicitly model the strategies of a fluent reader.

sign language acquisition Acquiring a manual language when one's oral language acquisition is compromised as a result of various disabilities.

silent period A period in which some Ln learners may stay silent for a while when they are first exposed to the Ln.

simile Similar to a metaphor in that it is used to describe one thing by making a comparison to something else, except that it uses the words "like" or "as" when comparing.

simple view of reading A straightforward outline of the relationship between language and literacy.

simplification and formulas period A period in which Ln learners use one- or two-word utterances like "me no __" to communicate or use the key words and omit the grammatical markers, or memorize chunks of language such as "Can I have __?" to communicate their basic needs.

single-system hypothesis Children initially develop only one system before they succeed in differentiating the lexical and grammatical systems of their ambient languages.

situated cognitive model of writing An approach that helps students with LI improve their writing skills, including planning, translating, reviewing, production, motivation, and social context.

situated practice A teaching practice that stresses that knowledge should build on students' experiences in real-world contexts, not in an isolated environment.

social language Everyday language.

social language register The oral language used in the everyday context.

sociolinguistic theory Emphasizing that the language use in communication is central to the linguistic process and to development.

sociopragmatic failure The social conditions placed on a language caused by different beliefs in social interaction.

sociopragmatics The social perceptions underlying a person's interpretation and performance of communicative acts.

sociopsycholinguistic transactional theory Readers produce meaning through the personal and world knowledge they bring to the act of reading.

specific disability model Students with LI differ in some underlying cognitive abilities.

speech acts A type of communication function in which we apologize, greet, request, promise, congratulate, complain, invite, compliment, or refuse.

splinter skills Exceptional skills that children with autism spectrum disorder may have.

spirants Sounds uttered with a continuous expulsion of breath.

spoken word recognition (SWR) The process by which a listener uses the acoustic-phonetic information available in the speech form, in conjunction with a variety of other forms of information that may be available, to access his or her lexicon.

spreading activation Lexicon is activated based on the strength of connections among words.

stabilization (see fossilization)

stops A consonant in which the vocal tract is blocked so that all airflow ceases.

story grammar (story structure) The elements of a narrative structure.

story macrostructure The degree of organization and number and type of story grammar elements.

story recounting A scaffolding process in which adults and children co-construct stories/narratives.

strategy-based instruction (SBI) An approach that teaches students reading comprehension by focusing explicitly on teaching them strategies to aid their understanding.

strengtheners Discourse markers (e.g., "really," "certainly," and "exactly").

structure strategy training (SST) A methods that teaches students how to use paragraphing and signaling cues to figure out the overall organization of the information they are reading.

subordination index figures The number of clauses for each T-unit in the sample are summed, and then divided by the number of T-units to obtain the subordination index for the sample.

sulcus A groove-like depression on the brain's surface that separates the gyri.

suprasegmental phonology (or prosodic properties) Rhythm, tone, pitch, stress, intonation, and length.

syllogisms Deductive reasoning.

symbolic thinking Talking and thinking about things that are beyond immediate experience or environment.

synapses A junction between two nerve cells, which allows a neuron to pass information to another cell.

syncretic literacy A transformative form of literacy practice in which children blend familiar practices (learned at home and in community) with new forms (learned at school).

synonyms Words that have almost the same meaning as other words.

syntactic bootstrapping Using context cues to determine the meaning of an unfamiliar verb.

syntactical knowledge The knowledge of how words and phrases are combined to form sentences.

syntax Sentence structure in a language.

system model Focusing on changing the environment to facilitate the communication of students with LI.

target language Language being learnt.

temporal lobe The brain area that controls auditory and visual memories, language, some hearing and speech, and some behavior.

text talk A method that is often used for young children as an effective vocabulary teaching method in which teachers ask students questions regarding the ideas in a text, talk about them and make connections among them as the reading moves along, thus enhancing vocabulary development.

theme comprehension The ability to derive a more general message from a passage of text.

theory of mind The ability to understand others' mental status.

third space A conceptual classroom space for learning that draws on the discourse of formal teaching as well as that of the students.

thresholds theory There are two thresholds in multilingual development. The first threshold is reached when a child can avoid the negative consequences of multilingualism. The second threshold is a level required to experience the possible positive benefits of multilingualism.

top-down reading process Higher level cognitive functions such as concepts and inferences influence lower level processes.

transfer strategy A Ln strategy in which Ln learners apply their L1 knowledge to the Ln.

transformative pedagogy (TP) A pedagogy that supports the critical discourse analysis practice in diverse classrooms and transforms an individual's learning over time.

transformed practice True learning transpires when students not only use knowledge appropriately, but they also demonstrate a significant level of creativity and innovation and are able to put meaning to work in other contexts.

translanguage The use of L1 and Ln alongside each other in the classroom.

transparency When scripts (such as letters) of a writing system correspond more closely to the sounds. For example, the letters in the word *c-a-t* correspond more closely to the sounds /k/-/æ/-/t/ than 猫 (cat) to *mao*.

trilingual first language acquisition (TFLA) Acquiring three first languages simultaneously from birth or during early childhood.

trill The pronunciation of a consonant, especially *r*, with rapid vibration of the tongue against the hard or soft palate or the uvula.

truncation Deletion of syllables.

T-unit A main clause with all the subordinate clauses and nonclausal phrases attached to or embedded in it.

turnabout A speaker not only comments on what has just been said but also adds a request to get the conversational partner to respond again.

type/token ratio (TTR) The total number of words in a given utterance or a written text is often referred to as the number of tokens. The token/type ratio means the proportion of the number of total words and the total types of words in an utterance or written text.

unanalyzed chunks Direct imitations of adult speech that appear to be multiword phrases.

unanalyzed wholes (see unanalyzed chunks)

unbound morpheme (see free morpheme)

underextension Using words to refer to only a subset of possible referents.

universal grammar (UG) The universal human capacity that guides language making and production.

unpacking period A period in which Ln learners begin to analyze the memorized chunks of language from the simplification and formulas period and break them down into Ln (target language) grammar.

usage-based theory of language acquisition A perspective that argues that as children repeatedly and increasingly use their awareness of social conventions to engage with other people, their general language abilities emerge.

utterance Units of thought or ideas.

velars Consonants articulated with the back part of the tongue touching or near the soft palate, such as /ɡ/ in *good* and /k/ in *king*.

verbal dyspraxia Expressive phonological difficulties.

visual cortex   The brain part that is in charge of the initial recognition of the visual pattern of a word.

vocables   (see idiomorphs)

vocabulary spurt   A rapid increase in vocabulary size.

vocal play   A period of phonological development between 16 and 30 weeks, when infants explore with vowel-like and consonant-like sounds by making squeals, growls, and fiction sounds.

weak central coherence theory   Individuals with autism are biased to process information locally.

weakeners   Discourse markers (e.g., "sort of" and "I think").

Wernicke's area   The brain area that is in charge of language comprehension (or processing meaning).

word web   A visual representation resembling a web of concepts and related ideas with connecting lines to show relationships.

writers' workshop   A method of writing instruction that involves four principles: students will write about their own lives, use a consistent writing process, work in authentic ways, and foster writing independence.

zone of proximal development   The level that is ahead of students' current developmental level.

References

Acredolo, L. and Goodwyn, S. (2002). *Baby Signs: How to Talk with Your Baby before Your Baby Can Talk*. Rev. edn. Chicago: Contemporary Books.

Adams, M. J. (1990). *Beginning to Read: Thinking and Learning about Print*. Cambridge, MA: MIT Press.

Aitchison, J. (2012). *Words in the Mind: An Introduction to the Mental Lexicon*. Oxford: Wiley-Blackwell.

Albarriba, J. and Bauer, L. (2004). The distinctiveness of emotion concepts: a comparison between emotion, abstract, and concrete words. *American Journal of Psychology*, 117: 389–410.

Alfassi, M. (1998). Reading for meaning: the efficacy of reciprocal teaching in fostering reading comprehension in high school students in remedial reading classes. *American Educational Research Journal*, 35: 309–332.

Alfieri, L., Brooks, P. J., Aldrich, N. J., and Tenenbaum, H. R. (2011). Does discovery-based instruction enhance learning? *Journal of Educational Psychology*, 103(1): 1–18.

Altarriba, J. and Basnight-Brown, D. M. (2011). The acquisition of concrete, abstract, and emotion words in a second language. *International Journal of Bilingualism*, 16(4): 446–452.

Alvermann, D. E. (2006). Struggling adolescent readers: a cultural construction. In A. McKeough, L. M. Philipps, V. Timmons, and J. L. Lupart (eds), *Understanding Literacy Development: A Global View*. Mahwah, NJ: Lawrence Erlbaum.

American Speech-Language-Hearing Association (1993). *Definitions of Communication Disorders and Variations*. At http://www.asha.org/docs/html/RP1993-00208.html (accessed Mar. 2014).

Apel, K., Wilson-Fowler, B., Briono, O., and Perrin, N. A. (2011). Metalinguistic contributions to reading and spelling in second and third grade students. *Read Writ*, 25: 1283–1305.

Archibald, L. M. D. (2008). The promise of nonword repetition as a clinical tool. *Canadian Journal of Speech-Language Pathology and Audiology*, 32(1): 21–28.

Ashmore, R. A. (2001). *Promoting the Gift of Literacy: 101 Lesson Plans for Oral and Written Language*. Boston: Allyn & Bacon.

Aslin, R. N. and Pisoni, D. B. (1980). Some developmental processes in speech perception. In G. H. Yeni-Komshian, J. F. Kavanagh, and C. A. Ferguson (eds), *Child Phonology*, vol. 2: *Perception*. New York: Academic Press.

Aslin, R. N., Jusczyk, P. W. and Pisoni, D. B. (1998). Speech and auditory processing during infancy: constraints on and precursors to language. In D. Kuhn and R. Siegler (eds), *Cognition, Perception and Language*, vol. 2 of W. Damon (gen. ed.), *Handbook of Child Psychology* (pp. 147–198). New York: Wiley.

Baba, J. (2010). Interlanguage pragmatics study of indirect complaint among Japanese ESL learners. *Sino-US English Teaching*, 7(12): 23–32.

Baker, C. (2011). *Foundations of Bilingual Education and Bilingualism*. Bristol: Multilingual Matters.

Baker, S. E. and MacIntyre, P. D. (2000). The role of gender and immersion in communication and second language orientation. *Language Learning*, 50(2): 311–341.

Ball, A. F. (1996). Expository writing patterns of African American students. *English Journal*, 85(1): 27–36.

Barnett, W. S., Yarosz, D., Thomas, J., Jung, K., and Blanco, D. (2007). Two-way and monolingual English immersion in preschool education: an experimental comparison. *Early Childhood Research Quarterly*, 22(3): 277–293.

Barratt-Pugh, C. (2000). Literacy in more than one language. In C. Barratt-Pugh and M. Rohl (eds), *Literacy Learning in the Early Years* (pp. 172–196). Philadelphia: Open University Press.

Barton, M. E., and Tomasello, M. (1991). Joint attention and conversation in mother-infant sibling triads. *Child Development*, 62: 517–529.

Bartsch, K., Wright, J. C., and Estes, D. (2009). Young children's persuasion in everyday conversation: tactics and attunement to others' mental states. *Social Development*, 19(2): 394–417.

Bates, E. (1976). *Language and Context: The Acquisition of Pragmatics*. New York: Academic Press.

Bates, E., Bretherton, I, and Snyder, L. (1988). *From First Words to Grammar: Individual Differences and Dissociable Mechanisms*. Cambridge: Cambridge University Press.

Bates, E., Dale, P., and Thal, D. (1995). Individual differences and their implications for theories of language development. In P. Fletcher and B. MacWhinney (eds), *The Handbook of Child Language*. Oxford: Blackwell.

Batshaw, M. L. (2002). *Children with Disabilities*. 5th edn. Baltimore: Paul H. Brookes.

Bauer, D. J., Goldfield, B.A., and Reznik, J. S. (2002). Alternative approaches to analyzing individual differences in the rate of early vocabulary acquisition. *Applied Psycholinguistics*, 23: 313–335.

Bear, D. R., Invernizzi, M., Templeton, S., and Johnson, F. (2008). *Words Their Way: Word Study for Phonics, Vocabulary, and Spelling Instruction*. Upper Saddle River, NJ: Pearson.

Beck, I. L. and McKeown, M. G. (2001). Text talk: capturing the benefits of reading aloud experiences for young children. *Reading Teacher*, 55(1): 10–20.

Beck, I. L., McKeown, M. G., and Kucan, L. (2002). *Bring Words to Life: Robust Vocabulary Instruction*. New York: Guilford Press.

Becker, J. A. (1994). Pragmatic socialization: parental input to preschoolers. *Discourse Processes*, 17(1): 131–148.

Benko, S. L. (2012–2013). Scaffolding: an ongoing process to support adolescent writing development. *Journal of Adolescent and Adult Literacy*, 56(4): 291–300.

Berk, L. E. (2009) *Child Development*. Boston: Allyn & Bacon.

Berko, J. (1958). The child's learning of English morphology. *Word*, 14: 150–177.

Berman, R. A. (2007). Developing linguistic knowledge and language use across adolescence. In E. Hoff and M. Shatz (eds), *Blackwell Handbook of Language Development* (pp. 347–367). Oxford: Blackwell.

Bernardini, P. and Schlyster, S. (2004). Growing syntactic structure and code-mixing in the weaker language: the ivy hypothesis. *Bilingualism: Language and Cognition*, 7 (1): 49–69.

Bertelson, P. (1993). Reading acquisition and phonemic awareness testing: how conclusive are data from Down's syndrome? (Remark on Cossu, Rossini, and Marchall, 1993.) *Cognition*, 48: 281–283.

Bhatia, T. K. and Ritchie, W. (2013). *The Handbook of Bilingualism and Multilingualism*. Oxford: Wiley-Blackwell.

Bialystok, E. (1988). Levels of bilingualism and levels of linguistic awareness. *Developmental Psychology*, 24(4): 560–567.

Bialystok, E. (1991). *Language Processing in Bilingual Children*. Cambridge: Cambridge University Press.

Bialystok, E. (2002). Acquisition of literacy in bilingual children: a framework for research. *Language Learning*, 52: 159–199.

Bialystok, E. and Hakuta, K. (1994). *In Other Words: The Science and Psychology of Second Language Acquisition*. New York: Basic Books.

Bialystok, E. and Martin, M. M. (2004). Attention and inhibition in bilingual children: evidence from the dimensional change card sort task. *Developmental Science*, 7(3): 325–339.

Bialystok, E., Majumder, S., and Martin, M. M. (2003). Developing phonological awareness: is there a bilingual advantage? *Applied Psycholinguistics*, 24: 27–44.

Bialystok, E., Luk, G., and Kwan, E. (2005). Bilingualism, biliteracy, and learning to read: interactions among languages and writing systems. *Scientific Studies of Reading*, 9(1): 43–61.

Biancarosa, C. and Snow, C. (2006). *Reading Next: A Vision for Action and Research in Middle and High School Literacy: A Report to Carnegie Corporation of New York*. 2nd edn. Washington, DC: Alliance for Excellent Education.

Bickerton, D. (1981). The language bioprogram hypothesis. *Behavioral and Brain Sciences*, 7: 173–221).

Bickerton, D. (1984). *Roots of Language*. Ann Arbor, MI: Karoma.

Bickerton, D. (1988). Creole languages and the bioprogram. In F. J. Newmeyer (ed.), *Linguistics: The Cambridge Survey* (pp. 268–284). Cambridge: Cambridge University Press.

Bishop, D. V. M. (1994). Grammatical errors in specific language impairment: competence or performance limitations? *Applied Psycholinguistics*, 15: 507–550.

Bishop, D. V. M. (2008). Specific language impairment, dyslexia, and autism: using genetics to unravel their relationship. In C. F. Norbury, J. B. Tomblin, and D. V. M. Bishop (eds), *Understanding Developmental Language Disorders: From Theory to Practice* (pp. 67–78). New York: Psychology Press.

Bishop, D. V. M. and Snowling, M. J. (2004). Developmental dyslexia and specific language impairments: same or different? *Psychological Bulletin*, 130: 858–886.

Bissex, G. L. (1980). *Gnys at Wrk: A Child Learns to Write and Read*. Cambridge, MA: Harvard University Press.

Bittman, M., Rutherford, L., and Lens, J. B. (2011). Digital natives? New and old media and children's outcomes. *Australian Journal of Education*, 55(2): 161–175.

Black, K. M. (1979). Hereditary factors in language acquisition. Paper presented at the Annual Meeting of the Orton Society, Indianapolis, Oct. 30–Nov. 3.

Blake, R. and Cutler, C. (2003). AAE and variation in teachers' attitudes: a question of school philosophy? *Linguistics and Education*, 14: 163–194.

Blanton, R. E., Levitt, J. G., Peterson, J.R., et al. (2004). Gender differences in the left inferior frontal gyrus in normal children. *Neuroimage*, 22(2): 626–636.

Bleses, D., Basboll, H., and Vach, W. (2011). Is Danish difficult to acquire? Evidence from Nordic past-tense studies. *Language and Cognitive Processes*, 26(8): 1193–1231.

Bloom, L. (1970). *Language Development: Form and Function of Emerging Grammars*. Cambridge MA: MIT Press.

Bloom, L. (1995). Foreword. In B. Hart and T. Risley, *Meaningful Differences in the Everyday Experiences of Young American Children*. Baltimore: Paul H. Brookes.

Bloom, L. and Tinker, E. (2001). The intentionality model and language acquisition: engagement, effort and the essential tension in development. *Monographs of the Society for Research in Child Development*, 66(4): 1–91.

Blum-Kulka, S. and Snow, C. (eds) (2002). *Talking to Adults*. Mahwah, NJ: Lawrence Erlbaum.

Bochner, J. H., Christie, K., Hauser, P. C., and Searls, J. M. (2011). When is a difference really different? Learners' discrimination of linguistic contrasts in American Sign Language. *Language Learning*, 61(4): 1302–1327.

Borkowski, J. G. (1992). Metacognitive theory of writing. *Journal of Learning Disabilities*, 25(4): 253–257.

Bornstein, M. H., Hahn, C. S., and Haynes, O. M. (2004). Specific and general language performance across early childhood: stability and gender considerations. *First Language*, 24: 267–304.

Bos, C., Mather, N., Dickerson, S., Podhajski, B., and Chard, D. (2001). Perceptions and knowledge of preservice and inservice educators about early reading instruction. *Annuals of Dyslexia*, 51: 97–120.

Bosch, L. and Sebastián-Gallés, N. (1997). Native-language recognition abilities in 4-month-old infants from monolingual and bilingual environments. *Cognition*. 65: 33–69.

Bosch, L. and Sebastián-Gallés, N. (2005). Developmental changes in the discrimination of vowel contrasts in bilingual infants. In J. Cohen, K. T. McAlister, K. Rolstad, and J. MacSwan (eds), *Proceedings of the 4th International Symposium on Bilingualism* (pp. 354–363). Somerville, MA: Cascadilla Press.

Bosman, J. (2012). Britannica is reduced to a click. *New York Times*, Mar. 14.

Bouchard, C., Trudeau, N., Sutton, A, Boudreault, M.-C, and Deneault, J. (2009). Gender differences in language development in French Canadian children between 8 and 30 months of age. *Applied Psycholinguistics*, 30(4): 685–707.

Bradley, R., Corwyn, R. McAdoo, P., and Coll, C. G. (2001). The home environments of children in the United States. Part 1: Variations by age, ethnicity, and poverty status. *Child Development*, 72: 1844–1867.

Braxton, B. (2007). Read-alouds: choosing right book. *Teacher Liberian*, 34(3): 52–53.

Brice, A. E. and Brice, R. G. (2009). *Language Development: Monolingual and Bilingual Acquisition*. Boston: Allyn & Bacon.

Brown, A. L. and Palincsar, A. S. (1987). Reciprocal teaching of comprehension strategies: a natural history of one program for enhancing learning. In J. Borkowski and L. D. Day (eds), *Cognition in Special Education: Comparative Approaches to Retardation, Learning Disabilities, and Giftedness*. Norwood, NJ: Ablex.

Brown, D. W. (2009). *In Other Words: Lessons on Grammar, Code-Switching, and Academic Writing*. Portsmouth, NH: Heinemann.

Brown, H. D. (2000). *Principles of Language Learning and Teaching*. 4th edn. White Plains, NY: Pearson Education.

Brown, H. and Cambournes, B. (1990). *Read and Retell*. Portsmouth, NH: Heinemann.

Brown, J. R., Donelan-McCall, N., and Dunn, J. (1996). Why talk about mental states? The significance of children's conversations with friends, siblings, and mothers. *Child Development*, 67: 836–849.

Brown, S. and Attardo, S. (2008). *Understanding Language Structure, Interaction, and Variation: An Introduction to Applied Linguistics and Sociolinguistics for Nonspecialists*. Michigan: University of Michigan Press.

Brozo, W. G. (2010). The role of content literacy in an effective RTI program. *Reading Teacher*, 64(2): 147–150.

Bruck, M. and Genesee, F. (1995). Phonological awareness in young second language learners. *Journal of Child Language*, 22: 307–342.

Burman, D. D., Bitan, T., and Booth, J. R. (2008). Sex differences in neural processing of language among children. *Neuropsychologia*, 46: 1349–1362.

Burns, T. C., Yoshida, K. A., Hill, K., and Werker, J. F. (2007). The development of phonetic representation in bilingual and monolingual infants. *Applied Psycholinguistics*, 28: 455–474.

Byrne, B. (1993). Learning to read in the absence of phonemic awareness? (A comment on Cossu, Rossini, and Marchal, 1993.) *Cognition*, 48: 285–288.

Cain, K. (2003). Text comprehension and its relation to coherence and cohesion in children's fictional narratives. *British Journal of Developmental Psychology* 21: 335–351.

Cain, K., Oakhill, J., Barnes, M. A., and Bryant, P. (2001). Comprehension skill, inference-making ability, and their relation to knowledge. *Memory and Cognition*, 29(6): 850–859.

Calkins, L. M. (1994). *The Art of Teaching Writing*. New edn. Portsmouth, NH: Heinemann.

Campbell, B. C. (2011). An introduction to the special issue on middle childhood. *Human Nature*, 22: 247–248.

Caravolas, M. (2004). Spelling development in alphabetic writing systems: a cross-linguistic perspective. *European Psychologist*, 9(1): 3–14.

Carhill, A., Suárez-Orozco, C., and Páez, A. (2008). Explaining English language proficiency among adolescent immigrant students. *American Educational Research Journal*, 45(4): 1155–1179.

Carle, E. (1989). *The Very Busy Spider*. New York: Philomel Books.

Carle, E. (1996). *The Grouchy Ladybug*. New York: HarperCollins.

Carle, E. (2009). *The Very Hungry Caterpillar*. New York: Philomel Books.

Carreker, S. H., Neuhaus, G. F., Swank, P. R., Johnson, P., Monfils, M. J., and Montemayor, M. L. (2007). Teachers with linguistically informed knowledge of reading subskills are associated with a Matthew effect in reading comprehension for monolingual and bilingual students. *Reading Psychology*, 28(2): 187–212.

Carroll, J. B. (1990). Cognitive abilities in foreign language aptitude: then and now. In T. S. Parry and C. W. Stansfield (eds), *Language Aptitude Reconsidered* (pp. 11– 29). Englewood Cliffs, NJ: Prentice Hall.

Casanave, C. P. (2003). *Controversies in Second Language Writing: Dilemmas and Decisions in Research and Instruction*. Ann Arbor: University of Michigan Press.

Caspi, J. (2011). *Sibling Development: Implications for Mental Health Practitioners*. New York: Springer.

Cecil, N. L. (1988). Black dialect and academic success: a study of teacher expectations. *Reading Improvement*, 25: 34–38.

Chapman, R. S. (2003). Language and communication in individuals with Down syndrome. In L. Abbeduto (ed.), *International Review of Research in Mental Retardation: Language and Communication*, vol. 27 (pp. 1–34). New York: Academic Press.

Charity-Hudley, A. H. and Mallinson, C. (2010). *Understanding English Language Variation in U.S. Schools*. New York: Teachers College Press.

Charniak, E. (1972). Toward a model of children's story comprehension. Doctoral dissertation, MIT, Cambridge, MA.

Cheng, C.-X., Wang, M., and Perfetti, C. (2011). Acquisition of compound words in Chinese-English bilingual children: decomposition and cross-language activation. *Applied Psycholinguistics*, 32(3): 583–600.

Chomsky, N. (1975). *Reflections on Language*. New York: Random House.

Christophe, A., Millotte, S., Bernal, S., and Lidz, J. (2008). Bootstrapping lexical and syntactic acquisition. *Language and Speech*, 51(1–2): 61–75.

Cicirelli, V.G. (1976). Mother-child and sibling-sibling interactions on a problem-solving task. *Child Development*, 47: 588–596.

Clancy, P., Jacobsen, T., and Silva, M. (1976). The acquisition of conjunction: a cross-linguistic study. *Papers and Reports on Child Language Development*, 12: 71–80.

Clark, E. V. (1988). Lexical innovations: how children learn to create new words. In M. B. Franklin and S. S. Barten (eds), *Child Language: A Reader* (pp. 118–129). New York: Oxford University Press.

Coates, J. (1993). The acquisition of gender-differentiated language. In J. Coates (ed.), *Women, Men and Language: A Sociolinguistic Account of Gender Differences in Language* (pp. 143–167). 2nd edn. Harlow: Pearson Education.

Cohen, A. D. and Horowitz, R. (2002). What should teachers know about bilingual learners and the reading process. In J. H. Sullivan (ed.), *Literacy and the Second Language Learner*, vol. 1. Greenwich, CT: Information Age.

Coiro, J. (2003). Reading comprehension on the internet: expanding our understanding of reading comprehension to encompass new literacies. *Reading Teacher*, 56: 458–464.

Coll, C. C. and Szalacha, L. A. (2004). The multiple contexts of middle childhood. *Future of Children*, 14(2): 81–97.

Collier, V. P. (1987) Age and rate of acquisition of second language for academic purposes. *TESOL Quarterly*, 21(4): 617–641.

Conboy, B. T. and Thal, D. (2006). Ties between the lexicon and grammar: cross-sectional and longitudinal studies of bilingual toddlers. *Child Development*, 77: 712–735.

Connelly, V., Gee, D., and Walsh, E. (2007). A comparison of keyboarded and hand written compositions and the relationship with transcription speed. *British Journal of Educational Psychology*, 77: 479–492.

Connor, C. M. and Craig, H. K. (2006). African American preschoolers' language, emergent literacy skills, and use of African American English: a complex relation. *Journal of Speech, Language, and Hearing Research*, 49: 771–792.

Copley, J. V. (2000). *The Young Child and Mathematics*. Washington, D.C: National Association for the Education of Young Children.

Cossu, G., Rossini, F., and Marshall, J. C. (1993). When reading is acquired but phonemic awareness is not: a study of literacy in Down Syndrome. *Cognition*, 46: 129–138.

Costa, A. (2009). Foreword. In E. R. Johnson, *Academic Language! Academic Literacy! A Guide for K-12 Educators* (pp. v–vii). Thousand Oaks, CA: Corwin.

Cote, L. R. (2001). Language opportunities during mealtimes in preschool classrooms. In D. K. Dickinson and P. O. Tabors (eds), *Beginning Literacy with Language* (pp. 205–221). Baltimore: Paul H. Brookes.

Craig, H. K. and Washington, J. A. (1994). The complex syntax skills of poor, urban African American preschoolers at school entry. *Language Speech and Hearing Services in Schools*, 25: 181–190.

Crais, E. (2007). Gesture development from an interactionist perspective. In R. Paul (ed.), *Language Disorders from a Developmental Perspective* (pp. 141–162). Mahwah, NJ: Lawrence Erlbaum.

Creese, A. and Blackledge, A. (2010). Translanguaging in the bilingual classroom: a pedagogy for learning and teaching? *Modern Language Journal*, 94(1): 103–115.

Crosser, S. (1994). When young children are afraid. *Daycare and Early Education*, 22(1): 7–11.

Cruz-Ferreira, M (2006). *Three Is a Crowd? Acquiring Portuguese in a Trilingual Environment*. Bristol: Multilingual Matters.

Cummins, J. (1981). The role of primary language development in promoting educational success for language minority students. In California State Department of Education (ed.), *Schooling and Language Minority Students: A Theoretical Framework*. Los Angeles: Evaluation, Dissemination and Assessment Center, California State University.

Cummins, J. (2000). *Language, Power, and Pedagogy: Bilingual Children in the Crossfire*. Bristol: Multilingual Matters.

Cunningham, P. M. and Hall, D. P. (2009). *Making Words First Grade: 100 Hands-on Lessons for Phonemic Awareness, Phonics and Spelling*. Boston: Pearson.

Cunningham-Andersson, U. and Andersson, S. (1999). *Growing up with Two Languages: A Practical Guide*. New York: Routledge.

Curdt-Christiansen, X. L. (2013). Implicit learning and imperceptible influence: syncretic literacy of multilingual Chinese children. *Journal of Early Childhood Literacy*, 13(3): 348–370.

Curenton, S. M. (2011). Understanding the landscapes of stories: the association between preschoolers' narrative comprehension and production skills and cognitive abilities. *Early Child Development and Care*, 18(6):791–808.

Curenton, S. M. and Justice, L. (2004). African American and Caucasian preschoolers' use of decontextualized language: literate language features in oral narratives. *Language Speech and Hearing Services in Schools*, 35: 240–253.

Curtis, S. (1977). Genie: a psycholinguistic study of a modern-day "wild child." New York: Academic Press.

Curwood, J. S., Magnifico, A. M., and Lammers, J. C. (2013). Writing in the wild: writers' motivation in fan-based affinity spaces. *Journal of Adolescent and Adult Literacy*, 56(8): 677–685.

Cusworth, R. and Simons, R. (1997). *Beyond the Script: Drama in the Classroom*. Newtown, NSW: Primary English Teaching Association.

Dale, P., Price, T., Bishop, D., and Plomin, R. (2003). Outcomes of early language delay, I: Predicting persistent and transient language difficulties at 3 and 4 years. *Journal of Speech, Language and Hearing Research*, 46: 544–560.

Damianova, M. K., Lucas, M., and Sullivan, G. B. (2012). Verbal mediation of problem solving in pre-primary and junior primary school children. *South African Journal of Psychology*, 42(3): 445–455.

Davidson, C. (2011). Seeking the green basilisk lizard: acquiring digital literacy practices in the home. *Journal of Early Childhood Literacy*, 12(1): 24–45.

Dehart, G. B., Sroufe, L. A. and Cooper, R. G. (2004). *Child Development: Its Nature and Course*. Boston: McGraw-Hill Higher Education.

de Boysson-Bardies, B. (1999). *How Language Comes to Children: From Birth to Two Years*. Cambridge, MA: MIT Press.

De Houwer, Annick (2009). *An Introduction to Bilingual Development*. Bristol: Multilingual Matters.

DeTemple, J. M. (2001). Parents and children reading books together. In D. K. Dickinson and P. O. Tabors (eds), *Beginning Literacy with Language: Young Children Learning at Home and School* (pp. 205–221). Baltimore: Paul H. Brookes.

DeThorne, L. S., Petrill, S. A., Chanell, R. W., Campbell, R. J., Deater-Deckard, K., Thompson, L. A., and Vandenbergh, D. J. (2008). Genetic effects on children's conversational language use. *Journal of Speech, Language, and Hearing Research*, 51: 423–435.

De Vries Guth, N. and Pratt-Fartro, T. (2010). *Literacy Coaching to Build Adolescent Learning: Five Pillars of Practice*. Thousand Oaks, CA: Corwin.

Dewaele, J.-M. (2000). Trilingual first language acquisition: exploration of a linguistic "miracle." *La Chouette*, 31: 41–46.

Dewaele, J.-M. (2012). *Emotions in Multiple Languages*. New York: Palgrave Macmillan.

Diaz, C. J. and Makin, L. (2002). Literacy as social practice. In L. Makin and C. J. Diaz (eds), *Literacies in Early Childhood* (pp. 3–14). Sydney: Maclennan & Petty.

Dickar, M. (2004). "Words is changing' everyday": language and literacy in the urban contact zone. In B. R. C. Barrel, R. F. Hammett, J. S. Mayher, and G. M. Pradle (eds), *Teaching English Today: Advancing Change in the Secondary Curriculum* (pp. 68–80). New York: Teachers College Press.

Dickinson, D. and McCabe, A. (2001). Bringing it all together: the multiple origins, skills, and environmental supports of early literacy. *Learning Disabilities Research and Practice*, 16: 186–202.

Dodd, B., Hemsley, G, and Holm, A. (2006). Diverse but not different: the lexical skills of two primary age bilingual groups in comparison to monolingual peers. *International Journal of Bilingualism*, 10(4): 453.

Dodd, B., So, L., and Li, W. (1996). Symptoms of disorder without impairment: the written and spoken errors of bilinguals. In B. Dodd, R. Campbell, and L. Worrall (eds), *Evaluating Theories of Language: Evidence from Disordered Communication* (pp. 119–136). London: Whurr.

Donahue, M. L., Pearl, R., and Herzog, A. (1997). Mothers' referential communication with preschoolers: effects of children's syntax and mothers' beliefs. *Journal of Applied Developmental Psychology*, 18(1): 133–147.

Döpke, S. (2000). Generation of and retraction from crosslinguistically motivated structures in bilingual first language acquisition.

Bilingualism: Language and Cognition, 3: 209–226.

Dörnyei, Z. (2003). *Attitudes, Orientations, and Motivations in Language Learning*. Oxford: Blackwell.

Dwyer, E. J. and Isbell, R. (1990). Reading aloud to students. *Educational Digest*, 56 (1): 70–71.

Eccles, J. S. (1999). The development of children ages 6 to 14. *The Future of Children*, 9(2): 30–44.

Eckman, F. R. (1981). On the naturalness of interlanguage phonological rules. *Language Learning*, 27: 315–330.

Edwards, J. (2010). *Language Diversity in the Classroom*. Bristol: Multilingual Matters.

Ehren, B. J. (2005). Looking for evidence-based practice in reading comprehension instruction. *Topics in Language Disorders*, 25 (4): 310–321.

Ellis, N. C. (1994). *Implicit and Explicit Learning of Languages*. New York: Academic Press.

Enguidanos, T. and Ruiz, N. T. (2008). Shared reading for older emergent readers in bilingual classrooms. *Focus on Exceptional Children*, 40(5): 4–16.

Erbaugh, M. S. (1992). The acquisition of Mandarin. In D. I. Slobin (ed.), *The Crosslinguistic Study of Language Acquisition*, vol. 3 (pp. 373–455). Hillsdale, NY: Lawrence Erlbaum.

Everett, D. L. (2009). *Don't Sleep, There Are Snakes: Life and Language in the Amazonian Jungle*. New York: Vintage.

Everett, D. L. (2012). *Language: The Cultural Tool*. New York: Pantheon.

Fabiano-Smith, L. and Goldstein, B. A. (2010). Phonological acquisition in bilingual Spanish–English speaking children. *Journal of Speech, Language, and Hearing Research*, 53: 160–178.

Feltmate, K., and Kay-Raining Bird, E. (2008). Language learning in four bilingual children with Down syndrome: a detailed analysis of vocabulary and morphosyntax. *Canadian Journal of Speech-Language Pathology and Audiology*, 32: 6–20.

Fenson, L., Dale, P., Reznick, S., Thal, D., Bates, E., Hartung, J., Pethick, S., and Reilly, J. (1993). *The MacArthur Communicative Development Inventories* San Diego, CA: Singular.

Fernald, A., Marchman, V. A., and Weisleder, A. (2013). SES differences in language processing skill and vocabulary are evident at 18 months. *Developmental Science*, 16(2): 234–248.

Ferris, D. R. and Hedgcock, J. S. (2014). *Teaching L2 Composition: Purpose, Process, and Practice*. 3rd edn. New York: Routledge.

Fletcher, P. (2001). Specific language impairment. In M. Barrett (ed.), *The Development of Language* (pp. 349–371). Hove: Psychological Press.

Freire, P. (1983). *Pedagogy in Process: The Letters to Guinea-Bissau*. New York: Continuum.

Freire, P. and Maccedo, D. (1987). *Literacy: Reading the Word and the World*. London: Routledge & Kegan Paul.

Gadamer, H.-G. (1993). Wie weit schreibt Sprache das Denken vor? [How far does speaking direct thinking?] In *Gesammelte Werke, Band 2: Hermeneutik II: Wahrheit und Methode: Ergänzungen, Register* (p. 205). Tübingen: Mohr Siebeck.

Gambrell, L. B. (2009). Forword. In L. M. Morrow, *Literacy Development in the Early Years: Helping Children Read and Write*. Boston: Pearson.

Ganger, J. and Brent, M. R. (2004). Reexamining the vocabulary spurt. *Developmental Psychology*, 40: 621–632.

García-Pérez, R. M., Hobson, R. P., and Lee, A. (2008). Narrative role-taking in autism. *Journal of Autism Developmental Disorder*, 38: 156–168

Gardner, R. C. (2010). *Motivation and Second Language Acquisition: The Socio-educational Model*. New York: Peter Lang.

Gardner, R. C. and Lambert, W. E. (1972). *Attitudes and Motivation in Second Language Learning*. Rowley, MA: Newbury House.

Gardner-Neblett, N., Pungello, E. P., and Iruka, I. U. (2011). Oral narrative skills: implications for the reading development of African American children. *Child Development Perspectives*, 6(3): 218–224.

Gass, M. and Selinker, L. (2001). *Second Language Acquisition. An Introductory Course*. 3rd edn. Mahwah, NJ: Lawrence Erlbaum.

Garton, A. and Pratt, C. (1989). *Learning to Be Literate: The Development of Spoken and Written Language*. Oxford: Basil Blackwell.

Gass, M. and Selinker, L. (2008). *Third Language Acquisition. An Introductory Course*. 3rd edn. Mahwah, NJ: Lawrence Erlbaum.

Gathercole, V. C. M. and Thomas, E. M. (2005). Minority language survival: input factors influencing the acquisition of Welsh. In *Proceedings of the 4th International Symposium on Bilingualism* (pp. 852–874). Somerville, MA: Cascadilla Press.

Gawlitzek-Maiwald, I. and Tracy, R. (1996). Bilingual bootstrapping. *Linguistics*, 34: 901–926.

Gazzaniga, M. (1998). *The Mind's Past*. Berkeley: University of California Press.

Gee, J. P. (2011). *An Introduction to Discourse Analysis: Theory and Method*. 3rd edn. New York: Routledge.

Geist, K., McCarthy, J., Rodgers-Smith, A., and Porter, J. (2008). Integrating music therapy services and speech-language therapy services for children with severe communication impairments: a co-treatment model. *Journal of Instructional Psychology*, 35(4): 386–399.

Gelman, S. A. and Tare, M. P. (2011). Bilingual parents' modeling of pragmatic language use in multiparty interactions. *Applied Psycholinguistics*, 32(4): 761–780.

Giambo, D. A. and Szecsi, T. (2005). Parents can guide children through the world of two languages. *Childhood Education*, 81(3): 164–165.

Gildersleeve-Neumann, C. and Davis, B. (1998). Learning English in a bilingual preschool environment: change over time. Paper presented at the Annual Convention of the American Speech-Language-Hearing Association, San Antonio, Texas.

Gillam, R. B. and Gillam, S. L. (2011). An introduction to the discipline of communication sciences and disorders. In R. B. Gillam, T. P. Marquardt, and F. N. Martin (eds), *Communication Sciences and Disorders: From Science to Clinical Practice* (pp. 3–26). 2nd edn. Sudbury, MA: Jones & Bartlett.

Gillam, R. B. and Petersen, D. B. (2011). Language disorders in school-age children. In R. B. Gillam, T. P. Marquardt, and F. N. Martin (eds), *Introduction to Communication Sciences and Disorders: From Science to Clinical Practice* (pp. 437–459). 2nd edn. Sudbury, MA: Jones & Bartlett.

Gillam, R. B., Marquardt, T. P., and Martin, F. N. (2011). *Communication Sciences and Disorders: From Science to Clinical Practice*. 2nd edn. Burlington, MA: Jones & Bartlett.

Gillon, G. (2000). The efficacy of phonological awareness intervention for children with spoken language impairment. *Language, Speech, and Hearing Services in Schools*, 31: 126–141.

Gillon, G. (2002). Follow-up study investigating benefits of phonological awareness intervention for children with spoken language impairment. *International Journal of Language and Communication Disorders*, 37(4): 381–400.

Gilman, P. (1993). *Something from Nothing*. New York: Scholastic Press.

Girbau, D. and Schwartz, R. G. (2008). Phonological working memory in Spanish–English bilingual children with and without specific language impairment. *Journal of Communication Disorders*, 41: 124–145.

Gleason, J. B. (2009). *The Development of Language*. New York: Pearson.

Godley, A. and Escher, A. (2012). Bidialectal African American adolescents' beliefs about spoken language expectations in English classrooms. *Journal of Adolescence and Adult Literacy*, 55(8): 704–713.

Goldin-Meadow, S. (2011). What modern-day gesture can tell us about language evolution? In K. Gibson and M. Tallerman (eds), *Oxford Handbook of Language Evolution*. Oxford: Oxford University Press.

Goldman, S. (2008). Brief report: narratives of personal events in children with autism and developmental language disorders: unshared memories. *Journal of Autism Developmental Disorders*, 38: 1982–1988.

Goldman, S. R. (2012). Adolescent literacy: learning and understanding content. *The Future of Children*, 22(2): 89–116.

Goldstein, B. and Iglesias, A. (1996). Phonological patterns in normally developing Spanish-speaking 3- and 4-year-olds of Puerto Rican descent. *Language, Speech, and Hearing Services in Schools*, 27: 82–90.

Goldstein, B. and Washington, P. (2001). An initial investigation of phonological patterns in 4-year-old typically developing Spanish–English bilingual children. *Language, Speech, and Hearing Services in Schools*, 32: 153–164.

Goldstein, B. A., Fabiano, L., and Washington, P. S. (2005). Phonological skills in predominantly English-speaking, predominantly Spanish-speaking, and Spanish–English bilingual children. *Language, Speech, and Hearing Services in Schools*, 36: 201–218.

Gollan, T. H., Forster, K. I., and Frost, R. (1997). Translation priming with different scripts: masked priming with cognates and noncognates in Hebrew–English bilinguals. *Journal of Experimental Psychology, Learning, Memory, and Cognition*, 23: 1122–1139.

Gombert, J. E. (1993). Metacognition, metalanguage and metapragmatics. *International Journal of Psychology*, 28: 571–580.

Gombert, J.-E. (2002). Children with Down syndrome use phonological knowledge in reading. *Reading and Writing*, 15: 455–469.

González, N. (2005). *I Am My Language: Discourses of Women and Children in Borderlands*. Tucson: University of Arizona Press.

Goodman, J. C., Dale, P. S., and Li, P. P. (2008). Does frequency count? Parental input and the acquisition of vocabulary. *Journal of Child Language*, 35(3): 515–531.

Goodwyn, S. W. and Acredolo, L. P. (1998). Encouraging symbolic gestures: effects on the relationship between gesture and speech. In J. Iverson and S. Goldin-Meadows (eds), *The Nature and Functions of Gesture in Children's Communication*. San Francisco: Jossey-Bass.

Gorman, B. K., Fiestas, C. E., Peña, E. D., and Clark, M. R. (2011). Creative and stylistic devices employed by children during a storybook narrative task: a cross-cultural study. *Language, Speech, and hearing Sciences in Schools*, 42: 167–181.

Graham, S. (2009–2010). Want to improve children's writing? *American Educator* 33(4): 20–40.

Graves, M. F., August, D., and Mancilla-Martines, J. (2013). *Teaching Vocabulary to English Language Learners*. New York: Teachers College Press.

Greenspan, S I. (2007). *Great Kids: Helping Your Babies and Children Develop the Ten Essential Qualities for a Healthy, Happy Life*. Philadelphia: Da Capo Press.

Gregory, E. (2008). *Learning to Read in a New Language*. Los Angeles: Sage.

Gregory, E., Long, S., and Volk, D. (eds) (2004). *Many Pathways to literacy: Young Children Learning with Siblings,*

Grandparents, Peers and Communities. London: Routledge.

Grice, P. (1975). Logic and conversation. In P. Cole and J. Morgan (eds), *Syntax and Semantics*, vol. 3. New York: Academic Press.

Grimm, H. and Weinert, S. (1990). Is the syntax development of dysphasic children deviant and why? New findings to an old question. *Journal of Speech and Hearing Research*, 33: 220–228.

Grosjean, F. (1989). Early bilingual development, one language or two? *Journal of Child Language*, 16: 161–179.

Grosjean, F. and Li, P. (2013). *The Psycholinguistics of Bilingualism*. Oxford: Wiley-Blackwell.

Gut, U. (2000a). *Bilingual Acquisition of Intonation: A Study of Children Speaking German and English*. Tübingen: Max Niemeyer.

Gut, U. (2000b). Cross-linguistic structures in the acquisition of intonational phonology by German–English bilingual children. In S. Döpke (ed.), *Cross-Linguistic Structure in Simultaneous Bilingualism* (pp. 201–225). Amsterdam: John Benjamins.

Gutiérrez-Clellen, V. F., Simon-Cerejido, G., and Erickson Leone, A. (2009). Code-switching in bilingual children with specific language impairment. *International Journal of Bilingualism*, 13: 91–109.

Habib, M., Rey, V., Daffaure, V., Camps, R., Espesser, R., Joly-Pottuz, B., and Demonet, J. (2002). Phonological training in children with dyslexia using temporally modified speech: a three-step pilot investigation. *International Journal of Language and Communication Disorders*, 37: 289–308.

Halliday, M. A. K. (1986). *Learning How to Mean: Explorations in the Development of Language*. New York: Elsevier.

Halliday, M. A. K. (2003). *On Language and Linguistics*. London: Continuum.

Hammer, C. S., Lawrence, F. R., and Miccio, A. W. (2007). Bilingual children's language abilities and early reading outcomes in head start and kindergarten. *Language, Speech, and Hearing Services in Schools*, 38: 237–248.

Hammer, C. S., Komaroff, E., Rodriguez, B. L., Lopez, L. M., Scarpino, S. E., and Goldstein, B. (2012). Predicting Spanish–English bilingual children's language abilities. *Journal of Speech, Language, and Hearing Research*, 55: 1251–1264.

Hart, B. and Risley, T. R. (1995). *Meaningful Differences in the Everyday Experience of Young American Children*. Baltimore: Paul H. Brookes.

Hayes, J. R. (1996). A new framework for understanding cognition and affect in writing. In C. M. Levy and S. Ransdell (eds), *The Science of Writing: Theories, Methods, Individual Differences and Applications* (pp. 1–27). Mahwah, NJ: Lawrence Erlbaum.

Hayes, J. R. and Flower, L. S. (1980). Identifying the organization of writing processes. In L. Gregg and E. R. Steinberg (eds), *Cognitive Processes in Writing* (pp. 3–30). Hillsdale, NJ: Lawrence Erlbaum.

Hayiou-Thomas, M. E., Harlaar, N., Dale, P. S., and Plomin, R. (2010). Preschool speech, language skills, and reading at 7, 9, and 10 years: etiology of the relationship. *Journal of Speech, Language, and Hearing Research*, 53: 311–332.

He, T.-H. and Wang, W.-L. (2009). Invented spelling of EFL young beginning writers and its relation with phonological awareness and grapheme-phoneme principle. *Journal of Second Language Writing*, 18(1): 44–56.

Heath, S. B. (1982). What no bedtime story means: narrative skills at home and school. *Language in Society*, 2: 49–76.

Heath, S. B. (1983). *Ways with Words: Language, Life, and Work in Communities and Classroom*. New York: Cambridge University Press.

Heilmann, J., Miller, J., and Nockerts, A. (2010). Using language sample databases. *Language, Speech, and Hearing Sciences in Schools*, 4:, 84–95.

Hesketh, L. J. and Chapman, R. S. (1998). Verb use by individuals with Down syndrome. *American Journal on Mental Retardation*, 103: 288–304.

Hess, L. J. and Fairchild, J. I. (1988). Model, analyze, practice (MAP): a language therapy model for learning disabled adolescents. *Child Language Teaching and Therapy*, 4: 325–338.

Hewitt, R. (1982). *White Talk Black Talk: Inter-racial Friendship and Communication amongst Adolescents*. Cambridge: Cambridge University Press.

Hinds, J. (1990). Inductive, deductive, quasi-inductive; expository writing in Japanese, Korean, Chinese, and Thai. In U. Connor and A. M. Johns (eds), *Coherence in Writing:*

Research and Pedagogical Perspectives (pp. 87–109). Alexandria, VA: TESOL.

Hirsch, E. (2003). Reading comprehension requires knowledge of words and the world: scientific insights into the fourth-grade slump and the nations' stagnant comprehension score. *American Educator*, 27(1): 10–29.

Hoff, E. (2009). *Language Development*. Belmont, CA: Wadsworth.

Hoffmann, C. (2001). Toward the description of trilingual competence. *International Journal of Bilingualism*, 5(1): 1–17.

Hoffman, C. and Stavans, A. (2007). The evolution of trilingual codeswitching from infancy to school age: the shaping of trilingual competence through dynamic language dominance. *International Journal of Bilingualism*, 11(1): 55–72.

Hoffman, C. and Ytsma, J. (eds) (2004). *Trilingualism in Family, School and Community*. Bristol: Multilingual Matters.

Holm, A. and Dodd, B. (1999). A longitudinal study of the phonological development of two Cantonese-English bilingual children. *Applied Psycholinguistics*, 20: 349–76.

Hornberger, N. (2003). *Continua of Biliteracy: An Ecological Framework for Educational Policy, Research, and Practice in Multilingual Settings*. Bristol: Multilingual Matters.

Horton-Ikard, R. and Weismer, S. E. (2007). A preliminary examination of vocabulary and word learning in African American toddlers from middle and low socioeconomic status homes. *American Journal of Speech-Language Pathology*, 16: 381–392.

Huang, H. and Hanley, R. (1994). Phonological awareness and visual skills in learning to read Chinese and English. *Cognition*, 54: 73–98.

Huang, S., Willson, V., and Eslami, Z. (2012). The effects of task involvement load on L2 incidental vocabulary learning: a meta-analytic study. *Modern Language Journal*, 96(4): 544–557.

Hudson, J. and Shapiro, I. (1991). From knowing to telling: the development of children's scripts, stories, and personal narratives. In A. McCabe and C. Peterson (eds), *Developing Narrative Structure* (pp. 89–136). Hillsdale, NJ: Lawrence Erlbaum.

Hughes, D. I., McGillivray, I., and Schmidek, M. (1997). *Guide to Narrative Language: Procedures for Assessment*. Eau Claire, WI: Thinking.

Hulit, L. M. and Howard, M. R. (2006). *Born to Talk: An Introduction to Speech and Language Development*. Boston: Pearson.

Huttenlocher, J. Aasilyeva, M., Cymerman, E., and Levine, S. (2002). Language input and child syntax. *Cognitive Psychology*, 45(3): 337–374.

Huttenlocher, J., Haight, W., Bryk, A., Seltzer, M., and Lyons, T. (1991). Early vocabulary growth: relations to language input and gender. *Developmental Psychology*, 27: 236–248.

Iluz-Cohen, P. and Walters, J. (2012). Telling stories in two languages: narratives of bilingual preschool children with typical ad impaired language. *Bilingualism: Language and Cognition*, 15(1): 58–74.

Ingram, D. (1981). *Procedure for the Phonological Abilities of Children's Language*. Baltimore: University Park Press.

Iverson, J. M., Capirci, O., Longobardi, E., and Caselli, M. C. (1999). Gesturing in mother–child interactions. *Cognitive Development*, 14: 57–75.

Jacobson, P. F. (2012). The effects of language impairment on the use of direct object pronouns and verb inflections in heritage Spanish speakers: a look at attrition, incomplete acquisition and maintenance. *Bilingualism: Language and Cognition*, 15 (1): 22–38.

Jacobson, P. F. and Walden, P. R. (2013). Lexical diversity and omission errors as predictors of language ability in the narratives of sequential Spanish–English bilinguals: a cross-language comparison. *American Journal of Speech-Language Pathology*, 22: 554–565.

Janks, H. (2014). *Doing Critical Literacy: Texts and Activities for Students and Teachers*. New York: Routledge.

Jia, G. and Fuse, A. (2007). Acquisition of English grammatical morphology by native Mandarin-speaking children and adolescents: age-related differences. *Journal of Speech, Language, and Hearing Research*, 50: 1280–1299.

Johansson, V. (2008). Lexical diversity and lexical density in speech and writing: developmental perspective. *Working Papers* (Lund University), 53: 61–79.

Johnson, D. D. (2001). *Vocabulary in the Elementary and Middle School*. Boston: Allyn & Bacon.

Johnson, E. R. (2009). *Academic Language! Academic Literacy! A Guide for K-12 Educators*. Thousand Oaks, CA: Corwin.

Johnson, J. S. and Newport, E. L. (1989). Critical period effects in second language learning: the influence of maturational state on the acquisition of English as a second language. *Cognitive Psychology*, 21: 60–99.

Johnston, J. C., Durieux-Smith, A., and Bloom, K. (2005). Teaching gestural signs to infants to advance child development: a review of the evidence. *First Language*, 25: 235–251.

Johnston, J. R. and Wong, M. Y. A. (2002). Cultural differences in beliefs and practices concerning talk to children. *Journal of Speech, Language, and Hearing Research*, 45: 916–926.

Jones, C. P. and Adamson, L. B. (1987). Language use in mother-child and mother-child–sibling interactions. *Child Development*, 58: 356–366.

Joshi, R. M., Binks, E., Hougen, M., Dahlgren, M. E., Ocker-Dean, E., and Smith, D. L. (2009). Why elementary teachers might be inadequately prepared to teaching reading. *Journal of Learning Disabilities*, 42(5): 392–402.

Jusczyk, P. W., Luce, P. A., and Charles-Luce, J. (1994). Infant's sensitivity to phonotactic patterns in the native language. *Journal of Memory and Language*, 33: 630–645.

Justice, L. M., Meier, J., and Walpole, S. (2005). Learning new words from storybooks: an efficacy study with at-risk kindergartners. *Language, Speech, and Hearing Services in Schools*, 36(1):17–32.

Justice, L. M., Kaderavek, J. N., Fan, X., Sofka, A., and Hunt, A. (2009). Accelerating preschoolers' early literacy development through classroom-based teacher–child storybook reading and explicit print referencing. *Language, Speech, and Hearing Services in Schools*, 40: 67–85.

Justice, L. M., Bowles, R., Pence, K., and Gosse, C. (2010). A scalable tool for assessing children's language abilities within a narrative context: the NAP (Narrative Assessment Protocol). *Early Child Research Quarterly*, 25: 218–234.

Kapantzoglou, M., Restrepo, M. A., and Thompsona, M. S. (2012). Dynamic assessment of word learning skills: identifying language impairment in bilingual children. *Language, Speech, and Hearing Services in Schools*, 43: 81–96.

Kaplan, R. B. (1966). Cultural though patterns in intercultural education. *Language Learning*, 16: 1–20.

Kavale, K. A. and Forness, S. R. (1985). *The Science of Learning Disabilities*. San Diego: College Hill Press.

Kay-Raining Bird, E. (2007). The case for bilingualism in children with Down syndrome. In R. Paul (ed.), *Language Disorders from a Developmental Perspective: Essays in Honor of Robin S. Chapman* (pp. 249–275). Mahwah, NJ: Lawrence Erlbaum.

Kegl, J. (2002). Language emergence in a language-ready brain. In G. Morgan and B. Woll (eds), *Directions in Sign Language Acquisition* (pp. 207–254). Amsterdam: John Benjamins.

Kegl, J., Senghas, A., and Coppola, M. (1999). Creation through contact: sign language emergence and sign language change in Nicaragua. In M. DeGraff (ed.), *Language Creation and Language Change: Creolization, Diachrony, and Development* (pp. 179–237). Cambridge, MA: MIT Press.

Kell, T. (2009). Using fan fiction to teach critical reading and writing skills. *Teacher Librarian*, 37(1): 32–35.

Kellerman, J. (1981). *Helping the Fearful Child*. New York: Norton.

Kent, R. D. (1976). Anatomical and neuromuscular maturation of the speech mechanism: evidence from acoustic studies. *Journal of Speech and Hearing Research*, 19: 421–447.

Kidd, D. C. and Castano, E. (2013). Reading literary fiction improves theory of mind. *Science*, 342(6156): 377–380. At www.sciencemag.org (accessed Mar. 2014).

Kim, S. J. (2012). Critical literacy in east Asian literacy classrooms. *Perspectives on Global Development and Technology*, 11: 131–144.

King, K. and Fogle, L. (2006). Raising bilingual children: common parental concerns and current research. *Center for Applied Linguistics Digest* (Apr.).

Klima, E. S. and Bellugi, U. (1979). *The Signs of Language*. Cambridge, MA: Harvard University Press.

Kohnert, K. and Derr, A. (2012). Language intervention with bilingual children. In B. A.

Goldstein (ed.), *Bilingual Language Development and Disorders in Spanish-English Speakers* (pp. 337–356). Baltimore: Paul H. Brookes.

Kohnert, K., Windsor, J., and Miller, R. (2004). Crossing borders: recognition of Spanish words by English-speaking children with and without language impairment. *Applied Psycholinguistics*, 25(4): 543.

Kondrad, R. and Jaswal, V. K. (2012). Explaining the errors away: young children forgive understandable semantic mistakes. *Cognitive Development* 27: 126–135.

Krashen, S. (1981). *Second Language Acquisition and Second Language Learning*. Englewood Cliffs, NJ: Prentice Hall.

Krashen, S. (1988). Comprehensible output? *System*, 26: 175–182.

Kress, G. (1997). *Before Writing: Rethinking the Paths to Literacy*. London: Routledge.

Kubota, R. (2010). Cross-cultural perspectives on writing: contrastive rhetoric. In N. H. Hornberger and S. L. McKay (eds), *Sociolinguistics and Language Education* (pp. 265–289). Bristol: Multilingual Matters.

Kuhl, P. K., Feng-Ming, T., and Huei-Mei, L. (2003). Foreign-language experience in infancy: effects of short-term exposure and social interaction on phonetic learning. *Proceedings of the National Academy of Sciences*, 100(15): 9096–9101.

Kupersmitt, J. and Berman, R. A. (2001). Linguistic features of Spanish-Hebrew children's narratives. In L. Verhoeven and S. Strömqvist (eds), *Narrative Development in a Multilingual Context* (pp. 277–317). Amsterdam: John Benjamins.

Kyle, J. G. and Woll, B. (1985). *Sign Language: The Study of Deaf People and Their Language*. Cambridge: Cambridge University Press.

Lamme, L. L. (1984). *Growing up Writing: Sharing with Your Children the Joys of Good Writing* (pp.16–17). Washington, DC: Acropolis.

Landau, B. and Gleitman, L. R. (1985). *Language and Experience: Evidence from the Blind Child*. Cambridge, MA: Harvard University Press.

Larson, J. and Marsh, J. (2003). *Making Literacy Real: Theories and Practices for Learning and Teaching*. London: Sage.

Lau, S. M. C. (2012). Reconceptualizing literacy in ESL classrooms. *Reading Teacher*, 65(5): 325–329.

Lave, J. and Wenger, E. (1991). *Situated Learning: Legitimate Peripheral Participation*. Cambridge: Cambridge University Press.

Lee, K.-O. and Lee, Y.-G. (2008). An Event-Structural Account of Passive Acquisition in *Korean Language and Speech*, 51(1–2): 133–149.

Lenneberg, E. H. (1967). *Biological Foundations of Language*. New York: John Wiley.

Leonard, L. B. (1998). *Children with Specific Language Impairment*. Cambridge, MA: MIT Press.

Leopold, W. (1970). *Speech Development of a Bilingual Child. A Linguist Record*. New York: AMS Press.

Lewin, T. (2009). In a digital future, textbooks are history. *New York Times*, August 9.

Lewis, C. S. (1996). *Of Other Worlds: Essays and Stories*. New York: Harcourt Brace & World.

Li, P. (2013). Successive language acquisition. In F. Grosjean and P. Li (eds), *The Psycholinguistics of Bilingualism* (p. 157). Oxford: Wiley-Blackwell.

Liberman, L. Y., Shanlweiler, D., Fischer, F. W., and Carter, B. (1997). Explicit syllable and phoneme segmentation in the young child. *Journal of Experimental Child Psychology*, 18: 201–212.

Lindsey, K., Manis, F., and Bailey, C. (2003). Prediction of first-grade reading in Spanish-speaking English-language learners. *Journal of Educational Psychology*, 95: 482–494.

Liontas, J. I. (2002). Reading between the lines: detecting, decoding, and understanding idioms in second language. In J. H. Sullivan (ed.), *Literacy and the Second Language Learner* (pp. 177–216). Greenwich, CT: Information Age.

Loeb, D., Stoke, C., and Fey, M. (2001). Language changes associated with FastForWord-Language: evidence from case studies. *American Journal of Speech-Language Pathology*, 10: 216–230.

Loizou, E. Kyriakides, E., Hadjicharalambous, M. (2001). Children's knowledge of genre and ability to carry on for different communication needs. *European Early Childhood Education Research Journal*, 19(1): 63–77.

Long, M. (1990). Maturational constraints on language development. *Studies in Second Language Acquisition*, 12: 251–258.

Long, M. H. (2003). Stabilization and fossilization in interlanguage development. In C. J. Doughty and M. H. Long (eds), *The Handbook of Second Language Acquisition* (pp. 487–535). Oxford: Blackwell.

Lonigan, C., Burgess, S., and Anthony, J. (2000). Development of emergent literacy and early reading skills in preschool children: evidence from a latent-variable longitudinal study. *Developmental Psychology*, 26: 596–613.

Lopez, J. K. (n.d.). Funds of knowledge: teachers can use "funds of knowledge," the knowledge students gain from their family and cultural backgrounds, to make their classrooms more inclusive. Website of Learn NC, University of North Carolina School of Education, athttp://www.learnnc.org/lp/pages/939 (accessed Mar. 2014).

Lord, C. and Paul, R. (1997). Language and communication in autism. In D. J. Cohen and F. R. Volkmar (eds), *Handbook of Autism and Pervasive Development Disorders*. New York: John Wiley.

Lugo-Neris, M. J., Jackson, W. C., and Goldstein, H. (2010). Facilitating vocabulary acquisition of young English language learners. *Language, Speech, and Hearing Services in Schools*, 41: 314–327.

Lung, F.-W., Chiang, T.-L., Lin, S.J., Feng, J.-Y., Chen, P.-F., and Shu, B.-C. (2011). Gender differences of children's developmental trajectory from 6 to 60 months in the Taiwan birth cohort pilot study. *Research in Developmental Disabilities*, 32(1): 100–106.

Lust, B. (2006). *Child Language: Acquisition and Growth*. Cambridge: Cambridge University Press.

Lyman-Hager, M. A., Johns, A., Nocon, H., and Davis, J. N. (2002). Literacy in digital environments: connecting communities of language learners. In J. H. Sullivan (ed.), *Literacy and the Second Language Learner* (pp. 261–279). Greenwich, CT: Information Age.

Lyytinen, H., Erskine, J., Tolvanen, A., Torppa, M., Poikken, A, and Lyytinen, P. (2006). Trajectories of reading development: a follow-up from birth to school age children with and without risk for dyslexia. *Merrill-Palmer Quarterly*, 52: 514–546.

Maccoby, E. E. (1992). *The Two Sexes: Growing up Apart, Coming Together*. Cambridge, MA: Belknap Press.

MacWhinney, B. and Bates, E. (1989). *The Crosslinguistic Study of Sentence Processing*. Cambridge: Cambridge University Press.

Magiste, E. (1979). The competing linguistic systems of the multilingual: a developmental study of decoding and encoding processes. *Journal of Verbal Learning and Verbal Behavior*, 18: 79–89.

Makin, l., Campbell, J., and Diaz, C. (1995). *One Childhood Many Languages: Guidelines for Early Childhood Education in Australia*. Pymble, NSW: Harper Educational.

Marchand-Martella, N. E., Martella, R. C., Modderman, S. L., Petersen, H. M., and Pan, S. (2013). Key areas of effective adolescent literacy programs. *Education and Treatment of Children*, 36(1): 161–184.

Marchman, V. A., Martinez-Sussmann, C., and Dale, P. S. (2004). The language-specific nature of grammatical development evidence from bilingual language learners. *Developmental Science*, 7(2): 212–224.

Manolitsi, M. and Botting, N. (2011). Language abilities in children with autism and language impairment: using narrative as an additional source of clinical information. *Child Language Teaching and Therapy*, 27(1): 39–55.

Manzo, A. V., Manzo, U. C., and Estes, T. H. (2001). *Context Area Literacy: Interactive Teaching for Active Learning*. New York: John Wiley.

Martello, J. (2002). many roads through many modes: becoming literate in early childhood. In L. Makin and C. J. Diaz (eds), *Literacies in Early Childhood: Changing Views, Changing Practice* (pp. 35–52). Sydney: MacLennan & Petty.

Martinez, M. A. (1987). Dialogues among children and between children and their mothers. *Child Development*, 58: 1035–1043.

Martin-Jones, M. and Jones, K. (2000). Multilingual literacies. In M. Martin-Jones and K. Jones (eds), *Multilingual Literacies: Reading and Writing Different Worlds* (pp. 1–15). Amsterdam: John Benjamins.

Martins, M. A. and Silva, C. (2006). The impact of invented spelling on phonemic awareness. *Learning and Instruction*, 16: 41–56.

Marvin, C. (1994). Cartalk! Preschool children's conversation en route home from school. *Language, and Hearing Sciences in the School*, 25(3): 146–155.

Marvin, C. A. and Cline, K. D. (2010). Bus talk: a preliminary analysis of children's decontextualized talk. *Communication Disorders Quarterly*, 31(3): 170–182.

Mayberry, R. I. (2007). When timing is everything: age of first-language acquisition effects on second-language learning. *Applied Psycholinguistics*, 28(3): 537–549.

Mayberry, R. I. (2010). Early language acquisition and adult language ability: what sign language reveals about the critical period for language. In M. Marschark and P. E. Spencer (eds), *The Oxford Handbook of Deaf Studies, Languages, and Education*. Oxford: Oxford University Press.

Mayberry, R. I. and Squires, B. (2006). Sign language: acquisition. In E. Lieven (ed.), *Language Acquisition*, vol. 11 of K. Brown (gen. ed.), *Encyclopedia of Language and Linguistics*, 2nd edn (pp. 291–296). Oxford: Elsevier.

Mayberry, R. I., Lock, E., and Kazmi, H. (2002). Linguistic ability and early language exposure. *Nature*, 417: 38.

Maynard, A. E. (2004). Sibling interactions. In U. P. Gielen and J. Roopnarine (eds), *Childhood and Adolescence, Cross-Cultural Perspectives and Applications* (pp. 229–252). Westport, CT: Praeger.

McBride-Chang, C., Shu, H., Zhou, A., Wat, C.-P., and Wagner, R. K. (2003). Morphological awareness uniquely predicts young children's Chinese character recognition. *Journal of Educational Psychology*, 95(4): 734–751.

McCauley, R. J. and Fey, M. E. (2006). *Treatment of Language Disorders in Children*. Baltimore: Paul H. Brookes.

McCombs, B. L and Marzano, R. J. (1990). Putting the self in self-regulated learning: the self as agent in integrating skill and will. *Educational Psychologist* 25: 51–70.

McCutchen, D. (1996). A capacity theory of writing: working memory in composition. *Educational Psychology Review*, 8(3): 299–325.

McCutchen, D., Abbott, R. D., Green, L. B., Beretvas, S. N., Cox, S., et al. (2002). Beginning literacy: links among teacher knowledge, teacher practice, and student learning. *Journal of Learning Disabilities*, 35: 69–86.

McDevitt, T. M. and Ormrod, J. E. (2010). *Child Development and Education*. Upper Saddle River, NJ: Merrill.

McGee, A. and Johnson, H. (2003). The effect of inference training on skilled and less skilled comprehenders. *Educational Psychology*, 23(1): 49–59.

McGee, L. M., Richgels, D. J., and Charlesworth, R. (1986). Emerging knowledge of written language: learning to read and write. In S. Kilmer (ed.), *Advances in Early Education and Day Care: A Research Annual*, vol. 4. London: JAI Press.

McGregor, K. K. (2009). Semantics in child language disorder. In R. G. Schwarts (ed.), *Handbook of Child Language Disorders* (pp. 365–387). New York: Psychology Press.

McLaughlin, B. (1978). *Second language Acquisition in Childhood*. Hillsdale, NJ: Lawrence Erbaum.

McLaughlin, B. (1990). The relationship between first and second languages: language proficiency and language aptitude. In B. Harley, P. Allen, J. Cummins, and M. Swain (eds), *The Development of Second Language Proficiency* (pp. 158–178). New York: Cambridge University Press.

McNabb, M. L. (2005–2006). Navigating the maze of hypertext. *Educational Leadership*, 63(4): 76–79.

McNabb, M. L., Thurber, B. B., Dibuz, P., McDermott, and Lee, C. A. (2006). *Literacy Learning in Networked Classrooms: Using the Internet with Middle-Level Students*. Newark, DE: International Reading Association.

McQuillan, J. (1998). The use of self-selected and free voluntary reading in heritage language programs: a review of research. In S. D. Krashen and J. McQuillan (eds), *Heritage Language Development* (pp. 73–87). Culver City, CA: Language Education Associates.

Mehrabian, A. (1981). *Silent Messages*. Belmont, CA: Wadsworth.

Meisel, J. M. (2006). The bilingual child. In T. K. Bhatia and W. C. Ritchie, *The Handbook of Bilingualism* (pp. 91–144). Oxford: Blackwell.

Miller, J. F. (1995). Individual differences in vocabulary acquisition in children with Down syndrome. In C. Epstein, T. Hassold, I. Lott, L. Nadel, and D. Patterson (eds), *Etiology and Pathogenesis of Down Syndrome: Proceedings of the International Down Syndrome Research Conference* (pp. 93–103). New York: Wiley-Liss.

Mills, K. A. (2010). A review of the "digital turn" in the new literacy studies. *Review of Educational Research*, 80(2): 246–271.

Mills, M. T., Watkins, R. V., Washington, J. A., Nippold, M., and Schneider, P. (2013). Structural and dialectal characteristics of the fictional and personal narratives of school-age African American children. *Language, Speech and Hearing Services in Schools*, 44(2): 211–223.

Moats, L. C. (1994). The missing foundation in teacher education. *American Education*, 19(2): 43–51.

Moats, L. C. and Foorman, B. R. (2003). Measuring teachers' content knowledge of language and reading. *Annuals of Dyslexia*, 53: 23–45.

Moats, L. C. and Lyon, G. R. (1996). Wanted: teachers with knowledge of language. *Topics in Language Disorders*, 16: 73–86.

Moerk, E. L. (1980). Relationships between parental input frequencies and children's language acquisition: a reanalysis of Brown's data. *Journal Of Child Language*, 7(1): 105–118.

Moll, L. C., Amanri, C., Neff, D., and Gonzalez, N. (1992). Funds of knowledge for teaching: using a qualitative approach to connect homes and classrooms. *Theory into Practice*, 31(2): 132–142.

Montanari, S. (2005). "Sol! 'GANDA, cute!": a longitudinal study of language choice in a developing trilingual child. In J. Cohen, K. T. McAlister, K. Rolstad, and J. MacSwan (eds), *Proceedings of the 4th International Symposium on Bilingualism* (pp. 1662–1678). Somerville, MA: Cascadilla Press.

Montanari, S. (2008). Pragmatic differentiation in early trilingual development. *Journal of Child Language*, 36(3): 597–627.

Montgomery, J. W., Magimairaj, B. M., and O'Malley, M. H. (2008). Role of working memory in typically developing children's complex sentence comprehension. *Journal of Psycholinguistic Research*, 37: 331–356.

Morales, M., Mundy, P., and Rojas, J. (1998). Following the directions of gaze and language development in 6-month-olds. *Infant Behavior and Development*, 21: 373–377.

Morgan, G. and Kegl, J. (2006). Nicaraguan sign language and theory of mind: the issue of critical period and abilities. *Journal of Child Psychology and Psychiatry*, 47: 811–819.

Morrow, L. M. (2012). *Literacy Development in the Early Years: Helping Children Read and Write*. Boston: Pearson.

Mourssi, A. (2012). The impact of reflection and metalinguistic feedback in SLA: a qualitative research in the context of post graduates. *International Journal of Language Learning and Applied Linguistics*, 1(1): 128–146.

Mui, S. and Anderson, J. (2008). At home with the Johars: another look at family literacy. *Reading Teacher*, 62(3): 234–243.

National Center for Education Statistics (2009). *National Assessment of Educational Progress, NAEP Trends in Academic Progress*. NCES 2009-479. Washington, DC: US Department of Education.

National Center for Education Statistics (2010). *National Assessment of Educational Progress*. At http://nces.ed.gov/nationsreportcard/ (accessed Mar. 2014).

National Center for Educational Statistics (2011). *The Nations' Report Card: Reading 2011*. NCES 2012-457. Washington, DC: US Department of Education.

National Governors Association Center and Council of Chief State School Officers (2010). *Common Core State Standards*. Washington, DC: National Governors Association Center for Best Practices and Council of Chief State School Officers.

National Institute of Child Health and Human Development Early Child Care Research Network. (2005). Pathways to reading: the role of oral language in the transition to reading. *Developmental Psychology*, 41: 428–442.

National Institute on Deafness and Other Communication Disorders (2014). Statistics on voice, speech, and language. At http://www.nidcd.nih.gov/health/statistics/Pages/vsl.aspx (accessed Mar. 2014).

Nelson, K. (1973). *Structure and Strategy in Learning to Talk*. Chicago: University of Chicago Press.

Nelson, K. (2007). *Young Minds in Social Worlds: Experience, Meaning, and Memory*. Cambridge, MA: Harvard University Press.

Nelson, N. W. (2010). *Language and Literacy Disorders: Infancy through Adolescence*. Boston: Allyn & Bacon.

Neuman, S. B. and Wright, J. S. (2007). *Reading with Your Young Child*. New York: Scholastic.

Neville, H. J., Coffey, S. A., Lawson, D. S., Fisher, A., Emmorey, K., and Bellugi, U. (1997). Neural systems mediating American Sign Language: effects of sensory experience and age of acquisition. *Brain and Language*, 57: 285–308.

New London Group (1996). A pedagogy of multiliteracies: designing social futures. *Harvard Educational Review*, 66(1): 60–92.

Newport, E. L. (2002). Critical periods in language development. In L. Nadel (ed.), *Encyclopedia of Cognitive Science*. London: Macmillan/Nature.

Newport, E. L. and Aslin, R. N. (2000). Innately constrained learning: blending old and new approaches to language acquisition. In S. A. F. Howell and T. Keith-Lucas (eds), *Proceedings of the 24th Annual Boston University Conference on Language Development* (pp. 1–21). Somerville, MA: Cascadilla Press.

Newport, E. L., Bavelier, D., and Neville, H. J. (2001). Critical thinking about critical periods: perspectives on a critical period for language acquisition. In E. Dupoux (ed.), *Language, Brain and Cognitive Development: Essays in Honor of Jacques Mehler* (pp. 481–502). Cambridge, MA: MIT Press.

Newport, E. L., Gleitman, H., and Gleitman, L. (1977). Mother, please, I'd rather do it myself. In C. Snow and C. Ferguson (eds), *Talking to Children* (pp. 109–150). Cambridge: Cambridge University Press.

Nijakowska, J. (2008). An experiment with direct multisensory instruction in teaching word reading and spelling to Polish dyslexic learners of English. In J. Kornos and E. H. Kontra (eds), *Language learners with Special Needs: An International Perspective* (pp. 130–157). Bristol: Multilingual Matters.

Nippold, M. A. (2007). *Later Language Development: School-Age Children, Adolescents, and Young Adults*. 3rd edn. Austin: Pro-ed.

Nippold, M. A. (2009). School-age children talk about chess: does knowledge drive syntactic complexity? *Journal of Speech, Language, and Hearing Research*, 52: 856–871.

Nolan, J. S. (2008). School and extended family in the transmission and revitalisation of Gallo in Upper-Brittany. *Journal of Multilingual and Multicultural Development*, 29(3): 216–234.

Nuske, N. J. and Bavin, E. L. (2011). Narrative comprehension in 4–7-year-old children with autism: testing the Weak Central Coherence account. *International Journal of Language Communication Disorders*, 46(1): 108–119.

Nuttall, C. (1996). *Teaching Reading Skills in a Foreign Language*. London: Heinemann.

O'Brien, D. and Scharber, C. (2008). Digital literacies go to school: potholes and possibilities. *Journal of Adolescent and Adult Literacy*, 52(1): 66–68.

Ochs, E. (1997). Cultural dimensions of language acquisition. In N. Coupland and A. Jawroski (eds), *Sociolinguistics: A Reader* (pp. 430–437). New York: St Martin's Press.

Ochs, E. and Schieffelin, B. (1984). Language acquisition and socialization: three developmental stories and their implications. In R. LeVine and R. Shweder (eds), *Culture Theory: Essays on Mind, Self, and Emotion* (pp. 276–321). New York: Cambridge University Press.

Oller, D. K. (2000). *The Emergence of the Speech Capacity*. Mahwah, NJ: Lawrence Erlbaum.

Oller, D. K. (2005). The distributed characteristic in bilingual learning. In J. Cohen, K. T. McAlister, K. Rolstad, and J. MacSwan (eds), *Proceedings of the 4th International Symposium on Bilingualism* (pp. 1744–1749). Somerville, MA: Cascadilla Press.

Oller, D. K. and Cobo-Lewis, A. B. (2002). The ability of bilingual and monolingual children to perform phonological translation. In D. K. Oller and R. E. Eliers (eds), *Language and Literacy in Bilingual Children* (pp. 255–278). Bristol: Multilingual Matters.

Olsen-Fulero, L., and Conforti, J. (1983). Child responsiveness to mother questions of varying type and presentation. *Journal of Child Language*, 10: 495–520.

Orellana, M.F., Dorner, L., and Pulido, L. (2003). Accessing assets: immigrant youth's work as family translator or "para-phrasers." *Social Problems*, 50(4): 5005–5024.

Orfanidou, E., Adam, R., Morgan, G., and McQueen, J. M. (2011). Recognition of signed and spoken language: different sensory inputs, the same segmentation procedures. *Journal of Memory and Language*, 62(3): 272–283.

Ortiz, E. A. (2009). The influence of family structures and the role of siblings on early language development of Latino preschool children. Doctoral dissertation, Utah State University, Logan.

Oshima-Takane, Y., Goodz, E., and Derevensky, J. L. (1996). Birth order effects on early language development: do second born children learn from overheard speech? *Child Development*, 67: 621–634.

Ostad, S. A. and Sorensen, P. M. (2007). Private speech and strategy-use patterns: bidirectional comparisons of children with and without mathematical difficulties. *Journal of Learning Disabilities*, 40(1): 2–14.

Otto, B. W. (2009). *Language Development in Early Childhood*. Upper Saddle River, NJ: Pearson.

Ouellette, G. and Sénéchal, M. (2008a). Pathway to literacy: a study of invented spelling and its role in learning to read. *Child Development*, 79(4): 899–913.

Ouellette, G. and Sénéchal, M. (2008b). A window into early literacy: exploring the cognitive and linguistic underpinnings of invented spelling. *Scientific Studies of Reading*, 1(2): 195–219.

Ovando, C. J., Combs, M. C., and Collier, V. P. (2006). *Bilingual and ESL Classrooms: Teaching in Multicultural Contexts*. Boston: McGraw Hill.

Owens, R. E. (2012). *Language Development: An Introduction*. Boston: Pearson.

Özçalişkan, S., Gentner, D., and Goldin-Meadow, S. (2013). Do iconic gestures pave the way for children's early verbs? *Applied Psycholinguistics*, 1–20.

Padilla, A. M. and Lindholm, K. (1984). Child bilingualism: the same old issues revisited. In Martinez, J. L., Jr, and Mendoza, R. H. (eds), *Chicano Psychology* (pp. 369–408). Orlando: Academic Press.

Palincsar, A. S. and Brown, A. L. (1984). Reciprocal teaching of comprehension-fostering and comprehension-monitoring activities. *Cognition and Instruction* 1: 117–175.

Palmer, B. C., Shackelford, V. S., Miller, S. C., and Leclere, J. T. (2007). Bridging two worlds: reading comprehension, figurative language instruction, and the English-language learner. *Journal of Adolescent and Adult Literacy*, 50(4): 258–267.

Paradis, J. (2010). The interface between bilingual development and specific language impairment. *Applied Psycholinguistics*, 31: 227–252.

Paradis, J. and Genesee, F. (1996). Syntactic acquisition in bilingual children: autonomous or interdependent? *Studies in Second Language Acquisition*, 18: 1–25.

Parsons, T. D., Rizzo, A. R., van der Zaag, C., McGee, J. S, and Buckwalter, J. G. (2005). Gender differences and cognition among older adults. *Aging Neuropsychology and Cognition*, 12(1): 78–88.

Patterson, J. L. (2002). Relationships of expressive vocabulary to frequency of reading and television experience among bilingual toddlers. *Applied Psycholinguistics*, 23(4): 493–508.

Paul, R. (2007). *Language Disorders from Infancy through Adolescence: Assessment and Intervention*. 3rd edn. St. Louis, MO: Mosby.

Pavlenko, A (2008). Emotion and emotion-laden words in the bilingual lexicon. *Bilingualism: Language and Cognition*, 11: 147–164.

Pearson, B. Z. (2007). Social factors in childhood bilingualism in the United Stages. *Applied Psycholinguistics*, 28: 399–410.

Pearson, B. Z. (2008). *Raising a Bilingual Child*. New York: Random House.

Pearson, B. Z., Fernandez, S. C., and Oller, D. K. (1995). Cross-language synonyms in the lexicons of bilingual infants: one language or two? *Journal of Child Language*, 22: 345–368.

Pearson, B. Z., Fernandez, S., Lewedag, V., and Oller, D. K. (1997). Input factors in lexical learning of bilingual infants (age 10–30 months). *Applied Psycholinguistics*, 18: 41–58.

Peck, M., Askov, E. N., and Fairchild, S. H. (1980). Another decade of research in handwriting: progress and prospect in the 1970's. *Journal of Educational Research*, 73: 282–298.

Pelliteri, J. (2000). Music therapy in the special education setting. *Journal of Educational and Psychological Consultation*, 11: 379–391.

Peña, E. D. and Bedore, L. M. (2009). Bilingualism in child language disorder. In R. G. Schwarts (ed.), *Handbook of Child Language Disorders* (pp. 281–307). New York: Psychology Press.

Pence, K. L. and Justice, L. M. (2008). *Language Development from Theory to Practice*. Upper Saddle River, NJ: Pearson.

Phillips, L. M., Norris, S. P., Osmond, W. C., and Maynard, A. M. (2002). Relative reading achievement: a longitudinal study of 187 children from first through sixth grades. *Journal of Educational Psychology*, 94(1): 3–13.

Piaget, J. (1962). *Play, Dreams and Imitation in Childhood*. New York: Norton.

Pine, J. M. (1995). Variation in vocabulary development as a function of birth order. *Child Development*, 66: 272–281.

Pinker, S. (1984). *Language Learnability and Language Development*. Cambridge, MA: Harvard University Press.

Plomin, R. and Kovas, Y. (2005). Generalist genes and learning disabilities. *Psychological Bulletin*, 131: 592–617.

Plowman, L., McPake, J. and Stephen, C. (2010). The technologisation of childhood? Young children and technology in the home. *Children and Society*, 24(1): 63–74.

Poplack, S. (1980). Sometimes I start a sentence in English y termino en Espanõl: towards a typology of code-switching. *Linguistics*, 18: 581–618.

Powell, R. and Rightmyer, E. C. (2011). *Literacy for All Students: An Instructional Framework for Closing the Gap*. New York: Routledge.

Purcell-Gates, V. (2001). Emergent literacy is emerging knowledge of written, not oral language. *New Directions for Child and Adolescent Development*, 92: 7–22.

Quay, S. (1995). The bilingual lexicon: implications for studies of language choice. *Journal of Child Language*, 22: 369–387.

Quay, S. (2001). Managing linguistic boundaries in early trilingual development. In J. Cenoz and F. Genesee (eds), *Trends in Bilingual Acquisition* (pp. 149–199). Amsterdam: John Benjamins.

Quay, S. (2008). Dinner conversations with a trilingual two-year-old: language socialization in a multilingual context. *First Language*, 28: 5–33.

Ramey, S. L. and Ramey, C. T. (1999). *Going to School: How to Help Your Child Succeed*. Goddard Press.

Rauch, D. P., Naumann, J., and Jude, N. (2012). Metalinguistic awareness mediates effects of full biliteracy on third-language reading proficiency in Turkish–German bilinguals. *International Journal of Bilingualism*, 16(4): 402–418.

Ray, J. (2002). Treating phonological disorders in a multilingual child: a case study. *American Journal of Speech-Language Pathology*, 11: 305–315.

Reich, P. A. (1986). *Language Development*. Englewood Cliffs, NJ: Prentice Hall.

Reilly, J., Losh, M., Bellugi, U., and Wulfeck, B. (2004). "Frog, where are you?" Narratives in children with specific language impairment, early focal brain injury, and Williams syndrome. *Brain and Language*, 88: 229–247.

Reynolds, J. F., Dorner, L. M., and Orellana, M. F. (2011). Siblings as cultural educators and socializing agents. In J. Caspi (ed.), *Sibling Development: Implications for Mental Health Practitioners*. New York: Springer.

Richards, P.O., Thatcher, D. H., Shreeves, M., Timmons, P., and Barker, S. (1999). Don't let a good scare frighten you: choosing and using quality chillers to promote reading. *Reading Teacher*, 52(8): 830–840.

Richgels, D. J. (1995). Invented spelling ability and printed word learning in kindergarten. *Reading Research Quarterly*, 30: 96–109.

Ringbom, H. (1987). *The Role of the First Language in Foreign Language Learning*. Bristol: Multilingual Matters.

Rinvolucri, M. (1996). *Grammar Games: Cognitive, Affective and Drama Activities for EFL Students*. Cambridge: Cambridge University Press.

Rogers, R. (2011). Critical approaches to discourse analysis in educational research. In R. Rogers (ed.), *An Introduction to Critical Discourse Analysis in Education* (pp. 1–20). 2nd edn. New York: Routledge.

Rogoff, B. (1990) *Apprenticeship in Thinking: Cognitive Development in Social Context*. Oxford: Oxford University Press.

Romaine, S. (1995). *Bilingualism*. Oxford: Blackwell.

Romero, G. (1983). Print awareness of the preschool bilingual Spanish–English speaking child. Doctoral dissertation, University of Arizona.

Rondal, J. A. (2000). Bilingualism in mental retardation: some prospective views. *Child Development and Disabilities*, 26: 57–64.

Ronjat, J. (1913). *Le développement du langue observé chez un enfant bilingue* [The development of language observed with a bilingual child]. Paris: Champion.

Ross, S. H., Oetting, J. B., and Stapleton, B. (2004). Preterite had plus V-ed: a developmental narrative structure of African American English. *American Speech*, 79: 167–193.

Ruddell, R. B. (2009). *How to Teach Reading to Elementary and Middle School Students: Practical Ideas from Highly Effective Teachers*. Boston: Allyn & Bacon.

Rutherford, W. (1982). Markedness in second language acquisition. *Language Learning*, 32: 85–108.

Sacks, O. (1989). *Seeing Voices: A Journey into the World of the Deaf*. Berkeley: University of California Press.

Salameh, E.-K., Nettelbladt, U., and Norlin, K. (2003). Assessing phonologies in bilingual Swedish-Arabic children with and without language impairment. *Child Language Teaching and Therapy*, 19: 338–364.

Santrock, J. W. (2007). *Adolescence*. Boston: McGraw Hill.

Scarborough, H. (2001). Connecting early language and literacy to later reading (dis)abilities: evidence, theory and practice. In S. Neuman and D. Dickinson (eds), *Handbook of Family Literacy* (pp. 97–110). New York: Guilford Press.

Schecter, S. and Bayley, R. (2002). *Language and Cultural Practice: Mexicanos en el norte*. Mahwah, NJ: Lawrence Erlbaum.

Schecter, S. and Bayley, R. (2004). Language socialization in theory and practice. *International Journal of Qualitative Studies in Education*, 17(5): 605–625.

Schieffelin, B. B. (1979). Getting it together: an ethnographic approach to the study of the development of communicative competence. In E. Ochs and B. B. Schieffelin (eds), *Developmental Pragmatics* (pp. 73–108). New York: Academic Press.

Schober-Peterson, D. and Johnson, C. J. (1991). Non-dialogue speech during preschool interactions. *Journal of Child Language*, 18: 153–170.

Schwartz, M. and Shaul, Y. (2013). Narrative development among language-minority children: the role of bilingual versus monolingual preschool education. *Language, Culture and Curriculum*, 26(1): 36–51.

Schwartz, R. (ed.) (2009). *Handbook of Child Language Disorders*. New York: Psychology Press.

Selinker, L. (1972). Interlanguage. *International Review of Applied Linguistics*, 10: 209–231.

Senghas, A. and Coppola, M. (2001). Children creating language: how Nicaraguan Sign Language acquired a spatial grammar. *Psychological Science*, 12: 323–328.

Shanker, J. L. and Cockrum, W. A. (2009). *Locating and Correcting Reading Difficulties*. Boston: Allyn & Bacon.

Shaywitz, S. E. and Shaywitz, B. A. (2004). Neurobiologic basis for reading and reading disability. In P. McCardle and V. Chhabra (eds), *The Voice of Evidence in Reading Research* (pp. 417–442). Baltimore: Brookers.

Sheridan, C. (2000). Children's literature and literacy learning. In C. Barratt-Pugh and M. Rohl (eds), *Literacy learning in the Early Years* (pp. 105–128). Philadelphia: Open University Press.

Shulman, C. and Guberman, A. (2007). Acquisition of verb meaning through syntactic cues: a comparison of children with autism, children with specific language impairment (SLI) and children with typical language development (TLD). *Journal of Child Language*, 34(2): 411–423.

Skarakis-Doyle, E. and Dempsey, L. (2008). Assessing story comprehension in preschool children. *Topics in Language Disorders*, 28(2): 131–148.

Silliman, E. R. and Scott, C. M. (2009). Research-based oral language intervention routes to the academic language of literacy. In S. Rosenfield and V. Berninger (eds), *Implementing Evidence-Based Academic Interventions in School Settings* (pp. 107–145). New York: Oxford University Press.

Simard, D. (2004). Using diaries to promote metalinguistic reflection among elementary school students. *Language Awareness*, 13(1): 34–48.

Simard, D. and Wong, W. (2004). Language awareness and its multiple possibilities for the L2 classroom. *Foreign Language Annuals*, 37: 96–110.

Simard, D., French, L., and Fortier, V. (2007). Elicited metalinguistic reflection and second language learning: Is there a link? *System*, 35: 509–522.

Singer, M. A, and Goldin-Meadow, S. (2005). Children learn when their teacher's gesture and speech differ. *Psychological Science*, 16(2): 86–89.

Singleton, J. L. and Newport, E. L. (2004). When learners surpass their models: the acquisition of American Sign Language from inconsistent input. *Cognitive Psychology*, 49(2): 370–407.

Sinka, I. and Schelletter, C. (1998). Morphosyntactic development in bilingual children. *International Journal of Bilingualism*, 2(3): 301–326.

Sipe, L. R. (2001). Invention, conventions, and intervention: the teachers' role. *Reading Teacher*, 55 (3): 264–273.

Slobin, D. I. (1982). Universal and particular in the acquisition of language. In E. Wanner and L. R. Gleitman (eds), *Language Acquisition: The state of the Art*. Cambridge: Cambridge University Press.

Slobin, D. I. (1985). Crosslingusitic evidence for the language-making capacity. In D. I. Slobin (ed.), *The Crosslinguistic Study of Language Acquisition*, vol. 2: *Theoretical Issues* (pp. 1157–1256). Hillsdale, NJ: Lawrence Erlbaum.

Smith, S. D. (2007). Genes, language development, and language disorders. *Mental Retardation and Developmental Disabilities Reviews*, 13: 96–105.

Smith, C. and Tager-Flusberg, H. (1982). Metalinguistic awareness and language development. *Journal of Experimental Child Psychology*, 34: 449–468.

Smitherman, G. (1994). "The blacker the berry, the sweeter the juice:" African American student writers. In A. H. Dyson (ed.), *The Need for Story: Cultural Diversity in Classroom and Community* (pp. 80–101). Urbana, IL: National Council of Teachers of English.

Snow, C. and Moje, E. (2010). Why is everyone talking about adolescent literacy? *Phi Delta Kappan*, 91(6): 66–69.

Snow, C. E., Burns, M. S., and Griffin, P. (eds) (1998). *Preventing Reading Difficulties in Young Children*. Washington, DC: National Academy Press.

Soler, E. A. and Martínez-Flor, A. (2008). Pragmatics in foreign language contexts. In E. A. Soler and A. Martínez-Flor (eds), *Investigating Pragmatics in Foreign Language Learning, Teaching and Testing* (pp. 3–21). Bristol: Multilingual Matters.

Soodak, L. (2003). Classroom management in inclusive settings. *Theory into Practice*, 42(4): 327–333.

Souto-Manning, M. (2013). On children as syncretic natives: disrupting and moving beyond normative binaries. *Journal of Early Childhood Literacy*, 13(3): 371–394.

Spear-Swerling, L. and Brucker, P. O. (2003). Teachers' acquisition of knowledge about English word structure. *Annuals of Dyslexia*, 53: 72–103.

Stark, R. E. (1986). Prespeech segmental feature development. In P. Fletcher and M. Garman (eds), *Language Acquisition* (pp. 149–173). Cambridge: Cambridge University Press.

Steelman, L., Powell, B., Werum, R., and Carter, S. (2002). Reconsidering the effects of sibling configuration: recent advances and challenges. *Annual Review of Sociology*, 28: 243–269.

Stein, N. L. (1988). The development of children's storytelling skills. In M. B. Frankling and S. S. Barten (eds), *Child Language: A Reader* (pp. 282–297). New York: Oxford University Press.

Stevens, L. P. and Bean, T. W. (2007). *Critical Literacy: Context, Research, and Practice in the K-12 Classroom*. Thousand Oaks, CA: Sage.

Stoel-Gammon, C. (1998). The role of babbling and phonology in early linguistic development. In: A. M. Wetherby, S. F. Warren, and J. Reichle (eds), *Transitions in Prelinguistic Communication* (pp. 87–110). Baltimore: Paul H. Brookes.

Stoel-Gammon, C. and Cooper, J. (1984). Patterns of early lexical and phonological development. *Journal of Child Language*, 11: 247–271.

Stone, K. (1981). Marchen to fairy tales: an unmagical transformation. *Western Folklore*, 40: 232–244.

Storch, S., and Whitehurst, R. (2002). Oral language and code-related precursors to reading: Evidence from a longitudinal structural model. *Developmental Psychology*, 38: 934–947.

Street, B. V. and Lefstein, A. (2007). *Literacy: An Advanced Resource Book for Students*. London: Routledge.

Suleiman, M. F. and Moore, R. (1995). Figures of speech, symbolism and the communicative process in the multilingual classroom. Paper presented at the Annual Meeting of the Speech and Communication Association of Puerto Rico, San Juan.

Sullivan, J. H. (2002). The second language educators' challenge: learning about literacy. In J. H. Sullivan (ed.), *Literacy and the Second Language Learner* (pp. ix–xi). Greenwich, CT: Information Age.

Summers, C., Bohman, T. M., Gillam, R. B., Peña, E. D., and Bedore, L. M. (2010). Bilingual performance on nonword repetition in Spanish and English. *International Journal of Language Communication Disorders*, 45(4): 480–493.

Sutherland-Smith, W. (2002). Weaving the literacy web: changes in reading from page to screen. *Reading Teacher*, 55(7): 662–669.

Swain, M. (1972). Bilingualism as a first language. PhD dissertation, University of California, Irvine.

Swain, M. (1995). Three functions of output in second language learning. In G. Cook and B. Seidhofer (eds), *Principles and Practice in Applied Linguistics: Studies in Honour of H. G. Widdowson* (pp. 125–144). Oxford: Oxford University Press.

Taback, S. (1999). *Joseph Had a Little Overcoat*. New York: Viking Children's Books.

Tabors, P. O., Páez, M., and López, L. (2003). Dual language abilities of bilingual four-year olds: initial findings from the early childhood study of language and literacy development of Spanish-speaking children. *NABE Journal of Research and Practice*, 1: 70–91.

Tabors, P. O., Roach, K. A. and Snow, C. E. (2001). Home language and literacy environment: final results. In D. K. Dickinson and P. O. Tabors (eds), *Beginning Literacy with Language* (pp. 111–138). Baltimore: Paul H. Brookes.

Tager-Flusberg, H. (2001). Language development in atypical children. In M. Barrett (ed.), *The Development of Language* (pp. 311–348). Hove: Psychological Press.

Tager-Flusberg, H., Rogers, S., Cooper, J., Landa, R., Lord, C., Paul, R., Rice, M., Stoel-Gammon, C., Wetherby, A., and Yoder, P. (2009). Defining spoken language benchmarks and selecting measures of expressive language development for young children with autism spectrum disorders. *Journal of Speech, Language, and Hearing Research*, 52: 643–652.

Tallal, P., Miller, S., and Fitch, R. H. (1993). Neurobiological basis of speech: a case for the pre-eminence of temporal processing. In P. Tallal, A. M. Galaburda, R. R. Llinas, and C. von Euler (eds), *Annals of the New York Academy of Sciences: Temporal Information Processing in the Nervous System*. New York: New York Academy of Sciences.

Tare, M. P. (2008). The development of pragmatic differentiation skills in preschool-aged bilingual children. Doctoral dissertation, University of Michigan.

Teale, W. H. (1982). Toward a theory of how children learn to read and write "naturally." *Language Arts*, 59(6): 555–570.

Tenenbaum, H. and Leaper, C. (1998). Gender effects on Mexican-descent parents' questions and scaffolding during toy play: a sequential analysis. *First Language*, 18: 129–147.

Terry, N. P., Mills, M. T., Bingham, G. E., Mansour, S., and Marencin, N. (2013). Oral narrative performance of African American prekindergarteners who speak nonmainstream American English. *Language, Speech, and Hearing Sciences in Schools*, 44: 291–306.

Tharp, R.G. and Gallimore, R. (1988). Rousing schools to life. *American Educator*, 13(2): 20–25, 46–52.

Tomasello, M. (2003). *Constructing a Language: A Usage-Based Theory of Language Acquisition*. Cambridge, MA: Harvard University Press.

Tomasello, M. (2008). *Origins of Human Communication*. Cambridge, MA: MIT Press.

Tomasello, M. and Mannle, S. (1985). Pragmatics of sibling speech to one-year-olds. *Child Development*, 56: 911–917.

Tomlinson, C. and Lynch-Brown, C. (1996). *Essentials of Children's Literature*. Boston: Allyn & Bacon.

Tompkins, G. E. (2009). *50 Literacy Strategies: Step by Step*. Boston: Allyn & Bacon.

Treiman, R. (1985). Onsets and rimes as units of spoken syllables: evidence from children. *Journal of Experimental Child Psychology*, 19: 181–191.

Tucha, O., Tucha, L., and lange, K. W. (2008). Graphonomics, automaticity and handwriting assessment. *Literacy*, 42(3): 145–155.

Uccelli, P. and Páez. M. M. (2007). Narrative and vocabulary development of bilingual children from kindergarten to first grade:

developmental changes and associations among English and Spanish skills. *Language, Speech, and Hearing Services in Schools*, 38: 225–236.

Uchikoshi, Y. (2005). Narrative development in bilingual kindergarteners: can *Arthur* help? *Developmental Psychology*, 41(3): 464–478.

Undheim, J. O. and Nordvik, H. (1992). Socio-economic factors and sex differences in an egalitarian educational system: academic achievement in 16-year-old Norwegian students. *Scandinavian Journal of Educational Research*, 36(2): 87–98.

US Census Bureau, 2012. At http://www.census.gov/# (accessed Mar. 3014).

US Department of Health and Human Services. (2003). *Head Start FACES 2000: A Whole-Child Perspective on Program Performance*. Washington, DC.

Van Horn, L. (2008). *Reading Photographs to Write with Meaning and Purpose, Grade 4-12*. Newark, DE: International Reading Association.

Van Kleeck, A. (1994). Metalinguistic development. In G. P. Wallack and K. G. Butler (eds), *Language Learning Disabilities in School-Age Children and Adolescents: Some Principles and Applications* (pp. 53–98). New York: Merrill.

Vallar, G. and Papagno, C. (1993). Preserved vocabulary acquisition in Down's syndrome: the role of phonological short-term memory. *Cortex*, 29: 467-483.

Vasilyeva, M., Huttenlocher, J., and Waterfall, H. (2006). Effects of language intervention on syntactic skill levels in preschoolers. *Developmental Psychology*, 42(1): 164–174.

Veltman, C. (1981). Anglicization in the United States: the importance of parental nativity and language practice. *International Journal of Society and Language*, 32: 65–84.

Verhoeven, L. and Strömqvist, S. (2001). *Narrative Development in a Multilingual Context*. Amsterdam: John Benjamins.

Verhoeven, L. and Van Leenuwe, J. (2011). Role of gender and linguistic diversity in word decoding development. *Learning and Individual Differences*, 21(4): 359–367.

Verhoeven, L., Steenge, J., and van Balkom, H. (2012). Linguistic transfer in bilingual children with specific language impairment. *International Journal of Communication Disorders*, 47(2): 176–183.

Verhoeven, L., Steenge, J., van Weerdenburg, M., and van Balkom, H. (2011). Assessment of second language proficiency in bilingual children with specific language impairment: a clinical perspective. *Research in Developmental Disabilities*, 32: 1798–1807.

Viberg, A (2001). Age-related and L2-related features in bilingual narrative development in Sweden. In L. Verborven and S. Strömqvist (eds), *Narrative Development in a Multilingual Context* (pp. 87–128). Amsterdam: John Benjamins.

Volk, D. (2013). Contradictions, clashes, cominglings: the syncretic literacy projects of young bilinguals. *Anthropology and Education Quarterly*, 44(3): 234–252.

Volterra, V. and Taeschner, T. (1978). The acquisition and development of language by bilingual children. *Journal of Child Language*, 5: 311–326.

Vygotsky, L. S. (1986). *Thought and Language*, ed. A. Kozulin. Cambridge, MA: MIT Press.

Walker, D., Greenwood, C., Hart, B., and Carta, J. (1994). Prediction of school outcomes based on early language production and socioeconomic factors. *Child Development*, 65: 606–621.

Walsh, M. (2003). "Reading" pictures: what do they reveal? Young children's reading of visual texts. *Reading*, 37(3): 123–130.

Walters, S. (2011). Masking, mediators and agency: bilingual children and learning to read. *Journal of Research in Reading*, 34(4): 384–401.

Wang, M., Yang, C., and Cheng, C.-X. (2009). The contributions of phonology, orthography, and morphology in Chinese–English biliteracy acquisition. *Applied Psycholinguistics*, 30: 291–314.

Wang, Q. and Leichtman, M. D. (2000). Same beginnings, different stories: a comparison of American and Chinese children's narratives. *Child Development*, 71: 1329–1346.

Wang, X.-L. (2008). *Growing up with Three Languages: Birth to Eleven*. Bristol: Multilingual Matters.

Wang, X.-L. (2009). *Bilingual Family Newsletter*. Bristol: Multilingual Matters.

Wang, X.-L. (2010). A comparative study of how moral values are conveyed in contemporary Chinese, English, and French children's books. Paper presented at the Fifth

Conference of Asia Pacific Network for Moral Education, Nagasaki, Japan, June 11-13.

Wang, X.-L. (2011a). *Learning to Read and Write in the Multilingual Family.* Bristol: Multilingual Matters.

Wang, X.-L. (2011b). Teaching children to read and write in more than one orthography: tips for parents. *Multilingual Living*, September 26, 2011.

Wang, X.-L. (forthcoming). *Keeping up with Three Languages: Adolescence.* Bristol: Multilingual Matters.

Wang, X.-L. and Eberhard, P. (2006). Helping second language learners construct meaning through hand gestures. *International Journal of Learning*, 12(3): 227–236.

Wang, X.-L., Bernas, R., and Eberhard, P. (2002). Variations in maternal support to children's early literacy development in Chinese and Native American families: implications for early childhood educators. *International Journal of Early Childhood*, 34(1): 9–23.

Wang, X.-L., Eberhard, L., and Bernas, R. (2014). Gestures can enhance the narrative ability of children with learning disabilities. *International Journal of Literacies*, 20: 1–23.

Wang, X.-L., Mylander, C. and Goldin-Meadow, S. (1993). Language and environment: a cross-cultural study of the gestural communication systems of Chinese and American deaf children. *Belgian Journal of Linguistics*, 8: 167–185.

Wang, X.-L., Mylander, C., and Goldin-Meadow, S. (1995). The resilience of language: mother-child interaction and its effect on the gesture systems of Chinese and American deaf children. In K. Emmorey and J. S. Reilly (eds), *Language, Gesture, and Space* (pp. 411–434). Hillsdale, NJ: Lawrence Erlbaum.

Wang, X-L., Mylander, C., and Goldin-Meadow, S. (1996). Cross-cultural study of mother/child interaction in Chinese and American families. In M. Cusinato (ed.), *Research on Family Resources and Needs across the World* (pp. 363–374). Milan: Edizioni Universitarie di Lettere Economia Diritto.

Wanner, P. J. (1996). A study of the initial codeswitching stage in the linguistic development of an English–Japanese bilingual child. *Japan Journal of Multilingualism and Multiculturalism*, 2: 20–40.

Warrick, N., Rubin, H., and Rowe-Walsh, S. (1993). Phoneme awareness in language delayed children: comparative studies and intervention. *Annals of Dyslexia*, 43: 153–173.

Washington, J. A. and Thomas-Tate, S. (2009). How research informs cultural-linguistic differences in the classroom. In S. Rosenfield and V. Berninger (eds), *Implementing Evidence-Based Academic Interventions in School Settings* (pp. 147–163). New York: Oxford University Press.

Weber-Fox, C. and Neville, H. (1996). Maturational constraints on functional specializations for language processing: ERP and behavioral evidence in bilingual speakers. *Journal of Cognitive Neuroscience*, 8: 231–256.

Weizman, Z. O. and Snow, C. E. (2001). Lexical input as related to children's vocabulary acquisition: effects of sophisticated exposure and support for meaning. *Developmental Psychology*, 37(2): 265–279.

Werker, J. and Tees, R. C. (2005). Speech perception as a window for understanding plasticity and commitment in language systems of the brain. *Developmental Psychology*, 46: 233–251.

Westby, C. E. (1994). The effects of culture on genre, structure, style of oral and written texts. In G. Wallach and K. Butler (eds), *Language Learning Disabilities in School-Age Children and Adolescents* (pp. 180–218). New York: Macmillan.

Wheeler, R. and Swords, R. (2010). *Code-Switching Lessons: Grammar Strategies for Linguistically Diverse Writers.* Portsmouth, NH: Heinemann.

White, E. J., Genesee, F., and Steinhauer, K. (2012). Brain responses before and after intensive second language learning: proficiency based changes and first language background effects in adult learners. *PloS One*, 7(12): e52318.

White, N. L., Anderson, N. L., and Carrico, H. (2009). *Linking Assessment to Reading Comprehension Instruction: A Framework for Actively Engaging Literacy Learners, K-8.* Boston: Pearson.

Whiteman, S. D., Bernard, J. M. B., and Jensen, A. C. (2011). Sibling influence in human development. In J. Caspi (ed.), *Sibling Development: Implications for Mental Health Practitioners* (pp. 1–15). New York: Springer.

Whitworth, N. (2002). Speech rhythm production in three German–English bilingual families. In D. Nelson (ed.), *Leeds Working Papers in Linguistics and Phonetics*, vol. 9 (pp. 175–205). Leeds: Leeds Metropolitan University.

Windsor, J. and Kohnert, K. (2004). In search of common ground – Part 1: Lexical performance by linguistically diverse learners. *Journal of Speech. Language, and Hearing Research*, 47: 877–890.

Wiggins, D. G. (2007). Pre-K music and the emergent reader: promoting literacy in a music-enhanced environment. *Early Childhood Education Journal*, 35(1): 55–64.

Winsler, A., Carlton, M. P., and Barry, M. J. (2000). Age-related changes in preschool children's systematic use of private speech in a natural setting. *Journal of Child Language*, 27: 665–687.

Witte-Townsend, D. L. and DiGiulio, E. (2004). Something from nothing: exploring dimensions of children's knowing through the repeated reading of favourite books. *International Journal of Children's Spirituality*, 9(2): 127–142.

Witzel, N. O. and Forster, K. I. (2012). How L2 words are stored: the episodic L2 hypothesis. *Learning, Memory, and Cognition*, 38(6): 1608–1621.

Wolfe, P. (2001). *Brain Matters: Translating Research into Classroom*. Alexandria, VA: Association for Supervision and Curriculum Development.

Wollak, B. A. and Koppenhaver, D. A. (2011). Developing technology-supported, evidence-based writing instruction for adolescents with significant writing disabilities. *Assistive Technology Outcomes and Benefits*, 7(1): 1–23.

Wong-Fillmore, L. (1983). The language learner as an individual: implications of research on individual differences for the ESL teacher. In M. Clarke and J. Handscomb (eds), *On TESOL'82: Pacific Perspectives on Language Learning and Teaching* (pp. 157–173). Washington, DC: Teachers of English to Speakers of Other Languages.

Wong-Fillmore, L. (2007). *Resource: Academic Language*. Sonoma, CA: SCOE.

Woollett, A. (1986). The influence of older siblings on the language environment of young children. *British Journal of Developmental Psychology*, 4(3): 235–245.

Yeong, S. H. M. and Liow, S. J. R. (2012). Development of phonological awareness in English–Mandarin bilinguals: a comparison of English-L1 and Mandarin-L1 kindergarten children. *Journal of Experimental Child Psychology*, 112: 111–126.

Yip, V. and Matthews, S. (2008). Lexical development in Cantonese–English bilingual children. Poster presented at the Eleventh Congress of the International Association for the Study of Child Language, Edinburgh, July 28–August 1.

Zehr, M. A. (2010). Reading aloud to teens gains favor among teachers. *Education Week*, at edweek.org, Jan. 4 (accessed Mar. 2014).

Zukow, P. G. (1989). Siblings as effective socialization agents: evidence from Central Mexico. In P. G. Zukow (ed.), *Sibling Interaction across Cultures: Theoretical and Methodological Issues* (pp. 79–105). New York: Springer.

Index